Revolt Against
the
Modern World

Other Books by Julius Evola

Eros and the Mysteries of Love (1983)
The Yoga of Power (1992)
The Hermetic Tradition (1995)
The Doctrine of Awakening (1995)

Revolt Against the Modern World

Julius Evola

Translated from the Italian
by Guido Stucco

Inner Traditions International
Rochester, Vermont

Inner Traditions International
One Park Street
Rochester, Vermont 05767

LIBRARY OF CONGRESS CATALOGING-IN-PUBLICATION DATA

Evola, Julius, 1898–1974.
    [Rivolta contro il mondo moderno. English]
    Revolt agaisnt the modern world : politics, religion and social order of the
Kali Yuga / Julius Evola ; translated from the Italian by Guido Stucco.
      p.   cm.
    Includes index.
    ISBN 0-89281-506-X
    1. History—Philosophy.   I. Title.
    D16.8.E8513 1995
    901–dc20   95–24561
                                          CIP

Printed and bound in the United States

10 9 8 7 6 5 4 3 2 1

Text design and layout by Charlotte Tyler
This book was typeset in Times with Bodega Sans Old Style and Times as a display face

Distributed to the book trade in Canada by Publishers Group West (PGW), Toronto, Ontario
Distributed to the book trade in the United Kingdom by Deep Books, London
Distributed to the book trade in Australia by Millennium Books, Newtown, N.S.W.
Distributed to the book trade in New Zealand by Tandem Press, Auckland

To the

1st Battaglione Carabinieri Paracadutisti "Tuscania" :

Caesarem Vehis!

Contents

⊷ Part One ⊶

The World of Tradition

Genesis and Face of the Modern World

A Short Introduction to Julius Evola

H. T. Hansen[1]

Julius Evola (1898–1974) is still relatively unknown to the English-speaking world, even in the traditional circles surrounding René Guénon, of whom he was his leading Italian representative. The major reason for this is that until recently little of Evola's work had been translated into English. This situation is being remedied by Ehud Sperling, president of Inner Traditions International. In addition to *Eros and the Mysteries of Love: The Metaphysics of Sex* published in 1983, Inner Traditions has also brought out two of Evola's most important books, *The Yoga of Power*, on Tantrism, and *The Hermetic Tradition*, on alchemy. Following *Revolt Against the Modern World*, Inner Traditions will also republish Evola's masterful work on Buddhist asceticism, *The Doctrine of Awakening*.[2]

Evola received some recent attention in *Gnosis* magazine, where Robin Waterfield attempted to present a well-balanced view of him, which drew immediate protest.[3] Evola's known sympathies for Italian Fascism and National Socialism,

1. A version of this article, translated by E. E. Rehmus, first appeared in *Theosophical History* 5 (January 1994): 11–22, and is reprinted here with the kind permission of the editor.

    Dr. Hansen, a native of Austria, studied law and received his Ph.D. in 1970. After working in the export trade, he has, since 1989, been exclusively engaged in writing book introductions and translating works in esotericism and philosophy. He is also a partner in the Ansata Verlag in Interlaken, Switzerland, one of the foremost publishers of the esoteric in the German-speaking world. Apropos this article, Dr. Hansen knew Julius Evola personally and has also devoted many years to researching Evola's life and writings.
2. *The Yoga of Power: Tantra, Shakti, and the Secret Way*, trans. Guido Stucco (Rochester, Vt., 1992); *The Hermetic Tradition: Symbols and Teachings of the Royal Art*, trans. E. E. Rehmus (Rochester, Vt., 1995); *The Doctrine of Awakening: The Attainment of Self-Mastery According to the Earliest Buddhist Texts*, trans. H. E. Musson (1951; reprint, Rochester, Vt., 1995).
3. "Baron Julius Evola and the Hermetic Tradition," *Gnosis* 14, (winter 1990): 12–17.

to which we will return in this article, were recalled. There is also Richard H. Drake's essay "Julius Evola and the Ideological Origins of the Radical Right in Contemporary Italy," which contributed a great deal to Evola's negative image in the English-speaking world, and Thomas Sheehan's "Myth and Violence: The Fascism of Julius Evola and Alain de Benoist."[4] That Evola, on the other hand, had been from his youth in constant personal contact and correspondence with Mircea Eliade and the famous Tibetologist Giuseppe Tucci, is less well known.

But who actually was Julius Evola? His career was many-sided: As a philosopher he belongs among the leading representatives of Italian Idealism; as a painter and poet he is counted as one of the founders of Italian Dadaism; as a cultural historian and critic of our times, in addition to his *Revolt Against the Modern World,* he also translated Oswald Spengler's *Decline of the West,* as well as Bachofen, Weininger, and Gabriel Marcel; as a patron of literature he was the publisher and translator of Ernst Jünger and Gustav Meyrink, whom he introduced into Italy; to some he might appear as an *éminence grise* in politics, for Mussolini apparently wanted to implement some of Evola's ideas to create more freedom from the restrictions of National Socialism, and today, as then, right- and even some left-wing groups adopt him against his intentions; his important activities in the UR Group and many of his books testify to his understanding of alchemy and magic, and it is reported that Mussolini stood in considerable awe of Evola's "magical powers."

Ultimately, no definite answer to the question of who he was can readily be given, for Evola was apparently (to others) all of these things and yet (to himself) none of them. He saw himself as a member of the *kṣatriya* or "warrior" class, who goes his way heedless of the praise or blame of others while simply wanting to do "what must be done, without thinking of success or failure." Only one thing was of primary importance: the "Above." For him transcendence was the be-all and end-all. From above derived all reasons for what happens below, and everything below must in turn be aligned to the above. Every thought and thing had to be judged as to whether it led upward. Only this resolute striving for the true foundation of all things can explain Evola's many nearly incomprehensible judgments and outlooks. His first aim was to turn toward transcendence and be liberated from Earth. Hence his constant attacks on "chthonic" religions, because they are *terrestrial* cults and not *celestial* religions. In these terrestrial cults, the Earth is the "Great Mother" and she alone has priority since she gives protection and help. Heaven, which in practically

---

4. Richard H. Drake, "Julius Evola and the Ideological Origins of the Radical Right in Contemporary Italy," in Peter H. Merkl, ed., *Political Violence and Terror: Motifs and Motivations* (Berkeley, Calif., 1986); Thomas Sheehan, "Myth and Violence: The Fascism of Julius Evola and Alain de Benoist," *Social Research* 48: 45–73.

all cultures is regarded as male because it makes the womb of the earth fertile through the sun and rain, is therefore in those cults nearly insignificant beside her. And if one worships the earth, striving upward for heavenly transcendence is of no avail. Evola's path, however, is neither a search for consolation nor an abandonment of the self to the mother goddess with its consequent loss of the self. For Evola the earthly is not the path that leads to active liberation, to "awakening." On the contrary, it strengthens the "sleep" in which one gropes to return to the mother's womb. Evola values only the continuum of consciousness, the enduring presence, and the awakening of the thousand eyes as the essentials for achieving liberation.

What Joscelyn Godwin wrote about René Guénon is also true of Evola's esoteric work:

> Mystical experience and religious devotion are certainly intrinsic elements of the spiritual path, but as Guénon never tired of emphasizing, the ultimate realization of a human being is through knowledge.
>
> Some may find this whole approach too intellectual, but they cannot deny that the Traditionalist's discipline of metaphysics cuts like a razor through the sloppy thinking and sentimentality prevalent among "New Age" types. It sets standards of integrity against which other spiritual teachings either stand or fall. It assumes from the outset that the absolute truth has always been there for the finding, so it has no time for the fumblings of Western philosophy, so-called, nor for a science whose basic dogma is that man is still searching for the truth. And it incidentally forces a revaluation of all the modern ideals that most North Americans take for granted, such as individualism, equality, evolution and progress. One looks at the world with new eyes once one has passed through a Traditionalist re-education.[5]

Since the chthonic or "Earth" religions go hand in hand with mother cults and their feminine leadership, Evola saw every matriarchal culture as further evidence of "deterioration." It was neither misogyny nor "patriarchism" that led him to this, but simply an intense striving for liberation from earthly bondage. In his eyes this liberation is all that matters; everything else is meaningless alongside it. To achieve this goal, no sacrifice is too great for him. Even one's own death becomes a "triumphal death," insofar as one is aware of it as a sacrifice undergone for this liberation. Who perishes in battle in this spirit is "godly," because for him the outer struggle is merely a symbol for the inner struggle against enslavement to earth. It is only from such a viewpoint that today we can grasp Evola's acceptance of the Hindu practice of *satī*.

5. *Gnosis* 7 (spring 1988): 23-24.

He sees it as the highest of devotions, precisely because it places perfect purity of purpose ahead of mere greed for life.

So asceticism is for Evola not a woeful and painful stifling of unlived passion, but simply a "technique" for setting the self free, a conscious step undertaken because one is aware of the Higher. He does not trust in grace and waiting, but wants to liberate himself through his own power. Consciousness therefore precedes unconsciousness, and to avoid any misunderstanding, Evola sharply differentiates the idea of higher consciousness from lower consciousness. A crystal-clear wakefulness characterizes the first, and surrender and self-sacrifice the latter. This is why Evola so often warns us about spiritualism and the usual "occult streams." These, he maintains, quoting Guénon, are even more dangerous than materialism. "Because of its primitivity and intellectual short-sightedness," materialism protected men from their own unconsciousness. In this regard, Guénon pointed out that rationalism, materialism, and positivism at first blocked the way for men to what lay *above* them, whereupon the occult streams now open them to what lies *below* them. And of course, this is why Evola also fights against the psychoanalysis of Freud and Jung, both of whom demand that one open oneself to the unconscious, allowing it to act, so as to receive clues for the meaning of unconscious phenomena. Here we must emphasize that Evola's path is not intended to be psychotherapeutic. On the contrary, his path demands the absolute mental health of a person who has already reached "individuation." He puts it in these words: "In most cases today the personality is an exercise, something not yet in existence, which one must first strive to acquire." If we cannot overcome the problems of this life, how can we hope to be ready for the much greater problems of Life and what lies beyond it?

Such emphasis on the "above" and on "reaching upward" helps to explain Evola's constant reference to "high" and "low," "pure" and "impure." Higher is simply that which bears "more transcendence" in itself or strives toward it. This is the only thing that justifies his positive evaluation of authority and the original priest-kings. Since they stood in immediate touch with the "overworld," it was only natural that they should command others who were more earth-arrested. According to Evola the entire Indian caste system, from *brāhmaṇa* to *śūdra,* was based in ancient times on this hierarchy of participation in the Absolute. And in aristocratic Rome, the patricians, who were in charge of the rites pertaining to the overworld, therefore ruled the plebeians, who worshiped earthly gods and mother goddesses.

That ideas of "high" and "low" are relative and ultimately invalid is clear enough. Nor does Evola endorse dualism. Such "hierarchical" evaluations may be necessary in our world, which demands clear-cut ideas if we wish to express ourselves clearly, but for Evola the key to Life beyond life, to initiation—that is, to the beginning, to the origin—is precisely the ultimate oneness of above and below, spirit and matter (as well as spiritual and worldly power), subject and object, myth and history, inner and outer, and thereby also word and deed. According to Evola this unity that does not recognize "other" was the sign of the original, the "godly" man. For this man, looking inward was the same as looking outward, and every "word" through the "magic imagination" was simultaneously the fulfillment of the imagined. As it was said of the ancients: they still knew the "true names" of things. Thought was visually perfect and hence one with the will.

Let us turn to another aspect of Evola's weltanschauung with which we are already acquainted from Hinduism, namely, the idea of involution as opposed to evolution. Not upward development but downward disintegration characterizes Evola's picture of history. We are engaged not in climbing but in sliding. For most of us this thought is so strange that an immediate "instinctual" negative reaction is rather natural. We might reject the idea of involution in the same way that Darwin's theory of evolution, which originated the belief in progress in the first place, was "instinctively" rejected in the last century. Evola took these thoughts of involution from Guénon's traditional worldview. The fundamental key to understanding this view is quite clear, for here again Evola sees the struggle as being between "above" and "below," between "higher" or "Uranian" (Uranus in Greek mythology is the personification of heaven, the principle of divine origination) and "lower" or "chthonic" peoples, whereby in the course of time the matter-bound "sons of the earth" became stronger and stronger and the "portion of transcendence" became ever more trivialized. So it is only a question then of choosing from which "ideological" standpoint one is to consider history, whether to regard it as Evola does—as involution—or as evolution along with the moderns, for whom scholarly and material achievements are more important than spiritual liberation.

For this reason Evola's thinking goes very much against the spirit of the times, which sees his position as a challenge and naturally declares war on it. Are not many of our most cherished beliefs and universally unquestioned opinions about democracy, monarchy, the caste system, slavery, and the emancipation of women unequivocally attacked by it? Before countering that attack, however, we should remember to cast an eye over exactly the same attitudes that have prevailed for millennia in many societies (in Japan up to 1945). Even Dante's *De monarchia* breathes this spirit.

Evola's rebukes spare no one—not even those who would be his bravest disciples. Since he does not regard himself as master, he can recognize no student. His thinking cannot be considered a teaching because he did not invent it; no one invented it; the Tradition has a transcendental origin. Evola wants only to lay down a "testimony" written for those who are "different"—*l'uomo differenziato*—those who are of the type that does not belong to this time.

Evola especially rejects "intellectuals" who, to be sure, frequently treasure his work, but for the wrong reason: their interest is purely of the intellect and therefore superficial. The understanding that Evola wants requires a fundamental inner change before anything else. Only then will it become an inner experience and bring with it knowledge and power simultaneously. He was well acquainted with the dangers of intellectualism, for he himself had been an engineering student, acquitting himself with the highest grades. He broke off his studies just before his doctorate, however, because he "did not wish to be bourgeois, like his fellow students." He said again and again that he valued qualities of character that were much higher than abstract intellect or "empty," that is, nontranscendental, artistic creativity. Both are but pretexts to entrench the ego in its own devices.

Nor was it of great importance for Evola whether the perfect world that he described had ever existed or would exist. The idea behind it, the principle for which the traditional world is always striving, was enough for him. That in practice this principle was fulfilled only in form, or not even that, was immaterial, for as long as the principle remained recognizable, at least the possibility of self-transcendence for men continued to present itself. In this sense one can speak of a "utopia," in which the idea is worth more than its puritanical realization. And this argument is valid not only for the traditional world but also for the modern. For religion, neighborly love, and democracy are likewise utopias in this sense. Nor has "utopia" here any negative overtones, for without its incredibly strong suggestive power no one would strive for a hyperbiological goal.

Later on Evola also rejected the idea of involving himself in recreating this traditional world today. He wanted, as we have said, only to transmit a "testimony," so that some, who "stand outside this world," could have a fixed point.

Nor can we reproach him for not mourning the past. Past and future are much the same to him; only the traditional principles are important, and these stand clearly outside time and space. That these were lasting principles he never doubted in the least. Therefore, in *Cavalcare la tigre* (Ride the Tiger), his main book for the "others," for those "who are different," he stressed that this "different" person should *not* turn his back on the world. On the contrary, he should seat himself on the very back of this ferocious, predatory world and rush forward with him. For as long as one keeps sitting on top of the running beast, one need not fear its claws and teeth. When the beast then becomes tired and weak from its wild running and lies down, one can then overcome it. "Manage so that what you can do nothing against, also can do nothing against you," and "you can do anything as long as you are sure that you can do without it," were his expressions.

We can correctly ascribe one danger to Evola's work that is not necessarily his fault. Since he is always talking about the grandiose, that which is stirring and noble, and never of the bondings of compassion and love, he could easily be mistaken for a seeker of the superman and the Titans. But that is exactly what Evola wants to avoid. He distinguishes quite carefully between the path of the hero and the path of the Titan. It is not the thought of power derived from the strengthening of the ego that Evola preaches, but on the contrary, the transcendence of the ego. Ordinary individuality must be dissolved. That is what is necessary in the struggle for freedom from bondage and the overcoming of passion. As long as one continues to strive for (true and unusurped) power *(śakti),* one neither has it nor can use it. In order to acquire it, one must be able to put oneself beyond it, to be free of it. As Evola says in the introduction to his three-volume work on magic *(Introduzione alla magia),* power is feminine. She comes to the strongest. Just as the waters around the bridge piles thrust and accumulate, so power collects around those who stand independently and are unconcerned about it. The power-greedy ego must be conquered and turned to something infinitely greater than itself.

Evola was born on May 19, 1898, the son of a noble Sicilian family, and had a strong, dogmatically Catholic upbringing. When he was still very young he joined the circle of rebellious poets around Marinetti (founder of Futurism) and Papini, who fascinated him with their iconoclastic, revolutionary outlook. Papini brought him into contact with all the new directions of art and streams of fashion, but also with Oriental wisdom and especially with Meister Eckhart. After voluntary war service as an officer candidate in the artillery, which left him untouched because of lack of any significant military action, Evola began to occupy himself with occult teachings. Drug experiences (to which he never returned) certainly gave him new ideas, but they also intensified an already present crisis so that he voluntarily planned to end his life.

His urge for the Absolute had crossed over to an urge for disintegration. In this he seems to have been influenced by his greatest models, namely Otto Weininger and Carlo Michelstaedter, for both had committed suicide early in their lives. Michelstaedter, in particular, had demonstrated both the insignificance and illusion of this world and this life with its continual longing for something that can never be satisfied. Here also is the origin of Evola's striving for self-sufficiency, independence from everything, and self-liberation. But a passage from the Buddhist Pali canon saved him from the catastrophe. This passage in the *Majjhima Nikāya* (1.1) says that whoever believes that extinction is extinction, understands extinction as extinction, thinks of extinction, truly believes extinction to be extinction and rejoices in extinction, that person does not know extinction.

Evola's involvement with Dadaism goes back to his relationship with its founder Tristan Tzara, who wanted to establish a new vision of the world rather than merely an avant-garde art movement. His aim was absolute liberation through the complete turning around of all logical, ethical, and aesthetic categories. He sought the union of order and disorder, of ego and non-ego, of yea- and nay-saying. Evola saw Dadaism therefore as the self-liberation through art into a higher freedom.

A "philosophical" period followed, which lasted until 1927. It led to the writing of three main books. These works follow the track laid down by the strong influence of Nietzsche and Stirner and were mainly directed against the then fascist "court philosophers" such as Giovanni Gentile.

But contacts with Theosophy, which he soon sharply condemned, and especially John Woodroffe (Arthur Avalon) also fall in this period.[6] An especially profound influence on him was Arturo Reghini, who was in fact the one who introduced him to the Western tradition. This led to the famous UR Group, with its "magic as science of the ego." "Magic" was understood to be the active taking up of a traditional initiation practice, and profound studies of alchemy, Buddhism, and Taoism complemented his practical experiences in the UR Group.

But along with these interests Evola was also looking for "an arena open to more opportunities," namely, politics. He wanted to create a spiritual foundation in the prevailing climate of the New Order, Fascism, and to strengthen what in his eyes were the positive possibilities in bringing back the idea of the ancient Roman Empire while avoiding its negative traits (totalitarianism, the emphasis on the masses). He set about doing this by first creating the periodical *La Torre*, which after ten issues had to be put on the shelf. By order of Mussolini no print shop was allowed to print it any longer. Evola's criticism therein had been belligerent. After being reminded that Mussolini thought otherwise about something he wrote, *"Tanto peggio per Mussolini"* (Too bad for Mussolini). At this time, therefore, in spite of his sympathies for Fascism, he was obliged to move about Rome with bodyguards.

Here we find ourselves in the middle of the key question as to why Evola suffers from a negative image—not only in the English-speaking world—despite many of his opponents' appreciation for his esoteric works. For starters, there is his undoubted sympathy for Fascism, National Socialism and racism, but let us also make some distinctions. First, there is the spirit of the times to take into consideration, under whose spell authors more famous than Evola, such as Ezra Pound and Knut Hamsun, also fell. In his defense, on no account must we forget Evola's numerous critical newspaper articles written during the entire Fascist epoch, inclusive of wartime, an accomplishment that under a totalitarian regime demanded personal courage by anyone's standards. Of course a comprehensive study of this question is not possible

---

6. A comprehensive study of Evola's involvement with Theosophy is planned for a future issue of *Theosophical History*.

here. But a couple of original quotations from those times should suffice to indicate the direction of Evola's criticism. (A study conducted to that end is the lengthy introduction to the German edition of Evola's major political work: *Uomini e rovine* (Men Amidst Ruins). Evola's criticism naturally consisted mainly of the fact that he failed to see in Fascism any spiritual root or direction toward the transcendent: the "plebeian," the "bourgeois," the "bureaucratic" elements were simply too strong.

As early as 1925 (Fascism in Italy was by then already in power), Evola had written in the antifascist magazine *Lo Stato Democratico* (no. 17) in reference to Fascism: "if one considers the type of (our actual) ruler and state that should truly embody the principle of freedom, then they present themselves as mere caricatures and grotesque parodies." And he makes his attitude clear in the very first issue of *La Torre* under the title "Identity Card":

> Our magazine was not created to "whisper" something to Fascism or into the ear of M. P. Mussolini, for neither Fascism nor Mussolini would know what to do with it. Rather, our publication was created for the purpose of defending *principles*, which for us will always be the same absolutely, independently, whether we are in a communistic, anarchistic, or republican regime.

Then Evola discusses the principles of hierarchy, of the need to anchor everything in the transcendental, and of spiritual imperial thought. He goes further—highlighting in italics: *"To the extent that Fascism follows these principles and defends them, to exactly that same extent can we consider ourselves to be fascist. And that is all."*

We have failed to mention that Evola was never a member of the Fascist Party. But exactly because he did not see his ideas fulfilled in Fascism, he turned to National Socialism, which in his opinion seemed of much more consequence, as it continued to speak, rhetorically at least, of its own spiritual roots, of holy runes, and so on. But here as well, Evola failed to find what he sought, for it was precisely the masses that stood as a point of reference at the center of Nazism and *not* the transcendent state or empire. A quote from "Orizzonte Austriaco" in the Fascist newspaper *Lo Stato* (January 1935) states this unequivocally:

> Nationalistic Socialism has clearly renounced the ancient, aristocratic tradition of the state. It is nothing more than a semi-collective nationalism that levels everything flat in its centralism, and it has not hesitated to destroy the traditional division of Germany into principalities, lands and cities, which have all enjoyed a relative autonomy. (22–29)

At the time Evola was repeatedly on lecture tours in Germany, and he was observed by the SS, who kept a dossier on him in the Correspondence Administration Department of Himmler's personal staff. In this dossier document number AR-126 says of him:

> The ultimate and secret goal of Evola's theories and projects is most likely an *insurrection of the old aristocracy* against the modern world, which is foreign to the idea of nobility. Thus the first German impression, that he was a "reactionary Roman," was correct: His overall character is marked by the feudal aristocracy of old. His learnedness tends toward the dilettante and pseudoscientific.
>
> Hence it follows that National Socialism sees nothing to be gained by putting itself at the disposal of Baron Evola. His political plans for a Roman-Germanic Imperium are utopian in character and moreover likely to give rise to ideological entanglements. As Evola has also only been tolerated and hardly supported by Fascism, there is not even a tactical need to assist him from our side. It is therefore suggested:
>
> 1. Not to give any concrete support of Evola's present efforts to establish a secret international order and a special publication intended for that purpose.
> 2. To stop his public effectiveness in Germany, after this lecture series, without deploying any special measures.
> 3. To prevent him from advancing to leading departments in party and state.
> 4. To have his propagandistic activity in neighboring countries carefully observed.

In response to this report, a short letter of August 11, 1938 (letter no. AR-83), puts it laconically: "Reichsführer SS Heinrich Himmler has taken note of the opinions expressed in the report on Baron Evola's lectures and strongly agrees with the ideas and proposals set forth in the final paragraph."

To put a period to the question of Evola and Fascism there is an important impartial voice. Renzo de Felice, an authority on Fascism and Mussolini, writes in *Der Faschismus: Ein Interview* (Stuttgart, 1977): "Who is Evola? It was no accident that he was an outsider during the entire era of Fascism, that he never held a position in the Fascist Party . . . and the Fascists themselves, at least many of them, criticized and mistrusted him."

In Evola's comments on the racial question we must also make distinctions. In particular, he introduces a new three-part classification of race that distinguishes between race of body (which is the usual bare-bones notion of race), race of soul (the character, style of living, emotional attitude toward the environment and society), and race of spirit (type of religious experience and attitude toward "traditional" values). Therefore, as Mussolini expressed it on the occasion of an encounter with Evola, this classification was comparable to Plato's division of the population into three groups: the broad masses, the warriors, and the wise men.[7]

Because the race of the spirit is the one that is most difficult to understand and even Evola himself did not always define it the same way, we will quote from his article "L'equivoco del razzismo scientifico" (The Misunderstanding of Scientific Racism):

> We would like to make it clear that to us spirit means neither frivolous philosophy nor "Theosophy," nor mystical, devotional withdrawal from the world, but is simply what in better times the wellborn have always said were the marks of *race*: namely, straightforwardness, inner unity, character, courage, virtue, immediate and instant sensitivity for all values, which are present in every great human being and which, since they stand well beyond all chance-subjected reality, they also dominate. The current meaning of race, however, which differs from the above by being a construction of "science" and a piece out of the anthropological museum, we leave to the pseudointellectual bourgeoisie, which continues to indulge in the idols of nineteenth-century Positivism.[8]

Evola's views on race made him well known in Italy for the first time, but they also brought him into opposition with the government. No less than Guido Landra, the powerful leader of the race studies section of the Folk Culture Ministry, copublisher of the official newspaper *La difesa della razza* (The Defense of Race), and coauthor of the official Fascist "race manifesto" of 1938, criticized Evola sharply:

> And that is the weakest point in Evola's teaching: that an Aryan can have the soul of a Jew or vice-versa. And that therefore unfair measures could be taken against a Jew, even though he might possess the soul of an Aryan—this seems to us theoretically untenable. The practical acceptance of such a principle would have terrible consequences for racism, and certainly be of exclusive benefit to the Jew.[9]

As the leading theoretician of race, Landra roundly condemned Evola's views in the

---

7. Mussolini consulted Evola about counterbalancing the Nazi pure-body-and-blood racial idea with Evola's soul-spirit view, which was more in line with his own thinking.
8. *Vita Italiana* 30 (September 1942).
9. *Vita Italiana* 31 (February 1943): 151.

government paper: "[and] that article 'Misunderstanding of Scientific Racism' by Evola, is the outstanding document of and monument to the present campaign, which has been unleashed against racism in Italy."[10]

Evola's position on the merely biological understanding of race is evident in this quote from 1931:

> The error of certain extreme "racists" who believe that the return of a race to its ethnic purity *ipso facto* also means rebirth for a people, rests exactly on this: they deal with men as if they were dealing with the racially pure or pure-blood caste of a cat or a horse or a dog. The preservation or restoration of the racial unity (taking its narrowest meaning) can mean everything when you deal with an animal. But with men it is not so . . . it would be far too easy if the simple fact of belonging to one race that has been kept pure, already conferred, without being or doing anything else, some "quality" in the higher sense.[11]

Let us examine Evola and Judaism. On the one hand, there are really incriminating statements of Evola's concerning individual Jews and he even, among other things, republished the infamous *Protocols of the Elders of Zion,* whose spurious character he must have known. In this regard he is quite in step with the style of the times. Evola was judging thereby not the Jewish people as such, whose spiritual attainments, such as the Kabbalah, he esteemed highly, but only "Judaism" as a "spiritual direction" when he alleged that it was from that we had been led to the despised modern times.

But even here Evola does not go blindly ahead; rather, he makes a distinction. For example, in his booklet *Tre aspetti del problema ebraico* (Three Aspects of the Jewish Problem) he writes:

> . . . in the concrete course of development of modern civilization the Jew can be seen as a power, who collectively with others has worked to create our "civilized," rationalistic, scientistic, and mechanistic modern decadence, but on no account can he be marked as its single, far-reaching cause. To believe such a thing would be very stupid. The actual truth is that one would rather fight against personified powers than against abstract principles or universal phenomena, because you can also fight them practically. So the world had turned en masse against the Jew, as he seemed to show in his being a typical form that one finds, however, in much wider regions and even in nations that are practically untouched by Jewish immigration.[12]

10. *La difesa della razza* 6 (November 1942): 20.
11. *Vita Nova* (July 1931).
12. *Tre aspetti del problema ebraico* (Rome, 1936).

And in his introduction to the *Protocols of the Elders of Zion* he says (p. xix): "We must say at once that in this matter we personally cannot follow a certain fanatical anti-Semitism, especially that which sees the Jews everywhere as *deus ex machina* and by which one finally leads oneself into a kind of trap."

And in 1942 he wrote in his abovementioned article "L'equivoco del razzismo scientifico":

> For it is useless to try to conceal it from ourselves: this very day, people are asking themselves if, in the end, the Jew is not being presented as a kind of scapegoat, because there are so often cases, in which the qualities that our doctrine ascribes to the Jew, also impertinently pop up in 100% "aryan" stock-market speculators, profiteers, price-hikers, parvenus and—why not—even journalists, who do not hesitate to use the most twisted and treacherous means purely for polemics.

And there is also the impartial keynote of the historian of Fascism Renzo de Felice, who confirms the above:

> We see ourselves compelled to state in the cultural sector, as well as in the political, that from a certain point of view, the most worthy of respect were those who were confirmed racists. Thereby, however, we do not mean—let this be clearly understood—a Landra or a Cogni, those pallid and obsequious vestals of Nazi racism, but an Evola, an Acerbo, each of whom had his own way that he followed to the very end, in dignity and even in earnestness. And that, contrary to the many who chose the way of the lie, abusing and smoke-screening each and every cultural and moral value. . . . Evola for his part also completely refused any racial theorizing of a purely biological kind, which went so far as to draw to himself the attacks and sarcasms of a Landra, for example. This does not mean that the "spiritual" theory of race is acceptable, but it had at least the merit of not totally failing to see certain values, to refuse the German aberrations and the ones modeled after them and to try to keep racism on a plane of cultural problems worthy of the name.[13]

These few quotations should suffice to shed some light on Evola's outlook.

In 1945, while Evola was living in Vienna and working through the SS-confiscated archives and documents of Freemasonry and various magical groups, he was so severely wounded in a Russian bombing attack that he remained paralyzed to the end of his life. During air attacks, Evola had the habit of not going to the bomb

---

13. *Storia degli Ebrei Italiani sotto il Fascismo* (History of Italian Jews under Fascism [Milan, 1977]): 465.

shelters, but instead working in his office or walking about the streets of Vienna. He wanted, as he said, "calmly to question his fate."

After several years' hospital stay in Austria and then in Italy (the war had ended in the meantime) Evola returned to his native city, Rome. Apparently he left his dwelling only once and was promptly arrested by the police on charges of "glorification of Fascism" and "intellectually inciting secret combat troops" in 1951. After several months of examination, however, the trial ended with a complete acquittal. In his famous self-defense (published by the Fondazione Julius Evola in Rome, undated) he indicated that the same incriminating statements could also be found in Aristotle, Plato, and Dante, and that they would also have to be charged.

Nevertheless, he still continued to be visited by right-wing young people and addressed as "maestro." But Evola always declined to occupy himself with everyday politics and concerned himself only with fundamental principles. His late work, *Cavalcare la tigre* (Rome and Milan, 1961), even calls for an *apoliteia*—for an attitude that goes against politics by placing itself spiritually above the political. Evola's later books include his work on original Buddhism, *The Doctrine of Awakening* (1943; first English edition, London, 1951), a strongly ascetic work written amid the chaos of World War II that speaks for his withdrawal from the politics of that time. His *Metaphysics of Sex* appeared in Rome in 1958. A critical analysis of Fascism and Nazism from the point of view of the right, *Il Fascismo* (Rome, 1964), a book on the German poet Ernst Jünger, some collections of essays, and finally his autobiography, *Il cammino del cinabro* (Milan, 1963), mark the limit of his work.

In this introduction, although we have been able to provide only a few details, it can be seen than an evaluation of Evola, who published in all twenty-five books, approximately three hundred longer essays, and more than one thousand newspaper and magazine articles, is not an easy task. Lately it has been pointed out, for example by Giano Accame in *Il Fascismo immenso e rosso* (Rome, 1990), that Evola's thinking bears a strong resemblance to the fundamental observations of Herbert Marcuse (Evola was much earlier, however), which may explain the new interest in Evola in leftist circles. In recent times a number of dissertations in various universities in Italy and France have also been written about him.

The Austrian poet Joseph Roth described Franz Grillparzer as "an anarchistic individualistic reactionary." By way of conclusion, I would like to suggest the same as a description that is also quite fitting for Evola.

Translated from the German by E. E. Rehmus

Translator's Preface

*R*ivolta contro il mondo moderno was first published in 1934, and followed by later editions in 1951 and in 1970. Two works with similar themes that influenced Evola were Oswald Spengler's *Decline of the West* (1918) and René Guénon's *The Crisis of the Modern World* (1927), both of which Evola translated into Italian.

Evola agreed with Spengler's criticism of the progressive and evolutionist myth and with his rejection of the modern "linear" understanding of history. Spengler argued that there is no such thing as one global civilization, but rather a plurality of civilizations, following one another according to the cyclical pattern of birth-growth-decline. Spengler often spoke of the aging of cultures in terms of the succession of the four seasons; the winter of our contemporary Western world is characterized by "pure intellectuality," by the advent of machinery, the power of money, the government of the masses, growing skepticism and materialism. Evola, who had adopted the cyclical view of history proper to Tradition, agreed with Spengler's assessment of our times but criticized him for failing to recognize the metaphysical nature of the cyclical laws and for lacking, like Nietzsche, any transcendent and traditional reference points. Evola also did not deem satisfactory Spengler's distinction between culture and civilization, the former being the early stage, the latter being the crepuscular phase of a historical cycle; in *Revolt Against the Modern World* Evola emphasized the irreconcilable antithesis, or rather the dualism between the two terms.

René Guénon's *The Crisis of the Modern World* was a very important influence on Evola's *Revolt*. In his work, Guénon discussed the relationship between action and contemplation, criticized democracy and individualism, and argued that we are living in the "Dark Age" (Kali Yuga). Evola picked up these themes and developed them further, supplying several historical examples to back up his thesis. While Evola is undoubtedly indebted to Guénon for several seminal ideas, it would be wrong to assume that he is just the Italian epigone of Guénon, with whom he disagreed on matters such as the correct relationship between action and contemplation, the role

of Catholicism as a future catalyst of traditionalist forces, and the hierarchical relationship between priesthood and regality in traditional civilizations.

In *Revolt Against the Modern World* Evola intended to offer some guidelines[1]
for a morphology of civilizations and for a philosophy of history, as well as to advocate a psychologically and intellectually detached stance toward the modern world,
which he regarded as decadent. In *Revolt* the reader will find strong criticism of the
notions of equality and democracy, which in turn led Evola to praise the role that the
caste system, feudalism, monarchy, and aristocracy have played in history. Regardless of whether one agrees with these views or not, the fact remains that a mere
sociopolitical assessment of *Revolt* would totally miss the essence and the scope of
Evola's thought.

The content of this text, as well as the rest of Evola's work, have been reviewed
mainly from a political perspective.[2] Unfortunately, as I have said elsewhere,[3] the
spiritual and metaphysical foundations of Evola's thought still need to be subjected
to a thorough review. Evola is not first and foremost a right-wing, reactionary political thinker, but rather a leading representative of that Esoteric Spirituality that has
always existed in many forms in or alongside every civilization, age and religious
tradition; therefore, when Evola deals with socio-political issues, he is just following
the premises of his metaphysical and religious convictions, and not the other way
around. This is why in order to understand Evola fully it is first necessary to confront
his suggestive religious thought. It has rightly been said:

> Esotericism is present today more than ever. In the modern era, its te-
> nacious permanence appears as a counterpart to our scientific and secu-
> larized vision of the world, but it would be simplistic and mistaken to
> explain its longevity by a need to react against the reigning episteme.
> More than a reaction, it is perhaps one of the possible forms assumed
> by one of the two poles of the human spirit in order to actualize itself,

1. Evola did *not* mean to engage in an exhaustive interpretation of cultures as Spengler did in his *Decline of
   the West* or like Ulick Varange in his unsystematic and obscurely written *Imperium* (1948). In his autobiography Evola wrote: "Naturally, in order to give an exhaustive treatment to the subject matter contained
   in *Rivolta*, each of the topics would have deserved to be discussed in a separate book rather than being
   summarily outlined in those little chapters." *Il cammino del cinabro* (Milan, 1963), 127.
2. See for instance the essay by Anna Jellamo, "Julius Evola, il pensatore della tradizione" in F. Ferraresi
   ed., *La destra radicale* (Milan, 1984), 214–47; the review by Furio Jesi, *Cultura di Destra* (Milan, 1979),
   89–102; Italo Mancini, *Il pensiero negativo e la nuova destra* (Milan, 1983); the impartial review by
   Richard Drake in *The Revolutionary Mystique and Terrorism in Contemporary Italy* (Bloomington, Ind.,
   1989), 116–34.
3. Julius Evola, *The Yoga of Power*, trans. Guido Stucco (Rochester, Vt., 1983), ix. For a more detailed
   account of Evola's life and works see Richard Drake, "Julius Evola and the Ideological Origins of the
   Radical Right in Contemporary Italy," in *Political Violence and Terror: Motifs and Motivations*, ed. Peter
   Merkl (Berkeley and Los Angeles, 1986), 61–89.

namely mythic thought, the other pole being what is called rational thought, which in the West is modeled on a logic of the Aristotelian type.[4]

The reader will notice that spiritual and religious themes are found throughout the book, such as a critique of theism and of Christianity, which Evola had formulated a few years earlier in a harsher tone in his *Imperialismo Pagano* (1927); the endorsement of the cyclical view of time and the rejection of the Judeo-Christian linear view[5]; the relationship between action and contemplation; views on the afterlife,[6] initiation, and asceticism; the clash between the spiritual and religious beliefs of various civilizations (it does not take long to find out where Evola's sympathy lies); transcendence; and Tradition.

Evola's negative assessment of empirical reality and his intense dislike of common man (the charges of "misogyny," "misanthropy," and "solipsism,"[7] are just labels behind which is usually found a psychological attitude rather than an articulated metaphysical weltanschauung such as Evola's, as his readers themselves will see) and of ordinary, everyday life, led him to espouse what Italo Mancini rebuffed as "ontological classism" and *contemptus mundi,*[8] which explains why his political view are so unpopular and controversial. According to Evola, human beings are fundamentally and inherently unequal; they do not have, nor should they enjoy the same dignity and rights and, therefore, a sociopolitical hierarchy is best suited to express the differentiation between human beings. Much could and ought to be said against this view.[9] In fact, many people will undoubtedly frown upon what they regard as authoritarian, fascist, and reactionary views. But when Evola writes: "there is a mortal nature and an immortal one; there is the superior realm of 'being' and the inferior realm of 'becoming,'"[10] and when he talks about "absolute" values, he is

---

4. A. Faivre & J. Needleman, eds., *Modern Esoteric Spirituality,* vol. 21 in the series *World Spirituality: An Encyclopedic History of the Religious Quest* (New York, 1992), xiv. For a positive assessment of the role of esoteric culture in the West, see E. Tiryakian, "Toward the Sociology of Esoteric Culture," *American Journal of Sociology* 78 (1971): 491–512.

5. The Judeo-Christian worldview opposes the cyclical view of time because it firmly believes that the history of the world is framed within two unrepeatable events, namely, Creation and Judgment.

6. The afterlife was truly one of Evola's main interests. He outlined his views on the matter in several of his works, such as *Introduzione alla magia* and in the essays he published in an Italian Baptist periodical, *Bilychnis,* between 1925 and 1931; see Julius Evola, *I saggi di Bilychnis* (Padua, 1970).

7. For the way in which Evola developed his philosophical views after overcoming the solipsism ("a rather inadequate term") of Idealist epistemology, see his *Il cammino del cinabro* (Milan, 1963), 39–62.

8. Italo Mancini, *Il pensiero negativo e la nuova destra,* 57–58.

9. See the brilliant analysis by Tomislav Sunic, *Against Democracy and Equality: The European New Right* (New York, 1987).

10. See p. 3.

upholding the primacy of Being, just as the pre-Socratic school of the Eleatics, Plato, Plotinus, and medieval Jewish, Christian, and Muslim theology, not to mention many schools of Hinduism and of Buddhism, did before him. And by openly professing a *contemptus mundi,* he is endorsing the worldview of some of the ascetical paths to enlightenment of the major world religions. Also, if his anthropology upholds a nega- tive and unfavorable view of mankind, is that also not found in Sartre's play *No Exit* ("Hell is other people"), in much Protestant theology (especially the neo-orthodox views formulated by Karl Barth in his *Epistle to the Romans*) and in the Buddhist view of human nature?[11] Thus, if Evola is "wrong" or guilty of antisocial opinions, he seems to be in good company.

I think that the peculiarity of *Revolt* lies in three features: rejection of dialogue; affirmation of traditional (not in the usual, conservative sense of the word) and abso- lute values; and bi-polar thinking (not dualism).

First, by rejecting dialogue with modernity and with fellow human beings, and by denying that dialogue is a means to arrive at the truth (the opposite spirit from that which animated Lacordaire, a follower of Voltaire who eventually became a Do- minican friar and who said: "What really matters to me is not to prove my opponent wrong, but to join him in a higher, encompassing truth"), Evola shifts the focus from sociopolitical affairs and interpersonal relationships back to self-questioning ("The unexamined life is not worth living") and to the cultivation of the inner life, away from life's busy and noisy crossroads.[12] This shift is likely to produce an indignant chorus of protests from the ranks of liberal and humanist thinkers in the theological, political, and social arenas: "Immoral!" "Selfish!" "Irresponsible individualism!" In accordance with Socrates' implication that the cultivation of one's soul *($ \dot{\epsilon}\pi\iota\mu\dot{\epsilon}\lambda\epsilon\iota\alpha$ $\psi\upsilon\chi\hat{\eta}\varsigma$)* is man's chief duty,[13] Evola's entire literary production may be regarded as a quest for, and as an exposition of, the means employed in Western and Eastern traditions to accomplish such a noble task.

Secondly, it is refreshing to hear in our day and age somebody saying *apertis verbis,* "This is the truth," or "These are absolute values," when cultural and ethical relativism, as well as philosophical and religious pluralism, have become the un- touchable dogmas and the hermeneutical a priori in contemporary academic dis- course. Evola's critics may well disagree, but today there is much hunger for solid,

---

11. For an exposition of the doctrines of early Buddhism, see Evola's *The Doctrine of Awakening,* trans. H. E. Musson. (London, 1951; reprint forthcoming from Inner Traditions).

12. See "Of the Flies of the Market-Place," in Nietzsche's *Thus Spoke Zarathustra,* trans. J. Hollingdale (New York, 1961), 78–81.

13. "Most excellent man, are you not ashamed to care for the acquisition of wealth and for reputation and honor, when you neither care nor take any thought for wisdom and truth and the perfection of your soul?" *Apology* 29E.

unshakable beliefs, for "objectivity" (to use a word that is much discounted today), and for foundationalist thinking, whether the "high priests" of progress and of dialogue like it or not.[14] Evola's *Revolt* may be food for such hungry souls.

Finally, Evola's metaphysics, which was greatly influenced by German Idealism (which Evola claimed to have successfully overcome), is based on the notion of "immanent transcendence." This view is opposed to any kind of religious dualism such as that of transcendence vs. immanence, heaven vs. hell, good vs. evil. Instead, Evola espouses a phenomenological dualism that could be characterized as "bipolarism" and in which Tradition is contrasted with modernity, solar civilizations and spirituality with lunar civilization and spirituality, the aristocratic world and values with the plebeian world and values, the caste system with the democratic system, masculine spirituality with feminine spirituality, and enlightenment and liberation with rebirth and permanence in *saṁsāra*.

The reader of *Revolt* may or may not agree with the theses contained in this book, but one thing must be acknowledged: Evola's weltanschauung is coherent and holistic. Though it may not be "prophetic," it is an act of remembrance: "Remember that I have remembered / and pass on the tradition."[15]

Dept. of Theological Studies
Saint Louis University
Saint Louis, Missouri

14. For a critique of contemporary cultural relativism, see Allan Bloom, *The Closing of the American Mind*, (New York, 1987).
15. Ezra Pound, *Cantos*. (New York, 1970), Canto LVXXX, p. 506.

Foreword

For quite some time now it has become almost commonplace to talk about the "decline of the West" and the crisis of contemporary civilization, its dangers, and the havoc it has caused. Also, new prophecies concerning Europe's or the world's future are being formulated, and various appeals to "defend" the West are made from various quarters.

In all this concern there is generally very little that goes beyond the amateurishness of intellectuals. It would be all too easy to show how often these views lack true principles, and how what is being rejected is often still unconsciously retained by those who wish to react, and how for the most part people do not really know what they want, since they obey irrational impulses. This is especially true on the practical plane where we find violent and chaotic expressions typical of a "protest" that wishes to be global, though it is inspired only by the contingent and terminal forms of the latest civilization.

Therefore, even though it would be rash to see in these phenomena of protest something positive, they nevertheless have the value of a symptom; these phenomena clearly illustrate that beliefs that were once taken for granted today no longer are, and that the idyllic perspectives of "evolutionism" have come of age. An unconscious defense mechanism, however, prevents people from going beyond a certain limit; this mechanism is similar to the instinct found in sleepwalkers who lack the perception of height as they amble about. Some pseudointellectual and irrational reactions seem to have no other effect than to distract modern humans and prevent them from becoming fully aware of that global and dreadful perspective according to which the modern world appears as a lifeless body falling down a slope, which nothing can possibly stop.

There are diseases that incubate for a long time and become manifest only when their hidden work has almost ended. This is the case of man's fall from the ways of what he once glorified as civilization par excellence. Though modern men[1] have come to perceive the West's bleak future only recently, there are causes that have been active for centuries that have contributed to spiritual and material degeneration. These causes have not only taken away from most people the possibility of revolt and the return to normalcy and health, but most of all, they have taken away the ability to understand what true normalcy and health really mean.

Thus, no matter how sincere the intention animating those who today attempt to revolt and to sound the alarm may be, we should not cherish false hopes concerning the outcome. It is not easy to realize how deep we must dig before we hit the only root from which the contemporary, negative forms have sprung as natural and necessary consequences. The same holds true for those forms that even the boldest spirits do not cease to presuppose and to employ in their ways of thinking, feeling, and acting. Some people "react"; others "protest." How could it be otherwise considering the hopeless features of contemporary society, morality, politics, and culture? And yet these are only "reactions" and not *actions,* or positive movements, that originate from the inner dimension and testify to the possession of a foundation, a principle, or a center. In the West, too many adaptations and "reactions" have taken place. Experience has shown that nothing that truly matters can be achieved in this way. What is really needed is not to toss back and forth in a bed of agony, but to awaken and get up.

Things have reached such a low point nowadays that I wonder who would be capable of assessing the modern world as a whole, rather than just some of its particular aspects (such as "technocracy" or the "consumer society"), and of understanding its ultimate meaning. This would be the real starting point.

In order for this to happen, it is necessary to leave the deceptive and magical "circle" and be able to conceive *something else,* to acquire new eyes and new ears in order to perceive things that have become invisible and mute with the passing of time. It is only by going back to the meanings and the visions that existed before the establishment of the causes of the present civilization that it is possible to achieve an absolute reference point—the key for the real understanding of all modern deviations—and at the same time to find a strong defense and an unbreakable line of resistance for those who, despite everything, will still be standing. The only thing that matters today is the activity of those who can "ride the wave" and remain firm in their principles, unmoved by any concessions and indifferent to the fevers, the convulsions, the superstitions, and the prostitutions that characterize modern

---

1. I say among "modern men" since the idea of a *downfall* and a progressive abandonment of a higher type of existence, as well as the knowledge of even tougher times in the future for the human races, were well known to traditional antiquity.

generations. The only thing that matters is the silent endurance of a few, whose impassible presence as "stone guests" helps to create new relationships, new distances, new values, and helps to construct a pole that, although it will certainly not prevent this world inhabited by the distracted and restless from being what it is, will still help to transmit to someone the sensation of the truth—a sensation that could become for them the principle of a liberating crisis.

Within the limits of my possibilities, this book hopes to be a contribution to such a task. Its main thesis is the idea of the decadent nature of the modern world. Its purpose is to present evidence supporting this idea through reference to the spirit of universal civilization, on the ruins of which everything that is modern has arisen; this will serve as the basis of every possibility and as the categorical legitimization of a revolt, since only then will it become clear what one is reacting *against,* but also and foremost, *in what name.*

By way of introduction I will argue that no idea is as absurd as the idea of progress, which together with its corollary notion of the superiority of modern civilization, has created its own "positive" alibis by falsifying history, by insinuating harmful myths in people's minds, and by proclaiming itself sovereign at the crossroads of the plebeian ideology from which it originated. How low has mankind gone if it is ready and willing to apotheosize a *cadaverous wisdom?* For this is how we should regard the perspective that refuses to view modern and "new" man as decrepit, defeated, and crepuscular man, but which rather glorifies him as the overcomer, the justifier, and as the only really living being. Our contemporaries must truly have become blind if they really thought they could measure everything by their standards and consider their own civilization as privileged, as the one to which the history of the world was preordained and outside of which there is nothing but barbarism, darkness, and superstition.

It must be acknowledged that before the early and violent shakings through which the inner disintegration of the Western world has become evident, even in a material way, the plurality of civilizations (and therefore the relativity of the modern one) no longer appears, as it once used to, as a heterodox and extravagant idea. And yet this is not enough. It is also necessary to be able to recognize that modern civilization is not only liable to disappear without a trace, like many others before it, but also that it belongs to a type, the disappearance of which has merely a contingent value when compared with the order of the "things-that-are" and of every civilization founded on such an order. Beyond the mere and secular idea of the "relativism of civilizations," it is necessary to recognize a "dualism of civilizations." The considerations that follow will constantly revolve around the opposition between the modern and the traditional world, and between modern and traditional man; such an opposition is *ideal* (that is, morphological and metaphysical) and both beyond and more than a merely historical opposition.

As far as the historical aspect is concerned, it is necessary to indicate the width of the horizons confronting us. In an antitraditional sense, the first forces of decadence began to be tangibly manifested between the eighth and the sixth centuries B.C., as can be concluded from the sporadic and characteristic alterations in the forms of the social and spiritual life of many peoples that occurred during this time. Thus, the limit corresponds to so-called historical times, since according to many people, whatever occurred before this period no longer constitutes the object of "history." History is replaced by legends and myths and thus no hard facts can be established, only conjectures. The fact remains, however, that according to traditional teachings, the abovementioned period merely inherited the effects of even more remote causes; during this period, what was presaged was the *critical* phase of an even longer cycle known in the East as the "Dark Age," in the classical world as the "Iron Age," and in the Nordic sagas, as the "Age of the Wolf."[2] In any event, during historical times and in the Western world, a second and more visible phase corresponds to the fall of the Roman Empire and to the advent of Christianity. A third phase began with the twilight of the feudal and imperial world of the European Middle Ages, reaching a decisive point with the advent of humanism and of the Reformation. From that period on, the forces that once acted in an isolated and underground fashion have emerged and led every European trend in material and spiritual life, as well as in individual and collective life in a downward trajectory, thus establishing one phase after another of what is usually referred to as the "modern world." From then on, the process has become increasingly rapid, decisive, and universal, forming a dreadful current by which every residual trace of a different type of civilization is visibly destined to be swept away, thus ending a cycle and sealing the collective fate of millions.

This is the case as far as the historical aspect is concerned, and yet this aspect is totally relative. If everything that is "historical" is included in what is "modern," then to go beyond the modern world (which is the only way to reveal its meaning), is essentially a process of traveling beyond the limits that most people assign to "history." It is necessary to understand that in this direction, we no longer find anything that is susceptible again to becoming "history." The fact that positive inquiry was not able to make history beyond a certain period is not at all a fortuitous circumstance, nor is it due to a mere uncertainty concerning sources and dates or to the lack of

2. R. Guénon, *La Crise du monde moderne* (Paris, 1927), 21.

vestigial traces. In order to understand the spiritual background typical of every nonmodern civilization, it is necessary to retain the idea that the opposition between historical times and "prehistoric" or "mythological" times is not the *relative* opposition proper to two homogeneous parts of the same time frame, but rather the *qualitative* and *substantial* opposition between times (or experiences of time) that are *not* of the same kind. Traditional man did not have the same experience of time as modern man; he had a supertemporal sense of time and in this sensation lived every form of his world. Thus, the modern researchers of "history" at a given point encounter an interruption of the series and an incomprehensible gap, beyond which they cannot construct any "certain" and meaningful historical theory; they can only rely upon fragmentary, external, and often contradictory elements—unless they radically change their method and mentality.

On the basis of these premises, the opposition of the traditional world to the modern world is also an ideal one. The character of temporality and of "historicity" is essentially inherent only to one of the two terms of this opposition, while the other term, which refers to the whole body of traditional civilizations, is characterized by the feeling of what is beyond time, namely, by a contact with metaphysical reality that bestows upon the experience of time a very different, "mythological" form based on rhythm and space rather than on chronological time.[3] Traces of this qualitatively different experience of time still exist as degenerated residues among some so-called primitive populations. Having lost that contact by being caught in the illusion of a pure flowing, a pure escaping, a yearning that pushes one's goal further and further away, and being caught in a process that cannot and does not intend to be satisfied in any achievement as it is consumed in terms of "history" and "becoming"—this is indeed one of the fundamental characteristics of the modern world and the limit that separates two eras, not only in a historical sense but most of all in an ideal, metaphysical, and morphological sense.

Therefore, the fact that civilizations of the traditional type are found in the past becomes merely accidental: the modern world and the traditional world may be regarded as two universal types and as two a priori categories of civilization. Nevertheless, that accidental circumstance allows us to state with good reason that wherever a civilization is manifested that has as its center and substance the temporal element, there we will find a resurgence, in a more or less different form, of the same attitudes, values, and forces that have defined the modern era in the specific sense of the term; and that wherever a civilization is manifested that has as its center

---

3. J. Evola, *L'arco e la clava* (Milan, 1968), chap. 1.

and substance the supernatural element, there we will find a resurgence, in more or less different forms, of the same meanings, values, and forces that have defined archaic types of civilization. This should clarify the meaning of what I have called the "dualism of civilization" in relation to the terms employed ("modern" and "traditional") and also prevent any misunderstandings concerning the "traditionalism" that I advocate. "These did not just happen once, but they have always been" (ταῦτα δὲ ἐμενετο, μὲν οὐδὲ ποτε ἔστι δὲ ἀεί). The reason behind all my references to nonmodern forms, institutions, and knowledge consists in the fact that they are more transparent symbols, closer approximations, and better examples of what is prior and superior to time and to history, and thus to both yesterday and tomorrow; it is these alone that can produce a real renewal and a "new and perennial life" in those who are still capable of receiving it. Only those capable of this reception may be totally fearless and able to see in the fate of the modern world nothing different or more tragic than the vain arising and consequential dissolution of a thick fog, which cannot alter or affect in any way the free heaven.

So much for the fundamental thesis. At this point, by way of introduction, I would like briefly to explain the "method" I have employed.

The above remarks will suffice to show how little I value all of what in recent times has officially been regarded as "historical science" in matters of religion, ancient institutions, and traditions, nor do I need refer to what I will say later concerning the origin, the scope, and the meaning of modern "knowledge." I want to make it clear that I do not want to have anything to do with this order of things, as well as with any other that originates from modern mentality; and moreover, that I consider the so-called scientific and positive perspective, with all its empty claims of competence and of monopoly, as a display of ignorance in the best of cases. I say "in the best of cases": I certainly do not deny that from the detailed studies of the "scholars" of different disciplines what may emerge is useful (though unrefined) material that is often necessary to those who do not have other sources of information or who do not have the time or intention to dedicate themselves to gather and to examine what they need from other domains. And yet, at the same time, I am still of the opinion that wherever the "historical" and "scientific" methods of modern man are applied to traditional civilizations, other than in the coarser aspect of traces and witnesses, the results are almost always distortions that destroy the spirit, limit and alter the subject matter, and lead into the blind alleys of alibis created by the prejudices of the modern mentality as it defends and asserts itself in every domain. Very rarely is this destructive and distorting work casual; it almost always proceeds, even though indirectly, from hidden influences and from suggestions that the "scientific" spirits, considering their mentality, are the last to know.

The order of things that I will mainly deal with in this present work, generally speaking, is that in which all materials having a "historical" and "scientific" value are the ones that matter the least; conversely, all the mythical, legendary, and epic elements denied historical truth and demonstrative value acquire here a superior validity and become the source for a more real and certain knowledge. This is precisely the boundary that separates the traditional doctrine from profane culture. In reference to ancient times this does not apply to the forms of a "mythological" or superhistorical life such as the traditional one; while from the perspective of "science" what matters in a myth is whatever historical elements may be extracted from it. From the perspective that I adopt, what matters in history are all the mythological elements it has to offer, or all the myths that enter into its web, as integrations of the "meaning" of history itself. Not only the Rome of legends speaks clearer words than the historical Rome, but even the sagas of Charlemagne reveal more about the meaning of the king of the Franks than the positive chronicles and documents of that time, and so on.

The scientific "anathemas" in regard to this approach are well known: "Arbitrary!" "Subjective!" "Preposterous!" In my perspective there is no arbitrariness, subjectivity, or fantasy, just like there is no objectivity and scientific causality the way modern men understand them. All these notions are unreal; all these notions are outside Tradition. Tradition begins wherever it is possible to rise above these notions by achieving a superindividual and nonhuman perspective; thus, I will have a minimal concern for debating and "demonstrating." The truths that may reveal the world of Tradition are not those that can be "learned" or "discussed"; either they are or they are not.[4] It is only possible to *remember* them, and this happens when one becomes free of the obstacles represented by various human constructions, first among which are all the results and the methods of specialized researchers; in other words, one becomes free of these encumbrances when the capacity for *seeing* from that nonhuman perspective, which is the same as the traditional perspective, has been attained. This is one of the essential "protests" that should be made by those who really oppose the modern world.

Let me repeat that in every ancient persuasion, traditional truths have always been regarded as *nonhuman*. Any consideration from a nonhuman perspective, which

---

4. "Those who are skilled in the Tao do not dispute about it; the disputatious are not skilled in it." *Tao te Ching*, 81. See also the traditional Aryan expressions concerning the texts that are "impossible to master and impossible to measure . . ." Further on, we read "The teachings differing from that of the Vedas that spring up and die out bear no fruit and are false, because they are of a modern date." W. Doniger and B. Smith, trans., *The Laws of Manu* (New York, 1991), 12.94.96 [also referred to in the text as the *Manudharmaśāstra*].

is "objective" in a transcendent sense, is a traditional consideration that should be made to correspond to the traditional world. Universality is typical of this world; the axiom, *"quod ubique, quod ab omnibus et quod semper"* characterizes it. Inherent to the idea of "traditional civilization" is the idea of an equivalence or homology of its various forms realized in space and time. The correspondences may not be noticeable from the outside; one may be taken aback by the diversity of several possible and yet equivalent expressions; in some case the correspondences are respected in the spirit, in other cases only formally and nominally; in some cases there may be more complete applications of principles, in others, more fragmentary ones; in some there are legendary expressions, in others, historical expressions—and yet there is always something constant and central that characterizes the same world and the same man and determines an identical opposition vis-à-vis everything that is modern.

Those who begin from a particular traditional civilization and are able to integrate it by freeing it from its historical and contingent aspects, and thus bring back the generative principles to the metaphysical plane where they exist in a pure state, so to speak—they cannot help but recognize these same principles behind the different expressions of other equally traditional civilizations. It is in this way that a sense of certainty and of transcendent and universal objectivity is innerly established, that nothing could ever destroy, and that could not be reached by any other means.

In the course of this book I will refer to various Eastern and Western traditions, choosing those that exemplify through a clearer and more complete expression the same spiritual principle or phenomenon. The method that I use has as little in common with the eclecticism or comparative methodology of modern scholars as the method of parallaxes, which is used to determine the exact position of a star by reference to how it appears from different places. Also, this method has as little in common with eclecticism—to borrow an image of Guénon's—as the multilingual person's choice of the language that offers the best expression to a given thought.[5] Thus, what I call "traditional method" is usually characterized by a double principle: ontologically and objectively by the principle of correspondence, which ensures an essential and functional correlation between analogous elements, presenting them as simple homologous forms of the appearance of a central and unitary meaning; and epistemologically and subjectively by the generalized use of the principle of induction, which is here understood as a discursive approximation of a spiritual intuition, in which what is realized is the integration and the unification of the diverse elements encountered in the same one meaning and in the same one principle.

5. R. Guénon, *Le Symbolisme de la croix* (Paris, 1931), 10.

In this way I will try to portray the sense of the world of Tradition as a unity and as a universal type capable of creating points of reference and of evaluation different from the ones to which the majority of the people in the West have passively and semiconsciously become accustomed; this sense can also lead to the establishment of the foundations for an eventual revolt (not a polemical, but real and positive one) of the spirit against the modern world.

In this regard I hope that those who are accused of being anachronistic utopians unaware of "historical reality" will remain unmoved in the realization that the apologists of what is "concrete" should not be told: "Stop!" or "Turn around!" or "Wake up!" but rather:

> Go ahead! Achieve all your goals! Break all the dams! Faster! You are unbound. Go ahead and fly with faster wings, with an ever greater pride for your achievements, with your conquests, with your empires, with your democracies! The pit must be filled; there is a need for fertilizer for the new tree that will grow out of your collapse.[6]

In the present work I will limit myself to offering guiding principles, the application and the adequate development of which would require as many volumes as there are chapters; thus, I will point out only the essential elements. The reader may wish to use them as the basis for further ordering and deepening the subject matter of each of the domains dealt with from the traditional point of view by giving to them an extension and a development that the economy of the present work does not allow for.

In the first part I will trace directly a kind of doctrine of the categories of the traditional spirit; I will indicate the main principles according to which the life of the man of Tradition was manifested. Here the term "category" is employed in the sense of a normative and a priori principle. The forms and the meanings indicated should not be regarded as "realities" proper, inasmuch as they are or have been "realities," but rather as ideas that must determine and shape reality and life, their value being independent from the measure in which their realization can be ascertained, since it will never be perfect. This should eliminate the misunderstandings and the objections of those who claim that historical reality hardly justifies the forms and the meanings (more on which later). Such a claim could eventually be validated without reaching the conclusion that in this regard, everything is reduced to make-believe, utopias, idealizations, or illusions. The main forms of the traditional life as categories enjoy the same dignity as ethical principles: they are valuable in and of them-

6. G. De Giorgio, "Crollano le torri," *La Torre*, no. 1 (1930): 5.

selves and only require to be acknowledged and willed so that man may hold steadily to them and with them measure himself and life, just like traditional man has always and everywhere done. Thus, the dimension of "history" and of "reality" has here merely an illustrative and evocative scope for values that even from this point of view, may not be any less actual today and tomorrow than what they could have been yesterday.

The historical element will be emphasized in the second part of this work, which will consider the genesis of the modern world and the processes that have led to its development. Since the reference point, however, will always be the traditional world in its quality as symbolical, superhistorical, and normative reality, and likewise, since the method employed will be that which attempts to understand what acted and still acts behind the two superficial dimensions of historical phenomena (space and time), the final outcome will be the outline of a metaphysics of history.

In both parts I think that sufficient elements have been given to those who, today or tomorrow, already are or will be capable of an awakening.

PART ONE

The World of Tradition

The skillful masters (of the Tao) in old times, with a subtle and exquisite penetration, comprehended its mysteries and were deep (also) so as to elude men's knowledge . . . Shrinking, looked they like those who wade through a stream in winter; irresolute, like those who are afraid of all around them; . . . evanescent like ice that is melting away; unpretentious like wood that has not been fashioned into anything; vacant like a valley, and dull like muddy water. . . .

Who can make the muddy water clear? Who can secure the condition of rest? . . .

They who preserve this method of the Tao do not wish to be full of themselves. It is through their not being full of themselves that they can afford to seem worn and not appear to be new and complete.

—*Tao te Ching,* 15
(from R. Van Over, *Chinese Mystics*)

1

The Beginning

In order to understand both the spirit of Tradition and its antithesis, modern civilization, it is necessary to begin with the fundamental doctrine of the *two natures*. According to this doctrine there is a physical order of things and a metaphysical one; there is a mortal nature and an immortal one; there is the superior realm of "being" and the inferior realm of "becoming." Generally speaking, there is a visible and tangible dimension and, prior to and beyond it, an invisible and intangible dimension that is the support, the source, and true life of the former.

Anywhere in the world of Tradition, both East and West and in one form or another, this knowledge (not just a mere "theory") has always been present as an unshakable axis around which everything revolved. Let me emphasize the fact that it was *knowledge* and not "theory." As difficult as it may be for our contemporaries to understand this, we must start from the idea that the man of Tradition was aware of the existence of a dimension of being much wider than what our contemporaries experience and call "reality." Nowadays, after all, reality is understood only as something strictly encompassed within the world of physical bodies located in space and time. Certainly, there are those who believe in something beyond the realm of phenomena. When these people admit the existence of something else, however, they are always led to this conclusion by a scientific hypothesis or law, or by a speculative idea, or by a religious dogma; they cannot escape such an intellectual limitation. Through his practical and immediate experiences, modern man, no matter how deep his "materialistic" or "spiritual" beliefs may be, develops an understanding of reality only in relation to the world of physical bodies and always under the influence of his direct and immediate experiences. This is the real materialism for which our contemporaries should be reproached. All the other versions of materialism that are formulated in scientific or in philosophical terms are only secondary phenomena. The worst type of materialism, therefore, is not a matter of an opinion or of a "theory," but it consists in the fact that man's *experience* no longer extends to nonphysical realities. Thus, the majority of the intellectual revolts against "materialistic" views are only vain reactions against the latest peripheral effects stemming from remote and deeper causes. These causes, incidentally, arose in a different historical context from the one in which the "theories" were formulated.

The experience of traditional man used to reach well beyond these limits, as in the case of some so-called primitive people, among whom we still find today a faint echo of spiritual powers from ancient times. In traditional societies the "invisible" was an element as real, if not *more* real, than the data provided by the physical senses. Every aspect of the individual and of the social life of the people belonging to these societies was influenced by this experience.

On the one hand, from the perspective of Tradition, what today is usually referred to as "reality," was only a species of a much wider genus. On the other hand, invisible realities were not automatically equated with the "supernatural." Traditionally speaking, the notion of "nature" did not correspond merely to the world of bodies and of visible forms—the object of research of contemporary, secularized science—but on the contrary, it corresponded essentially to part of an invisible reality. The ancients had the sense of a dark netherworld, populated by obscure and ambiguous forces of every kind (the demonic soul of nature, which is the essential substratum of all nature's forms and energies) that was opposed to the superrational and sidereal brightness of a higher region. Moreover, the term *nature* traditionally included everything that is merely human, since what is human cannot escape birth and death, impermanence, dependence, and transformation, all of which characterize the inferior region. By definition, "that which is" has nothing to do with human and temporal affairs or situations, as in the saying: "The race of men is one thing, and the race of the gods is quite another." This saying retains its validity even though people once thought that the reference to a superior, otherworldly domain could effectively lead the integration and the purification of the human element in the direction of the nonhuman dimension. Only the nonhuman dimension constituted the essence and the goal of any truly traditional civilization.

The world of being and the world of becoming affect things, demons, and men. Every hypostatic representation of these two regions, whether expressed in astral, mythological, theological, or religious terms, reminded traditional man of the existence of the two states; it also represented a symbol to be resolved into an inner experience, or at least in the foreboding of an inner experience. Thus, in Hindu, and especially in Buddhist tradition, the idea of *saṁsāra*—the current that dominates and carries away every form of the inferior world—refers to an understanding of life as blind yearning and as an irrational identification with impermanent aggregates. Likewise, Hellenism saw nature as the embodiment of the eternal state of "deprivation"

4

of those realities that, by virtue of having their own principle and cause outside of themselves, flow and run away indefinitely *(ἀεὶ ρεοντα)*. In their becoming, these realities reveal a primordial and radical lack of direction and purpose and a perennial limitation.[1] According to these traditions, "matter" and "becoming" express the reality that acts in a being as an obscure necessity or as an irrepressible indetermination, or as the inability to acquire a perfect form and to possess itself in a law. What the Greeks called *ἀναηκαῖον* and *ἄπειρον,* the Orientals called *adharma.* Christian Scholastic theology shared similar views, since it considered the root of every unredeemed nature in terms of *cupiditas* and of *appetitus innatus.* In different ways, the man of Tradition found in the experience of covetous identification, which obscures and impairs "being," the secret cause of his existential predicament. The incessant becoming and the perennial instability and contingency of the inferior region appeared to the man of Tradition as the cosmic and symbolical materialization of that predicament.

On the other hand, the experience of *asceticism* was regarded as the path leading to the other region, or to the world of "being," or to what is no longer physical but metaphysical. Asceticism traditionally consisted in values such as mastery over oneself, self-discipline, autonomy, and the leading of a unified life. By "unified life" I mean an existence that does not need to be spent in search of other things or people in order to be complete and justified. The traditional representations of this other region were solar symbols, heavenly regions, beings made of light or fire, islands, and mountain peaks.

These were the two "natures." Tradition conceived the possibility of being born in either one, and also of the possibility of going from one birth to another, according to the saying: "A man is a mortal god, and a god is an immortal man."[2] The world of Tradition knew these two great poles of existence, as well as the paths leading from one to the other. Tradition knew the existence of the physical world and the totality of the forms, whether visible or underground, whether human or subhuman and demonic, of *ὑπερκοσμία,* a "world beyond this world." According to Tradition, the former is the "fall" of the latter, and the latter represents the "liberation" of the former. The traditional world believed spirituality to be something beyond life and death. It held that mere physical existence, or "living," is meaningless unless it approximates the higher world or that which is "more than life," and unless one's highest ambition consists in participating in *ὑπερκοσμία* and in obtaining an active and

---

1. See Plotinus, *Enneads,* 1.8.4–7; 6.6.18.
2. Heraclitus, frag. 62 Diels; *Corpus Hermeticum* 12.1.

final liberation from the bond represented by the human condition. According to Tradition, every authority is fraudulent, every law is unjust and barbarous, every institution is vain and ephemeral unless they are ordained to the superior principle of Being, and unless they are derived from above and oriented "upward."

The traditional world knew divine kingship. It knew the bridge between the two worlds, namely, initiation; it knew the two great ways of approach to the transcendent, namely, heroic action and contemplation; it knew the mediation, namely, rites and faithfulness; it knew the social foundation, namely, the traditional law and the caste system; and it knew the political earthly symbol, namely, the empire.

These are the foundations of the traditional hierarchy and civilization that have been completely wiped out by the victorious "anthropocentric" civilization of our contemporaries.

2

Regality

Every traditional civilization is characterized by the presence of beings who, by virtue of their innate or acquired superiority over the human condition, embody within the temporal order the living and efficacious presence of a power that comes from above. One of these types of beings is the *pontifex,* according to the inner meaning of the word and according to the original value of the function that he exercised. *Pontifex* means "builder of bridges," or of "paths" (*pons,* in ancient times, also meant "path") connecting the natural and the supernatural dimensions. Moreover, the *pontifex* was traditionally identified with the king *(rex).* Servius, a late fourth-century commentator on Virgil's works, reports: "The custom of our ancestors was that the king should also be *pontifex* and priest." A saying of the Nordic tradition reads: "May our leader be our bridge."[1] Thus, real monarchs were the steadfast personification of the life "beyond ordinary life." Beneficial spiritual influences used to radiate upon the world of mortal beings from the mere presence of such men, from their "pontifical" mediation, from the power of the rites that were rendered efficacious by their power, and from the institutions of which they were the center. These influences permeated people's thoughts, intentions, and actions, ordering every aspect of their lives and constituting a fit foundation for luminous, spiritual realizations. These influences also made propitious the general conditions for prosperity, health, and "good fortune."

In the world of Tradition the most important foundation of the authority and of the right *(ius)* of kings and chiefs, and the reason why they were obeyed, feared, and venerated, was essentially their transcendent and nonhuman quality. This quality was not artificial, but a powerful reality to be feared. The more people acknowledged the ontological rank of what was prior and superior to the visible and temporal dimension, the more such beings were invested with a natural and absolute sovereign power. Traditional civilizations, unlike those of decadent and later times,

---

1. See the *Mabinogion.*

completely ignored the merely political dimension of supreme authority as well as the idea that the roots of authority lay in mere strength, violence, or natural and secular qualities such as intelligence, wisdom, physical courage, and a minute concern for the collective material well-being. The roots of authority, on the contrary, always had a metaphysical character. Likewise, the idea that the power to govern is conferred on the chief by those whom he rules and that his authority is the expression of the community and therefore subject to its decrees, was foreign to Tradition. It is Zeus who bestows the $\theta \acute{\epsilon} \mu \iota \sigma \tau \epsilon \varsigma$ on kings of divine origin, whereby $\theta \acute{\epsilon} \mu \iota \varsigma$, or "law from above," is very different from what constitutes $\nu \acute{o} \mu o \varsigma$, which is the political law of the community. The root of every temporal power was spiritual authority, which was almost a "divine nature disguised in human form." According to an Indo-European view, the ruler is not "a mere mortal," but rather "a great deity standing in the form of a man."[2] The Egyptian pharaoh was believed to be the manifestation of Ra or of Horus. The kings of Alba and of Rome were supposed to be the incarnations of Zeus; the Assyrian kings, of Baal; the Persian shahs, of the god of light. The Nordic-Germanic princes were believed to derive from the race of Tiuz, of Odin, and of the Aesir; and the Greek kings of the Doric-Achaean cycle were called $\delta \iota o \tau \rho \epsilon \psi \acute{\epsilon} \epsilon \varsigma$ or $\delta \acute{\iota} o \gamma \epsilon \nu \acute{\epsilon} \epsilon \varsigma$ in reference to their divine origin. Beyond the variety of mythical and sacred expressions, the recurrent view of kingship is expressed in terms of an "immanent transcendence" that is present and active in the world. The king—who was believed to be a sacred being and not a man—by virtue of his "being," was already the center and the apex of the community. In him was also the supernatural strength that made his ritual actions efficacious. In these actions people could recognize the earthly counterpart of supernatural "ruling," as well as the supernatural support of life in the world of Tradition.[3] For this reason, kingship was the supreme form of government, and was believed to be in the natural order of things. It did not need physical strength to assert itself, and when it did, it was only sporadically. It imposed itself mainly and irresistibly through the spirit. In an ancient Indo-Aryan text it is written: "The dignity a god enjoys on earth is splendid, but hard to achieve for the weak. Only he who sets his soul on this objective, is worthy to become a king."[4] The ruler appears as a "follower of the discipline that is practiced by those who are gods among men."[5]

In Tradition, kingship was often associated with the solar symbol. In the king, people saw the same "glory" and "victory" proper to the sun and to the light (the

---

2. *The Laws of Manu*, 7.8.
3. Conversely, in Greece and in Rome, if the king was found unworthy of the priestly office, he could no longer be king.
4. *Nitisara*, 4.4.
5. Ibid., 1.63.

symbols of the superior nature), which every morning overcome darkness. "Everyday he rises on Horus's throne, as king of the living, just like his father Ra [the sun]." And also: "I have decreed that you must eternally rise as king of the North and of the South on the seat of Horus, like the sun." These sayings from the ancient Egyptian royal tradition bear a striking similarity to the sayings of the Persian tradition, in which the king is believed to be "of the same stock as the gods": "He has the same throne of Mithras and he rises with the Sun"; he is called *particeps siderum* and "Lord of peace, salvation of mankind, eternal man, winner who rises in company of the sun." In ancient Persia the consecrating formula was: "Thou art power, the force of victory, and immortal . . . Made of gold, thou rise, at dawn, together with Indra and with the sun." In the Indo-Aryan tradition, in reference to Rohita, who is the "conquering force" and who personifies an aspect of the radiance of the divine fire (Agni), we find: "By coming forward, he [Agni] has created kingship in this world. He has conferred on you [Rohita] majesty and victory over your enemies."[6] In some ancient Roman representations, the god Sol (sun) presents the emperor with a sphere, which is the symbol of universal dominion. Also, the expressions *sol conservator* and *sol dominus romani imperii*, which are employed to describe Rome's stability and ruling power, refer to the brightness of the sun. The last Roman profession of faith was "solar," since the last representative of the ancient Roman tradition, the emperor Julian, consecrated his dynasty, his birth, and royal condition to the brightness of the sun,[7] which he considered to be a spiritual force radiating from the "higher worlds." A reflection of the solar symbol was preserved up to the time of Ghibelline emperors—one may still speak of a *deitas solis* in reference to Frederick II of Hohenstaufen.

This solar "glory" or "victory" in reference to kingship was not reduced to a mere symbol, but rather denoted a metaphysical reality. Eventually it came to be identified with a nonhuman operating force, which the king did not possess in and by himself. One of the most characteristic symbolic expressions of this idea comes from the Zoroastrian tradition, wherein the *hvareno* (the "glory" that the king possesses) is a supernatural fire characterizing heavenly (and especially solar) entities that allows the king to partake of immortality and that gives him witness through victory. This victory must be understood in such a way that the two meanings, the first mystical, the second military (material), are not mutually exclusive but rather complementary.[8] Among non-Persian people, this *hvareno* was later confused with "fate" (τύχη). With this meaning it reappeared in the Roman tradition in the form of the

---

6. *Atharva Veda*, 13.1.4–5.
7. Emperor Julian, *Hymn to King Helios*, 131b.
8. Concerning the *hvareno*, see *Yasht* (19): "We sacrifice to the awesome kingly Glory made by Mazda; most conquering, highly working, that possesses health, wisdom and happiness, and is more powerful to destroy than all other creatures." *The Avesta Major Portions*, ed. and trans. Rev. E. G. Busch (1985).

"royal fate" that the Caesars ritually transmitted to each other, and in which the people recognized an active, "triumphal" undertaking of the personified destiny of the city (τύχη πόλεως), determined by the ritual of their appointment. The Roman regal attribute *felix* must be referred to this context and to the possession of an extranormal *virtus*. In the Vedic tradition we find a parallel notion: Agni-Vaishvanara is conceived as a spiritual fire that leads the conquering kings to victory.

In ancient Egypt the king was not called merely "Horus," but "fighting Horus" (Hor aha), to designate the victorious and glorious character of the solar principle present in the monarch. The Egyptian pharaoh, who was believed to descend from the gods, was "enthroned" as one of them, and later on in his life he was periodically reconfirmed in his role through rituals that reproduced the victory of the solar god Horus over Typhon-Set, a demon from the netherworld.[9] These rites were thought to have such a power as to evoke the "force" and the "life" that supernaturally encompassed the king's person. The hieroglyphic for "force" *(uas)* is the scepter handled by gods and kings alike. In the oldest texts, the scepter is portrayed as the zigzag bolt of lightning. The regal "force" thus appears as a manifestation of the dazzling, heavenly force. The combination of signs represented the concept of "life-force" *(anshus)*, form a word for "fiery milk," which is the nourishment of the immortals. This word is not without relation to *uraeus,* the divine flame, at times life-giving, at other times dangerously destructive, which crowns the head of the Egyptian king in the shape of a serpent.

In this traditional formulation, the various elements converge in the idea of a nonterrestrial power or fluid *(sa)*. This power consecrates and gives witness to the solar, triumphant nature of the king, and "gushes" forth from one king to the other, thus guaranteeing the uninterrupted and "golden" sequence in the divine lineage, which is legitimately appointed to the task of *regere*. Interestingly enough, the theme of "glory" as a divine attribute is found even in Christianity, and according to mystical theology the beatific vision takes place within the "glory of God." Christian iconography used to portray this glory as a halo around the person's head, thus visibly representing the meaning of the Egyptian *uraeus* and of the glowing crown of the Persian and Roman solar kings.

According to a Far Eastern tradition, the king, as a "son of heaven" who is believed to have nonhuman origins, enjoys the "mandate of heaven" *(tien ming)*, which implies the idea of a real and supernatural force. This force that comes "from heaven," according to Lao-tzu, acts without acting *(wei wu wei)* through an immate-

---

9. One phase of these rites was the "walking in circles," reproducing the journey of the sun. Along the king's path an animal dear to Typhon was sacrificed as a magical, ritual evocation of Horus's victory over Typhon-Set.

rial presence, or by virtue of just being present.[10] It is as invisible as the wind, and yet its actions are as ineluctable as the forces of nature. When this power is unleashed, the forces of common men, according to Meng-tzu, bend under it as blades of grass under the wind.[11] Concerning *wu wei,* a text says:

> By its thickness and substantiality, sincerity equals earth; and by its height and splendor it equals heaven. Its extent and duration are without limit. He who possesses this sincerity, without showing himself, he will shine forth, without moving he will renovate others; without acting, he will perfect them.[12]

Only such a man, "is able to harmonize the opposing strands of human society, to establish and to maintain moral order in the country."[13]

Established in this force or "virtue," the Chinese monarch *(wang)* performed the supreme role of a center, or of a third power between heaven and earth. The common assumption was that the fortunes and misfortunes of the kingdom, as well as the moral qualities of his subjects (it is the "virtue" in relation to the "being" of the monarch, and not his "actions," that carries positive or negative influences on them), secretly depended on the monarch's behavior. The central role exercised by the king presupposed that the king maintained the aforesaid "triumphal" inner way of being. In this context, the meaning of the famous saying, "Immutability in the middle," may correspond to the doctrine according to which, "in the immutability of the middle, the virtue of heaven is manifested."[14] If this principle was implemented as a general rule, nothing could have changed the arranged course of human events or those of the state.[15]

In general, the fact that the king's or chief's primary and essential function consisted in performing those ritual and sacrificial actions that constituted the center of gravity of life is a recurrent idea in a vast cycle of traditional civilizations, from pre-

---

10. *Tao te Ching,* 37.
11. *Lun-yu,* 12.18. In the *Chung-yung* it is written that the secret actions of heaven are eminently immaterial: they are "without sound or scent" and as subtle as the "lightest feather." Ezra Pound, trans., *Chung Yung: The Unwobbling Pivot* (New York, 1969), 33.6.
12. Ibid., 26.5–6.
13. Ibid., 31.1.
14. *Lun-yu* (6.27): "The due medium is virtue. This is the highest attainment. For a long time few people have reached it."
15. The Chinese distinguished between the imperial function and the emperor's person. The imperial function is believed to be divine and to transfigure the person invested with it. When the emperor is enthroned he renounces his personal name and adopts instead an imperial name. He is not so much a person as a neutral element, one of the forces of nature, or something like the sun or a polar star. A natural catastrophe or a popular rebellion signify that the individual has betrayed the principle, which nevertheless still stands. These events are a heavenly sign of the emperor's decadence; not of the imperial function, but of the individual himself.

Columbian Peru to the Far East, and including Greek and Roman cities. This idea confirms the inseparability of royal office from priestly or pontifical office. According to Aristotle, "the kings enjoy their office by virtue of being the officiating priests at their community's worship."[16] The first duty of the Spartan kings was to perform sacrifices, and the same could be said about the first kings of Rome and of many rulers during the imperial period. The king, empowered with a nonterrestrial force with its roots in something that is "more than life," naturally appeared as one who could eminently actualize the power of the rites and open the way leading to the superior world. Thus, in those traditional forms of civilization in which there was a separate priestly class, the king, because of his original dignity and function, belonged to this class and was its true leader. In addition to early Rome, this situation was found both in ancient Egypt (in order to make the rites efficacious, the pharaoh repeated daily the prayer that was believed to renew the divine force in his person) and in Iran, where, as Xenophon recalls,[17] the king, who according to his function was considered the image of the god of light on earth, belonged to the caste of Magi and was its leader. On the other hand, if among certain people there was the custom of deposing and even of killing the chief when an accident or a catastrophe occurred—for this seemed to signify a decrease in the mystical force of "good fortune" that gave one the right to be chief[18]—this custom gives witness to the same order of ideas, although in the form of a superstitious degeneration. In the Nordic racial stocks up to the time of the Goths, and notwithstanding the principle of royal sacredness (the king was considered as an Aesir and as a demigod who wins in battle thanks to the power of his "good fortune"), an inauspicious event was understood not so much as the absence of the mystical power of "fortune" abiding in the king, but rather as the consequence of something that the king, as a mortal man, had done, thus compromising the objective effectiveness of his power. It was believed, for instance, that the consequence for failing to implement the fundamental Aryan virtue of always telling the truth, and thus being stained by lies, caused the "glory," or the mystical efficacious virtue, to abandon the ancient Iranian king, Yima.[19] All the way up to the Carolingian Middle Ages and within Christianity itself, local councils of bishops were at times summoned in order to investigate what misdeed perpetrated by a representative of the temporal or ecclesiastical authority could have caused a given calamity. These are the last echoes of the abovementioned idea.

16. Aristotle, *Politics* 6.5.2.
17. *Cyropaedia*, 8.26.
18. In *La Mentalité primitive* (Paris, 1925), Lévy-Bruhl showed that "primitive peoples" believed that "a catastrophe disqualified the leader."
19. *Yasht*, 19.34–38. The *hvareno* withdraws three times following the triple dignity of Yima as a priest, warrior, and shepherd.

The monarch was required to retain the symbolic and solar dignity of *invictus* (*sol invictus, ἥλιος ανίκητος*), as well as the state of inner equilibrium that corresponds to the Chinese notion of "immutability in the middle"; otherwise the force and its prerogatives would be transferred to another person who could prove worthy of it. I will mention in this context a case in which the concept of "victory" became a focal point of various meanings. There is an interesting ancient saga of Nemi's King of the Woods, whose royal and priestly office was supposed to be conferred on the person capable of catching him by surprise and slaying him. J. G. Frazer tracked down numerous traditions of the same kind all over the world.

In this context, the physical combat aspect of the trial, if it had to occur, is only the materialistic transposition of some higher meaning, and it must be related to the general view of "divine judgments" (more on which later). Concerning the deepest meaning of the legend of Nemi's king-priest, it must be remembered that according to Tradition, only a "fugitive slave" (esoterically speaking, a being who had become free from the bonds of his lower nature), armed with a branch torn off a sacred oak, had the right to compete with the Rex Nemorensis (King of the Woods). The oak is the equivalent of the "Tree of the World," which in other traditions is frequently adopted as a symbol designating the primordial life-force and the power of victory.[20] This means that only a being who has succeeded in partaking of this force may aspire to take the place of the Rex Nemorensis. Concerning this office, it must be observed that the oak and the woods, of which Nemi's priest-king was *rex*, were related to Diana. In turn, Diana was the "bride" of the king of the woods. In some ancient, eastern Mediterranean traditions, the great goddesses were often symbolized by sacred trees. From the Hellenic myth of the Hesperides, to the Nordic myth of the goddess Idun, and to the Gaelic myth of Magh-Mell, which was the residence of very beautiful goddesses and of the "Tree of Victory," it is possible to notice traditional symbolic connections between women or goddesses, forces of life, immortality, wisdom, and trees.

Concerning the Rex Nemorensis, we can recognize in the symbols employed that the notion of kingship derives from having married or possessed the mystical force of "life," of transcendent wisdom and immortality that is personified both by the goddess and by the tree.[21] Nemi's saga, therefore, incorporates the general symbol, which is found in many other myths and traditional legends, of a winner or of a

---

20. The *aśvattha* tree of the Hindu tradition has its roots in heaven, or in the invisible dimension (*Kaṭha Upaniṣad* 6.1–2; *Bhaghavadgītā*, 15.1–2). In the first of these texts, the tree is related to the vital force (*prāna*) and to the "thunderbolt." Since the tree is related to the power of victory, the *aśvattha* is considered the ally of Indra, the warrior god, slayer of *Vṛtra*.

21. In the Egyptian tradition the "name" of the pharaoh was written by the gods on the sacred tree *ashed*, thus becoming "perennial." In the Persian tradition there is a relationship between Zarathustra who was, among the Parsis, the prototype of the divine king, and a heavenly tree planted on top of a mountain.

hero who possesses a woman or a goddess. The goddess appears in other traditions either as a guardian of the fruits of immortality (see the female figures in relation to the symbolical tree in the myths of Heracles, Jason, Gilgamesh, and so on), or as a personification of the occult force of the world, of life and of nonhuman knowledge, or as the embodiment of the principle of sovereignty (the knight or the unknown hero of the legend, who becomes king after taking as his bride a mysterious princess).[22]

Some of the ancient traditions about a female source of royal power[23] may also be interpreted in this fashion; their meaning, in that case, is exactly opposite to gynaecocracy, which will be discussed later. As far as the tree is concerned, interestingly enough, even in some medieval legends it is related to the imperial ideal; the last emperor, before dying, will hang the scepter, the crown, and the shield in the "Dry Tree," which is usually located in the symbolical region of "Prester John," just like the dying Roland hung his unbreakable sword in the tree. This is yet another convergence of symbolical contents, for Frazer has shown the relationship existing between the branch that the fugitive slave must break off Nemi's sacred oak in order to fight with Nemi's king and the branch Aeneas carried to descend, while alive, into the invisible dimension. One of the gifts that Emperor Frederick II received from the mysterious Prester John was a ring that renders invisible and victorious the one who wears it. Invisibility, in this context, refers to the access to the invisible realm and to the achievement of immortality; in Greek traditions the hero's invisibility is often synonymous with his becoming immortal.

This was the case of Siegfried in the *Niebelungen* (6), who through the same symbolic virtue of becoming invisible, subjugates and marries the divine woman Brynhild. Brynhild, just like Siegfried in the *Siegdrifumal* (4–6), is the one who bestows on the heroes who "awaken" her the formulas of wisdom and of victory contained in the runes.

Remnants of traditions, in which we find the themes contained in the ancient saga of the King of the Woods, last until shortly beyond the end of the Middle Ages. They are always associated with the old idea, according to which a legitimate king is capable of manifesting in specific, concrete and almost experimental ways, the signs of his supernatural nature. The following is just one example: prior to the Hundred Years War, Venice asked Philip of Valois to demonstrate his actual right to be king

---

22. The Roman tradition of the gens Julia, which traced its origins to Venus victrix and to Venus genitrix, shared this perspective. In the Japanese tradition, until a few years ago, the origin of the imperial power was attributed to a solar deity (Amaterasu Omikami), and the focal point of the ceremony of enthronement *(dajo-sai)* represented the contact the emperor established with her through the "offering of new food."

23. In ancient India, for instance, the essence of royalty was condensed in a divine or semidivine woman (Śrī, Lakṣmī, Padmā) who chose and "embraced" the king, thus becoming his bride, notwithstanding the king's human wives.

in one of the following ways. The first way, victory over a contender whom Philip was expected to fight to the death in an enclosed area, reminds us of the Rex Nemorensis and of the mystical testimony inherent in every victory.[24] As far as the other examples are concerned, we read in a text dating back to those times:

> If Philip of Valois is, as he affirms, the true king of France, let him prove the fact by exposing himself to hungry lions; for lions never attack a true king; or let him perform the miraculous healing of the sick, as all other true kings are wont to do. If he should fail, he would own himself to be unworthy of the kingdom.[25]

A supernatural power, manifested through a victory or through a thaumaturgical virtue, even in times like Philip's, which are no longer primordial times, is thus inseparably connected with the traditional idea of real and legitimate kingship.[26] Aside from the factual adequacy of single individuals to the principle and to the function of kingship, what remains is the view that "what has led people to venerate so many kings were mainly the divine virtues and powers, which descended on the kings alone, and not on other men as well." Joseph de Maistre wrote:[27]

> God makes kings in the literal sense. He prepares royal races; maturing them under a cloud which conceals their origin. They appear at length crowned with glory and honor; they take their places; and this is the most certain sign of their legitimacy. The truth is that they arise as it were of themselves, without violence on their part, and without marked deliberation on the other: it is a species of magnificent tranquillity, not easy to express. Legitimate usurpation would seem to me to be the most appropriate expression (if not too bold), to characterize these kinds of origins, which time hastens to consecrate.[28]

24. Later on, I will expound the notion that in this context appears in a materialistic form. Traditionally the winner was believed to incarnate a nonhuman energy; in him there were two phases of the same act: he was the point of convergence of a "descent" and of an "ascent."

25. Marc Bloch, *The Royal Touch* (New York, 1961), i–ii.

26. Tradition also ascribed the thaumaturgical virtue to the Roman emperors Hadrian and Vespasian (Tacitus, *Historiae*, 4.81). Among the Carolingians it is still possible to find a residue of the idea that the supernatural power penetrated even the royal clothes. Beginning with Robert the Pius (French dynasty) and Edward the Confessor (English dynasty) until the age of revolutions, the thaumaturgical power was transmitted from one royal generation to the other. The power at first could heal all diseases, but with the passing of time it could only heal a few. C. Agrippa (*De occulta philosophia*, 3.35) wrote: "Righteous kings and pontiffs represent God on earth and partake of his power. If they touch the sick, they heal them from their diseases."

27. Joseph de Maistre, *Essay on the Generative Principle of Constitutions* (reprint, New York, 1977), 19–20.

28. In this passage of de Maistre, we find again the mystical view of victory, since "taking their place" is considered "the most certain sign of their legitimacy."

3

Polar Symbolism;
the Lord of Peace and Justice

It is possible to connect the integral and original understanding of the regal function with a further cycle of symbols and myths that point back in the same one direction through their various representations and analogical transpositions.[1]

As a starting point, we may consider the Hindu notion of the *cakravartin*, or "universal king." The *cakravartin* may be considered the archetype of the regal function of which various kings represent more or less complete images or even particular expressions whenever they conform to the traditional principle. *Cakravartin* literally means "lord" or "spinner of the wheel." This notion brings us back again to the idea of a center that corresponds also to an inner state, to a way of being, or better yet, to the way of Being.

Actually the wheel also symbolizes *saṁsāra* or the stream of becoming (the Hellenes called it κύκλος τῆς γενὲσεως, the "wheel of generation," or κύκλος ἀνάγκης, "the wheel of Fate"). Its motionless center signifies the spiritual stability inherent in those who are not affected by this stream and who can organize and subject to a higher principle the energies and the activities connected to the inferior nature. Then the *cakravartin* appears as the *dharmarāja*, the "Lord of the Law," or the "Lord of the Wheel of the Law."[2] According to Confucius: "The practice of government by means of virtue may be compared to the polestar, which the multitudinous stars pay homage to while it stays in its place."[3] Hence the meaning of the

---

1. See R. Guénon's *Le Roi du monde* (Paris, 1927), in which several corresponding traditions have been gathered and interpreted. [English trans. *The Lord of the World* (Ellingstring, 1983).]

2. According to this tradition, the "wheel" has also a "triumphal" meaning: its appearance as a heavenly wheel is the visible sign of conquerors' and rulers' destinies. Like a wheel, the chosen one will go forth, sweeping away and dominating everything on his path (see the legend of the "Great Magnificent One" in *Dīgha Nikāya*, 17). As far as the organizing function is concerned, we may recall the Vedic image of the "cosmic order's *(ṛta)* bright and terrible chariot which confounds the enemies." *Ṛg Veda*, 2.23.3.

3. *The Analects,* trans. R. Dawson (Oxford, 1993), 2.1.

concept of "revolution," which is the motion occurring around an "unmoved mover," though in our modern day and age it has become synonymous with subversion.

In this sense royalty assumes the value of a "pole," by referring to a general traditional symbolism. We may recall here, besides Midgard (the heavenly "middle abode" described in Nordic traditions), Plato's reference to the place where Zeus holds counsel with the gods in order to reach a decision concerning the fate of Atlantis: "He accordingly summoned all the gods to his own most glorious abode, which stands at the center of the universe and looks out over the whole realm of change."[4] The abovementioned notion of *cakravartin* is also connected to a cycle of enigmatic traditions concerning the real existence of a "center of the world" that exercises this supreme function here on earth. Some fundamental symbols of regality had originally a close relationship with these ideas. One of these symbols was the scepter, the main function of which is analogically related to the "axis of the world."[5] Another symbol is the throne, an "elevated" place; sitting still on the throne evokes, in addition to the meaning of stability connected to the "pole" and to the "unmoved mover," the corresponding inner and metaphysical meanings. Considering the correspondence that was originally believed to exist between the nature of the royal man and the nature produced by initiation, in the classical Mysteries we find a ritual consisting of sitting still on a throne. This ritual appears to have been very important since it was sometimes equated with initiation itself. The term τεθρονισένος, enthroned, is often synonymous with τελετεσμένος, "initiate."[6] In fact, in some instances, in the course of an initiation the θρονισμός, or royal enthronement, preceded the experience of becoming one with the god.

The same symbolism is embodied in the ziggurat, the Assyrian-Babylonian terraced pyramid, as well as in the master plan of the capital of the Persian kings (as in Ecbatana) and in the ideal image of the *cakravartin's* royal palace. In these places we find the architectural expression of the cosmic order complete in its hierarchy and in its dependence upon an unmoved center. From a spatial perspective this center corresponded, within the building itself, to the king's throne. Similar to Hellas, in India we find forms of initiation that employ the ritual of the so-called *maṇḍala*. These forms dramatize the gradual ascent of the initiate from the profane and demonic space to a sacred space, until he reaches a center. A fundamental ritual symbolizing this journey is called *mūkatābhiṣaka* and it consists in being crowned or in being given a tiara; he who reaches the "center" of the *maṇḍala* is crowned as king because he is now believed to be above the interplay of the forces at work in the

---

4. *Critias*, 121.
5. R. Guénon, *Autorité spirituelle et pouvoir temporel* (Paris, 1929), 137.
6. V. Magnien, *Les Mystères d'Eleusis* (Paris, 1929), 196.

inferior nature.[7] It is interesting that the ziggurat, the sacred building towering above the city-state of which it was the center, was called "cornerstone" in Babylon and "link between heaven and earth" in Lhasa;[8] the theme of the "rock" and of the "bridge" is pretty much summed up in the Far Eastern expression: "third power between Heaven and Earth."

The importance of these traces and correlations should not be overlooked. Moreover, "stability" has the same double dimension; it is at the center of the Indo-Aryan formula for consecration of the kings:

> Remain steady and unwavering . . . Do not give in. Be strong like a
> mountain. Stay still like the sky and the earth and retain control of power
> at all times. The sky, the earth and the mountains are unmoved as un-
> moved is the world of living beings and this king of men.[9]

In the formulas of the Egyptian royalty, stability appears as an essential attribute that complements the attribute of "power-life" already present in the sovereign. And just as the attribute of "vital-force," the correspondence of which with a secret fire has already been emphasized, "stability" too has a heavenly counterpart. Its hieroglyphic, *djed,* conveys the stability of the "solar gods resting on pillars or on light beams."[10] These examples bring us back to the system of initiations, since they are much more than abstract ideas; like "power" and "vital-force"; "stability" too, according to the Egyptian tradition, is simultaneously an inner state of being and an energy, a *virtus* that flows from one king to the next, and which sustains them in a supernatural way.

Moreover, the "Olympian" attribute and the attribute of "peace" are connected to the condition of "stability" in the esoteric sense of the word. Kings "who derive their power from the supreme god and who have received victory at his hands," are "lighthouses of peace in the storm."[11] After "glory," centrality ("polarity"), and stability, peace is one of the fundamental attributes of regality that has been preserved until relatively recent times. Dante talked about the *imperator pacificus,* a title previously bestowed on Charlemagne. Obviously, this is not the profane and social peace pursued by a political government—a kind of peace that is at most an external consequence—but rather an inner and positive peace, which should not be divorced from the "triumphal" element. This peace does not convey the notion of cessation, but rather that of the highest degree of perfection of a pure, inner and withdrawn activity. It is a calm that reveals the supernatural.

---

7. G. Tucci, *Teoria e pratica dei mandala* (Rome, 1949), 30–32; 50–51.
8. C. Dawson, *The Age of the Gods* (New York, 1933), 6.2.
9. *Ṛg Veda,* 10.173.
10. Moret, *Royauté pharaonique,* 42–43.
11. *Corpus Hermeticum,* 18.10–16.

According to Confucius a man destined to be a ruler (the "virtuous"), unlike ordinary men, "rests in rectitude and is stable and unperturbed"; "the men of affairs enjoy life, but the virtuous prolongs it."[12] Hence that great calm that conveys the feeling of an irresistible superiority and terrifies and disarms the adversary without a fight. This greatness immediately evokes the feeling of a transcendent force that is already mastered and ready to spring forward; or the marvelous and yet frightful sense of the *numen*.[13] The *pax romana et augusta*, which is connected to the transcendent sense of the *imperium*, may be considered one of the several expressions of these meanings in the context of a universal historical realization. Conversely, the ethos of superiority over the world, of dominating calm and of imperturbability combined with readiness for absolute command, which has remained the characteristic of various aristocratic types even after the secularization of nobility, must be considered an echo of that element that was originally the regal, spiritual, and transcendent element.

The *cakravartin*, besides being the "Lord of Peace," is "Lord of the Law" (or cosmic order, *ṛta*) and "Lord of Justice" *(dharmarāja)*. "Peace" and "justice" are two more fundamental attributes of royalty that have been preserved in Western civilization until the time of the Hohenstaufens and Dante, even though the political aspect predominated over the higher meaning presupposing it.[14] Moreover, these attributes were also found in the mysterious figure of Melchizedek, king of Salem, one of the many representations of the function of the "universal king." Guénon has pointed out that in Hebrew, *mekki-tsedeq* means "king of justice," while Salem, of which he is king, is not a city, but rather "peace," at least according to Paul's exegesis.[15] Tradition upholds the superiority of Melchizedek's royal priesthood over Abraham's. It is not without a deep reason that Melchizedek was present in the enigmatic medieval allegory of the "three rings," and that he declared that neither Christianity nor Islam know any longer which is the true religion; moreover, the "royal religion of

---

12. *The Analects*, 6.21.

13. In ancient times the fulgurating power, symbolized by the broken scepter and by the pharaoh's *uraeus*, was not a mere symbol; likewise many acts found in court ceremonies were not mere expressions of formalism and servile adulation of the pharaoh, but rather were induced by spontaneous sensations awakened in the subjects by the royal *virtus*. Somebody visited an Egyptian king of the Twelfth Dynasty, and later recalled: "When I came close to His Highness I prostrated myself and lost consciousness before Him. The god addressed me with friendly words, but I felt like I was suddenly blinded. I couldn't think straight, my body went limp; my heart gave way and I knew the difference between life and death." G. Maspero, *Les Contes populaires de l'Egypte ancienne* (Paris, 1889), 123. See also *The Laws of Manu*, (7.6): "Like the Sun, he burns eyes and hearts and no one on earth is able even to look at him."

14. Frederick II recognized that "justice" and "peace" are the foundation on which all kingdoms are built. "Justice" during the Middle Ages was often confused with "truth" and indicated the ontological dignity of the imperial principle. See A. De Stefano, *L' idea imperiale di Federico II* (Florence, 1927), 74. Among the Goths, truth and justice were often portrayed as regal virtues par excellence. These are all traces of the doctrine of the origins.

15. Heb. 7:1–3.

Melchizedek" was often upheld by the Ghibelline ideology in the struggle against the Church.

At this level, the expression "king of justice" is the equivalent of the previously mentioned *dharmarāja,* designating the "universal king." From this expression we may gather that in this context, "justice" and "peace" do not have a secular meaning. In fact, *dharma* in Sanskrit also means "proper nature of," or the law typical of a certain being; the correct reference concerns the particular primordial legislation that hierarchically orders, in a system oriented upwards, every function and form of life according to the nature of every being *(svadharma),* or "according to justice and truth." Such a notion of justice is also characteristic of the Platonic view of the state; this view, rather than an abstract "utopian" model, should be regarded in many aspects as an echo of traditional orientations from an even more distant past. In Plato the idea of justice *(δικαιοσύνη),* of which the state should be the embodiment, is closely related to that of *οἰκειοπραγία* or *cuique suum,* that is, with the principle according to which everybody should fulfill the function typical of his or her own nature. Thus the "king of justice" is also the primordial legislator, or he who instituted the castes, assigned the offices, and established the rites; or, in other words, he who determined the ethical and sacred system that was called *dharmanga* in Aryan India, and that in other traditions was the local ritual system that determined the norms for regulating individual and collective life.

This presupposes that the royal condition enjoys a higher power of knowledge. The capability to deeply and perfectly understand the primordial laws of human beings is the basis of authority and of command in the Far East. The Mazdean royal "glory" *(hvorra-i-kayani)* is also the virtue of a supernatural intellect. And while according to Plato[16] the philosophers *(οἱ σοφοί)* should be at the top of the hierarchy of the true state, for him the abovementioned traditional idea takes on an even more specific form. For Plato, wisdom or "philosophy" is understood as the knowledge of "that which is," rather than the knowledge of illusory visible forms. The philosopher is one who can effectively formulate laws conforming to justice precisely because he has the direct knowledge of that which is supremely real and normative. The conclusion Plato draws is:

> Until philosophers are kings, or the kings and princes of this world have the spirit and power of philosophers, and political greatness and wisdom meet in one, and these commoner natures who pursue either to the exclusion of the other are compelled to stand aside, cities will never have rest from their evils, nor the human race itself.[17]

16. *The Republic,* 5.18; 6.1.
17. *The Republic,* trans. B. Jowett (New York, 1937), 473.

4

The Law, the State,
the Empire

The traditional society's view of both the law and the state is closely related to the order of ideas that I have been discussing so far. Generally speaking, a transcendent realism is the presupposition of the traditional notion of the law. Especially in Aryan formulations, the notion of law has an intimate relationship with the notions of truth, reality, and stability inherent to "that which is." In the Vedas, the term *ṛta* often has the same meaning as *dharma;* it not only signifies the order found in the world (the world as order, or κόσμος), but it has a deeper meaning whenever it designates truth, law, or reality, just as its opposite, *anṛta,* designates falsehood, evil, or unreality. Thus, the world of the law and consequently of the state came to be equated with the world of truth and of reality in the eminent sense of the word.

As a natural consequence, traditional man either ignored or considered absurd the idea that one could talk about laws and the obedience due them if the laws in question had a mere human origin—whether individual or collective. Every law, in order to be regarded as an objective law, had to have a "divine" character. Once the "divine" character of a law was sanctioned and its origin traced back to a nonhuman tradition, then its authority became absolute; this law became then something ineffable, inflexible, immutable and beyond criticism. Thus, every transgression of such law was regarded not so much as a crime against society, but rather and foremost as sacrilege or as an act of impiety (ἀσέβεια), or as an act that jeopardized the spiritual destiny of the person who disobeyed it as well as of the people with whom that person was socially related. This is why, up to and including medieval civilization, rebellion against authority and the imperial law was considered as serious a crime as religious heresy. Thus the rebels were considered just like heretics, namely, as the enemies of their own natures and as beings who contradict the law of their very own being.[1] Aryan India employed a special expression to designate those who broke the caste law: they were called "the fallen ones," or "the lapsed" (more on which later). The usefulness of the law in the modern sense of the word, that is, its collective and empirical usefulness, was never the true criterion adopted in ancient times; not that this aspect was never considered, but it was rather thought to be an accessory or a consequential aspect in every law, once a law was sanctioned as true. After all, there are different views of what constitutes usefulness. The notion of usefulness is the ultimate materialistic criterion of modern society, though that was not the case in traditional societies, which rather regarded it as a means to be employed in the function of a higher purpose. But for a law to be considered useful it was necessary to appear as something other than a mere and repealable creation of the human will. Once it was established that its authority originated "from above," its usefulness and efficacy were definitively acknowledged. This certainty was never questioned, even in those cases in which experience, in the most immediate and unrefined meaning of the word, did not confirm and even proved such a law to be wrong somehow, since as the saying goes, "the web of 'Heaven's way' is complex and incomprehensible." This is why in the traditional world the creation of a system of laws and rituals was always attributed to divine legislators or to divine mediators; these beings, in turn, were considered as various forms or apparitions of the "lord of the center," or "king of justice," the forms being determined by different geographical areas and by different populations. And even when in more recent times the electoral system was introduced, tradition retained a partial formal existence when the people's decision was not considered to be sufficient; in that case, in order for new laws to be finally ratified, it was necessary to obtain the approval of the pontifexes and to make sure that the diviners ascertained whether these laws enjoyed the gods' approval.[2]

Moreover, laws and institutions, as in the case of all traditional civilizations, were both "from above" and oriented upwards. A political, economic, and social order created merely for the sake of temporal life is exclusively characteristic of the modern world, that is, of the antitraditional world. Traditionally the state had a transcendent meaning and purpose that were not inferior to the ones the Catholic Church claimed for itself in the West as a manifestation of, and a path to, the "world above." The very term "state," in Latin *status*, from the Greek ἰστάναι, "to stay," empirically may have derived from the form of social life taken up by nomadic populations

---

1. De Stefano, *L'idea imperiale di Federico II*, 75–79.
2. "Cities did not inquire whether the institutions which they had adopted were useful or not: these institutions had been established because it so pleased religion . . . Originally the higher rule on which the social order was founded was not self-interest." Fustel de Coulanges, *La Cité antique* (Paris, 1900), 365. (Up to Frederick II we still find the idea that the laws, to which the emperor himself is subjected, derive immediately not from men or from the people, but from God himself. De Stefano, *L'idea imperiale*, 57.)

once they permanently settled down; however, it may also point to a higher meaning, namely, to an order concerned with hierarchical participation in a spiritual "stability" as opposed to the contingent, unstable, changeable, chaotic, and particularistic character of a naturalistic existence. This order constituted the accurate reflection of the world of being in the world of becoming, hence the words pronounced in the course of a Vedic royal consecration: "This world of the living is steady, and so is this king of the people." In this way, traditional states and empires often employed the symbols of "centrality" and of "polarity" that have been associated with the archetype of regality.

Thus, while the ancient Chinese empire was called the Middle Empire and the seat of the world according to Nordic legends was called Midgard, the "middle abode" or center of the world, the capital of the Incas' solar empire was called Cuzco, or "navel" of the world. Likewise in ancient Greece, Delphi enjoyed the same designation as the center of Doric civilization. It would be easy to find analogous references in different civilizations, all pointing to the ancient meaning of traditional states and organizations. Generally speaking, in prehistoric times the symbolism of "sacred stones" already points to the same order of ideas, the alleged fetishism of the cult of the stones partially being a mere fancy of modern researchers. The *omphalos,* or sacred stone, is not a naive representation of the shape of the world; its meaning in Greek ("navel") brings it back to the idea of a "center," of a "stable point"; and it can also be related to what may be called *sacred geography:* the "sacred stone" is often found, and not without reason, in selected ritual places that served as traditional centers in relation to a given historical cycle or to a given people.[3] The meaning of the "sacred stone" was often that of a "foundation from above," especially when the stone was "from the sky," namely, an aerolith. Some examples are the *lapis niger* of the ancient Roman tradition and the "stone of destiny," the black, fatal stone figuring in the British and Celtic traditions, which was important for its alleged ability to recognize legitimate kings among various pretenders to the throne.[4] Following the same order of ideas, in Wolfram von Eschenbach's view the Grail was a mysterious "divine stone" that also had the power of revealing who was worthy of the royal dignity.[5] Hence, the obvious meaning of the trial consisting in being able to draw a sword from a stone (Theseus in Hellas, Sohrab in Persia, King Arthur in ancient Britannia, and so on).

The doctrine of the two natures—which is the foundation of the traditional view of life—is also reflected in the relationship that exists between the state and the

---

3. R. Guénon, *Roi du monde,* chap. 9.
4. J. L. Weston, *The Quest of the Holy Grail* (London, 1913), 12–13.
5. See J. Evola, *Il mistero del Graal e l'idea imperiale ghibellina* (Rome, 1972).

people *(demos)*. The idea that the state derives its origin from the *demos* and that the principle of its legitimacy and its foundation rests upon it is an ideological perversion typical of the modern world and essentially represents a regression; with this view we regress to what was typical of naturalistic social forms lacking an authentic spiritual chrism. Once this direction was taken, an inevitable downward spiraling occurred, which ended with the triumph of the collectivistic world of the masses and with the advent of radical democracy. This regression proceeds from a logical necessity and from the physical law of gravity that affects falling bodies. According to the traditional view, on the contrary, the state was related to the people, just as the Olympian and Uranian principles are related to the chthonic and "infernal" world; or as "idea," "form," or *voûç*, are related to "matter," "nature," or *ὕλη;* or as the luminous, masculine, differentiating, individualizing, and life-giving principle is related to the unsteady, promiscuous, and nocturnal feminine principle. Between these two poles there is a deep tension, which in the traditional world was resolved in the sense of a transfiguration and of the establishment of an order from above. Thus, the very notion of "natural rights" is a mere fiction, and the antitraditional and subversive use of that is well documented. There is no such thing as a nature that is "good" in itself and in which the inalienable rights of an individual, which are to be equally enjoyed by every human being, are preformed and rooted. Even when the ethnic substance appears to be somewhat "well defined," in other words, when it presents some elementary forms of order, these forms (unless they are residues and traces of previous formative actions) do not have a spiritual value in and of themselves unless by participating in a higher order, such as when they are assumed in the state or an analogous traditional organization, they are first consecrated as being from above. In the end, the demos's substance is always *demonic* (in the ancient, non-Christian, and amoral sense of the word); it always requires a catharsis or a liberation before it can act as a force *(δύναμις)* and as the material of a traditional political system, and before it can favor the development of a differentiated and hierarchical order of dignity over and beyond a naturalistic substratum.

In this regard we shall see that the main principle upon which the differentiation between people and the hierarchy of the traditional castes is built has not been political or economical, but spiritual; and thus was developed an authentic system of participations as well as the progressive stages of a conquest and a victory of the cosmos over chaos. In addition to the four major castes, the Indo-Aryan tradition knew a broader and more significant distinction that points to the duality of natures; I am referring to the distinction between the *ārya* or *dvīja* and the *śūdra*. The former were the "nobles" or "the twice-born," who represented the "divine" element *(daivya)*. The latter were beings who belong to nature, and thus who represent the promiscu-

24

ous substratum of the hierarchy that was gradually overcome by the formative influence exercised within the higher castes, from the heads of the households to the brāhmaṇa.[6] Strictly speaking, this influence was the original meaning of the state and of the law within the world of Tradition; it had a meaning of supernatural "formation," even where it did not manifest itself immediately in visible ways, because of either incomplete applications of the principle or later materialistic and degenerative processes.

These premises are the foundation upon which the potential affinity between the principle of every state and that of *universality* is founded; wherever an action takes place that is aimed at constituting life beyond the limits of nature and of contingent and empirical existence, it is unavoidable that some forms not connected to the particular will manifest themselves. The dimension of that which is universal may appear in different aspects and different degrees in various civilizations and traditional organizations. The "formative process" always encounters resistance from matter, which in its determinations caused by time and space acts in a differentiating and particularistic sense in relation to the effective historical application of the one principle that in itself is superior and antecedent to these manifestations. Nevertheless, there is no form of traditional organization—which despite any local characteristics, any empirical exclusivism, any "autochthonism" of the cults and institutions it jealously defends—that does not hide a higher principle; this principle is actualized whenever the traditional organization reaches the heights of the idea of the empire. Thus, there are occult ties of sympathy and of analogy between the individual traditional formations and something unique, indivisible, and perennial, and these ties are portrayed in many ways. Once in a while it is possible to detect in certain historical institutions (such as monarchies and empires) an esoteric and universal core that transcends the specific geographical and historical dimensions of said institutions, thus culminating in a unity of a higher kind; such are the imperial peaks of the world of Tradition. Ideally, one same line runs from the traditional idea of law and state to that of empire.

We have seen that the opposition between the higher castes (which are characterized by rebirth) and the inferior caste of the *śūdra* was considered by the Indo-Aryans as an opposition between the "divine" and the "demonic" element. In Iran the higher castes were believed to correspond to emanations of the heavenly fire descended to earth, and more specifically upon three distinct "peaks"; after the "glory"

---

6. Often the caste of the *śūdra*, or servants, was considered to be "demonic" *(asurya)* in opposition to the caste of the *brāhmaṇa*, which was considered to be "divine" *(daivya)* and at the peak of the hierarchy of the "twice-born."

(hvareno), the supreme form that was embodied in kings and priests, such supernatural fire descended hierarchically to castes or classes of the warriors and of the patriarchical wealthy leaders (rathaestha and vastriya-ishuyant) until it reached and "glorified" the lands occupied by Aryan descent.[7]

In the ancient Persian tradition, this was the background against which a metaphysical view of the empire was formulated in the terms of a reality unrelated to space and time. There are two possibilities: on the one hand there is the ashavan, the pure, the "faithful" on earth and the blessed in heaven. The ashavan is one who boosts the power of the principle of light here on earth, in the domain proper to him. The ashavan is exemplified by the members of three classes: the lords of the ritual and of fire, who exercise an invisible power over occult influences; the warriors, whose job is to fight against barbarians and impious people; and finally, those who work on the dry and arid land, whose job is a militia, since fertility is almost a victory that increases the mystical virtus of the Aryan land.

On the other hand, opposed to the ashavan, are the anashvan, the impure ones, those without law, or those who oppose the principle of light. In this context, the empire as a traditional system governed by the "king of kings" corresponds to what the principle of light has successfully snatched from the snares of the principle of darkness; the limit of the empire is illustrated by the myth of the hero Shaoshan, the universal lord of a future, complete, and victorious kingdom of "peace."[8]

A similar idea is found in the legend according to which the emperor Alexander the Great contained the onslaught of the peoples of Gog and Magog by building an iron wall. These people may represent in this context the "demonic" element that in the traditional hierarchies was successfully subjugated; one day these people will flood the earth in pursuit of conquest but they will ultimately be challenged by figures who, according to medieval sagas, will embody the archetype of the leaders of the Holy Roman Empire.[9] A similar idea is expressed in some Nordic traditions with the image of the bulwarks that protect the "middle abode" (the legendary Midgard) from the elementary powers and that one day will be overpowered during the "twilight of the gods" (the ragna-rokkr).[10] The relationship between aeternitas and

---

7. In Yasht (19.9) it is said that the "glory" belongs "to the Aryan people who have already been born and who are yet to be born, and to the holy Zarathustra." This reminds us of the notion of "men of the primordial tradition" (paoiryo-thaesha), which was considered the true Aryan religion in every age, before and after Zarathustra.

8. Bundahesh, 30.10; Yasht, 29.89–90.

9. This deed of Alexander the Great is described in the Koran (18:93), in which he is called Dhul-Qarnain. Gog and Magog are also found in the Hindu tradition with the similar names of the demons Koka and Vikoka, who will be destroyed at the end of the present age by Kalki-avatara, yet another messianic-imperial figure. See my Il mistero del Graal e l'idea imperiale ghibellina.

10. Gylfaginning, 8.42; Voluspa, 82.

imperium is also found in the Roman tradition; hence the transcendent, nonhuman character with which the notion of *regere* is associated; this is why the pagan world credited the gods for the greatness of Rome, the city of the eagle and of the axe. According to another view endowed with a deeper meaning, the "world" will not end as long as the Roman Empire existed. This idea is connected to the function of mystical salvation attributed to the empire, provided that the "world" is not understood in physical or political terms but rather in terms of "cosmos" and of a dam of order and stability containing the disruptive forces of chaos.[11]

In relation to this theme, the Byzantine continuation of the Roman ideal acquires a particular meaning owing to the markedly theological and eschatological nature animating that ideal. The empire, which even in this context is conceived as an image of the heavenly kingdom, is willed and preordained by God. In the empire the earthly sovereign (the $\beta\alpha\sigma\iota\lambda\varepsilon\acute{\nu}\varsigma$ $\alpha\nu\tau\sigma\kappa\rho\acute{\alpha}\tau\omega\rho$) is himself an image of the Lord of the universe; as the Lord himself, the sovereign is alone and without a second. He presides over both the temporal and the spiritual domains and his formal right is universal. This right extends even over people who have an autonomous government and who are not directly subjected to the real imperial power (any such government being considered "barbaric" and not "according to justice," since it has a mere naturalistic foundation). The subjects of the empire are the "Romans" *($\rho\omega\mu\alpha\hat{\iota}o\iota$)*, no longer in an ethical and juridical sense, but in the sense of a superior dignity and chrism, since they live in the pax guaranteed by a law that is a reflection of the divine law. The imperial ecumene sums up the order of "salvation" as well as that of the law in the higher sense of the word.[12]

The ideal of the empire reemerged one more time in the Ghibelline Middle Ages with the same metahistorical content, that is, as a supernatural universal institution created by Providence as a *remedium contra infirmitatem peccati* in order to straighten the fallen human nature and direct people to eternal salvation. This ideal was for all practical purposes paralyzed both by the Church and by historical circumstances, which precluded its comprehension as well as its effective realization according to its higher meaning. Dante, for instance, from a traditional point of view was correct in claiming for the empire the same origins and supernatural destiny of the Church. He was also correct in talking about the emperor as one who, "owning

---

11. The dynamic interplay between the two opposite principles was represented in Aryan India during the feast of *gavām-ayana*, during which a black *śūdra* wrestled against a white Aryan for the possession of a solar symbol. One of the Nordic myths tells about a knight in white armor who fights against a knight in black armor; the knight in black wins the contest, but will eventually be vanquished once and for all by a king.

12. On an analogous basis in Islam we find the geographical distinction between Dar al-Islam, or "Land of Islam," ruled by divine laws, and Dar al-Harb, or "Land of War," the inhabitants of which must be brought into Dar al-Islam by means of *jihad* or "holy war."

everything and no longer wishing for anything else," is free of concupiscence, and who can therefore allow peace and justice to reign and thus strengthen the active life of his subjects; after the original sin, this life can no longer resist the seductions of *cupiditas* unless a higher power controls it and directs it.[13]

Although he expressed traditionally correct views about the empire, Dante Alighieri was unable to carry these ideas beyond the political and material plane. In Dante's view, the emperor's "perfect possession" is not an inner possession, typical of "those who are" but it is rather a territorial possession. Also, the *cupiditas* that he abhors is not the root of an unregenerated life tied to the law of becoming and lived out in a naturalistic state, but rather the *cupiditas* of the princes competing for power and riches. Again, according to him, "peace" is that of the "world," which constitutes the anticipation of a different order beyond that of the empire and of a contemplative life in an ascetical Christian sense.

Tradition lives on, however, although only in faint echoes. With the Hohenstaufen dynasty Tradition had a last bright flicker; eventually the empires would be replaced by "imperialisms" and the state would be understood only as a temporal, national, particularistic, social, and plebeian organization.

13. Dante, *Convivium*, 4.5.4; *De monarchia*, 1.11, 11–14.

5

The Mystery of the Rite

As the king by divine right was the center of the traditional state, two elements, rite and faithfulness *(fides),* connected particular components and activities within the social order to this center and allowed individuals to partake of the transcendent influence emanating from the sovereign.

The rite was the original cement binding together traditional organizations, whether large or small, considered in their nonnaturalistic dimension. The rite was first of all the prerogative of the king; second, of the aristocratic or priestly classes and of the magistrates (whom the Greeks called οἱ ἐν ιτέλε, "those whose responsibility is to perform sacrifices")[1]; and finally, of the *patres,* or heads of households. Rites and sacrifices were regulated by detailed and strict traditional norms that left no room for anything arbitrary or subjective. The performance of rites and sacrifices was imperative, *ius strictum:* a ritual or sacrifice that was neglected or performed by an unqualified person, or performed in a way that did not conform to traditional rules, was considered a cause of misfortune for both individuals and society, since it unleashed dreadful powers both in the moral and in the material order. Conversely, in the classical world it was said that the priest in charge of the holy fire "saved" the city through his ritual, day after day.[2] In the Chinese tradition, to establish the rites was the first of the three most important things in the government of an empire, since the rites were the "channels by which we can apprehend the ways of Heaven."[3] In the Hindu tradition, the "sacrificial sites" were considered to be the seats of the "cosmic order" *(ṛta)* itself;[4] it is very significant that the expression *ṛta (artha,* in

---

1. F. de Coulanges, 211.
2. Pindar, *The Nemean Odes,* 11.1–5.
3. *Li-Chi,* 7.4.6: "It was on this account that the sages knew that the rules of ceremony could not be dispensed with, while the ruin of states, the destruction of families and the perishing of individuals are always preceded by their abandonment of the rules of propriety." According to the Indo-Aryan tradition, not only truth, order and asceticism, but ritual formulations and sacrifices as well are the foundations of all human organizations.
4. *Ṛg Veda,* 10.124.3.

Persian) appears in connection with analogous conceptions as the root of the Latin word *ritus,* "ritual action." In the ancient traditional way of life, both at an individual and at a collective level, every action was connected with a determined ritual element that acted as its support and as the transfiguring and guiding element "from above." The tradition of rites and sacrifices, which was often confused with the legislative tradition (hence the notion of *ius sacrum*), referred both in the private and in the public dimensions to a nonhuman being or to a being who had transcended the human condition. This can hardly be comprehended by the modern, secular mentality that views every ritual either as an "outdated" superstition or as a mere ceremony[5] to be appreciated merely for the sake of its symbolical, aesthetical, or emotional value. At this point I wish to discuss some of the aspects and meanings of this particular form of the traditional spirit.

As far as "sacrifice" is concerned, according to a text universally regarded as very old, Brahman, "which in the beginning constituted the entire universe, created a higher and more perfect form of itself" from which the "gods of the warriors" (Indra, Mitra, and so on) came into existence.[6]

The primordial power's ability to go beyond itself, an act that is credited with the origination of entities that are the heavenly archetypes of the divine and triumphal regality, is strictly connected with the nature of an entire class of sacrifices. A similar idea is found in a cycle of other myths in which we witness a fundamental identity between heroes and gods who fight victoriously against the personifications of the forces of chaos.[7] This is the same notion of a primordial power that reacts against itself, frees itself, and ascends to a higher plane of being that defines its peculiar divine aspect (the Upaniṣad's "highest and most perfect form of itself"). This plane of being often manifests itself in a law or in a principle of order. For example, the Chaldean hero Marduk, who overcame Tiamat, the demon of chaos, is a cosmic principle of order; in Hindu cosmogony, the vital force produces the "One" of creation through asceticism *(tapas tapyati).* In the Nordic tradition the same idea is expressed through Odin's sacrifice to the cosmic tree Yggdrasil, through which Odin draws out of the abyss the transcendent wisdom contained in the runes and puts it to good use[8]; also, in one specific version of this myth Odin, who is viewed as a king, through his sacrifice points the way that leads to Valhalla, namely, to the type of action that allows

---

5. The original meaning of the word "ceremony" cannot be established for certain. The word comes from the root *creo,* which is identical to the Sanskrit root *kṛ,* "to do," "to act," "to create"; it did not express a conventional celebration, but an authentically creative action.

6. *Bṛhad-āraṇyaka Upaniṣad,* 1.4.11.

7. In the *Bṛhad-āraṇyaka Upaniṣad,* (1.2.7–8) the primordial principle says: "Let my body become fit for sacrifice. Thanks to it I will acquire being." This sacrifice *(aśvamedha)* is related to the sun.

8. *Havamal,* 139.

a person to partake of the heroic, aristocratic, and Uranian immortality.[9]

According to its original meaning, the type of sacrifice to which I refer corresponds to either a similar action that generates a "god" or "hero," or to its repetition, which is connected to a sacrificial tradition centered on that particular god or hero; this repetition either renews the effective power of that god or reproduces it and develops it within the order of a given community. In the Egyptian tradition these meanings find a very important expression: according to a myth, Osiris is believed to be the one who taught mankind how to perform rites as well as the sacred art of temple construction. Osiris is also the god of rites since he himself, first among all the gods, went through sacrifice and experienced "death." His death and dismemberment by Set are related to his "being the first to penetrate the unknown of the otherworld and to his becoming a being who knows the great secret."[10] The myth is developed in the saga of Horus, son of Osiris, who resurrects his father. Horus finds the "proper rites" *(khu)* that give back to Osiris, who has gone into the otherworld or, strictly speaking, into the supernatural, the form that he previously had:

> Through death and rites, Osiris, the first among all beings, knew the mystery and a new life: this science and this life were the privilege of beings who were considered divine. It is from this perspective that Osiris was thought to have initiated both men and gods into sacred rituals. . . . He had shown to beings who inhabit the heavens and earth how to become a god.[11]

From then on, the cult belonging to all divine beings or deified beings consisted in reenacting the mystery of Osiris. This was true first of all for the king; the sacrificial mystery of Osiris was repeated not only in the ritual of the enthroning and in the solemn rite called *sed* repeated every thirty years, but also in the daily cult, which aimed at renewing in the pharaoh the transcendent influence associated with his function. The king publicly acknowledged his kingship and paid homage to Osiris by "piecing him back together" and by ritually renewing his death and victory. The king was called "Horus who shapes the father (Osiris)" and also: "The giver of life, or he who through the rite makes divine life arise in a regal fashion, like the sun."[12] The

---

9. *Ynglingasaga*, 10. Somebody pointed out that the name of the Eddic Tree, Yggdrasil, "the roots of which cannot be found by any mortal being" (*Havamal*, 139–40), seems to denote the instrument employed to sacrifice Yggr, "the Terrible," which is one of Odin's names.

10. A. Moret, *Royauté pharaonique*, 148.

11. Ibid., 149.

12. Ibid., 149; 153–61; 182–83. See also the expression of Ramses II: "I am a son who shapes the head of his own father and who gives life to the one who generated him," (127). The king's entrance into the throne room *(paduat)* corresponded to entering the otherworld *(duat)*, namely, that of sacrificial death and transcendence.

sovereign became "Horus" who resuscitated Osiris or was the resurrected Osiris himself. Similarly, in the Mysteries the initiates often took their name from the god who had founded those same Mysteries, since the initiation reproduces the same act that constitutes the essence of the god, thus determining an analogical similarity of natures; sometimes this similarity is figuratively described as "incarnation" or "generation."

What has been said also applied to the rite in general, that is, to the rite dedicated to the "hero" or to the founding father to whom the traditional patrician family lines often attributed their nonmaterial origins as well as the principle of their rank and of their rights; it also applied to the rite dedicated to the cult of the founders of an institution, of a legislation, or of a city who were believed to be nonhuman beings. In these instances too it was believed that in the origins an action analogous to a sacrifice took place that produced a supernatural quality that remained as a potential spiritual legacy within the stock as the "soul" of those institutions, laws, or foundations. In these cases, rites and various ceremonies helped to actualize and to nourish that original influence, which by virtue of its own nature, appeared to be a principle of well-being, good fortune, and "happiness."

Having clarified the meaning of a relevant body of traditional rites allows me to establish an important point. There are two elements within the traditions of those civilizations or of those castes characterized by a Uranian chrism. The first element is a materialistic and a naturalistic one; it consists of the transmission of something related to blood and race, namely, a vital force that originates in the subterranean world together with the elementary, collective, and ancestral influences. The second element is "from above," and it is conditioned by the transmission and by the uninterrupted performance of rites that contain the secret of a certain transformation and domination realized within the abovementioned vital substratum. The latter element is the higher legacy that confirms and develops the quality the "divine forefather" has either established *ex novo* or attracted from another world. This quality originates the royal stock, the state, the city or the temple, and the caste, the gens or the patrician family according to the supernatural dimension that acts as a "form" shaping chaos. Both of these elements were found in the higher types of traditional civilizations. This is why the rites could appear to be "manifestations of the heavenly law,"[13] according to a Chinese saying.

The unfolding of the ritual action par excellence in its most complete form (e.g., the Vedic sacrifice) reveals three distinct phases. First of all, there was a ritual and spiritual purification on the part of the person performing the sacrifice that put him in real contact with invisible forces and facilitated the possibility of his dominating

13. *Chung–yung*, 27.6.

them. What followed was an evocative process that produced a saturation of these energies either within the person performing the sacrifice, within the victim, or within both—or even within a third element that varied according to the structure of the rite. Finally, there was an action that induced a crisis (for example, the slaying of the victim) and that "actualized" the presence of the god out of the substance of the evoked influences.[14] With the exception of those cases in which the rite is aimed at creating a new entity destined to be the "soul" or the "genius" of a new tradition, a new city, or a new temple (traditionally even the construction of cities and temples had a supernatural counterpart),[15] what took place was something similar to the *releasing* and the *resealing* of hidden forces. In other words, what took place was the evocative renewal of the contact with the infernal forces that acted as the substratum of a primordial deification, as well as with the violence that freed and elevated them to a higher form. This explains the danger believed to be associated with the repetition of a traditional rite and also the reason why the person performing the sacrifice was called "virile hero."[16] A rite that fails or that goes wrong or that deviates in any way from its original form, wounds and defaces a "god": it is *sacrilegium*. Once a law has been altered, the seal of a supernatural dominion is broken and dark, ambiguous, and dreadful forces are unleashed. Even neglecting a rite has a similar effect: it lessens the presence of the "god" in the relationship with those who are guilty of such neglect and it strengthens those energies that were tamed and restrained in the "god" himself; in other words, it opens the doors to chaos. Conversely, a correctly performed and diligent sacrificial action was reputed to be the support that men and gods provide for each other in their mutual interest.[17] The fate awaiting those who no longer have any rite is the "infernal regions"; they fall from the supernatural order they had partaken of into the states of the lower nature. It has been said that only the sacrificial action does not create a "bond."

Olympiodorus wrote that the whole world is one great symbol, since it reflects invisible realities through sensible forms. Plutarch wrote: "Among the things that

---

14. *Introduzione alla magia* (Rome, 1951), 3.281.

15. With regard to a new city, it is the formation of that τυχή πόλεως that in those civilizations of a higher type was identified with the "royal fortune" (τυχή βασίλεως). To consider such entities simply as "personified abstractions" is to adopt the perspective of profane knowledge. In ancient Egypt the divine king presided over the rites related to the construction of new temples; he even performed in a symbolical and ritual fashion the first steps in the construction process. To the vulgar construction materials, he also added gold and silver which symbolize the divine element that he bestowed, by virtue of his presence and of his rite, upon the visible construction as its soul. In this regard he acted in the spirit of an "eternal deed" and in some inscriptions it is written: "The king permeated the ground that will become the abode of the gods."

16. *Ṛg Veda*, 1.40.3.

17. *Bhagavadgītā*, 3.11. In another text it is said that the sacrifice is the food of the gods and the "principle of their lives." *Śatapatha Brāhmaṇa*, 8.1.2, 10.

belong to a higher order there are secret connections and correspondences, just like in the order of natural phenomena: these connections cannot be recognized other than through experience, traditions and universal consensus."[18] A characteristic expression of Jewish esotericism is:

> Through the impulse from below there is a stirring above, and through the impulse from above there is a stirring higher up still. Thus by the impulse of the smoke [of sacrifice] from below the lamp is kindled above and when this is kindled all the other lamps are kindled and all the worlds are blessed from it. Thus by the impulse of the sacrifice is the mainstay of the world and the blessing of all worlds.[19]

This may be considered the general profession of faith of traditional civilizations. According to modern man, both causes and effects are relegated to the physical plane, framed within time and space. According to traditional man the physical plane merely contains effects; nothing takes place in this world that did not originate first in the next world or in the invisible dimension. In this sense too, it is possible to see how the rite takes hold and affects the development of all actions, destinies, and ways of traditional life. In traditional societies the action par excellence consisted in shaping events, relations, victories, and defense mechanisms through the rite, that is, in preparing *causes* in the invisible dimension. Any material action not connected to this supreme action was impaired by a radical contingency; the very soul of an individual was inadequately protected from the dark and elusive forces acting within human passions, thoughts, and inclinations and behind the scenes of nature and of history.

All things considered, it is difficult to label as "fanciful" the fact that traditionally the performance of the rite was considered one of the fundamental principles in the hierarchical differentiation of people, and generally speaking, it was closely associated with every authority within the state, the gens, and the family itself. It is possible to reject the traditional world en bloc, but it is not possible to deny the intimate logical connection of all its parts, once its foundation has been properly understood.

18. Plutarch, *De sera num. vindicta*, 28.
19. *Zohar*, trans. H. Sperling and M. Simon (London, 1933), 2.244a.

6

On the Primordial Nature
of the Patriciate

The Indo-Aryan civilization exemplifies one of the most thorough applications of the foregoing principles. In this civilization, the *brāhmaṇa* caste was not at the top of the social hierarchy by virtue of its material strength or its wealth, or even of its para-ecclesiastical organization; only the sacrificial rite, which was its privilege, determined its higher status vis-à-vis other castes. By permeating those who performed them with some kind of dreadful and beneficial psychic power, the rite and the sacrifice allowed the *brāhmaṇa* to partake of the same nature as the evoked powers; not only would this quality abide in that person forever, making him directly superior to and revered and feared by others, but it would also be transmitted to his descendants. Having entered into the bloodstream as some sort of transcendent legacy, this quality would become the characteristic feature of a race that is activated in individuals by the rite of initiation.[1] The dignity of a caste was determined both by the difficulty and by the usefulness of the functions it exercised. Because of the abovementioned presuppositions, in the world of Tradition nothing was cherished more than the spiritual influences that the rite could activate through its necessitating action; nothing appeared as difficult as entering into a real and active relationship with the invisible forces that were ready to overcome the imprudent person who dared to confront them without possessing the necessary qualifications and knowledge. For this reason the *brāhmaṇa* caste, despite the fact that it was scattered throughout India, could evince the respect of the masses and enjoy a prestige that no tyrant ever enjoyed, no matter how well armed.[2]

In China as well as in Greece and ancient Rome, the patriciate was essentially characterized by the possession and by the practice of those rites that were

---

1. The *brāhmaṇa*, who was compared to the sun, was often thought to be substantiated by a radiant energy or splendor *(tejas)* that he drew from his vital force through his "spiritual knowledge." *Śatapatha Brāhmaṇa,* 13.2.6, 10.
2. Concerning the foundation of the *brāhmaṇa's* authority, see *The Laws of Manu* 9.313–17.

connected to the divine power emanating from the founder of a family. In China, only the patricians practiced the rites *(yi-li)*, while the plebeians merely had customs *(su)*. There is a Chinese saying: "The rites are not the legacy of ordinary people," which corresponds to the famous saying of Appius Claudius: *"Auspicia sunt patrum."* A Latin expression characterized the plebeians as *gentem non habent:* people who have no rites nor ancestors. This is why in ancient Rome the patricians viewed the plebeians' lifestyle and sexual coupling as similar to that of wild animals *(more ferarum)*. Thus, the supernatural element was the foundation of the idea of a traditional patriciate and of legitimate royalty: what constituted an ancient aristocrat was not merely a biological legacy or a racial selection, but rather a sacred tradition. In fact, even an animal may have biological and racial purity. After all, in the caste system the laws of blood, heredity, and endogamic restrictions did not apply only to the *brāhmaṇa* but to the other castes as well. It was not in this sense that the plebeian was said to lack ancestors: the true principle of the differentiation between patricians and plebeians was that the ancestors of the plebeian and of the slave were not "divine ancestors" *(divi parentes)* like the ancestors of the patrician stocks. No transcendent quality or "form" entrusted to a rigorous and secret ritual tradition was transmitted to them through the blood. The plebeians lacked that power through which the members of the aristocracy could directly celebrate their own cults or be members of the priestly class (as was the case in the ancient classical world, in ancient Northern and Germanic races, in the Far East, and so on). The plebeians did not have the privilege of the second birth that characterized the *ārya* (the noble) and the *Manudharmaśāstra*[3] does not hesitate to say that even an *ārya* is not superior to the *śūdra* until he has been born again. The plebeians were not purified by any of the three heavenly fires that in ancient Iran were believed to act as the occult souls of the three higher castes in the empire. The plebeians also lacked the "solar" element that in ancient Peru characterized the race of the Incas. The plebeians' promiscuity had no limits; they had no true cult of their own, and in a higher sense they had no founding father *(patrem ciere non possunt)*.[4] Therefore the plebeians' religion could not help but have a collective and chthonic character. In India their religion was characterized by frenzied and ecstatic forms more or less connected to the substratum of pre-Aryan races. In the Mediterranean civilizations, the plebeians' religion was characterized by the cult of the mothers and by subterranean forces instead of the luminous forms of the heroic and Olympian tradition. The plebeians, who in ancient Rome were called "children of the Earth," had a religious devotion to the feminine deities of the earth. Even in China, the official aristocratic religion stood in

---

3. *Laws of Manu*, 2.39; 103; 157–58; 172.
4. In the mythical account of the establishment of the castes as it was handed down by the *brāhmaṇa*, while to each of the three higher castes corresponds a group of deities, this is not the case of the *śūdra*, who do not have any god of their own to whom they may pray and offer sacrifices.

contrast with the practices of those who were often called "obsessed" *(ling-pao)*, and with the popular cults of a Mongolian and shamanic type.

We find the supernatural conception of the aristocracy also in ancient Teutonic traditions, not only because in these traditions every leader was at the same time the high priest of his people and of his lands, but also because claiming as an ancestor a divine being was enough to separate a family from all the others; a king was then chosen exclusively from among the members of these privileged families. This is why the king enjoyed a different dignity from that enjoyed, for instance, by a military leader (*dux* or *heritzogo*) who was occasionally appointed in military situations on the basis of his recognized individual talents. It seems that ancient Norwegian kings celebrated the rites by themselves, without the help of the priestly class. Even among the so-called primitive populations those who had not been initiated were looked down upon by their own people and excluded from all the military and political privileges of their clan. Before undergoing rites that were destined to transform one's innermost nature and that were often associated with hard trials and a with a period of isolation, a person was not considered to be a true man but was rather seen as belonging to the same class as women, children, and animals. An individual became a member of the group of true men who control the community only through the new life awakened in him by initiation, almost as if he partook of a "mystery" or joined an order.[5] Once an individual partakes of this new life, which is almost "unrelated to the old one," he receives a new name, a new language, and new attributions. Thus, authors such as H. Schurtz have rightfully seen in this the germ of true political unity; this insight corroborates what I have said before concerning the plane proper to any traditional state, which is different from the plane typical of any unity built on merely naturalistic premises. These "virile groups" (in German, *Männerbunde*) to which one is admitted after a regeneration that truly confers manhood and differentiates a person from all other members of the community, enjoy power *(imperium)* and an undisputed prestige.[6]

Only in recent times has aristocracy, like royalty, taken on a mere secular and political character. In the beginning, aristocracy and royalty were based on character, race, honor, valor, and faithfulness, on *noblesse d'épée* and on *noblesse de coeur*. In later times a plebeian view of the aristocracy arose that denied even the privileges of blood and tradition.

A typical example of the latter view is the so-called aristocracy of culture, or the

---

5. Hutton Webster, *Primitive Secret Societies* (Italian trans., Bologna, 1921).

6. Concerning virility in an eminent and not naturalistic sense, we may refer to the Latin term *vir* as opposed to *homo*. G. B. Vico (*The New Science*, 3.41) had already remarked that this term implied a special dignity, since it designated not only a man to be married with a patrician woman, but also the nobility, the magistrates *(duumviri, decemviri)*, the priests *(quindicemviri, vigintiviri)*, judges *(centemviri)*, because "the term *vir* indicated wisdom, priesthood and kingship, as I have previously demonstrated that it formed one thing in the person of the first fathers in the state constituted by families."

aristocracy of intellectuals that arose as a by-product of bourgeois civilization. During a census taken in the reign of Frederick the Great, the head of an ancient German noble family humorously replied, *"Analphabet wegen des höhen Adels,"* in reference to the ancient notion of the British lords who were considered "experienced in the law and learned, even though they may not know how to read." The truth is that in the context of a normal hierarchical view, the principle that determined the precise ontological and essential differences between people and was at the basis of the notion of aristocracy and of its privileges was never "intellectuality" but rather "spirituality." The tradition was preserved, though in an attenuated form, up to the time of the knightly nobility where it was embodied in a somewhat ascetical and sacral aspect in the great medieval orders. At that point the nobility already had its main reference point in the sacred, not in but outside itself and in a separate class, namely, the clergy, although the clergy represented a spirituality that was still a far cry from the spirituality of the primordial elites.

The ritual and sacral element was the foundation of the authority of both the higher castes and of the father in the ancient patrician family. In Western Aryan societies such as Greece and Rome, the *pater familiae* originally enjoyed a status similar to that of the priest-king. The term *pater* was synonymous with king (hence the words *rex, ἄναξ, βασιλεύς*); it conveyed the idea of a spiritual authority as well as that of power and majestic dignity. According to some views with which I totally concur, the state is an application on a larger scale of the same principle that in the beginning constituted the patrician family. Therefore the *pater,* though he was the military leader and the lord of justice of his relatives and slaves, *in primis et ante omnia* was the person entrusted with performing those traditional rites and sacrifices proper to every family, the rites and sacrifices that constituted its nonhuman legacy.

This legacy, which emanated from the founding father, was represented by fire (for example, the thirty fires of the thirty families surrounding the central fire of Vesta, in ancient Rome). This fire, which was fed with special substances and lit according to specific rituals and secret norms, was supposed to be kept burning at all times by every family as the living and tangible witness of its divine legacy. The father was the virile priest in charge of tending to the sacred family fire, but he was also one who must have appeared like a "hero" to his children, relatives, and servants; or like the natural mediator of every efficacious relationship with the supernatural; or like the supreme vivifier of the mystical force of the ritual, which was present in the substance of fire; or like the incarnation of "order," as Agni was to the Indo-Aryans; or like the principle that "brings the gods to us"; or like "the firstborn from order"; or like "the son of strength";[7] or like "he who leads us away from this

7. *Ṛg Veda,* 1.1.7–8; 1.13.1; 10.5.7; 8.3.8.

38

world, to higher dimensions, into the world of the right action."[8] The *pater*'s main responsibility was to prevent the "fire from going out" so that it might continue to reproduce, perpetuate, and nourish the mystical victory of the ancestor;[9] this responsibility to the fire was the manifestation of the "regal" component of his family, with the *pater* being the "lord of the spear and of the sacrifice." In this way the *pater* really constituted the center of the family; the entire rigorous constitution of traditional paternal rights flowed from this center as a natural consequence, and it subsisted even when the awareness of its primordial foundation was lost. In ancient Rome, anyone who like the *pater* had the *ius quiritium* (the right to the bear the lance and to perform sacrifices), also had the right to own land; his privileges could never be abrogated. He spoke on behalf of the gods and on account of power. Just like the gods, he expressed himself through symbols and signs. He was immaterial. Originally, it was not possible *(nulla auctoritas)* to prosecute a patrician legally, since he was regarded as a minister of the gods, just like the king in recent times. If the patrician committed a crime in his *mundus,* the Curia would only declare that he did something wicked *(improbe factum).* His rights over his relatives were absolute: *ius vitae necisque.* His superhuman character made it natural for him to sell and even to put to death his own children, at his own discretion.[10] It was in this spirit that the articulations of what Vico rightly called "natural heroic rights" or "divine rights of heroic people" were formulated.

According to a patrician tradition the rite, which corresponded to a "Uranian" component, enjoyed primacy over other elements of the same tradition that were related to nature; this can be established from several aspects of the ancient Greco-Roman laws. It has rightfully been said that:

> In antiquity what united the members of a family was something more powerful than birth, feelings and physical strength: it was the cult of the hearth and of the ancestors. This cult shaped the family into a united body, both in this world and in the next. The ancient family was more a religious than a natural association.[11]

---

8. *Atharva Veda* 6.120.1. The expression refers to *gārhapatya-agni* which, among the three fires, is that of the *pater* or head of the household.

9. "The father is the household's fire." *Laws of Manu,* 2.231. To keep fueling the sacred fire is the duty of the *dvīja,* the twice-born, who constitute the three higher castes (2.108). It is not possible now to elaborate beyond this brief reference to the traditional cult of fire. Later on I will discuss the role that men and women played in the cult of the fire, in the family and in social life.

10. Concerning the abovementioned expressions, see M. Michelet, *Histoire de la république romaine* (Paris, 1843), 1.138, 144–46. Similar elements are even found in more recent traditions. The British lords in the beginning were considered to be demigods and on the same footing with the king. According to a law promulgated by Edward I, they enjoyed the privilege of simple homicide.

11. F. de Coulanges, *Cité antique,* 105.

The common ritual constituted the true bond of the family's unity and often even of the gens itself. If an outsider was allowed to participate in the common rite, he thereby became an adoptive son who enjoyed those privileges that could also be taken away from a biological son guilty of neglecting the rite of his family, or from a son who was interdicted from participating in it. This obviously meant that according to the traditional idea, rite rather than blood had the power to unite or to differentiate people.[12] In India, Greece, and Rome, a woman had to mystically join her future husband's family or gens through the rite; the bride, before being a man's bride, was the bride of Agni or the mystical fire. Those who were allowed to participate in the cult proper of a patrician stock were thereby allowed to enjoy an ennobling mystical participation that conferred upon them some of the privileges of that particular stock, while at the same time they committed their future offspring to it. Consequently, it is possible to understand the sacred aspect of the feudal principle as it previously emerged in ancient Egypt, since through the mystical "gift of life" emanating from him, the king gathered around himself a body of faithful subjects who were elevated to the priestly dignity. Analogous ideas can be found in Peru among the Incas, the "Children of the Sun," and to a certain extent, even among the Japanese feudal nobility.

In India one finds the idea—which should be reduced to the doctrine of the "sacrifices" in general—of a family line of male descendants (primogeniture) that is strictly related to the problem of immortality. The firstborn—who alone has the right to invoke Indra, the heavenly warrior god—is seen as the one whose birth frees the father of his debt to the ancestors; thus, it is said that the firstborn "frees" or "saves" *(trayate)* the ancestors in the world beyond. The firstborn, standing on the "battle-field" represented by this earthly existence, confirms and continues the line of influence that constitutes the ancestors' substance and that is carried on in the blood-stream as a purifying fire. It is significant that the firstborn is believed to have been generated in order to fulfill a "duty" to this ritual commitment that is not affected by human feelings or ties.

It is not impossible, therefore, that in some cases a family derived by adaptation from a superior and purely spiritual type of unity found in older times. For instance, Lao-tzu[13] hinted that the family arose at the end of a relationship of direct participation, through blood, with the original spiritual principle. A similar idea still echoes as

---

12. In Rome there were two types of marriage, one related to the chthonic and the other to the Uranian component of Roman civilization. The first type was a secular and practical marriage, in which the woman was considered mere property to be transferred to the *manum viri;* the second type was a ritual and sacred marriage, a *confarreatio,* a sacrament or sacred union *(hierogamos).* The Hellenistic equivalent of the *confarreatio* was the *eggineois;* the sacral element that abided in the *agape* was considered to be so important that without it the validity of the marriage could be challenged.

13. *Tao te Ching,* 18.

a residue in the priority acknowledged by several traditions of spiritual paternity over natural paternity, or of a "second birth" versus natural birth. In ancient Rome, for instance, we could refer to the inner aspect of the dignity conferred at the time of adoption, which was understood as an immaterial and supernatural filiation that was believed to take place under the aegis of "Olympian" deities; at one point in time adoption was also chosen as the basis for the continuation of the imperial function. According to an ancient Hindu text:

> That his mother and father produced him through mutual desire and he was born in the womb, he should regard as his mere coming into existence. But the birth that a teacher produces for him . . . is real, free from old age and free from death.[14]

In this way natural relationships not only are secondary, but they may also be reversed; thus according to the same text, "the *brāhmaṇa* who brings about the Vedic birth of an older person and who teaches him his own duties becomes his father, according to law, even if he is himself a child."[15] Wherever the law of *patria potestas* was considered from a social and juridical point of view to be absolute and almost superhuman, such a law could enjoy this spiritual character only if it had (or if it originally had) such a justification in the order of spiritual paternity, and also if it was related to blood ties as the "soul" is related to the "body" within the organic unity of the family stock. I will not dwell further on these concepts; however, it is noteworthy that a body of ancient beliefs also postulates the idea of a unity that is not merely biological but psychospiritual as well. Thus the guilt of a family member was believed to affect the entire family;[16] also, according to this idea, a family member may redeem another or carry out an act of vengeance on behalf of another, and so on.

In all of these aspects one finds repeated confirmation of the view according to which traditional institutions were ordered "from above" and were not based on nature but on sacred legacies and on spiritual actions that bind, free, and "shape" nature. In the divine dimension what counts is the blood *(θεοὶ σύναιμοι)* and the family *(θεοὶ εγγενεῖς)*. The state, the community, the family, bourgeois feelings, duties in the modern (profane, human, and social) sense of the word—all these are human "fabrications," things entirely made up and existing outside the realm of traditional reality, in the world of shadows. The light of Tradition did not know any of these things.

---

14. *Laws of Manu*, 2.147–48.
15. *Laws of Manu*, 2.150.
16. Deut. 5:7.

7

Spiritual Virility

S o far I have discussed the roles that the Sacred, the gods, the priestly class, and
the rites played in traditional societies. In the world of Tradition, these things
hardly correspond to categories typical of the domain of "religion" in the current
sense of the word, based as it is on the notion of deities conceived as self-sufficient
beings and the notion of God as a personal being who providentially rules the universe. Moreover, the cult is essentially characterized by an affective disposition and
by a sentimental and devotional relationship of the "believer" to this Supreme Being
or deities. In this type of relationship the moral law plays a fundamental role.

One would look in vain for "religion" in the original forms of the world of Tradition. There are civilizations that never named their gods or attempted to portray them—
at least this is what is said about the ancient Pelasgians. The Romans themselves, for
almost two centuries, did not portray their deities; at most, they represented them with
a symbolical object. What characterizes the primordial times is not "animism" (the
idea that an "anima" is the foundation of the general representation of the divine and
of the various forces at work in the universe) but rather the idea or perception of pure
powers,[1] adequately represented by the Roman view of the *numen*. The *numen,* unlike the notion of *deus* (as it later came to be understood), is not a being or a person,
but a sheer power that is capable of producing effects, of acting, and of manifesting
itself. The sense of the real presence of such powers, or *numina*, as something simultaneously transcendent and yet immanent, marvelous yet fearful, constituted the substance of the original experience of the "sacred."[2] A well-known saying of Servius
emphasizes that in the origins, "religion" consisted in nothing else but *experience.*[3]
Even though more conditioned points of view were not excluded from exotericism
(those traditional forms reserved for the common people), "inner doctrines" were

---

1. G. F. Moore, *Origin and Growth of Religion* (London, 1921).
2. R. Otto *(The Holy)* has employed the term "numinous" (from *numen*) to designate the content of the
experience of the sacred.
3. *"Maiores enim expugnando religionem totum in experientia collocabunt." Ad georgicas,* 3.456

characterized by the teaching that the personal forms of deities, variously objectified, are only symbols of superrational and superhuman ways of being. As I have said, the center consisted in the real and living presence of these states within an elite, or in the ideal of their realization through what in Tibet is called the "direct path," and which generally corresponds to initiation conceived as an ontological change of nature. The saying from the Upaniṣads that best represents the traditional "inner doctrine" is: "So whoever worships another divinity than his Self, thinking: 'He is one and I another,' he knows not. He is like a sacrificial animal for the gods."[4]

With regard to the rite there was nothing "religious" about it and little or no devout pathos in those who performed it. The rite was rather a "divine technique," a determining action upon invisible forces and inner states similar in spirit to what today is obtained through physical forces and states of matter. The priest was simply a person who, by virtue of his qualification and the *virtus* intrinsic to the rite itself, was capable of producing results through this technique. "Religion" was the equivalent of the *indigitamenta* of the ancient Roman world, namely, of the body of formulations used with different *numina*. Thus it is easy to see that prayers, fears, hopes, and other feelings displayed before what has the character of *numen* had as little meaning and effect upon it as if one of our contemporaries were to employ prayers when confronting a machine. Instead, what was at stake was to be able to understand such relationships so that once a cause was established through a correctly performed rite, a necessary and constant effect would ensue on the plane of "powers" and invisible forces and states of being. Thus, the law of action reigned supreme. But the law of action is also the law of freedom; no bond can be spiritually imposed on beings who neither hope nor fear, but rather act.

Thus in the older Indo-Aryan view of the world only the *brāhmaṇa* caste, consisting as it did of superior natures, could tower over everybody else since it ruled over the power of the rite, or of Brahman, understood in this context as the vital and primordial principle. The "gods" themselves, when they are not personifications of the ritual action (that is, beings who are actualized or renewed by this action), are spiritual forces that bow before this caste.[5] According to the Far Eastern tradition, the person who has authority also enjoys the dignity of a "third power between Heaven and Earth."[6] In ancient Egypt, even the "great gods" could be threatened with destruction by priests who knew special sacred incantations.[7] "Kemotef" ("his mother's

---

4. *Bṛhad-āraṇyaka Upaniṣad* 1.4.10.
5. Somebody remarked that in the Hindu tradition the religious deed par excellence appears to have been thought of in terms of a magical procedure or of a quasi-mechanical operation, the good or bad outcome of which depended entirely on the person engaging in it; in this context, morality had no role to play.
6. *Chung-yung*, 24.1; 23.1; 31.1, 3, 4.
7. Porphyry did not fail to contrast this kind of attitude toward the divine with the attitude of fearful religious worship that emerged in some features of the Greco-Roman cult. *Epistula Anebo*, 29.

bull") was a title of the Egyptian king, emphasizing that as a man, the king possesses the primordial substance; he affects the divine more than being affected by it. One of the formulations recited by the Egyptian kings before the performance of the rites was: "O gods, you are safe if I am safe; your doubles are safe if my double is at the head of all living doubles; everybody lives if I live."[8] Formulations of glory, power, and total identification are recited by the soul "rendered like Osiris" in the course of its trials; these trials in turn can be assimilated to various degrees of solar initiation. Similar traditions are perpetuated wherever in Alexandrian literature mention is made of the "holy race of people without kings," a race "autonomous and immaterial" that "acts without being acted upon."[9] This race is believed to be endowed with a "sacred science centuries old" that is proper to "the lords of the spirit and of the temple," and communicated only to kings, princes, and priests; this science is related to the rituals of the pharaohs and later on it came to be known in the Western world as Ars Regia.[10]

In the higher forms of the luminous Aryan spirituality, whether in Greece, ancient Rome, or the Far East, the role played by doctrine was minimal: only the rituals were mandatory and absolutely necessary. Orthodoxy was defined through rituals and practices and not through dogmas and theories. Sacrilege and impiety ($\dot{\alpha}\sigma\dot{\epsilon}\beta\epsilon\iota\alpha$) did not consist in "not believing" but rather in neglecting rites. This does not amount to "formalism"—as modern historians, who are more or less influenced by a Protestant mentality, would have us believe—but rather to the pure law of spiritual action. In the Doric-Achaean ritual, the relationship with the divine was not based on feelings but on an attitude characterized by *do ut des*.[11] Even the gods presiding over funerals were not treated very "religiously"; they did not love men, nor were they loved by them in return. The reason behind their cult was to propitiate them and to prevent them from exercising an unfavorable action. The *expiatio* itself originally had the character of an objective operation, such as the medical procedure for an

---

8. This explains why the first generation of Egyptologists was led by devotional religion to recognize in the features of pharaonic regality those of the Antichrist or of the *princeps huius mundi*.

9. This obviously corresponds to the principle of "acting without acting," which according to the Taoist tradition is "Heaven's Way"; accordingly, "those without kings" correspond to those whom Lao-tzu called "skillful masters" of the Tao (*Tao te Ching*, 15) and to the Iranian "men of the primordial law."

10. See J. Evola, *The Hermetic Tradition*, trans. E. E. Rehmus (Rochester, Vt., 1994). Even though the king may be called "son of the Sun," or "son of Heaven" this does not contradict the abovementioned views, since such concepts do not evoke creationist and dualistic concepts. Rather, these views convey the idea of a descent that is the "continuation" of the same one influence, spirit or emanation. Agrippa remarked (*De occulta philosophia*, 3.36) that it is like "the univocal generation in which the son is similar to the father in all regards, and having been generated according to the human species, he is the same as the one who generated him."

11. J. E. Harrison, *Prolegomena to the Study of the Greek Religion* (Cambridge, 1903), 162.

infection, without resembling either a punishment or an act of repentance on the part of a soul. The formulations employed by every patrician family and by every ancient city in their relationship with the forces controlling their destinies, had been previously employed by their divine forefathers to overcome spiritual forces *(numina)*. Thus, these formulations were merely the legacy of a mystical domain; they were not the effusion of feelings but a supernaturally efficacious weapon, provided that not a single technique was changed in the course of the rite.[12]

Wherever the traditional principle was applied in its entirety it is possible to find, in its hierarchical differentiations, a transcendent virility that finds its best symbolical expression in the synthesis of the two attributes of the Roman patrician class, namely, the lance and the rite. There one also finds beings who are *reges sacrorum,* innerly free, and often consecrated by Olympian immortality. With regard to invisible and divine forces these beings exercise the same function of centrality and the same role that leaders exercise among human beings. A very long downward path or degenerated process unwinds from this "peak" to what is currently and commonly considered "religion" and "priesthood."

The world of "animism" represents a fall from and an attenuation of the world perceived under the species of "powers" and of *numina*. This attenuation and degeneration was destined to increase with the shift from a world in which "souls" were inherent in things and in the elements to a world in which the gods were conceived as persons in an objective sense rather than as figurative allusions to nonhuman states, forces, and possibilities. When the efficacy of the rite disappeared, man was motivated to give a mythological individuality to those forces with which he had previously dealt according to simple relationships of technique or which, at most, he had conceived under the species of symbols. Later on man conceived these forces in his own image, thus limiting human possibilities; he saw in them personal beings who were more powerful than he was, and who were to be addressed with humility, faith, hope, and fear, not only to receive protection and success, but also liberation and *salus* (in its double meaning of health and salvation). The hyperrealistic world that was substantiated with pure and sheer action was replaced with a subreal and confused world of emotions, imagination, hopes, and fears; this world became increasingly "human" and powerless as it followed various stages of the general involution and alteration of the primordial tradition.

Only vis-à-vis this decadence is it possible to distinguish the regal and the priestly functions. Even when a priestly class ruled without departing from the pure tradi-

12. Cicero, *De haruspicina responsio,* 11.23; Arnobius, *Adversus nationes* (The Case Against the Pagans), 4.31.

tional spirit, as in the case of ancient India, it had a much more "magical" and regal rather than religious character, in the usual sense of the word "religious."

When I say "magical," I do not mean what today the majority of people think when they hear the term "magic," which is almost always discredited by prejudices and counterfeits. Nor do I refer to the meaning the term acquires when referred to the *sui generis* empirical science typical of antiquity, which was rather limited in its scope and effects. Magic in this context designates a special attitude toward spiritual reality itself, an attitude of centrality that is closely related to regal tradition and initiation.

Secondly, it does not make sense to emphasize the relationship between the magical attitude, the pure ritual, the impersonal, direct, and "numinous" perception of the divine and the way of life of savage tribes, which according to the Judeo-Christian mentality are still unaware of "true religiosity." In most cases, savage tribes should not be considered as precivilized states of mankind, but rather as extremely degenerated forms of remnants of very ancient races and civilizations. Even though the abovementioned particulars are found among savage tribes and are expressed in materialistic, dark, and shamanic forms, this should not prevent us from recognizing the meaning and the importance they assume once they are brought back to their true origins. Likewise, "magic" should not be understood on the basis of those wretched and degenerated remnants, but rather on the basis of the forms in which it was preserved in an active, luminous, and conscious way. These forms coincide with what I have called the "spiritual virility" of the world of Tradition. It does not come as a surprise that most noted modern "historians of religion" have no idea whatsoever about this concept; the confusions and the prejudices found in their highly documented works are most unfortunate.

8

The Two Paths in the Afterlife

At this point it is necessary to discuss the connection between the order of ideas I have outlined so far and the problem of one's destiny in the afterlife. In this context too, reference should be made to teachings that have almost entirely been lost in recent times.

The belief that everybody's soul is immortal is rather odd; very little evidence of it can be found in the world of Tradition. In Tradition, a distinction was made between true immortality, which corresponded to participation in the Olympian nature of a god, and mere survival; also, various forms of possible survival came into play and the problem of the postmortem condition of each individual was analyzed, always taking into consideration the various elements present in the human aggregate, since man was far from being reduced to the simple binomial "soul-body."

What continuously emerges in various forms in ancient traditions is the teaching that in man, in addition to the physical body, there are essentially three entities or principles, each endowed with its own character and destiny. The first principle corresponds to the conscious "I" typical of the waking state, which arose with the body and was formed in parallel with its biological development; this is the ordinary personality. The second principle was called "demon," *"manes,"* *"lar,"* and even "double." The third and last principle corresponds to what proceeds from the first entity after death; for most people, it is the "shadow."

As long as a person belongs to "nature," the ultimate foundation of a human being is the daemon or "demon," ($\delta\alpha\acute{\iota}\mu\omega\nu$ in Greek); in this context the term does not have the evil connotation Christianity bestowed upon it. When man is considered from a naturalistic point of view, the demon, could be defined as the deep force that originally produced consciousness in the finite form that is the body in which it lives during its residence in the visible world. This force eventually remains "behind" the individual, in the preconscious and in the subconscious dimensions, as the foundation of organic processes and subtle relations with the environment, other beings, and with past and future destiny; these relations usually elude any direct perception. In this regard, in many traditions the demon corresponds to the so-called double, which is perhaps a reference to the soul of the soul or the body itself; this "double" has also often been closely associated with the primordial ancestor or with the totem conceived as the soul and the unitary life that generated a stock, a family, a *gens,* or a tribe, and therefore it has a broader sense than the one given to it by some schools of contemporary ethnology. The single individuals of a group appear as various incarnations or emanations of this demon or totem, which is the "spirit" pulsating in their blood; they live in it and it lives in them, though transcending them, just as the matrix transcends the particular forms it produces out of its own substance. In the Hindu tradition the demon corresponds to that principle of man's inner being called *liṅga-śarīra.* The word *liṅga* contains the idea of a generating power; hence, the possible derivation of *genius* from *genere,* which means to act in the sense of begetting; and hence, the Roman and Greek belief that the *genius* or *lar* (demon) is the same procreating force without which a family would become extinct. It is also very significant that totems have often been associated with the "souls" of selected animal species, and that especially the snake, essentially a telluric animal, has been associated in the classical world with the idea of demon or of *genius.* These two instances bear witness to the fact that in its immediacy this force is essentially subpersonal, and belongs to nature and to the infernal world. Thus, according to the symbolism of the Roman tradition, the seat of the *lares* is underground; they are in the custody of a female principle, Mania, who is the Mater Larum.

According to esoteric teachings, at the death of the body an ordinary person usually loses his or her personality, which was an illusory thing even while that person was alive. The person is then reduced to a *shadow* that is itself destined to be dissolved after a more or less lengthy period culminating in what was called "the second death."[1] The essential vital principles of the deceased return to the totem, which is a primordial, perennial, and inexhaustible matter; life will again proceed from this matter and assume other individual forms, all of which are subject to the same destiny. This is the reason why totems, *manes, lares,* or *penates* (the gods of

---

1. The Egyptian tradition referred to those who are damned in the afterlife judgment as "twice dead." They become the victims of the infernal monster Amam ("The Devourer") or Am-mit ("The Corpse Eater"). The Egyptian *Book of the Dead* contains formulations designed to help a person "to elude the second death in the next world." "Judgment" is just an allegory. It is rather an impersonal and objective process, as the symbol of the scale weighing the "hearts" of the deceased seems to suggest, since nothing could prevent a scale from being weighed down by the greater weight. As far as the "sentencing" is concerned, it also presupposes the inability to realize some possibilities of immortality granted in the postmortem; these possibilities are alluded to by some traditional teachings, from Egypt to Tibet, and described in their respective "Books of the Dead." Also, see the Aztec traditions concerning the "trials" undergone by the deceased and the magical formulas employed by them.

48

the Roman people, "to whom we owe the breath within us and by whom we possess our bodies and our power of thought"[2]) were identified with the *dead;* the cult of the ancestors, the demons, and the invisible generating force that is present in everybody was often confused with the cult of the dead. The "souls" of the deceased continued to exist in the *dii manes* into whom they were dissolved, but also in those forces of the stock, the race, or the family in which the life of these *dii manes* was manifested and perpetuated.

This teaching concerns the naturalistic order. There is, however, a second teaching relating to a higher order and a different, more privileged, aristocratic, and sacred solution to the problem of survival after death. It is possible to establish a connection here with the ideas expressed above concerning those ancestors who, through their "victory," bestowed a sacred legacy upon the ensuing patrician generations that re-enact and renew the rite.

The "heroes" or demigods to whom the higher castes and the noble families of traditional antiquity traced their lineage were beings who at death (unlike most people or unlike those who had been defeated in the trials of the afterlife) did not emanate a "shadow" or the larva of an ego that was eventually destined to die anyway; instead, they were beings who had achieved the self-subsistent, transcendent, and incorruptible life of a "god." They were those who "had overcome the second death." This was possible because they had more or less directly imposed upon their own vital force that change of nature I mentioned before when talking about the transcendent meaning of "sacrifice." Ancient Egyptian traditions clearly articulated the task of creating out of the *ka* (another name for the "double" or the "demon") some kind of new incorruptible body *(sahu)* that was supposed to replace the physical body and "stand on its own feet" in the invisible dimension. In other traditions it is possible to find the identical concept under the names of "immortal body," "body of glory," or "resurrection body." Therefore, if in their traditions the Greeks of Homer's time (as in the first Aryan period when the Vedas were written) did not contemplate the survival of the soul alone, but instead, believed the survivors (those who had been "kidnapped" or "made invisible" by the gods and who had settled in the "island of the blessed," where there is no death) retained soul and body in an indissoluble unity, this should not be understood as a coarse materialistic representation, as many historians of religion today are inclined to believe, but as the symbolic expression of the idea of an "immortal body" and the condition for immortality; this idea enjoyed its classical formulation in Far Eastern esotericism, and more specifically, in operative Taoism. The Egyptian *sahu,* created by the rite, thanks to which the deceased can go on to live in the company of solar gods, indicates a body that has achieved a

2. Macrobius, *Saturnalia,* 3.4.

high degree of knowledge, power, and glory and that has thus become everlasting and incorruptible. This body is referred to in the following formulation: "Your soul lives, your body germinates eternally at Ra's command without any diminution or defect, just like Ra's." In this context the attainment of immortality or the victory over adverse powers of dissolution is related to wholeness, namely, to the inseparability of the soul from the body—better yet, from a body that does not undergo decay. There is a very suggestive Vedic formula: "Leaving behind every fault, go back home. Filled with splendor, be reunited with your body."[3] The Christian dogma of the "resurrection of the flesh" that will take place on Judgment Day is the last echo of this idea, which can be traced back to prehistoric times.[4]

In these instances death did not represent an end but a fulfillment. It was a "triumphal death" bestowing immortality and was the reason why in some Hellenic traditions the deceased was called "hero" and dying was called "generating demigods" (ἥρωα γίνεσθαι); or why the deceased was portrayed wearing a crown (often put on his head by the goddesses of victory) made with the same myrtle that identified those who were going to be initiated into the Eleusinian Mysteries; or why in the Catholic liturgical language the day of death is called *dies natalis* (day of birth); or why in Egypt the tombs of the deceased who had been dedicated to Osiris were called "houses of immortality," and the afterlife was conceived as "the land of triumph"; or why in ancient Rome the emperor's "demon" was worshiped as divine, and why the kings, legislators, victorious generals, and founders of those institutions or traditions that were believed to involve an action and a conquest beyond nature were worshiped as heroes, demigods, gods, and avatars of different deities. The sacred foundation of the authority the elders enjoyed in several ancient civilizations lies in similar ideas. People saw in the elders, who were closer to death, the manifestation of the divine force that was thought to achieve its full liberation at death.[5]

Thus, as far as the destiny of the soul after death is concerned, there are two opposite paths. The first is the "path of the gods," also known as the "solar path" or Zeus's path, which leads to the bright dwelling of the immortals. This dwelling was variously represented as a height, heaven, or an island, from the Nordic Valhalla and Asgard to the Aztec-Inca "House of the Sun" that was reserved for kings, heroes, and nobles. The other path is that trodden by those who do not survive in a real way, and who slowly yet inexorably dissolve back into their original stocks, into the

---

3. *Rg Veda*, 10.14.8.
4. D. Merezhkovsky (*Dante* [Bologna, 1939]), wrote: "In Paleolithic times soul and body were believed to be inseparable; united in this world they remained joined together in the next world too. As strange as it may seem, cave men knew a 'resurrection of the flesh' which a Socrates and a Plato, with their 'immortality of the soul,' seem to have forgotten."
5. Such a justification of the authority of the leaders is still preserved among some primitive populations.

"totems" that unlike single individuals, never die; this is the life of Hades, of the "infernals," of Niflheim, of the chthonic deities.[6] This teaching is found in the Hindu tradition where the expressions *deva-yāna* and *pitṛ-yāna* signify "path of the gods," and "path of the ancestors" (in the sense of *manes*), respectively. It is also said: "These two paths, one bright and the other dark, are considered eternal in the universe. In the former, man goes out and then comes back; in the latter he keeps on returning." The first path "leading to Brahman," namely, to the unconditioned state, is analogically associated with fire, light, the day, and the six months of the solar ascent during the year; it leads to the region of thunderbolts, located beyond the "door of the sun." The second path, which is related to smoke, night, and the six months of the sun's descent leads to the moon, which is the symbol of the principle of change and becoming and which is manifested here as the principle regulating the cycle of finite beings who continuously come and go in many ephemeral incarnations of the ancestral forces.[7] According to an interesting symbolism, those who follow the lunar path become the food of the *manes* and are "sacrificed" again by them in the semen of new mortal births. According to another significant symbol found in the Greek tradition, those who have not been initiated, that is to say, the majority of people, are condemned in Hades to do the Danaïdes' work; carrying water in amphorae filled with holes and pouring it into bottomless barrels, thus never being able to fill them up; this illustrates the insignificance of their ephemeral lives, which keep recurring over and over again, pointlessly. Another comparable Greek symbol is Ocnus, who plaited a rope on the Plains of Lethe. This rope was continually eaten by an ass. Ocnus symbolizes man's activity, while the ass traditionally embodies the "demonic" power; in Egypt the ass was associated with the snake of darkness and with Am-mit, the "devourer of the dead."

In this context we again find the basic ideas concerning the "two natures" that I discussed in the first chapter. But here it is possible to penetrate deeper into the meaning of the existence in antiquity not only of two types of divinities, (the former Uranian and solar, the latter telluric and lunar), but also of the existence of two

6. Among Assyrian-Babylonian people we find conceptions of a larval state, similar to the Hellenic Hades, awaiting the majority of people after death. Also, see the Jewish notion of the dark and cold *sheol* in which the deceased, including prestigious figures such as Abraham and David, led an unconscious and impersonal existence. The notion of torments, terrors and punishments in the afterlife (like the Christian notion of "hell") is very recent and extraneous to the pure and original forms of Tradition; in these forms we find only the difference between the aristocratic, heroic, solar, and Olympian survival for some, and the dissolution, loss of personal consciousness, larval life, or return into the cycle of generation for the others. In various traditions (e.g., in Egypt and in ancient Mexico) the fate of the postmortem of those who underwent the latter destiny was not even considered.

7. In *Maitrāyaṇī Upaniṣad* (6.30) the "path of the ancestors" is also called "the path of the Mother," more on which later. See also *Bhagavadgītā*, 8.24–26.

essentially distinct types (at times even opposed to each other) of rite and cult.[8] A civilization's degree of faithfulness to Tradition is determined by the degree of the predominance of cults and rituals of the first type over those of the second type. Likewise, the nature and the function of the rites proper to the world of "spiritual virility" is specified.

A characteristic of what today goes by the name of the "science of religions" is that whenever by sheer chance it finds the right key to solve a "mystery," it reaches the conclusion that this key is good to solve all mysteries. Thus, when some scholars learned about the idea of the totem, they began to see totems everywhere. The "totemic" interpretation was shamelessly applied to the forms found in great civilizations, since some scholars thought that the best explanation for them could be derived from earlier studies on primitive tribes. Last but not least, a sexual theory of the totem eventually came to be formulated.

I will not say that the shift from the totems of those primitive populations to a traditional regality was a historical development; at most, it was an evolution in an ideal sense. A regal or an aristocratic tradition arises wherever there is dominion *over* the totems and not dominion *of* the totems, and wherever the bond is inverted and the deep forces of the stock are given a superbiological orientation by a supernatural principle in the direction of an Olympian "victory" and immortality. To establish ambiguous promiscuities that make individuals more vulnerable to the powers on which they depend as natural beings, thus allowing the center of their being to fall deeper and deeper into the collective and into the prepersonal dimensions and to "placate" or to propitiate certain infernal influences, granting them their wish to become incarnated in the souls and in the world of men—this is the essence of an inferior cult that is only an extension of the way of being of those who have no cult and no rite at all. In other words, it is the characteristic of the extreme degeneration of higher traditional forms. To free human beings from the dominion of the totems; to strengthen them; to address them to the fulfillment of a spiritual form and a limit; and to bring them in an invisible way to the line of influences capable of creating a destiny of heroic and liberating immortality—this was the task of the aristocratic cult.[9] When human beings perse-

---

8. All the main characteristics of the Greek religion are related to the opposition between chthonic and Olympian deities. The opposition was not merely between Hades, Persephone, Demeter, Dionysus and Zeus, Hera, Athena, Apollo. It was not just a matter of the difference between two orders of gods, but also of the opposition between radically different cults; the consequences of this opposition affected even the smallest details of the daily cult. In the second part of this work I will show an analogous opposition, including its development, in other civilizations.

9. In some traditions there is the belief in two demons: a divine and friendly demon (the "good demon" or ἀγαθός δαίμων) and an earthly demon, subjected to the body and to passions. The former may represent transformed influences, or the "triumphal" heredity that the individual can confirm and renew or betray whenever he gives in to his inferior nature, expressed by the other demon.

vered in this cult, the fate of Hades was averted and the "way of the Mother" was barred. Once the divine rites were neglected, however, this destiny was reconfirmed and the power of the inferior nature became omnipotent again. In this way, the meaning of the abovementioned Oriental teaching is made manifest, namely, that those who neglect the rites cannot escape "hell," this word meaning both a way of being in this life and a destiny in the next. In its deepest sense, the duty to preserve, nourish, and develop the mystical fire (which was considered to be the body of the god of the families, cities, and empires, as well as, according to a Vedic expression, the "custodian of immortality"[10]) without any interruption concealed the ritual promise to preserve, nourish, and develop the principle of a higher destiny and contact with the overworld that were created by the ancestor. In this way this fire is most intimately related to the fire, which especially in the Hindu and in the Greek view and, more generally speaking, in the Olympian-Aryan ritual of cremation, burns in the funeral pyre; this fire was the symbol of the power that consumes the last remains of the earthly nature of the deceased until it generates beyond it the "fulgurating form" of an immortal.[11]

10. Concerning the relationship between the fire tended by noble families and a divine survival, see *The Laws of Manu*, 2.232.
11. This form is the same superindividual form of the divine ancestor or of the god into whom the limited consciousness of the individual becomes transformed; this is why in Greece the name of the deceased sometimes was substituted with the name of the founding father of his stock. We may also refer to the Zen koan: "Show me the face you had before you were born."

9

Life and Death of Civilizations

In those areas in which Tradition retained all of its vitality the dynastic succession of sacred kings represented an axis of light and of eternity within the temporal framework, the victorious presence of the supernatural in the world, and the "Olympian" component that transfigures the demonic element of chaos and bestows a higher meaning to state, nation, and race. Even in the lower strata of society, the hierarchical bond created by a conscious and virile devotion was considered a means to approach, and to participate in, the supernatural.

In fact, invested with authority from above, the simple law acted as a reference and a support that went beyond mere human individuality for those who could not light the supernatural fire for themselves. In reality, the intimate, free, and effective dedication of one's entire life to traditional norms, even when a full understanding of their inner dimension was not present to justify such an adherence, was enough to acquire objectively a higher meaning: through obedience, faithfulness, and action in conformity with traditional principles and limitations an invisible force shaped such a life and oriented it toward that supernatural axis that in others (in those privileged few at the top of the hierarchy) existed as a state of truth, realization, and light. In this manner, a stable and lively organism was formed that was constantly oriented toward the overworld and sanctified in power and in act according to its hierarchical degrees in the various domains of thinking, feeling, acting, and struggling. Such was the climate of the world of Tradition.

All of the exterior life was a rite, namely, an approximation, more or less efficacious and depending on individuals and groups, to a truth that the exterior life cannot produce by itself, but that allows a person to realize one's self in part or entirely, provided it is lived in a saintly way. These people lived the same life that they led for centuries; they made of this world a ladder in order to achieve liberation. These peoples used to think, to act, to love, to hate, and to wage war on each other in a saintly way; they had erected the one temple among a great number of other temples through which the stream of the waters ran. This temple was the bed of the river, the traditional truth, the holy syllable in the heart of the world.[1]

At this level to leave the parameters of Tradition meant to leave the true life. To abandon the rites, alter or violate the laws or mix the castes corresponded to a regression from a structured universe (cosmos) back into chaos, or to a relapse to the state of being under the power of the elements and of the totems—to take the "path leading to the hells" where death is the ultimate reality and where a destiny of contingency and of dissolution is the supreme rule.

This applied to both single individuals and to entire peoples. Any analysis of history will reveal that just like man, civilizations too, after a dawn and an ensuing development, eventually decline and die. Some people have attempted to discover the law responsible for the decline of various civilizations. I do not think that the cause or causes can be reduced to merely historical and naturalistic factors.

Among various writers, de Gobineau is the one who probably better demonstrates the insufficiency of the majority of the empirical causes that have been adduced to explain the decline of great civilizations. He showed, for instance, that a civilization does not collapse simply because its political power has been either broken or swept away: "The same type of civilization sometimes endures even under a foreign occupation and defies the worst catastrophic events, while some other times, in the presence of mediocre mishaps, it just disappears." Not even the quality of the governments, in the empirical (namely, administrative and organizational) sense of the word, exercises much influence on the longevity of civilizations. De Gobineau remarked that civilizations, just like living organisms, may survive for a long time even though they carry within themselves disorganizing tendencies in addition to the spiritual unity that is the life of the one common Tradition; India and feudal Europe, for example, show precisely the absence of both a unitary organization and a single economic system or form of legislation on the one hand and a marked pluralism with repeatedly recurring antagonisms on the other.[2]

Not even the so-called corruption of morals, in its most profane and moralistically bourgeois sense, may be considered the cause of the collapse of civilizations; the corruption of morals at most may be an effect, but it is not the real cause. In almost every instance we have to agree with Nietzsche, who claimed that wherever the preoccupation with "morals" arises is an indication that a process of decadence is

1. G. De Giorgio, "Azione e contemplazione," *La Torre,* no. 2 (1930).
2. J. de Gobineau, *The Inequality of Human Races.*

already at work; the *mos* of Vico's "heroic ages" has nothing to do with moralistic limitations. The Far Eastern tradition especially has emphasized the idea that morals and laws in general (in a conformist and social sense) arise where "virtue" and the "Way" are no longer known:

> When the Tao was lost, its attributes appeared; when its attributes were lost, benevolence appeared; when benevolence was lost, righteousness appeared; and when righteousness was lost, the proprieties appeared. Now propriety is the attenuated form of filial piety and good faith, and is also the commencement of disorder.[3]

As far as the traditional laws are concerned, taken in their sacred character and in their transcendent finality, then just as they had a nonhuman value, likewise they could not be reduced in any way to the domain of morality in the current sense of the word. Antagonism between peoples or a state of war between them is in itself not the cause of a civilization's collapse; on the contrary, the imminent sense of danger, just like victory, can consolidate, even in a material way, the network of a unitary structure and heat up a people's spirit through external manifestations, while peace and well-being may lead to a state of reduced tension that favors the action of the deeper causes of a possible disintegration.[4]

The idea that is sometimes upheld against the insufficiency of these explanations is that of race. The unity and the purity of blood are believed by some to be the foundation of life and the strength of a civilization; therefore, the mixing and the ensuing "poisoning" of the blood are considered the initial cause of a civilization's decline. This too is an illusion, which among other things, lowers the notion of civilization to a naturalistic and biological plane, since this is the plane on which race is thought of in our day and age. Race, blood, hereditary purity of blood: these are merely "material" factors. A civilization in the true, traditional sense of the word arises only when a supernatural and nonhuman force of a higher order—a force that corresponds to the "pontifical" function, to the component of the rite, and to the principle of spirituality as the basis of a hierarchical differentiation of people—acts upon these factors. At the origin of every true civilization there lies a "divine" event (every great civilization has its own myth concerning divine founders): thus, no human or naturalistic factor can fully account for it. The adulteration and decline of civilizations is caused by an event of the same order, though it acts in the opposite, degenerative sense. When a race has lost contact with the only thing that has and can

---

3. *Tao te Ching*, 38, in R. Van Over, ed., *Chinese Mystics* (New York, 1973), 22.
4. For a critique of these alleged causes of the decline of civilizations, see de Gobineau's *The Inequality of Human Races.*

provide stability, namely, with the world of "Being"; and when in a race that which forms its most subtle yet most essential element has been lost, namely, the inner race and the race of the spirit—compared to which the race of the body and of the soul are only external manifestations and means of expression[5]—then the collective organisms that a race has generated, no matter how great and powerful, are destined to descend into the world of contingency; they are at the mercy of what is irrational, becoming, and "historical," and of what is shaped "from below" and from the outside.

Blood and ethnic purity are factors that are valued in traditional civilizations too; their value, however, never justifies the employment, in the case of human beings, of the same criteria employed to ascertain the presence of "pure blood" in a dog or in a horse—as is the case in some modern racist ideologies. The "blood" or "racial" factor plays a certain role not because it exists in the "psyche" (in the brain and in the opinions of an individual), but in the deepest forces of life that various traditions experience and act upon as typical formative energies. The blood registers the *effects* of this action, yet it provides through heredity a material that is preformed and refined so that through several generations, realizations similar to the original ones may be prepared and developed in a natural and spontaneous way. It is on this foundation—and on this foundation only—that, as we shall see, the traditional world often practiced the heredity of the castes and willed endogamous laws. If we refer, however, to the Indo-Aryan tradition in which the caste system was the most rigorously applied, simply to be born in a caste, though necessary, was not considered enough; it was necessary for the quality virtually conferred upon a person at birth to be actualized by initiation. I have already mentioned that according to the *Manudharmaśāstra*, unless a man undergos initiation or "second birth," even though he may be an Aryan, he is not superior to a *śūdra*. I also related how three special differentiations of the divine fire animated the three hierarchically higher Persian *pishtra*, and that definite membership in one of them was sealed at the moment of initiation. Even in these instances we should not lose sight of two factors being present, and never mistake the formative element for the element that is formed, nor the conditioning for the conditioned factor. Both the higher castes and traditional aristocracies, as well as superior civilizations and races (those that enjoy the same status that the consecrated castes enjoy vis-à-vis the plebeian castes of the "children of the Earth") cannot be explained by blood, but *through* the blood, by something that goes beyond blood and that has a metabiological character.

When this "something" is truly powerful, or when it constitutes the deeper and

---

5. For a more detailed account of race and of the relationship between the somatic, soul, and spiritual race, see my *Sintesi di dottrina della razza* (Milan, 1941).

most stable nucleus of a traditional civilization, then that civilization can preserve and reaffirm itself—even when ethnical mixtures and alterations occur (no matter how destructive they may be)—by reacting on the heterogeneous elements, and shaping them, by reducing them slowly but gradually to their own type, or by regenerating itself into a new, vibrant unity. In historical times there are a number of cases of this: China, Greece, Rome, Islam. Only when a civilization's generating root "from above" is no longer alive and its "spiritual race" is worn out or broken does its decline set in, and this in tandem with its secularization and humanization.[6]

When it comes to this point, the only forces that can be relied upon are those of the blood, which still carries atavistically within itself, through race and instinct, the echo and the trace of the departed higher element that has been lost; it is only in this way that the "racist" thesis in defense of the purity of blood can be validly upheld—if not to prevent, at least to delay the fatal outcome of the process of dissolution. It is impossible, however, to really prevent this outcome without an inner awakening.

Analogous observations can be made concerning the value and the power of traditional forms, principles, and laws. In a traditional social order there must be somebody in whom the principle upon which various institutions, legislations, and ethical and ritual regulations are based is truly active; this principle, though, must be an objective spiritual realization and not a simulacrum. In other words, what is required is an individual or an elite to assume the "pontifical" function of lords and mediators of power from above. Then even those who can only obey but who cannot adopt the law other than by complying with the external authority and tradition are able intuitively to know *why* they must obey; their obedience is not sterile because it allows them to participate effectively in the power and in the light. Just as when a magnetic current is present in a main circuit and induced currents are produced in other distinct circuits, provided they are syntonically arranged—likewise, some of the greatness, stability, and "fortune" that are found in the hierarchical apex pass invisibly into those who follow the mere form and the ritual with a pure heart. In that case, the tradition is firmly rooted, the social organism is unified and connected in all of its parts by an occult bond that is generally stronger than external contingencies.

When at the center, however, there is only a shallow function or when the titles of the representatives of the spiritual and regal authority are only nominal, then the

6. We may here consider A. J. Toynbee's thesis (*A Study of History* [London, 1934]) according to which, a few exceptions notwithstanding, there have never been civilizations that have been killed, but only civilizations that have committed suicide. Wherever the inner strength exists and does not abdicate, then difficulties, dangers, an adverse environment, attacks from the outside, and even invasions may become a stimulus or a challenge that induces that inner strength to react in a creative way. Toynbee saw in these external elements the conditions for the advent and for the development of civilizations.

pinnacle dissolves and the support crumbles.[7] A highly significant legend in this regard is that of the people of Gog and Magog, who symbolize chaotic and demonic forces that are held back by traditional structures. According to this legend, these people attack when they realize that there is no longer anybody blowing the trumpets on that wall upon which an imperial type had previously arrested their siege, and that it was only the wind that produced the sounds they were hearing. Rites, institutions, laws, and customs may still continue to exist for a certain time; but with their meaning lost and their "virtue" paralyzed they are nothing but empty shells. Once they are abandoned to themselves and have become secularized, they crumble like parched clay and become increasingly disfigured and altered, despite all attempts to retain from the outside, whether through violence or imposition, the lost inner unity. As long as a shadow of the action of the superior element remains, however, and an echo of it exists in the blood, the structure remains standing, the body still appears endowed with a soul, and the corpse—to use an image employed by de Gobineau—walks and is still capable of knocking down obstacles in its path. When the last residue of the force from above and of the race of the spirit is exhausted, in the new generations nothing else remains; there is no longer a riverbed to channel the current that is now dispersed in every direction. What emerges at this point is individualism, chaos, anarchy, a humanist hubris, and degeneration in every domain. The dam is broken. Although a semblance of ancient grandeur still remains, the smallest impact is enough to make an empire or state collapse and be replaced with a demonic inversion, namely, with the modern, omnipotent Leviathan, which is a mechanized and "totalitarian" collective system.

From prehistoric times to our own day and age this is what "evolution" has been all about. As we shall see, from the distant myth of divine regality through the descent from one caste to the next, mankind will reach the faceless forms of our contemporary civilization in which the tyranny of the pure demos and the world of the masses is increasingly and frightfully reawakening in the structures of mechanization.

---

7. According to the Hindu tradition, the four great ages of the world, or *yugas,* depend on the kings's state: the Dark Age (Kali Yuga) corresponds to the state in which the regal function is "asleep"; the Golden Age corresponds to the state in which the king reproduces the symbolic actions of the Aryan gods.

10

Initiation and Consecration

Having defined the essence of both the pinnacle and center of a traditional civilization, it is necessary to describe briefly some of its external features that refer to already conditioned existential situations. This will enable me to indicate the origin of the first alteration of the world of Tradition.

The regal idea occurs in an already weakened form when it no longer becomes incarnated in beings who are naturally above human limitations, but rather in beings who must develop this quality within themselves. In the ancient Hellenic tradition, such a distinction corresponded analogically to that between a "god" (Olympian ideal) and a "hero." In terms of the Roman tradition this distinction was formally sanctioned through the titles of *deus* and *divus*, the latter always designating a man who had become a god, the former designating a being who had always been a god. According to tradition, in Egypt the regal race of the θέοι was replaced by that of the ἡμίθεοι (who correspond to the "heroes"), who in turn precede in time the race of the νέκυες, an expression subject to being referred mainly to human leaders. What emerges in this context is a situation in which there is a certain distance between the person and the function being exercised: in order for a person to embody a certain function what is required is a specific action capable of producing in him a new quality; this action may appear either in the form of an initiation or of an investiture (or consecration). In the first case this action has a relatively autonomous and direct character; in the second case it is mediated, or it takes place from the outside through a priestly caste distinct from the regal caste.

As far as the regal initiation is concerned, it will suffice to repeat what has been said about the ritual, sacrificial, and triumphal actions that reenact those deeds attributed to a god or a hero with the intent of actualizing, evoking, or renewing the corresponding supernatural influences. This occurred in a very specific way in ancient Egypt. As I have said, the king at his enthronement reenacted the "sacrifice" that made Osiris a transcendent divinity; this rite was used not only as a way to renew the quality of a nature that was already divine by birth, but also and foremost as an initiation aimed at arousing the dimension of transcendence in the man who was destined to be king and at granting him "the gift of life." As far as the details of similar rites are concerned, I will limit myself to describing the rite that in the Eleusinian Mysteries corresponded to the bestowal of the regal title.[1]

The future "king" first spends some time in solitary confinement. Then he must swim across a river through blood and vortices—in other words, he crosses the "stream of generation" by means of his own strength, leaving behind on the riverbank his old body, soul, and personality. The river is later crossed again by boat,[2] and the king wears animal skins. These skins apparently signified totemic powers that emerged as a consequence of the suspension of the ephemeral, external I, powers that also represented the powers of the community; this symbolism was meant to establish a contact and an identification with the supernatural dimension. In the Bacchic ritual, after devouring the victims the Corybantes wore their skins; this was meant as an identification with the god represented by the sacrificial victims and as the act of taking on his strength and nature; the Egyptian initiate too wore the skin of a victim representing Set. Thus, the overall symbolism of the new phase of the ritual probably refers to the achievement of a state in which one can undertake the symbolic crossing, thanks to which he will be qualified to become the leader, even after assuming certain powers related to the subterranean and vital dimension of the collective organism.

The future "king" eventually reaches the other bank of the river and now must climb to the top of a mountain. Darkness surrounds him, but the gods help him to climb the path and to rise several levels. We notice here a recurrence of well-known symbols: the dry land or island, the mountain or the height. Moreover, we find the

---

1. My primary source is the reconstruction of the Eleusinian Mysteries proposed by V. Magnien in his *Les Mystères d'Eleusis*.
2. Because of their traditional character, each of these phases could generate innumerable comparisons. Crossing the waters, together with the symbol of navigating, is one of the most recurrent themes. The ship is one of the symbols ascribed to Janus, which later on was incorporated into the Catholic pontifical symbolism. The Chaldean hero Gilgamesh who walks on the "sun's path" and on the "mountain path," must cross the ocean in order to reach a divine garden where he will find the gift of immortality. The crossing of a great river and a number of various trials consisting in encounters with animals (totems), storms, and the like, is also found in both the ancient Mexican and Nordic-Aryan (crossing of the river Thund in order to arrive in Valhalla) journey after death. The crossing of the waters is found in the Nordic saga of the hero Siegfried, who says: "I can lead you there [to the 'island' of the divine woman Brunhild, a land 'known to Siegfried alone'] riding the waves. I am accomplished in the true ways of the sea" (*Niebelungenlied*, 6); and it is also found in the Vedas where the king Yama, conceived as the "Sun's son" and as the first among the beings who have found their way to the otherworld, is called "he who has gone far out into the sea." (*Ṛg Veda*, 10.14.1–2; 10.10.1). The symbolism of the crossing is very frequent in Buddhism, while in Jainism we find the expression *tīrthaṃkara* ("ford-builder").

idea of planetary influences (the "rings" may correspond to the Platonic seven "wheels of destiny") that one must overcome by climbing all the way to the symbolic region of the fixed stars, which represent the states of the pure world of being. This corresponds to the passage from the Lesser to the Greater Mysteries and to the old distinction between the lunar and telluric rite and the solar and Olympian rite. The person who is to be initiated is welcomed by other kings and by the highest dignitaries; he walks into an illuminated temple in order to establish contact with the divine; he is reminded to fulfill the main duties of a king; he finally receives the robes and the insignia of his dignity and sits on the throne.

In Egypt, the rite of regal initiation included three separate moments corresponding to the abovementioned phases; first came a purification; then the rite of the reception of the supernatural fluid symbolized by the crown (*uraeus*) or by the double crown (the crown was often called the "great sorceress," who "establishes at the right and at the left hand of the king the gods of eternity and of stability"); and finally, the "ascent" to the temple representing the "otherworld" *(paduat)* and the "embrace" of the solar god, which was the definitive consecration that sanctified this new immortalizing birth and his divine nature and by virtue of which the Egyptian king appeared as the "son" of the same god.

The Eleusinian rite is one of the most complete rites of "regal" initiation; allegedly each of the symbols employed therein corresponded to a particular inner experience. Though at this time I do not intend to describe the means through which similar experiences were induced or what they were all about,[3] I wish to emphasize that in the world of Tradition, initiation in its highest forms was conceived as an intensely real operation that was capable of changing the ontological status of the individual and of grafting onto him certain forces of the world of Being, or of the overworld. The title of *rex* (in Greek, βασιλεύς) at Eleusis testified to the acquired supernatural dimension that potentially qualified the function of the leader. The fact that at the time of the Eleusinian Mysteries this title certainly did not go together with effective political authority was due to the decadence of ancient Hellas. Because of this decadence, the ancient regal dignity was retained on a different plane than that of royal power, which by then had fallen into profane hands.[4] This did not

---

3. See *Introduzione alla magia* (Milan, 1952) and also my other work, *The Hermetic Tradition*. It has been suggested that the requirement for the regal dignity consists in the control of the *manas* (the inner and transcendent root of the five senses), which is also a requirement for the successful practice of yoga and asceticism. See *The Laws of Manu*, 7.44.
4. As far as Rome is concerned we may notice the shift from the integral notion of regality to the narrower notion of *rex sacrorum*, the king's competence being limited to the sacral dimension. This shift was justified to the degree to which the king had to engage in military matters.

prevent temporal sovereigns in ancient times, however, from aspiring to achieve the dignity of an initiatory king, which was very different from the dignity that they actually enjoyed. Thus, for instance, when Hadrian and Antoninus were already Roman emperors, they received the title of "king" only after being initiated at Eleusis. According to concordant testimonies, the quality bestowed by initiation is distinct from and unrelated to any human merit: all of the human virtues combined could not produce this quality, just as, to a certain extent, no human "sin" could affect it.[5] An echo of this notion was preserved in the Catholic view according to which the priestly dignity, which is transmitted sacramentally, cannot be effaced by any moral sin committed by the person endowed with it, since it remains in that person as an *indoles indelebilis,* an "indelible mark" ("You are a priest forever," Ps. 110:4). Moreover, as in the case of the Mazdean notion of "glory" and of the Chinese notion of "virtue," the priestly dignity corresponded to an objective power. In ancient China a distinction was made between those who were naturally endowed with "knowledge" and "virtue" (those who are capable of "fulfilling Heaven's law with calm and imperturbability and no help from the outside" are at the pinnacle, and are "perfected" and "transcendent" men) and those who achieved them "by disciplining themselves and by returning to the rites."[6] The discipline *(sieu-ki)* that is suitable to the latter men and that is the equivalent of initiation was considered only as a means to the real creation of that "superior man" *(kiun-tze)* who could legitimately assume the function proper to the supreme hierarchical apex by virtue of the mysterious and real power inherent in him. The distinctive feature of what makes one a king is more evident when a consecration rather than an initiation occurs; for instance, only the characteristic special investiture that turns the already crowned Teutonic prince into the *romanorum rex* can bestow upon him the authority and the title of leader of the Holy Roman Empire. Plato wrote: "In Egypt no king is allowed to rule without belonging to the priestly class; if by any chance a king of another race rises to power through violence, he eventually needs to be initiated into this class."[7]

Likewise, Plutarch wrote that "A king chosen from among the warriors instantly became a priest and shared in the philosophy that is hidden for the most part in myths and stories that show dim reflections and insights of the truth."[8] The same was true

---

5. "Just as fire instantly burns up the fuel that it touches with its brilliant energy, so a man who knows the Veda burns up all evil with the fire of his knowledge." *The Laws of Manu,* 11.246. Also: "A priest who retains the *Ṛg Veda* in his memory incurs no guilt at all, even if he destroys these three worlds or eats food taken from anyone whatever" (11.262).
6. *Analects,* 12.1; 14.45.
7. *Statesman,* 290d–e.
8. *De Iside et Osiride,* 9.

for the Parsis; it was precisely because the Persian Great Kings were elevated to the dignity of "magi" at the time of their enthronement and thus reunited the two powers that Iran did not experience conflicts or antagonisms between royalty and priesthood during the better period of its tradition. At the same time it must be noted that traditionally, while those who had received the initiation were kings, the opposite was also true, namely, the fact that often the initiation and the priestly function itself were considered a prerogative of kings and of aristocratic castes. For instance, in the *Homeric Hymn to Demeter* (verse 270 ff.), the goddess allegedly restricted to the four Eleusinian princes and to their descendants the "celebration of the cult and the knowledge of sacred orgies," by virtue of which "at death one does not incur the same fate as others." Ancient Rome struggled for a long time against the plebeian prevarication, and insisted that the priests of the higher collegia and especially the consuls (who originally enjoyed a sacred character themselves) were to be chosen only from patrician families. In this context, the need for a unitary authority was affirmed together with the instinctive acknowledgment that such an authority has a stronger foundation in those cases in which the race of the blood and the race of the spirit converge.

Let us now examine the case of kings who have not been raised to a superindividual dignity through initiation but rather through an investiture or a consecration that is mediated by a priestly caste; this form is typical of more recent, historical times. The primordial theocracies did not derive their authority from a church or from a priestly caste. The Nordic kings were kings immediately by virtue of their divine origin, and just like the kings of the Doric-Achaean period, they were the only celebrants of sacrificial actions. In China the emperor received his mandate directly "from heaven." Until recently in Japan, the ritual of enthronement took place in the context of the individual spiritual experience of the emperor, who established contact with the influences of the regal tradition without the presence of an officiating clergy. Even in Greece and in Rome the priestly collegia did not "make" kings through their rites, but limited themselves to exercising the divinatory science in order to ascertain whether the person appointed to exercise the regal function "was found pleasing to the gods"; in other words, it was an issue of acknowledgment and not of investiture, as in the ancient Scottish tradition concerning the so-called Stone of Destiny. Conversely, at the origins of Rome the priesthood was conceived as some kind of emanation of the primitive regality and the king himself promulgated the laws regulating the cult. After Romulus, who was himself initiated to the divinatory art, Numa delegated the typically priestly functions to the collegium of the *flamines*, which he himself instituted;[9] at the time of the empire, the priestly body was again

---

9. Cicero, *On the Nature of the Gods*, 3.2. Livy, *The History of Rome*, 1.20.

subjected to the authority of the Caesars, just like the Christian clergy later became subjected to the Byzantine emperor. In Egypt, until the Twenty-first Dynasty, the king delegated a priest (designated as "the king's priest," *nutir hon*) to perform the rites only sporadically, and the spiritual authority itself always represented a reflection of the royal authority. The paleo-Egyptian *nutir hon* parallels the role often played in India by the *purohita,* who was a *brāhmaṇa* employed at court and in charge of performing fire sacrifices. The Germanic races ignored consecration up to the Carolingian era; Charlemagne crowned himself, and so did Ludovicus and Pius, who later crowned his own son, Lothar, without any direct involvement on the part of the pope. The same holds true for the earlier forms of all traditional civilization, including the historical cycles of pre-Colombian America, and especially for the Peruvian dynasty of the "solar masters" or Incas.

On the contrary, when a priestly caste or a church claims to be the exclusive holder of that sacred force that alone can empower the king to exercise his function, this marks the beginning of an involutive process. A spirituality that in and of itself is not regal, and conversely, a regality that is not spiritual, eventually emerged; this spirituality and this regality enjoyed separate existences. Also, a "feminine" spirituality and a material virility began to coexist jointly with a lunar "sacredness" and a material "solarity." The original synthesis, which corresponded to the primordial regal attribute of the "glory" or of the celestial "fire" of the "conquerors," was dissolved and the plane of absolute centrality was lost. We shall see later on that such a split marks the beginning of the descent of civilizations in the direction that has led to the genesis of the modern world.

Once the fracture occurred, the priestly caste portrayed itself as the caste in charge of attracting and transmitting spiritual influences, but without being capable of constituting their dominating center within the temporal order. This dominating center, instead, was virtually present in the quality of a warrior or a nobleman of the king to whom the rite of consecration communicated these influences (the "Holy Spirit" in the Catholic tradition) so that he may assume them and actualize them in an efficient form. Thus, in more recent times it is only through this priestly mediation and through a rite's *virtus deificans* that the synthesis of the regal and priestly dimensions is reconstituted, a synthesis that is supposed to be the supreme hierarchical peak of a traditional social order. It is only in this way that the king again can be something more than a mere mortal.

Likewise, in the Catholic ritual the dress a king was supposed to wear before the rite of the investiture was simply a "military" dress; it is only in later times that a king began to wear the "regal dress" during the ceremony and began the tradition of sitting on an "elevated place" that had been reserved for him in the church. The rigorously symbolical meaning of the various phases of the ceremony has been preserved almost up to modern times. It is significant to find in older times the recurrent use of the expression "regal religion," for which the enigmatic figure of Melchizedek was often evoked; already in the Merovingian era in reference to the king we find the formula: *"Melchizedek noster, merito rex atque sacerdos."* The king, who during the rite took off the dress that he previously put on, was believed to be one who "leaves the mundane state in order to assume the state of *regal religion.*" In A.D. 769 Pope Stephanus III reminded the Carolingians that they were a sacred race and a royal priesthood: *"Vos gens sancta estis, atque regales estis sacerdotium."* Regal consecration was bestowed through anointing; back in those times this rite differed from the rite of consecration of bishops only in a few minor details, and therefore the king became as holy as a priest before men and God. Anointing, which belonged to the Jewish tradition and which was eventually taken up again by Catholicism, was the habitual rite employed to transfer a being from a profane into a sacred world;[10] according to the Ghibelline ideal it was thanks to his virtue that the consecrated person became a *deus-homo, in spiritu et virtute Christus domini, in una eminentia divinificationis—summus et instructor sanctae ecclesiae.* Therefore it was said that "the king must stand out from the mass of lay people, since he participates in the priestly function by his having been anointed by consecrated oil." The anonymous author of York wrote: "The king, the Christ [anointed] of the Lord, cannot be regarded as being a layman." In the sporadic emergence of the idea that the rite of regal consecration has the power to erase every sin committed, including those that involved the shedding of blood, we find an echo of the abovementioned initiatory doctrine concerning the transcendence of the supernatural quality vis-à-vis any human virtue or sin.

In this chapter I have discussed initiation in relation to the positive function of regality, even when considered in material terms. I have also mentioned instances in which the initiatory dignity separated itself from that function, or better, instances in which that function separated itself from the initiatory dignity by becoming secularized and by taking on a merely warrior or political character. Initiation must also be considered, however, as an independent category of the world of Tradition without a necessary relation to the exercise of a visible function at the center of a society. Initiation (high-level initiation, not to be confused with initiation that is related to the regimen of the castes or to the traditional professions and the various artisan guilds) has defined, in and of itself, the action that determines an ontological transformation

---

10. David was anointed by Samuel, "and the spirit of the Lord came upon David from that day forward." 1 Sam. 16:13. In some medieval texts the oil of regal consecration was assimilated to the oil used to consecrate prophets, priests, and martyrs. During the Carolingian era, the bishop at the time of consecration pronounced the words: "May God in his mercy grant you the crown of glory; may He pour upon you the oil of the grace of the Holy Spirit, which He poured upon His priests, kings, prophets, and martyrs."

of man. High-level initiation has generated initiatory chains that were often invisible and subterranean and that preserved an identical spiritual influence and an "inner doctrine" superior to the exoteric and religious forms of a historical tradition.[11] There are even instances in which the initiate has enjoyed this distinct character in a normal civilization and not only during the ensuing period of degeneration and inner fracture of the traditional unity. This character has become necessary and all-pervasive, especially in Europe in these latter times because of the involutive processes that have led both to the organization of the modern world and to the advent of Christianity (hence the merely initiatory character of the hermetic *rex*, of the Rosicrucian emperor, and so on).

---

11. For a definition of the specific nature of initiatory realization, see chapter 14 in my *L'arco e la clava*.

11

On the Hierarchical Relationship
Between Royalty and Priesthood

If on the one hand the original synthesis of the two powers is reestablished in the person of the consecrated king, on the other hand, the nature of the hierarchical relationships existing in every normal social order between royalty and priestly caste (or church), which is merely the mediator of supernatural influences, is very clearly defined: regality enjoys primacy over the priesthood, just as, symbolically speaking, the sun has primacy over the moon and the man over the woman. In a certain sense this is the same primacy over Abraham's priesthood that was traditionally attributed to the priestly regality of Melchizedek, who performed sacrifices in the name of the Almighty, the God of Victory ("God Most High who delivered your foes into your hand," Gen. 14:20). As I have said, the medieval apologists of the Ghibelline ideal occasionally referred to the symbol of Melchizedek when laying claim, over and against the Church, to the privileges and to the supernatural dignity of the monarchy.[1]

When referring to thoroughly traditional civilizations, it is helpful to employ Aryan or Indo-Aryan texts in order to emphasize that even in a civilization that appears to be characterized mainly by the priestly caste, the notion of the correct relationship between the two dignities was preserved to a large extent. In these texts, which I have previously quoted, it is said that the stock of the warrior deities arose from Brahman as a higher and more perfect form than Brahman itself. Reading on: "This is why nothing is greater than the warrior nobility *(kṣatram);* the priests *(brāhmaṇa)* themselves venerate the warrior when the consecration of the king occurs."[2]

---

1. In the Middle Ages, the mysterious figure of the royal Prester John replicated somewhat the figure of Melchizedek, while at the same time being related to the idea of a supreme center of the world. There is a legend according to which Prester John sent a salamander's skin, fresh water, and a ring that bestowed victory and invisibility to "Frederick"; this legend expresses the confused belief in a relationship between the medieval imperial authority and some kind of transmission of the authority found in that center.
2. *Bṛhad-āraṇyaka Upaniṣad,* 1.4.11.

In the same text, the priestly caste that was assimilated to that Brahman (understood here in an impersonal manner and in an analogous sense to what in Christianity is considered to be the power, or *dunamis,* of the Holy Spirit), which is in its safekeeping, was represented as a mother or as a maternal matrix *(yoni)* in relation to the warrior or regal caste. This is particularly meaningful. The regal type is presented here according to its value as male principle, which surpasses, individuates, masters, and rules "triumphantly" over the spiritual force, which is conceived of as a mother and as a female. Reference was made to ancient traditions concerning a type of regality that was attained by marrying a divine woman, often portrayed as a mother (this symbolizes incest, whereby the Egyptian king, in a broader context, was given the title of "his mother's bull"). We are led again to the same point. Therefore, even when the rite of investiture is considered necessary, this does not establish or acknowledge the subordination of the king per se to the priestly caste. After the race of beings who are by nature more than mere human beings became extinct, a king was, prior to his consecration, simply a "warrior," provided that he did individually rise to something higher through other means.[3] But in the rite of consecration the king, rather than receiving, *assumes* a power that the priestly class does not own but rather has in custody; this power is then supposed to rise to a "higher form" that it did not possess before. Also, in consecration the virile and warrior quality of the person to be initiated frees itself and rises to a higher plane;[4] it then acts as an axis or as a pole of the sacred force. This is why the officiating priest must "worship" the king whom he consecrates, although the latter, according to a text, owes to the *brāhmaṇa* the respect owed to a mother. In the *Manudharmaśāstra* itself, although the primacy of the *brāhmaṇa* is upheld, the latter is compared to the water and to the stone, while the *kṣatriya* is compared to the fire and to iron. The text goes on to say that "rulers do not prosper without priests and priests do not thrive without rulers," and that "the priest is said to be the root of the law, and the ruler is the peak."[5] Odd as it may seem, these ideas originally were not totally alien to Christianity itself. According to the testi-

---

3. In the Hindu tradition there are plenty of instances of kings who already posses or eventually achieve a spiritual knowledge greater than that possessed by the *brāhmaṇa*. This is the case, for instance, of King Jaivala, whose knowledge was not imparted by any priest, but rather reserved to the warrior caste *(kṣatram);* also, in *Bṛhad-āraṇyaka Upaniṣad* (4.3.1) King Janaka teaches the *brāhmaṇa* Yājñavalkya the doctrine of the transcendent Self.

4. In a text called *Pañcaviṁśati Brāhmaṇa* (18.10.8) we read that although in the regal consecration the formulations employed are the same as those inherent to the *brāhmaṇa* (the priestly caste), the latter has to be subjected to the *kṣatram* (the regal-warrior caste). The qualities that characterize the aristocrat and the warrior (rather than the priest strictly speaking) and that, once integrated in the sacred, reproduce the "solar" peak of spirituality, are the foundation of the well-known fact that in the highest traditions the priests, in the higher sense of the word, were chosen only from among the patrician families; initiation and the transmission of transcendent knowledge was reserved to these families alone.

5. *The Laws of Manu,* 11.321–22; 11.83–84.

mony of Eginhard, after Charlemagne was consecrated and hailed with the formula, "Long life and victory to Charles the Great, crowned by God, great and peaceful emperor of the Romans!" the pope "prostrated himself *(adoravit)* before Charles, according to the ritual established at the time of the ancient emperors."[6] In the time of Charlemagne and of Louis the Pius, as in the time of the Christian Roman and Byzantine emperors, the ecclesiastical councils were summoned, authorized, and presided over by the prince, to whom the bishops presented the conclusions they had reached, not only in matters of discipline but in matters of faith and doctrine as well, with the formula: "O Your Lordship and Emperor! May your wisdom integrate what is found lacking, correct what is against reason. . . ."[7] Almost as in an echo this bears witness to the fact that the ancient primacy and an undeniable authority over the priesthood, even in matters of wisdom, was attributed to the ruler. The liturgy of power, typical of the primordial tradition, still subsists. It was not a pagan, but Bossuet, a Catholic bishop (1627–1704), who declared in modern times that the sovereign is the "image of God" on earth and who exclaimed: "You are divine though you are subject to death, and your authority does not die!"[8]

When the priestly caste, however, by virtue of the consecration that it administers demands that the regal authority should recognize the hierarchical superiority[9] of the priesthood ("unquestionably, a lesser person is blessed by a greater," Heb. 7:7) and be subjected to it—such was, in Europe, the Church's claim during the struggle for the investitures—this amounts to a full-blown heresy, totally subversive of traditional truths. In reality, as early as in the dark ages of prehistory we can detect the first episodes of the conflict between regal and priestly authority, since they both claimed for themselves the primacy that belongs to what is prior and superior to each of them. Contrary to common opinion, in the beginning this contrast was not motivated at all by a yearning for political hegemony; the cause of this conflict had a deeper root in two opposing spiritual attitudes. According to the prevalent form he was destined to assume after the differentiation of dignities, the priest is by definition always an interpreter and a mediator of the divine: as powerful as he may be, he will always be aware of addressing God as his Lord. The sacred king, on the other hand, feels that he belongs to the same stock as the gods; he ignores the feeling of religious subordination and cannot help but be intolerant of any claim to supremacy

---

6. De Coulanges, *Transformations de la royaute pendant l'époque Carolingienne* (Paris, 1892), 315–16. The *Liber pontificalis* says: *"Post laudes ad Apostolico more antiquorum principum adoratus est."*

7. We may recall here that it was the emperor Sigismund who summoned the Council of Constance (A.D. 1413) on the eve of the Reformation in order to purify the clergy from schisms and anarchy.

8. *Oeuvres oratoires,* 4.362.

9. This Pauline expression can be contrasted with the symbolism of Jacob who struggles against the angel of the Lord and forces him to bless him. (Gen. 32:27).

advanced by the priesthood. Later times witnessed the emergence of forms of an antitraditional anarchy that was manifested mainly in two ways: either as a royalty that is a mere temporal power in rebellion against spiritual authority; or as a spirituality of a "lunar" character in rebellion against a spirituality embodied by kings who were still aware of their ancient function. In both instances, heterodoxy was destined to emerge from the ruins of the traditional world. The first path will lead to the hegemony of the "political" element, the secularization of the idea of the state, the destruction of every authentic hierarchy, and last but not least, to the modern forms of an illusory and materialistic virility and power that are destined to be swept away by the power of the world of the masses in its collectivist versions. The second path will run parallel to the first; it will initially be manifested through the advent of the "civilization of the Mother" and through its pantheist spirituality, and later on through the varieties of what constitutes devotional religion.

The Middle Ages were the theater of the last great episode in the abovementioned conflict between the religious universalism represented by the Church and the regal ideal, embodied, though not without some compromises, in the Holy Roman Empire. According to the regal ideal, the emperor is really the *caput ecclesiae*, not in the sense that he takes the place of the head of the priestly hierarchy (the pope), but in the sense that only in the imperial function may the force that is represented by the Church and that animates Christianity efficaciously impose its dominion. In this context,

> The world, portrayed as a vast unitary whole represented by the Church, was perceived as a body in which the single members are coordinated under the supreme direction of the Emperor, who is at the same time the leader of the realm and of the Church.[10]

The emperor, although he was constituted as such by the rite of investiture that followed the other investitures relative to his secular aspect of Teutonic prince, claimed to have received his right and his power directly from God and claimed to acknowledge only God above himself; therefore the role of the head of the priestly hierarchy who had consecrated him could logically be only that of a mere mediator, unable— according to the Ghibelline ideal—to revoke by means of excommunication the supernatural force with which the emperor had been endowed. Before the Gregorian interpretation subverted the very essence of the ancient symbols, the old tradition

---

10. A. Solmi, *Stato e Chiesa secondo gli scritti politici da Carlomagno al Concordato di Worms* (Modena, 1901), 156. For the entire duration of the Roman Empire in the East, the Church was always a state institution dependent on the emperor, who exercised a universal rule. The beginning of the priestly usurpation can be traced back to the declarations of Pope Gelasius I (ca. 480).

was upheld in lieu of the fact that the Empire had always and everywhere been compared to the sun as the Church had been compared to the moon. Moreover, even at the times of her highest prestige, the Church attributed to herself an essentially feminine symbolism (that of a mother) in relation to the king, whom she viewed as her "son"; the Upaniṣads' designation (the *brāhmaṇa* as the mother of the *kṣatram*) appears again in this symbolism, this time in concomitance with the supremacist fancies of a gynaecocratic civilization marked by an antiheroic subordination of the son to the mother and by an emphasis on the mother's privileges. After all, based on what I have discussed so far, it is clear that the very assumption of the title of *pontifex maximus* by the head of the Christian religion, the pope, turned out to be more or less a usurpation, since *pontifex magnus* was originally a function of the king and of the Roman Augustus. Likewise, the characteristic symbols of the papacy, the double keys and the ship, were borrowed from the ancient Roman cult of Janus. The papal tiara itself derives from a dignity that was not religious or priestly, but essentially initiatory, and from the dignity proper of the "Lord of the Center" or of the "sovereign of the three worlds." In all this we can visibly detect a distortion and an abusive shift of dimension that, although they occurred in a hidden way, are nevertheless real and testify to a significant deviation from the pure traditional ideal.

12

Universality and Centralism

The ideal of the Holy Roman Empire points out the decadence the principle of *regere* [ruling] is liable to undergo when it loses its spiritual foundation. I will here anticipate some of the ideas I intend to develop in the second part of this work.

In the Ghibelline ideal of the Holy Roman Empire, two beliefs were firmly upheld: that the *regnum* had a supernatural origin and a metapolitical and universal nature, and that the emperor as the *lex animata in terris* and as the peak of the *ordinatio ad unum,* was *aliquod unum quod non est pars* (Dante) and the representative of a power transcending the community he governed; in the same way the Empire should not be confused with any of the kingdoms and nations that it encompassed, since in principle it was something qualitatively other, prior, and superior to each of them.[1] There was no inconsistency—as some historians would have us believe—in the medieval contrast between the absolute right (above all places, races, and nations) the emperor claimed for himself by virtue of having been regularly invested and consecrated, and the practical limitations of his material power vis-à-vis the European sovereigns who owed him obedience. The nature of the plane of every universal function that exercises an all-encompassing unifying action is not a material one; as long as such a function does not assert itself as a mere material unity and power, it is worthy of its goals. Ideally speaking, the various kingdoms were not supposed to be united to the Empire through a material bond, whether of a political or a military nature, but rather through an ideal and spiritual bond, which was expressed by the characteristic term *fides,* which in Medieval Latin had both a religious meaning and the political and moral meaning of "faithfulness" or "devotion." The *fides* elevated to the dignity of a sacrament *(sacramentum fidelitatis)* and the principle of all honor was the

---

1. "The Emperor was entitled to the obedience of Christendom, not as a hereditary chief of a victorious tribe, or feudal lord of a portion of the earth's surface, but as solemnly invested with an office. Not only did he excel in dignity the kings of the earth: his power was different in its nature; and so, far from supplanting or rivalling theirs, rose above them to become the source and needful condition of their authority in their several territories, the bond which joined them in one harmonious body." James Bryce, *The Holy Roman Empire* (London, 1889), 114.

cement that unified the various feudal communities. "Faithfulness" bound the feudal lord to his prince, who was himself a feudal lord of a higher rank; moreover, in a higher, purified, and immaterial form, "faithfulness" was the element required to bring back these partial units *(singulae communitates)* to the center of gravity of the Empire, which was superior to them all since it enjoyed such a transcendent power and authority that it did not need to resort to arms in order to be acknowledged.

This is also why, in the feudal and imperial Middle Ages, as well as in any other civilization of a traditional type, unity and hierarchy were able to coexist with a high degree of independence, freedom, and self-expression.

Generally speaking and especially in typically Aryan civilizations, there were long periods of time in which a remarkable degree of pluralism existed within every state or city. Families, stocks, and gentes made up many small-scale states and powers that enjoyed autonomy to a large degree; they were subsumed in an ideal and organic unity, though they possessed everything they needed for their material and spiritual life: a cult, a law, a land, and a militia. Tradition, the common origin, and the common race (not just the race of the body, but the race of the spirit) were the only foundations of a superior organization that was capable of developing into the form of the Empire, especially when the original group of forces spread into a larger space when it needed to be organized and unified; a typical example is the early history of the Franks. "Frank" was synonymous with being free, and the bearer, by virtue of one's race, of a dignity that in their own eyes made the Franks superior to all other people: *"Francus liber dicitur, quia super omnes gentes alias decus et dominatio illi debetur"* (Turpinus). Up to the ninth century, sharing the common civilization of and belonging to the Frank stock were the foundations of the state, although there was no organized and centralized political unity coextensive with a national territory as in the modern idea of a state. Later on, in the Carolingian development that led to establishment of the Empire, Frank nobility was scattered everywhere; these separated and highly autonomous units, which still retained an immaterial connection with the center, constituted the unifying vital element within the overall connection, like cells of the nervous system in relation to the rest of the organism. The Far Eastern tradition in particular has emphasized the idea that by leaving the peripheral domain, by not intervening in a direct way, and by remaining in the essential spirituality of the center (like the hub of the wheel effecting its movement), it is possible to achieve the "virtue" that characterizes the true empire, as the single individuals maintain the feeling of being free and everything unfolds in an orderly way. This is possible because by virtue of the reciprocal compensation resulting from the invisible direction being followed, the partial disorders or individual wills will eventually contribute to the overall order.[2]

2. *Tao te Ching*, 3, 66.

This is the basic idea behind any real unity and any authentic authority. On the contrary, whenever we witness in history the triumph of a sovereignty and of a unity presiding over multiplicity in a merely material, direct, and political way—intervening everywhere, abolishing the autonomy of single groups, leveling in an absolutist fashion every right and every privilege, and altering and imposing a common will on various ethnic groups—then there cannot be any authentic imperial power since what we are dealing with is no longer an organism but a mechanism; this type is best represented by the modern national and centralizing states. Wherever a monarch has descended to such a lower plane, in other words, wherever he, in losing his spiritual function, has promoted an absolutism and a political and material centralization by emancipating himself from any bond owed to sacred authority, humiliating the feudal nobility, and taking over those powers that were previously distributed among the aristocracy—such a monarch has dug his own grave, having brought upon himself ominous consequences. Absolutism is a short-lived mirage; the enforced uniformity paves the way for demagogy, the ascent of the people, or demos, to the desecrated throne.[3] This is the case with tyranny, which in several Greek cities replaced the previous aristocratic, sacral regime; this is also somewhat the case with ancient Rome and with Byzantium in the leveling forms of the imperial decadence; and finally, this is the meaning of European political history after the collapse of the spiritual ideal of the Holy Roman Empire and the ensuing advent of the secularized, nationalist monarchies, up to the age of "totalitarianism" as a terminal phenomenon.

It is hardly worth talking about the great powers that arose from the hypertrophy of nationalism that was inspired by a barbaric will to power of a militaristic or economic type and that people called "empires." Let me repeat that an empire is such only by virtue of higher values that have been attained by a given race, which first of all had to overcome itself and its naturalistic particularities; only then will a race become the bearer of a principle that is also present in other peoples endowed with a traditional organization, although this principle is present only in a potential form. In this instance the conquering material action presents itself as an action that shatters the diaphragms of empirical separation and elevates the various potentialities to the one and only actuality, thus producing a real unification. The principle "die and become," which resembles being hit by "Apollo's thunderbolt" (C. Steding), is the elementary requirement for every stock striving to achieve an imperial mission and dignity; this is exactly the opposite of the morality of so-called sacred selfishness displayed by various nations. To remain limited by national characteristics in order to dominate on their basis other peoples or other lands is not possible other than through a temporary violence. A hand, as such, cannot pretend to dominate the other organs of

---

3. R. Guénon, *Autorité spirituelle et pouvoir temporel,* 112.

the body; it can do so, however, by ceasing to be a hand and by becoming *soul*, or in other words, by rising up again to an immaterial function that is able to unify and to direct the multiplicity of the particular bodily functions, being superior to each one of them considered in and of themselves. If the "imperialist" adventures of modern times have failed miserably, often bringing to ruin the peoples that promoted them, or if they have been transformed into calamities of different kinds, the cause is precisely the absence of any authentically spiritual, metapolitical, and metanationalistic element; that is replaced instead with the violence of a stronger power that nonetheless is of the same nature as those minor powers it attempts to subdue. If an empire is not a *sacred* empire it is not an empire at all, but rather something resembling a cancer within a system comprised of the distinct functions of a living organism.

This is what I think about the degeneration of the idea of *regere* once it has become secularized and separated from the traditional spiritual basis: it is merely a temporal and centralizing idea. When considering yet another aspect of this deviation, one will notice that it is typical of all priestly castes to refuse to acknowledge the imperial function (as was the case of the Roman Church at the time of the struggle over the investitures) and to aim at a deconsecration of the concept of state and of royalty. Thus, often without realizing it, the priestly caste contributed to the formation of that lay and "realistic" mentality that unavoidably was destined to rise up against priestly authority itself and to ban any of its effective interferences in the body of the state. After the fanaticism of the early Christian communities, which originally identified the ruling Caesar's empire with Satan's kingdom, the greatness of the *aeternitatis Romae* with the opulence of the Babylonian prostitute, and the lictorian conquests with a *magnum latrocinium;* and after the Augustinian dualism, which contrasted state institutions with the *civitas dei* and considered the former as sinful *(corpus diaboli)* and unnatural devices—the Gregorian thesis eventually upheld the doctrine of the so-called natural right in the context of which regal authority was divested of every transcendent and divine character and reduced to a mere temporal power transferred to the king by the people. According to this thesis, a king is always accountable to the people for his power, as every positive state law is declared contingent and revocable vis-à-vis that "natural right."[4] As early as the thirteenth century, once the Catholic doctrine of the sacraments was defined, regal anointing was discontinued and ceased to be considered, as it had been previously, almost on the same level as priestly ordination. Later on, the Society of Jesus often

---

4. I have discussed the real meaning of the primacy of the "natural law" over the positive and political laws (a primacy that is also employed as an ideological weapon by all kinds of subversive movements) in my edition of selected passages of J. J. Bachofen's *Myth, Religion and Mother Right* and in my *L'arco e la clava,* chap. 8.

accentuated the antitraditional lay view of royalty (even though they sided with the absolutism of those monarchies that were subservient to the Church, the Jesuits in some cases went as far as legitimizing regicide[5]), in order to make it clear that only the Church enjoys a sacred character and that therefore every primacy belongs to her alone. As I have already mentioned, however, exactly the opposite came true. The spirit that was evoked overcame those who evoked it. Once the European states became the expressions of popular sovereignty and found themselves governed merely by economic principles and by the acephalous organizations (such as the Italian city-republics) that the Church had indirectly sponsored in their struggle against imperial authority, they became self-subsistent entities. These entities eventually became increasingly secularized and relegated everything that had to do with "religion" to an increasingly abstract, privatistic, and secondary domain and even used "religion" as an instrument to pursue their own goals.

The Guelph (Gregorian-Thomist) view is the expression of an emasculated spirituality to which a temporal power is superimposed from the outside in order to strengthen it and render it efficient; this view eventually replaced the synthesis of spirituality and power, of regal supernaturality and centrality typical of the pure traditional idea. The Thomist worldview attempted to correct such an absurdity by conceiving a certain continuity between state and Church and by seeing in the state a "providential" institution. According to this view, the state cannot act beyond a certain limit; the Church takes over beyond that limit as an eminently and directly supernatural institution by perfecting the overall sociopolitical order and by actualizing the goal that *excedit proportionem naturalis facultatis humanae*. While this view is not too far off from traditional truth, it unfortunately encounters, in the order of ideas to which it belongs, an insurmountable difficulty represented by the essential difference in the types of relationship with the divine that are proper to regality and to priesthood respectively. In order for a real continuity, rather than a hiatus, to exist between the two successive degrees of a unitary organization (Scholasticism identified them with state and Church), it would have been necessary for the Church to embody in the supernatural order the same spirit that the *imperium,* strictly speaking, embodied on the material plane; this spirit is what I have called "spiritual virility." The "religious" view typical of Christianity, however, did not allow for anything of this sort; from Pope Gelasius I onward the Church's claim was that since Christ had come, nobody could be king and priest at the same time. Despite her hierocratic claims, the Church does not embody the virile (solar) pole of the spirit, but the feminine (lunar) pole. She may lay claim to the key but not to the scepter. Because of her

5. R. Fülöp-Miller, *Segreto della potenza dei Gesuiti* (Milan, 1931), 326–33.

role as mediatrix of the divine conceived theistically, and because of her view of spirituality as "contemplative life" essentially different from "active life" (not even Dante was able to go beyond this opposition), the Church cannot represent the best integration of all particular organizations—that is to say, she cannot represent the pinnacle of a great, homogeneous *ordinatio ad unum* capable of encompassing both the peak and the essence of the "providential" design that is foreshadowed, according to the abovementioned view, in single organic and hierarchical political unities.

If a body is free only when it obeys its soul—and not a heterogeneous soul—then we must give credit to Frederick II's claim, according to which the states that recognize the authority of the Empire are free, while those states that submit to the Church, which represents *another* spirituality, are the real slaves.

13

The Soul of Chivalry

As I have previously indicated, not only regality but traditional nobility as well was originally characterized by a spiritual element. As we did for regality, let us consider the case in which this element is not the natural but rather the acquired possession of nobility. It follows that we find a gap analogous to that which exists between initiation and investiture. Investiture corresponds to what in the West was knightly ordination and to what in other areas was the ritual initiation typical of the warrior caste; initiation (a realization of a more direct, individual, and inner nature) corresponds to heroic action in a traditional, sacral sense, which is connected to doctrines such as that of the "holy war" and of the *mors triumphalis.*

I will discuss the second possibility later. In this context I will only discuss the spirit and the mystery of medieval knighthood as an example of the first possibility.

To begin with, we must be aware of the difference that existed during the European Middle Ages between the feudal and knightly aristocracy. The former was connected to a land and to faithfulness *(fides)* to a given prince. Knighthood, instead, appeared as a superterritorial and supernational community in which its members, who were consecrated to military priesthood, no longer had a homeland and thus were bound by faithfulness not to people but, on the one hand, to an ethics that had as its fundamental values honor, truth, courage, and loyalty[1] and, on the other hand, to a spiritual authority of a universal type, which was essentially that of the Empire. Knighthood and the great knightly orders of the Christian ecumene were an essential part of the Empire, since they represented the political and military counterpart of what the clergy and the monastic orders represented in the ecclesiastical order. Knighthood did not necessarily have a hereditary character: it was possible *to become a*

---

1. Concerning the cult of truth, the knights' oath was "In the name of God, who does not lie!" which corresponded to the Aryan cult of truth. According to this cult, Mithras was the god of all oaths and the Iranian mystical "glory" was believed to have departed from King Yima the first time he lied. In *The Laws of Manu* (4.237), we read: "By telling a lie, a sacrifice slips away."

knight as long as the person wishing to become one performed feats that could demonstrate both his heroic contempt for attachment to life as well as the abovementioned faithfulness (in both senses of the term). In the older versions of knightly ordination, a knight was ordained by another knight without the intervention of priests, almost as if in the warrior there was a force "similar to a fluid" that was capable of creating new knights by direct transmission; a witness to this practice is found in the Indo-Aryan tradition of "warriors ordaining other warriors." Later on, a special religious rite was developed, aimed at ordaining knights.

This is not all; there is a deeper aspect of European chivalry worth mentioning. The knights dedicated their heroic deeds to a *woman;* this devotion assumed such extreme forms in European chivalry that we should regard them as an absurd and aberrant phenomenon, if taken literally. To avow unconditional faithfulness to a woman was one of the most recurrent themes in chivalrous groups; according to the "theology of the castles" there was little doubt that a knight who died for his "woman" shared the same promise of blessed immortality achieved by a crusader who had died to liberate the Temple. In this context, faithfulness to God and to a woman appear to coincide. According to some rituals, the neophyte knight's "woman" had to undress him and lead him to the water, so that he could be purified before being ordained. On the other hand, the heroes of daring feats involving a "woman," such as Tristan and Lancelot, are simultaneously knights of King Arthur committed to the quest for the Grail, and members of the same order of "heavenly knights" to which the Hyperborean "Knight of the Swan" belonged.

The truth is that behind all this there were esoteric meanings that were not disclosed to the judges of the Inquisition or to ordinary folks; thus, these meanings were often conveyed in the guise of weird customs and of erotic tales. In a number of instances what has been said about the knight's "woman" also applies to the "woman" celebrated by the Ghibelline "Love's Lieges,"[2] which points to a uniform and precise traditional symbolism. The woman to whom a knight swears unconditional faithfulness and to whom even a crusader consecrates himself; the woman who leads to purification, whom the knight considers his reward and who will make him immortal if he ever dies for her—that woman, as it has been documented in the case of the "Worshipers of Love" or "Love's Lieges," is essentially a representation of "Holy Wisdom," or a perceived embodiment, in different degrees, of the "transcendent, divine woman" who represents the power of a transfiguring spirituality and of a life unaffected by death. This motif, in turn, is part of a complete traditional system; there is, in fact, a vast cycle of sagas and myths in which the "woman" is portrayed

2. See J. Evola, *The Yoga of Power,* trans. Guido Stucco (Rochester, Vt., 1993), 205–9; and J. Evola, *Eros and the Mysteries of Love: The Metaphysics of Sex* (Rochester, Vt., 1983), 195–202.

according to this value. The same theme runs through the stories of Hebe, a perennial youth who becomes the spouse of the hero Heracles in the Olympian domain; of Idun (whose name means "rejuvenation," "renewal") and of Gunnlöd, holder of the magic potion Odhaerir, who attempt in vain to attain Freya, goddess of light, who is constantly yearned for by "elemental beings"; of Brynhild, whom Odin appoints as the earthly bride of a hero who will dare go through the flickering flame surrounding her hall;[3] of the woman of the "Land of the Living" and of the "Victorious One" (Boagad) who attracts the Gaelic hero Conall Cearnach; of the Egyptian women who offer the "key of life" and the lotus of resurrection; of the Aztec Teoya-miqui who leads the fallen warriors to the "House of the Sun"; of the "well-shaped, strong, and tall-formed maidens who make the soul of the righteous go above the Kivad bridge and who place it in the presence of the heavenly gods themselves";[4] of Ardvi Sura Anahita, "strong and holy, who proceeds from the god of light," and of whom one asks for "the glory which belongs to the Aryan race and to the holy Zarathustra," as well as wisdom and victory;[5] of the "bride" of Gesar, the Tibetan hero, who is an emanation of "the conquering Dolma," not without relation to the double meaning of the Sanskrit term *śakti*, which means both "bride" and "power"; to the *fravashi*, divine women who, like the Valkyrie, are simultaneously transcendental parts of the human soul and beings who "bestow victory on those who invoke them, favors on those who love them, health on those who are ill."[6] This theme helps us to penetrate the esoteric dimension of some of the chivalrous literature about the "woman" and her cult. In the Indo-Aryan tradition it is said:

> Verily, not for love of kṣatrahood [in a material sense] is kṣatrahood dear, but for love of the soul [the principle of the Self which is "light and immortality"] kṣatrahood is dear . . . Kṣatrahood has deserted him who knows kṣatrahood in anything else but the Soul.[7]

The same idea may constitute the background of the particular aspect of chivalry that I have considered in this context.

3. This is mentioned in the *Eddas: Gylfaginning*, 26, 42; *Havamal*, 105; *Sigrdifumal*, 4–8. Gunnlöd, like the Hellenic Hesperides, is the keeper of the *golden fruit* and of a divine potion. Sigrdifa, contrasted with Sigurd who "awakens" her, appears as a woman endowed with wisdom; she imparts to the hero the knowledge of the runes of victory. Finally we may recall in the Teutonic tradition the "wondrous woman" waiting on a mountain for "the hero who shines like the sun," and who will live forever with her. The ring of fire around the sleeping "woman" recalls the barrier that according to the Christian myth blocked the entrance to Eden after Adam's fall (Gen. 3:24).
4. They are the *fravashi* described in *Vendidad*, 19.30.
5. *Yashna*, 10.7.
6. *Yasht*, 12.23–24.
7. *Bṛhad-āraṇyaka Upaniṣad*, 2.5–6.

It is important to note that in some cases the symbolism of the "woman" may assume a negative, "gynaecocratic" character (see chapter 27) that is different from the character related to the core of chivalry that leads to the ideal of "spiritual virility" mentioned in the previous chapter. The persistent, repeated use of feminine characters, which is typical of cycles of a heroic type, in reality means nothing else but this: even when confronting the power that may enlighten him and lead him to something more than human, the only ideal of the hero and of the knight is that active and affirmative attitude that in every normal civilization characterizes a true man as opposed to a woman. This is the "mystery" that in a more or less hidden form has shaped a part of the chivalrous medieval literature and that was familiar to the so-called Courts of Love, since it was able to confer a deeper meaning to the often debated question whether a "woman" ought to prefer a "cleric" or a "knight."[8]

Even the odd declarations of some chivalrous codes, according to which a knight (who is believed to have a semi-priestly dignity or to be a "heavenly knight") has the right to make other people's women his own, including the women of his own sovereign, as long as he proves to be the strongest, and according to which the possession of a "woman" automatically derives from his victory—must be related to the meanings that I have discussed in the context of expounding the saga of the King of the Woods of Nemi, described in chapter 1.

We are entering here into an order of real experiences, and thus we must renounce the idea that these are just inoperative and abstract symbols. I must refer my readers to another work of mine, *The Metaphysics of Sex*,[9] where I said that the "initiatory woman" or "secret woman" could be evoked in a real woman; in this book I also explained that Eros, love, and sex were known and employed according to their real transcendent possibilities. Such possibilities were hinted at by several traditional teachings, so much so as to define a special path leading to the effective removal of the limitations of the empirical self and to the participation in higher forms of being. Existentially, the nature of the warrior was such as to present eventually a qualification for this path. I cannot, however, develop this point any further in this context.

Materialized and scattered fragments of an ancient symbolism are also found in other cases, such as the fact that the title of "knight" confers a special prestige and that the knight is in some cases so close to his horse that he shares both danger and glory with it and may become ritually demoted from his rank when he allows himself

---

8. Ricolfi (*Studi sui fedeli d'amore* [Milan, 1933]) remarked that "in the thirteenth century the divine intellect is usually portrayed in feminine, not masculine terms": it is called Wisdom, knowledge, or "Our Lady Intelligence." In some figurations the symbol of what is active was attributed to man; this expresses an ideal corresponding to the path of a "warrior" rather than that of a "cleric."

9. See note 2 above.

to be unsaddled. These facts may lead us beyond the merely material dimension, and may be related to other filiations of the ancient symbolism of the horse. The horse appears in the famous myths of Perseus and Bellerophon as a winged creature capable of taking to the sky, the riding of which constitutes a test for divine heroes. The symbolism becomes more evident in the Platonic myth where the outcome of the choice between the white and the black horse determines the transcendental destiny of the soul, represented by the charioteer,[10] and also in the myth of Phaëthon, who was flung into the river Eridanus by his horse's driving force as it drove the sun chariot through the sky. In its traditional association with Poseidon, the god of the fluid element, the horse played the role of a symbol of the elementary life-force; even in its relation with Mars—another equestrian god of classical antiquity—the horse was the expression of the same force, which in ancient Rome was subjected to the warrior principle. The meaning of two representations, which in this context have a particular importance, will now become clear. First, in some classical figurations the "hero-like" soul that was transfigured or made was presented as a knight or accompanied by a horse.[11] The second figuration is the so-called Kalki-avatara: according to the Indo-Aryan tradition, the force that will put an end to the "dark era" (Kali Yuga) will be embodied in the form of a white horse; it will destroy the evil people and particularly the *mlecchas*, who are warriors demoted in rank and disjoined from the sacred.[12] The coming of the Kalki-avatara to punish these people inaugurates the restoration of primordial spirituality. In another occasion, it would be interesting to follow the threads of these symbolical motifs from the Roman world all the way to the Middle Ages.

On a more relative and historical plane, European aristocratic chivalry enjoyed a formal institution through the rite of ordination as it was defined around the twelfth century. Following two seven-year periods in the service of a prince (from ages seven to fourteen, and then from fourteen to twenty-one), in which the youth was supposed to prove his loyalty, faithfulness, and bravery, the rite of ordination took place at a date that coincided with Easter or Pentecost,[13] thus suggesting the idea of

---

10. Plato, *Phaedrus*, 264b.
11. This is certainly the case of the bas-reliefs of Tanagris and Tirea; in the latter the soul, wearing nothing but a regal mantle, holds the horse by the bridle; nearby there is the very significant symbol of the tree with a serpent.
12. *Viṣṇu Purāṇa* 4.3.24.
13. On the Easter date, which was not chosen arbitrarily by Christians, and much earlier than the times of Jesus, many populations used to celebrate the rite of the "kindling of fire"; this was an element related to several traditions of a "solar" type. Concerning the two periods of seven years in the knightly novitiate, we should recall that a similar rhythm was followed in ancient Greece (Plato, *Alcibiades*, 1.121e) and not without reason: according to a traditional teaching, the number seven presided over the rhythms of the development of those forces acting within man and nature.

a resurrection or of a "descent of the Spirit." First came a period of fasting and penance, followed by a symbolic purification through a bath, so that, according to Redi, "these knights may lead a new life and follow new habits." Secondly (at times, this came first) came the "wake in arms": the person to be initiated spent the night in the church and prayed standing up or on his knees (sitting was strictly prohibited), so that God may help him achieve what was lacking in his preparation. Following the example of the neophytes of the ancient Mysteries, after the ritual bathing, the knight took on a white robe as a symbol of his renewed and purified nature; sometimes he even wore a black vest, reminding him of the dissolution of mortal nature, and a red garment, which alluded to the deeds he was supposed to undertake at the cost of shedding his blood.[14] Third came the priestly consecration of the arms that were laid on the altar and that concluded the rite by inducing a special spiritual influence that was supposed to sustain the "new life" of the warrior, who was now elevated to knightly dignity and turned into a member of the universal order represented by knighthood.[15] In the Middle Ages we witness a blossoming of treatises in which every weapon of the knight was portrayed as a symbol of spiritual or ethical virtues; symbols that were almost intended to remind him of these virtues in a visible way and to connect any chivalrous deed with an inner action.

It would be easy to indicate the counterpart of this in the mysticism of weapons found in other traditional civilizations. I will limit myself to the example of the Japanese warrior aristocracy, which considered the sword *(katana)* as a sacred object. In Japan, the making of a sword followed precise, unbreakable rules; when a blacksmith fabricated a sword, he had to wear ceremonial robes and to purify the forge. The technique for ensuring the sharpness of a blade was kept absolutely secret, and it was transmitted only from master to disciple. The blade of a sword was the symbol of the soul of the samurai[16] and the use of such a weapon was subject to precise rules; likewise, to train in its use and in the use of other weapons (such as the bow), because of their relation with Zen, could plunge a person into an initiatory dimension.

In the list of knightly virtues given by Redi, first came wisdom followed by faithfulness, liberality, and strength. According to a legend, Roland was an expert in theological science; he was portrayed engaging in a theological discussion with his

---

14. These three colors, sometimes found in the symbolism of three robes, are central in the Hermetic Ars Regia since they represent the three moments of the initiatory palingenesis; the "red" corresponds to "Gold" and to the "Sun."

15. If the term *adoubler* employed in the knightly ordination derives from the Anglo-Saxon *dubban,* "to strike" (in reference to the violent blow the consecrating person inflicted on the knight-to-be), this probably symbolizes the ritual "mortification" that the human nature of the knight had to undergo prior to sharing in the superior nature. In the secret language of the "Love's Lieges" we find mention of "being wounded" or "hit by death" or by Love or by the vision of the "Woman."

16. [Inazo Nitobe, *Bushido: The Warrior's Code.* (Burbank, Calif., 1975), 82–87.]

enemy Ferragus, before combat. Godfrey of Buillon was called by some of his contemporaries *lux monarchorum;* Hugh of Tabaria, in his *Ordene de Chevalrie* portrayed the knight as an "armed priest," who by virtue of his two dignities (military and priestly), has the right to enter a church and to keep the order in it with his sacred sword.[17] In the Indo-Aryan tradition we see members of the warrior aristocracy competing victoriously in wisdom with the *brāhmaṇa* (that is, with the representatives of the priestly caste, for example Ajataśatru vs. Gargya Balaki; Pravahana Jaivali vs. Āruṇi; Sanatkumāra vs. Nārada, etc.); becoming *brāhmaṇa,* or, just like other *brāhmaṇa,* being "those who tend to the sacred flame."[18] This confirms the inner character of chivalry and, in a wider sense, of the warrior caste in the world of Tradition.

With the decline of chivalry, the European nobility also eventually lost the spiritual element as a reference point for its highest "faithfulness," and thus became part of merely political organisms as in the case of the aristocracies of the national states that emerged after the collapse of the civilization of the Middle Ages. The principles of honor and of faithfulness continued to exist even when the noble was nothing but a "king's officer"; but faithfulness is blind when it does not refer, even in a mediated way, to something beyond the human dimension. Thus the qualities that were preserved in the European nobility through heredity eventually underwent a fatal degeneration when they were no longer renewed in their original spirit; the decline of the regal spirituality was unavoidably followed by the decline of nobility itself, and by the advent of the forces found in a lower order.

I have mentioned that chivalry, both in its spirit and in its ethics, is an organic part of the empire and not of the Church. It is true that the knight almost always included in his vows the defense of the faith. This should be taken as the generic sign of a militant commitment to something superindividual, rather than a conscious profession of faith in a specific and theological sense. Just by scraping a little bit off the surface, it becomes evident that the strongest "trunks" of the sprouting of knighthood derived their "sap" from orders and movements that had the odor of heresy to the Church, to the point of being persecuted by her. Even from a traditional point of view, the doctrines of the Albigenses cannot be considered to be perfectly orthodox; however, we cannot fail to notice, especially in reference to Frederick II and to the Aragonenses, a certain connection between the Albigenses and a current of chivalry that defended the imperial ideal against the Roman Curia, and which during the

---

17. Among the twelve palatines there was an armed priest, the bishop Turpinus. He invented the war cry: "Glory be to our nobility, Montjoie!" See also the legendary journey of King Arthur through Montjoie before he was solemnly crowned in Rome; it is highly significant that the real etymology of the word Montjoie was Mons Jovis, or Mount Olympus (this etymology was suggested to me by R. Guénon).
18. *Viṣṇu Purāṇa* 4.2.19.

Crusades ventured all the way to Jerusalem (not without a reason), which it conceived almost as the center of a higher spirituality than that which was incarnated in papal Rome.

The most characteristic case is that of the Knights Templar, ascetic warriors who gave up the pleasures of the world in order to pursue a discipline not practiced in the monasteries but on the battlefields, and who were animated by a faith consecrated more by blood and victory than by prayer. The Templars had their own secret initiation, the details of which, though they were portrayed by their accusers with blasphemous tinges, are very significant. Among other things, in a preliminary part of the ritual the candidates to the highest degree of Templar initiation were supposed to reject the symbol of the cross and to acknowledge that Christ's doctrine did not lead to salvation. The Templars were also accused of engaging in secret dealings with the "infidels" and of celebrating wicked rites. These were just symbols, as it was declared repeatedly, though in vain, at the Templars' trial. In all probability, this was not a case of sacrilegious impiety but of acknowledgment of the inferior character of the exoteric tradition represented by devotional Christianity, an acknowledgment that was required in order for one to be elevated to higher forms of spirituality. Generally speaking, as somebody has correctly remarked, the very name "Templars" bespeaks transcendence. "Temple" is a more august, comprehensive, and inclusive term than "church." The temple dominates the church. Churches fall in ruins, but the temple stands as a symbol of the kinship of religions and of the perennial spirit informing them.[19]

The Grail was another characteristic reference point of chivalry.[20] The saga of the Grail closely reflects the hidden ambition of the Ghibelline knights; this saga too has hidden motifs that cannot be ascribed to the Church or to Christianity alone. Not only does the official Catholic tradition not acknowledge the Grail, but the essential elements of the saga are related to pre-Christian and even Nordic-Hyperborean traditions. In this context I can only remind the reader that in the most important versions of the legend, the Grail is portrayed as a *stone* (stone of light and "luciferian

---

19. Concerning the ethos of the Knights Templar, in his *De laude novae militiae* (chap. 4), Saint Bernard wrote: "They live in pleasant fellowship in a frugal way, without getting married, begetting children or owning a thing of their own, including their will. . . . Usually they do not wear fancy clothes; they are covered with dust, their faces burnt by the sun, with a proud and severe look in their eyes. When preparing for battle they arm themselves with faith in the inside and with iron on the outside, without wearing adorned insignia or putting beautiful saddles on their horses. Their only decorations are their weapons which they use with bravery in the greatest dangers, without fearing the number or the strength of the enemy. They put all their trust in the Lord of Hosts, and as they fight for Him, they seek either a certain victory or a holy and honored death on the battlefield."

20. See my work, *Il mistero del Graal e l'idea imperiale ghibellina*.

stone") rather than as a mystical chalice; that the adventures related to the Grail, almost without exception, have a more heroic and initiatory rather than a Christian and eucharistic character; that Wolfram von Eschenbach refers to the Knights of the Grail as "Templeise"; and finally that the Templar insignia (a red cross on a white background) is found on the garment of some of the Grail knights and on the sail of the ship on which Perlesvaux (Parsifal) leaves, never to return. It is worth noting that even in the most Christianized versions of the saga one still finds extra-ecclesial references. It is said that the Grail as a bright chalice (the presence of which produces a magical animation, a foreboding, and an anticipation of a nonhuman life), following the Last Supper and Jesus' death, was taken by angels into heaven from where it is not supposed to return until the emergence on earth of a stock of heroes capable of safeguarding it. The leader of this stock instituted an order of "perfect" or "heavenly knights," dedicated to this purpose. The "myth" and the highest ideal of medieval chivalry was to reach the Grail in its new earthly abode and to belong to such an order, which was often identified with King Arthur's knights of the Round Table. Considering that the Catholic Church has descended directly and without any interruptions from primitive Christianity, and considering the fact that the Christianized Grail disappeared until that time a knightly rather than priestly order was to be instituted—this obviously testifies to the emergence of a different tradition than the Catholic and apostolic one. There is more: in almost all the texts dealing with the Grail, the symbol of the "temple" (still a very priestly one) is abandoned in favor of the symbol of the court or of a regal castle, as the mysterious, inaccessible, and well-protected place in which the Grail is kept. The central theme of the "mystery" of the Grail, besides the test of mending a broken sword, consists in a regal restoration; there is the expectation of a knight who will restore the prestige of a decadent realm and who will avenge or heal a king who is either wounded, paralyzed, or in a catatonic state. Crisscrossing references connect these themes both to the imperial myth and to the very idea of a supreme, invisible, and "polar" center of the world. It is obvious that in this cycle, which was important to the medieval chivalrous world, a particular tradition was at work. This tradition had little to do with that of the dominant religion, and although it occasionally adopted some elements from Christianity, maybe it did so the better to express, or conversely, to hide itself. The Grail is truly a myth of the "regal religion" that confirms what has been said about the secret soul of chivalry.

When looking at the outer domain relative to a general view of life and of ethics, the overall scope of the formative and correcting action that Christianity underwent because of the world of chivalry must be acknowledged. Christianity could not reconcile itself with the ethos of chivalry and espouse the idea of a "holy war" other than by betraying the principles of that dualistic and escapist spirituality that characterized it over and against the traditional and classical world. Christianity had to forget Augustine's words: "Those who can think of war and endure it without experiencing great sufferings have truly lost their sense of humanity"; the more radical expressions of Tertullian and his warning: "The Lord, by ordering Peter to put the sword back into the scabbard, has thereby disarmed soldiers";[21] the martyrdom of saints Maximilian and Theogon, who preferred to die rather than to serve in the army; and Saint Martin's words prior to battle: "I am a soldier of Christ; I am not allowed to draw the sword." Christianity also had to bestow on the chivalrous principle of honor a very different understanding than what the Christian principle of love could allow for; moreover, it had to conform to a type of morality that was more heroic and pagan than evangelical. It also had to "close an eye" to expressions such as John of Salisbury's: "The military profession, both worthy and necessary, has been instituted by God himself"; and it even had to come to see war as a possible ascetical and immortalizing path.

Moreover, it was thanks to this very deviation of the Church from the main themes of primitive Christianity that during the Middle Ages Europe came to know the last image of a world that in many aspects was of a traditional type.

---

21. Augustine, *The City of God*, 19.7; Tertullian, *De corona*, 11.

14

The Doctrine of the Castes

The caste system is one of the main expressions of the traditional sociopolitical order, a "form" victorious over chaos and the embodiment of the metaphysical ideas of stability and justice. The division of individuals into castes or into equivalent groups according to their nature and to the different rank of activities they exercise with regard to pure spirituality is found with the same traits in all higher forms of traditional civilizations, and it constitutes the essence of the primordial legislation and of the social order according to "justice." Conformity to one's caste was considered by traditional humanity as the first and main duty of an individual.

The most complete type of caste hierarchy, the ancient Indo-Aryan system, was visibly inspired by the hierarchy of the various functions found in a physical organism animated by the spirit. At the lower level of such an organism there are the undifferentiated and impersonal energies of matter and of mere vitality; the regulating action of the functions of the metabolism and of the organism is exercised upon these forces. These functions, in turn, are regulated by the will, which moves and directs the body as an organic whole in space and time. Finally, we assume the soul to be the center, the sovereign power and the "light" of the entire organism. The same is true for the castes; the activities of the slaves or workers (śūdras) were subordinated to the activities of the bourgeoisie (vaiśya); higher up in the hierarchy we find the warrior nobility (kṣatriya); and finally the representatives of the spiritual authority and power (the brāhmaṇa, in the original sense of the word, and the leaders as pontifices). These groups were arranged in a hierarchy that corresponded to the hierarchy of the functions within a living organism.

Such was the Indo-Aryan sociopolitical system, which closely resembled the Persian system; the latter was articulated into the four pishtra of the Lords of fire (athreva), of the warriors (rathaestha), of the heads of the family (vastriya-fshuyant), and of the serfs assigned to manual labor (huti). An analogous pattern was found in other civilizations up to the European Middle Ages, which followed the division of people into servants, burghers, nobility and clergy. In the Platonic worldview, the castes corresponded to different powers of the soul and to particular virtues: the rulers *(ἄρχοντες)*, the warriors *(φύλακες or ἐπικουροί)* and the workers *(demiurgoi)* corresponded respectively to the spirit *(νοῦς)* and to the head, to the animus *(θυμοιδές)* and to the chest, and to the faculty of desire *(ἐπιθυμητικόν)* and to the lower organs of the body regulating sex and the functions of excretion. In this way, as stated by Plato, the external order and hierarchy correspond to an inner order and hierarchy according to "justice."[1] The idea of organic correspondence is also found in the well-known Vedic simile of the generation of the various castes from the distinct parts of the "primordial man" or *puruṣa*.[2]

The castes, more than defining social groups, defined functions and typical ways of being and acting. The correspondence of the fundamental natural possibilities of the single individual to any of these functions determined his or her belonging to the corresponding caste. Thus, in the duties toward one's caste (each caste was traditionally required to perform specific duties), the individual was able to recognize the normal explication as well as the development and the chrism of his or her own nature[3] within the overall order imposed "from above." This is why the caste system developed and was applied in the traditional world as a natural, agreeable institution based on something that everybody regarded as obvious, rather than on violence, oppression, or on what in modern terms is referred to as "social injustice." By acknowledging his own nature, traditional man knew his own place, function, and what would be the correct relationship with both superiors and inferiors; hence, if a *vaiśya* did not acknowledge the authority of a *kṣatriya*, or if a *kṣatriya* did not uphold his superiority in regards to a *vaiśya* or a *śūdra*, this was not so much considered a fault but as the result of ignorance. A hierarchy was not a device of the human will but a law of nature and as impersonal a physical law as that according to which a lighter fluid floats on top of a denser fluid, unless an upsetting factor intervenes. There was a firmly upheld principle according to which "Those who want to institute a process at variance with human nature cannot make it function as an ethical system."[4]

What upsets modern sensitivity the most about the caste system is the law of

---

1. "Justice is produced in the soul, like health in the body, by establishing the elements concerned in their natural relations of control and subordination; whereas injustice is like disease and means that this natural order is inverted." Plato, *Republic,* trans. B. Jowett, 444a, b.
2. *Rg Veda* 10.90.10–12. This fourfold division became a threefold division when nobility was thought to encompass both the warrior and the spiritual dimensions and practiced in those areas in which residues of this original situation existed. This division corresponds to the Nordic division into *jarls, karls,* and *traells* and to the Hellenistic division into *eupatrids, gheomors,* and *demiurgs.*
3. *Bhagavadgītā* (18.41): "The works of Brahmins, Kshatriyas, Vaisyas and Sudras are different in harmony with the three powers of their born nature." *The Bhagavad Gita,* trans J. Mascaró (New York, 1962).
4. *Chung-yung,* 13.1. Plato defined the concept of "justice" along similar lines *(Republic,* 432d, 434c).

heredity and preclusion. It seems "unfair" that fate may seal at birth one's social status and predetermine the type of activity to which a man will consecrate the rest of his life and which he will not be able to abandon, not even in order to pursue an inferior one, lest he become an "outcast," a pariah shunned by everybody.

When seen against the background of the traditional view of life, however, these difficulties are overcome. The closed caste system was based on two fundamental principles: the first principle consisted of the fact that traditional man considered everything visible and worldly as the mere effects of causes of a higher order. Thus, for example, to be born according to this or that condition, as a man or a woman, in one caste rather than in another, in one race instead of another, and to be endowed with specific talents and dispositions, was not regarded as pure chance. All of these circumstances were explained by traditional man as corresponding to the nature of the principle embodied in an empirical self, whether willed or already present transcendentally in the act of undertaking human birth. Such is one of the aspects of the Hindu doctrine of *karma;* although this doctrine does not correspond to what is commonly meant by "reincarnation,"[5] it still implies the generic idea of the preexistence of causes and the principle that "human beings are heirs of karma." Similar doctrines were not typical of the East alone. According to a Hellenistic teaching, not only "the soul's quality exists before any bodily life; it has exactly what it chose to have," but "the body has been organized and determined by the image of the soul which is in it."[6] Also, according to some Persian-Aryan views that eventually found their way to Greece and then to ancient Rome, the doctrine of sacred regality was connected to the view that souls are attracted by certain affinities to a given planet corresponding to the predominant qualities and to the rank of human birth; the king was considered *domus natus* precisely because he was believed to have followed the path of solar influences.[7] Those who love "philosophical" explanations should remember that Kant's and Schopenhauer's theory concerning the "intelligible character" (the "noumenal" character that precedes the phenomenal world) relates to a similar order of ideas.

---

5. The idea that the same personal principle or spiritual nucleus has already lived in previous human lives and that it will continue to do so ought to be rejected. R. Guénon launched a devastating critique of this idea in his *L'Erreur spirite* (Paris, 1923). I followed suit in my *The Doctrine of Awakening*. Historically, the belief in reincarnation is related to the weltanschauung typical of the substratum of pre-Aryan races and of the influence exercised by them; from a doctrinal point of view it is a simple popular myth, and not the expression of an "esoteric" knowledge. In the Vedas the idea of reincarnation is not found at all.

6. Plotinus, *Enneads*, 3.4.5; 1.1.1. Plato wrote: "No guardian spirit will cast lots for you, but you shall choose your own destiny. Let him to whom the first lot falls choose first a life to which he will be bound of necessity." *Republic*, 617e.

7. See Plato's *Phaedrus*, 10.15–16, 146–48b; and Emperor Julian's *Hymn to King Helios*, 131b. However, the nature of the elements that determine a given birth is as complex as the nature of the elements that constitutes a human being, who is the sum of various legacies. See my *Doctrine of Awakening*.

And so, given these premises and excluding the idea that birth is a casual event, the doctrine of the castes appears under a very different light. It can be said therefore that birth does not determine nature, but that nature determines birth; more specifically, a person is endowed with a certain spirit by virtue of being born in a given caste, but at the same time, one is born in a specific caste because one possesses, transcendentally, a given spirit. Hence, the differences between the castes, far from being artificial, unfair, and arbitrary, were just the reflection and the confirmation of a preexisting, deeper, and more intimate inequality; they represented a higher application of the principle *suum cuique.*

In the context of a living tradition, the castes represented the natural "place" of the earthly convergence of analogous wills and vocations; also, the regular and closed hereditary transmission forged a homogeneous group sharing favorable organic, vitalistic, and even psychic proclivities in view of the regular development on the part of single individuals of the aforesaid prenatal determinations or dispositions on the plane of human existence. The individual did not "receive" from the caste his own nature; rather, the caste afforded him the opportunity to *recognize* or remember his own nature and prenatal will, while at the same time presenting him with a kind of occult heritage related to the blood so that he would be able to realize the latter in a harmonious way. The characteristics, the functions, and the duties of the caste constituted the traces for the regular development of one's possibilities in the context of an organic social system. In the higher castes, initiation completed this process by awakening and inducing in the single individual certain influences that were already oriented in a supernatural direction.[8] The *ius* of the single individual, namely, those prerogatives and distinct rights inherent to each of these traditional articulations, not only allowed this transcendental will to be in harmony with a congenial human heredity, but also allowed everybody to find in the social organism a condition that really corresponded to their own nature and to their deepest attitudes; such a condition was protected against any confusion and prevarication.

When the sense of personality is not focused on the ephemeral principle of human individuality, which is destined to leave behind nothing but a "shadow" at death, all this seems very natural and evident. It is true that much can be "achieved" in a lifetime, but "achievements" mean absolutely nothing from a higher point of view (from a point of view that knows that the progressive decay of the organism will eventually push one into nothingness) when they do not actualize the preexisting will that is the reason for a specific birth; such a prenatal will cannot be easily altered

---

8. "Just as good seed, sown in a good field, culminates in a birth, so the son born from an Aryan father in an Aryan mother deserves every transformative ritual. . . . Seed sown in the wrong field perishes right inside it; and a field by itself with no seed also remains barren." *The Laws of Manu,* 10.69.71.

by a temporary and arbitrary decision taken at a given point of one's earthly journey. Once this is understood, the necessity of the castes will become clear. The only "self" modern man knows and is willing to acknowledge is the empirical self that begins at birth and is more or less extinguished at death. Everything is reduced by him to the mere human individual since in him all prior recollections have disappeared. Thus we witness the disappearance of both the possibility of establishing contact with those forces of which a given birth is just the effect, and the possibility of rejoining that nonhuman element in man, which being situated before birth, is also beyond death; this element constitutes the "place" for everything that may eventually be realized beyond death itself and is the principle of an incomparable sense of security. Once the rhythm has been broken, the contacts lost, and the great distances precluded to the human eye, all the paths seem open and every field is saturated with disorderly, inorganic activities that lack a deep foundation and meaning and are dominated by temporal and particularistic motivations and by passions, cheap interests, and vanity. In this context, "culture" is no longer the context in which it is possible to actualize one's being through serious commitment and faithfulness; it is rather the locus for "self-actualization." And since the shifting sands of that nothingness without a name and tradition that is the empirical human subject have become the foundation of that self-actualization, the claim to equality and the right to be, as a matter of principle, anything one chooses to be is therefore carried forward and strenuously advocated in modern society. No other difference is acknowledged to be more right and truer than that which is "achieved" through one's efforts and "merit" according to the terms of various vain, intellectual, moral, or social beliefs typical of these recent times. In the same way, it is only natural that the only things left are the limits of the most coarse physical heredity, which have become the signs of incomprehensible meanings and which are endured or enjoyed according to each case, as a caprice of fate. It is also natural that personality and blood traits, social vocation and function are all elements that have become increasingly discordant to the point of generating states of real, tragic, inner and outer conflict; from a legal and ethical perspective, they have also led to a qualitative destruction, to a relative leveling, to equal rights and duties, and to an equal social morality that pretends to be imposed on everyone and to be valid for all people in the same way, with total disregard for single natures and for different inner dignities. The "overcoming" of the castes and of the traditional sociopolitical orders has no other meaning. The individual has achieved all his "freedom"; his "chain" is not short, and his intoxication and his illusions as a restless puppet have no limits.

The freedom enjoyed by the man of Tradition was something very different. It did not consist in discarding but in being able to rejoin the deeper vein of his will, which was related to the mystery of his own existential "form." In reality, that which corresponds to birth and to the physical element of a being reflects what can be called, in a mathematical sense, the resultant [the vectorial sum] of the various forces or tendencies at work in his birth; in other words, it reflects the direction of the stronger force. In this force there may be inclinations of minor intensity that have been swept away and that correspond to talents and tendencies that on the plane of individual consciousness are distinct from both their own organic preformation and the duties and environment of one's caste. These instances of inner contradiction within a traditional political order regulated by the caste system must be considered an exception to the rule; they become predominant, though, in a society that no longer knows the castes and, in general, in distinct social organisms in which there is no law to gather, preserve, and shape talents and qualifications in view of specific functions. Here we encounter a chaos of existential and psychic possibilities that condemns most people to a state of disharmony and social tension; we can see plenty of that nowadays. Undoubtedly, there may have been a margin of indetermination even in the case of traditional man, but this margin in him only served to emphasize the positive aspect of these two sayings: "Know yourself" (complemented by the saying "nothing superfluous"), and "Be yourself," which implied an action of inner transformation and organization leading to the elimination of this margin of indetermination and to the integration of the self. To discover the "dominating" trait of one's form and caste and to will it, by transforming it into an ethical imperative[9] and, moreover, to actualize it "ritually" through faithfulness in order to destroy everything that ties one to the earth (instincts, hedonistic motivations, material considerations, and so on)—such is the complement of the abovementioned view that leads to the second foundation of the caste system in its closeness and stability.

On the other hand, we must keep in mind that aspect of the traditional spirit according to which there was no object or function that in itself could be considered as superior or inferior to another. The true difference was rather given by the *way* in which the object or the function was lived out. The earthly way, inspired by utilitarianism or by greed *(sakāma-karma)*, was contrasted with the heavenly way of the one who acts without concern for the consequences and for the sake of the action itself *(niṣkāma-karma)*, and who transforms every action into a rite and into an "offering." Such was the path of *bhakti*, a term that in this context corresponds more to the virile sense of medieval *fides* than to the pietistic sense that has prevailed in the theistic idea of "devotion." An action performed according to this type of *bhakti* was

---

9. The only modern thinker who has come close to this view, yet without being aware of it, was Nietzsche; he developed a view of absolute morality with a "naturalistic" basis.

compared to a fire that generates light and in which the matter of the act itself is consumed and purified. The degree to which the act was freed from matter, detached from greed and passion, and made self-sufficient (a "pure act," to employ analogically an Aristotelian expression) defined the hierarchy of activities and consequently the hierarchy of the castes or other bodies that corresponded to them as "functional classes."

Given these premises, which were not theoretical but experiential and thus at times not even openly expressed, the aspiration to go from one kind of activity to another (and therefore from one caste to another), which from a superficial and utilitarian perspective may be considered by some as a worthier and more advantageous step, was hardly considered in the traditional world, so much so that the heredity of functions was spontaneously established even where there were no castes, but only social groups. Every type of function and activity appeared equally as a point of departure for an elevation in a different and vertical rather than horizontal sense; and not in the temporal, but in the spiritual order. In this regard, by being in their own caste, in faithfulness to their own caste and to their own nature, in obedience not to a general morality but to their morality, or to the morality of their own caste, everyone enjoyed the same dignity and the same purity as everybody else; this was true for a *śūdra* as well as for a king. Everybody performed their function within the overall social order, and through their own peculiar *bhakti* even partook of the supernatural principle of this same order. Thus it was said: "A man attains perfection when his work is worship of God, from whom all things come and who is in all."[10] The god Kṛṣṇa declared: "In any way that men love me in the same way they find my love: for many are the paths of men, but they all in the end come to me."[11] And also: "In liberty from the bonds of attachment, do thou therefore the work to be done: for the man whose work is pure attains indeed the Supreme."[12] The notion of *dharma,* or one's peculiar nature to which one is supposed to be faithful,[13] comes from the root *dṛ* ("to sustain," "to uphold") and it expresses the element of order, form, or cosmos that Tradition embodies and implements over and against chaos and becoming. Through *dharma* the traditional world, just like every living thing and every being, is upheld; the dams holding back the sea of pure contingency and temporality stand firm; living beings partake of stability. It is therefore clear why leaving one's caste and mixing castes or even the rights, the duties, the morality, and the cults of each

---

10. *Bhagavadgītā,* 18.46.

11. Ibid., 4.11. In 17.3 it is stated that the "devotion" of a man must be conformed to his nature.

12. Ibid., 3.19. See also *The Laws of Manu,* 2.9: "For the human being who fulfills the duty declared in the revealed canon and in tradition wins renown here on earth and unsurpassable happiness after death."

13. *Bhagavadgītā,* 18.47: "Greater is thine own work, even if this be humble, than the work of another, even if this be great. When a man does the work God gives him, no sin can touch this man."

caste was considered a sacrilege that destroys the efficacy of every rite and leads those who are guilty of it to "hell,"[14] that is, to the realm of demonic influences that belong to the inferior nature. The people guilty of crossing the "caste line" were considered the only "impure" beings in the entire hierarchy; they were pariahs, or "untouchables" because they represented centers of psychic infection in the sense of an inner dissolution. In India only the people "without a caste" were considered outcasts, and they were shunned even by the lowest caste, even if they had previously belonged to the highest caste; on the contrary, nobody felt humiliated by his own caste and even a *śūdra* was as proud of and as committed to his own caste as a *brāhmaṇa* of the highest station was to his. Generally speaking, the idea of contamination did not concern only the individual of a higher caste who mixed with a member of a lower caste; even the latter felt contaminated by such mixture.[15] When gold and lead are mixed together, they are both altered; they both lose their own nature. Therefore it was necessary for *everybody* to be themselves. Thus, mixing subverted the traditional order and opened the door to infernal forces by removing what Goethe called the "creative limitation." The goal was the transfiguration of the "form," which was obtained through *bhakti* and *niṣkāma-karma*, namely, through action as rite and as oblation; the alteration, the destruction of the "form," no matter the way it was carried out, was considered as a degrading form of escapism. The outcast was just the vanquished—in the Aryan East he was called a *fallen one, patitas*.

This was the second principle on which the caste system was founded; it was a thoroughly spiritual foundation, since India, which implemented this system in one of its strictest versions (even to the point of becoming sclerotic), never had a centralized organization that could impose it by means of a political or economic despotism. Moreover, it is possible to find expressions of this second foundation even in the Western forms of Tradition. It was a classical idea, for instance, that perfection cannot be measured with a material criterion, but that it rather consists in realizing one's nature in a thorough way. The ancients also believed that materiality only represents

14. Ibid., 1.42–44. In relation to the duty of remaining faithful to the specific function and to the customs of one's caste, we may recall the characteristic episode in which Rama killed a serf *(śūdra)* who practiced asceticism, thus usurping a privilege of the priestly caste. Also we may recall the traditional teaching according to which the "Iron Age" or "Dark Age" will be inaugurated when the serfs will practice asceticism; this seems indeed a sign of our times, as some plebeian ideologies have come to see in "labor" a particular kind of asceticism.

15. Within certain limits, the idea of contamination did not apply to women; men of higher castes could marry women of lower castes without being contaminated. Traditionally the woman did not relate to a caste in a direct way but rather through her husband. *The Laws of Manu* (9.22): "When a woman is joined with a husband in accordance with the rules, she takes on the very same qualities that he has, just like a river flowing down into the ocean." This is, however, no longer the case when the existential traditional structures lose their vital force.

the inability to actualize one's form, since matter ($\H{\upsilon}\lambda\eta$) was depicted in Plato and Aristotle's writings as the foundation of undifferentiation and of an evasive instability that causes a thing or being to be incomplete in itself and not to correspond to its norm and "idea," (that is, to its *dharma*). In the Roman deification of the "limit" (*termen* or *terminus*) implemented through the elevation of the god Terminus to the highest dignity (he was even associated with the Olympian god Jupiter) as a principle of order and also as the patron saint of the "limits"; in the tradition (susceptible of being interpreted in terms of higher meanings) according to which he who knocked down or removed a single one of the territorial boundary stones was an accursed being to be killed on sight by anybody; and in the Roman oracle that announced that the era of the destruction of the limits erected against human greed will also be the *saeculum* of the "end of the world"[16]—in all these elements we find the esoteric reverberation of the same spirit. Plotinus wrote: "Each several thing must be a separate thing; there must be acts and thoughts that are our own; the good and evil done by each human being must be his own."[17] The idea that to comply perfectly with one's own specific function leads to an identical participation in the spirituality of the whole, conceived as a living organism, can be traced back to the best Greco-Roman traditions; later on it eventually became part of the *organic* vision of the Germanic-Roman civilization of the Middle Ages.

The presuppositions for the sense of joy and pride in one's own profession (such that any job, no matter how humble it was, could be performed as an "art), which have been preserved in some European peoples until recent times as an echo of the traditional spirit, are not any different, after all. The ancient German peasant, for instance, experienced his cultivating the land as a title of nobility, even though he was not able to see in this work, unlike his Persian counterpart, a symbol and an episode of the struggle between the god of light and the god of darkness. The members of the medieval corporations and guilds were as proud of their professional tradition as the nobility was proud of its bloodline. And when Luther, following Saint Thomas, taught that to go from one profession to another in order to enhance one's position in the social hierarchy ran contrary to God's law because God assigns to each and every one his or her own state, and therefore people must obey Him by remaining where they are and that the only way to serve God consists in doing one's best at one's job, the tradition was faithfully preserved in these ideas, and the best spirit of the Middle Ages was reflected, although with the limitations inherent in a theistic and devotional schema.

---

16. The meaning of this oracle converges with the Hindu teaching according to which the Dark Age (Kali Yuga), which is the end of a cycle (Mahā Yuga), corresponds to a period of unrestrained intermingling of the castes and to the decline of the rites.

17. *Enneads*, 3.1.4.

Prior to the advent of the civilization of the Third Estate (mercantilism, capitalism), the social ethics that was religiously sanctioned in the West consisted in realizing one's being and in achieving one's own perfection within the fixed parameters that one's individual nature and the group to which one belonged clearly defined. Economic activity, work, and profit were justified only in the measure in which they were necessary for sustenance and to ensure the dignity of an existence conformed to one's own estate, without the lower instinct of self-interest or profit coming first. Hence, we encounter a character of active impersonality in this domain as well.

It has been noted that in the caste hierarchy, relationships like those occurring between potentiality and act were reenacted. In the superior caste, the same activity that in the inferior caste presented itself in a more conditioned form was manifested in a more pure, complete, and freer manner as an idea. This allows us to take issue with the modern demagogical ideas concerning an alleged "flocklike mindedness" of individuals who lived in traditional societies, and concerning the alleged lack of that sense of dignity and freedom of every individual that only modern, "evolved" mankind is supposed to have achieved. In fact, even when the hierarchical position of the individual did not proceed from the spontaneous acknowledgment of one's own nature and one's faithfulness to it, the subordination of the inferior to the superior, far from being an indolent acquiescence, was almost the symbolical and ritual expression of a faithfulness and a devotion to one's particular ideal and to a higher form of being that the inferior could not directly and organically live out as his own nature *(svadharma)*, but which he could still consider as the center of his own actions precisely through his devotion and active subordination to a higher caste.[18] Moreover, although in the East to leave one's caste was only allowed in exceptional cases and a fugitive was far from being considered a free man, it was still possible to create certain causes through the way one conducted oneself in thought, word, and deed. These causes, by virtue of the analogy with the principle or with the hierarchy to which one was subjected, could produce a new way of being that corresponded to that principle or to that hierarchy.[19] Besides the *bhakti* or *fides* that is aimed directly

---

18. "If we say that people of this sort ought to be subject to the highest type of man, we intend that the subject should be governed not to his own detriment but on the same principle as his superior, who is himself governed by the divine element within him. It is better for everyone to be subject to a power of godlike wisdom residing within himself, or failing that, imposed from without." Plato, *Republic*, 590d.

19. In *The Laws of Manu*, while on the one hand it is written: "Even if he is set free by his master, a servant is not set free from slavery; for since that is innate in him, who can take it from him?" (8.414); on the other hand we read: "The servant's duty and supreme good is nothing but obedience to famous priestly householders, who know the Veda. If he is unpolluted, obedient to his superiors, gentle in his speech, without a sense of 'I,' and always dependent on the priests and the other twice-born castes, he attains a superior birth in the next life" (9.334–5). And also (10.42): "By the powers of their seed and their asceticism, in age after age these castes are pulled up or pulled down in birth among men here on earth."

at the Supreme Principle, that is, at the Unconditioned, the *bhakti* that was centered on some other high principle was thought to have the real and objective power to resolve the elements of the one who had nourished it (following the fulfillment of his own *dharma*) into this same principle,[20] and thus to make that person ascend, not exteriorly and artificially (as is the case in the disorder and careerism of modern society), but from within, in a profound and organic way, from a lower to a higher degree of the spiritual hierarchy as a reflection of the passage of the transcendental principle of being from one possibility to another.

Regarding that kind of social order that had its center in a sovereign and lasted up to the time of the Holy Roman Empire, there survives the principle (upheld by Celsus against the dualism of early Christianity) according to which the subjects may demonstrate their faithfulness to God through faithfulness to their ruler. The view of the subject as a being connected to the person of his sovereign through a sacred and freely chosen vow is an ancient Indo-European view. In the traditional world, this *fides* or personal devotion went beyond political and individual boundaries, and even acquired the value of a path leading to liberation. Cumont, in reference to Iran, observed that

> The subjects dedicated to their deified kings not only their actions and words, but their very thoughts. Their duty was a complete abandonment of their personality in favor of those monarchs who were held the equal of gods. The sacred militia of the mysteries was nothing but this civic morality viewed from the religious standpoint. It confounded loyalty with piety.[21]

This loyalty, in the brightest and most luminous forms of Tradition, was credited with the power of producing the same fruits faith is supposed to produce. Not too many years ago, the Japanese general Nogi, who had prevailed at Port Arthur against his Russian foes, killed himself with his wife after the death of his emperor in order to follow him in the afterlife.

All of this is self-evident since I have said that *faithfulness* is the second cornerstone of every traditional organization, in addition to the rite and an elite that embodies transcendence. This is the force that, as a magnet, establishes contacts, creates a

---

20. We may recall Plotinus's teaching: "When we cease to live, our death hands over to another principle this energy of our own personal career. That principle (of the new birth) strives to gain control, and if it succeeds it also lives and itself, in turn, possesses a guiding spirit." *Enneads*, 3.1.3. In this instance, this "guiding spirit" corresponds to the principle that has been made the object of one's active and loyal *bhakti*.

21. F. Cumont, *The Oriental Religions in Roman Paganism*, 20.

psychic atmosphere, stabilizes the social structure, and determines a system of coordination and gravitation between the individual elements and the center. When this fluid, which is rooted in freedom and in the spiritual spontaneity of the personality, fails, the traditional organism loses its elementary power of cohesion, paths become precluded, subtler senses atrophied, the parts dissociated and atomized. The consequence of this degeneration is the immediate withdrawal of the forces from above, which thus abandon men to themselves, leaving them free to go where they wish according to the destiny that their actions create and that no superior influence will ever be able to modify again. This is the mystery inherent in decadence.

15

Professional Associations
and the Arts; Slavery

When viewed as a relationship between potentiality and act, hierarchy allowed the same motif established at the top to be reproduced in the activities of the different castes or social organisms; though on the plane of different (more or less spiritual) paths of fulfillment, each one retained in its own way the same upward orientation. This is why in the more complete traditional forms, the "sacred" was a light that shone not only on what today are the profane sciences, arts, and professions, but on trades and various material activities as well. By virtue of the analogical correspondences existing between the various planes, the sciences, activities, and skills of the lower plane could traditionally be considered as symbols of a higher nature and thus help to communicate the meaning hidden in the latter, since it was already present in the former, even though in a potential form.[1]

In the domain of knowledge, the presupposition was of a system of sciences fundamentally different in their premises and methodologies from modern ones. Every modern, profane science corresponds in the world of Tradition to a "sacred" science that had an organic, qualitative character and considered nature as a whole in a hierarchy of degrees of reality and forms of experience in which the form connected to the physical senses is just one among others. It is precisely in this way that the system of transpositions and symbolic and ritual participations was made possible. This was the case in cosmology and in related disciplines: for instance, ancient alchemy was not at all a primitive chemistry and ancient astrology was not at all (as it is mistakenly assumed today) a superstitious deification of the heavenly bodies and of their movements, but a knowledge of the stars so organized as to be able to constitute a science of purely spiritual and metaphysical realities expressed in a symbolic

---

1. R. Guénon, *La Crise du monde moderne*, 108–15.

form. The world of Tradition knew in these same terms a physiology, parts of which are still preserved in the East (for example, the knowledge of anatomy and physiology presupposed by Chinese acupuncture; Japanese ju-jitsu; and some aspects of Hindu hatha-yoga). In this physiology, the consideration of the material aspect of the human organism represented only a particular chapter, becoming part of the general science of the correspondences between macrocosm and microcosm, human world and elemental world. Ancient medicine proceeded from these same premises as a "sacred science" in which "health" appeared as a symbol of "virtue"; virtue in turn was considered a superior form of health and due to the ambiguity of the term soter, he who "saves" was on a higher plane of the same type as he who "heals."

The development of the physical and practical aspect of knowledge in these traditional sciences must naturally appear as limited when compared and contrasted with modern sciences. The cause of this, however, was a correct and healthy hierarchy in which the interests of traditional man were arranged; in other words, he did not give to the knowledge of external and physical reality more importance than it deserved or than was necessary.[2] What mattered the most in a traditional science was the anagogic element, namely, the power to "lead to higher planes" that was virtually present in the knowledge relative to a given domain of reality; this element is totally lacking today in modern profane sciences. The latter, in reality, may act and have acted exactly in the opposite direction: the worldview from which they originate and on which they are based is such as to affect human interiority in a dissolving and negative way—in other words, they are centrifugal.[3]

Coming back to our subject matter, analogous considerations to the previous ones may be extended to the domain of the arts, understood both as real arts and as the activities of professional artisans. Concerning the former, only in periods of decadence did the world of Tradition come to know the emancipation of the purely "aesthetic," subjective, and human element that characterizes modern arts. In the figurative arts, even prehistoric findings (such as the civilization of the Cro-Magnon and of the reindeer) show the inseparability of the naturalistic element from a magical and symbolical intention; an analogous dimension was present also in later, more developed civilizations. The "theater" corresponded to reenactments of the Mysteries, to the "sacred dramas" and, in part, to the ludi of classical antiquity, more on which later. Ancient poetry had close ties with the art of telling the future and with sacred inspiration; poetic verse, in fact, was associated with incantation (see the ancient

2. Very appropriately O. Spann defines modern knowledge as "the knowledge of what is not worthy of being known." Religionsphilosophie (Vienna, 1948), 44.
3. Concerning the illusions nourished by some in regard to modern science, see my Cavalcare la tigre (Milan, 1962).

meaning of the word *carmen*). As far as literature is concerned, the symbolic and initiatory element (which proceeded from a conscious intention and also from infraconscious influences grafted onto the creative spontaneity of single individuals and of various groups) throughout the Middle Ages often influenced not only the myth, saga, and traditional fairy tale, but the epic stories and chivalrous and erotic literature as well. The same applies to music, dance, and rhythm; Lucian reports that dancers, who were assimilated to priests, had a knowledge of the "sacred mysteries of the Egyptians,"[4] as the science of the *mudrās*, the symbolic, magical gestures that play an important role in Hindu rituals and ascetical paths affected the dance, the mime and pantomime of that civilization. Again, these were various expressions of the same one intent: "one temple, sculptured in a forest of temples."

With specific regard to professional and artisanal activities, a typical example is given in the art of construction and building (their moral transpositions in the Gospels are well known), which occasioned even higher and initiatory interpretations. In the ancient Egyptian tradition, construction was regarded as a regal art, so much so that the king himself performed in a symbolic sense the first acts of the building of the temples in the spirit of an "eternal work of art." While on the one hand people today are nowadays puzzled when it comes to explaining how achievements that require a superior knowledge of mathematics and engineering were possible in antiquity, on the other hand what emerges are unquestionable signs of a priestly art in the orientation, placement, and other aspects of ancient buildings, especially temples and, later on, cathedrals. The symbolism of masonry established analogical connections between the "little art" on the one hand and the "great art" and the "great work" on the other within secret associations that in the beginning could claim links with the corresponding medieval professional corporations. This is also partially true in the case of the arts of the blacksmiths, weavers, navigators, and farmers. Concerning the latter, just as Egypt knew the ritual of regal constructions, likewise the Far East knew the ritual of regal plowing[5] and, in a symbolic transposition of the farming art, generally speaking, man himself was considered as a field to be cultivated, and the initiate as the cultivator of the field in an eminent sense.[6] (The echo of this has been preserved in the very origins of the modern term "culture" in its reductive, intellectualistic, and petit bourgeois meaning.)

The ancient arts, after all, were traditionally "sacred" to specific deities and heroes, always by virtue of analogical reasons, and thus they presented themselves

---

4. Lucian of Samosata, *On Dance*, 59. The "dance of the seven veils," which are removed one at a time until the dancer is totally nude, repeats on its own plane a precise initiatory schema.
5. *Li Chi*, 4.1.13; 17.3.20.
6. J. Evola, *The Hermetic Tradition*, chap. 22.

as potentially endowed with the possibility of "ritually" transforming physical activities into symbolic actions endowed with a transcendent meaning.

In reality, in the caste system not only did every profession or trade correspond to a vocation (hence the double meaning preserved in the English term "calling");[7] not only was there something to be found in every product as a "crystallized tradition" that could be activated by a free and personal activity and by an incomparable skill; not only were the dispositions developed in the exercise of a trade and acknowledged by the social organism transmitted through the blood as congenital and deep attitudes—but something else was present as well, namely, the transmission, if not the real initiation, of at least an "inner tradition" of the art that was preserved as a sacred and secret thing *(arcanum magisterium),* even though it was partly visible in the several details and rules, rich with symbolical and religious elements that were displayed in the traditional guilds (whether Eastern, Mexican, Roman, medieval, and so on).[8] Being introduced to the secrets of an art did not correspond to the mere empirical or rational teachings of modern man: in this domain certain cognitions were credited with a nonhuman origin, an idea expressed in a symbolic form by the traditions concerning the gods, the demons, or the heroes (Balder, Hermes, Vulcan, Prometheus) who originally initiated men into these arts. It is significant that Janus, who was also the god of initiation, was the god of the Collegia Fabrorum in Rome; in relation to this we find the idea that mysterious congregations of blacksmiths who came to Europe from the East, also brought with them a new civilization. Moreover, it is significant that in the locations where the oldest temples of Hera, Cupra, Aphrodite-Venus, Heracles-Hercules, and Aeneas were built, quite often it is possible to find archaeological evidence of the working of copper and bronze; and finally, it is significant that the Orphic and Dyonisiac mysteries were associated with the themes of the art of weaving and spinning. This order found its most complete fulfillment in examples found especially in the East, where the achievement of an effective mastery in a given art was just a symbol, a reflection, and a sign; in fact, it was the counterpart of a fulfillment and a parallel inner realization.

Even in those areas in which the caste system did not have the rigor and the determination exemplified by Aryan India, something resembling it was developed in a spontaneous way in relation to inferior activities. I am referring to the ancient corporations or artisan guilds that were omnipresent in the traditional world, and that

7. In the language of the *campagnonagge,* in which these traditions were preserved, the word *vocation* was always synonymous with occupation: instead of asking a person what his occupation was, he was asked what was his "vocation."

8. The medieval "manuals" that have been preserved often mention mysterious practices that were associated with the process of construction itself; they also relate legends according to which masters of the art were killed because they betrayed the oath of secrecy.

in the case of ancient Rome date back to prehistoric times, reproducing on their own plane the typical makeup of the patrician gens and family. It is the art and the common activity that provide a bond and an order replacing those that in higher castes were provided by the aristocratic tradition of blood and ritual. This does not imply that the collegium and the corporation lacked a religious character and a virile, semimilitary constitution. In Sparta the cult of a "hero" represented the ideal bond between the members of a given profession, even in the case of an inferior one.[9] Just like every city and gens, in Rome every corporation (originally consisting of free men) had its own demon or *lar;* it had a temple consecrated to it and a correlative, common cult of the dead, that determined a unity in life and in death; it had its own sacrificial rites performed by the *magister* on behalf of the community of the *sodales* or *collegae,* who celebrated certain events or holy days in a solemn, mystical way through feasts, agapes, and games. The fact that the anniversary of the collegium or corporation *(natalis collegi)* coincided with the anniversary of its patron deity *(natalis dei)* and of the "inauguration" or consecration of the temple *(natalis templi),* indicates that in the eyes of the *sodales* the sacred element constituted the center from which the inner life of the corporation originated.[10]

The Roman corporation is a good example of the virile and organic aspect that often accompanies the sacred dimension in traditional institutions; it was hierarchically constituted *ad exemplum rei publicae* and animated by a military spirit. The body of *sodales* was called *populus* or *ordo,* and just like the army and the people at solemn gatherings, it was divided into *centuriae* and *decuriae.* Every *centuria* had its leader, or centurion, and a lieutenant *(optio),* just like in the legions. To differentiate them from the masters the other members had the name of *plebs* and *corporati,* but also *caligati* or *milites caligati* like simple soldiers. And the *magister,* besides being the master of the art and the priest of the corporation in charge of his "fire," was the administrator of justice and the overseer of the behavior of the members of the group.

Analogous characteristics were found in the medieval professional communities, especially in Germanic countries: together with the community of the art, a religious and ethical element bound the members of the Gilden and of the Zunften. In these corporate organizations, the members were bonded together "for life" more as in a common rite than on the basis of the economic interests and mere productive goals; the effects of intimate solidarity, which affected man as a whole and not just

9. Herodotus, *The Histories,* 6.60.
10. According to a tradition, Numa, by instituting the collegia, intended for "every profession to celebrate its own cult" (Plutarch, *Numa,* 17). In India too each profession pursued by the inferior castes often corresponded to a special cult of divine or legendary patrons; this practice is also found in Greece, among Nordic people and the Aztecs, in Islam, and so on.

his particular aspect as an artisan, permeated everyday life in all of its forms. As the Roman professional collegia had their own *lar* or demon, the German guilds, which were constituted as small-scale images of cities, also had their own "patron saint," altar, common funerary cult, symbolic insignia, ritual commemorations, ethical laws, and leaders (Vollenossen), who were supposed to regulate the art and guarantee compliance with the general norms and duties regulating the lives of the members of the corporation. The requirement for being admitted to the guilds was a spotless name and an honorable birth; people who were not free and those belonging to foreign races were not admitted. Typical of these professional associations were the sense of honor, purity, and impersonal character of their work, almost according to the Aryan canons of *bhakti* and of *niṣkāma-karma:* everybody performed their work silently, setting their own person aside, while still remaining active and free human beings; this was an aspect of the great anonymity typical of the Middle Ages and of every great traditional civilization. Something else was shunned, namely, anything that could generate illicit competition or a monopoly, thus contaminating the purity of the art with mere economic concerns; the honor of one's guild and the pride in the activity characterizing it constituted the firm, immaterial bases of these organizations. While not formally hereditary, these organizations often became so, thereby demonstrating the strength and the naturalness of the principle responsible for generating the castes.[11] In this way, even in the order of inferior activities connected to matter and to material conditions of life it was possible to find the reflection of the way of being of a purified and free action endowed with its own *fides* and living soul, which freed it from the bonds of selfishness and ordinary interests. In the corporations there was a natural and organic connection between the caste of the *vaiśya* (in modern terms, "management") and the caste of the *śūdras,* namely, the working class.

Considering the spirit of an almost military solidarity that was both felt and willed, and whereby the *vaiśya* was the equivalent of a manager and the *śūdra* an employee, both of whom worked in the same company, the Marxist antithesis between capital and labor, between employers and employees, at that time would have been inconceivable. Everybody attended their own function and stayed in their own place. Especially in the German guilds, the faithfulness of the inferior was the counterpart of the pride the superior took in the subordinates' zeal and efficiency. In this context too, the anarchy of "rights" and "demands" did not arise until the inner spiritual orientation died out and the action performed in purity was supplanted by one

---

11. In Rome the professional guilds became hereditary during the third century A.D. From that time on, every member of a corporation passed on to his heirs not only a biological legacy, but his profession and his property as well, provided that they too followed in his footsteps. This succession was enforced by the state, however, and thus we can no longer speak of an authentic conformity of the castes to the traditional spirit.

motivated by materialistic and individualistic concerns, and by the multiform and vain fever brought about by the modern spirit and a civilization that has turned economics into a guiding principle (daemon) and a destiny.

When the inner strength of a *fides* is no longer present, then every activity is defined according to its purely material aspect; also, equally worthy paths are replaced with an effect-driven differentiation dictated by the type of activity being performed. Hence, the sense of intermediary forms of social organization, such as ancient slavery. As paradoxical as it may first appear in the context of those civilizations that largely employed the institution of slavery, it was *work* that characterized the condition of a slave, and not vice versa. In other words: when the activity in the lower strata of the social hierarchy was no longer supported by a spiritual meaning, and when instead of an "action" there was only "work," then the material criterion was destined to take over and those activities related to matter and connected to the material needs of life were destined to appear as degrading and as unworthy of any free human being. Therefore "work" *(ponos)* came to be seen as something that only a slave would engage in, and it became almost a sentence; likewise, the only *dharma* possible for a slave was work. The ancient world did not despise labor because it practiced slavery and because those who worked were slaves; on the contrary, since it despised labor, it despised the slave;[12] since those who "worked" could not be anything but slaves, the traditional world willed slavery into being and it differentiated, instituted, and regulated into a separated social class the mass of those people whose way of being could only be expressed through work.[13] Labor as *ponos*, an

12. [The translator of this work has come across a passage that he regards worth quoting in this context: "Around 1820 an astrologer says to the young hero of Stendhal's *Charterhouse of Parma:* 'In a century perhaps nobody will want idlers any more.' He was right. It ill becomes anyone today to admit that he lives without working. Since Marx and Proudhon, labor has been universally accepted as a positive social value and a philosophical concept. As a result, the ancients' contempt for labor, their undisguised scorn for those who work with their hands, their exaltation of leisure as the sine qua non of a 'liberal' life, the only life worthy of a man, shocks us deeply. Not only was the worker regarded as a social inferior; he was base, ignoble. It has often been held, therefore, that a society like the Roman, so mistaken about what we regard as proper values, must have been a deformed society, which inevitably paid the price of its deformity. . . . And yet, if we are honest, we must admit that the key to this enigma lies within ourselves. True, we believe that work is respectable and would not dare to admit to idleness. Nevertheless, we are sensitive to class distinction and, admit or not, regard workers and shopkeepers as people of relatively little importance. We would not want ourselves or our children to sink to their station, even if we are a little ashamed of harboring such sentiments. Therein lies the first of six keys to ancient attitudes toward labor: contempt for labor equals social contempt for laborers." Paul Veyne, ed., *A History of Private Life*, vol. 1, *From Pagan Rome to Byzantium*, trans. Arthur Goldhammer (Cambridge, Mass., 1987), 118–19.]

13. Aristotle (*Politics*, 1.4) based slavery on the presupposition that there are men who are only fit for physical labor, who therefore must be dominated and directed by others. According to this order of ideas, a distinction was made between "barbarians" and "Hellenes." Likewise, the Hindu caste of the *śūdras* originally corresponded to the stratum of the black aboriginal race, the "enemy race" dominated by the Aryans, which had no other choice but to serve those who were "twice-born."

obscure effort strictly dictated by need, was the opposite of *action*, the former representing the material, heavy, dark pole, the latter the free pole of human possibilities detached from need. Free men and slaves, after all, represented the social crystallization of those two ways of performing an action—either according to matter, or ritually—that I have already discussed; we do not need to look elsewhere to find the basis for the contempt for work and of the view of hierarchy typical of the constitutions of an intermediate type. In such a world, speculative action, asceticism, contemplation (sometimes even "play" and war) characterized the pole of action vis-à-vis the servile pole of work.

Esoterically speaking, the limitations that slavery put on the possibilities of an individual who happened to be born in this condition correspond to the nature of his given "destiny," of which slavery should be considered sometimes the natural consequence. On the plane of mythological transpositions, the Jewish tradition is not too far from a similar view when it considers work as a consequence of Adam's fall and, at the same time, as an "expiation" of this transcendental fault taking place in human existence. On this basis, when Catholicism tried to turn work into an instrument of purification it partially echoed the general idea of the ritual offering of an action conformed to one's nature (in this context: the nature of "fallen man" according to the Judeo-Christian view of life) as a path of liberation.

In antiquity, the vanquished were often assigned the functions of slaves. Was this barbarian-style materialism? Yes and no. Once more, we should not forget the truth that permeated the traditional world: nothing happens on this earth that is not the symbol and the parallel effect of spiritual events, since between spirit and reality (hence, power too) allegedly there was an intimate relationship. As a particular consequence of this truth, it has already been mentioned that winning or losing were never considered as mere coincidences. There still remains today among primitive populations the ancient belief that the person afflicted by misfortunes is always a guilty person; the outcomes of every struggle and every war are always mystical signs, or the results of a "divine judgment," and therefore capable of revealing or unfolding a human destiny. Starting with this presupposition, it is possible to go further and establish a transcendental convergence of meanings between the traditional view of the "vanquished" and the Jewish view of the "sinner," as they both inherit a fate befitting the *dharma* of the slave, namely, work. This convergence is inspired by the fact that Adam's "fault" is associated with a defeat he suffered in a symbolical event (the attempt to come into possession of the fruit of the "Tree"), which may yet have had a victorious outcome. We know of myths in which the winning of the fruits of the Tree or of things symbolically equivalent (the "woman," the "golden fleece," etc.) is achieved by other heroes (Heracles, Jason, Siegfried) and does not lead them to damnation, as in the Judeo-Christian myth, but rather to immortality or to a transcendent knowledge.[14]

If the modern world has disapproved of the "injustice" of the caste system, it has stigmatized much more vibrantly those ancient civilizations thast practiced slavery; recent times boast of having championed the principle of "human dignity." This too is mere rhetoric. Let us set aside the fact that Europeans reintroduced and maintained slavery up to the nineteenth century in their overseas colonies in such heinous forms as to be rarely found in the ancient world; what should be emphasized is that if there ever was a civilization of slaves on a grand scale, the one in which we are living is it. No traditional civilization ever saw such great masses of people condemned to perform shallow, impersonal, automatic jobs; in the contemporary slave system the counterparts of figures such as lords or enlightened rulers are nowhere to be found. This slavery is imposed subtly through the tyranny of the economic factor and through the absurd structures of a more or less collectivized society. And since the modern view of life in its materialism has taken away from the single individual any possibility of bestowing on his destiny a transfiguring element and seeing in it a sign and a symbol, contemporary "slavery" should therefore be reckoned as one of the gloomiest and most desperate kinds of all times. It is not a surprise that in the masses of modern slaves the obscure forces of world subversion have found an easy, obtuse instrument to pursue their goals; while in the places where it has already triumphed, the vast Stalinist "work camps" testify to how the physical and moral subjection of man to the goals of collectivization and of the uprooting of every value of the personality is employed in a methodical and even satanic way.

In addition to the previous considerations concerning work as art in the world of Tradition, I will briefly mention the organic, functional, and consistent quality of the objects produced, by virtue of which the Beautiful did not appear as something separated or distinct from a certain privileged category of artistic objects and the mere utilitarian and mercantile character of the objects was totally lacking. Every object had its own beauty and a qualitative value, as well as its own function as a useful object. With regard to art in the traditional world,

> While on the one hand what occurred was *(a)* the prodigy of the unification of the opposites, *(b)* the utter compliance with a set of established rules in which every personal élan appears to be sacrificed and suffocated and *(c)* the authentic arising of spirituality within an authentic, personal creation;[15]

14. See the introduction of my *Hermetic Tradition*.
15. G. Villa, *La filosofia del mito secondo G. B. Vico* (Milan, 1949), 98–99.

on the other hand it could be rightly said that:

> Every object did not have the imprint of an individual artistic personal-
> ity, as happens today with the so-called artistic objects; yet while re-
> vealing a "choral" taste, which makes of the object one of many, infi-
> nite expressions, it had the seal of a spiritual genuineness that prevented
> it from being called a "copy."[16]

Such products bore witness to one stylistic personality whose creative activity developed through centuries; even when a name, whether real, fictitious, or symbolic was known, this was considered irrelevant. Anonymity, not of a subpersonal but of a superpersonal character, was therefore upheld; on this soil what was born and proliferated in all the domains of life were artisans' creations that were far from both a shallow, plebeian sense of utility and an extrinsic, afunctional, "artificial" beauty; this scission reflects the overall inorganic character of modern civilization.

16. Ibid., 102.

16

Bipartition of the Traditional
Spirit; Asceticism

Having explained the spirit that animated the caste system, it is now necessary to discuss the path that is above the castes and is directed at implementing the realization of transcendence—in analogous terms to those of high initiation, yet *outside* the specific and rigorous structures characterizing it. On the one hand, the pariah is a person without a caste, the one who has "lapsed" or who has eluded the "form" by being powerless before it, thus returning to the infernal world. The ascetic, on the other hand, is a being above the caste, one who becomes free from the form by renouncing the illusory center of human individuality; he turns toward the principle from which every "form" proceeds, not by faithfulness to his own nature and by participation in the hierarchy, but by a direct action. Therefore, as great as was the revulsion harbored by every caste toward the pariah in Aryan India, so, by contrast, was the veneration felt by everybody for a person who was above the castes. These beings, according to a Buddhist image, should not be expected to follow a human *dharma*, just as one who is trying to kindle a fire ultimately does not care what kind of wood is being employed, as long as it is capable of producing fire and light.

Asceticism occupies an ideal intermediary state between the plane of direct, Olympian, and initiatory regality and the plane of rite and of *dharma*. Asceticism also presents two features or qualifications that from a broader perspective may be considered as qualifications of the same traditional spirit. The first aspect of the ascetic path is action, understood as heroic action; the second aspect is asceticism in the technical sense of the word, especially with reference to the path of contemplation. Beyond complete traditional forms and in more recent times some civilizations have arisen that were inspired in different degrees by either one of these two poles. Later on we shall see what role the two aspects have played in the dynamism of historical forces, even on the plane that is related to the ethnic and racial factor. In order to grasp the spirit of an ascetical tradition at a pure state it is necessary to leave out of consideration the meanings that have been associated with the term *asceticism* in the world of Western religiosity. Action and knowledge are two fundamental human faculties; in both domains it is possible to accomplish an integration capable of removing human limitations. The asceticism of contemplation consists of the integration of the knowing faculty (achieved through detachment from sensible reality) with the neutralization of individual rationalizing faculties and with the progressive stripping of the nucleus of consciousness, which thus becomes "free from conditionings" and subtracts itself from the limitation and from the necessity of any determination, whether real or virtual. Once all the dross and obstructions are removed *(opus remotionis),* participation in the overworld takes place in the form of a vision or an enlightenment. As the peak of the ascetical path, this point also represents at the same time the beginning of a truly continuous, progressive ascent that realizes states of being truly superior to the human condition. The essential ideals of the ascetical path are the universal as knowledge and knowledge as liberation.

The ascetical detachment typical of the contemplative path implies "renunciation." In this regard, it is necessary to prevent the misunderstanding occasioned by some inferior forms of asceticism. It is important to emphasize the different meanings that renunciation assumed in higher forms of ancient and Eastern asceticism on the one hand, and in most of Western and especially Christian asceticism on the other hand. In the latter, renunciation often assumed the character of a repression and of a "mortification"; the Christian ascetic becomes detached from the objects of desire not because he no longer has any desire, but in order to mortify himself and to "escape temptation." In the former, renunciation proceeds from a natural distaste for objects that are usually attractive and yearned for; this distaste is motivated by the fact that one directly desires—or better, wills—something the world of conditioned experience cannot grant. In this case, what leads to renunciation is the natural nobility of one's desire rather than an external intervention aimed at slowing down, mortifying, and inhibiting the faculty of desire in a vulgar nature. After all, the emotional phase, even in its purest and noblest forms, is only found at the introductory levels in higher forms of asceticism; in later stages, it is consumed by the intellectual fire and by the arid splendor of pure contemplation.

A typical example of contemplative asceticism is given by early Buddhism in its lack of "religious" features, its organization in a pure system of techniques, and in the spirit that animates it, which is so different from what anyone may think about asceticism. First of all, Buddhism does not know any "gods" in the religious sense of the word; the gods are believed to be powers who also need liberation, and thus the "Awakened One" is acknowledged to be superior to both men and gods. In the Buddhist canon it is written that an ascetic not only becomes free from human bonds, but from divine bonds as well. Secondly, moral norms, in the original forms of Buddhism, are purported to be mere instruments to be employed in the quest for the objective realization of superindividual states. Anything that belongs to the world of "believing," of "faith," or that is remotely associated with emotional experiences is shunned. The fundamental principle of the method is "knowledge": to turn the knowledge of the ultimate nonidentity of the Self with anything "else" (whether it be the monistic All or the world of Brahmā, theistically conceived) into a fire that progressively devours any irrational self-identification with anything that is conditioned. In conformity to the path, the final outcome, besides the negative designation (*nirvāṇa* = "cessation of restlessness"), is expressed in terms of "knowledge," *bodhi*, which is knowledge in the eminent sense of superrational enlightenment or liberating knowledge, as in "waking up" from sleep, slumber, or a hallucination. It goes without saying that this is not the equivalent of the cessation of power or of anything resembling a dissolution. To dissolve ties is not to become dissolved but to become free. The image of the one who, once freed from all yokes, whether human or divine, is supremely autonomous and thus may go wherever he pleases, is found very frequently in the Buddhist canon together with all kinds of symbols of a virile and warrior type, and also with constant and explicit reference not so much to nonbeing but rather to something superior to both being and nonbeing. Buddha, as it is well known, belonged to an ancient stock of Aryan warrior nobility and his doctrine (purported to be the "*dharma* of the pure ones, inaccessible to an uninstructed, average person") is a very far cry from any mystical escapism. Buddha's doctrine is permeated by a sense of superiority, clarity, and an indomitable spirit, and Buddha himself is called "the fully Self-Awakened One," "the Lord."[1]

The Buddhist renunciation is of a virile and aristocratic type and is animated by an inner strength; it is not dictated by need but is consciously willed, so that the person practicing it may overcome need and become reintegrated into a perfect life. It is understandable that when our contemporaries, who only know a life that is mixed with nonlife that in its restlessness presents the irrational traits of a "mania," hear mention of *nirvāṇa* (in reference to the condition experienced by the Awakened One), namely, of an extinction of mania corresponding to what the Germans call "more than living" *(mehr als Leben)* and to a superlife, they cannot help but equate *nirvāṇa* with "nothingness": for non-mania *(nir-vāṇa)* means nonlife, or nothingness. After all, it is only natural that the modern spirit has relegated the values cherished by higher asceticism to the things of the "past."

1. J. Evola, *The Doctrine of Awakening.*

A Western example of pure contemplative asceticism is given by Neoplatonism. With the words, "The gods ought to come to me, not I to them,"[2] Plotinus indicated a fundamental aspect of aristocratic asceticism. Also, with the sayings, "It is to the gods, not to good men that we are to be made like," and, "Our concern, though, is not to be out of sin, but to be god,"[3] Plotinus has definitely overcome the limitations posed by morality, and has employed the method of inner simplification ($\dot{\alpha}\pi\lambda\omega\sigma\iota\varsigma$) as a way to become free from all conditionings in that state of metaphysical simplicity from which the vision[4] will eventually arise. By means of this vision—"having joined as it were center to center"[5]—what occurs is the participation in that intelligible reality that compared to which any other reality may be characterized as more nonlife than life,[6] with the sensible impressions appearing as dreams[7] and the world of bodies as the place of radical powerlessness and of the inability to be.

Another example is given by the so-called Rhineland mysticism that was capable of reaching metaphysical peaks towering above and beyond Christian theism. Tauler's *Entwerdung* corresponds to Plotinus's $\dot{\alpha}\pi\lambda\omega\sigma\iota\varsigma$ and to the destruction of the element of "becoming" (or saṁsāric element) that Buddhism regarded as the condition necessary to achieve "awakening." The aristocratic view of contemplative asceticism reappears in the doctrine of Meister Eckhart. Like Buddha, Eckhart addressed the noble man and the "noble soul" whose metaphysical dignity is witnessed by the presence of a "strength," a "light," and a "fire" within it—in other words, of something before which even the deity conceived as a "person" (i.e., theistically) becomes something exterior. The method he employed consisted essentially of detachment from all things (Abegescheidenheit), a virtue that according to Eckhart is above love, humility, or mercifulness, as he explained in his sermon *On Detachment*.[8] The principle of "spiritual centrality" was affirmed: the true Self is God, God is our real center and we are external only to ourselves. Fear, hope, anguish, joy, and pain, or anything that may bring us out of ourselves, must be allowed to seep into us. An action dictated by desire, even when its goal is the kingdom of heaven itself, eternal life, or the beatific vision, must not be undertaken. The path suggested by Eckhart leads from the outside to the inside, beyond everything that is mere "im-

---

2. Porphyry, *The Life of Plotinus*, 10.
3. Plotinus, *Enneads*, 1.2.7; 1.2.6.
4. Ibid., 1.6.9.
5. "For here too when the centers have come together they are one, but there is duality when they are separate." Ibid., 6.9.10.
6. "The perfect life, the true, real life, is in that transcendent intelligible reality, and other lives are incomplete traces of life, not perfect or pure and no more life than its opposite." Ibid., 1.4.3.
7. Ibid., 3.6.6.
8. *Meister Eckhart: The Essential Sermons, Commentaries, Treatises and Defense*, trans. E. Colledge and B. McGinn. (New York, 1982), 286.

age"; beyond things and what represents the quality of a thing (Dingheit); beyond forms and the quality of form (Formlichkeit); beyond essences and essentiality. From the gradual extinction of all images and forms, and eventually of one's own thoughts, will, and knowledge, what arises is a transformed and supernatural knowledge that is carried beyond all forms *(überformt)*. Thus one reaches a peak in respect to which "God" himself (always according to his theistic view) appears as something ephemeral, that is, as a transcendent and uncreated peak of the Self without which "God" himself could not exist. All the typical images of the religious consciousness are swallowed up by a reality that is an absolute, pure possession, and that in its simplicity cannot help but to appear terrifying to any finite being. Once again we find a solar symbol: before this barren and absolute substance, "God" appears as the moon next to the sun. The divine light in comparison with the radiance of this substance pales, just as the sun's light outshines the moon's.

After this brief mention of the meaning of contemplative asceticism, it is necessary to say something about the other path, namely, the path of action. While in contemplative asceticism we find a mostly inner process in which the theme of detachment and the direct orientation toward transcendence are predominant, in the second case we have an immanent process aimed at awakening the deepest forces of the human being and at bringing them to the limit, thus causing a superlife to spring from life itself in a context of absolute intensity; this is the heroic life according to the sacred meaning often displayed in the traditional Eastern and Western worlds. The nature of such a realization causes it to present simultaneously an outer and an inner, a visible and an invisible aspect; conversely, pure contemplative asceticism may also lie entirely in a domain that is not connected to the external world by something tangible. When the two poles of the ascetical path are not separated and neither one becomes the "dominating" trait of a particular type of civilization, but on the contrary, both poles are present and joined together, then the ascetical element feeds in an invisible way the forces of "centrality" and "stability" of a traditional organism, while the heroic element enjoys a greater relationship with the dynamism and the force animating its structures.

In relation to the path of action, in the next two chapters I will discuss the doctrine of the holy war and the role played by games in antiquity. I will further develop the topic of heroic action given the interest it should evoke in Western man who, by virtue of his own nature, is more inclined to act than to contemplate.

17

The Greater and the Lesser Holy War

C onsidering that in the traditional view of the world every reality was a symbol and every action a ritual, the same was true in the case of war; since war could take on a sacred character, "holy war" and "the path to God" became one and the same thing. In more or less explicit forms, this concept is found in many traditions: a religious aspect and a transcendent intent were often associated with the bloody and military deeds of traditional humanity.

Livy relates that the Samnite warriors looked like initiates;[1] similarly, among savage populations the magical and the warrior elements are often intermingled. In ancient Mexico the bestowal of the title of commander *(tecuhtli)* was subordinated to the successful outcome of difficult trials of an initiatory type; also, until recent times the Japanese warrior nobility (the samurai) was to a large degree inspired by the doctrines and asceticism of Zen, an esoteric form of Buddhism.

The ancient worldview and myths, in which the theme of antagonism repeatedly occurred, automatically propelled the elevation of the art of war to a spiritual plane. This was the case of the Persian-Aryan tradition and also of the Hellenic world, which often saw in material warfare the reflection of a perennial cosmic struggle between the spiritual Olympian-Uranian element of the cosmos on the one hand, and the Titanic, demonic-feminine unrestrained elements of chaos on the other hand. This interpretation is possible especially in those instances where war was associated with the idea of the empire, and also because of the transcendent meaning this concept evoked; it was then translated into a very powerful idea. The symbolism of Heracles' labors, he being the hero fighting on the side of the Olympian forces, was applied to as late a figure as Frederick I of Hohenstaufen.

---

1. "Sacratos more Samnitium milites eoque candida veste et paribus candore armis insignes." *History of Rome,* 9.44.9. And also: "They had also called in the aid of the gods by submitting the soldiers to a kind of initiation into an ancient form of oath (*ritu quodam sacramenti vetusta velut initiatis militibus*)." Ibid., 10.38.2.

Special views concerning one's fate in the afterlife introduce us to the inner meanings of warrior asceticism. According to the Aztec and Nahua races, the highest seat of immortality—the "House of the Sun" or the "House of Huitzilopochtli"— was reserved not only for sovereigns but for heroes as well; as far as ordinary people were concerned, they were believed to slowly fade away in a place analogous to the Hellenic Hades. The Nordic-Aryan mythology conceived Valhalla as the seat of heavenly immortality reserved for the heroes fallen on the battlefield, in addition to nobles and free men of divine origin. This seat was related to the symbolism of "heights" (as Glitnirbjorg, the "resplendent mountain," or Hmninbjorg, the "heavenly mountain," the highest divine mountain on whose peaks an eternal brightness shines beyond the clouds), and was often identified with Asgard, namely, with the Aesir's seat located in the Middle Land (Mitgard); the Lord of this seat was Odin-Wotan, the Nordic god of war and victory. According to a particular myth, Odin was the king who with his sacrifice showed to the heroes the path that leads to the divine dwellings where they will live forever and be transformed into his "sons."[2] Thus, according to the Nordic races, no sacrifice or cult was more cherished by the supreme god and thought to bear more supernatural fruits than the one celebrated by the hero who falls on the battlefield; from a declaration of war to its bloody conclusion, the religious element permeated the Germanic hosts and inspired the individual warrior as well. Moreover, in these traditions we find the idea that by means of a heroic death the warrior shifted from the plane of the material, earthly war to the plane of struggle of a transcendent and universal character. The hosts of heroes were believed to constitute the so-called Wildes Heer, the mounted stormtroopers led by Odin who take off from the peak of Mount Valhalla and then return to rest on it. In the higher forms of this tradition, the host of the dead heroes selected by the Valkyrie for Odin, with whom the Wildes Heer eventually became identified, was the army the god needed in order to fight against the *ragna-rokkr*, the "twilight of the gods" that has been approaching for a very long time.[3] It is written: "There is a very large number of dead heroes in Valhalla, and many more have yet to come, and yet they will seem too few when the wolf comes."[4]

What has been said so far concerns the transformation of the war into a "holy war." Now I wish to add some specific references found in other traditions.

---

2. *Ynglingasaga*, 10.
3. The term *ragna-rokkr* is found in the *Lokasenna* (39), and it literally means "twilight of the gods." More often we encounter the term *ragna-rok* (*Voluspa*, 44), which signifies the "doom" or the "end of the gods." The term *ragna-rokkr* became prevalent because from the twelfth or thirteenth century on, Norse writers adapted it instead of *ragna-rok*. The Nordic view of the Wildes Heer corresponds to the Iranian view of Mithras, the "sleepless warrior," who at the head of the fravashi leads the fight against the enemies of the Aryan religion (*Yashna*, 10.10).
4. *Gylfaginning*, 38.

In the Islamic tradition a distinction is made between two holy wars, the "greater holy war" *(el-jihadul-akbar)* and the "lesser holy war" *(el-jihadul-ashgar)*. This distinction originated from a saying *(hadith)* of the Prophet, who on the way back from a military expedition said: "You have returned from a lesser holy war to the greater holy war." The greater holy war is of an inner and spiritual nature; the other is the material war waged externally against an enemy population with the particular intent of bringing "infidel" populations under the rule of "God's Law" (al-Islam). The relationship between the "greater" and the "lesser holy war," however, mirrors the relationship between the soul and the body; in order to understand the heroic asceticism or "path of action," it is necessary to recognize the situation in which the two paths merge, "the lesser holy war" becoming the means through which "a greater holy war" is carried out, and vice versa: the "little holy war," or the external one, becomes almost a ritual action that expresses and gives witness to the reality of the first. Originally, orthodox Islam conceived a unitary form of asceticism: that which is connected to the *jihad* or "holy war."

The "greater holy war" is man's struggle against the enemies he carries within. More exactly, it is the struggle of man's higher principle against everything that is merely human in him, against his inferior nature and against chaotic impulses and all sorts of material attachments.[5] This is expressly outlined in a text of Aryan warrior wisdom: "Know Him therefore who is above reason; and let his peace give thee peace. Be a warrior and kill desire, the powerful enemy of the soul."[6]

The "enemy" who resists us and the "infidel" within ourselves must be subdued and put in chains. This enemy is the animalistic yearning and instinct, the disorganized multiplicity of impulses, the limitations imposed on us by a fictitious self, and thus also fear, weakness, and uncertainty; this subduing of the enemy is the only way to achieve inner liberation or the rebirth in a state of a deeper inner unity and "peace" in the esoteric and triumphal sense of the word.

In the world of traditional warrior asceticism the "lesser holy war," namely, the external war, is indicated and even prescribed as the means to wage this "greater

---

5. R. Guénon, *Le Symbolisme de la croix*, 77. In reference to the *Bhagavadgītā*, a text written in the form of a dialogue between the warrior Arjuna and the Lord Kṛṣṇa, Guénon wrote: "Kṛṣṇa and Arjuna, who represent respectively the Self and the empirical ego, or personality and individuality, or the unconditioned *ātman* and the living soul *(jivātmā)*, climbed into the same chariot, which is the vehicle of Being, considered in its manifested state. As Arjuna fights on, Kṛṣṇa drives the chariot without becoming involved in the action. The same meaning is also found in various Upaniṣads; 'the two birds sitting in the same tree,' and 'the two birds who entered into a cave.' Al Hallaj said: 'We are two souls joined together within the same body.'"

The famous seal found in the Knights Templar tradition (a horse mounted by two knights wearing a helmet and a spike, and underneath the inscription *sigillum militum Christi*) may be interpreted along the same lines.

6. *Bhagavadgītā* 3.43.

holy war"; thus in Islam the expressions "holy war" *(jihad)* and "Allah's way" are often used interchangeably. In this order of ideas action exercises the rigorous function and task of a sacrificial and purifying ritual. The external vicissitudes experienced during a military campaign cause the inner "enemy" to emerge and to put up a fierce resistance and a good fight in the form of the animalistic instincts of self-preservation, fear, inertia, compassion, or other passions; those who engage in battles must overcome these feelings by the time they enter the battlefield if they wish to win and to defeat the outer enemy or the "infidel."

Obviously the spiritual orientation and the "right intention" *(niya),* that is, the one toward transcendence (the symbols employed to refer to transcendence are "heaven," "paradise," "Allah's gardens" and so on), are presupposed as the foundations of *jihad,* lest war lose its sacred character and degenerate into a wild affair in which true heroism is replaced with reckless abandonment and what counts are the unleashed impulses of the animalistic nature.

It is written in the Koran: "Let those who would exchange the life of this world for the hereafter fight for the cause of Allah; whether they die or conquer, We shall richly reward them."[7] The presupposition according to which it is prescribed, "When you meet the unbelievers in the battlefield strike off their heads, and when you have laid them low, bind your captives firmly";[8] or, "Do not falter or sue for peace when you have gained the upper hand,"[9] is that "the life of this world is but a sport and a pastime"[10] and that "whoever is ungenerous to this cause is ungenerous to himself."[11] These statements should be interpreted along the lines of the evangelical saying: "Whoever wishes to save his life shall lose it; but whoever loses his life for my sake shall find it" (Matt. 16:25). This is confirmed by yet another Koranic passage: "Why is it that when it is said to you: 'March in the cause of Allah,' you linger slothfully in the land? Are you content with this life in preference to the life to come?"[12] "Say: 'Are you waiting for anything to befall us except victory or martyrdom?'"[13]

Another passage is relevant as well: "Fighting is obligatory for you, as much as you dislike it. But you may hate a thing although it is good for you, and love a thing although it is bad for you. Allah knows but you do not."[14] This passage should also be connected with the following one:

7. *Koran* 4:76.
8. Ibid., 47:4.
9. Ibid., 47:37.
10. Ibid.
11. Ibid., 47:38.
12. Ibid., 9:38.
13. Ibid., 9:52.
14. Ibid., 2:216.

They were content to be with those who stayed behind: a seal was set upon their hearts, leaving them bereft of understanding. But the Apostle and the men who shared his faith fought with their goods and their persons. These shall be rewarded with good things. They shall surely prosper. Allah has prepared for them gardens watered by running streams, in which they shall abide forever. That is the supreme triumph.[15]

This place of "rest" (paradise) symbolizes the superindividual states of being, the realization of which is not confined to the postmortem alone, as the following passage indicates: "As for those who are slain in the cause of Allah, He will not allow their works to perish. He will vouchsafe them guidance and ennoble their state; He will admit them to the Paradise He has made known to them."[16] In the instance of real death in battle, we find the equivalent of the *mors triumphalis* found in classical traditions. Those who have experienced the "greater holy war" during the "lesser holy war," have awakened a power that most likely will help them overcome the crisis of death; this power, having already liberated them from the "enemy" and from the "infidel," will help them avoid the fate of Hades. This is why in classical antiquity the hope of the deceased and the piety of his relatives often caused figures of heroes and of victors to be inscribed on the tombstones. It is possible, however, to go through death and conquer, as well as achieve, the superlife and to ascend to the "heavenly realm" while being alive.

The Islamic formulation of the heroic doctrine corresponds to that formulated in the *Bhagavadgītā*, in which the same meanings are expressed in a purer way. The doctrine of liberation through pure action, which is expounded in this text, is declared to be "solar" in origin and is believed to have been communicated by the founder of the present cycle to dynasties of sacred kings rather than to priests (*brāhmaṇa*).[17]

The piety that keeps the warrior Arjuna[18] from going to battle against his enemies, since he recognizes among them his own relatives and teachers, is characterized by the *Bhagavadgītā* as "lifeless dejection." The text adds: "Strong men do not know despair, for that wins neither heaven nor earth."[19] The promise is the same: "In death thy glory in heaven, in victory thy glory on earth. Arise therefore, with thy soul

---

15. Ibid., 9:88–89.
16. Ibid., 47: 5–7.
17. *Bhagavadgītā*, 4.1–2.
18. Arjuna has the title of Gudakesha, which means "Lord of sleep." Thus, he represents a warrior version of the "Awakened One"; Arjuna also ascended a "mountain" (in the Himalayas) to practice asceticism and to achieve superior warrior skills. In the Iranian tradition the attribute of "sleepless" was referred in an eminent sense to the god of light, Ahura-Mazda (*Vendidad,* 19.20) and to Mithras (*Yashna,* 10.10).
19. *Bhagavadgītā*, 2.2.

ready to fight."[20] The inner attitude—the equivalent of the Islamic *niya*—that is capable of transforming the "lesser war" into a "greater holy war" is described in clear terms: "Offer to me all thy works and rest thy mind on the Supreme. Be free from vain hopes and selfish thoughts, and with inner peace fight thou thy fight."[21] The purity of this type of action, which must be willed for its own sake, is also celebrated in clear terms: "Prepare for war with peace in thy soul. Be in peace in pleasure and pain, in gain and in loss, in victory or in the loss of a battle. In this peace there is no sin."[22] In other words: you will not stray from the supernatural direction by fulfilling your *dharma* as a warrior.[23]

The relationship between war and "the path to God" is present in the *Gītā* too, though the metaphysical rather than the ethical aspect is more heavily stressed: the warrior reproduces somewhat the deity's transcendence. The teaching Kṛṣṇa imparts to Arjuna concerns first of all the distinction between what is pure and undying and that which, as a human and naturalistic element, only appears to exist:

> The unreal never is: the Real never is not. This truth indeed has been seen by those who can see the true. Interwoven in his creation, the Spirit is beyond destruction. No one can bring to an end the Spirit which is everlasting. . . . If any man thinks he slays, and if another thinks he is slain, neither knows the ways of truth. The Eternal in man cannot kill: the Eternal in man cannot die. . . . He does not die when the body dies . . . these bodies have an end in their time; but he remains immeasurable, immortal. Therefore, great warrior, carry on thy fight.[24]

The consciousness of the irreality of what can be lost or caused to be lost as ephemeral life and as mortal body (the equivalent of the Islamic view that this life is just a sport and a pastime) is associated with the knowledge of that aspect of the divine according to which this aspect is an absolute power before which every conditioned existence appears as a negation; this power becomes naked and dazzles in a terrible theophany precisely in the act of destruction, in the act that "negates the negation,"

20. Ibid., 2.37.
21. Ibid., 3.30.
22. Ibid. 2.38. In the Chinese tradition mention is made of the brave and virile warrior who "regards equally defeat and victory" and of his noble countenance, which is unaffected by "tumultuous passions": "When I journey inward I find a pure heart; even if I had to face a thousand or ten thousand enemies, I march against them without any fear." Mencius, 3.2.
23. *The Laws of Manu* (5.98): "When a man is killed by upraised weapons in battle, in fulfillment of the duty of a ruler, instantly he completes both a sacrifice and the period of pollution caused by his death." Also (7.89): "Kings who try to kill one another in battle and fight to their utmost ability, never averting their faces, go to heaven."
24. *Bhagavadgītā*, 2.16–20.

in the whirlwind that sweeps away every finite life, either destroying it or making it arise again in a transhuman state.

In order to free Arjuna from doubt and from the "soft bond of the soul," Kṛṣṇa says:

> I am the life of all living beings, and the austere life of those who train their souls. And I am from everlasting the seed of eternal life. I am the intelligence of the intelligent. I am the beauty of the beautiful. I am the power of those who are strong, when this power is free from passions and selfish desires. I am desire when this is pure, when this desire is not against righteousness.[25]

In the end, having abandoned all personifications, Kṛṣṇa manifests himself in the "wonderful and fearful form before which the three worlds tremble," "vast, reaching the sky, burning with many colors, with wide open mouths, with vast flaming eyes."[26] Finite beings—as lamps outshone by a much greater source of light, or as circuits pervaded by a much greater current—give way, disintegrate, melt, because in their midst there is now a power transcending their form, that wills something infinitely greater than anything that as individual agents they may will by themselves. This is why finite beings "become," being transformed and going from the manifested into the unmanifested, from the material to the immaterial. On this basis the power capable of producing the heroic realization is clearly defined. The values are overturned: death becomes a witness to life, and the destructive power of time displays the indomitable nature hidden inside what is subject to time and death. Hence the meaning of these words uttered by Arjuna at the moment in which he experiences the deity as pure transcendence:

> As roaring torrents of waters rush forward into the ocean, so do these heroes of our mortal world rush into thy flaming mouths. And as moths swiftly rushing enter a burning flame and die, so all these men rush to thy fire, rush fast to their own destruction.[27]

Kṛṣṇa also added:

> I am all-powerful Time which destroys all things, and I have come here to slay these men. Even if thou dost not fight, all the warriors facing thee shall die. Arise therefore! Win thy glory, conquer thy enemies,

25. Ibid., 7.9–11.
26. Ibid., 11.20, 24.
27. Ibid., 11.28–29.

and enjoy thy kingdom. Through fate of their own karma I have doomed them to die: be thou merely the means of my work . . . tremble not, fight and slay them. Thou shalt conquer thy enemies in battle.[28]

In this way we find again the identification of war with "the path to God." The warrior evokes in himself the transcendent power of destruction; he takes it on, becomes transfigured in it and free, thus breaking loose from all human bonds. Life is like a bow and the soul like an arrow, the target being aimed at is the Supreme Spirit; another text of the same Hindu tradition says that what matters is to become united with the Supreme, as an arrow is united with its target.[29] This is the metaphysical justification of war and the transformation of the lesser into the greater holy war. It also sheds further light on the meaning of the traditions concerning the transformation, in the course of the battle, of a warrior or a king into a god. According to an Egyptian tradition, Ramses Merianun was transformed in the battlefield into the god Amon, and said: "I am like Baal in his own time"; when his enemies recognized him in the mêlée, they cried out: "This is not a man; he is Satkhu, the Great Warrior; he is Baal in the flesh." In this context Baal is the equivalent of the Vedic Śiva and Indra; of the solar god Tiuz-Tyr, who is represented by a sword and by the rune Y, which is the ideogram of resurrection ("a man with raised arms"); and of Odin-Wotan, the god of battles and of victories. It should not be forgotten that both Indra and Wotan are conceived of as gods of order and as the overseers of the world's course (Indra is called "the one who stems the tides"; as the god of the day and of clear skies he also exhibits Olympian traits). What we find in these examples is the general theme of war being justified as a reflection of the transcendent war waged by "form" against chaos and the forces of the inferior nature that accompany it.

Further on, I will discuss the classical Western forms of the "path of action." As far as the Western doctrine of the "holy war" is concerned, I will refer here only to the Crusades. The fact that during the Crusades men who fought the war intensely and experienced it according to the same spiritual meaning were found on both sides demonstrates the true unity between people who shared the same traditional spirit; a unity that can be preserved not only through differences of opinion but also through the most dramatic contrasts. In their rising up in arms against each other, Islam and Christianity gave witness to the unity of the traditional spirit.

The historical context in which the Crusades took place abounds with elements capable of conferring upon them a potential symbolical and spiritual meaning. The

---

28. Ibid., 11.32–34.

29. *Mārkaṇḍeya Purāṇa,* 42.7.8. Along these lines we may understand the "solar" transfiguration of the divine hero Karna described in the *Mahābhārata:* from his body, fallen on the battlefield, a thunderbolt of light tears the heavenly vault and pierces the "sun."

conquest of the "Holy Land" located "beyond the sea" in reality had many more connections with ancient traditions than it was first thought; according to these traditions, "in the ancient East, where the sun rises, there lies the happy region of the Aesir and in it, the city of Ayard, where there is no death and where journeyers enjoy a heavenly peace and eternal life."[30] Moreover, the struggle against Islam, by virtue of its nature, shared from the beginning several common traits with asceticism: "It was not a matter of fighting for earthly kingdoms, but for the kingdom of God: the Crusades were not a human, but a divine affair; consequently they should not be considered like all other human events."[31] The holy war was at that time the equivalent of a spiritual war and of "a cleansing that is almost a purgatorial fire that one experiences before death," to use an expression found in a chronicle of those times. Popes and preachers compared those who died in the Crusades to "gold tested three times and purified seven times in the furnace"; the fallen warriors were believed to find grace with the supreme Lord. In his *De laude novae militiae*, Saint Bernard wrote:

> Whether we live or die, we belong to the Lord. What a glory it is for you to emerge from the battle crowned with victory! But what a greater glory it is to win on the battlefield an immortal crown. . . . What a truly blessed condition, when one can wait for death without any fear, yearning for it and welcoming it with a strong spirit![32]

The crusader was promised a share in the "absolute glory" and "rest" in paradise (in the coarse language of the time: *conquerre lit en paradis*), which is the same kind of supernatural rest mentioned in the Koran.

Likewise, Jerusalem, the military objective of the Crusades, appeared in the double aspect of an earthly and of a heavenly city,[33] and thus the Crusade became the equivalent in terms of heroic tradition of a "ritual," a pilgrimage, and the "passion" of the *via crucis*. Moreover, those who belonged to the orders that contributed the most to the Crusades—such as the Knights Templar and the Knights of Saint John—were men who, like the Christian monks or ascetics, learned to despise the vanity of this life; these orders were the natural retirement place for those warriors

---

30. B. Kugler, *History of the Crusades* (Milan, 1887). This region appears as one of the representations of the symbolic "center of the world"; in this context, though, it is mingled with motifs proper to the Nordic tradition, considering that Ayard is Asgard, the Aesir's seat described in the Eddic saga, which is often confused with Valhalla.
31. J. Michaud, *The History of the Crusades* (Milan, 1909).
32. Saint Bernard, *De laude novae militiae*.
33. In the Judeo-Christian belief system, Jerusalem was often considered as an image of the mysterious Salem ruled by Melchizedek.

who were weary of the world, who had seen and experienced just about everything, and who had directed their spiritual quest toward something higher. The teaching that *vita est militia super terram* was instilled in these knights in an integral, inner, and outer fashion. Through prayers they readied themselves to fight and to move against the enemy. Their matins was the trumpet; their hair shirts, the armor they rarely took off; their fortresses, the monasteries; the trophies taken from the infidels, the relics and the images of saints. A similar kind of asceticism paved the way for that spiritual realization that was also related to the secret dimension of chivalry.

The military defeats the crusaders suffered, after an initial surprise and perplexity, helped to purify the Crusades from any residue of materialism and to focus on the inner rather than on the outer dimension, on the spiritual rather than on the temporal element. By comparing the unfortunate outcome of a Crusade with that of an unnoticed virtue, which is appreciated and rewarded only in the next life, people learned to see something superior to both winning and losing and to put all their values in the ritual and "sacrificial" aspect of an action as an end in itself, which is performed independently from the visible earthly results as an oblation aimed at deriving the life-giving "absolute glory" from the sacrifice of the human element.

Therefore, in the Crusades we find the recurrence of the main meanings of expressions such as: "Paradise lies under the shade of the swords," and "The blood of the heroes is closer to God than the ink of the philosophers and the prayers of the faithful," as well as the view of the seat of immortality as the "island of heroes," (or Valhalla) and as the "court of heroes." What occurs again is the same spirit that animated the warrior in Zoroastrian dualism. By virtue of this spirit, the followers of Mithras assimilated the exercise of their cult to the military profession; the neophytes swore by an oath *(sacramentum)* similar to that required of the recruits in the army; and once a man joined the ranks of the initiates, he became part of the "sacred militia of the invincible god of light."[34]

Moreover, it must be emphasized that during the Crusades the realization of universality and of supernationalism through asceticism was eventually achieved. Leaders and nobles from all lands converged into the same sacred enterprise, above and beyond their particular interests and political divisions, to forge a European solidarity informed by the same ecumenical ideal of the Holy Roman Empire. The main strength of the Crusades, was supplied by chivalry, which as I have already remarked, was a supernational institution whose members had no homeland because they would go anywhere they could to fight for those principles to which they swore unconditional faithfulness. Since Pope Urban II referred to chivalry as the community of

---

34. F. Cumont, *The Oriental Religions in Roman Paganism*, xv–xvi.

those who "show up everywhere a conflict erupts, in order to spread the terror that their weapons evoke in defense of honor and justice," he expected chivalry to answer the call to a holy war. Thus, here too we find a convergence of the inner and outer dimensions; in the holy war the individual was afforded the experience of a meta-individual action. Likewise, the teaming up of warriors for a purpose higher than their own race, national interests, or territorial and political concerns was an external expression of the overcoming of all particularities, already an ideal of the Holy Roman Empire.[35] In reality, *if* the universality connected with the asceticism of the pure spiritual authority is the condition for an invisible traditional unity that exists over and above any political division within the body of a unitary civilization informed by the cosmic and by the eternal (in respect of which everything that is pathos and human inclination disappears and the dimension of the spirit presents the same characteristic of purity and power as the great forces of nature); and *when* this universality is added to "universality as action"—then we arrive at the supreme ideal of the empire, an ideal whose unity is both visible and invisible, material and political, as well as spiritual. Heroic asceticism and the untameability of the warrior vocation strengthened by a supernatural direction are the necessary instruments that allow the inner unity to be analogically reflected in the outer unity, namely, in the social body represented by many peoples that are organized and unified by the same one great conquering stock.

Moreover, those who love to contrast the past with our recent times should consider what modern civilization has brought us to in terms of war. A change of level has occurred; from the warrior who fights for the honor and for the right of his lord, society has shifted to the type of the mere "soldier" that is found in association with the removal of all transcendent or even religious elements in the idea of fighting.

To fight on "the path to God" has been characterized as "medieval" fanaticism; conversely, it has been characterized as a most sacred cause to fight for "patriotic" and "nationalistic" ideals and for other myths that in our contemporary era have eventually been unmasked and shown to be the instruments of irrational, materialistic, and destructive forces. It has gradually become possible to see that when "country" was mentioned, this rallying cry often concealed the plans of annexation and oppression and the interests of monopolistic industries; all talk of "heroism" was done by those who accompanied soldiers to the train stations. Soldiers went to the front to experience war as something else, namely, as a crisis that all too often did

35. An analogous form of universality "through action" was achieved to a large degree by the ancient Roman civilization. Even the Greek city-states experienced something higher than their political particularisms "through action," that is, through the Olympic games and through the league of the Hellenic cities against the "barbarians."

not turn out to be an authentic and heroic transfiguration of the personality, but rather the regression of the individual to a plane of savage instincts, "reflexes," and reactions that retain very little of the human by virtue of being below and not above humanity.[36]

The era of nationalism has known a worthy surrogate for the two great traditional culminations that are the universality of spiritual authority and heroic universality: I am referring to imperialism. Although in society the act of one who takes over somebody else's goods by force, whether out of envy or out of need, is considered to be reprehensible, a similar behavior in the relationships between nations has been considered as a natural and legitimate thing; it has consecrated the notion of fighting; and it has constituted the foundation of the "imperialistic" ideal. It was thought that a poor nation "lacking living space" has every right, if not the duty, to take over the goods and the lands of other people. In some instances the conditions leading to expansion and to "imperialist conquest" have been fabricated ad hoc. A typical example has been the pursuit of demographical growth, inspired by the password "There is power in numbers." Another example, more widespread and denoting a lower mentality since it is exclusively controlled by economic and financial factors, is that of overproduction. Once a nation experiences an excess of production and the demographical or commercial "need for space," it desperately requires an outlet. When the outlet of a "cold war" or diplomatic intrigues are no longer sufficient, what ensues are military expeditions that in my view rank much lower than what the barbaric invasions of the past may have represented. Such an upheaval, which has recently assumed global proportions, is accompanied by hypocritical rhetoric. The great ideas of "humanity," "democracy," and "the right of a people to self-determination," have been mobilized. From an external point of view, not only is the idea of "holy war" considered "outdated," but also the understanding of it that people of honor had developed; the heroic ideal has now been lowered to the figure of the

---

36. The reading of the so-called war novels written by E. M. Remarque (especially *All Quiet On the Western Front*) reveals the contrast between the patriotic idealism and rhetoric on the one hand and the realistic results of the experience of the war among European youth. An Italian officer, in the aftermath of World War I wrote: "When war is seen at a distance it may have idealistic and knightly overtones for the enthusiastic souls and some sort of choreographic beauty for aesthetes. It is necessary that future generations learn from our generation that there is no fascination more false and no legend more grotesque than that which attributes to war any virtue or influence on progress, and an education that is not based on cruelty, revolution and brutishness. Once stripped of her magical attractive features, Bellona is more disgusting than Alcina, and the youth who died in her arms have shivered in horror at her touch. But we had to go to war." V. Coda, *Dalla Bainsizza al Piave*. It was only in the earlier works of Ernst Jünger, inspired by his personal experiences as a soldier in the German army, that we find again the idea that these processes may change polarity and that the most destructive aspects of modern technological war may condition a superior type of man, beyond the patriotic and "idealist" rhetoric as well as beyond humanitarianism and antimilitarism.

policeman because the new "crusades" have not been able to find a better flag to rally around than that of the "struggle against the aggressor." From an inner point of view, beyond all this rhetoric, what proved to be decisive was the brute, cynical will to power of obscure, international, capitalist, and collectivist powers. At the same time "science" has promoted an extreme mechanization and technologization of war, so much so that today war is not a matter of man against man but of machines against man. Rational systems of mass extermination are being employed (through indiscriminate air raids, atomic weapons, and chemical warfare) that leave no hope and no way out; such systems could once have been devised only to exterminate germs and insects. In contrast to "medieval superstitions" that refer to a "holy war," what our contemporaries consider sacred and worthy of the actual "progress of civilization" is the fact that millions of human beings, taken away en masse from their occupations and vocations (which are totally alien to the military vocation), and literally turned into what military jargon refers to as "cannon fodder," will die in such events.

18

Games and Victory

In classical antiquity games *(ludi)* had a sacred character and they therefore became typical expressions of the traditional path of action. *"Ludorum primum initium procurandis religionibus datum,"* wrote Livy. It was considered dangerous to neglect the sacred games *(negligere sacra certamina);* thus, if the state's funds were depleted, the games were simplified but never suppressed. An ancient Roman law required the *duoviri* and the *aediles* to have the games celebrated in honor of the gods. Vitruvius wanted every city to be endowed with its own theater, *deorum immortalium diebus festis ludorum spectationibus,* and originally the person presiding over the games in the Circus Maximus was also the priest of Ceres, Liber, and Libera. In any event, the person in charge of the games in Rome was always a representative of the official patrician religion; in the case of some games (such as the Salii's), special priestly colleges were formed for the occasion. The games were so closely related to pagan temples that Christian emperors had no choice but to keep them open, since shutting them down would have caused those games to be canceled; these games even outlasted most ancient Roman institutions, and eventually ended with the Roman Empire itself. An agape to which demons were invited *(invitatione daemonum)* usually closed the games, signifying a ritual participation of the people in the mystical force associated with them.[1] Augustine reported that *"ludi scenici . . . inter res divinas a doctissimis conscribuntur."*[2]

The games assumed the character of *res divinae,* and they have been replaced today by contemporary sports and by the plebeian infatuation with them. In the Hellenic tradition the institution of the most important games bore a close relationship with the idea of the struggle of Olympian, heroic, and solar forces against natural and elemental forces. The Pythian games in Delphi celebrated Apollo's triumph over Python and the victory of this Hyperborean god in the contest with other gods.

---

1. Cassius Dio, *Roman History*, 51.1.
2. Augustine, *De civitate dei*, 4.26.

Likewise, the Olympian games were related to the idea of the triumph of the heav-enly race over the race of Titans. Heracles, the demigod who was the ally of the Olympian hosts in the struggle against the Giants, was believed to have instituted the Olympian games[3] and to have symbolically taken the olive branch with which the winners were crowned from the land of the Hyperboreans.[4] These games had a rigorously virile character; women were absolutely forbidden to attend them. Be-sides, it was not a coincidence that in the Roman arenas several numbers and sacred symbols appeared repeatedly: the three, in the *ternae summitates metarum* [the tops of the three columns] and in the *tres arae trinis Diis magnis potentibus valentibus* [three altars for the triple gods, the Great, the Potent, the Prevailing] that Tertullian[5] attributed to the great Samothracian Triad; the five in the five *spatia* of the Domitian racetracks; the zodiac's twelve in the number of doors from which the chariots en-tered and exited in the early empire; the seven in the annual games at the time of the Republic, in the number of altars of the planetary gods in the Circus Maximus[6] (with the sun's pyramid at the top), in the total number of rounds of a complete race, and in the "eggs," "dolphins," or "tritons" located in each of these seven *curricula.*[7] Bachofen has noticed that the egg and the triton symbolically referred to the fundamental dual-ism of the powers at work in the world; the egg represented the generating matter that encompasses every potentiality, while the triton or sea horse, sacred to Poseidon-Neptune and a frequent symbol of the waves, expressed the same fecundating phal-lic and telluric power whereby, according to a tradition reported by Plutarch, the current of the waters of the Nile was thought to represent the fecundating sperm of the primordial male spilled on Isis, herself a symbol of the land of Egypt. This duality was reflected in the very location where the ancient games and *equiria* [horse races dedicated to Mars] were held. Tarquinius had his circus built in the valley between the Aventine and the Palatine, which was sacred to Murcia (a feminine-telluric god-dess); the tracks of the *equiria* began at the Tiber's banks and the finish line was marked with swords planted into Mars' field. Thus, heroic and virile symbols were found at the end of the tracks *(telos)* while the feminine and the material element of generation, namely, flowing waters or whatever was sacred to chthonic deities, was found at the beginning of and alongside the tracks.

In this way, action took place in the context of material symbols representing higher meanings, so that "the magical method and technique" hidden in the *ludi*

---

3. Pindar, *The Olympian Odes*, 3; 10.42; Diodorus, 4.14.
4. Pindar, *The Olympian Odes*, 3.13; Pliny the Elder, *Historia naturalis*, 16.240.
5. Tertullian, *De spectaculis*, 8.
6. Lidius, *De mensibus*, 1.4.12.
7. The undeniable symbolism of various details found in Roman circuses is one of the traces of the presence of "sacred" knowledge in the ancient construction art.

(which always began with solemn sacrifices and were often celebrated to invoke divine powers at times of an imminent national danger) could have a greater efficacy. The impetus of the horses and the vertigo of the race through seven rounds, which was also compared with and consecrated to the sun's "journey" in the sky,[8] evoked the mystery of the cosmic current at work in the "cycle of generation" according to the planetary hierarchy. The ritual slaying of the victorious horse, which was consecrated to Mars, should be connected to the general idea of "sacrifice"; it seems that the force that was consequently unleashed was for the most part directed by the Romans to increase the crops in an occult fashion, *ad frugum eventum.* (This sacrifice may be considered as the equivalent of the Indo-Aryan *aśvamedha,* which originally was a magical, ritual, propitiating power.) The Roman ritual was celebrated in extraordinary occasions, for instance at the time of declaration of war or after a victory. Two horsemen entered into the arena, one from the east and the other from the west, to engage in mortal combat; the original colors of the two factions, which were the same colors of the Orphic cosmic egg—white symbolizing winter and red symbolizing summer (or better, the former symbolizing the lunar-chthonic power, the latter the solar-Uranian power[9])—evoked the struggle of the two great elemental forces. Every goal, *meta sudans,* was considered as a "living" thing *(λίθος ἔμψυχος);* the altar erected in honor of the god Consus ("He who gathers in," a demon who fed on the blood spilled in the violent games, or *munera)* at one of the finish lines of the circus, which was unveiled only on the occasion of the games, appeared as the outlet of infernal forces, just like its Etruscan counterpart, *puteal.* Higher up, statues of triumphant deities were erected, which referred to the opposite Uranian principle, so that the circus was transformed into a council of *numina (daemonum concilium)*[10] whose invisible presence was ritually sanctioned by seats left purposefully vacant. Thus, what on the one hand appeared as the unfolding of action in an athletic, competitive, or scenic event, on the other hand was elevated to the plane of a magical evocation. The risk inherent in this evocation was real in a wider order than that of the lives of the participants in the *certamina,* whose victory renewed and strengthened in the individual and in the collectivity the victory of the

8. In antiquity the god Sol had a temple in the middle of the circus; the circuit races were sacred to this god who was represented as steering the chariot of the sun. In Olympia there were twelve rounds *(dodekagnamptos,* see Pindar, *Olympian Odes,* 2.50) that represented the position of the sun in the zodiac. Cassius Dio relates that the Roman circus represented the sequence of the four seasons.

9. These Roman games are connected with analogous traditions found in other Indo-European stocks. During the feast of Mahāvrata, which was celebrated in ancient India during the winter solstice, a representative of the white and divine Aryan caste fought against a representative of the dark caste of the *śūdras* for the possession of an object symbolizing the sun. In an ancient Nordic saga we find the periodic combat between two knights, one riding a white and the other a black horse, in the proximity of a symbolic tree.

10. "The concourse of demons," in Tertullian, *De spectaculis,* 8.

Uranian forces over the infernal forces, a victory that became transformed into a principle of "destiny." For instance, Apollo's games were instituted on the occasion of the Punic Wars as a protection against the danger foretold by the oracle; they were repeated to ward off an epidemic of plague, and eventually they came to be celebrated periodically. Thus, during the parade preceding the games, the images *(exuviae)* of the Capitol gods, protectors of Rome, were solemnly carried from the Capitol to the circus in consecrated chariots *(tensae)*; special regard was paid to the *exuviae* of Jovis Optimi Maximi (the thunderbolt, the scepter surmounted by the eagle, and the golden crown), which were also the symbols of the *imperium*. This was done with the assumption that the same occult power inherent in Roman sovereignty witnessed to and participated in the games consecrated to it *(ludi Romani)* or that it was involved in them. The magistrate who was elected to preside over the games led the parade that carried the divine symbols as if he were a conqueror: he was surrounded by his people and followed by a public slave holding over his head a crown of oak leaves encrusted with gold and diamonds. It is probable that in the early games the quadriga was a symbol of Jupiter's attributes and an insignia of triumphal royalty; an ancient quadriga of Etruscan origins kept in a Capitoline temple was considered by the Romans as a pledge of their future prosperity.

This explains why those games that were not performed according to tradition were looked down upon as unorthodox sacred rituals; if their representation were upset by an accident or interrupted for any reason, it was considered an omen of bad luck and a curse, and the games had to be started all over again in order to "placate" the divine powers. Conversely, according to a famous legend, when the people, following a surprise attack by the enemy, left the games (which in the meantime were not interrupted) in order to take up arms, they found the enemy miraculously routed by a supernatural power that was later on identified with the power evoked by the rite of the game dedicated to the savior Apollo.[11] If the games were often consecrated to "Victories" that personified the triumphant power, their purpose was to renew the life and presence of such a power, to nourish it with the new energies that were awakened and that imparted the same direction. This explains why, in specific reference to the *certamina* and to the *munera*, the winner appeared to be endowed with a divine character and at times to be a temporary incarnation of a deity. In Olympia, in the moment of triumph, the winner was thought to be an incarnation of the local Zeus, and the public acclamation to the victorious gladiator was incorporated into the ancient Christian liturgy: εις αιῶνας ἀπό αἰῶνος [forever and ever].[12]

---

11. Macrobius, *The Saturnalia*, 1.17.25. See also the Platonic saying: "Their victory [the Olympian winners] is the nobler, since by their success the whole commonwealth is preserved." *Republic*, 465d.

12. Tertullian, *De spectaculis*, 25.

What should really be considered in this context is what kind of inner (besides ritual and magical) meaning the event may have had for the individual. What has been said about the notion of "holy war" applies in this context as well: the heroic exaltation found in competition and in victory, once it was given a ritual meaning, became the imitation of, or the introduction to, that higher and purer impetus the initiate used to defeat death. This explains the frequent references to the *certamina,* to the games of the circus, and to the figures of winners in classical funerary art; all these references immortalized in an analogical way the highest hope of the deceased, and visibly portrayed the kind of action most likely to help him overcome Hades and obtain the glory of an eternal life in a way conforming to the traditional path of action. What we find over and over again in sarcophagi, funerary urns, and classical bas-reliefs are the images of a "triumphal death": winged Victories open the doors of the otherworld's domain, or uphold the medallion of the deceased or crown him with the evergreen that usually crowns the heads of the initiates. In the context of the Pindaric celebration of the divinity of victorious wrestlers, the Enagogues and the Promachi were portrayed as mystical deities leading the souls to immortality. And vice versa: in Orphism, every victory (Nike) became the symbol of the victory of the soul over the body, and those who achieved initiation were called the "heroes" of a dramatic and endless struggle. What in the myth is the expression of a heroic life, constitutes the model of an Orphic life; therefore in the sepulchral images, Heracles, Theseus, the Dioscuri, Achilles, and others are designated as Orphic initiates: $\sigma\tau\rho\alpha\tau\acute{o}\varsigma$ (*militia* in Latin) is the term designating the host of initiates, and $\mu\nu\alpha\sigma\acute{\iota}\sigma\tau\rho\alpha\tau\sigma\varsigma$ the term designating the Mystery's hierophant. Light, victory, and initiation were eventually represented next to each other in several Hellenic monuments. Helios, as the rising sun (alias Aurora) is a Nike and is endowed with a triumphal chariot; other Nikai were Teletes, Mystis, and other deities or personifications of the transcendent rebirth. When we go from the symbolic and esoteric to the magical aspect, it should be noted that the competitions and the warrior dances celebrated on the occasion of a hero's death (the Roman equivalent were the *ludi* celebrated at the funerals of major figures) had the purpose of awakening a mystical, saving force that was supposed to accompany and strengthen him during the crisis that occurred at the moment of death. People also paid homage to the heroes by periodically repeating the contests that followed their funerals.

All this is typical of a traditional civilization qualified by the "pole" of action rather than by the "pole" of contemplation: action as spirit and spirit as action. As far as Greece is concerned, I have already mentioned that in Olympia, action in the form of "games" exercised a unifying function beyond the particularism of the city-states similar to that function manifested through action as "holy war," as in the case of the supernatural phenomenon of the Crusades or, in the context of Islam, during the period of the First Caliphate.

There are plenty of elements that enable us to perceive the innermost aspect of such traditions. I have pointed out that in antiquity the notions of soul, of "double" or daemon, and later on of Furies or Erinyes, and finally of the goddess of death and the goddess of victory were often confused in the same one notion, so much so as to establish the notion of a deity who is simultaneously goddess of battles and a transcendental element of the human soul.

This was the case, for instance, with the notions of *fylgja* (Nordic tradition) and of the *fravashi* (Iranian). The *fylgja,* which literally means "the escort," was conceived as a spiritual entity dwelling in every man; she may be perceived in special times, for instance at the time of death or of mortal danger. The *fylgja* was confused with the *hugir,* the equivalent of the soul, but was also believed to be a supernatural power *(fylgjukoma),* namely, the spirit of both the individual and of his stock *(kynfylgja).* But the *fylgja* was often portrayed as the equivalent of the *valkyrie,* who in turn was conceived as an entity of "fate" leading the individual to victory and to a heroic death. The same was true for the *fravashi* of the ancient Iranian tradition, the terrifying goddesses of war who "give victory, health, and good Glory to those who invoke them," while appearing as "the inner power in every being that maintains it and makes it grow and subsist"[13] and as "the everlasting and deified souls of the dead"[14] in relation to the mystical power of the stock, as in the Hindu *pitṛ* and in the Latin *manes.*

I have already discussed this kind of "life's life," or deep-seated power of life hidden behind the body and the state of finite consciousness. Here it will suffice to say that one's guiding principle *(δαîμον)* or "double" transcends every personal and particular form in which it is manifested; thus, the abrupt and sudden shift from the ordinary state of individuated consciousness to the state characterized by such a principle would usually have the meaning of a destructive crisis, which effectively takes place after death. If we conceive that in some special circumstances the double may "burst" into one's conscious "I" and manifest itself according to its destructive transcendence, the meaning of the first of the abovementioned assimilations will become apparent; hence the "double" (or man's guiding principle) and the deity of death that manifests itself (e.g., as a valkyrie) at the moment of death or in circumstances of mortal danger, become one and the same. In the asceticism of a religious and mystical type, self-mortification, renunciation of one's self, and devotion to God are the preferred means that are employed to induce and to overcome the abovementioned crisis. According to the other path to transcendence, however, the

13. *Yasht,* 13.23–24; 66–67.
14. *Zend Avesta,* trans. S. Darmesteter, in *Sacred Books of the East,* ed. M. Moeller (Oxford, 1883), 179.

means to induce this crisis consist in the active exaltation and awakening of the element of "action" in a pure state. At an inferior level dance was used as a sacred method to attract and to manifest various divinities and invisible powers through the ecstasy of the soul: this was the orgiastic, shamanistic, Bacchic, Maenadic, and Corybantic theme. In ancient Rome too there were sacred priestly dances performed by the Luperchi and by the Arvali; the words of the Arvali's hymnal "Help us, O Mars; dance! dance!" already show the relationship between dance and war, which was sacred to Mars.[15] Another life, unleashed by the rhythm, was grafted onto the life of the dancer, representing the emergence of the abyssal root of the previous life dramatized by the *lari* as *lares ludentes* or as Cureti[16] by the Furies, by the Erinyes, and by the wild spiritual entities that have attributes similar to Zagreus ("Great-hunter-who-destroys-everything-on-his-path"). These were manifestations of the guiding principle in its fearful and active transcendence. At a higher level there were the games as *munera*, namely, as sacred games, and war. In the clear-minded in-ebriation and in the heroic élan generated in the struggle and in the tension for victory (in the games, but especially in war), Tradition recognized the opportunity to undergo an analogous experience: it appears that even etymologically, *ludere* conveyed the idea of "untying," which esoterically referred to the ability usually found in competition to untie the individual bond and to reveal deep-seated powers. Hence a further assimilation through which the guiding principle and the goddess of death not only are identical to the Furies and to the Erinyes, but to the goddesses of war known as the Valkyrie, virgin warriors who magically strike the enemy with a frantic panic *(herfjoturr),* and to the *fravashi,* who are "terrible, omnipotent powers who attack impetuously."

These powers were eventually transformed into goddesses such as Victory or Nike, into the *lar victor,* into the *lar Martis et pacis triumphalis,* and into *lares,* who in Rome were considered as "demigods who have founded the city and instituted the Empire."[17] This further transformation corresponds to the positive outcome of such experiences. Just as the "double" signified the deep power at a latent state in relation to the external consciousness; just as the goddess of death dramatized the sensa-

---

15. The name of yet another priestly college (the Salii) is usually derived from *salire* or *saltare* ("to climb" or "to jump"). According to the Muslim mystic Jelaluddin Rumi, "He who knows the power of dance dwells in God, since he knows that love slays."

16. E. Saglio, *Dictionnaire des antiquities grecques et romains d'après les textes et les monuments,* 6.947. The Cureti, armed dancers who engaged in orgies *(arkesteres aspidephoroi),* were regarded as demigods endowed with the power to initiate and also as the "child's rearers" or *pandotrophoi* (See J. E. Harrison, *Themis* [Cambridge, 1912], 23–27), that is, as the mentors of the new principle that emerges through similar experiences.

17. E. Saglio, *Dictionnaire,* 6.944.

tion of the manifestation of this power as a principle of crisis for the essence of the empirical self; and just as the Furies and the Erinyes or the *lares ludentes* reflected a particular way for this power to become unleashed and to burst out—likewise, the goddess Victoria and the *lar victor* expressed the triumph over this power, the "two merging into one," and the triumphant passage to the state that lies beyond the danger of the formless ecstasy and dissolution occurring at the precise frantic moment of action.

Moreover, wherever the actions of the spirit take place within the body of real actions and events (unlike what takes place in the domain of contemplative asceticism), a real parallelism can be established between the physical and the metaphysical, the visible and the invisible; therefore those actions can appear as the occult counterpart of warrior feats or of competitive events, that have a real victory as their climax. Then the material victory reflects a corresponding spiritual event that has determined it alongside the previously disclosed paths of the energies connecting the inside to the outside; in other words, it appears as the real sign of an initiation and of a mystical epiphany taking place simultaeously. The warrior and the military leader who faced the Furies and Death in a real way, met them simultaneously within himself, in his spirit, under the form of dangerous manifestations of powers emerging from his abyssal nature; by triumphing over them, he achieved victory.[18] This is why in classical traditions every victory often acquired a sacred meaning; in the *imperator,* in the hero, and in the leader who was acclaimed victorious on the battlefield—just as in the winner of the sacred *ludi*—it was possible to detect the abrupt manifestation of a mystical force that transformed him and made him more than a human being. One of the warrior customs practiced by the Romans, which is susceptible to an esoteric interpretation, was the act of carrying the victorious general on shields. Ennius (239–169 B.C.) had previously assimilated the shield to the vault of heaven (*altisonum coeli clupeum)* and the shield was sacred in the temple of the Olympian Jupiter. In the third

18. The Nordic view, according to which battles are won thanks to the Valkyrie, expresses the idea that the outcome of a fight is determined by these powers rather than by human strength in a materialistic and individualistic sense. In the ancient Roman world we often find the idea of the manifestation of a transcendent power. This manifestation was sometimes expressed through the voice of the god Faunus that was heard by the troops before a battle and that filled the enemy with a holy terror. We also find the idea that it is sometimes necessary to sacrifice a leader in order to actualize this presence, according to the general meaning of ritual slayings; this was the rite of *devotio,* the sacrifice of the leader that unleashed infernal powers and the genius of terror onto the enemy. The minute the leader died, the panic and horror that corresponded to the power liberated from the body was manifested; this horror could be compared to the *herfjoturr,* the panic and terror that were magically transmitted by the unleashed Valkyrie to the enemy. One of the last echoes of similar meanings was found in the Japanese kamikaze during World War II; the word *kamikaze* referred to the suicide pilots unleashed against the enemy, and it means "divine wind." On the fuselages of their planes there was the inscription: "You are gods who are free from all human yearnings."

century the title of *imperator* became one and the same with that of *victor* and the ceremony of triumph, more than a military parade, was a sacred ceremony in honor of the supreme Capitoline god. The winner appeared as the living image of Jupiter and proceeded to put into the hands of this god the triumphal laurel of his victory. The triumphal chariot was the symbol of Jupiter's cosmic quadriga and the insignia of the leader corresponded to those of the god. The symbolism of "Victories," Valkyries, or analogous entities leading the souls of the fallen heroes to the "heavens," or the symbolism of a triumphant hero who, like Heracles, receives from Nike the crown reserved for those who partake of the Olympian immortality, becomes clear and completes what has been said so far about the holy war. We are in the context of traditions in which victory acquires the meaning of immortality similar to that bestowed in an initiation, and in which Victory appears as the mediatrix because of either her participation in transcendence or the manifestation of transcendence into a body of power. The Islamic idea according to which the warriors slain in a "holy war" *(jihad)* have never really died[19] should be referred to the same principle.

Last but not least, the victory of a leader was often regarded by the Romans as a separate entity *(numen)*, the mysterious life of which constituted the focus of a special cult; feasts, sacred games, rituals, and sacrifices were destined to renew its presence. The Victoria Caesaris is the best example of this. Being the equivalent of an initiatory or "sacrificial" action, every victory was believed to generate an entity that was distinct from the destiny and from the particular individuality of the mortal being from which it derived; just as in the case of the victory of the divine ancestors, this entity was believed to be capable of establishing a line of special spiritual influences. And as in the case of the cult of the divine ancestors, such influences needed to be confirmed and developed through rites acting in accord with the laws of sympathy and analogy. Therefore, it was mainly through games and competitions that the *victoriae* as *numina* were periodically celebrated. The regularity of this competitive cult, which was decreed by law, had the power to materialize a "presence" that was ready to join the forces of the race in an occult fashion and lead them toward a good outcome in order to transform new victories into the means necessary for the revelation, and for the strengthening of the energy of the original victory. Thus, in Rome, once the celebration of the deceased Caesar was confused with that of his victory, and once regular games were dedicated to

19. See the enigmatic saying in the Koran (2:153): "Do not say that those who were slain in the cause of Allah are dead; they are alive, although you are not aware of them." Plato also wrote: "And of those who are slain in the field, we shall say that all who fell with honor are of that golden race, who when they die, according to Hesiod, 'Dwell here on earth, pure spirits, beneficent, Guardians to shield us mortal men from harm.'" (*Republic*, 468e).

the Victoria Caesaris, it became possible to see in him a "perennial winner."[20]

The cult of Victory, believed to predate history,[21] may be considered, generally speaking, as the secret soul of the Roman greatness and *fides*. Since the times of Augustus, the statue of the goddess Victory had been placed on the altar of the Roman Senate; according to a traditional custom, any senator heading for his seat was expected first to approach that altar in order to burn some incense on it. That force was thus believed to preside invisibly over the deliberations of the Curia: hands were raised toward it when an oath of faithfulness was pronounced upon the advent of a new Caesar, and also on every January third when solemn vows were made for the well-being of the emperor and for the prosperity of the empire. This was the most resilient Roman cult, and the last to fall under the onslaught of Christianity.

No belief was more strongly upheld by the Romans than the belief that the divine powers were responsible for creating Rome's greatness and for supporting its *aeternitas*[22] and, consequently, that a war, before being won on the battlefields, had to be won or at least actuated in a mystical way. Following the defeat at Lake Trasimene (217 B.C.), Fabius told his soldiers: "Your fault consists in having neglected the sacrifices and in having ignored the declarations of the augurs rather than in having lacked courage or ability."[23] It was also an article of faith that in order to take a city it was necessary first to cause its tutelary god to abandon it.[24] No war was initiated without sacrifices; a special college of priests *(fetiales)* was entrusted with the rites pertaining to war. The bottom line of the Roman art of war was not to be forced to fight if the gods were opposed to it. Themistocles said: "The gods and heroes performed these deeds, not us."[25] Again, the real focus of everything was the *sacrum*. Supernatural actions were invoked to assist human actions and to infuse in them the mystical power of Victory.[26]

---

20. Cassius Dio, *Roman History,* 45.7.
21. Dionysius of Halicarnassus, 1.32.5.
22. Cicero, *De natura deorum,* 2.3.8; Plutarch, *Life of Romulus,* 1.8.
23. Livy, *History of Rome,* 17.9; 31.5; 36.2; 42.2. Plutarch tells us: "To such a degree did the Romans make everything depend upon the will of the gods, and so intolerant were they of any neglect of omens and ancestral rites, even when attended by the greatest success, considering it of more importance for the safety of the city that their magistrates should reverence sacred things than that they should overcome their enemies." *Marcellus,* 4.4.
24. Macrobius, *Saturnalia,* 3.9.2. Servius, *Ad Aeneidem,* 2.244.
25. Herodotus, *The Persian Wars,* 8.109.19.
26. In savage populations we still find characteristic echoes of these views, which should not be considered "superstitious" provided they are properly contextualized and interpreted. According to these populations, war, in the last analysis, is a confrontation between warlocks. Victory goes to those who have the more powerful "war medicine" with every other apparent factor, including the equal courage of the warriors, being just a consequence.

Since I have mentioned action and heroism as traditional values, it is expedient to underline the difference between them and the forms that, a few exceptions notwithstanding, can be seen in our day and age. The difference consists, once again, in the lack of the dimension of transcendence, and thus of an orientation that, even when it is not dictated by pure instinct and blind force, does not lead to a true "opening" but rather generates qualities that are destined to bestow on the empirical subject only a dark and tragic splendor. In the case of ascetical values we find an analogous alteration that deprives asceticism of every enlightening element as one goes from the notion of asceticism to that of ethics, especially in relation to moral doctrines such as the Kantian and the Stoic ethical systems. Every morality (in its higher versions, such as Kant's "autonomous morality"), is nothing but secularized asceticism; as such it is only a surviving stump and it lacks a real foundation. Thus, the critique of the modern "free spirits," Nietzsche included, could easily dismiss the values and the imperatives of the morality improperly designated as "traditional" ("improperly," because in a traditional civilization no morality enjoyed an autonomous dimension). Our contemporaries, however, have fallen to an even lower level in the shift that occurred from the "autonomous" and categorically imperative morality to a utilitarian and "social" morality affected by a fundamental relativity and contingency.

As is the case with asceticism in general, when heroism and action are not aimed at leading back one's personality to its true center, they are nothing but an artificial "device" that begins and ends with man; as such they do not acquire a meaning or a value beyond that of sensation, exaltation, and frantic impulsiveness. Such is, almost without exception, the case of the modern cult of action. Even when everything is not reduced to a cultivation of "reflexes" and to a control of elementary reactions, as in the case of war on the frontline (considering the advanced degree of mechanization of the modern varieties of action), it is almost inevitable for man to seek out and to feed himself with existentially liminal experiences wherever they are to be found. Moreover, the plane is often shifted to collective and subpersonal forces, the incarnation of which is furthered by the "ecstasy" associated with heroism, sport, and action.

The heroic myth based on individualism, voluntarism, and a superman attitude constitutes a dangerous deviation in our modern era; on its basis the individual,

> Precluding to himself all possibilities of extraindividual and extrahuman development, assumes—by virtue of a diabolical construction—the principle of his insignificant physical will as an absolute reference point and assails the external "phantasm" by opposing to it the phantasm of his own self. It is ironic that when confronting this contaminating insanity, he who realizes what game these poor and more or less heroic

individuals are playing, recalls Confucius' advice according to which
every reasonable person has the duty to safeguard his own life in view
of the development of the only possibilities by virtue of which a man
truly deserves to be called a man.[27]

The fact remains that modern man needs these degraded and desecrated forms of
action as if they were some kind of drug; he needs them to elude the sense of his
inner emptiness, to be aware of himself, and to find in exasperated sensations the
surrogate for the true meaning of life. One of the characteristics of the Western
"Dark Age" (Kali Yuga) is a sort of Titanic restlessness that knows no limitations
and that induces an existential fever and awakens new sources of elation and of
stupefaction.

Before continuing, I need to mention an aspect of the traditional spirit that is
related to the Law and to the views expounded so far. I am talking about various
ordeals of character and so-called divine judgments.

Quite often the test of truth, right, justice, and innocence was made to depend on
a trial that consisted of a decisive action *(experimentum crucis)*. Just as the law was
traditionally believed to have a divine origin, likewise injustice was considered to be
a violation of the divine Law and to be detectable through the outcome of a human
action that had been given an adequate orientation. A Germanic custom consisted of
delving into the divine will through the test of arms as a particular form of oracle
mediated by action; the idea that originally was at the basis of the custom of challenging somebody to a duel is not very different. Starting with the principle: *"de
coelo est fortitudo" (Annales Fuldenses),* this principle was eventually extended to
feuding states and nations. A battle as late as that of Fonteney (A.D. 841) was conceived as a "divine judgment" that was invoked to establish the rights of two brothers both claiming the legacy of Charlemagne. When a battle was fought in this spirit,
it followed special rules: the winner was forbidden to loot and to exploit strategically
and territorially the successful outcome, and both sides were expected to tend equally
to the fallen and to the wounded. According to the general view that was preserved
through the entire Carolingian period, however, even when the idea of a specific
proof was not required, victory and defeat were felt to be signs "from above" establishing justice or injustice, truth or guilt. In the legend of the combat between Roland
and Ferragus and in analogous themes of chivalrous literature, we can see that during the Middle Ages people believed that the test of arms was the criterion capable
of assessing the truer faith.

In other instances the trial consisted in the induction of a paranormal phenomenon.

---

27. G. De Giorgio, "La contemplazione e l'azione," *La Torre*, no. 7 (1930).

This was the case of classical antiquity too: according to a Roman tradition, a vestal virgin suspected of sacrilege demonstrated her own innocence by carrying water from the Tiber River in a sieve. There was also the custom, which is not confined to the degenerative forms that have survived among savage populations, of challenging a suspect who claimed his or her own innocence to ingest a poison or a substance inducing vomit; if the substance induced the usual effects, the charge was validated. During the Middle Ages analogous voluntary ordeals were found not only in the context of temporal justice, but in the sacred domain too; monks and even bishops agreed to submit themselves to such a criterion in order to establish the truth of their claims in matters of doctrine.[28] Even torture, which was conceived as a means to interrogate prisoners, was originally related to the notion of "divine judgment." Truth was believed to have an almost magical power; it was a common belief that no torture could undermine the inner truth of an innocent person and of somebody who was telling the truth.

There is a clear connection between all this and the mystical character traditionally associated with "victory." In these trials, including the trial of arms, God was "called" as a witness by the participants in order for them to receive from Him a supernatural sign that would then be used as a judgment. It is possible to rise from the lower level of these naive theistic representations to the purer form of the traditional idea, according to which truth, law, and justice ultimately appear as the manifestations of a metaphysical order conceived as a *reality* that the state of truth and of justice in man has the power to evoke in an objective way. In antiquity the overworld was conceived of as a reality in the higher sense of the word, superior to the laws of nature and capable of manifesting itself in this world every time one opened oneself to it without reservations and concern for one's self; in the next stage the individual entered into certain psychic states (the already mentioned heroic, competitive state that "unties" the extreme tension of the ordeal and of the danger being faced) that were destined to open the closed human "circuits" to wider "circuits," and through which it was possible to generate unusual and apparently miraculous effects. This view explains and gives the proper meaning to traditions and customs such as the abovementioned ones. In the order of these customs, truth and reality, might and law, victory and justice formed one thing having the supernatural as their center of gravity.

These views were destined to be regarded as pure superstition wherever

---

28. Around the year A.D. 506, during the reign of Emperor Athanasius, a Catholic bishop proposed to an Arian bishop to undergo the test of fire in order to determine which one of the two faiths was the true one. After the Arian refused, the Catholic entered the fire and exited unscathed. This power was also attributed to the priests of Apollo: *super ambustam ligni struem ambulantes, non aduri tradebantur* says Pliny (7.2). The same idea is also found on a higher plane: according to the ancient Iranian idea, at the "end of the world" all people will have to go through a fiery current; the "righteous" will not be harmed but the evil ones will be consumed by the flames. *Bundahesh*, 30.18.

"progress" systematically deprived the human virtues of any possibility of establishing an objective contact with a superior order of things. Once man's strength was thought to be on the same level as that of animals, that is, as the faculty of mechanical action in a being who is not at all connected to what transcends him as an individual, the trial of strength obviously becomes meaningless and the outcome of every competition becomes entirely contingent and lacking a potential relation with an order of higher "values." Once the ideas of truth, law, and justice were turned into abstractions or social conventions; once the sensation, thanks to which in Aryan India it was possible to say, "The earth has truth as its foundation," was forgotten; once every perception of these "values" as objective and almost physical apparitions of the supernatural amid the network of contingencies was lost—then it is natural to wonder how truth, law, and justice could possibly influence the determination of the phenomena and facts that science, until recently, has decreed not to be susceptible to modification.[29] Nowadays, decisions with regard to what is true or right as well as matters of innocence and guilt are left to the clamor of pettifoggers, the laborious promulgation of legal documents, the lengthy paragraphs of laws that are "equal for everybody" and made omnipotent by the secularized states and the plebeian masses who rule themselves without kings and self-appointed rulers. Conversely, the proud self-assurance with which traditional man reacted valiantly and superindividually against the unrighteous, armed with faith and the sword, and the spiritual impassibility that placed him in an a priori, absolute relation to a supernatural power not subject to the power of the elements, sensations, and natural laws—all these things have come to be considered mere "superstitions."

In this context too, the decline of traditional values has been followed by their inversion; an inversion that can be seen at work wherever the modern world makes a profession of "realism" and seems to take up again the idea of an identity of victory and law with the principle "might is right." Since this is might in the highest material sense of the word—or better, if we refer to war in its most recent forms, in an almost *demonic* sense (since the technical and industrial potential has become the most decisive factor)—then we can see that discussions about "values" and righteousness are merely rhetorical. Such rhetoric is employed through big words and a hypocritical declamation of principles as a means in the service of an ugly will to power. This is a particular upheaval characterizing the last times, more on which later.

29. I said "until recently" because modern metapsychical researches have established the existence of paranormal powers latent in man that can become objectively manifested and modify the network of physical and chemical phenomena. In addition to the fact that it would have been unlikely for the practice of "divine judgment" to be continued for such a long time if no extranormal phenomenon were ever produced, the said metapsychical findings ought to modify the common opinion regarding the "superstitious" variations of the so-called divine trials.

19

Space, Time, the Earth

I have previously pointed out that the difference between traditional and modern man is not simply a matter of mentality and type of civilization; rather, the difference concerns the experiential possibilities available to each and the way in which the world of nature is experienced according to the categories of perception and the fundamental relationship between I and not-I. For traditional man space, time, and causality had a very different character than they have in the experience of modern man. The mistake of epistemology from Kant on is to assume that these fundamental forms of human experience have always remained the same, especially those with which we are most familiar in recent times. On the contrary, even in this aspect it is possible to notice a deep transformation that reflects the general involutive process at work in history. With this said, I will limit myself to discussing the difference in the perception of space and time.

As I mentioned in the foreword, my main contention is that time in traditional civilizations was not a linear, "historical" time. Time and becoming are related to what is superior to time; in this way the perception of time undergoes a spiritual transformation.

In order to clarify this point it is necessary to explain what time means today. Time is perceived as the simple irreversible order of consecutive events; its parts are mutually homogeneous and therefore can be measured in a quantitative fashion. Moreover, a distinction is made between "before" and "later" (namely, between past and future) in reference to a totally relative (the present) point in time. But whether an event is past or future, whether it takes place in one or another point in time, does not confer upon it any special quality; it merely makes it a dateable event, that's all. In other words, there is some kind of reciprocal indifference between time and its contents. The temporality of these contents simply means that they are carried along by a continuous current that never inverts its course and in which every moment, while being different from all others, is also equal to all others. In the most recent scientific theories (such as Minkowski's and Einstein's) time even loses this particular character.

Scientists talk about the relativity of time, of time as space's "fourth dimension" and so on; this means that time becomes a mathematical order per se that is absolutely indifferent with regard to events, which may thus be located in a "before" rather than in an "after," depending on the reference system being adopted.

The traditional experience of time was of a very different kind; time was not regarded quantitatively but rather qualitatively; not as a series, but as rhythm. It did not flow uniformly and indefinitely, but was broken down into cycles and periods in which every moment had its own meaning and specific value in relation to all others, as well as a lively individuality and functionality. Each of these cycles or periods (the Chaldean and Hellenic "great year"; the Etruscan or Latin *saeculum;* the Iranian aeon; the Aztec "suns"; the Hindu *kalpas*) represented a complete development forming closed and perfect units that were identical to each other; although they reoccurred they did not change nor did they multiply, but rather followed each other, according to Hubert-Mauss's fitting expression, as a "series of eternities."[1] Since this wholeness was not quantitative but organic, the chronological duration of the *saeculum* was ephemeral. Quantitatively different periods of time were regarded as equal, provided that each of them contained and reproduced all the typical phases of a cycle. And so, certain numbers such as seven, nine, twelve, and one thousand were traditionally employed not to express quantities, but rather typical structures of rhythm; thus they had different durations though they remained symbolically equivalent.

Accordingly, instead of an indefinite chronological sequence, the traditional world knew a hierarchy based on analogical correspondences between great and small cycles; the result was a sort of reduction of the temporal manifold to the supertemporal unity.[2] Since the small cycle reproduced analogically the great cycle, this created the possibility of participation in ever greater orders and in durations increasingly free from all residues of matter or contingency, until what was reached was some kind of space-time continuum.[3] By ordering time "from above" so that every duration was

---

1. Hubert-Mauss, *Mélange d'histoire religieuse,* 207. According to the Chaldeans, the universe's eternity was divided into a series of "great years" in which the same events keep on recurring, just like winter and summer keep on recurring every "small year." If some time periods were sometimes personified as divinities or as divinities' organs, this was yet another expression of the idea of the cycle as an organic unity.
2. "The durations of traditional time may be compared to numbers that in turn are regarded as the enumeration of lower unities or as sums capable of serving as units for the composition of higher numbers. Continuity is given to them by the mental operation that synthesizes their elements." Ibid., 202.
3. This idea is reflected in the Hindu view according to which a year on the earth corresponds to a day for some lesser gods; while a year of these gods' lives corresponds to a day for gods occupying a higher hierarchical level, until we reach the days and nights of Brahman, which express the cyclical unfolding of the cosmic manifestation. See *The Laws of Manu* 1.64–74. In the same text it is written that these cycles are repeated by the Supreme Lord "as if he were playing"; this expresses the irrelevance and the antihistoricity of the repetition in comparison to the immutable and eternal element that is manifested in it. We may also recall the biblical saying: "For a thousand years in your sight are as yesterday, now that it is past. . . ." Ps. 90:4.

divided into several cyclical periods reflecting such a structure, and by associating to specific moments of these cycles the celebrations, rituals, or festivities that were destined to reawaken or to reveal the corresponding meanings, the traditional world actively promoted a liberation and a transfiguration; it arrested the confused flow of the "waters" and created in them a transparency in the current of becoming, thus revealing immobile metaphysical depths. Therefore, it should not come as a surprise that the base calendar that measured time in ancient times had a sacred character and that it was entrusted to the wisdom of the priestly castes and that the hours of the day, the days of the week, and given days of the year were considered sacred to certain deities or associated with specific destinies. After all, as a residue of this notion, Catholicism developed a liturgical year spangled with religious festivities and with days marked by sacred events; in this liturgical year we can still find an echo of that ancient view of time that was measured by ritual, transfigured by the symbol, and shaped into the image of a "sacred history."

The fact that stars, stellar periods, and given points in the course of the sun were traditionally utilized to determine the units of rhythm hardly lends support to the so-called naturalistic interpretations of time; in fact, the traditional world never "deified" the natural or heavenly elements, but on the contrary, these elements were thought fit to convey divine forces in an analogical fashion: "There is in the heavens a great multitude of gods who have been recognized as such by those who survey the heavens not casually, nor like cattle."[4] Therefore, we can assume that the position of the sun in the course of the year was primordially the center and the beginning of an organic system (of which the calendar notation was just another aspect) that established constant interferences and symbolical and magical correspondences between man, cosmos, and supernatural reality.[5] The two arches of the ascent and the descent of the solar light during the year appear to be the most apt to express the sacrificial meaning of death and rebirth, as well as the cycle constituted by the dark descending path and by the bright ascending path.

I will discuss later the tradition according to which the area that today corresponds to the Arctic regions was the original homeland of the stocks that created the main Indo-European civilizations. It is possible that when the Arctic freeze occurred, the division of the year into one long night and one long day highly dramatized the perception of the sun's journey in the sky, and thus made it one of the best ways to express the abovementioned metaphysical meanings, substituting them with what was referred

---

4. Emperor Julian, *Hymn to King Helios*, 148c.
5. From a traditional point of view, great reservations should be expressed about the theory of H. Wirth concerning a sacred series derived in primordial times from the astral movement of the sun as "god-year"; this series, according to Wirth, was the basis for the measurement of time, for the signs and for the roots of a common prehistoric language and also for meanings related to the cult.

to in more remote periods as a pure, though not yet solar, "polar" symbolism.

Considering that the constellations of the zodiac, which were articulations of the "god-year," were used to identify the "moments" of the sun's position in the sky, the number twelve is repeatedly found as one of the most apt "rhythms" to express anything that may have the meaning of a "solar" fulfillment. This number is also found wherever a center was established that in one way or another embodied or attempted to embody the Uranian-solar tradition, or wherever myths or legends have portrayed the type of an analogous regency through figurations or symbolical personifications.[6] But in the course of the solar journey along the twelve points of the zodiac, one point in particular acquires a special meaning, and that is the critical one corresponding to the lowest point on the ellipsis (winter solstice), which marks the end of the descent, the beginning of the reascent, and the separation of the dark and the bright periods. According to figurations formulated in remote prehistory, the "god-year" is portrayed in this context as the "axe" or as the "god-axe" who splits in half the circular symbol of the year (or other equivalent symbols): from a spiritual perspective this marks the typically "triumphant" moment of solarity and the beginning of a "new life" and of a new cycle *(natalis dii solis invicti)*. This moment was represented in various myths as the victorious outcome of the struggle of a solar hero against creatures manifesting the dark principle; these creatures were often represented by the sign of the

6. The number twelve, characterizing the signs of the zodiac, which correspond to the Hindu *āditya*, appears in the number of chapters of *The Laws of Manu*; in the twelve great Namshan of the circular council of the Dalai Lama; in the twelve disciples of Lao-tzu (originally two, who in turn initiated another ten); in the number of the priests of several Roman collegia (such as the Arvali and the Salii); in the number of the ancilia established by Numa in return for the sign of the heavenly protection he received (twelve is also the number of vultures that gave to Romulus rather than Remus the right to give his name to the city; twelve were also the lictorians instituted by Romulus), and in the altars dedicated to Janus; in the twelve disciples of Christ and in the twelve gates of the heavenly Jerusalem; in the twelve great Hellenic and Roman deities; in the twelve judges of the Egyptian *Book of the Dead;* in the twelve jasper towers built on the Taoist sacred mountain named Kuen-Lun; in the twelve main Aesir and their corresponding dwellings or thrones in the Nordic tradition; in the twelve labors of Heracles; in the number of days of Siegfried's journey and in twelve kings subjected to him; in the twelve main knights sitting at King Arthur's Round Table; and in the twelve palatines of Charlemagne. The list could go on and on.

Traditionally the number seven refers to rhythms of development, of formation and of fulfillment in man, the cosmos, and the spirit. As far as the spiritual dimension is concerned, see the seven trials found in many initiations; the seven deeds of Rostan; the seven days Buddha spent under the "bodhi tree"; the seven cycles of seven days each necessary to learn the doctrine, according to some Buddhist traditions. While the days of biblical "creation" were believed to be seven, these "days" corresponded to the millennia of the Iranian-Chaldean traditions; these millenia were cycles, the last of which was considered a cycle of "consummation," that is, of fulfillment and resolution or destruction in a solar sense. See R. Guénon, *Le Symbolisme de la croix*. Thus the week corresponds to the great hebdomadary of the ages of the world, just as the solar year corresponds to the cosmic "great year." There are also many references to the development and duration of some civilizations, such as the six *saecula* of life attributed to the Roman world, the seventh being the *saeculum* of its demise; the number of the first kings of Rome; the ages of the first Manus of the present cycle according to the Hindu tradition, and so on.

zodiac in which the winter solstice happened to fall in that particular year.

The dates corresponding to stellar positions in the sky (such as the solstice), which were apt to express higher meanings in terms of a cosmic symbolism, are preserved almost identically in the various forms assumed by Tradition and passed on from one people to another. Through a comparative study it is possible and very easy to point out the correspondence and the uniformity of feasts and of fundamental calendar rhythms through which the Sacred was introduced into the fabric of time, thus breaking its duration into many cyclical images of an eternal history that various natural phenomena contributed to recall and to mark the rhythm.

In the traditional view, moreover, time presented a magical aspect. Since by virtue of the law of analogical correspondences every point of a cycle had its own individuality, duration consisted in the periodical succession of manifestations typical of certain influences and powers: it presented times that were favorable and unfavorable, auspicious and inauspicious. This qualitative element of time played the main role in the science of the rite; the parts of time could not be considered indifferent to the things to be performed and thus presented an active character that had to be reckoned with.[7] Every rite had its own appointed "time"; it had to be performed at a particular moment, outside of which its virtue was diminished or paralyzed, and could even produce the opposite effect. In many ways we can agree with Hubert-Mauss, who said that the ancient calendar marked the periodicity of a system of rites. More generally, there were disciplines (such as the science of divination) that attempted to establish whether a given time or period was auspicious or not for the performance of a given deed; I have already mentioned the attention given to this matter in Roman military enterprises.

This is not "fatalism"; it rather expresses traditional man's constant intent to prolong and to integrate his own strength with a nonhuman strength by discovering the times in which two rhythms (the human rhythm and the rhythm of natural powers), by virtue of a law of syntony—of a concordant action and of a certain correspondence between the physical and the metaphysical dimensions—are liable to become one thing, and thus cause invisible powers to act. In this way the qualitative view of time is confirmed. Within time every hour and every aspect has it sacred aspect and its "virtue"; also, acting within time on the higher, symbolical, and sacral plane[8] there are cyclical laws that actualize in an identical fashion an "uninterrupted chain of eternity."

---

7. Concerning this future, see the characteristic expressions of Macrobius, *Saturnalia*, 1.15.

8. Such a plane should not be confused with the magical plane, although the latter, in the last analysis, presupposes an order of knowledge deriving more or less directly from the former. A separate group consists of those rites and those celebrations, which despite their cyclical character, do not find real correspondences in nature but are rather originated by fatal events connected to a given race.

The considerations that follow from these premises are very important. If traditionally, empirical time was measured by a transcendent time that did not contain events but meanings; and if this essentially metahistorical time must be considered as the context in which myths, heroes, and traditional gods lived and "acted"—then an opposite shift acting "from below" must also be conceived. In other words, it is possible that some historically real events or people may have repeated and dramatized a myth, incarnating metahistorical structures and symbols whether in part or entirely, whether consciously or unconsciously. Thereupon, by virtue of this, these events or beings shift from one time to the other, becoming new expressions of preexisting realities. They belong to both times; they are characters and events that are simultaneously real and symbolical, and on this basis they can be transported from one period to another, before or after their real existence, as long as one is aware of the metahistorical element they represent. This is the reason why some of the findings of modern scholars concerning the alleged historicity of events or characters of the traditional world, much of their obsession to separate what is historical from what is mythical or legendary, some of their doubts about the "childish" traditional chronology, and finally their belief in so-called euhemerism, can most decisively be said to lack solid foundations. In these cases—as I have previously argued—myth and antihistory represent the path leading to a deeper knowledge of what we regard as "history."

Moreover, it is in this same order of ideas that we must look for the true meaning of the legends concerning characters who became "invisible," who "never died," and who are destined to "reawaken" or to manifest themselves at the end of a given time (cyclical correspondence) such as Alexander the Great, King Arthur, "Frederick," King Sebastian. The latter are all different incarnations of the same one theme transferred from reality into superreality. The Hindu doctrine of the avatars, the periodical divine incarnations who assume different personalities but who nevertheless express the same function, must be interpreted along these lines.

If traditional man had an experience of time essentially different from that of modern man, it follows that analogous considerations must be made concerning the experience of space. Space is considered today as the simple "container" of bodies and of motions, totally indifferent to both. It is homogeneous: a particular area of it is the objective equivalent of another one, and the fact that a thing is found—or that an event may take place—in one point of space rather than in another, does not confer any particular quality to the intimate nature of that thing or of that event. I am referring here to what space represents in the immediate experience of modern man and not to certain recent physical-mathematical views of space as a curved and nonhomogeneous, multidimensional space. Moreover, beside the fact that these are mere mathematical schemata (the value of which is merely pragmatic and without correspondence to any real experience), the different values that the points of each of these spaces represent when considered as "intensive fields" are referred only to matter, energy, and gravitation, and not to something extraphysical or qualitative.

In the experience of traditional man, on the contrary, and even in its residues (at times present among some savage populations), space is alive and saturated with all kinds of qualities and intensity. The traditional idea of space is often confused with the same idea of "vital ether" (the *ākāśa* or *mana*), which is a mystical, all-pervasive substance-energy, more material than immaterial, more psychic than physical, often conceived as "light," and distributed according to various saturations in various regions; thus, each of these regions seems to possess its own virtues and to participate essentially in the powers that reside in it so as to make every place a fatidic space endowed with its own intensity and occult individuality. In the well-known expression of Epimenides of Knossos (sixth century B.C.) that was quoted by Paul in his speech in the Areopagus: "In him we live and move and have our being" (Acts 17:28), if we substitute for the word "him" the word "divine" or "sacred" or "numinous," it may be employed to express what traditional man often saw instead of the space of the moderns, which is ultimately an abstract and impersonal "place" filled with objects and motions.

It is not possible in this context to discuss all of what in the traditional world was based on such an experience of space. I will limit myself to references in the two distinct orders mentioned above, namely, the magical and the symbolical.

Space in antiquity has constantly provided the basis for the most characteristic expressions of the metaphysical dimension. The heavenly and the earthly regions, high and low, the vertical and horizontal axis, left and right, were all categories that provided the material for a typical, highly significant, and universal symbolism, one of the most famous forms of which was the symbolism of the cross. There may well have been a relationship between the two-dimensional cross and the four cardinal points; between the three-dimensional cross and the schema derived by adding to these points the dimensions of "above" and "below." Still this does not lend any support whatsoever to the naturalistic and geo-astronomical interpretations of ancient symbols. At this point it is helpful to repeat what has been said concerning the astral element of the calendars, namely, that when the cross is found in nature this means that "true symbolism, far from being artificially devised by man, is found in nature itself; or better, nature in its entirety is nothing but a symbol of transcendent realities."[9]

When we shift to the magical plane, every direction in space corresponded to given "influences" that were often portrayed as supernatural beings or as spirits; this knowledge not only helped to establish important aspects of the augural science and

9. R. Guénon, *Le Symbolisme de la croix*. Also J. Evola, *The Hermetic Tradition*.

of geomancy (see the characteristic development of this discipline in the Far East), but also the doctrine of the sacred orientations in the rite and the arrangement of the temples (the art of orientation of the cathedrals was preserved in Europe up to the Middle Ages), always in conformity with the law of analogies and with the possibility, afforded by this law, to extend the human and the visible element into the cosmic and invisible dimension. Just as one moment of traditional time did not correspond to another because of the action (especially a ritual one) that had to be undertaken, likewise there was not a point, a region, or a place of traditional space that corresponded to another. This was the case in an even wider sense owing to the fact that some rites required subterranean places or caves, while others required mountain peaks, and so on. In fact there was such a thing as a real (that is, not arbitrary, but conformed to physical transpositions of metaphysical elements) *sacred geography* that inspired the belief in "sacred" lands and cities, in the traditional centers of spiritual influence on earth, and also in environments consecrated so as to "vitalize" any action oriented to the Transcendence taking place within them. Generally speaking, in the world of Tradition the location of the temples and of many cities was not casual, nor did it obey simple criteria of convenience; their construction was preceded by specific rites and obeyed special laws of rhythm and of analogy. It is very easy to identify those elements that indicate that the space in which the traditional rite took place was not space as modern man understands it but rather a living, fatidic, magnetic space in which every gesture had a meaning and in which every sign, word, and action participated in a sense of ineluctability and of eternity, thus becoming transformed into a kind of decree of the Invisible. And yet the space in which the rite occurs should be regarded as a more intense kind of space in the general perception of the man of Tradition.

I will now briefly discuss the "myths" with which, according to our contemporaries, ancient man embellished the various elements and aspects of nature. The truth is that here we find once more that opposition between hyperrealism and humanism that separates what is traditional from what is modern.

The "experience of nature," as it is understood by modern man, namely, as a lyrical, subjectivist pathos awoken in the sentiments of the individual at the sight of nature, was almost entirely absent in traditional man. Before the high and snowy peaks, the silence of the woods, the flowing of the rivers, mysterious caves, and so on, traditional man did not have poetic and subjective impressions typical of a romantic soul, but rather real sensations—even though at times confused—of the supernatural, of the powers *(numina)* that permeated those places; these sensations were translated into various images (spirits and gods of the elements, waterfalls, woods, and so on) often determined by the imagination, yet not arbitrarily and subjectively, but according to a necessary process. In other words, we may assume that in traditional man the power of the imagination was not merely confined to either the material images corresponding to sensible data or arbitrary and subjective images, as in the case of the reveries or dreams of modern man. On the contrary, we may conclude that in traditional man the power of the imagination was free, to a high degree, from the yoke of the physical senses, as it is nowadays in the state of sleep or through the use of drugs; this power was so disposed as to be able to perceive and translate into plastic forms subtler impressions of the environment, which nonetheless were not arbitrary and subjective. When in the state of dream a physical impression, such as the pressure of the blankets, is dramatized with the image of a falling rock, this is obviously the case of a fantastic and yet not arbitrary production: the image arose out of necessity, independently from the I, as a symbol that effectively corresponds to a perception. The same holds true for those fantastic images primordial man introduced in nature. Primordial man, in addition to physical perception, also had a "psychic" or subtle perception of things and places (corresponding to the "presences" found in them) that was generated by a power of the imagination free from the physical senses and responsible for determining in it corresponding symbolical dramatizations: for example, gods, demons, elementals, and spirits ruling over places and phenomena. It is true that there have often been different personifications according to the multiform power of the imagination of various races and sometimes even of different people; but a trained eye is able to see a unity behind this variety, just as a person who is awake is immediately able to see unity in the variety of impressions created by the diversity of symbols in the dreams of different people. These images are nevertheless equivalent once they are reduced to their common objective cause and perceived in a distinct way.

Far from being fantastic poetical tales drawn from nature, or better, from those material representations of nature that modern man can perceive, the myths of the ancients and their fantastic fundamental figurations originally represented an *integration* of the objective experience of nature. The myths also represented something that spontaneously penetrated into the fabric of sensible data, thus completing them with lively and at times even visible symbols of the subtle, "demonic," or sacred element of space and time.

These considerations concerning the traditional myths and the special relation they have with the sense of nature must naturally be applied to every traditional myth. It must be acknowledged that every traditional mythology arises as a necessary process in the individual consciousness, the origin of which resides in real, though unconscious and obscure, relationships with a higher reality; these relationships are then dramatized in various ways by the power of the imagination. Therefore, not only naturalistic or "theological" myths but historical ones as well should not be regarded as arbitrary inventions totally devoid of an objective value with regard to facts or people, but rather as integrations that did not occur casually. These integrations eventually revealed the superhistorical content that may be found to varying degrees in those historical individuals and events. Therefore, the eventual lack of correspondence of the historical element with a myth demonstrates the untruth of history rather than that of the myth; this thought occurred to Hegel too, when he spoke about the "impotence [Ohnmacht] of nature."

What has been said so far relates to the presence of some kind of existential situation concerning the basic relationship between the I and the not-I. This relationship has lately been characterized by a set and rigid separation. It so appears that in the origins, the borders between I and not-I were potentially fluid and unstable, and in certain cases they could partially be removed. When that happened, either one of two possibilities could occur: the possibility of incursions of the not-I (of "nature" in the sense of its elemental forces and its psychism) into the I, or an incursion of the I into the not-I. The first possibility explains what have been called the *perils of the soul.* It is the idea that the unity and the autonomy of the person may be threatened and affected by processes of possession and of obession; hence the existence of rituals and various institutions that have as their goal the spiritual defense of the individual or of the collectivity and the confirmation of the independence and the sovereignty of the I and of its structures.[10]

The general presupposition for the efficacy of a body of magical procedures was that the second possibility, which consists of the removal of the boundaries and of the ensuing incursions in the opposite direction (of the I into the not-I), could take place. Since the two possibilities shared the same basis, the advantages of the latter had as a counterpart the existential risks derived from the former.

We should remember that during the last times, following the progressive materialization of the I, both possibilities have disappeared. The active and positive (magic) possibility has disappeared everywhere but in few insignificant and marginal residues. As far as the "perils of the soul" are concerned, modern man, who boasts to have finally become free and enlightened, and who laughs at everything that in traditional antiquity derived from that different relationship between I and not-I, is really deceiving himself to think he is safe from them. Those dangers have only assumed a different form, which disguises them; modern man is open to the complexes of the "collective unconscious," to emotive and irrational currents, to collective influences and to ideologies with consequences far more harmful and deplorable than those found in other eras and deriving from different influences.

---

10. This should refer mainly to civilizations of a higher kind. When talking about the earth, I will mention the existence of an opposite orientation in the primitive connections between man and earth.

Returning to what I have expounded before, I would like to say something about the ancient meaning of the earth and of its properties.

From a traditional point of view, between man and his land, between blood and soil, there existed an intimate relationship of a living and psychic character. Since a given area had a psychic individuality in addition to its geographic individuality, those who were born in it were bound to be deeply affected by it. From a doctrinal point of view we must distinguish a double aspect in this state of dependency, the former naturalistic, the latter supernaturalistic, which leads us back to the abovementioned distinction between "totemism" and the tradition of a patrician blood that has been purified by an element from above.

The former aspect concerns beings who do not go beyond empirical and ordinary life. In these beings the collective predominates, both as a law of blood and stock and as law of the soil. Even if the mystical sense of the region to which they belong is awakened, such a sense does not go beyond mere "tellurism"; though they may know a tradition of rites, these rites have only a demonic and totemic character and they contribute to strengthening and renewing rather than overcoming and removing, the law by virtue of which the individual does not have a life of his own and is thus destined to be dissolved into the subpersonal stock of his blood. Such a stage may be characterized by an almost communist, and at times even matriarchical social organization of the clan or of the tribe. What we find in it, however, is what in modern man has either become extinguished or has become nationalistic or romantic rhetoric, namely, the *organic* and *living* sense of one's own land, which is a direct derivation of the qualitative experience of space in general.

The second aspect of the traditional relationship between a man and his land is very different. Here we find the idea of a supernatural action that has permeated a given territory with a supernatural influence by removing the demonic telluric element of the soil and by imposing upon it a "triumphal" seal, thus reducing it to a mere substratum for the powers that transcend it. We have already found this idea in the ancient Iranian belief that the "glory," the celestial, living, and "triumphal" fire that is the exclusive legacy of kings, pervades the lands that the Aryan race has conquered and that it possesses and defends against the "infidels" and the forces working for the god of darkness. After all, even in more recent times, there has been an intimate and not merely empirical relationship between spear and plough, between nobility and the farmers. It is significant that Aryan deities such as Mars or Donar-Thor were simultaneously deities of war and of victory (over "elemental natures" in the case of Thor) and of the soil, presiding over its cultivation. I have already mentioned the symbolical and even initiatory transpositions that surrounded the "cultivator" and the memory of it that remains in the derivation of the word "culture."

Another characteristic expression lies in the fact that in every higher form of tradition, private ownership of the land as private property was an aristocratic and sacred privilege; the only people who could lay claim to the land were those who had rites in the specific patrician sense I mentioned in chapter 6, namely, those who are the living bearers of a divine element (in Rome this right belonged only to the *patres,* the lords of the sacrificial fire; in Egypt it belonged only to the warriors and the priests). The slaves, those without family names and tradition, were not thought to be qualified to own land because of their social status. For instance, in the ancient Nahua-Aztec civilization, two distinct and even opposite types of property coexisted. One was an aristocratic, hereditary, and differentiated type, that was transmitted together with one's family's social status; the second was popular and plebeian, of a promiscuous type, like the Russian *mir.* This opposition can be found in several other civilizations and is related to that which existed between the Uranian and the chthonic cults. In traditional nobility a mysterious relationship was established between the gods or the heroes of a particular gens and that very land; it was through its *numina* and with a net accentuation of the meaning (originally not only material) of ownership and lordship that the gens was connected to its own land, so much so that, due to a symbolical and possibly magical transposition, its limits (the Greek ἕρκος and the Roman *herctum*) were regarded as sacred, fatal, and protected by gods of order such as Zeus and Jupiter; these are almost the equivalent, on another plane, of the same inner limits of the noble caste and of the noble family. We can say that at this level the limits of the land, just like the spiritual limits of the castes, were not limits that enslaved but that preserved and freed. Thus, we can understand why exile was often regarded as a punishment of a seriousness hardly understood today; it was almost like dying to the gens to whom one belonged.

The same order of ideas is confirmed in the fact that in several traditional civilizations, to settle in a new, unknown, or wild land and to take possession of it was regarded as an act of creation and as an image of the primordial act whereby chaos was transformed into cosmos; in other words, it was not regarded as a mere human deed, but rather as an almost magical and ritual action believed to bestow on a land and on a physical location a "form" by bathing such land in the sacred and by making it living and real in a higher sense. Thus, there are examples of the ritual of taking possession of lands and of territorial conquests, as in the case of the *landnama* in ancient Iceland or in the Aryan celebration of a territory through the establishment in it of an altar with fire.[11]

In China the assignment of a fief, which turned a patrician into a prince, implied,

---

11. M. Eliade, *Manuel d'histoire des religions* (Paris 1949), 345; see *The Myth of the Eternal Return* (Princeton, 1954). Eliade correctly remarked that at the time of the expansion of the Christian ecumene, to raise or plant a cross (today this is done with a flag) in every new country added to this ecumene.

among other things, the duty to maintain a sacrificial ritual for one's divine ancestors (who thus became the protectors of the territory) and for the god of this piece of land, who was "created" for the benefit of the prince himself. Moreover, if in the ancient Aryan law the firstborn was entitled to inherit the father's property and lands—often with the bond of inalienability—the property belonged to him essentially because he was regarded as the one who perpetuated the ritual of the family as the *pontifex* and the βασιλεύς of his own people, and as the one whose responsibility it was to tend the sacred fire and not let it be put out, since the fire was considered the body or life of the divine ancestor. We must also consider that the legacy of the rite and that of the earth formed one whole, filled with meaning. The *odel*, the *mundium* of free Northern-Aryan men, in which the ideas of possession of the land, nobility, warrior blood, and divine cult were aspects of an unbreakable synthesis, was an example of this. In inheriting the ancestral land, there existed an unspoken and express commitment toward it, almost as a counterpart of the duty toward the divine and aristocratic legacy that was passed on through the blood and that alone had originally introduced the right to property. The last traces of these values can be found in the feudal Middle Ages.

Even though during this time the right to property no longer belonged to the type of the aristocrat of sacred origins who was surrounded only by equals or by inferiors, as in the traditional forms of the origins found in the oldest constitution of the German people, and even though an aristocratic warrior class came to own the right to the land, nevertheless, the counterpart of such a right was the capability of a superindividual, though not sacred, dedication. The assignment of a fief implied, from the Franks on, the commitment on the part of the feudal lord to be faithful to his prince, that is, to exercise that *fides* that had a heroic and religious as well as a political and military value *(sacramentum fidelitatis)*. This *fides* represented readiness to die and to sacrifice (i.e., a connection to a superior order) in a mediated way rather than immediately (as in the case of sacred aristocracy), sometimes without a metaphysical insight, although always with the virile superiority over the naturalistic and individualistic element and with a well-developed ethics of honor. Thus, those who are prone to consider not only the contingent and historical element, but also the meaning that social institutions assume on a higher plane, may detect in the feudal regimes of the Middle Ages traces of the traditional idea of the aristocratic and sacred privilege of ownership of the land, the idea according to which to own and be lord of a land (the inalienable right of superior stocks) is a spiritual and not merely a political title and commitment. Even the feudal interdependence between the state of the people and the state of the lands had a special meaning. Originally the state of the people determined the state of the territorial property; depending on whether a man was more or less free, more or less powerful, the land he inhabited assumed either this or that character, which was validated by various titles of nobility. The state of the lands reflected therefore the state of the people. On this basis, the dependency that arose between the ideas of ownership and land became so intimate that later on the sign often appeared as a cause and the state of a people not only was indicated but determined by that of the lands; moreover, the social status and the various hierarchical and aristocratic dignities were incorporated in the soil.[12]

Thus I agree wholeheartedly with the idea expressed by Coulanges according to which the apparition of the "will," in the sense of an individualistic freedom, of those who own the land to divide their property, break it up, and separate it from the legacy of blood and the rigorous norms of the paternal right and primogeniture, truly represents one of the characteristic manifestations of the degeneration of the traditional spirit. More generally, when the right of property ceases to be the privilege of the two higher castes and shifts to the two lower castes (the merchants and the serfs), what de facto occurs is a virtual naturalistic regression, and therefore man's dependency on the "spirits of the land" is reestablished; in the case of the solar traditionalism of the lords of the soil, superior "presences" transformed these "spirits" into zones of favorable influences and into "creative" and preserving limits. The land, which may also belong to a merchant (the owners of the capitalist, bourgeois age may be regarded as the modern equivalent of the ancient merchant caste) or to a serf (our modern worker), is a desecrated land; in conformity with the interests typical of the two inferior castes, which have succeeded in taking the land away from the ancient type of "feudal lords," the land is only valued from an economic point of view and it is exploited as much as possible with machines and with other modern technical devices. That being the case, it is natural to encounter other typical traits of a degeneration such as the property increasingly shifts from the individual to the collectivity. Parallel with the collapse of the aristocratic title to the lands and the economy having become the main factor, what emerges first is nationalism, which is followed by socialism and finally by Marxist communism. In other words, there is a return to the rule of the collective over the individual that reaffirms the collectivist and promiscuous concept of property typical of inferior races as an "overcoming" of private property and as nationalization, socialization, and proletarization of goods and of lands.

12. M. Guizòt, *Essais sur l'histoire de France* (Paris, 1868).

20

Man and Woman

To complete these considerations on traditional life, I will now briefly discuss the sexual dimension.

In this context too we find that in the traditional worldview, realities corresponded to symbols and actions to rites; what derives from these correspondences are the principles for understanding the sexes and for regulating the relationships that are necessarily established between men and women in every normal civilization.

In traditional symbolism, the supernatural principle was conceived as "masculine" and the principle of nature and of becoming as "feminine." In Hellenic terms the "one" *(τò ἕv)*, which is "in itself," complete, and self-sufficient, is regarded as masculine. Conversely, the dyad, the principle of differentiation and of "other-than-self," and thus the principle of desire and of movement, is regarded as feminine. In Hindu terms (according to the Sāṃkhya *darśana*), the impassible spirit *(puruṣa)* is masculine, while *prakṛti*, the active matrix of every conditioned form, is feminine. The Far Eastern tradition has expressed equivalent concepts through the cosmic duality of *yin* and *yang*, whereby *yang*, the male principle, is associated with the "virtue of heaven" and *yin*, the feminine principle, with the principle of the "earth."[1]

Considered in and of themselves, the two principles are in opposition to each other. But in the order of the creative formation that I have repeatedly identified as the soul of the traditional world, and that was destined to develop historically in relation to the conflict between various races and civilizations, they are transformed into elements of a synthesis in which both retain a distinctive function. This is not the place to show that behind the various representations of the myth of the "fall" we often find the idea of the male principle's identification with and loss in the feminine principle until the former has acquired the latter's way of being. In any event, when

---

1. Further metaphysical and mythical references are found in J. Evola, *Eros and the Mysteries of Love:* among the philosophers of the Sung dynasty we find the teaching that Heaven "produces" men while the Earth "produces" women; therefore woman must be subjected to man as the Earth is subjected to Heaven.

this happens, when that which is naturally a self-subsistent principle succumbs to the law of that which does not have its own principle in itself by giving in to the forces of "desire," then it is appropriate to talk about a "fall." On the plane of human reality, the diffidence that various traditions have nurtured toward women is based precisely on this belief; the woman is often considered as a principle of "sin," impurity, and evil, as well as a temptation and a danger for those who are in search of the supernatural.

Nevertheless, it is possible to consider another possibility that runs counter to the direction of the "fall," and that is to establish the correct relationship between the two principles. This occurs when the feminine principle, whose force is centrifugal, does not turn to fleeting objects but rather to a "virile" stability in which she finds a limit to her "restlessness." Stability is then transmitted to the feminine principle to the point of intimately transfiguring all of its possibilities. What occurs in these terms is a synthesis in a positive sense. What is needed therefore is a radical "conversion" of the feminine principle to the opposite principle; moreover, it is absolutely necessary for the masculine principle to remain wholly itself. Then, according to metaphysical symbols, the female becomes the "bride" and also the "power" or instrumental generating force that receives the primordial principle of the immobile male's activity and form: as in the doctrine of Śakti, which can also be found in Aristotelianism and in Neoplatonism, though expressed in different terms. I have mentioned the Tantric-Tibetan representations that are very significant in this regard, in which the male "bearer-of-the-scepter" is immobile, cold, and substantiated with light while the substance of Śakti, which envelops it and uses it as its axis, is a flickering flame.[2]

These meanings constitute the foundation of the traditional teachings concerning the human sexes. This norm obeys the principle of the caste system and it also emphasizes the two cardinal tenets of *dharma* and of *bhakti*, or *fides:* self-subsistent nature and active dedication.

If birth is not a matter of chance, then it is not a coincidence for a being to "awaken" to itself in the body of a man or a woman. Here too, the physical difference should be viewed as the equivalent of a spiritual difference; hence a being is a man or a woman in a physical way only because a being is either masculine or feminine in a transcendental way; sexual differentiation, far from being an irrelevant factor in relation to the spirit, is the sign that points to a particular vocation and to a distinctive *dharma*.

---

2. In the erotic symbolism of these traditions the same meaning is expressed through the figuration of the divine couple as they engage in the so-called *viparīta-maithuna,* an intercourse in which the male is still while the *śakti* moves her body.

We know that every traditional civilization is based on the will to order and give "form," and that the traditional law is not oriented toward what is unqualified, equal, and indefinite, or in other words, toward that impersonal mix in which the various parts of the whole become promiscuously or atomically similar, but rather intends these parts to be themselves and to express as perfectly as possible their own typical nature. Therefore, particularly with regard to the genders, man and woman are two different types; those who are born as men must realize themselves as men, while those who are born as women must realize themselves as women, overcoming any mixture and promiscuity of vocations. Even in regard to the supernatural vocation, man and woman must both have their own distinctive paths to follow, which cannot be altered without them turning into contradictory and inorganic ways of being.

I have already considered the way of being that corresponds eminently to man; I have also discussed the two main paths of approach to the value of "being a principle to oneself," namely, action and contemplation. Thus, the warrior (the hero) and the ascetic represent the two fundamental types of pure virility. In symmetry with these types, there are also two types available to the feminine nature. A woman realizes herself as such and even rises to the same level reached by a man as warrior and ascetic only as lover and mother. These are bipartitions of the same ideal strain; just as there is an active heroism, there is also a passive heroism; there is a heroism of absolute affirmation and a heroism of absolute dedication. They can both be luminous and produce plenty of fruits, as far as overcoming human limitations and achieving liberation are concerned, when they are lived with purity and in the sense of an offering. This differentiation of the heroic strain determines the distinctive character of the paths of fulfillment available to men and women. In the case of women the actions of the warrior and of the ascetic who affirm themselves in a life that is beyond life, the former through pure action and the latter through pure detachment, correspond to the act of the woman totally giving of herself and being entirely for another being, whether he is the loved one (the type of the lover—the Aphrodistic woman) or the son (the type of the mother—the Demetrian woman), finding in this dedication the meaning of her own life, her own joy, and her own justification. This is what *bhakti* or *fides,* which constitute the normal and natural way of participation of the traditional woman, really mean, both in the order of "form" and even beyond "form" when it is lived in a radical and impersonal way. To realize oneself in an increasingly resolute way according to these two distinct and unmistakable directions; to reduce in a woman all that is masculine and in a man everything that is feminine; and to strive to implement the archetypes of the "absolute man" and of the "absolute woman"—this was the traditional law concerning the sexes according to their different planes of existence.

Therefore, a woman could traditionally participate in the sacred hierarchical order only in a mediated fashion, through her relationship with a man. In India women did not have their own initiation even when they belonged to a higher caste: before they got married they did not belong to the sacred community of the noble ones (*ārya*) other than through their fathers, and when they were married, through their husbands, who also represented the mystical head of the family.[3] In Doric Hellas, the woman in her entire life did not enjoy any rights; before getting married, her κύριος was her father. In Rome, in conformity with a similar spirituality, a woman, far from being "equal" to man, was juridically regarded as a daughter of her own husband *(filiae loco)* and as a sister of her own children *(sororis loco);* when she was a young girl, she was under the *potestas* of her father, who was the leader and the priest of his own gens; when she married, according to a rather blunt expression she was *in manu viri*. These traditional decrees regulating a woman's dependency can also be found in other civilizations;[4] far from being unjust and arrogant, as the modern "free spirits" are quick to decry, they helped to define the limits and the natural place of the only spiritual path proper to the pure feminine nature.

I will mention here some ancient views that expressly describe the pure type of the traditional woman, who is capable of an offering that is half human and half divine. In the Aztec-Nahua tradition the same privilege of heavenly immortality proper to the warrior aristocracy was partaken of by the mothers who died while giving birth, since the Aztecs considered this sacrifice on the same level as the one made by those who die on the battlefield. Another example is the type of the traditional Hindu woman, a woman who in the deepest recesses of her soul was capable of the most extreme forms of sensuality and yet who lived by an invisible and votive *fides*. By virtue of this *fides*, that offering that was manifested in the erotic dedication of her body, person, and will culminated in another type of offering—of a different kind and way beyond the world of the senses. Because of this *fides* the bride would leap into the funerary pyre in order to follow the man whom she had married into the

---

3. "Apart from their husbands women cannot sacrifice or undertake a vow or fast; it is because a wife obeys her husband that she is exalted in heaven." *The Laws of Manu* 5.155. It is not possible in this context to discuss the meaning of female priesthood and to explain why it does not contradict the abovementioned example. Female priesthood traditionally had a lunar character; rather than representing another path available to women, it expressed an affirmation of feminine *dharma* as an absolute elimination of any personal principle so as to make room for the voice of the oracle and of the god. Further on I will discuss the alteration proper of decadent civilizations in which the lunar, feminine element usurps the hierarchical peak. We must also consider the sacral and initiatory use of women in the "path of sex."

4. In an ancient Chinese text, the *Niu-kie-tsi-pien* (5) we read: "When a woman leaves the house of her father to join the house of her husband, she loses everything, including her name. She does not own anything in her own right; whatever she has and whatever she is belongs to her husband." And in the *Niu-hien-shu* it is said that a woman must be in the house "as a shadow and as a mere echo." Quoted in S. Trovatelli, *Le civilta e le legislazioni dell'antico Oriente* (Bologna, 1890), 157–58.

next life. This traditional sacrifice, which was regarded as a sheer "barbarism" by Europeans and by Westernized Hindus and in which the widow was burnt alive with the body of the dead husband, is called *sati* in Sanskrit, from the root *as* and the prefix *sat* (being), from which the word *satya* (the truth) comes; *sati* also signifies "gift," "faithfulness," "love."[5] Therefore this sacrifice was considered as the supreme culmination of the relationship between two beings of a different sex and as the sign of an absolute type of relationship, from the point of view of truth and superhumanity. In this context man provides the role of the support for a liberating *bhakti,* and love becomes a door and a pathway. According to the traditional teaching the woman who followed her husband in death attained "heaven"; she was transformed into the same substance as her deceased husband[6] since she partook of that transfiguration (which occurred through the incineration of the material body) into a divine body of light, symbolized among Aryan civilizations by the ritual burning of the cadaver.[7] We find an analogous renunciation of life on the part of Germanic women if their husbands or lovers died in battle.

I have previously suggested that, generally speaking, the essence of *bhakti* consists of indifference toward the object or the means of an action, that is, in pure action and in a selfless attitude. This helps us understand how the ritual sacrifice of a widow (*sati*) could have been institutionalized in a traditional civilization such as the Hindu. Whenever a woman gives herself and even sacrifices herself only because of a stronger and reciprocated bond of human passion toward another being, her actions are still on the level of ordinary events; only when her dedication can support and develop itself without any other external motivation whatsoever, does she truly participate in a transcendent dimension.

In Islam the institution of the harem was inspired by these motivations. In Christian Europe it would take the idea of God for a woman to renounce her public life and to withdraw to a cloistered life; and even in this case, this was the choice of only a very few. In Islam a man sufficed to provide such a motivation and the cloistered life of the harem was considered as a natural thing that no wellborn woman would ever criticize or intend to avoid; it seemed natural for a woman to concentrate all her life on one man only, who was loved in such a vast and unselfish way as to allow

---

5. Analogous customs are also found among other Indo–European stocks: among the Thracians, the Greeks, the Scythians, and Slavs. In the Inca civilization the suicide of widows, though it was not decreed by a law, was nevertheless common practice; those women who had not the courage to commit suicide or believed they had good reasons not to commit it, were despised by their community.

6. "The woman who is not unfaithful to her husband but restrains her mind and heart, speech, and body reaches her husband's worlds after death, and good people call her a virtuous woman." *The Laws of Manu* 9.29.

7. "In this fire the gods offer a person. From this oblation the man arises having the color of light." *Bṛhad-āraṇyaka Upaniṣad* 4.2.14. See also Proclus, *In Timeum,* 5.331b; 2.65b.

other women to share in the same feeling and to be united to him through the same
bond and the same dedication. What surfaces in all this is the character of "purity,"
which is considered to be essential in this path. A love that sets conditions and requires the reciprocated love and the dedication of a man was reputed to be of an
inferior kind. On the other hand, a real man could not know love in this way other
than by becoming feminine, thus losing that inner self-sufficiency thanks to which a
woman finds in him a support and something that motivates and excites her desire to
totally give herself to him. According to the myth Śiva, who was conceived as the
great ascetic of the mountain peaks, turned Kāma (the god of love) into ashes with a
single glance when the latter tried to awaken in him passion for his bride, Pārvatī.
Likewise, there is a profound meaning in the legend about the Kalki-avatara, which
talks about a woman who could not be possessed by anybody because the men who
desired her and fell in love with her turned into women as the result of their passion.
As far as the woman is concerned, there is true greatness in her when she is capable
of giving without asking for anything in return; when she is like a flame feeding
itself; when she loves even more as the object of her love does not commit himself,
does not open himself up, and even creates some distance; and finally, when the
man is not perceived by her as a mere husband or lover, but as her lord. The spirit
animating the harem consisted in the struggle to overcome jealousy and thus the
passionate selfishness and the woman's natural inclination to possess the man. A
woman was asked to commit herself to the harem from her adolescence to her old
age and to be faithful to a man who could enjoy other women beside herself and
possess them all without "giving" himself to any one in particular. In this "inhuman"
trait there was something ascetical and even sacred.[8] In this apparent reification of
woman, she experienced a true possession, an overcoming, and even a liberation
because vis-à-vis such an unconditional *fides*, a man, in his human appearance, was
just a means to higher ends; thus she discovered new possibilities to achieve higher
goals. Just as the rule of the harem imitated the rule of the convents, likewise the
Islamic law regulating a woman's life (according to the possibilities of her own nature, without excluding, but on the contrary, including and even exasperating the life
of the senses) elevated her to the same plane of monastic asceticism.[9] To a lesser

8. In *The Laws of Manu* it is written: "A girl, a young woman or even an old woman should not do anything
independently, even in her own house. In childhood a woman should be under her father's control, in
youth under her husband's, and when her husband is dead, under her sons'" (5.147–48). And also: "A
virtuous wife should constantly serve her husband like a god, even if he behaves badly, freely indulges his
lust, and is devoid of any good qualities" (5.154).
9. The sacral offering of the body and of virginity itself has been sanctioned in a rigorous form in what
amounts to yet another cause of scandal for our contemporaries, namely, in sacred prostitution, which
was practiced in ancient Syrian, Lician, Lidian, and Theban temples. The woman was not supposed to
offer her virginity out of a passional motive toward a given man; she was supposed to give herself to the
first man who tossed her a sacred coin within the sacred enclosure, as if it were a sacred offering to the

degree, an analogous attitude in a woman should be considered the natural presupposition in those civilizations, such as Greece and Rome, in which the institution of concubinage enjoyed a sort of regular character and was legally acknowledged as a way to complement the monogamic marriage and in which sexual exclusivism was overcome.

It goes without saying that I am not referring here to the harem or analogous institutions in mere materialistic terms. I have in mind what the harem meant to the pure traditional idea, and the superior possibility inspiring these institutions. It is the task of Tradition to create solid riverbeds, so that the chaotic currents of life may flow in the right direction. Free are those people who, upon undertaking this traditional direction, do not experience it as a burden but rather develop it naturally and recognize themselves in it so as to actualize through an inner élan the highest and most "traditional" possibility of their own nature. The others, those who blindly follow the institutions and obey and live them without understanding them are not what we may call "self-supported" beings: although devoid of light, their obedience virtually leads them beyond their limitations as individuals and orients them in the same direction followed by those who are free. But for those who follow neither the spirit nor the form of the traditional riverbed, there is nothing but chaos; they are the lost, the "fallen" ones.

This is the case of our contemporaries as far as the woman is concerned. And yet it was not possible that a world that has "overcome" (to employ a Jacobin term) the caste system by returning to every human being his or her own "dignity" and "rights" could preserve some sense of the correct relationship between the two sexes. The emancipation of women was destined to follow that of the slaves and the glorification of people without a caste and without traditions, namely, the *pariah*. In a society that no longer understands the figure of the ascetic and of the warrior; in which the hands of the latest aristocrats seem better fit to hold tennis rackets or shakers for cocktail mixes than swords or sceptres; in which the archetype of the virile man is represented by a boxer or by a movie star if not by the dull wimp represented by the intellectual, the college professor, the narcissistic puppet of the artist, or the busy and dirty money-making banker and the politician—in such a society it was only a matter of time before women rose up and claimed for themselves a "personality" and a "freedom" according to the anarchist and individualist meaning usually associated with these words. And while

---

goddess of the temple. A woman was supposed to get married only after this ritual offering of her body. Herodotus (*The Histories*, 1.199) noted that: "The woman goes with the first man who throws her a coin, and rejects no one. When she has gone with him, and so satisfied the goddess, she returns home, and from that time forth no gift however great will prevail with her."

traditional ethics asked men and women to be themselves to the utmost of their capabilities and express with radical traits their own gender-related characteristics—the new "civilization" aims at leveling everything since it is oriented to the formless and to a stage that is truly not beyond but on this side of the individuation and differentiation of the sexes.

What truly amounts to an abdication was thus claimed as a "step forward." After centuries of "slavery" women wanted to be themselves and to do whatever they pleased. But so-called feminism has not been able to devise a personality for women other than by imitating the male personality, so that the woman's "claims" conceal a fundamental lack of trust in herself as well as her inability to be and to function as a real woman and not as a man. Due to such a misunderstanding, the modern woman has considered her traditional role to be demeaning and has taken offense at being treated "only as a woman." This was the beginning of a wrong vocation; because of this she wanted to take her revenge, reclaim her "dignity," prove her "true value" and compete with men in a man's world. But the man she set out to defeat is not at all a real man, only the puppet of a standardized, rationalized society that no longer knows anything that is truly differentiated and qualitative. In such a civilization there obviously cannot be any room for legitimate privileges and thus women who are unable and unwilling to recognize their natural traditional vocation and to defend it (even on the lowest possible plane, since no woman who is sexually fulfilled ever feels the need to imitate and to envy man) could easily demonstrate that they too virtually possess the same faculties and talents—both material and intellectual—that are found in the other sex and that, generally speaking, are required and cherished in a society of the modern type. Man for his part has irresponsibly let this happen and has even helped and "pushed" women into the streets, offices, schools, and factories, into all the "polluted" crossroads of modern culture and society. Thus the last leveling push has been imparted.

And wherever the spiritual emasculation of materialistic modern man did not tacitly restore the primacy (typically found in ancient gynaecocratic communities) of the woman as *hetaera*, ruling over men enslaved by their senses and at her service, the results have been the degeneration of the feminine type even in her somatic characteristics, the atrophy of her natural possibilities, the suppression of her unique inner life. Hence the types of the woman-*garçonne* and the shallow and vain woman, incapable of any élan beyond herself, utterly inadequate as far as sensuality and sinfulness are concerned because to the modern woman the possibilities of physical love are often not as interesting as the narcissistic cult of her body, or as being seen with as many or as few clothes as possible, or as engaging in physical training, dancing, practicing sports, pursuing wealth, and so on. As it is, Europe knew very little about the purity of the offering and about the faithfulness of the one who gives her all without asking anything in return; or about a love strong enough so as not to be exclusivist. Besides a purely conformist and bourgeois faithfulness, the love Europe has celebrated is the love that does not tolerate the other person's lack of commitment. Now when a woman, before consecrating herself to a man, pretends that he belongs to her body and soul, not only has she already "humanized" and impoverished her offering, but worse yet, she has begun to betray the pure essence of femininity in order to borrow characteristics typical of the male nature—and possibly the lowest of these: the yearning to possess and lay claims over another person, and the pride of the ego. After that, everything else came tumbling down in a rush, following the law of acceleration. Eventually, because of the woman's increased egocentrism, men will no longer be of interest to her; she will only care about what they will be able to offer to satisfy her pleasure or her vanity. In the end she will even incur forms of corruption that usually accompany superficiality, namely, a practical and superficial lifestyle of a masculine type that has perverted her nature and thrown her into the same male pit of work, profits, frantic activity, and politics.

The same holds true for the results of the Western "emancipation" of women, which is on its way to infecting the rest of the world faster than a plague. Traditional woman or the absolute woman, in giving herself, in her living for another, in *wanting* to be only for another being with simplicity and purity fulfilled herself, belonged to herself, displayed her own *heroism,* and even became superior to ordinary men. Modern woman in wanting to be for herself has destroyed herself. The "personality" she so much yearned for is killing all semblance of female personality in her.

It is easy to foresee what will become of the relationship between the sexes, even from a material point of view. Here too, like in magnetism, the higher and stronger the creative spark, the more radical the polarity; the more a man is a man, the more a woman is a woman. What could possibly go on between these mixed beings lacking all contact with the forces of their deepest nature? between these beings for whom sex is reduced to the physiological plane? between these beings who, in the deepest recesses of their souls, are neither men nor women, or who are masculine women or feminine men, and who claim to have reached full sexual emancipation while truly having only regressed? All relationships are destined to have an ambiguous and crumbling character: the comradely promiscuities and morbid "intellectual" sympathies such as are commonplace in the new communist realism. In other words, modern woman will be affected by neurotic complexes and all the other complexes upon which Freud constructed a "science" that is truly a sign of our times. The possibilities of the world of the "emancipated" woman are not dissimilar: the avant-gardes of this world (North America and Russia) are already present, and give interesting and very meaningful testimonies to this fact.[10]

All this cannot but have repercussions on an order of things that goes way beyond what our contemporaries, because of their recklessness, will ever suspect.

10. According to some statistics gathered in the 1950s (C. Freed and W. Kroger), an estimated 75 percent of North-American women are "sexually anesthetized," while their "libido" has allegedly shifted in the direction of exhibitionist narcissism. In Anglo-Saxon women, the neurotic and typically feminine sexual inhibition was typical of their culture and was due to their being victims of a false ideal of "dignity" in addition to the prejudices of puritan moralism. The reaction of the so-called sexual revolution has only led the masses to a regimen of quick, easy, and cheap sex treated as an item of consumption.

21

The Decline of Superior Races

The modern world is far from being threatened by the danger of underpopulation; the cry of alarm some political leaders have launched in the past with the absurd slogan "there is power in numbers," is totally unfounded. The truth is that we are facing an opposite danger: the constant and untrammeled increase of population in purely quantitative terms. The deterioration of the population affects only those stocks that should be considered the bearers of the forces that preside over the demos and the world of the masses and that contribute to any authentic human greatness. When I criticized the racist worldview I mentioned that occult power when present, alive, and at work constitutes the principle of a superior generation that reacts on the world of quantity by bestowing upon it a form and quality. In this regard, one can say that the superior Western races have been agonizing for many centuries and that the increasing growth in world population has the same meaning as the swarming of worms on a decomposing organism or as the spreading of cancerous cells: cancer is an uncontrolled hypertrophy of a plasma that devours the normal, differentiated structures of an organism after subtracting itself from the organism's regulating laws. This is the scenario facing the modern world: the regression and the decline of fecundating (in the higher sense of the term) forces and the forces that bear forms parallels the unlimited proliferation of "matter," of what is formless, of the masses.

This phenomenon must be related to what I have mentioned in the previous chapter concerning the sexes and concerning the relationship between men and women in this day and age, since they affect the issue of procreation and its meaning. If it is true that the modern world seems destined not to know any longer what the absolute woman and the absolute man are all about, and if in this world the sexualization is incomplete, that is, limited to the corporeal plane—then it must seem natural that the superior and even transcendent dimensions of sex, known by the world of Tradition in multiple forms, have been lost, and that this loss may affect the regimen of sexual unions and the possibilities offered by them either as a pure erotic experience or in view of a procreation that may not exhaust itself in a simple, opaque biological event.

The world of Tradition effectively knew a sexual *sacrum* and a magic of sex. What constantly transpires in countless symbols and customs from all parts of the world is the acknowledgment of sex as a creative and primordial force, rather than as a generative power.

In the woman, abyssal powers of passion and light, of danger and disintegration, were evoked.[1] The chthonic power—namely, the Earth—lived in her while Heaven lived in man. Everything that is experienced by ordinary men in the form of peri-pheral sensations and passional and corporeal impulses was assumed in an organic and conscious way. Generation was decreed[2] and the being who was generated was willed as the "child of duty," namely, as one who must undertake and nourish the supernatural element of his stock and the liberation of the ancestor, and who must receive and pass on to future generations strength, life, and stability. Today, all this has become an inane fancy; men, instead of being in control of sex are controlled by it and wander about like drunkards without having the least clue as to what takes place in the course of their embraces, and without seeing the guiding principle acting behind their quest for pleasure or behind their own passions. Without people being aware of any of this, beyond and often against their own will, what comes into existence as a result of their intercourse is a new being who will have no spiritual continuity and, as in the case of the most recent generations, even without the pale residue constituted by bourgeois affective bonds.

This being the case, it is no wonder the superior races are dying out before the ineluctible logic of individualism, which especially in the so-called contemporary "higher classes," has caused people to lose all desire to procreate. Not to mention all the other degenerative factors connected to a mechanized and urbanized social life and especially to a civilization that no longer respects the healthy and creative limitations constituted by the castes and by the traditions of blood lineage. Thus proliferation is concentrated in the lower social classes and in the inferior races where the animal-like impulse is stronger than any rational calculation and consideration. The unavoidable effects are a *reversed selection* and the ascent and the onslaught of inferior elements against which the "race" of the superior castes and people, now exhausted and defeated, can do very little as a spiritually dominating element.

1. J. Evola, *Eros and the Mysteries of Love,* especially chapters 5 ("Sacred Ceremonies and Evocations") and 6 ("Sex in the Realm of Initiations and Magic").
2. In the Upaniṣads there are some expressions that describe sexual intercourse: "With power and glory I give you glory." Also: "This man *(ama)* am I; that woman *(sa),* thou! That woman thou, this man am I. I am the heaven; thou the earth! Come, let us two together clasp! Together let us semen mix, a male, a son for to procure." (*Bṛhad-āraṇyaka Upaniṣad* 6.4.8; 6.4.20–22.)

Though today people talk more frequently about "population control" in view of the catastrophic effects of the demographical phenomenon that I have compared to a cancer, this still does not address the essential issue, since a differentiated and qualitative criterion does not come into play at all. But those who oppose population control on the basis of traditionalist and pseudomoralistic ideas, which nowadays amount to mere prejudices, are guilty of an even greater obtuseness. If what really matters is the greatness and the might of a stock, it is useless to be concerned about the material quality of fatherhood unless an equal concern for its spiritual dimension is present as well in the sense of superior interests, of the correct relationship between the sexes, and above all, of what is really meant by *virility*—of what it still signifies on a plane that is not merely naturalistic.

After exposing the decadence of modern woman, we must not forget that man is mostly responsible for such a decadence. Just like the plebeian masses would have never been able to make their way into all the domains of social life and of civilization if real kings and real aristocrats would have been in power, likewise, in a society run by real men, woman would never have yearned for or even been capable of taking the path she is following today. The periods in which women have reached autonomy and preeminence almost always have coincided with epochs marked by manifest decadence in ancient civilizations. Thus, the best and most authentic reaction against feminism and against every other female aberration should not be aimed at women as such, but at men instead. It should not be expected of women that they return to what they really are and thus reestablish the necessary inner and outer conditions for a reintegration of a superior race, when men themselves retain only the semblance of true virility.

If all efforts to reawaken the spiritual dimension of sexuality fail, and if the form of virility is not separated from what has become an amorphous and promiscuous spiritual substance, then everything is in vain. The virility that is physical, phallic, muscular, and animal is lifeless and does not contain any creative germ in the superior sense. Phallic man deceives himself by thinking that he dominates; the truth is that he is passive and is always susceptible to the subtler power of women and to the feminine principle.[3] The differentiation of the sexes is authentic and absolute only in the spirit.

In all superior types of Tradition, man has always been considered the bearer of the lineage of the Uranian, solar principle; this principle transcends the mere "blood" principle, which is lost as soon as it converges into the feminine lineage. Its development is favored by the fertile ground represented by a pure woman belonging to a

---

3. J. Evola, *Eros and the Mysteries of Love.*

higher caste, but in any event, it always remains the qualifying principle that bestows a form and that orders the feminine generating substance.[4] This principle is related to the same supernatural element, to the power that can "make the current ascend upward" and of which "victory," "fortune," and prosperity of a particular stock are usually the consequences. Hence the symbolical association (which did not have an obscene, but rather a real and deep meaning), typical of ancient traditional forms,[5] of the male organ with ideas of resurrection, asceticism, and energies that confer the highest powers. As an echo of superior meanings found even among savage populations, we find expressed in clear terms the idea that only the initiate is a true male, and that initiation marks in an eminent way one's entrance into virility; this means that prior to initiation, the individuals, notwithstanding their physical appearance, "have not yet turned into men," and even if they are old they belong to the same group of children and women and are deprived of all the privileges of the clan's virile elites. When the superbiological element that is the center and the measure of true virility is lost, people can call themselves men, but in reality they are just eunuchs and their paternity simply reflects the quality of animals who, blinded by instinct, procreate randomly other animals, who in turn are mere vestiges of existence.

If the expired civilization is propped up so as to make it look alive, and if men are treated like rabbits or stallions, their unions being carefully and rationally planned, let no one be fooled; what they will generate will either be a civilization of very beautiful animals destined to work, or, if the individualistic and utilitarian element predominates, a stronger law will lead the races toward the path of regression or extinction according to the same inexorability of the law of entropy and the degradation of energy. What will then be registered by future historians is only one of the several aspects of the "decline of the West" that are today very much in evidence.

4. "Of the seed and the womb, the seed is said to be more important, for the offspring of all living beings are marked by the mark of the seed. Whatsoever sort of seed is sown in a field prepared at the right season, precisely that sort of seed grows in it, manifesting its own particular qualities." *The Laws of Manu*, 9.35–36. On this basis the caste system even practiced hypergamy: the man from a higher caste was allowed to marry women of lower castes, no matter how high his caste was (*The Laws of Manu*, 3.13). It is possible to find among savage populations the idea of the duality of the blood and the spirit that is passed on exclusively through the male lineage.

5. In the Hindu tradition the male semen is often called *vīrya*, a term that in texts describing ascetical practices (especially Buddhist) is also used to designate that "upward-streaming" force that has the power of spiritually renewing all the human faculties. As a sign of distinction Śaivite ascetics and yogis carry the *phallus* emblem around their necks. The reason why in places like Lydia, Phrygia, and Etruria tombs were ornate with phalli or with statues of an ithyphallic form was to express the association between the virile force and the power of resurrection. Likewise, in ancient Hellenism, the ithyphallic Hermes represented the resurrected primordial man "who did, does, and will stand" through the various phases of the manifestation (Hippolytus, *Philosophumena*, 5.8.14). An echo of this reverberates in an ancient Roman superstition that regarded the phallus as an amulet capable of warding off fascinations and nefarious influences.

By way of introduction to the second part of this work, let me make a final point that is directly related to what I have previously mentioned concerning the relationships between spiritual virility and devotional religiosity. From these last considerations what has emerged is that what in the West goes by the name of "religion" truly corresponds to an essentially "feminine" orientation. The relationship with the supernatural, conceived in a personalized form (theism) as dedication, devotion, and inner renunciation of one's own will before the divine hypostasis presents the typical traits of the path on which a feminine nature may realize itself.

Moreover and, generally speaking, if the feminine element corresponds to the naturalistic element, then it is easy to see why in the world of Tradition the inferior castes and races (in which the naturalistic element was more predominant than in those castes and races governed by the power of aristocratic rituals and divine heritage) benefitted from the participation in a higher order precisely through relationships of a "religious" type. Thus, even "religion" could have a place and exercise its function within the whole hierarchy, though subordinated and relative to higher forms of spiritual realization such as initiation and the various types of higher asceticism.

Following the mixing of the castes or of analogous social bodies and the coming to power of the inferior social strata and races, it was unavoidable that their spirit triumphed even in this regard; that any relationship with the supernatural would be conceived exclusively in terms of "religion"; that any other higher form came under suspicion and was even stigmatized as sacrilegious and demonic. This feminization of spirituality was already foreshadowed in ancient times. Wherever it prevailed, it determined the first alteration of the primordial tradition in the races.

The object of the considerations I will articulate in the second part of my work is to analyze this process of decadence together with all those processes that have led to the collapse of primordial humanity; through these the genesis and face of the "modern world" will become manifest.

PART TWO

Genesis and face of the Modern World

Many things are known by the Wise. They foresee many things: the decline of the world and the end of the Aesir.

—*Voluspa*, 44

I reveal to you a secret. The time has come when the Groom will crown the Bride. But where is the crown? In the North . . . And whence comes the Groom? From the Center, where the heat generates the Light and turns towards the North . . . where the Light becomes radiant. What are the people living in the South doing? They have fallen asleep in the heat; but they will reawaken in the storm and many among them will be terrified unto death.

—J. Boehme, *Aurora*, 2.11.43

Introduction

I would like to point out the difference between the methodology employed in the first part of this work and the methodology adopted in the second part.

In the first part, which had a morphological and typological character, I attempted to draw from various testimonies those elements that were more suitable for characterizing, in a universal and metahistorical fashion, the nature of the traditional spirit and the traditional view of the world, of man, and of life. Therefore, I neglected to examine the relationship between the chosen elements and the overall spirit of the different historical traditions to which they belonged. Those elements that in the context of a particular and concrete tradition did not conform to the traditional spirit were considered to be absent and unable to influence the value and the meaning of the rest of the elements. I did not even attempt to determine up to what point certain attitudes and historical institutions had truly been "traditional" in the spirit rather than just the form.

Now my approach is going to be different. I will attempt to follow the dynamic unfolding of the traditional and antitraditional forces in history, and therefore it will no longer be possible to apply the same methodology; it will be impossible to isolate and to bring out some particular elements in the complex of various historical civilizations because of their "traditional potential." The overall spirit of a given civilization and the way it has concretely utilized all of the elements included in it, will now become the relevant and specific object of my discussion. The synthetic consideration of the forces at work will replace my analysis, which had previously isolated the valid elements. I will attempt to discover the "dominating factor" within the various historical complexes and to determine the value of the different elements, not in an absolute and abstract way, but according to the action they exercised within a given civilization.

While so far I have attempted to integrate the historical and particular element with the ideal, universal, and "typical" element, I will henceforth attempt to integrate the ideal element with the real one. The latter integration, just like the former, more than following the methods and the results of the researches of modern critical historiography, is going to be based mainly on a "traditional" and metaphysical perspective, on the intuition of a sense that cannot be deduced from the individual elements but that presupposes them; by beginning from this sense it is possible to grasp the different instrumental and organic roles that such elements may have played in various eras of the past and in the different historically conditioned forms.

Therefore, it may happen that whatever has been left out in the first integration will become prominent in the second integration, and vice versa; in the framework of a given civilization some elements may be valued and considered to be decisive, while in other civilizations they are present but in the background and deemed to be irrelevant.

This warning may be helpful to a certain category of readers. To shift from the consideration of Tradition as metahistory to the consideration of Tradition as history implies a change of perspectives; it causes the same elements to be valued differently; it causes united things to become separated and separated things to unite according to whatever the contingencies of history may determine from case to case.

22

The Doctrine of the Four Ages

Although modern man until recently has viewed and celebrated the meaning of the history known to him as epitomizing progress and evolution, the truth as professed by traditional man is quite the opposite. In all the ancient testimonies of traditional humanity it is possible to find, in various forms, the idea of a regression or a fall: from originally higher states beings have stooped to states increasingly conditioned by human, mortal, and contingent elements. This involutive process allegedly began in a very distant past; the term that best characterizes it is the Eddic term *ragna-rokkr,* "the twilight of the gods." In the traditional world this teaching was not expressed in a vague and generic form, but rather was articulated in the organic doctrine of the four ages, which can be found with a large degree of uniformity in different civilizations. According to Tradition, the actual sense of history and the genesis of what I have labeled, generally speaking, as the "modern world," results from a process of gradual decadence through four cycles or "generations."

The best known form of the doctrine of the four ages is that which was typical of the Greco-Roman tradition. Hesiod wrote about four eras symbolized by four metals (gold, silver, bronze, and iron), inserting between the last two a fifth era, the era of the "heroes," which as we shall see, had only the meaning of a partial and special restoration of the primordial state.[1] The Hindu tradition knows the same doctrine in the form of four cycles, called respectively, Satya Yuga (or Kṛta Yuga), Tretā Yuga, Dvāpara Yuga, and Kali Yuga (or Dark Age),[2] together with the simile of the failing, during each of these, of one of the four hoofs or supports of the bull symbolizing *dharma,* or the traditional law. The Persian version of this myth is similar to the Hellenic version: the four ages are known and characterized by gold, silver, steel, and an "iron compound." The Chaldean version articulated this same view in almost identical terms.

1. Hesiod, *Works and Days,* 5.109 ff.
2. *The Laws of Manu,* 1.81–83.

In particular, we can find a more recent simile of the chariot of the universe represented as a quadriga led by the supreme god; the quadriga is carried along a circular course by four horses representing the elements. The four ages were believed to correspond to the alternate predominance of each of these horses, which then leads the others according to the more or less luminous and rapid symbolic nature of the element that it represents.[3] This view reappears, although in a special transposition, in the Hebrew tradition. In one of the prophetic writings[4] mention is made of a very bright statue with the head made of gold, the chest and the arms of silver, the belly and the thighs of copper, the legs and the feet, of iron and tile. This statue's four parts represent the four "kingdoms" that follow one another, beginning with the golden kingdom of the "king of kings" who has received "dominion, strength, power, and glory from the god of Heaven." If Egypt knew the tradition mentioned by Eusebius concerning three distinct dynasties consisting respectively of gods, demigods, and *manes,* we can see in them the equivalent of the first three ages (golden, silver, and bronze). Likewise, the ancient Aztec traditions speak about five suns or solar cycles, the first four of which correspond to the elements and in which, as in the Eurasian traditions, one finds portrayed the catastrophes of fire, water (flood), and the struggles against giants characterizing the cycle of "heroes" that Hesiod added to the other four—in this we may recognize a variation of the same teaching, the memory of which may also be found more or less fragmentarily among other populations.

Upon examining the meaning of each of these periods, it is opportune to anticipate some general considerations, since the abovementioned view is in open contrast with the modern views concerning prehistory and the primordial world. To uphold with Tradition that in the beginning there were no animal-like cavemen, but rather "more-than-human" beings, and that in ancient prehistory there was no "civilization" but an "era of the gods";[5] this to many people—who in one way or another believe in the gospel of Darwinism—amounts to pure and simple "mythology." Since I have not invented this mythology myself, however, critics still have to explain its existence, that is, the fact that according to the most ancient testimonies and writings there is no memory that may lend support to "evolutionism"; what is found in them instead is the opposite, in other words, the recurrent idea of a better, brighter, and superhuman ("divine") past. These same testimonies also know very little about "animal origins"; constant mention is made rather of the original relationship between men and deities; and a memory is kept alive of a primordial state of immortality together with the idea that the law of death appeared at one particular moment,

---

3. Dio Chrysostom, *Orationes,* 36.39.
4. Daniel 2:31–45.
5. Cicero, *De legibus* 2.11: *"Antiquitas proxime accedit ad deos"* (Ancient times came very close to the gods).

almost as an unnatural fact or as an anathema. In two characteristic testimonies, the cause of the "fall" was identified with the mixing of the "divine" race with the human race, which was regarded as inferior; in some texts that "sin" is compared to sodomy and to sexual mating with animals. On the one hand there is the biblical myth of the Ben Elohim, "the children of the gods," who mated with the "daughters of men," with the consequence that in the end, "all mortals led depraved lives on earth."[6] On the other hand there is the Platonic myth of the inhabitants of Atlantis, conceived as the descendants and disciples of the gods, who lost the divine element and eventually allowed their human nature to become predominant because of their repeated intermingling with human beings.[7] Tradition, in more recent eras, developed a variety of myths referring to races as bearers of civilization and to the struggles between divine races and animal, cyclopic, or demonic races. They are the Aesir against the Elementarwesen; the Olympians and the heroes against giants and monsters of the darkness, the water, and the earth. They are the Aryan *deva* fighting against the *asura*, "the enemies of the divine heroes"; they are the Incas, the dominators who impose their solar laws on the aborigines who worshipped "Mother Earth"; they are the Tuatha dé Danaan, who, according to Irish legends overcame the dreadful race of the Fomors; and so on. On this basis it can be argued that even though the traditional teaching retains the memory of the existence of stocks that could even correspond to the animalistic and inferior types described in the theory of evolution (this was the substratum predating the civilizations created by superior races), evolutionism mistakenly considers these animal-like stocks to be absolutely primordial, while they are so only relatively.

Another mistake of evolutionism is to conceive of some forms of miscegenation that presuppose the emergence of *other* races that are superior either as civilizations and biological specimens or as products of "evolution." These races had their own origins; because so much time has elapsed (as in the case of the "Hyperborean" and the "Atlantic" races) and because of geophysical factors, these races have left very few traces of their existence and what remains is difficult to spot by those who are merely seeking archaeological and paleontological traces accessible to profane research.

On the other hand, it is significant that populations that still live in the alleged original, primitive, and "innocent" state provide little comfort to the evolutionist

---

6. Gen. 6: 4–13.
7. Plato, *Critias*, 110c; 120d–e; 121a–b: "As long as the divine element in their nature survived, they obeyed the laws and loved the divine to which they were akin. But when the divine element in them became weakened by frequent admixture with mortal stock, and their human traits became predominant, they ceased to be able to carry their spiritual legacy with moderation."

hypothesis. These stocks, instead of evolving, tend to become extinguished, thereby demonstrating themselves to be the degenerate residues of cycles the vital potential of which has long since been exhausted; in other words, they are heterogeneous elements and remnants left behind by the mainstream of humanity. This was the case of the Neanderthal man, who in his extreme morphological brutishness closely resembles the "ape-man." Neanderthal man mysteriously disappeared in a given period and the races that followed (Aurignacian man and especially Cro-Magnon man), and that represented a superior type (so much so that we can recognize in it the stock of several contemporary human races), cannot be considered further "evolutionary stages" of this vanished type. The same goes for the Grimaldi race, which also became extinct, and for the many "primitive" populations still in existence: they are not "evolving," but rather becoming extinct. Their "becoming civilized" is not an "evolution" but almost always represents a sudden mutation that affects their vital possibilities. There are species that retain their characteristics even in conditions that are relatively different from their natural ones; other species in similar circumstances instead become extinct; otherwise what takes place is racial mixing with other elements in which no assimilation or real evolution occurs. The result of this interbreeding closely resembles the processes that follow Mendel's laws concerning heredity: once it disappears in the phenotype, the primitive element survives in the form of a separated, latent heredity that is capable of cropping up in sporadic apparitions, even though it is always endowed with a character of heterogeneity in regard to the superior type.

Evolutionists believe they are "positively" sticking to the facts. They ignore that the facts per se are silent, and that if interpreted in different ways they can lend support to the most incredible hypotheses. It has happened, however, that someone, though fully informed of all the data that are adduced to prove the theory of evolution, has shown these data to support the opposite thesis, which in more than one respect corresponds to the traditional teaching. I am referring to the thesis according to which man is not alone in being far from a product of the "evolution" of animal species, but many animal species must be considered as the offshoots or as the "abortions" of a primordial impulse; only in the racially superior human species does this primordial impulse find its direct and adequate manifestation.[8] There are also ancient myths about the struggle between divine races and monstrous entities or animal-like demons that allegedly took place before the advent of the human race (humanity at its earliest stage). These myths may refer to the struggle of the primordial

8. Douglas Dewar, *The Transformist Illusion* (1957).

human principle against its intrinsic animalistic potentialities, which were eventually isolated and left behind, so to speak, in the form of certain animal stocks. As far as the alleged "ancestors" of mankind (such as the anthropoid and the Ice Man) are concerned, they could represent the first casualties in the above-mentioned struggle or the best human elements that have been mixed together with or swept away by animal potentialities. If in totemism, which is found in inferior societies, the notion of the mythical collective ancestor of the clan is often confused with that of the demon of a given animal species, this appears to reflect the memory of a similar stage of promiscuity.

Although this is not the proper context to raise the issues related to anthropogenesis, which are to a certain degree of a transcendent nature, the absence of human fossils and the sole presence of animal fossils in remote prehistory may be interpreted to mean that primordial mankind (provided that we may call primordial "man" a type that would be very different from historical mankind) was the last form of life to undergo the process of materialization, which process endowed the earlier, animal-like human species with an organism capable of being.

We may recall here that in some traditions there is the memory of a primordial race characterized by "weak" or "soft bones." For instance Lieh-tzu, when talking about the Hyperborean region in which the present cycle began, mentioned that the inhabitants of this region have "soft bones." In more recent times, the fact that superior races that came from the North did not bury but cremated their dead, is just another factor that needs to be considered when facing the dilemma caused by the absence of pieces of bones.

Somebody may object: "There is no trace whatsoever of this fantastic mankind!" Besides being somewhat naive to think that superior beings could not have existed without leaving behind traces such as ruins, utensils, weapons, and so on, it must be noted that in relatively recent eras there are residues of cyclopic works, though not all of them are typical of a civilized society (the circle at Stonehenge; enormous stones put in a precarious and miraculous equilibrium; the *pedra cansada* in Peru; the colossus of Tiuhuanac and the like). The archaeologists are baffled as to what means were employed just to gather and transport the necessary material. Going back in time, not only should we not conveniently forget what has already been admitted or at least not excluded a priori (that is, the existence of ancient lost lands and also that some lands were formed in recent geological eras), but we should also wonder whether it is fair to exclude a priori that a race in direct spiritual contact with cosmic forces ever existed (as tradition claims to be the case in the origins) just because it did not work on materials such as stone or metal, like those races that no longer have the means to act in accord with the power of the elements and beings.

Rather, it seems to me that the "caveman" is itself a legend: it seems that "primitive" man did not employ caves (many of which betray a sacred orientation) as animal-like dwellings but as places of a cult that has remained in this form even in undoubtedly "civilized" eras (such as the Greek-Minoan cult of caves and the ceremonies and the initiatory retreats on Mount Ida); it is only natural to find therein only traces, as a natural protection of the site, which in other sites the combined work of time, men, and the elements did not leave behind for our contemporaries.

According to a very basic traditional idea, generally speaking, the state of knowledge and of civilization was the natural state, if not of mankind in general, at least of certain primordial elites; and knowledge was not constructed and acquired just as true kingship did not originate from below. Joseph de Maistre, after remarking that what Rousseau and his epigones assumed to be the "natural" state (in reference to savages) is only the last stage of brutishness of some stocks that have either been scattered or suffered the consequences of some primordial act of degradation that affected their deepest substance, correctly pointed out:

> As far as the development of science is concerned, we are blinded by a gross misunderstanding; that is, to assume a judgmental attitude toward those times in which men saw effects in the causes, on the basis of times in which men with effort ascended from the effects to the causes; in which people only care about effects; in which it is said that it is useless to be concerned about causes; and in which people have forgotten what a cause really means.[9]

In the beginning mankind not only possessed a science, but

> A very different science, which originated from above and was therefore very dangerous. This explains why in the beginning science was always mysterious and confined to the temples, in which it eventually became extinct *when the only thing this "flame" could do was to burn.*[10]

Thus, another science was slowly formed as a surrogate, namely, the merely human and empirical science of which our contemporaries are so proud and through which they have thought fit to judge everything that they consider to be civilization. This "science" merely represents the futile attempt to climb back up, through surrogates,

9. J. de Maistre, *Soires de St. Petersburg* (Paris, 1924), 1.63.
10. Ibid., 1.82. One of the things de Maistre points out is that the ancient languages are more essential, organic, and logical than modern ones; they reveal a hidden formative, nonhuman principle, especially when the ancient or "primitive" languages obviously contain fragments of even older languages that have either been lost or fallen into disuse, an eventuality hinted at by Plato himself.

from an unnatural and degenerated state (what is most sad is that it is no longer even perceived to be such) that did not characterize the origins at all.

In any event one must realize that these and similar indications will play a minimal role for those who are not determined to change their own frame of mind. Every epoch has its own "myth" through which it reflects a given collective climate. Today the aristocratic idea that mankind has higher origins, namely, a past of light and of spirit, has been replaced by the democratic idea of evolutionism, which derives the higher from the lower, man from animal, civilization from barbarism. This is not so much the "objective" result of a free and conscious scientific inquiry, but rather one of the many reflections that the advent of the modern world, characterized by inferior social and spiritual strata and by man without traditions, has necessarily produced on the intellectual and cultural plane. Thus we should not delude ourselves: some "positive" superstitions will always produce alibis to defend themselves. The acknowledgment of new horizons will be possible not through the discovery of new "findings," but rather through a new attitude toward these findings. Any attempt to validate even from a scientific perspective what the traditional dogmatic point of view upholds will generate results only among those who are already spiritually well disposed to accept this kind of knowledge.

23

The Golden Age

I will now engage in an ideal and morphological assessment of the cycles corresponding to the four traditional eras; further on I will discuss their geographical and historical trajectories.

First of all, the Golden Age: this era corresponds to an original civilization that was naturally and totally in conformity with what has been called the "traditional spirit." For this reason, in both the location and the stock that the Golden Age is historically and metahistorically associated with, we find symbols and attributes that characterize the highest function of regality—symbols of polarity, solarity, height, stability, glory, and life in a higher sense. In later epochs and in particular traditions, which are already mixed and scattered, the dominating (in a traditional sense) elites effectively appeared as those who still enjoyed or reproduced the state of being of the origins. This allows us—through a shift from the derivative to the integral, so to speak—to deduce also from the titles and the attributes of those dominating strata of society some elements that may help us to characterize the nature of the first era.

The first era is essentially the era of Being, and hence of truth in a transcendent sense.[1] This is evident not only from the Hindu designation of Satya Yuga (*sat* means being, hence *satya* or "truth") but also from the Latin name "Saturn," who is the king or god of the Golden Age. Saturn, who corresponds to the Hellenic Kronos, is a subtle reference to this idea, since in his name we find the Aryan root *sat*, "being," together with the attributive ending *urnus* (as in *nocturnus*).[2] As far as the era of Being or of spiritual stability is concerned, we shall see below that in several representations of the primordial site in which this cycle unfolded it is possible to find the symbols of "terra firma" surrounded by waters, or of the "island," the mountain, or the "middle land."

---

1. Purity of heart, justice, wisdom, and adherence to sacred institutions are qualities that characterized every caste during the first age. See *Viṣṇu Purāṇa* 1.6.
2. *Introduzione alla magia* (Genoa, 1955) 2.80 ff.

As the age of Being the first era is also the era of the Living in the eminent sense of the word. According to Hesiod, death—which for most people is truly an end that bequeaths Hades—made its appearance only during the last two ages (the Iron and Bronze ages). During Kronos's Golden Age "mortal people lived as if they were gods" *(ἰσός τε θεοὶ)*, and "no miserable old age came their way." That cycle ended, "but those men continue to live upon the earth *[τοὶ μεν . . . εἰσι]*" in an invisible way, "mantling themselves in dark mist and watching *[ἠέρα ἐσσαμένοι]* over mortal men";[3] these words allude to the previously mentioned doctrine according to which the representatives of the primordial tradition, as well as their original site, disappeared. In the realm of Yima, the Persian king of the Golden Age, before the new cosmic events forced him to withdraw into a "subterranean" refuge (the inhabitants of which were thus enabled to evade the dark and painful destiny befallen the new generations), there was "neither disease nor death."[4] Yima, "the brilliant, the most glorious of those yet to be born, the sunlike one of men," banished death from his kingdom.[5] Just as in Saturn's golden kingdom, according to both Romans and Greeks, men and immortal gods shared one common life, the rulers of the first of the mythical Egyptian dynasties were called θεοὶ, "gods," or "divine beings." According to a Chaldean myth, death reigns universally only in the postdiluvian era, in which the "gods" left death to men while keeping eternal life for themselves.[6] Tir na mBeo, the "Land of the Living," and Tir na nOg, the "Land of Youth," are the names in the Celtic traditions of an island or a mysterious Atlantic land the Druids believed to be the birthplace of mankind. In the saga *(ea)* . of Conall Cearnach where this land is identified with the "Land of the Victorious One" (Tir na Boadag), it is called "the Land of the Living, in which there is no death or old age."[7]

Moreover, the relationship that the first era always has with gold symbolizes what is incorruptible, solar, luminous, and bright. In the Hellenic tradition gold had a relationship with the radiant splendor of light and with everything that is sacred and

---

3. Hesiod, *Works and Days*, 5.108–202.
4. *Vendidad*, 2.5.
5. *Yasna*, 9.4. Immortality in this context should be regarded as the condition enjoyed by an indestructible soul; therefore there is no contradiction with the longevity that in other traditions characterizes the material or physical life of men during the first age.
6. *Gilgamesh*, 10. In Gen. 6:3, a finite life span (one hundred and twenty years) appeared only at a given moment, thus putting an end to a state of tension between the divine spirit and mankind; that moment corresponds to the beginning of the "Titanic" cycle (third age). In several traditions of primitive populations we find the idea that one never dies because of natural circumstances, since death is always an accident and a violent and unnatural event that should rather be explained through the intervention of adverse magical powers; in this belief we find an echo of the memory of the origins, although in a superstitious form.
7. P. W. Joyce, *Old Celtic Romances* (London, 1879), 106–11.

great;[8] thus anything that was bright, radiant, and beautiful was designated as "golden." In the Vedic tradition the "primordial germ," *hiranya-garbha,* was golden; it was also said: "For gold indeed is fire, light, and immortality."[9] In the Egyptian tradition the king was believed to be made of gold or of the same "solar fluid" the incorruptible body of the heavenly gods and the immortals was made of, so much so that the title "golden" applied to the king ("Horus made of gold") and designated his divine and solar origin, his incorruptibility and indestructibility. Plato believed gold to be the distinctive element that characterized the nature of the race of rulers.[10] From the golden top of Mount Meru, which was considered to be a "pole," the original homeland of mankind, and the Olympian seat of the gods; and from the golden top of the "ancient Asgard," which was believed to be the seat of the Aesir and of the divine Nordic kings located in the "Middle Abode";[11] to the "Pure Land" *(ching-t'u)* and to equivalent locations portrayed in Chinese traditions—time and time again we find the concept of the original cycle in which the spiritual quality symbolized by gold had its definitive and most eminent manifestation. We may also assume that in several myths that mention the deposit or the transmission of some golden object, reference is being made to the deposit or transmission of something closely related to the primordial tradition. According to the Eddic myth, immediately following the *ragna-rokkr* ("the twilight of the gods") a new race and a new sun will arise; then the Aesir will be brought together again, and they will discover the mysterious golden tablets that they possessed in the time of the origins.[12]

Equivalent ideas or further explicitations of the golden symbol during the first era are light, splendor, and the "glory," in that specific triumphal meaning that I already explained when discussing the concept of the Mazdean *hvareno.* According to the Persian tradition, the primordial land (Airyana Vaego) inhabited by the "seed" of the Aryan race and by Yima himself, who was called "The Glorious and the Radiant One," was regarded as "the first of the good lands and countries created by Ahura Mazda."[13] According to an equivalent figuration found in the Hindu tradition, the Sveta-dvīpa, the "white island or continent" situated in the north (just like Aztlan, the northern primordial seat of the Aztecs, which implies the idea of whiteness or brightness) is the place of *tejas,* of a radiant force, and inhabited by the divine

8. Pindar, *The Olympian Odes,* 1.1.
9. *Śatapatha Brāhmaṇa,* 13.4.7.
10. "The god who fashioned you mixed gold in the composition of those among you who are fit to rule, so that they are of the most precious quality." *Republic,* 415d. The golden symbol was applied again (468e) to the heroes, with an explicit reference to the primordial race.
11. Odin's royal palace in Asgard "shines like a room covered with gold, on the top of Gimle." *Voluspa,* 64.
12. *Gylfaginning,* 52.
13. *Vendidad,* 1.3.

Nārāyaṇa, who was regarded as "the light" or as "he in whom a great fire shines, radiating in every direction." The Thule mentioned by the Greeks was characterized as the "Land of the Sun." Someone said: *Thule ultima a sole nomen habens.*" Though the etymology of the word *Thule* is obscure and uncertain, it still signifies the idea the ancients had concerning this divine region and it points to the solar character of the "ancient Tlappallan," Tullan, or Tula (a contraction of *tonalan* = "the place of the Sun"), the original homeland of the Toltecs and the "paradise" of their heroes; it also points to the home of the Hyperboreans, since according to the sacred geography of ancient traditions, the Hyperboreans were a mysterious race that lived in an eternal light and whose region was believed to be the dwelling place and the homeland of the Delphic Apollo, who was the Doric god of light (φοῖβος ἀπόλλον, the "Pure and the Radiant One"), who was also represented as a "golden" god and as a god of the Golden Age.[14] There were stocks like the Boreads that were simultaneously priestly and kingly and who derived their dignity from the Apollonian land of the Hyperboreans.[15] Here too there are plenty of references that can be cited.

Cycle of Being, solar cycle, cycle of light as glory, cycle of the living in an eminent and transcendent sense—these are the characteristics of the first age, the Golden Age, or the "era of the gods" found in the traditional memories.

---

14. Callimachus, *Hymn to Apollo,* 34–35.
15. Diodorus Siculus, *Bibliotheca historica,* 2.11.

The Pole and the Hyperborean Region

A t this time it is important to consider a peculiar characteristic of the primordial age that allows us to associate with it very specific historical and geographical representations. I have previously discussed the symbolism of the "pole." This pole is either represented as an island or as terra firma and symbolizes spiritual stability (the seat of transcendent beings, heroes, and immortals) opposed to the contingency of the "waters"; or as a mountain or "elevated place" usually associated with Olympian meanings. In ancient traditions both of these representations were often associated with the "polar" symbolism that was applied to the supreme center of the world and thus to the archetype of any kind of *regere* in the supreme sense of the word.[1]

In addition to the symbol of the pole, there are some recurrent and very specific traditional data that indicate the North as the site of an island, terra firma, or mountain, the meaning of which is often confused with the location of the first era; in other words, we are confronted by a motif that simultaneously has a spiritual and a real meaning, pointing back to a time when the symbol was reality and the reality a symbol and history and metahistory were not two separated parts but rather two parts reflecting each other. This is precisely the point in which it is possible to enter into the events conditioned by time. Allegedly, according to tradition, in an epoch of remote prehistory that corresponds to the Golden Age or Age of Being, the symbolical island or "polar" land was a real location situated in the Arctic, in the area that today corresponds to the North Pole. This region was inhabited by beings who by virtue of their possession of that nonhuman spirituality (characterized by gold, "glory," light, and life) that in later times will be evoked by the abovementioned symbolism, founded the race that exemplified the Uranian tradition in a pure state; this race, in turn, was

---

1. R. Guénon, *Le Roi du monde,* chaps. 3, 4. The idea of a magnetic "polar" mountain, often located on an island, can be found in different forms and adaptations in Chinese, medieval Nordic, and Islamic legends. See E. Taylor, *Primitive Culture* (London, 1920).

the central and most direct source of the various forms and manifestations this tradition produced in other races and civilizations.[2]

The memory of this Arctic seat is the heritage of the traditions of many people, both in the form of real geographical references and in symbols of its function and its original meaning; these symbols were often elevated to a superhistorical plane, in other words they were applied to other centers that were capable of being considered as replicas of the former. For this reason there is often a confusion of memories, names, myths, and locations, but a trained eye will easily detect the single components. It is noteworthy to emphasize the interference of the Arctic theme with the Atlantic theme, of the mystery of the North with the mystery of the West, since the latter succeeded the original traditional pole as the main seat. We know that owing to an astrophysical cause, that is, to the tilting of the terrestrial axis, in every era there has been a change in climate. According to tradition, this inclination occurred at the specific moment in which the syntony of a physical and a metaphysical event occurred, as if to represent a state of disorder in the natural world that reflected an event of a spiritual nature. When Lieh-tzu described the myth of the giant Kung-Kung who shatters the "column of heaven," he was probably referring to such an event. In this Chinese tradition we also find other concrete references, such as the following one, though it is mixed together with details that describe later cataclysms:

> The pillars of heaven were shattered. The earth shook at its foundations. The northern skies descended lower and lower. The sun, the moon and the stars changed their course [their course appeared changed as a result of the tilting of the terrestrial axis]. The earth's surface cracked and the waters contained in its belly gushed forward and inundated various countries. Man was in a state of rebellion against Heaven and the universe fell victim to chaos. The sun darkened. The planets changed their course [because of the abovementioned shift in perspective] and the great harmony of heaven was destroyed.[3]

In any event, the freezing and the long night descended at a specific time on the polar region. Thus, when the forced migration from this seat ensued, the first cycle came to an end and a new cycle—the Atlantic cycle—began.

---

2. The hypothesis of an austral rather than a boreal origin can be ascribed to the traditions concerning Lemuria, which, however, is connected to a cycle so ancient that it cannot be adequately considered in this context. [For an interesting discussion of this theme see J. Godwin, *Arktos: The Polar Myth in Science, Symbolism and Nazi Survival* (Grand Rapids, Mich., 1993).]

3. *Lieh-tzu*, 5. Plato himself associated mythical catastrophes such as the one caused by Phaëthon with a "change in the course of the stars," that is, with the different appearance of the heavenly vault that resulted from the shift of the terrestrial axis.

Aryan texts from India, such as the Vedas and the *Mahābhārata* preserve the memory of the Arctic seat through astronomical and calendar-related allusions that cannot be understood other than through an actual reference to such a seat.[4] In the Hindu tradition the term *dvīpa*, which means "insular continent," is often used to designate different cycles by virtue of a spatial transposition of a temporal notion (cycle = island). Now, in the doctrine of the *dvīpa* we find meaningful recollections of the Arctic seat, even though they are mixed with other things. The above mentioned Śveta-dvīpa ("Island of Splendor") was situated in the Far North; the Uttara-Kuru are often mentioned as an original Northern race that originated from Jambu-dvīpa, the "polar" insular continent that is the first of the various *dvīpa* and, at the same time, the center of them all. Its memory is mixed with the memory of the Śaka-dvīpa, located in the "white sea" or "milky sea," namely, the Arctic Sea. In this place no deviation from the law from above occurred. According to the *Kūrma Purāṇa*, the seat of the solar Viṣṇu, symbolized by the "polar cross" (the hooked cross or swastika), coincides with the Śveta-dvīpa that the *Padma Purāṇa* claims to be the homeland, located beyond anything connected with saṁsāric fear and fret, of the great ascetics, the *mahāyogi,* and the "children of Brahman" (the equivalent of the "transcendent beings" who inhabited the northern regions, according to the Chinese tradition); these "great souls" live by Hari, who is Viṣṇu himself, represented as "blond" and "golden" and living by a symbolic throne "upheld by lions, which shines like the sun and radiates like fire." These are variations on the theme of the "Land of the Sun." As a reflection of this, on a doctrinal plane the *deva-yāna*, which is the way leading to solar immortality and to superindividual states of being—as opposed to the way or a return to the mani or to the Mothers—was called the "Way of the North": in Sanskrit, north *(uttara)* also means "the most elevated, or supreme region." Also, *uttara-yāna* (northern path) is the "ascending" path followed by the sun between the winter and summer solstices.[5] Among the Aryans from Iran we find more precise memories. Their original seat (Ariyana Vaego), created by the god of light and in which the "glory" dwells and where the king Yima allegedly met Ahura Mazda, was a land situated in the Far North. The tradition of the *Zend-Avesta* relates that Yima was warned in advance of the approaching of "fatal winters"[6] and that the "serpent of winter," the pet of the god of darkness, Angra Mainyu, came

---

4. G. B. Tilak, *The Arctic Home in the Vedas: Being Also a New Key to the Interpretation of Many Vedic Texts and Legends* (Poona, 1903).
5. In a Hindu rite *(anjali)*, the homage paid to traditional texts is performed while facing north (*The Laws of Manu* 2.70), as if in memory of the place of origin of the transcendent wisdom contained in them. In Tibet, the north is believed to be the origin of a very ancient spiritual tradition, of which the magical formulas of the indigenous Bön religion allegedly are the degenerated residues.
6. *Vendidad,* 2.20.

upon Ariyana Vaego; then "there were ten months of winter and two of summer," and "it was cold in the waters, on the earth, and frost covered the vegetation."[7] Ten months of winter and two months of summer: this is the climate of the Arctic regions.

The Nordic-Scandinavian tradition, notwithstanding its fragmentary nature, offers various testimonies that are often mixed together in a confused way. It is possible, however, to find analogous testimonies. The Asgard, the primordial golden seat of the Aesir, was located by those traditions in the Mitgard, which was the "Land in the Middle." This mythical land was in turn identified both with Gardarike, which is a semi-Arctic region, and with the "Green Island" or "Green Land," which, though portrayed in ancient cosmology as the first land to arise from the abyss Ginnungagap, is likely to be related with Greenland itself. Greenland, as the name itself suggests, seems to have had a rich vegetation and to have been unaffected by the Ice Age up to the time of the Goths. In the early Middle Ages we still find the idea that the northern regions were the original birthplace of all races and people.[8] Moreover, in the Eddic tales describing the struggle of the gods against destiny (rok), an eschatological struggle that they believed was going to affect their own homeland, it is possible to recognize some data that refer to the end of the first cycle; in these tales reminiscences of past events are mixed with apocalyptical themes. Here, just like in the Vendidad, we find the theme of a terrible winter. The breaking out of the natural elements was coupled with the dimming of the sun. According to the Gylfaginning: "First of all a winter will come called fimbul-winter [mighty or mysterious winter]. Then snow will drift from all directions. There will be great frosts and keen winds."[9]

In the Chinese tradition the country of "transcendent men" and the country of a "race of beings with soft bones" are often identified with the northern region: an emperor of the First Dynasty was thought to have resided in a country located north of the Northern Sea, in a boundless region spared by inclement weather and endowed with a symbolic mountain (Hu-Ling) and a water spring. This country was called "Far North"; Mu, another imperial type, was said to have been brokenhearted upon leaving it.[10] Analogously, Tibet retains the memory of Tshang Shambhala, the mystical "northern city," or city of "peace," also thought to be the island on which the

---

7. Ibid., 1.3–4.

8. Jordanes, *Historia Gotorum:* "Sandza insula quasi officina gentium aut certe velut nationum."

9. *Gylfaginning*, 51. The Eddic representation of the North as Niflheim, the "world of mist and darkness," inhabited by giants and by frost, was most likely developed in a later period by stocks that had already migrated to the South; likewise, the frozen Ariyana Vaego was regarded as the seat of the dark forces of the evil creation of Angra Mainyu, who personally came from the North to fight against Zarathustra. Vendidad, 19.1.

10. *Lieh–tzu*, 5.

hero Gesar was said to have been "born" (just like Zarathustra was born in the Ariyana Vaego). The masters of Tibetan traditions say that the "northern paths" lead the yogin to the great liberation.

The recurrent tradition concerning the origins that is found in North America, from the Pacific to the region of the Great Lakes, mentions the sacred land of the "Far North," situated by the "great waters," whence allegedly came the ancestors of the Nahuatlans, the Toltecs, and the Aztecs. I previously mentioned that the name of this land, Aztlan, just like the Hindu Śveta-dvīpa, denotes the idea of whiteness, or of white land. In the northern traditions there is the memory of a land inhabited by Gaelic races and situated by the Gulf of St. Lawrence called "Great Ireland" or Hvitramamaland, which means "homeland of white people"; the names Wabanaki and Abenaki found among the inhabitants of those regions derive from the word *wabeya*, which means "white."

Furthermore, some legends of central America mention four primordial ancestors of the Quiche race who are trying to return to Tulla, the region of light. When they get there they only find ice; also, the sun seldom appears. Then they scatter and move to the country of the Quiche.[11] This Tula or Tullan was the original homeland of the Toltecs' forefathers, who probably derived their tribal name from it and who eventually called "Tula" the center of the empire they established on the Mexican plateau. This Tula was also conceived as the "Land of the Sun" and was sometimes located east of North America, in the Atlantic; but this is probably due to the interference of the memory of a later location that was destined to perpetuate for some time the function of the primordial Tula (to which Aztlan probably corresponds) when the glacial weather descended upon it and when the sun disappeared;[12] the name Tula, which visibly corresponds to the Greeks' Thule, was also applied to other regions.

According to Greco-Roman traditions, Thule lay in the sea that derives its name from the god of the Golden Age, namely, the Cronium Sea, which corresponds to the

---

11. The four Quiche ancestors probably correspond to the Celtic idea of the "Island of the Four Lords," and to the Chinese idea of the faraway Ku-she island, inhabited by transcendent men and by four lords (R. Guénon, *Le Roi du monde*, 71–72). Guénon recalled the division of ancient Ireland into four kingdoms that allegedly reproduced the division proper of "a land situated farther North, today unknown and maybe gone forever" and the repeated occurrence in Ireland of the symbol of the "center" or "pole," which the Greeks called *omphalos*. I will add that the black Stone of Destiny, which designated legitimate kings and which was one of the mystical objects brought to Ireland by the race of the Tuatha dé Danaan, who themselves came from an Atlantic or North Atlantic land, had the same value as a regal "polar" symbol in the double meaning of the word.

12. Guénon, in his *Le Roi du monde* (ch. 10), made some astute observations on the relationship that traditionally existed between Thule and the figurations of the Big Dipper, which is connected with the polar symbolism.

northern region of the Atlantic;[13] a similar location was ascribed in later traditions to what became symbol and metahistory in the form of the Happy Islands, or the Islands of the Immortals,[14] or the Lost Island. This island, as Honorius Augustadumensis wrote, "is hidden from people's sight; sometimes it is discovered by chance, but when it is actively sought after, it cannot be found." Thule is confused with both the legendary Hyperborean homeland, situated in the Far North[15] and from which the original Achaean stocks brought the Delphic Apollo, and with the isle of Ogygia, "the sea's navel" located far away in the vast ocean.[16] Plutarch situated this island north of Great Britain and claimed that it was in proximity of the Arctic region where Kronos, the god of the golden region, is still asleep; in this location the sun sets only for one hour each day, and even then the darkness is not all-enveloping but looks more like a twilight, just like in the Arctic regions.[17] The confused notion of the bright northern night became the foundation of the notion of the land of the Hyperboreans as a place of perennial light, free of darkness. This representation and this memory were so vivid that an echo of it lasted until the end of the Roman civilization. After the primordial land was identified with Great Britain, it is said that the Constantius Chlorus (reigned A.D. 305–306) went there with his legions not so much to pursue trophies and military victories, but rather in order to visit the land that is "most sacred and closest to heaven"; to be able to contemplate the father of the gods (Kronos); and to enjoy a "day without a night," in other words to be able to anticipate the possession of the eternal light that is typical of imperial apotheosis.[18] Even when the Golden Age was projected into the future as the hope of a new *saeculum,* we can still find references to Nordic symbolism. According to Lactantius,[19] the mighty prince who will reestablish justice after the fall of Rome will come from the north *(ab extremis finibus plagae septemtrionalis);* the mystical and invincible Tibetan hero Gesar, who will reestablish a kingdom of justice and exterminate the usurpers, is expected to be

---

13. Pliny, *Historia naturalis,* 4.30.

14. According to Strabo (*Geographia,* 1.6.2), Thule was six days of navigation, north of (Great) Britain.

15. Callimachus, *Hymn to Apollo,* 4.281; Pliny, 4.89. Around the fourth century B.C., Hecateus of Abdera said that Great Britain was inhabited by "Hyperboreans," who are identified with the proto-Celts; these people were credited with erecting the prehistoric temple of Stonehenge.

16. *Odyssey,* 1.50; 12.244. Here too, because of the connections with Zeus's and the Hesperides' garden, there are several obvious interpolations with the memory of the later Atlantic seat.

17. Plutarch, *De facie in orbe lunae,* 26. Plutarch says that beyond other islands, further north, there the seat still exists in which Kronos, the god of the Golden Age, sleeps on a rock that shines like gold and where birds bring him ambrosia.

18. It is possible that Ogygia, composed of the Gaelic roots *og* ("young" and "sacred") and *iag* ("island"), refers to the "Sacred Land of Youth," to the Tir na mBeo, the "Land of the Living" spoken of in Nordic legends, which in turn corresponds to Avalon, the original seat of the Tuatha dé Danaan.

19. *The Divine Institutes,* 7.16.3. These emergences continue in the later mystical and hermetic literature. Besides Boehme, G. Postel in his *Compendium cosmographicum* says that "heaven" (a mystical and theological transposition of the primordial homeland) is found underneath the North Pole.

"reborn" in the north; Shambhala, the sacred northern city, will be the birth place of Kalki-avatara, the one who will put an end to the Dark Age; the Hyperborean Apollo, according to Virgil, will inaugurate a new golden and heroic age in the sign of Rome;[20] and so on.

After stating these essential points, I will not make further references to the law that connects physical and spiritual causes as it is applied to a plane upon which, between what may be characterized as a "fall" (the deviation of an absolutely primordial race) and the physical tilting of the terrestrial axis (which determined radical changes in climate and periodical natural disasters affecting entire continents), it is possible to have a foreboding of an intimate connection. I will only point out that ever since the polar seat became deserted it is possible to verify that progressive alteration and loss of the original tradition that will eventually lead to the Iron Age, or Dark Age, or Kali Yuga, or "era of the wolf" *(Edda)* and, strictly speaking, to modern times.

20. Virgil, *Eclogues,* 4.5–10.

25

The Northern-Atlantic Cycle

As far as the migration of the Northern primordial race is concerned, it is necessary to distinguish two great waves, the first moving from north to south, the second from west to east. Groups of Hyperboreans carrying the same spirit, the same blood, and the same body of symbols, signs, and languages first reached North America and the northern regions of the Eurasian continent. Supposedly, tens of thousands of years later a second great migratory wave ventured as far as Central America, reaching a land situated in the Atlantic region that is now lost, thereby establishing a new center modeled after the polar regions. This land may have been that Atlantis described by Plato and Diodorus; the migration and the reestablishment of a center help to explain the transpositions of names, symbols, and topographies that I have discussed in reference to the first two ages. In regard to this, it is fitting to talk about a Northern-Atlantic people and civilization.

From this Atlantic seat the races of the second cycle spread to the American (hence the previously mentioned memories of the Nahuatlans, Toltecs, and Aztecs concerning their original homeland), European, and African continents. Most likely these races reached the borders of western Europe in the early Paleolithic. These races supposedly corresponded to, among others, the Tuatha dé Danaan, the divine stock that came to Ireland from Avalon and who were led by Ogma Grian-aineach, the hero with a "sunny countenance," whose counterpart is the white and solar Quetzalcoatl, who came with his companions to America from the "Land situated beyond the Waters." Anthropologically speaking, these races correspond to Cro-Magnon man, who made his appearance toward the end of the glacial age in the western part of Europe (especially in the area of the French Cantabric civilization of Abri La Madeleine, Gourdain, and Altamira); Cro-Magnon man was clearly superior, both culturally and biologically, to the aboriginal Mousterian man of the Ice Age, so much so that somebody recently nicknamed the Cro-Magnon "the Greeks of the Paleolithic." As far as their origin is concerned, the similarity between their civilization and the civilization of the Hyperborean, which is found even in the vestiges of the people of the Far North (civilization of the reindeer), is very significant. Among other prehistoric traces of the same cycle are those found on the Baltic and Frisian-Saxon shores; in the Doggerland, in a region that has partly disappeared—the legendary Vineta—a center of this civilization was eventually established. Besides Spain, other migratory waves landed on West African shores;[1] later on, between the Paleolithic and the Neolithic and probably in conjunction with races of direct Northern descent, other people moved through the continents from northwest to southeast toward Asia, into the area many believe to be the cradle of the Indo-European race, and then further on, all the way to China;[2] other waves followed the North African shoreline all the way to Egypt or went by sea from the Balearic Islands to Sardinia and to the prehistoric sites in the Aegean Sea. More particularly, in Europe and in the Near East, the origin of the megalithic civilization of the dolmen and the so-called battle-axe people, which remains as enigmatic as that of Cro-Magnon, is very similar. This migration occurred in separate waves, through fluxes and refluxes, interbreeding, and conflicts with aboriginal or already mixed races. Thus, from north to south and from west to east, through diffusion, adaptation, or domination there arose civilizations that originally shared, to a certain degree, the same matrix, and often strains of the same spiritual legacy found in the conquering elites. Encounters with inferior races, which were enslaved to the chthonic cult of demons and mixed with the animal nature, generated memories of struggles that were eventually expressed in mythologized forms that always underline the contrast between a bright, divine type (an element of Northern origins) and a dark, demonic type. Through the institution of traditional societies by the conquering races a hierarchy was established that carried a spiritual, ethnic, and racial value; in India, in Iran, in Egypt, and even in Peru we find rather evident traces of this in the institution of the caste system.

I have said that originally the Atlantic center was supposed to reproduce the "polar" function of the Hyperborean seat and that this second center occasioned frequent confusion in traditions and in memories. This confusion should not prevent us from detecting in a later period, yet still falling within remote prehistory, a transformation of civilization and spirituality and a differentiation leading from the first to the second era (from the Golden Age to the Silver Age) that eventually prepared the way for the third era, the Bronze Age or Titanic Age; this age should be character-

---

1. This is the legendary kingdom of Uphaz and, in part, the prehistoric African civilization as it was imagined by Frobenius; by confusing the partial center with the original seat of which Uphaz was probably a colony, he identified it with the seat of the Platonic Atlantis. See L. Frobenius, *Die atlantische Götterlehre* (Jena, 1926).
2. In China there have been recent discoveries of the vestiges of a great prehistoric civilization, similar to the Egyptian-Minoan, which was likely created by these migratory waves.

ized as the "Age of Atlantis," considering that the Hellenic tradition regarded Atlas as related to the Titans by virtue of being Prometheus's brother.[3]

Anthropologically speaking, we must consider a first major group that became differentiated through idio-variation, or variation without mixing: this group was mainly composed of the migratory waves of a more immediate Arctic derivation and it made its last appearance in the various strains of the pure Aryan race. A second large group became differentiated through miscegenation with the aboriginal Southern races, with proto-Mongoloid and Negroid races, and with other races that probably represented the degenerated residues of the inhabitants of a second prehistoric continent, now lost, which was located in the South, and which some designated as Lemuria.[4] The second group includes the red-skinned race of the last inhabitants of Atlantis (according to Plato's mythical account, those who forfeited their pristine "divine" nature because of repeated unions with the human race); these people should be regarded as the original ethnic stock of several newer civilizations established by the migratory waves from west to east (the red race of Cretan-Aegeans, Eteicretes, Pelasgians, Lycians, Egyptians, Kefti, etc.),[5] and of the American civilizations. These latter people in their myths remembered the country of origin of their ancestors who had come from the divine Atlantic land "situated on the great waters." The name Phoenicians means "the Red Ones," and most likely it is another memory of the first Atlantic navigators of the Neolithic Mediterranean.

Two components must be considered both from an anthropological and from a spiritual point of view (the Northern and the Atlantic components) in the vast material concerning traditions and institutions found in this second cycle. The first component is immediately related to the Light of the North, and it retained for the most part the original Uranian and "polar" orientation; the second component reveals the transformation that occurred as a result of the contacts established with the Southern populations. Before considering the meaning of such a transformation, which constitutes the first alteration or, so to speak, the inner counterpart of the loss of the polar residence, it is necessary to emphasize another point.

Almost every people retains the memory of a catastrophe that ended the previous cycle of mankind. The myth of the Flood is the most frequent form employed to

3. While on the one hand the legend of Atlas holding the world on his shoulders depicts the sentence of the Titan Atlas, who according to some (Servius, *Ad Aeneidem*, 4.247) participated in the conflict against the Olympian gods, on the other hand it may represent a symbol indicating the function of "pole," support, and spiritual axis the Atlanteans inherited from the Hyperboreans. In his exegesis, the Christian theologian and Church father Clement of Alexandria wrote: "Atlas is an impassible pole; it may even be an immobile sphere, and maybe, in the best of cases, it alludes to the state of unmoved immortality."
4. See the works of H. Wirth for the attempt to utilize the researches on blood types in order to define the two races that emerged from the original stock.
5. A. Mosso, *Le origini della civilita' mediterranea* (Milan, 1910).

describe this memory; it is shared by many people: from the Persians and Mexicans to the Mayas, from the Chaldeans and Greeks to the Hindus and to the people who inhabited the Atlantic-African coastline, to the Celts and to the Scandinavian people. Moreover, its original content is a historical event; according to the tale of Plato and Diodorus it essentially represented the end of an Atlantic land. The center of the Atlantic civilization, to which its colonies were subordinated for a long time, sank into the sea in an era that by far predates the time that according to Hindu tradition, inaugurated the Dark Age; according to some traces of chronology built into the myth, this is what indeed happened. The historical memory of that center gradually disappeared in the civilizations that derived from it but in which elements of the ancient heritage were retained in the blood of the dominating castes, the roots of various languages, and also in social institutions, signs, rituals, and hierograms. In the Hebrew tradition, the theme of the tower of Babel, with the ensuing punishment represented by the "confusion of the various languages" (Gen. 11:7), may refer to the period in which the unitary tradition was lost and the various forms of civilization were dissociated from their common origin and could no longer understand each other after the catastrophe of the Flood ended the cycle of Atlantic mankind. The historical memory was often preserved in myth, that is, in metahistory. The West, in which Atlantis was located during its original cycle (when it reproduced and per-petuated the much older "polar" function), very often represented a nostalgic refer-ence point for the fallen ones. By virtue of a transposition onto a different plane, the waters that submerged the Atlantic land were called "waters of death," which the following postdiluvian generations, consisting entirely of mortal beings, must cross through initiation in order to be reintegrated with the divine state of the "dead," namely, with the lost race. On this basis, the well-known figurations of the "Island of the Dead" could be understood in a similar sense as transformations of the memory of the sunken insular continent.[6] The mystery of paradise and of places of immortal-ity in general was reconnected with the mystery of the West (and in some instances, of the North too), and thus it formed a body of traditional teachings the same way the theme of "Those Who Are Rescued from the Waters" and of "Those Who Do Not Drown In the Waters"[7] shifted from the real, historical sense (that referred to the

6. See D. Merezhkovsky, *Das Geheimnis des Westens* (Leipzig and Zurich, 1929), in which there are several valid references to what the rituals and the symbols of the Atlanteans might have been.
7. See for instance Yama, Yima, Noah, Deucalion, Shamashnapishtim, Romulus, the solar hero Karṇa in the epic *Mahābhārhata*, and so on. Just as Manu, son of Vivasvat, the heir of the solar tradition who survived the Flood and created the laws of a new cycle *(The Laws of Manu)* had for a brother Yama (compare with the Iranian Yima, the solar king who escaped the Flood too), who was "the god of the dead"; likewise Minos, whose name corresponds etymologically to Manu, often appears as the counterpart of Radamant, who is the king of the "Island of the Blessed" or of the "Heroes."

elites who escaped the catastrophe and went on to establish new traditional centers) to a symbolic meaning and appeared in the legends of prophets, heroes, and initiates. Generally speaking, the symbols proper to that primordial race surface again in enigmatic ways until relatively recent times, wherever traditional conquering kings and dynasties made their appearance.

Moreover, the Greeks often discussed the exact spot of the divine garden (θεῶν κῆπος), which was the original dwelling of the Olympian god Zeus,[8] and of the Garden of the Hesperides, "beyond the river Ocean"; according to some, the Hesperides were the daughters of Atlas, the king of the Western Island. It was precisely this garden that Heracles was supposed to find in that symbolic feat that has often been associated with his winning Olympian immortality, and having had Atlas as a guide, who alone "knows the dark depths of the sea."[9] Generally speaking, the Hellenic equivalent of the Northern, solar way or of the Indo-Aryan deva-yāna, was a western path or "Zeus's way," which led from the fortress of Kronos, located in the Island of the Heroes on the faraway sea, to the peaks of Mount Olympus.[10] According to the Chaldean tradition, it is in the West, "beyond the deep waters of death, which have no ford and which have not been crossed for the longest time" that the divine garden is to be found, in which the king Shamashnapishtim, the hero who escaped the Flood and who still retains the privilege of immortality, still reigns; this garden was reached by Gilgamesh who followed the western path of the sun in order to receive the gift of life.[11]

It is significant that the Egyptian civilization did not have a "barbaric" prehistory: it arose all of a sudden, so to speak, enjoying from the start a high level of sophistication. According to tradition, the first Egyptian dynasties were formed by a race that had come from the West, also known as the race of "Horus's companions" (shemsu Heru), or of those marked by the "sign of the first among the inhabitants of the western land," namely, Osiris. Osiris himself was believed to be the eternal king on "Yalu's Fields," in the "land of the sacred Amentet," beyond the "waters of death," which was thought to exist "in the far West," and which sometimes has been associated with the idea of a great insular land. The Egyptian funerary rite carried on the symbolism and the ancient memory: in this rite the ritual formula was "To the West!"

---

8. According to some (Piganiol, *Les Origines de Rome* [Paris, 1899]) the appearance of the Olympian gods next to the feminine deities of the earth was the result of the mixture of the cults of northern origin with the cults of southern origin.

9. Hesiod, *Theogony*, 215.

10. W. Ridgeway, *The Early Age of Greece* (Cambridge, 1901), correctly pointed out that the belief in western dwellings of immortality was typical of those people who used the essentially Northern-Aryan ritual of cremation and not merely of burial.

11. *Gilgamesh*, 10.65–77; 11.296–98.

and it included the crossing of the waters and a procession carrying the "sacred ark of the sun," that is, the ark of those who had been "rescued from the waters."[12] Moreover, the Chinese and Tibetan traditions mention the existence of a "western paradise" with trees bearing golden fruits, like the Hesperides' garden. There is also a frequent image of Mi-tu with a rope and the inscription: "He who draws [the souls] to the West."[13] On the other hand, the memory that was transformed into the myth of paradise is also found in Celtic and Gaelic sagas concerning the "Land of the Living," the Magh-Mell ("The Pleasant Plain"), or Avalon, which were otherworldy regions located in western lands. Avalon was believed to be the place in which the survivors of the race "from above," of the Tuatha dé Danaan, King Arthur himself, legendary heroes such as Conall, Oisin, Cuchulainn, Loegaire, Ogier the Dane, and others came to enjoy eternal life.[14] This mysterious Avalon is the equivalent of the Atlantic "paradise" described in American legends; it is the ancient Tlapallan or Tullan; it is the "Land of the Sun," or the "Red Land" to which both the white god Quetzalcoatl and legendary heroes such as the Toltec priest Huemac ("Great Hand") mentioned in the Codex Chimalpopoca, returned, as did the Tuatha to Avalon, thus disappearing from people's sight. According to Jewish folklore, Enoch went to a western place, "to the far end of the earth," in which there are symbolical mountains and divine trees guarded by the archangel Michael; these trees give life and salvation to the elect but are barred to mere mortals until the time of the Last Judgment.[15] The last echoes of this myth were kept secret until the Christian Middle Ages; the navigator monks of the monasteries of Saint Matthias and of Saint Albaeus allegedly found in a mysterious Atlantic land a golden city, which was believed to be the dwelling place of Enoch and Elijah, the prophets "who never died."

On the other hand, in the myth of the Flood the disappearance of the sacred land separated from continental land by a *mare tenebrosum*—the "Waters of Death"— may also assume a meaning that connects it to the symbolism of the "ark," to the preservation of the "germs of the Living"—the "Living" in an eminent and figura-

---

12. Just as among the Hellenes the localization of the dwelling of the immortals alternated between the North and the West, likewise in some ancient Egyptian traditions the Fields of Peace and the Land of Triumph that the deified soul of the deceased reached by first going through an existing passage in the "mountain," were also thought to be located in the North.

13. See *Lieh-tzu* (3) concerning the journey to the West made by the emperor Mu, who reached the "mountain" (Kuen-Lun) and met Si Wang Mu, the "Mother-Queen of the West."

14. Alan of Lille *(Prophetia anglicana Merlini)* compared the place where King Arthur disappeared with that in which Elijah and Enoch disappeared and from which they will return one day. In regard to the land of the Hyperboreans, classical antiquity believed in the existence of beings (often kings such as Kroisos) who were taken there by Apollo.

15. *Enoch*, 24.1–6; 25.4–6.

tive sense;[16] the disappearance of the legendary sacred land may also signify the passage of the center, which retains in an unadulterated way the primordial nonhuman spirituality, into the invisible, the occult, or the unmanifested. Hence, according to Hesiod, the beings of the first age, "who never died," would continue to exist as humankind's "invisible" guardians. Thus, the legend of the subterranean people or of the subterranean kingdom[17] is often the counterpart of the legend of the sunken land, island, or city; this legend is found among several populations.[18] When impiety began to run rampant on the earth, the survivors of previous eras moved to an "underground" location (in other words, they acquired an "invisible" existence) that is often situated in the mountains as a result of transpositions with the symbolism of the "heights."[19] These beings continue to exist on those mountain peaks until a new manifestation is made possible for them as the end of the cycle of decadence approaches. Pindar said that the road leading to the Hyperboreans can be found "neither by ship nor by marching feet,"[20] and that only heroes such as Perseus and Heracles were admitted to it. Montezuma, the last Mexican emperor, may enter Aztlan only after performing magical operations and undergoing a transformation of his physical body. Plutarch relates that the inhabitants of Northern regions could commune with Kronos (the king of the Golden Age) and with the inhabitants of the Far Northern region[21] only in their sleep. According to Lieh-tzu (2), those marvelous regions he mentions that are connected to the Arctic and the Atlantic seat, "you cannot reach by boat or carriage or on foot, only by a journey of the spirit."[22] According to the Tibetan lamas' teachings, Shambhala, the mystical Northern seat, is within everyone. This is how the testimonies concerning what once was a real location inhabited by nonhuman beings survived and assumed a metahistorical value, providing at the same

---

16. In the Chaldean redaction of the myth, the gods ordered Atrachasis to rescue the sacred writings of the previous era from the flood by "burying them": they were conceived as the "residual seeds" from which everything else will grow again.

17. According to the Iranian tradition, King Yima built a refuge *(vara)*, which is often portrayed as "subterranean," in order to save the seeds of all living things. *Vendidad,* 2.22.

18. See R. Guénon, *Le Roi du monde,* chaps. 7–8.

19. In the Irish sagas some of the Tuatha, after their defeat by the Milesians, withdrew to the "western paradise" of Avalon, others chose underground dwellings beneath mounds or hills *(sidhe),* hence the name Aes Sidhe, "the people of the hills." According to a Mexican tradition, in the caves of Chapultepec lies the entrance to the subterranean world into which King Huemac II disappeared and from which he will emerge one day in order to rebuild his kingdom.

20. Pindar, *The Pythian Odes,* 10.29.

21. Plutarch, *De facie in orbe lunae,* 26. In antiquity sleep was believed to neutralize the physical senses and to awaken the inner senses, thus naturally creating the conditions for contacts with the invisible dimension.

22. *The Book of Lieh-tzu,* trans. A. C. Graham (New York, 1960), 34.

time symbols of states beyond ordinary life, that can only be reached through initiation. Besides the symbol, we find the idea that the original center still exists in an occult and usually unreachable location (similar to what Catholic theology said about the Garden of Eden): only a change of state or of nature can open its doors to the generations living in the last ages.

This is how the second great transposition of metaphysics and history was established. In reality, the symbol of the West, just like that of the "pole," may acquire a universal value beyond all geographical and historical references. In the West, where the physical light that is subject to birth and to decline becomes extinguished, the unchanging spiritual light is kindled; there the journey of the "Sun's ship" toward the Land of the Immortals commences. And since this region lies where the sun disappears beyond the horizon, it was also conceived as subterranean or as underwater. This is straightforward symbolism directly inspired by natural observations and thus used by various populations, even by those that have no relation with Atlantic memories. This, however, does not mean that such a theme, situated within given limits determined by concomitant testimonies such as the ones I have presented, may not also have a historical character. What I mean is that among the countless forms assumed by the mystery of the West, a group may be isolated for which it is legitimate to assume that the origin of the symbol did not consist in the natural phenomenon of the course of the sun, but rather, by virtue of a spiritual transposition, in the distant memory of the disappeared Western land. In this regard, the surprising correspondence between American and European myths, especially Nordic and Celtic ones, constitutes a very decisive proof.

Secondly, "the mystery of the West" always marks a particular stage in the history of the spirit that is no longer the primordial one; it corresponds to a type of spirituality that cannot be considered to be primordial and therefore it is defined by the mystery of transformation. It is characterized by a dualism and by a discontinuous passage: a light is kindled, another fades away. Transcendence has gone underground. Supernature, unlike the original state, is no longer nature: it is the goal of an initiation and the object of a problematic quest. Even when considered in its general aspect "the mystery of the West" appears to be typical of those more recent civilizations, the varieties and destinies of which I will examine in the next chapter. It is connected to the solar symbolism rather than to the polar one; we have now entered the second phase of the primordial tradition.

26

North and South

In the first part of this work I pointed out the relationship between the solar symbolism and several traditional civilizations; this symbolism naturally occurs in a number of traces, memories, and myths connected to the primordial civilization. When considering the Atlantic cycle, however, we can distinguish a typical alteration and differentiation of the polar symbolism from the symbolism relating to the previous Hyperborean civilization. The Hyperborean stage may be characterized as that in which the luminous principle presents the characteristics of immutability and of centralism, which are, so to speak, typically "Olympian." These are the same characteristics proper to the Hyperborean god Apollo, who unlike Helios, does not represent the sun following its patterns of ascent and of descent over the horizon, but is rather the sun itself, the dominating and unchanging source of light. The swastika and other forms of the prehistoric cross that are found approximately at the beginning of the glacial period (like the other very ancient prehistoric solar symbol of the circle with an inner center that was sometimes represented by the colossal dolmen), originally seem to have had a connection with this early form of spirituality. In fact, the swastika is a solar symbol inasmuch as it represents a rotary movement around a determined and unmovable pivot corresponding to the center of another solar symbol, the circle.[1] There are different kinds of solar wheels and swastikas: circles, crosses, circles with crosses, and radiating circles; later on, there are axes with a swastika, double axes, and axes and other objects made with aeroliths arranged in a circular pattern; and then images of the "solar ship," associated with the axes or with the Apollonian-Hyperborean swan and reindeer; all of these symbols are the traces of the original stage of the northern tradition.

---

1. See R. Guénon, *Le Roi du monde*, chap. 2. From an analysis of the geographical distribution of the swastika on the earth prepared by T. Wilson (*The Swastika: The Earliest Known Symbol* in *Annual Report of the Smithsonian Institution*, 1896), while it seems that this sign was not proper only to the Indo-European races as it was supposed at first, nevertheless we find a distribution that largely corresponds to the Northern-Atlantic migrations to the west (America) and to the east (Europe).

There is also a different spirituality connected to the polar symbolism, though it emphasizes the relationship with the year (the year-god) and thus with a law of mutation, ascent, descent, death, and rebirth. The original theme, therefore, is distinct from what may be characterized as a "Dionysian" phase; here we find the influences proper to another principle, another cult, another stock of races, and another geographical region. We notice a differentiating transposition.

In order to classify this type of transposition we may consider the most significant point in time for the symbol of the sun as the "sun god," the winter solstice. Here a new element acquires an ever greater relevance; it is that element into which the light seems to disappear and from which it seems to rise again, almost by virtue of renewed contact with the original principle animating its own life. This symbol does not appear in the traditions of pure boreal stock, and if it does, it appears only in a very subordinated way; conversely, in the southern civilizations and races this symbol is predominant and it often acquires a central meaning. It is the feminine, telluric symbol, which is portrayed as the Mother (the Divine Woman), the Earth, or the Waters (or Serpent); these three characteristic expressions are equivalent to a great degree and are often related to one another (Mother Earth; the generating Waters; the Serpent of the Waters). The relationship established between the two principles (the Mother and the Sun) is what gives meaning to two different redactions of the symbolism, the first of which still retains traces of the "polar" tradition, while the second characterizes a new cycle, namely, the Silver Age, and a mingling (which is already a degeneration) of North and South.

From an abstract perspective, in those places in which solstices are celebrated there still is a connection with the "polar" symbolism (the vertical axis running from north to south), while the symbolism of the equinoxes is connected with the longitudinal (east-west) direction so much so that the predominance of either one of the two symbolisms in different civilizations, in and of itself, allows us to characterize whatever in them refers to either the Hyperborean or Atlantic heritage. In what may be more properly characterized as an Atlantic tradition and civilization, however, we find a mixed form. Here, together with the presence of the solstice symbolism, we still have a "polar" element; but in the predominance of the theme of the solar god who changes, and in the appearance and ensuing predominance of the figure of the Mother or of similar symbols during the solstices, we may detect the effects of yet another influence and of another type of civilization and spirituality.

Therefore, when the center consists of the solar male principle conceived of as life that arises and declines and that goes through winter and spring, or death and rebirth (as in the case of the so-called vegetation deities), while the identical and immutable principle is identified with the Universal Mother and with the Earth conceived as the eternal principle of every life, as the cosmic matrix and the inexhaustible source and seat of all energy—then we are truly confronted by a decadent civilization and by the second era, which is traditionally under the aegis of the water or of the moon. Conversely, wherever the sun continues to be conceived of in terms of uncreated and unprecedented pure light and "spiritual virility" following the lines of an Olympian meaning; and wherever people's attention focuses on the luminous and heavenly nature of the *fixed* stars, since they appear to be exempt from the law of rising and setting, which in the opposite view affects the sun as the year-god himself—then what we are witnessing are instances of the highest, purest, and most ancient spirituality (the cycle of the Uranian civilizations).

This is a very general and yet fundamental scheme. Generally speaking, we can distinguish between a Southern and a Northern Light; in the amount in which such an opposition has relatively well-defined traits within the mixed matter of what is historical and traceable back to very distant ages, it is possible to distinguish between a Uranian and a lunar spirituality, between "Arctic regions" and "Atlantis."

Historically and geographically, Atlantis does not correspond to the South, but to the West. The South corresponds to Lemuria, which I mentioned in passing, and some Negroid and Southern populations may be considered the last crepuscular remnants of this continent. Since until now, however, I have essentially followed the trajectory of the decline of the primordial Hyperborean civilization, I will discuss Atlantis only in reference to a phase of this decline; moreover, I will only consider the South in relation to the influence it exercised on primordial races and on Northern civilizations during the Atlantic cycle (but not only in it, provided we do not give to this expression a general, typological meaning) or in relation to intermediate forms, which have the double meaning of an alteration of the primordial heritage and of the elevation to higher forms of the chthonic and demonic themes typical of the southern aboriginal races. This is why I did not simply say "South," but "Southern Light," and why I will use the term "lunar spirituality" to characterize the second cycle, in reference to the moon as a bright and yet nonsolar symbol, which is almost similar to a "heavenly Earth," namely, to a purified land (South).

Because of numerous elements, there is no doubt that the themes of the Mother or Woman, the Waters, and the Earth all trace their origins to the South and are also recurrent, through transpositions and interpolations, in all the ensuing "Atlantic" traces and memories; this has misled some into thinking that the cult of the Mother was typical of the Northern-Atlantic civilization. According to a well-established idea, there is a connection between Mouru—one of the "creations" that, according to the *Zend-Avesta*,[2] came after the Arctic seat—and the "Atlantic" cycle, and therefore,

---

2. *Vendidad*, 1.4.

Mouru should be equated with the "Land of the Mother."[3] Moreover, if some have attempted to see in the prehistoric Magdalenian civilization (of an Atlantic origin) the original center from which a civilization—in which the Mother Goddess enjoyed such a predominant role that some could say that at the dawn of civilization the woman radiates such a bright light through religion that the male figure is confined to the shadows—spread throughout the Neolithic Mediterranean; and if some have claimed to have discerned in the Hiberic-Cantabric cycle the same characteristics of the lunar, Demetrian mystery that is dominant in the pre-Hellenic Pelasgic civilization—undoubtedly there must be some truth in this. After all, the name Tuatha dé Danaan, which is found in the Irish cycle and characterizes a divine race from the West, means "the people of the goddess Dana." The legends, the memories, and the metahistorical transpositions according to which a western island was the residence of a goddess, a queen, or a priestess-ruler, are numerous and very revealing. I previously mentioned some of these references. The custody of the golden apples (which may represent the traditional heritage of the first age and the symbol of the spiritual states proper to it) located in Zeus's western garden, according to the myth, became the responsibility not only of women, but of the daughters of Atlas, the Hesperides. According to some Gaelic sagas, the Atlantic Avalon was ruled by a regal virgin; also, the woman who appeared to Conall in order to lure him to the "Land of the Living" implied through symbols that this land was inhabited only by women and by children.[4] Hesiod declared that the Silver Age was characterized by a very long period of "infancy" under maternal tutelage;[5] this is the same idea, conveyed through the same symbolism. Even the designation "Silver Age" is a reminder of the lunar light and of a lunar, matriarchical era. In Celtic myths we find the recurrent theme of the woman who bestows immortality on the hero in the Western Island.[6] This corresponds to (1) the Hellenic legend of Calypso, daughter of Atlas, queen of the mysterious island of Ogygia, a divine woman who enjoyed immortality and gave it to those whom she chose;[7] (2) the theme

---

3. This was the opinion of H. Wirth. The term *mu* is often found in the Maya civilization, which may be considered a residue of the Southern cycle. The seat of this cycle was a very ancient continent that included Atlantis and perhaps stretched to the Pacific. It seems that in the Mayan tablets of the Troana Codex, mention is made of a certain Mu, a queen or divine woman who traveled west as far as Europe. Ma or Mu was also the name of the main Mother goddess of ancient Crete.

4. Joyce, *Old Celtic Romances*, 108.

5. Hesiod, *Works and Days*, 130–32.

6. In the medieval legend of monks who found a golden city and the prophets who never died in the middle of the Atlantic, mention is made of a statue of a woman in the middle of the sea, made of "copper" (Venus's metal) pointing the way.

7. *Odyssey*, 1.50; 7.245, 257; 22.336. We may connect this with what Strabo wrote (*Geographia*, 4.4.5) concerning the island close to Britain in which the cult of Demeter and Core was as predominant as in the Pelasgic Aegean basin. While Ovid made of Anna an Atlantean nymph, Anna or Anna Perenna is but a personification of the food that bestows immortality (in Sanskrit: *anna*), which is often associated with the western Elysium.

206

of the "virgin who sits on the throne of the seas" along the western path followed by Gilgamesh, and who is the goddess of wisdom and the guardian of life—a virgin who tends to be confused with the mother goddess Ishtar; (3) the Nordic myth of Idunn ("Land of the Ever Young") and of its apples that grant and renew eternal life; (4) the Far Eastern tradition concerning the "western paradise," in the aspect in which it is also called "Land of the Western Woman";[8] and finally, (5) the great Mexican tradition relative to the divine woman, mother of the great Huitzilopochtli, who remained the ruler of the sacred oceanic land of Aztlan. These are echoes that, directly or indirectly, refer to the same one idea; they are memories, symbols, and allegories that need to be dematerialized and regarded as universal references to a "lunar" spirituality, to a *regere*, and to the participation in a life that is not ephemeral, all of which have shifted from the solar and virile aegis to the lunar and "feminine" aegis of the Divine Woman.

It would probably be possible to reach the same conclusions through the Hellenic myth of Aphrodite—a goddess who in her Asiatic variations characterizes the Southern component of the Mediterranean civilizations—since according to Hesiod, Aphrodite was born from the foam that gathered about the severed genitals of the primordial heavenly deity Uranus, who some believe to represent both the Golden Age (like Kronos) and the Northern center. According to the tradition of the *Elder Edda,* the appearance of the feminine element ("of the three strong daughters of the giants") marks both the end of the Golden Age and the beginning of the first struggles between divine races (Aesir and Wanen), and later on between divine races and giants; these struggles, as we shall see later on, reflect the spirit of later epochs.

Considered in her elementary chthonic aspect, the woman, together with the earthly demons, was really the main object of the Southern aboriginal cults; this will be the source of the great Asiatic-Southern chthonic goddesses and of those goddesses who represent the monstrous steatopygic female idols of the early megalithic period. This goddess of the Southern Hemisphere, who is transfigured and reduced to a pure and almost Demetrian form, as exemplified in the Brassampouy caves inhabited by Aurignacian man, was introduced and became dominant in the new civilization of Western-Atlantic origin. Along the path of Atlantic colonizers, from the Neolithic to the Minoan period and from the Pyrenees to Egypt, we encounter female idols almost exclusively, while in the cult there were more priestesses than priests, or quite often, effeminate priests. The same motif is present in Thracia, Illyria,

---

8. The royal Mother of the West also appears in connection with the "mountain" Kuen-Lun; she possesses the elixir of immortality and according to the legend she bestows immortal life to kings such as Wang-Mu. In this Chinese view we find a contrast between two components; the pure western land, the seat of the mother, and the kingdom of Amitabha, from which women are rigorously excluded.

Mesopotamia, and even in some Northern and Celtic stocks all the way up to the time of the Germanic tribes, and especially in India where it has been preserved in some Southern forms of the Tantric cult and in the prehistoric traces of the civilization of Mohenjo-Daro; not to mention the most recent forms, which I will discuss later on in greater detail.

This is but a brief reference to the primordial chthonic roots of the Southern Light, which can be associated with the Southern component found in those civilizations, traditions, and institutions that emerged in the wake of the great migratory tides that moved from west to east; this is a disaggregating component, opposed to the original Olympian and Uranian type of spirituality connected with the races of a more immediate Northern descent (Northern-Atlantic) or with those races that were capable of retaining or of rekindling the fire of the primordial tradition even in an environment far removed from the influences of the original one.

By virtue of the occult relationship that exists between what takes place on the visible plane (which is apparently shaped according to external conditions) and that which conveys a deep and even spiritual meaning, we can refer to environmental and climatic factors in order to explain analogically the differentiation that occurred. The experience of the sun, of light, and of fire itself naturally acted in the Northern races as a liberating spirituality, especially during the long glacial winter; Uranian and solar, Olympian, or fiery figures also played a major role in the sacred symbolism of these races. Moreover, the rigorous climate, barren soil, and need for hunting as well as the need to migrate across unknown seas and continents naturally shaped those who innerly retained this spiritual experience of the sun, bright sky, and fire into warriors, conquerors, and navigators, and thus furthered that synthesis of virility and spirituality, the characteristic traces of which were retained in the Indo-European races.

In relation to this, it becomes easier to understand another aspect of the previously mentioned symbolism of sacred stones. The stone or the rock is an expression of the hardness, the sacred and ironlike spiritual firmness of those who are "Rescued from the Waters." The stone represents the main characteristic of those who eventually dominated in later times and who established the traditional centers following the Great Flood in places where the sign of the "center," the "pole," and "God's house" often reemerged in the symbolic stone as a variation of the omphalos.[9] Hence, the Hellenic theme of the second race, born from "stone" after the flood;[10] the idea that Mithras was believed to have been born from stone; that stones were believed to

---

9. R. Guénon, *Le Roi du monde*, chap. 10. The Hebrew term *baithel* or *bethel*, which corresponds to *omphalos*, means "the house of God."

10. Arnobius, *The Case Against the Pagans*, 11.5.

point out true kings or that they are found at the beginning of the Via Sacra (see the Roman *lapis niger*, or black stone); that sacred stones were the material from which fatal swords are made; and finally, that meteorites, or "stones from heaven," or "thunderbolts," were often turned into axes, the weapon and the symbol of prehistoric conquerors.

Conversely, it was only natural that in the South the object of the most immediate experience was not the solar *principle*, but rather its effects displayed in the luscious fertility of the Earth, and that the center shifted toward Mother Earth portrayed as Magna Mater while the symbolism shifted to chthonic deities or beings, to gods and goddesses of vegetation and of vegetal and animal fertility, while fire, once perceived as a divine, heavenly, and beneficial reality, eventually came to be perceived as something "infernal," ambiguous, and telluric. The favorable climate and the natural plentiness eventually induced most people to seek peace and rest and to cultivate the feeling of contemplation and of getting lost in nature, rather than an active pursuit of affirmation and self-transcendence.[11] Therefore, even in the order of what can be affected to a certain degree by external factors, while the Northern Light goes hand in hand, through solar and Uranian symbols, with a virile ethos and a warrior spirituality consisting of a harsh will to establish order and to dominate, conversely, in the Southern traditions the predominance of the chthonic theme and of the pathos of death and resurrection corresponds to a certain propensity to promiscuity, escapism, a sense of abandonment, and a naturalistic pantheism with sensual or mystical and contemplative overtones.[12]

In every historical epoch that follows the descent of the Northern races it is possible to detect the action of two opposing tendencies that can be traced, one way or another, back to the fundamental polarity of North-South. In every civilization that emerged later on it is possible to recognize the dynamic outcome of either the encounter or the clash of these two tendencies, which generated more or less lasting forms until the advent of forces and of processes that ushered in the later Bronze and

---

11. "To teach with kindly benevolence, not to lose one's temper and avenge the unreasonableness of others, that is the virile energy of the South that is followed by the well-bred man. To sleep on a heap of arms and untanned skins, to die unflinching and as if dying were not enough, that is the virile energy of the North that is followed by the brave man." *Chung-yung*, 10.4.

12. Having suggested that the symbolism of the solstices has a "polar" character, while the symbolism of the equinoxes is referred to the western and eastern direction and to the "Atlantic" civilization, I think it is interesting to consider the meaning of some equinoctial feasts in relation to the themes typical of Southern civilizations; in this regard the exegesis of Emperor Julian (*Hymn to the Mother of the Gods*, 173c–d; 175a–b) is very significant. When an equinox occurs, the sun seems to escape from its orbit and law and to get lost in the unlimited; at that time the sun is at its "antipolar" and "anti-Olympian" peak. This tendency toward evasion and escapism corresponds to the pathos of the promiscuous feasts that some people celebrated during the spring equinox in the name of the Great Mother; these feasts were sometimes connected with the myth of the "castration" of her solar son-lover.

Iron Ages. Not only within every single civilization but even in the struggle between various civilizations and in the advent of one tendency and in the demise of the other, deeper meanings will often surface; it will also be possible to notice again the advent or the demise of forces that are inspired by either one of these spiritual poles, with a greater or lesser reference to the ethnic lines that originally either knew the "Northern Light" or fell under the spell of the Mothers and of the Southern ecstasies.

27

The Civilization of the Mother

I n order to undertake this kind of research successfully, it is necessary to provide a
more exact typological characterization of the forms of civilization that followed
the primordial one. First of all, I will discuss the notion of the "civilization of the
Mother."[1] The characteristic trait of this civilization is a transposition into the metaphysical of the view of woman as the principle and substance of generation; a goddess expresses the supreme reality, while every being, conceived as a son or daughter, appears next to her as something conditioned, subordinated, lacking life in itself,
and ephemeral. This is the type of the great Asiatic-Mediterranean goddesses of
life, such as Isis, Asherat, Cybele, Tanit, and especially Demeter (Ceres to the Romans), a central figure in the Pelasgic-Minoan cycle. The representation of the solar
principle as a child resting on the lap of the Great Mother, suggesting that it was
generated from her; the Egyptian-Minoan representations of queens or divine women
holding the lotus and the key to life; Ishtar, celebrated by one of the most ancient
recorded hymns with the words: "There is no true god besides you," and who is often
referred to as Ummu ilani, "the Mother of the gods"; the various allusions, often with
cosmological transpositions, to an alleged primacy of the "night" principle over the
"day" principle arising from her bosom, and therefore of dark or lunar deities over
manifested and diurnal ones; the ensuing characteristic sense of the "occult" as destiny and as a fatalistic law from which nobody can escape; the priority, in some
archaic symbolisms (often connected with the lunar rather than with the solar measure of time) of the sign or of the god of the moon over that of the sun (see for
instance the primacy enjoyed by the Babylonian god Sin over Shamash) and the
inversion whereby the moon was sometimes portrayed as a masculine deity and the
sun as a feminine deity; the part assigned to the principle of the waters and to the
relative cult of the serpent and of analogous entities; and also, on a different plane,

---

1. A reading of Bachofen's *Das Mutterrecht* (1897) will show the extent to which I have employed the
findings of this scholar and the extent to which I have integrated them in a wider and more up-to-date
order of ideas.

the subordination of Adonis to Aphrodite, Virbius to Diana, some forms of Osiris (who was transformed from his original solar form into a lunar god of the waters) to Isis,[2] Iacchus to Demeter, the Asiatic Heracles to Milittas—all of these examples seem to point in the same direction. Little statues of the Mother with child dating back to the Neolithic are found everywhere in the Southern Hemisphere, from Mesopotamia to the Atlantic.

In the civilization of Crete, where the homeland was called "motherland" (μετρίς) rather than "fatherland" (πατρίς), which also exhibits a specific relation with the Atlantic-Southern civilization[3] and with the substratum of even more ancient cults in the South, the gods were believed to be mortal; just like summer, every year they underwent death. In Cretan civilization Zeus (Teshub) did not have a father, and his mother was the humid soil; the "woman" was therefore at the beginning, while the god himself was a "generated" and mortal being and his sepulcher was shown from generation to generation on Crete's Mount Iouktas.[4] Conversely, the unchanging feminine substratum of every form of life was believed to be immortal. According to Hesiod's *Theogony*, when the shadows of Chaos are dispersed, the black goddess Gaia (μέλαινα γαῖα), a feminine principle, makes her appearance. Gaia generates her own male or bridegroom *without a spouse*, after producing the "great mountains," the Ocean, and the Pontus; Gaia's entire divine offspring, which Hesiod lists following a tradition that should not be confused with that of the pure Olympian stock, is portrayed as a world subject to movement, change, and becoming.

On a lower plane, and on the basis of traces that have been preserved until the earliest recorded historical times, it is possible to recognize in some of the Asiatic Mediterranean cults ritual expressions that characterize this inversion of values. Take, for instance, the Sacchean and Phrygian festivals. The Sacchean festivals, which were celebrated in honor of the great Goddess, culminated in the slaying of a person who represented the male regal figure.[5] The dismissal of the virile element on the occasion of the celebration of the Goddess was also found in a dramatic way in the castra-

---

2. Plutarch, *De Iside et Osiride*, 41; 33. Diodorus Siculus (*Bibliotheca historica*, 1.27) related that in Egypt the queen enjoyed greater powers and was given higher honors than the king, to reflect the fact that Isis survived Osiris and that she was credited with the resurrection of the god and with the bestowal of many gifts to mankind (since she embodied the immortal principle and knowledge). I would add that this view reflects the decadence of the primordial Egyptian civilization.

3. Bachofen, *Mutterecht*, chap. 1. Herodotus says that originally the Licians (the primordial inhabitants of Crete) adopted their mothers' rather than their fathers' names.

4. Callimachus, *Hymn to Zeus*, 1.9–15.

5. Dio Chrysostom, *Orationes*, 4.66. Although the modern interpretations that see in this ritual the slaying of the "spirit of vegetation" are typical of the whims of the ethnologists, nevertheless we find a predominant chthonic character in these Sacchean rituals that is found among several other peoples. Philo of Biblos recalled that Kronos sacrificed his son after putting the regal robe on him; in this context, Kronos is not the king of the Golden Age, but he represents time, which in later ages gains power over all forms of life and from which the new Olympian stock manages to escape only thanks to a stone. The sacrifice recalls

tions performed during Cybele's Mysteries: sometimes the priests who felt possessed by the Goddess would go so far as emasculating themselves in order to resemble her and to become transformed into the female type, which was conceived as the highest manifestation of the sacred. Moreover, from the temples of Astarte and of Artemis at Ephesus to Hieropolis the priests were often eunuchs. Consider the following: (a) the Lydian Hercules, dressed as a woman, who for three years serves the imperious Omphales, who was a type of the divine woman like Seramis; (b) the fact that those who participated in some Mysteries consecrated to Heracles or to Dionysus often wore women's clothes; (c) the fact that priests dressed in women's clothes would keep watch in the sacred woods by some ancient Germanic trees; (d) the ritual inversion of sex whereby some statues of Nana-Ishtar in Susa and of Venus in Cyprus would display masculine features, and whereby women dressed as men and men dressed as women celebrated their cult;[6] and finally (e) the Pelasgic-Minoan offering of *broken* weapons to the Goddess and the usurpation of the sacred Hyperborean warrior symbol of the battle-axe by Amazonian figures and southern goddesses—all of these instances represent the fragmentary, materialized, and distorted echoes, none of them any less characteristic, of the overall view according to which (as the feminine became the fundamental symbol of sacredness, strength, and life) the masculine element and men in general came to be looked down upon as irrelevant, innerly inconsistent, ephemeral, of little value, and as a source of embarrassment.

Mater = Earth, *gremium matris terrae*. This equivalence suggests a main point, namely, that in the type of civilizations with Southern roots it is possible to include all the varieties of cults, myths, and rituals in which the chthonic theme predominates; in which the masculine element appears; and in which not only goddesses but gods of the earth, of growth, natural fertility, the waters, or the subterranean fire are to be found. The Mothers presided over the subterranean world and the occult, conceived of in terms of night and darkness and in opposition to *coelum*, which also suggests the generic idea of the invisible, though in its higher, luminous, and heavenly aspect. Moreover, there is a fundamental and well-known opposition between the Deus, the type of the luminous deities of the Indo-European pantheon,[7] and Al, who is the object of the demonic, ecstatic, and frenzied cult of the dark southern races that lack any

---

the ephemeral character of every life, even when it has a regal dignity. While in the Sacchean feasts the role of the king was played by a prisoner sentenced to death—just as, according to the truth of the Mother, everybody is sentenced to die at their birth—this may contain a deep meaning.

6. Macrobius, *Saturnalia*, 3.7.2. An analogous change of sex occurred at Argos during the feast of the Hibristics, and also in the marriage ritual that was retained in some ancient traditions or employed by some primitive populations that are the degenerated remnants of lost civilizations.

7. The "gods," according to Varro, are beings of light and the day. Heaven is at the origins of all things and it expresses the highest power. The root of Zeus, as that of Jupiter (the Deus Pater), is the same as that for *deva*, Dyaus, and similar words, that refer to the splendor of the sky and the brightness of the day.

contact with what is truly supernatural. In reality, the infernal-demonic element, or the elemental kingdom of the subterranean powers, defines the lower aspect of the cult of the Mother. In opposition to all this there is the "Olympian," immutable, and acosmic reality bathed in the light of a world of intelligible essences *(κόσμος νοητός)*, and sometimes dramatized in the form of gods of war, victory, splendor, or heavenly fire.

If in southern civilizations (in which the feminine, telluric cult predominates) burial was the prevalent funerary rite, while cremation was practiced among civilizations of northern and Aryan origin, this reflects the abovementioned view; namely, that the destiny of the individual was not to become purified from earthly residues and to ascend to heavenly regions, but rather to return to the depths of the Earth and to become dissolved into the chthonic Magna Mater, who was the source of his ephemeral life. This explains the subterranean rather than heavenly location of the kingdom of the dead, which is typical of the most ancient ethnic strata of the South. According to its symbolical meaning, the burial of the dead was characteristic of the cycle of the Mother.

Generally speaking, it is possible to establish a relationship between feminine spirituality and pantheism, according to which ultimate reality is conceived as a great sea into which the nucleus of an individual merges and becomes dissolved like a grain of salt. In pantheism, personality is an illusory and temporary manifestation of the one undifferentiated substance, which is simultaneously spirit and nature as well as the only reality; in this weltanschauung there is no room for any authentically transcendent order. It is necessary to add—and this will be a key factor when assessing the meaning of later cycles—that those forms in which the divine is conceived of as a person represent a mixed and yet similar thing;[8] in these forms we find a connection between the naturalistic relationship of generation and creation of man and the corresponding pathos of utter dependence, humility, passivity, surrender, and renunciation of one's will. Strabo's opinion (*Geographia*, 7.3.4), according to which prayer was taught to man by woman, is very significant in this regard.

I had previously suggested that the materialization of true virility is the inevitable counterpart of the femininization of spirituality. This motif, which will introduce further modifications of various civilizations during the Bronze or Iron Age, helps to characterize other aspects of the civilization of the Mother.

When we compare femininity with virility understood in material terms, such as physical strength, harshness, and violent affirmation, it is only natural that the woman, owing to her characteristics of sensitivity, self-sacrifice, and love—not to mention the mystery of procreation—was regarded as the representative of a higher prin-

---

8. I am referring to cases in which this attitude was not typical only of the inferior strata of a civilization and the exoteric aspect of a tradition, and in which it did not even occur in a given ascetical path as a transitory phase, but formed all relationships with the divine.

ciple; she was even able to acquire authority and to appear as an image of the universal Mother. Thus, it is not a contradiction that in some instances, spiritual and even social gynaecocracy did not appear in effeminate but in violent and bellicose societies. Indeed, the general symbol of the Silver Age and of the Atlantic cycle was not a demonically telluric or a coarsely naturalistic symbol (as in the case of the cycle of the coarse prehistoric feminine idols), but one in which the feminine principle was elevated to a higher form, almost like in the ancient symbol of the Moon as a purified or heavenly Earth *(οὐρανίη αιθερίη λῆ)*, and as such, ruling over anything terrestrial;[9] a spiritual or moral authority was therefore bestowed upon femininity that predominates over purely material and physical virile instincts and qualities.

We find this higher form in those regions where the entities that not only safeguard natural customs and laws, avenge sacrilege, and punish misdeeds (from the northern women to the Erinyes, Themis, and Dike), but that also mediate the gift of immortality are portrayed as female. This form was usually characterized as Demetrian and it was associated with chaste symbols of virgins or mothers who conceive without a male partner, or with goddesses of vegetal fertility and crops such as Ceres. A true opposition exists between the Demetrian and the Aphrodistic type. This differentiation may be associated with the opposition found in Far Eastern countries between the "Pure Land" inhabited by the "Western Woman" and the subterranean world of Emma-O; in the Hellenic traditions this opposition existed between the symbol of Athena and the symbol of the Gorgons whom she fights. The pure and peaceful Demetrian spirituality, portrayed as the moon's light, characterized the type of the Silver Age and, most likely, the cycle of the first Atlantic civilization; historically, however, it was not the original spirituality, but rather a product of an ensuing transformation.[10] Effective forms of gynaecocracy developed in those places where the symbol became a reality; traces of it can be found in the most ancient substratum of several civilizations.[11] Just as leaves are not born one from another but derive from the trunk, likewise, although man produces life, it is woman

---

9. "For Selene is the last of the heavenly spheres that Athena fills with wisdom; and by her aid Selene beholds the intelligible that is higher than the heavens, and adorns with its forms the realm of matter that lies below her, and thus she does away with its savagery and confusion and disorder." Emperor Julian, *Hymn to King Helios,* 150a.

10. Bachofen's views, which in many regards are true from a traditional point of view, should be rejected or at least integrated whenever they take as a reference point and assume as an original and even older element that which is connected with the Earth and with the Mother; these views posit something like a spontaneous evolution from the inferior to the superior in those cases in which there are forms of "mixture" between the inferior (the South) and the superior (the Hyperborean element).

11. A characteristic example is the légend of Jurupary, which reflects the sense of the recent Peruvian civilization. Jurupary was a hero who appeared in societies ruled by "women" to reveal a secret solar law, reserved to men alone, to be taught in every nation, against the ancient law of the mothers. Jurupary, like Quetzalcoatl, eventually withdrew to the sacred land situated east of America.

who begets it. The son does not perpetuate the race, but merely enjoys an individual existence circumscribed to the time and place in which he happens to live; real continuity abides in the feminine-motherly principle. Hence, as a consequence, the woman as mother was the center and the foundation of a people's or a family's laws and the genealogical transmission took place through the feminine bloodline. By transposition, if we go from the family to society at large, we arrive at structures of a collectivist and communist type. In reference to the unity of origin and to the maternal principle of which we are all the children, *aequitas* becomes *aequalitas;* relationships of universal brotherhood and equality are established; a sympathy reaching out beyond all boundaries and differences is affirmed; and a tendency to share whatever one possesses, which is considered to be a gift of Mother Earth, is encouraged. An echo of this motif is found in the fact that until recently, during festivals that celebrated chthonic goddesses and the return of men to the great Mother of Life (not without a revival of an orgiastic element typical of the lowest southern forms) all men felt themselves to be free and equal; caste and class distinctions no longer applied, but could freely be overturned; and a general licentiousness and pleasure in promiscuity tended to be rather widespread.

On the other hand, the so called "natural law" and common promiscuity typical of several savage populations of a totemic type (Africa and Polynesia), up to the so-called Slavic *mir*, almost always point to the typical context of the "civilization of the Mother," even in those places in which matriarchy was not found and where, rather than mixed-variations of the primordial boreal civilization, we find remnants of tellurism inherent to inferior autochthonous races. The communal theme, together with the ideal of a society that does not know wars and that is free and harmonious is found in various descriptions of the earlier ages, including the Golden Age and Plato's description of primordial Atlantis. But this, in my view, is merely due to mistaking a relatively recent memory with a more distant one. The "lunar" theme of peace and community in a naturalistic sense has little to do with those themes that characterized the first age.[12]

Once we eliminate this misunderstanding and bring them back to their true setting (namely, to the second age of the Mother, or Silver rather than Golden Age), the abovementioned memories concerning a primordial, peaceful, and communitarian world close to nature and without conflicts and divisions, become very significant.

---

12. The Saturnalia, by evoking the Golden Age in which Saturn reigned, celebrated the promiscuity and universal brotherhood that were believed to characterize this age. In reality, this belief represents a deviation from traditional truth, and the Saturn who was evoked was not the king of the Golden Age, but rather a chthonic demon; this can be established by the fact that he was represented in the company of Ops, a form of the earth goddess.

On the other hand, if we bring this order of ideas to its logical conclusion, we arrive at a morphological characterization of fundamental importance. In reference to what I have expounded in the first part of this work concerning the meaning of the primordial regality and the relationships between regality and priesthood, it is possible to see that the type of society ruled by a priestly class and yet dominated by "feminine" spirituality, which is characterized by the subordination of the spirit to priestly matters and the confinement of the regal function to a subordinated and material role—this type of society tends to be dominated by a gynaecocratic and lunar spirit or by a Demetrian form, especially if it is oriented toward the ideal of mystical unity and brotherhood. In opposition to a society articulated according to specific hierarchies and animated by a "triumphal" assumption of the spirit and culminating in regal superhumanity—this society reflects the truth of the Mother, but in one of its sublimated versions. This version is in line with what probably characterized the best period of the Atlantic cycle, which was reproduced and preserved in the colonies that developed from the Pelasgic populations into the cycle of the great Asiatic-Mediterranean goddesses of life.

Thus in myth and ritual, in the general views concerning life and the sacred, and in laws, ethics, and even social forms one finds specific elements. These elements can be found in the historical world only as fragments mixed together with other motifs, transposed to other planes, yet leading back, at least ideally, to the same basic orientation. This orientation corresponds to the Southern alteration of the primordial tradition and to the spiritual deviation from the "pole" that occurred, parallel to the change of location, in the mixed-variations of the original boreal stock and the civilizations of the "Silver Age." This is what must be held by those who accept the meanings of North and South—not only morphologically in relation to two universal types of civilization (it is always possible to limit oneself to this minimalist view), but also as points of reference—in order to integrate into a higher meaning the dynamics and the struggle of historical and spiritual forces in the development of recent civilizations, in the latest phase of the "twilight of the gods."[13]

---

13. A. Rosenberg in *The Myth of the Twentieth Century* (Munich, 1930), was right to claim, against Bachofen, that it is necessary to differentiate and not to put civilizations in a linear succession; that the "civilization of the Mother," which Bachofen thought to be the oldest stage from which Uranian and patriarchical societies "evolved" as superior and more recent forms, in reality was a heterogeneous, independent world, inhabited by other races that eventually clashed or came in contact with Nordic traditions. Rosenberg was also right to criticize Wirth's association, concerning the Northern-Atlantic cycle, of the solar cult with the cult of the Mother, which consistently presents chthonic and lunar, rather than solar, characteristics. Such confusions are driven by both the temporal distance between us and those events, and by their assumption of mythical forms; in many traditions the memories of the Arctic cycle are fused together with the memories of the Atlantic cycle.

28

The Cycles of Decadence
and the Heroic Cycle

In relation to the period preceding the Flood, the biblical myth mentions a race of "heroes of old, the men of renown" (Gen. 6:4), born of the union between the sons of heaven and the daughters of men. This union is an example of the miscegenation that caused the primordial spirituality to give way to the spirituality of the age of the Mother. The offspring of this union was the race of the Giants (Nephilim in Hebrew), whom the *Book of Enoch* refers to as "the people from the Far West." The biblical myth relates that the earth became filled with violence and wickedness, thus drawing upon itself the catastrophe of the Flood.

The myth of a fantastic "androgynous" race of powerful beings that the gods themselves feared constitutes another example of nonhuman races; in order to neutralize these beings, the gods broke them into two halves, into "male" and "female."[1] The symbolism of the "inimical pair," found in several traditions, sometimes refers to a similar division that destroys the power feared by the gods; this motif is susceptible to a historical and even a metaphysical interpretation. The primordial powerful and divine race of androgynous beings may be related with the period in which the Nephilim were "men of renown"; it is the race of the Golden Age. After this race, a new division occurred; the "One" generated the "Two," the couple, or the dyad. The first of the two elements is the Woman (Atlantis), the second is Man. This Man was no longer pure spirit and he eventually rebelled against the lunar symbolism by

---

1. Plato, *Symposium*, 189c2–d6. Concerning the theme of the "pair," we may recall that according to Plato the primordial woman Kleito generated three couples in the mythical Atlantis; this corresponds to the Mexican tradition describing the cycle of the Waters, Atonatiu, in which the serpent woman Ciuatcoatl generated a large number of twins. The Mexican cycle ended with a deluge that corresponds in the smallest details (survival of the seeds of all living things, the sending forth of a vulture that does not return and of a hummingbird that returns with a green branch in its beak) to the biblical account.

either affirming himself or by pursuing violent conquests and by attempting to usurp certain spiritual powers.

This is the myth of the Titans. They are the Giants. This is the Bronze Age. In Plato's *Critias* violence and injustice, yearning for power, and covetousness are the qualities ascribed to the degenerate inhabitants of Atlantis.[2] In another Hellenic myth it is said that "men living in primordial times [to which Deucalion, who survived the Flood, belonged] were filled with arrogance and pride; they were guilty of many crimes; they broke oaths and were merciless."

An essential feature of myth and symbol is that both are apt to convey multiple meanings, which must be separated in a clear-cut fashion and assigned methodically to different categories by means of adequate interpretations. This is also the case of the "inimical pair" and of the Titans.

On the basis of the duality Man-Woman (in the sense of a materialized virility and of a merely priestly spirituality), which is the premise of the new types of civilization derived by involution from the primordial civilization, it is possible to define the following types.

The first type of civilization is the Titanic one, in a negative sense, and refers to the spirit of a materialistic and violent race that no longer recognized the authority of the spiritual principle corresponding to the priestly symbol or to the spiritually feminine "brother" (e.g., Cain vs. Abel); this race affirmed itself and attempted to take possession, by surprise and through an inferior type of employment, of a body of knowledge that granted control over certain invisible powers inherent to things and people. Therefore, this represented an upheaval and a counterfeit of what could have been the privilege of the previous "glorious men," namely, of the virile spirituality connected to the function of order and of domination "from above." It was Prometheus who usurped the heavenly fire in favor of the human races, and yet he did not know how to carry it; thus the fire became his source of torment and damnation[3] until he was freed by another hero, Heracles, who was worthier and also one

---

2. "To the perceptive eye the depth of their degeneration was clear enough, but to those whose judgment of true happiness is defective, they seemed, in their pursuit of unbridled ambition and power, to be at the height of their fame and fortune." Plato, *Critias*.

3. The punishment met by Prometheus contains symbolic elements that reveal its esoteric meaning: an "eagle" ate his liver. The eagle or the sparrow hawk, birds of prey sacred to Zeus and to Apollo (in Egypt to Horus, among the Nordic people to Odin-Wotan, in India to Agni and Indra), were among the symbols of the regal "glory," in other words, of the divine fire that Prometheus stole. The liver was considered the seat of a feisty spirit and of the "irascible soul." The shift of the divine force onto the plane of merely human and impure qualities that are not adequate to it was what consumed Prometheus and was his punishment as well. I have already mentioned the double aspect in the symbolism of the Titan Atlas in which the idea of a "polar" function and of a punishment are seen as interchangeable.

reconciled with the Olympian principle (i.e., with Zeus) and its ally in the struggle against the Giants. The second race was "far worse than the other," both naturally (ρυὴν) and mentally (νόημα). According to Hesiod, as early as the end of the first age, it refused to pay respect to the gods and thus opened itself up to the influence of telluric forces (according to Hesiod, at the end of its cycle it became the race of subterranean demons, the ὑποχθόνιοι); it eventually produced a mortal generation characterized by pertinacity, physical strength, and an uncontrolled pleasure in violence, war, and power (this corresponds to Hesiod's Bronze Age, to the Persians' Iron Age, and to the biblical giants, or Nephilim).[4] According to yet another Hellenic tradition, Zeus is believed to have caused the Flood in order to extinguish the "fire" element that threatened to destroy the entire earth, as Phaëton, the son of the Sun, lost control of the quadriga that the frenzied horses had carried up into the sky. "Age of battle-axes, age of swords, age of wolves, until the world is ruined. Brothers will fight and kill each other": this is the prophecy contained in the *Edda*.[5] Men living in this age have hearts "as hard as iron." But no matter how scary these men may appear, they will fall victim to the black death and disappear into the "moldering domain [εὑρωέντα] of cold Hades."[6] While the biblical myth claims that the Flood put an end to this civilization, we may assume that the Atlantic cycle ended with a similar stock and that a similar civilization was eventually swept away by the oceanic catastrophe—and maybe because of the previously mentioned abuse of certain secret powers (Titanic black magic).

Generally speaking, according to the Northern tradition, the "Age of the Battle-Axes" opened the way to the unleashing of the elemental powers, that eventually swept away the divine race of the Aesir—in this context this race may be made to correspond with the race of the residual groups of the golden race and to the breaking down of the barriers of the "fortress at the center of the world," which express figuratively the creative limits established by the primordial "polar" spirituality. The emergence of women and of a no-longer virile spirituality heralded the "twilight of the Aesir" and the end of the golden cycle.[7] During this time, the dark strength that the Aesir themselves had nourished, after keeping it chained for a while—symbolized by the wolf Fenrir, or better, by two wolves—"grows tremendously."[8] This corresponds to the usurpation of the Titans, which was immediately followed by the revolt and the emergence of all the elemental powers, the Southern infernal fire, and

---

4. Hesiod, *Works and Days*, 129–42; 143–55.
5. *Gylfaginning*, 5.
6. Hesiod, *Works and Days*, 154.
7. *Gylfaginning*, 51.
8. Ibid., 34. From the mention that the two wolves were generated by a giantess (*Gylfaginning*, 12) we can see the inner connection between the various "stages of decadence."

the beings of the earth *(hrinthursen)* that used to be kept outside the walls of Asgard. The bond is broken. After the "Age of the Battle-Axe" (the Bronze Age) one of the two wolves "will swallow the sun. Then the other wolf will catch the Moon":[9] in other words, this is the end not only of the solar spirituality, but of the Demetrian, lunar spirituality as well. Odin, the king of the Aesir, falls, and Vidar himself, who succeeded in killing the wolf Fenrir, falls victim to its poison; in other words his own divine nature as an Aesir is corrupted by the lethal principle that is passed on to him by this wild creature. Fate or the twilight *(rok)* of the gods takes place with the collapse of the Bifrost bridge that connects heaven and earth;[10] this represents the earth abandoned to itself, lacking all connections with the divine element, following the rebellion of the Titans. This is the "Dark Age," or "Iron Age" that comes after the Bronze Age.

A more concrete reference is given by the concurrent witnesses of the oral and written traditions of several peoples that mention a frequent opposition between the representatives of the spiritual and the temporal (i.e., regal or warrior) powers, regardless of the special forms assumed by either one in adapting to different historical circumstances. This phenomenon was just another aspect of the process leading to the third age. The usurpation of the priestly caste was followed by the revolt of the warrior class and by its struggle against the priestly class for the achievement of supreme authority; this was the prelude to an even lower stage than that reached by a Demetrian and priestly society; this was the social equivalent of the Bronze Age and of the Titanic, Luciferian, or Promethean motif.

While the Titanic upheaval represented the degenerated (in a materialistic, violent, and almost individualistic sense) attempt to reinstate "virility," it nevertheless corresponded to an analogous deviation from the sacred female law that characterized the "Amazonian" phenomenon. From a symbolic point of view the Amazons and the generic type of armed goddesses can be understood, following Bachofen, as an abnormally empowered gynaecocracy, or as an attempt to react and to reinstate

---

9. Concerning the "wolf" and the "Age of the Wolf," here portrayed as synonymous with the Bronze Age and with the "Dark Age," we must keep in mind that this symbolism also has an opposite meaning: the wolf was associated with Apollo and with the light *(ly-kos, lyke)*, not only among the Hellenes, but also among the Celts. The positive meaning of the wolf appears in the Roman cycle, in which the wolf and the eagle appeared as the symbols of the "eternal city." In the exegesis of Emperor Julian (*Hymn to King Helios*, 154b) the wolf was associated with the solar principle in its regal aspect. The double meaning of the symbol of the wolf is but an example of the degeneration of an older cult, the symbols of which take on a negative meaning in the following age. The wolf—in the Nordic tradition—that was related to the primordial, warrior element takes on a negative meaning when this element loses control and becomes unleashed.

10. This bridge, which recalls the "pontifical" symbol mentioned in chapter 1, collapses when Muspell's sons "go and ride it"; the lord of Muspell is Surtr, who comes from the south to battle the Aesir. Thus, we have yet another mention of a southern location from which destructive forces will descend upon the world.

the ancient authority of the "feminine" or lunar principle against the male revolt and usurpation; this attempt, though, was carried out on the same plane as the violent masculine affirmation and in so doing it lost that spiritual element that alone established the primacy and the dignity of the Demetrian principle. Whether or not Amazonism enjoyed a historical and social reality, it is found throughout myths with constant traits, thus rendering it susceptible of characterizing analogically a certain type of civilization.

Thus, it is possible to prescind from the real appearance of women warriors in history or prehistory and understand Amazonism as the symbol of the reaction of a "lunar" or priestly spirituality (the feminine dimension of the spirit) that was unable to oppose the material or even temporal power (the masculine dimension of the spirit, which no longer acknowledged its laws, as for instance in the myth of the Titans) in any way other than in a material and temporal fashion, that is, by adopting the way of being of its opposite (the virile figure and strength of the "Amazon"). Thus, it is possible to refer to what I previously said concerning the alteration of the normal relationship between royalty and priesthood. In the abovementioned generalization there is Amazonism wherever there are priests who do not yearn *to be* kings, but rather *to dominate* kings.

There is a very revealing legend according to which the Amazons, who attempted in vain to conquer the symbolical "White Island" (the *leuke* island, which has an equivalent in several traditions), did not flee at the sight of a Titan-like figure, but rather at the sight of a *hero:* Achilles. They were also fought by other heroes such as Theseus, who can be considered the founder of the virile state of Athens, and by Bellerophon. The Amazons, who had usurped the Hyperborean battle-axe, came to the rescue of Venus's city, Troy, against the Achaeans; they were eventually exterminated by another hero, Heracles, the rescuer of Prometheus. Heracles grabbed from their queen the symbolic belt of Ares-Mars and the axe $(\lambda\alpha\beta\rho\acute{\upsilon}\varsigma)$ that was the symbol of the supreme power of the Lydian dynasty of the Heraclideans.[11] The meaning of Amazonism versus "Olympian" heroism will be discussed further on.

A second type of civilization must also be considered. The pair always come first. There is, however, a crisis, and the feminine primacy is upheld through a new principle, the Aphrodistic principle. The mother is replaced by the hetaera, the son by the lover, and the solitary virgin by the divine couple that, as I have suggested, in various mythologies often characterizes a compromise between two opposite cults. But the woman in this context (unlike in the Olympian synthesis) is not Hera, who was subordinated to Zeus although always scheming behind his back; we do not

---

11. In the Germanic sagas the same theme appeared in the conflict between the original figure of Brunhild, queen of the island, and Siegfried, who defeated her.

even have, as in the Far Eastern synthesis, the *yang* principle that retains its active and heavenly character vis-à-vis the *yin* principle, which is its feminine and earthly complement.

Instead, the chthonic and infernal nature penetrates the virile principle and lowers it to a phallic level. The woman now dominates man as he becomes enslaved to the senses and a mere instrument of procreation. Vis-à-vis the Aphrodistic goddess, the divine male is subjected to the magic of the feminine principle and is reduced to the likes of an earthly demon or a god of the fecundating waters—in other words, to an insufficient and dark power. From this theme derive, analogically and according to different adaptations, types of civilization that may be called Aphrodistic. This could be yet another meaning of the theory of eros that Plato associated with the myth of the androgynous beings whose power was shattered when they became "two," male and female. Sexual love arises between mortal beings from the deep-seated desire of the fallen male who realizes his inner insufficiency and who seeks, in the fulgurating ecstasis of orgasm, to reascend to the wholeness of the primordial "androgynous" state. In this sense, the erotic experience conceals a variation in the theme of the rebellion of the Titans with the only difference being that, due to its own nature, it takes place under the aegis of the feminine principle. It is easy to remark that a principle of ethical decadence and corruption must necessarily be connected with a civilization oriented in this sense, as it is apparent in the various festivals that up to relatively recent times were inspired by Aphroditism. If Mouru, the third creation of Ahura Mazda, which most likely corresponds to Atlantis, is seen as the Demetrian civilization, then the notion that the god of darkness set up various sins[12] as some kind of countercreation may refer to the following period of Aphrodistic degeneration in that civilization that is parallel to the Titanic upheaval itself; this is true especially if we consider the frequent associations between Aphrodistic goddesses and violent and brutally warlike divine figures.

It is well known that Plato established a hierarchy of the forms of eros, rising from the sensual and the profane up to the peaks of the sacred[13] and culminating in the eros through which "the mortal seeks to live forever and to become immortal."[14] In Dionysism, eros becomes "sacred frenzy," mystic orgiasm: it is the highest possibility inherent in this direction and it is aimed at undoing the bonds of matter and at producing a transfiguration through frenzy, excess, and ecstasis.[15] But if the symbol of Dionysus, who fights against the Amazons himself, reveals the highest ideal of

---

12. Such as unbelief, pride, sodomy, burial of the dead, witchcraft, and cremation. *Vendidad*, 1.12.
13. Plato, *Symposium*, 14–15; 26–29; *Phaedrus*, 244–45; 251–57b.
14. *Symposium*, 26.
15. For an in-depth analysis of this positive possibility of human sexuality, see my *Eros and the Mysteries of Love*.

this spiritual world, nevertheless it remains something inferior compared to what the third possibility of the new era will be: the heroic reintegration that alone is really detached from both the feminine and the telluric principle.[16] In fact, Dionysus was also represented as a demon of the infernal regions ("Hades is the same as Dionysus" said Heraclitus[17]), and was often associated with the principle of the waters (Poseidon) or with the underground fire (Hephaestus). Often he is found together with feminine figures of mothers, virgins, or goddesses of nature turned into lovers: Demeter and Core, Ariadne and Aridela, Semelis and Libera. The masculinity of the Corybantes, who often dressed as women, like the priests in the Phrygian cult of the Mother, was very ambiguous. The ecstatic and pantheistic orientation, associated with the sexual element, predominates in the Mystery or in the "sacred orgy"; frenzied contacts with the occult forces of the earth and maenadic and pandemic liberations occur in a domain that is simultaneously that of unrestrained sex, night, and death. If in Rome the Bacchanalia were originally celebrated by women and if in the Dionysian Mysteries women could play the role of priestesses and initiators; and if historically all the memories of Dionysian epidemics are essentially to be attributed to the feminine element—in all this we have a clear indication of the survival during this cycle too, of the theme of the woman's preeminence, not only in the coarsely Aphrodistic stage (in which she dominates through the bond that eros in its carnal form imposes upon phallic man), but also as the woman inducing an ecstasis that may also signify dissolution, destruction of the form, and therefore, attainment of the spirit, but only on condition of the renunciation of its possession in a virile form.

The third and last type of civilization to be considered is the civilization of the heroes. Hesiod mentions that following the Bronze Age and prior to the Iron Age, Zeus created a better lineage out of those races whose destiny was "to descend ingloriously to Hades." Hesiod called this lineage the race of "heroes" to whom it is given the possibility of attaining immortality and partaking, despite all, in a state similar to that of the primordial age.[18] In this type of civilization we find evidence of the attempt to restore the tradition of the origins on the basis of the warrior principle and of membership in the warrior caste. Indeed not all the "heroes" become immortal by escaping Hades; this is the fate of only some of them. And if we examine the body of Hellenic

---

16. Bachofen identified three stages in the cult of Dionysus that represent this god respectively as a chthonic being, a lunar nature, and a luminous god associated with Apollo, although with an Apollo conceived as the sun subject to change and passions. In this latter aspect Dionysus may fall into the group of heroes who vanquished the Amazons. More than in the Thracian-Hellenic myth, however, the highest possibility of the Dionysian principle was upheld in the Indo-Aryan myth of the *soma*, a heavenly and lunar principle that induces a divine intoxication *(mada)* and that is related with the regal animal, the eagle, and with a struggle against female demons.
17. Heraclitus, frag. B15 Diehl.
18. Hesiod, *Works and Days*, 156–73.

myths and the myths of other traditions, upon recognizing the affinity—hidden behind various symbols—of the deeds of the Titans with those of the heroes, we will realize that the hero and the Titans, after all, belong to the same stock; they are the daring ones who undertook the same transcendent adventure, which can either fail or succeed. The heroes who become immortal are those whose adventure succeeds; in other words, they correspond to those who are really capable of overcoming, thanks to an inner impulse toward transcendence, the deviation proper to the Titanic attempt to restore the primordial spiritual virility and the supremacy over the woman, that is, over the lunar spirit, both Aphrodistic and Amazonian; conversely, the other heroes, those who are not capable of realizing such a possibility conferred upon them by the Olympian principle, or Zeus—the same possibility to which Jesus referred when he said (Matt. 11:2): "The kingdom of heaven has been subject to violence and the violent are taking it by storm"[19]—descend to the same level as the race of the Titans and of the Giants, who were cursed with various punishments and afflictions as a result of their boldness and their corruption (of which they were guilty) in the "ways of the flesh on earth." As far as these relationships between the way of the Titans and that of the heroes is concerned, there is an interesting myth according to which once Prometheus was freed, he taught Heracles the way to reach the Garden of the Hesperides, where he would find the fruit that renders one immortal. Such a fruit, once obtained by Heracles, is taken back by Athena, who represents in this context the Olympian intellect, and put back "so that it may not be partaken of by anybody";[20] this probably means that the attainment of that fruit should be reserved for the stock to which it belongs and that it should not be desecrated by putting it at the disposal of the human race, as Prometheus intended to do.

Even in the heroic cycle we sometimes find the theme of the dyad, that is, of the pair, and of the Woman, but with a different meaning from that of the cases I discussed in the first part concerning the saga of the Rex Nemorensis, the "women" who appoint divine kings, the "women" of the chivalrous cycle, and so on. Concerning this different aspect, in which the same symbolism will appear to function differently, here it will suffice to say that the woman who embodies a vivifying principle (such as Eve, the "Living Woman," Hebe, and what derives from the relation of the divine women with the Tree of Life, etc.); or a principle of transcendent or enlightening wisdom (such as Athena, born from the mind of the Olympian Zeus, Heracles' guide; or the virgin Sophia, or the Lady Intelligence of the medieval "Love's Lieges," etc.); or a power (such as the Hindu *śaktis,* the goddess of the Morrigu's battles who

---

19. During his quest for the gift of everlasting life, the Chaldean hero Gilgamesh uses violence and threatens to knock down the door of the garden filled with "divine trees." A feminine figure, Sabitu, had closed this door to him.
20. Apollodorus, *Bibl.,* 2.122.

offers her love to solar heroes of the Celtic Ulster Cycle, etc.)—is the object of conquest, and does not take from the hero his virile character, but allows him to integrate it on a higher plane. A relevant motif in the cycles of the heroic type is that of the opposition to any gynaecocratic claim and to any Amazonian attempt to usurp power. This motif, together with the previous one, which is equally essential for a definition of the notion of "hero" and refers to an alliance with the Olympian principle and a struggle against the Titanic principle, had a very clear expression in the Hellenic cycle, especially in the figure of the Doric Heracles.

We have already seen that Heracles, like Theseus, Bellerophon, and Achilles, fights against the Amazons and eventually exterminates them. Though the Lydian Heracles falls for Omphale, the Doric Heracles proves to be a true μισόγυνος, an enemy of women. Since his birth, Hera, the earth goddess, is hostile to him; while still in his cradle he choked two snakes she had sent to kill him. Heracles has constantly to battle Hera without winning, but succeeds instead in wounding her and in taking her only daughter Hebe, the "perennial youth." If we consider other figures of this cycle in both East and West, we will always find these fundamental themes. Thus Apollo, whose birth had been prevented many times by Hera (it is significant that she was helped in this by Ares, the violent god of war), who had sent the serpent Python to kill him, eventually has to fight against Tatius, Hera's son, who can count on his mother's protection. In the ensuing struggle she is wounded by the Hyperborean hero, just like in the epic tale Aphrodite is wounded by Ajax. As uncertain as the final outcome may be of the saga of Gilgamesh, the Chaldean hero who set out to find the plant of immortality, the bottom line is that his story is the account of the struggle he waged against the goddess Ishtar, an Aphrodistic type of the Mother of Life. He turned her love down, reminding her of the fate of her former lovers; he finally slew the demonic animal that the goddess unleashed against him. In one of his actions that is considered "heroic and virile," Indra, who is the heavenly prototype of the hero, strikes the Amazonian and heavenly woman Uṣas with his thunderbolt while being at the same time the Lord of Śakti, whose name also means "power." And if Parsifal's departure caused his mother, who opposed his heroic vocation as a "heavenly knight,"[21] to die of grief; and if the Persian hero Rostam, according to the *Shanami*, must thwart the plot of the dragon that approached him in the disguise of a seductive woman before freeing a blind king who, thanks to Rostam, gains his sight back and is revealed to be the one who attempted to ascend to heaven with the help of "eagles"—in all this we find the same theme over and over again.

---

21. In the saga of the Grail, the sacred "heroic" type corresponds to the one who can sit in the empty place in the assembly of the knights without being struck by lightning.

Generally speaking, the seductive snares of a woman who tries to distract from a symbolic feat a hero who is conceived of as a slayer of Titans, monstrous beings, or rebellious warriors, or as a conqueror abiding by a higher law, is such a recurrent and popular theme as not to require individual examples. The element in these legends and sagas that must be firmly upheld, however, is that the woman's snares can be reduced to the plane of the flesh in the lowest sense of the word. If it is true that woman brings death and that man overcomes her through the spirit by passing from the phallic to the spiritual plane of virility, it must be added that the plot devised by the woman, or by the goddess, expresses in esoteric terms the snare represented by a form of spirituality that emasculates and tends to paralyze or to thwart any impulse toward the supernatural.

Lordship over the origins; not to be the original force but to possess it; the quality of the $\alpha\dot{\upsilon}\tau o\phi\upsilon\acute{\eta}\varsigma$ [to be a light unto oneself] and of the $\alpha\dot{\upsilon}\tau o\tau\acute{\epsilon}\lambda\epsilon\sigma\tau o\varsigma$ [to have oneself as an end], which in Hellas was often associated with the heroic ideal— these qualities have sometimes been represented through the symbolism of parricide or of incest; parricide in the sense of an emancipation, and of becoming one's own guiding principle; incest in an analogous sense, conveying the idea of possessing the prime generating matter.

Thus, as a reflection of the same spirit in the world of the gods, we find, for instance, the type of Zeus who killed his own father and possessed his mother Rhea, when in order to run away from him, she took the form of a snake. Indra himself, just like Apollo, who had killed the snake Python, slew the primordial serpent Ahi; he too was believed to have killed his heavenly father Dyaus. Even in the symbolism of the Hermetic Ars Regia we find the theme of the "philosophical incest."[22]

With regard to the two accounts of the solar symbolism previously employed to point out the differentiation of traditions, we may generally assume that the heroic myth is related to the sun, which is associated with a principle of change, not with change as such—as in the destiny of caducity and perennial redissolution into Mother Earth typical of the year-god—but in a way that tends to become free from this principle in order to become transfigured and reintegrated into an Olympian immutability and into a Uranian immortal nature.

The heroic civilizations that arose prior to the Iron Age (an age deprived of every real spiritual principle) and around the time of the Bronze Age, and that overcame both the Demetrian-Aphrodistic spirituality and the Titanic *hubris* thus bringing about the end of the Amazonian upheavals, represent partial resurrections of the Northern Light as well as instances of restoration of the golden Arctic cycle. It is

---

22. See J. Evola, *The Hermetic Tradition*, chap. 19.

very significant that among the feats that bestowed Olympian immortality upon Heracles we find the adventure of the Garden of the Hesperides. According to some traditions, in order to reach that garden Heracles went through the symbolic northern center "which neither ship nor marching feet may find,"[23] namely, the land of the Hyperboreans. Then Heracles, the "handsome victor" (χαλλίνικος), was believed to have carried away from this land the green olive leaf with which victors are crowned.[24]

In summary, I have reached a morphological determination of six basic types of civilization and tradition that came after the primordial one (the Golden Age). These are: Demetrism, representing the pure Southern Light (the Silver Age, Atlantic cycle, societies ruled by a priestly caste); Aphroditism as a degenerate version of Demetrism; and finally Amazonism, which was a deviated attempt at lunar restoration. On the other hand, we find Titanism (in a different, almost Luciferian context), which was a degeneration of the Northern Light (the Bronze Age, age of warriors and giants); Dionysism, as a deviated and emasculated masculine spirituality generating passive and promiscuous forms of ecstasis;[25] and finally, Heroism, as the restoration of the Olympian-solar spirituality and the overcoming of both the Mother and Titan figures. These are the fundamental structures to which, generally speaking, we can analytically reduce any mixed form of civilization arising in historical times during the cycle of the Dark Age or Age of Iron.

---

23. Pindar, *The Pythian Odes*, 10.2.
24. Pindar, *The Olympian Odes*, 3.
25. It is important to distinguish the valid elements that Dionysism may contain in the context of the so-called Way of the Left Hand (in relation to a special initiatory use of sex), from the meaning that Dionysism has in the context of a morphology of civilizations.

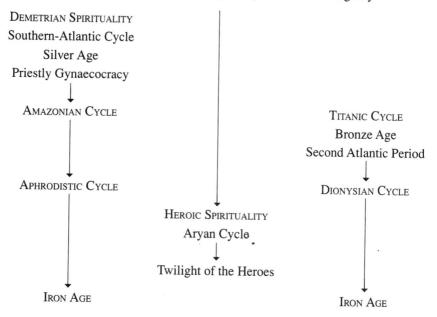

SOLAR SPIRITUALITY

Arctic Cycle of the Golden Age—Cycle of Divine Regality

DEMETRIAN SPIRITUALITY
Southern-Atlantic Cycle
Silver Age
Priestly Gynaecocracy
↓
AMAZONIAN CYCLE

APHRODISTIC CYCLE

TITANIC CYCLE
Bronze Age
Second Atlantic Period
↓
DIONYSIAN CYCLE

HEROIC SPIRITUALITY
Aryan Cycle
↓
Twilight of the Heroes

IRON AGE

IRON AGE

29

Tradition and Antitradition

THE AMERICAN CYCLE AND
THE EASTERN MEDITERRANEAN CYCLE

For obvious reasons I cannot include in the present work a metaphysics of history of the main ancient civilizations. I will limit myself to pointing out some of their most characteristic aspects and meanings, thus providing a common thread to those who want to pursue their own special research in any one of them.

In any event, my scope will be confined to the Western world, since outside our hemisphere the great majority of civilizations retained, in one way or another and until recent times, a traditional character ("traditional" in the widest sense of the term, which includes all of the previously described forms of civilization and associates them in a common opposition to the "humanist" cycle of the last ages), which they eventually lost due to the eroding action exercised upon them by Western countries that had themselves fallen victim to a degenerative process. Thus, in order to understand the processes that played a decisive role in the genesis of the modern world, it is necessary to look at the West.

The traces of the Northern and solar spirituality can be found in historical times mainly in the area of the Aryan civilizations. Considering the abuse that has been made of the term *aryan* in some contemporary milieus, such a term should be used with some reservations; in other words, it should not be made to correspond to a merely biological or ethnic concept (in this regard it would be more appropriate to talk about a boreal or Northern-Atlantic race, depending on the case at hand), but rather to the concept of a *race of the spirit*, whose correspondence to a physical race has varied from one civilization to another. "Aryan" corresponds more or less to "heroic"; the connection with the origins still exists as a dimmed legacy, but the decisive element is the tendency toward inner liberation and the reintegration in an active and combative form. The fact that in India the term *ārya* was the synonym of *dvīja*, "twice-born" or "regenerated," supports this point.[1]

Concerning the area proper to the Aryan civilization there is the interesting testimony of the *Aitareya Brāhamana*. This text relates that the struggle between the *deva*, the luminous deities, and the *asura*, the enemies of the divine heroes, began in the four regions of space. The region in which the *deva* triumphed and that received the name of *sa-eśa dig aparājita*, or "unconquered region," was the region situated between North and East, which corresponds to the direction of the Northern-Atlantic migration. On the other hand, the South has been considered in India as the region inhabited by demons, by the forces hostile to the gods and to the *āryas;* the "southern fire," of the ritual of three fires is aimed at exorcising these forces.[2] As far as the Western world is concerned, a reference can be made to the so-called battle-axe cultures that are usually associated with the megalithic culture of the dolmen. To the profane sciences, the original seat of these races still remains shrouded in mystery, like the seat of the first races that were clearly superior to Neanderthal man and who have been called the "Greeks of the Paleolithic." There is a connection between the appearance of the "battle-axe cultures" of the Neolithic and the more recent expansion of the Indo-European populations ("Aryans") in Europe; they are believed to have originated the political and military institutions and forms of government that opposed the Demetrian, peaceful, communitarian, and priestly type of culture and that often replaced it.[3]

Other civilizations in addition to the Aryan ones have displayed traces of the primordial tradition up to historical times. To follow closely the interplay of the two opposite themes of South and North, however, with reference to an ethnic element, would take us too far afield and cause us to formulate uncertain hypotheses.

In any event, with regard to pre-Columbian America, we must consider first of all the archaic substratum of a telluric, Southern cycle of civilization related to the Atlantean cycle. In this cycle we find the civilizations of the Maya, the Tiahuanac, and the Pueblo as well those of other stocks or minor centers; its traits are very similar to those that can be found in the prehistoric traces of some sort of Southern belt extending from the Pelasgian Mediterranean to the vestiges of the pre-Aryan civilization of Mohenjo-Daro (India) and to analogous traces in predynastic China.

Such a civilization is prevalently of a Demetrian, priestly type; solar symbols

---

1. For an overview of the notion of "Aryan," see my *Sintesi di dottrina della razza*.
2. In the *Ṛg Veda* the South is the direction of the sacrifice performed in honor of the forefathers *(pitṛ-yāna)*; conversely, the North is the direction of the sun and of the gods *(deva-yāna)*.
3. C. Dawson, *The Age of the Gods*.

survive together with a strong chthonic component, though in altered and weakened forms, so much so that one would search in vain for elements that are traceable to the principle of spiritual virility and Olympian superiority. This applies also to the civilization of the Maya where we find prominent figures of priests and deities who assume the insignia of supreme sovereignty and royalty. There is a very characteristic Mayan figure in the Dresden Codex of the god Kukulcán, adorned with the insignia of royalty and with a priest kneeling before him, performing a bloody and mortifying ritual on himself. The Demetrian principle thus leads to forms of a "religious" type, in which fasts and bodily mortifications characterize the fall of man from his original dignity. Though the Maya built an empire called "the Kingdom of the Great Snake" (*nachan* was a frequent and highly representative symbol of this civilization), it had a peaceful rather than a warrior and heroic character; the priestly sciences were highly developed, but once the empire reached a high stage of opulence, it slowly but increasingly degenerated into the forms of a hedonistic and Aphrodistic civilization. It seems that among the Maya originated the figure of the god Quetzalcoatl, who was a solar Atlantean god who came to be worshiped in an emasculated type of cult that was of a peaceful, contemplative, and self-mortifying nature. According to a tradition, one day Quetzalcoatl left his subjects and withdrew to the Atlantic seat whence he had come.

This should probably be related to the invasions of the races of the Nahuatlans, Toltecs, and finally of the Aztecs who overcame the Maya and their crepuscular civilization, forming new states. These are races that retain in a more distinct way the memory of Tula and Aztlan, that is, of the Northern-Atlantic seat, and thus can be considered part of a "heroic" cycle. Their last creation was the ancient Mexican empire, the capital of which (Tenochtitlan), according to a legend, was built on the site of an apparition of an eagle holding in its claws a snake. The same can be said of those Inca stocks who were sent as conquerors by the "sun" and who created the Peruvian empire after subjugating races of lower types of civilizations and their animistic and chthonic cults (which had survived in the lowest strata of society).[4] There is a very interesting legend about the race of the giants of Tiuhanac—whose heaven included only the moon (lunar cycle with its Titanic counterpart)—a race that killed the Sun's prophet only to be massacred and turned into stone by the ensuing apparition of the Sun; this legend can be related to the advent of the Incas. Generally speaking, there are numerous legends concerning the American white stocks of supernatural conquerors credited with creating various civilizations.[5] In Mexico, the following

---

4. According to an Inca law, every new king had the duty to increase the size of the empire and to replace the indigenous cults with the solar cult.

5. See L. Spence, *The Mythologies of Ancient Mexico and Peru* (London, 1914). Analogous legends are found in North America too. From scientific researches on the blood types applied to the problem of the race, it seems that among the Indians of North America and the Pueblos the blood remnants are more similar than that between Scandinavian people.

pairs of contrasting elements are very revealing: (1) a solar calendar opposed to a lunar one, which apparently belonged to the more ancient stratum of the aboriginal civilization and was mainly employed by the priestly caste; (2) an aristocratic and hereditary system of property that was opposed to a communist, plebeian type; and finally, (3) the opposition between the cult of fierce warrior deities, such as Uitzilopochtli and Tezcatlipoca, and the surviving traces of the cult of Quetzalcoatl. In the most distant memories of these civilizations we find again—as in the *Edda*— the theme of the struggle against the giants and a recent generation affected by the Flood. At the time of the Spanish invasion, the warrior civilization of these races showed a characteristic degeneration in the direction of a special and sinister version of Dionysism, which may be called frenzy of blood. The themes of holy war and heroic death as a sacrifice that confers immortality, which were found among the Aztecs as well as among northern European stocks or Arab people, in Central and South American civilizations were mixed with some kind of frenzy of human sacrifices; these sacrifices, even in the form of collective slaughters, were performed in order to maintain contact with the divine but with a dark, fierce exaltation derived from destroying life, the likeness of which is to be found nowhere else in the world.

As in the case of the Incan empire, other factors of a general degeneration coupled with internal political strife brought about the collapse of Mexican civilizations— which undoubtedly had a glorious and solar past—at the hands of a few groups of European adventurers. The vital and inner potential of these cycles had been depleted for a long time, and thus we cannot verify any subsistence or revival of the ancient spirit in the times following the conquest.

Nevertheless, morainic fragments of the ancient heritage endured for a longer time in the spirit and in the race of some North American stocks. In these tribes too, the heroic element was altered, thus generating forms of unprecedented cruelty and harshness. Nevertheless, for the most part, it is possible to subscribe to the view of Frithjof Schuon, who spoke about the

> singularly complete human type of the American Indian: his dignity, his pride, his moral uprightness and strength, his generosity and his heroism, which are all dimensions of an inner beauty represented both by the sun and by the eagle, command our respect and bespeak a spirituality without which these virtues would appear unintelligible and lacking a sufficient reason.[6]

A similar situation can be verified during the late Neolithic in Europe, with regard to warrior stocks that may appear somewhat barbaric when compared to the societies

---

6. F. Schuon, *Études traditionnelles* (1949), 3.64.

of a Demetrian and priestly type that they swept away, subdued, or absorbed. In these stocks, notwithstanding a certain involution, there are visible traces of the formative action of the previous cycle of Nordic spirituality; this is also the case, as I will try to document, of the epigones of several northern people during the age of the invasions.

As far as China is concerned, the ritual retained traces of an ancient dynastic transmission following the feminine line that was radically opposed to the spirit of the cosmocratic view, according to which the emperor embodied both the functions of male and of pole vis-à-vis the forces of the demos and of the world, and the spirit of one of the most rigorous types of paternal right ever seen. Even the recently discovered vestiges of a civilization similar to that of the Maya, which had a linear type of writing and was considered to be the unsuspected underground and most archaic stratum of the Chinese civilization, seem to suggest that a Demetrian-Atlantean phase[7] was followed by a solar cycle (how such a thing could have happened still needs to be determined) that was not able to erase all of its traces. We find an echo of this phase in the following elements: (1) those metaphysical views that show traces of the archaic idea in the assimilation of "Heaven" to a woman or mother, which was conceived as the original source of life; (2) the frequent recurrence of the primacy of the "left" over the "right" and in the opposition between a lunar and a solar calendar; (3) the telluric element of the popular cult of demons; (4) the shamanic ritual with its disorderly and frenzied expressions; and finally, (5) the practice of magical techniques, which were originally the almost exclusive prerogative of women, in opposition to the nonmystical and almost Olympian austerity of the official Chinese patrician and imperial religion. From an ethnical perspective, in the Far Eastern regions it is possible to recognize the encounter of two opposite currents: the first, which came from the North, was endowed with the characteristics of Ural-Altaic populations (in which there was a strong Aryan component), while the second originated in southeastern and austral regions. The periods in which the elements of the first current predominated, also corresponded to the periods of China's greatness; these times were characterized by a marked propensity toward war and by territorial expansion, both of which played a similar role in the Japanese cycle. An in-depth investigation would easily bring similar data to light. In ancient China the polar symbol of centrality played a prominent role; it was connected both to the view of the Middle Empire, which was underlined by local geographic elements, and to the recurrence of the ideas of the "middle way" and of "equilibrium" in views that influenced the ethical

---

7. See H. Schmidt, *Prähistorisches aus Ostasien* (1924), concerning the possibility of civilizing actions of a Western origin during the Neolithic in China.

plane and that originated a special (clear and ritualistic) attitude toward life. Just like in ancient Rome, the Chinese representatives of power embodied a religious type too: the type of the "priest" appeared only in a later period and in relation to exogenous cults. The foundation of the Chinese wisdom tradition, namely the *I Ching*, was attributed to a mythical king, Fo-hi, just like the main commentaries to this text were believed to have been written by princes and nobles rather than priests. The teachings found therein—which according to Fo-hi himself are traceable to a very ancient and not easily individuated past—were the common foundation of two more recent doctrines (Taoism and Confucianism) that seem to have very little in common, considering the different dimensions they address. These two doctrines represented a spiritual revival in a period of latent crisis and sociopolitical disintegration; Taoism contributed to the revival of the metaphysical element through initiatory and esoteric developments, while Confucianism helped to revive the ethical and ritualistic element. Thus, a regular traditional continuity was preserved in China in stable forms until relatively recent times.

The same holds true for Japan. Its traditional national form, Shintoism, exemplifies an influence that rectified and raised to a higher level a cultural milieu that partially derived from a primitive stratum (nothing relevant can be deduced from the presence of the isolated white stock of the Ainu). In historical times, at the heart of Shintoism we find the imperial idea and the identification of the imperial tradition with the divine tradition. "Obeying a command, I have descended from heaven," it says in the *Ko-gi-ki* about the founding father of the Japanese imperial dynasty. In a commentary by the prince Hakabon Itoe it is said:

> The sacred throne was created when Earth became separated from Heaven [that is, at the time of the dissolution of the primordial unity of the earthly and the divine realities—an echo of which is also found in the Chinese tradition; thus, quite often the ideograms representing "nature" and "heaven" are synonymous]. The Emperor descends from heaven; he is divine and sacred.

To the emperor was also attributed a "solar" principle, though with a confusing transposition of the feminine principle: his descendence came from the goddess Amaterasu Omikami.

On this basis the act of governing and of dominating formed one thing with the cult—the term *matsurigoto* signifies both government and "pursuit of religious affairs"; in the context of Shintoism, loyalty—unwavering faithfulness to the ruler (*ciughi*)—assumed a religious meaning and was at the basis of its ethics. Any reprehensible, low, or criminal deed was not thought of as a transgression of an abstract, "social" law, but rather as a betrayal, an act of disloyalty, and a disgrace: there were no "guilty" people in Japan, but rather "traitors," or people without honor.

These general values received a particular emphasis in the warrior nobility (*bushi* or *samurai*) and in its ethics (the *bushido*). The orientation of tradition in Japan was essentially active and even militaristic, but its counterpart consisted of an inner formation—the samurai's ethics had a warrior and ascetical character—and also sacred and ritual features; it remarkably resembled the elements typical of the feudal and knightly European Middle Ages. Besides Shintoism, Zen, which is an esoteric form of Buddhism, played a role in the formation of the samurai and also in the traditional formation of various aspects and customs of Japanese life, including the arts and crafts; the presence of sects that have practiced Buddhism in its most recent, weakened, and religious forms, such as Amidism (a devotional version of Buddhism), have not substantially modified the predominant character of the Japanese spirit. In Japan, together with *bushido* we also find the traditional idea of the warrior's sacrificial death, exemplified by the kamikaze, the suicide pilots of World War II.

Until recently, Japan has offered an example, unique in its kind, of the coexistence of a traditional orientation with the adoption, on a material plane, of the structures of modern technological society. In the aftermath of World War II, a millenary continuity was shattered and an equilibrium lost, thus marking the disappearance of the last state in the world that still recognized the principle of the "solar" regality of pure divine right. Because of the "Dark Age" and its laws, wherein technological and industrial potential as well as organized material power play a decisive role in the clash of world powers, the fate of this tradition has been sealed with the outcome of the last war.

As far as Egypt is concerned, it is possible to gather some data on the primordial history of its civilization. The tradition relative to a very ancient dynasty of "divine departed ones," who are confused with so-called Followers of the Ancient Horus (Shemsu Heru) and represented by the hieroglyphic of Osiris as the Lord of the "Sacred Western Land" and who was believed to have come from the West,[8] may reflect the memory of a primordial civilizing and conquering Atlantic stock. According to the title bestowed on divine kings, Horus is a god made of gold, like Apollo; in other words, he is connected to the primordial tradition. In Egypt we also find the symbolism of the "two" inimical brothers, Osiris and Set, and of their struggle. In the Egyptian tradition there is some evidence that would allow us to see in this struggle an ethnical counterpart, namely, the struggle between two stocks that at that time represented the spirit symbolized by each god. While Osiris's death at the hands of Set, in addition to the "sacrificial" meaning I discussed in the first part of this work,

---

8. E. A. Wallis Budge, *Egypt in the Neolithic and Archaic Periods* (London, 1902), 164–65.

may express on the historical plane a crisis that brought an end to the first age, called "Age of the gods," *(θεοί)*⁹—Osiris's resurrection as Horus could represent a restoration connected to the second Egyptian age, which the Greeks called "Age of the ἡμίθεοι," which corresponds to one of the forms of the "heroic" cycle mentioned by Hesiod. According to Tradition, this second age ended with Manes; the title Hor aha, "fighting Horus," which was bestowed on this king, may underscore this meaning.

The crisis that was initially overcome by the ancient Egyptians, however, must have reemerged later on with disaggregating results. One of the indications of this crisis is the democratization of the notion of immortality, which can be observed as early as the end of the Ancient Empire (Sixth Dynasty); another sign of this crisis is the alteration in the character of spiritual centrality and in the "immanent transcendence" of the pharaoh, who tends to become a mere representative of the deity. In later times we can witness in Egypt, in addition to the presence of the solar theme, the emergence of the chthonic, lunar theme, which was connected with the figure of Isis, the "Mother of all things," or the "Lady of the elements, who was born at the beginning of time."[10] In this regard, the legend in which Isis, who is conceived as an enchantress, wants to become herself "the Ruler of the world and a deity similar to the Sun (Ra) both in heaven and on earth," is highly significant. For this purpose Isis ambushed Ra as he sat on the "throne of the two horizons"; she caused a poisonous snake to bite him and thus the god allowed his "name" to pass on to her.

This is how the shift to the civilization of the Mother occurred. From a solar god Osiris turned into a lunar god, a god of the waters in a phallic sense, and into a god of wine (that is, of the Dionysian element), just as, at the advent of Isis, Horus degenerated to a mere symbol of the ephemeral world.[11] The pathos of Osiris's death and resurrection acquires mystical and escapist overtones in radical contrast to the impassive solar spirituality of the aristocratic cult of Ra and of "ancient Horus." Often the type of divine woman, of which Isis is an archetype, mediated the resurrection and eternal life; these are figures of virgins who carry the lotus symbolizing rebirth and the "key of life." This is reflected in ethics and in social customs in that Isis-like predominance of the woman and of the queen that Herodotus and Diodorus ascribed

---

9. The tradition reported by Eusebius mentions an interval of time following the "divine" dynasty, which was characterized by lunar months. There is also an undeniable relation between Set and the feminine element, both because Set was mainly conceived as a female and also because while Isis—who will be the chief goddess during the Egyptian decadence—was portrayed in search of the dead Osiris, by disobeying Horus she freed Set. See Plutarch, *De Iside et Osiride*, 13.

10. Apuleius, *Metamorphosis*, 11.5.

11. Plutarch, *De Iside et Osiride*, 33 (Osiris is associated with the waters); 41 (Osiris is associated with the lunar world); 33–34 (Osiris is associated with Dionysus and with the moist principle); 42 (Horus is associated with the terrestrial world). Osiris even came to be regarded as "Hysiris," namely as the son of Isis (34).

to the more recent Egyptian society and that found a typical expression in the dynasty of the so-called Divine Worshipers of the Nubian period.[12]

It is significant that corresponding to this, the center shifted from the regal to the priestly symbol. Around the time of the Twenty-first Dynasty, the Egyptian priests, instead of yearning to be at the service of the divine king, attempted to usurp the regal power; the Theban dynasty of regal priests was established at the expense of the pharaohs. Thus, what emerged was a priestly theocracy in lieu of the divine regality of the origins; this was another typical manifestation of the Southern Light. From this time on, the gods were regarded increasingly less as embodied presences and thus became transcendent beings whose efficacy is essentially mediated by the priest. The solar-magical stage declined, followed by a new "religious" stage: prayer replaced command; desire and sentimentalism replaced identification and magical techniques. For instance, while an ancient Egyptian sorcerer could say: "I am Ammon, who fertilizes his Mother. I am the Lord of the Sword, and I possess a great power. Do not rise up against me—I am Set! Do not touch me, for I am Horus!"; and while a man who had been made into the image of Osiris could say things like: "I arise like a living god," or "I am the Only One; my being is the being of all gods in eternity"; or, "If the Risen One wishes your death, O gods, you will certainly die; but if he wishes you to live, you shall live"; or, "You command the gods"; the last forms of Egyptian spirituality are marked by the emergence of the mystical élan and by supplications: "O Ammon, Lord of the Silent Ones, who heeds the call of the poor ones. I cry out to you in my torment . . . Truly you are the savior."[13] Thus the Egyptian cycle ended with a decadence taking place under the aegis of the Mother. According to Greek historians, it was from Egypt that the main Demetrian and chthonic cults reached the Pelasgians first and the Hellenes later.[14] In any event, Egypt was destined to play a role in the interplay of Mediterranean civilizations only as an Isis-type of civilization under the influence of a mostly "lunar" (as the Pythagorean) wisdom. Isis's and Serapis's mysteries and the royal hetaera Cleopatra were the best Egypt had to offer vis-à-vis the onslaught of Roman power.

---

12. The relationship was very different in ancient Egyptian society. Trovatorelli (*Civilta'e legislazione dell'antico Oriente*, 136–38) mentions the figure of Ra-em-ke; the royal woman is smaller than man, to indicate inferiority and submission, and she is represented prostrated behind him. Only in a later period Osiris assumed the abovementioned lunar character and Isis appeared as the "Living One" in the eminent sense of the word, and as the "mother of the gods." Traces of the earlier period are documented by Bachofen (*Mutterrecht*, 68) and by Herodotus (*The Histories*, 2.35), according to whom there were no priestesses in the cult of male or female deities.

13. Texts quoted by K. G. Bittner, *Magie, Mutter aller Kultur* (Munich, 1930), 140–43 and by Merezhkovsky, *Mystères de l'Orient*, 163.

14. Herodotus, *The Histories*, 2.50; 2.171.

If we go from Egypt to Chaldea and Assyria, we will find an even more distinct version of the theme of the Southern civilizations and of their materializations and alterations. In the more ancient substratum of those people, which was constituted by the Sumerian element, we find the characteristic theme of a primordial heavenly Mother ruling over various manifested deities as well as the theme of a "son" whom she generates without the need of father; this son was sometimes represented as a hero or as a "god" still subject to the law of death and resurrection. In the late Hittite civilization the goddess overcame the god and ended up absorbing the attributes of the god of war by presenting herself as an Amazonian goddess; in such a civilization there were also plenty of eunuch priests and armed priestesses of the Great Goddess. Chaldea lacked for the most part the idea of divine regality: with the exception of some minor influences from the Egyptian tradition, the Chaldean kings, even when they took on a priestly character, acknowledged themselves as being mere "vicars" of the deities and shepherds elected to watch over the human flock rather than divine natures. In that civilization the god of the city was given the title of king—either "my Lord" or "my Lady." The human king was entrusted by the god to rule over the city on his behalf, and was made a prince in the sense of a mere representative. His title of *en* was mainly a priestly one: he was the priest, the shepherd, and the vicar. The priestly caste remained a separate entity and it eventually ruled over the other castes. The yearly humiliation of the king in Babel, when he laid down his regal insignia before the statue of the god, put on the robes of a slave, and implored the god's mercy by confessing his "sins," is characteristic of this dominance; he was even flogged by the priest who represented the deity. The Babylonian kings were often portrayed as the "Mother's creation" (Ishtar-Mami); in Hammurabi's Code the king received his crown and scepter from the goddess. Ashurbanipal even said to her: "I implore from you the gift of life." The formula "Omnipotent Queen, merciful protector, there is no other refuge but Thee" was a characteristic confession of Babylonian spirituality and of the pathos with which it approached the sacred.[15]

The Chaldean science that represented the highest aspect of this cycle of civilization, exemplifies for the most part the lunar and Demetrian type: its science of the stars, unlike its Egyptian counterpart, was mostly concerned with the planets rather than with the fixed stars, and with the moon rather than with the sun (to the Babylonians the night was more sacred than the day; Sin, the god of the moon, dominated Shamash, the god of the sun). Babylonian astrology was a science heavily influenced by fatalism and the belief in the omnipotence of a cosmic law or "harmony," and character-

---

15. Egypt, unlike Babylon, ignored the notions of "sin" and "repentance"; Egyptians remained standing before their gods, while Babylonians prostrated themselves.

ized by little or no sense of an authentic kind of transcendence; in other words, it could not prescind from the naturalistic and antiheroic limitation in the dimension of the spirit. In the more recent civilization (the Assyrian), which descended from the same stock, we find characteristics typical of the Titanic and Aphrodistic cycles. In such a civilization, on the one hand we find the emergence of races and virile deities of a violent, coarsely sensual, cruel, and bellicose type; on the other hand, we find a spirituality culminating in Aphrodistic figurations such as the Great Mothers, to whom the male deities were subordinated. Although Gilgamesh represented the heroic, solar type who despises the Goddess and attempts to conquer the Tree of Life, his attempt failed: upon landing on the symbolic land ruled by Shamashnapishtim (the divine hero who survived the Flood), a serpent snatched away from him the gift of "perennial youth" that he had obtained (although with the intercession of a woman, the "Virgin of the Seas") and that he intended to bring back to men, "so that they too may enjoy eternal life." This may symbolize the inability on the part of a materialistic warrior race, such as the Assyrian, to ascend to a transcendent plane and thereby to be transformed into a stock of "heroes" fit to receive and to preserve the "gift of life" and to perpetuate the primordial tradition. Since the Assyrian-Chaldean calendar was lunar, however, as opposed to the Egyptian solar calendar, we also find in these civilizations traces of gynaecocracy of an Aphrodistic type. (See, for instance, the types like Semiramis, who was the real ruler of the kingdom of the Nile behind the effeminate Sardanapalus, almost as a reflection of the relationship between the divine couple composed by Ishtar and Ninip-Ador.) Even though it seems that in these races the woman originally played a dominant role and was only later overcome by man, this shift in power may be interpreted as the analogous sign of a wider movement that represented a further involution rather than a restoration. The replacement of the Chaldeans by the Assyrians in many regards marks the passage from a Demetrian stage to a "Titanic" stage, which was expressed more significantly in the Assyrian bellicosity and fierceness that followed the Chaldean lunar and astrological priesthood. It is very significant that a legend established a relationship between Nimrod, who was credited with the foundation of Niniveh and of the Assyrian empire, and the Nephilim and other types of antedeluvian "giants," who with their violence, "filled the earth with wickedness."

THE HEBREW CYCLE AND THE EASTERN ARYAN CYCLE

The failure of the attempt of the Chaldean hero Gilgamesh corresponds to the fall of Adam in the myth of another civilization within the Semitic cycle, the Hebrew civilization. Here we find a fundamental and characteristic motif: the transformation into *sin* of what in the Aryan version of the myth was regarded as a heroic, bold deed, often crowned by success, but that in Gilgamesh's myth had a negative outcome only because the hero was caught asleep. In the context of Hebrew Semitism, the one who attempts to take possession of the symbolic Tree is univocally transformed into a victim of woman's seduction and a sinner. The curse he has to suffer and the punishment that has been meted out to him by a jealous, terrible, and omnipotent god, follow him; there is no better hope, in the end, than that for a "redeemer" who will provide a vicarious atonement.

In the ancient Hebrew tradition there are also elements of a different type. Moses himself, though he owed his life to a woman of the royal family (i.e., pharaoh's daughter, Exod. 2:5), was conceived of as having been "rescued from the waters"; likewise, the events described in the book of Exodus are capable of esoteric interpretation. Besides Elijah and Enoch, Jacob too was a heroic type, because he fought an angel and won; in relation to this, even the name "Israel," which the angel gave him, conveys the idea of a "victory over the deity" (Gen. 32:29). These elements are still sporadic and reveal a curious oscillation, which is typical of the Jewish soul, between a sense of guilt, self-humiliation, deconsecration, and carnality and an almost Luciferian pride and rebelliousness. Maybe this could be explained by the fact that even the initiatory tradition, which is also found in Judaism (e.g., the Kabbalah) and which played an important role in the European Middle Ages, has some particularly involuted traits, which characterize it at times as an "accursed science."

The Jews originally conceived the otherworld as the dark and mute Sheol, or as some kind of Hades without the counterpart of an "Island of Heroes"; not even sacred kings such as David could escape it. This is the theme of the "way of the ancestors" (*pitṛ-yāna* in Hinduism), which in this context has special relevance as the idea of an ever greater distance between man and God. Even on this plane, however, we find a double characteristic. On the one hand, according to the ancient Hebrews, Jehovah is the true king; thus, the Jews saw in the full and traditional understanding of regal dignity a disparagement of God's privilege (whether historical or not, Samuel's opposition to the establishment of a monarchy is very significant). On the other hand, the Jewish people considered themselves to be a "chosen people" and "God's people," who had been promised dominion over all the other peoples and possession of all the riches of the earth. They even derived from the Iranian tradition the theme of the hero Saoshyant, who in Judaism became the "Messiah," retaining for some time the traits typical of a manifestation of the "Lord of Hosts."

Not without relation to all this, in ancient Judaism we find a very visible effort on the part of a priestly elite to dominate and coalesce a turbid, multiple, and turbulent ethnical substance by establishing the divine Law as the foundation of its "form," and by making it the surrogate of what in other people was the unity of the common fatherland and the common origins. From this formative action, which was connected to sacred and ritualistic values and preserved from the first redactions of the ancient Torah to the elaboration of the Talmuds, the Jewish type arose as that of a spiritual rather than a physical race.[16] But the original substratum was never totally eliminated, as ancient Jewish history shows in the form of the recurrent betrayals of God and his becoming reconciled with Israel. This dualism and the ensuing tension help to explain the negative forms that Judaism assumed in later times.

For Judaism, as in the case of other civilizations, the time frame between the seventh and the sixth century B.C. was characterized by upheaval. Once the military fortunes of Israel declined, defeat came to be understood as a punishment for "sins" committed, and thus an expectation developed that after a dutiful expiation Jehovah would once again assist his people and restore their power. This theme was dealt with in Jeremiah and in Isaiah. But since this did not happen, the prophetic expectations degenerated into an apocalyptic, messianic myth and in the fantastic eschatological vision of a Savior who will redeem Israel; this marked the beginning of a process of disintegration. What derived from the traditional component eventually turned into a ritualistic formalism and thus became increasingly abstract and separated from real life. To be aware of the role the Chaldean priestly sciences played in this cycle would allow one to connect to this source everything that was successively articulated in Judaism in the form of abstract thought and even of mathematical insights (up to and including Spinoza's philosophy and the modern "formal" physics in which the Jewish component is very strong). Moreover, a connection was established with a human type, who in order to uphold values that he cannot realize and that thus appear to him increasingly abstract and utopian, eventually feels dissatisfied and frustrated before any existing positive order and any form of authority (especially when we find in him, though in an unconscious way, the old idea according to which the state of justice willed by God is only that in which Israel rules) so as to be a constant source of disorder and of revolution. Finally we must consider another dimension of the Jewish soul: it is like somebody who, having failed to realize the values typical of the sacral and transcendent dimension in the course of the attempt to overcome the antithesis between spirit and "flesh" (which he exasperates in a characteristic way), eventually rejoices wherever he discovers the illusion and the irreality of those values and wherever he ascertains the failure of the yearning for redemption; this becomes for him some kind of alibi and self-justification. These are specific developments of the original "guilt" motif, which acted in a

---

16. Originally Israel was not a race, but a people, or an ethnical mixture of various elements. This was a typical case in which a tradition "created" a race, and especially a race of the soul.

disaggregating way as Judaism became increasingly secularized and widespread during the most recent Western civilization.

It is necessary to point out a characteristic moment in the development of the ancient Jewish spirit. The abovementioned period of crisis witnessed the loss of anything that was pure and virile in the ancient cult of Jehovah and in the warrior figure of the Messiah. Already in Jeremiah and in Isaiah there emerged a rebellious spirituality that condemned and disdained the hieratic, ritual element; such was the meaning of Hebrew "prophetism," which originally displayed traits that were very similar to the cults of inferior castes, and to the pandemic and ecstatic forms of the Southern races. The figure of the "seer" *(roeh)* was replaced by the figure of the one obsessed by the spirit of God.[17] Other features of prophetism were the pathos of the "servants of the Eternal," which replaced the proud and fanatical self-confidence of being "God's people," and also an equivocal mysticism with apocalyptic overtones. The latter feature, once freed from the ancient Hebrew context, played a relevant role in the general crisis that affected the ancient Western world. The Diaspora, or the scattering of the Jewish people, corresponded to the by-products of the spiritual dissolution of a cycle that did not have a "heroic" restoration and in which some sort of inner fracture promoted processes of an antitraditional character. There are ancient traditions according to which Typhon, a demon opposed to the solar God, was the father of the Hebrews; various Gnostic authors considered the Hebrew god as one of Typhon's creatures. These are references to a demonic spirit characterized by a constant restlessness, by an obscure contamination, and by a latent revolt of the inferior elements; when this substance returned to a free state and when it separated itself from the "Law," that is, from the tradition that had formed it, all these factors acted upon the Jewish substratum in a more dramatic and decisive way than in other people.

This is the origin of one of the main hotbeds of those forces that exercised an often unconscious, though negative influence during the last phases of the Western cycle of the Iron Age.

Even though it began relatively recently, I will briefly refer to another tradition, Islam, which originated among Semitic races and succeeded in overcoming those

---

17. Originally the prophets *(nebiim)* were possessed people who, through a natural disposition or through artificial means achieved a state of excitement in which they felt dominated and guided by a higher power, superior to their own wills. When they spoke it was no longer themselves but the spirit of God who made utterances. See J. Reville, *Le Prophétisme hébreux* (Paris, 1906). Thus the prophets were regarded by the priestly caste as raving lunatics; opposed to the prophet *(nabi)* originally there was the higher and "Olympian" figure of the seer *(roeh)*: "In former times in Israel, anyone who sent to consult God used to say: 'Come, let us go to the seer,' for he who is now called prophet was formerly called seer." 1 Sam. 9:9.

negative motifs. As in the case of priestly Judaism, the center in Islam also consisted of the Law and Tradition, regarded as a formative force, to which the Arab stocks of the origins provided a purer and nobler human material that was shaped by a warrior spirit. The Islamic law *(shariah)* is a divine law; its foundation, the Koran, is thought of as God's very own word *(kalam Allah)* as well as a nonhuman work and an "uncreated book" that exists in heaven *ab eterno*. Although Islam considers itself the "religion of Abraham," even to the point of attributing to him the foundation of the Kaaba (in which we find again the theme of the "stone," or the symbol of the "center"), it is nevertheless true that (*a*) it claimed independence from both Judaism and Christianity; (*b*) the Kaaba, with its symbolism of the center, is a pre-Islamic location and has even older origins that cannot be dated accurately; (*c*) in the esoteric Islamic tradition, the main reference point is al-Khadir, a popular figure conceived as superior to and predating the biblical prophets (Koran 18:59-81). Islam rejects a theme found in Judaism and that in Christianity became the dogma and the basis of the mystery of the incarnation of the Logos; it retains, sensibly attenuated, the myth of Adam's fall without building upon it the theme of "original sin." In this doctrine Islam saw a "diabolical illusion" *(talbis Iblis)* or the inverted theme of the fall of Satan (Iblis or Shaitan), which the Koran (18:48) attributed to his refusal, together with all his angels, to bow down before Adam. Islam also not only rejected the idea of a Redeemer or Savior, which is so central in Christianity, but also the mediation of a priestly caste. By conceiving of the Divine in terms of an absolute and pure monotheism, without a "Son," a "Father," or a "Mother of God," every person as a Muslim appears to respond directly to God and to be sanctified through the Law, which permeates and organizes life in a radically unitary way in all of its juridical, religious, and social ramifications. In early Islam the only form of asceticism was action, that is, *jihad,* or "holy war"; this type of war, at least theoretically, should never be interrupted until the full consolidation of the divine Law has been achieved. It is precisely through the holy war, and not through preaching or missionary endeavor, that Islam came to enjoy a sudden, prodigious expansion, originating the empire of the Caliphs as well as forging a unity typical of a race of the spirit, namely, the *umma* or "Islamic nation." Finally, Islam presents a traditional completeness, since the *shariah* and the *sunna*, that is, the exoteric law and tradition, have their complement not in a vague mysticism, but in full-fledged initiatory organizations *(turuq)* that are characterized by an esoteric teaching *(tawil)* and by the metaphysical doctrine of the Supreme Identity *(tawhid)*. In these organizations, and in general in the *shia*, the recurrent notions of the *masum*, of the double prerogative of the *isma* (doctrinal infallibility), and of the impossibility of being stained by any sin (which is the prerogative of the leaders, the visible and invisible Imams and, the *mujtahid*), lead back to the line of an unbroken race shaped by a tradition at a higher level than both Judaism and the religious beliefs that conquered the West.

If in India, which in ancient times was called *āryavarṇaḥ*, "land of the Aryans," the term *(varṇaḥ)* designating the caste also meant "color"; and if the serfs' caste of the *śūdras*, which was opposite to the castes of the Aryans, the race of the "twice-born" *(dvīja)*, was also called black race *(kṛṣṇa-varṇa)*, the inimical race *(dāsa-varṇaḥ)*, and the demonic race *(asura)*—in all this we can see the memory of the spiritual difference existing between two races that originally clashed, and also of the nature of the race that formed the higher castes. Apart from its metaphysical content, the myth of Indra—called *hari-yaka*, the "blond god," or "golden hair"—is liable to have a historical meaning. The god Indra was born despite his mother's wish to the contrary; eventually abandoned by her, he did not perish but found a glorious path. The myth of this luminous and heroic god who exterminated the multitudes of black *kṛṣṇa*, who subdued the color *dāsa* by causing the fall of the *dasyu* who wanted to ascend to "heaven," who assisted the Aryans, and who conquered ever greater territories with the help of his "white companions" is likely to have a historical meaning. Finally, in the feats of Indra, who fights against the serpent Ahi and the dreadful warlock Namuci (possibly an echo of the legendary struggle of the *devas* against the *asura*); in the fulguration of the goddess of the dawn "who wanted to be great"; and in the destruction of the demon Vṛtra and of his mother by Indra, who thereby "generated the Sun and heaven," namely, the Uranian, solar cult—we find mythical events that may contain allusions to the struggle between the cult of the Aryan conquerors against the demonic and magical (in the lower sense of the word) cults of aboriginal Dravidian, paleo-Malayan races. Moreover, since popular epics mention a primordial solar dynasty *(sūrya-vaṃśa)* that allegedly triumphed in India after it destroyed a lunar dynasty, this may well be an echo of the struggle against forms that are related to the Southern-Atlantic cycle.[18] The story of Paraśu-Rāma, the sixth avatar of Viṣṇu, who is a hero wielding the Hyperborean axe, who exterminated (after several incarnations) the rebellious warrior class during an era (Tretā Yuga) in which the ancestors of the Hindus still inhabited a northern region, and who prepared the way for the race of *brāhmaṇa*[19] from his northern seat; and even the tradition concerning Viṣṇu, also called the "golden god," who destroyed the

---

18. Some recent archaeological excavations have brought to light the vestiges of a pre-Aryan Hindu civilization similar to the Sumerian, which supplied the main elements to the civilizations of the southeastern Mediterranean cycle. In relation to the Aryan element, in India the attribute used for salvific deities and heroes is *hari* and *harit*, a term which means both "the golden one" (in relation to the primordial cycle: Apollo, Horus, etc.) and the "blond god."

19. *Mahābhārata; Viṣṇu Purāṇa,* 4.8.

mlecchas, the degenerated warrior stocks who had become alienated from the sacred[20]—are among the various themes that allude to the overcoming of degenerated forms and to the reaffirmation or restoration of a "heroic" type.

In historical India, however, we find traces of a modification that was probably due to the substratum of the autochthonous vanquished races. Thus, by virtue of a subtle action that undermined the original spirituality of the Aryan conquerors, and despite the subsistence of virile asceticism and heroic fulfillment, India eventually took the course of "contemplation" and of "priestly ways" instead of remaining rigorously faithful to the original regal and solar path. The period of greater tension extended to the time of Viśvāmitra, who incarnated the regal and priestly dignity and who exercised his authority over all the Aryan stocks living in the Punjab region. The following period, in which the Gangetic plains were invaded already marked a time of division.

The authority the priestly caste acquired in India may therefore be considered, as in the case of Egypt, a subsequent development, and it probably derived from the importance that the *purohita* (the *brāhmaṇa* working under the sacral king) slowly acquired as soon as the original dynasties decayed following the Aryans' settlement in the recently conquered territories; these dynasties eventually ranked as a mere warrior nobility vis-à-vis the priestly caste. Popular epics recall a prolonged and violent struggle between the priestly and warrior castes for the control of India.[21] The division, which took place in a later period, did not prevent the priests from having virile and regal traits or the warrior caste (originally called the regal caste, *rājanya*) from retaining its own spirituality, which in various instances triumphed over the priestly spirituality; in the warrior spirituality we often find specific traces of the original boreal element.

Moreover, the "Nordic" elements within the Indo-Aryan civilization were: (1) the austere type of the ancient *atharvan,* the "lord of fire," he who "first opened the paths through sacrifices," as well as the type of the *brāhmaṇa,* he who dominates the *brahman* and the gods through his formulas of power; (2) the doctrine of the absolute Self *(ātman)* of the early Upaniṣadic period, which corresponds to the impassible and luminous principle of Sāṃkhya; (3) the virile and conscious asceticism oriented to the Unconditioned that also characterized the Buddhist doctrine of awakening; (4) the doctrine of pure action and heroism expounded in the *Bhagavadgītā,* which was

---

20. Ibid., 4.3.
21. See for instance the *Mahābhārata* and the *Rāmāyaṇa.* There is an interesting tradition concerning a lunar dynasty, which through *soma,* was associated with the priestly caste and the telluric, vegetal kingdom. This dynasty usurped the solar ritual *(rājasūya),* became violent, and attempted to kidnap the divine woman Tara; this caused the outbreak of a war between gods and *asura. Viṣṇu-Purāṇa* 4.6.

credited with a solar origin and a regal heritage; (5) the Vedic view of the world as "order" *(ṛta)* and law *(dharma);* and (6) the patriarchical right, the cult of fire, the symbolically rich ritual of the cremation of the dead, the caste system, the cult of truth and honor, the myth of the universal sacred sovereign *(cakravartin).* In all these elements we find the traditional poles of "action" and "contemplation" closely intertwined and elevated to a higher meaning.

In India, in much older times, the southern component was found in everything that betrayed, unlike the purer and more spiritual elements of the Vedic cult, a kind of primacy of the imagination and a chaotic and tropical effusion of animal and vegetal symbols that eventually came to dominate the greater part of the external artistic and religious expressions of the Hindu civilization. Even though the Tantric cult in its Shaivite trajectories was purified and transformed into a superior type of magic[22] and into a doctrine of power, nevertheless, because of its deification of woman and its orgiastic elements, it represented the resurgence of a pre-Aryan and ancient root congenially akin to the Mediterranean-Asiatic civilizations dominated by the figure and the cult of the Mother.[23] It is possible that this root encompassed all those features that in Hindu asceticism have a mortifying character; allegedly the same ideal orientation connected it with what emerged among the Maya and the civilizations of Sumerian stock.[24]

On the other hand, the disintegration of the Aryan worldview began in India when the identity between the *ātman* and *brahman* was interpreted in a pantheistic sense that reflected the spirit of the South. Brahman was no longer conceived, as in the earlier period described in the *Atharva Veda* and in the Brāhmaṇas, as the spirit or the formless magical force characterized by an almost "mana-like" quality that the Aryan dominates and directs through his rite: *brahman* was instead conceived as the One and All from which all life forms proceed and into which they are redissolved. When it is interpreted in such a pantheistic fashion, the doctrine of the identity between *ātman* and *brahman* leads to the denial of the spiritual personality and is transformed into a ferment of degeneration and promiscuity: one of its corollaries will be the equality of all creatures. The doctrine of reincarnation, understood as the primacy of the destiny of a recurrent and yet ephemeral reappearance in the conditioned world *(saṁsāra)*—a doctrine not found in the early Vedic period—became predominant. Thus, asceticism aimed at achieving a liberation that had the meaning of escapism rather than a truly transcendent fulfillment.

Early Buddhism, which was originated by Prince Siddharta Gautama, an ascetic

22. J. Evola, *The Yoga of Power.*
23. J. Woodroffe, *Shakti and Shakta* (Madras, 1929).
24. M. Eliade, *Patanjali and Yoga* (New York, 1975).

from a warrior clan, may be considered in many ways as a reaction against these views as well as against the purely speculative interest and the ritualistic formalism that had become predominant in so many *brāhmaṇa* circles. The Buddhist doctrine of awakening, by declaring that the view of the identification of the self with nature, with the All, and even with the divinity theistically conceived (Brahma) is proper to "an uninstructed average person, taking no account of the pure ones, unskilled in the *dharma* of the pure ones, untrained in the *dharma* of the pure ones,"[25] firmly upheld the principle of an aristocratic asceticism oriented to an authentically transcendent goal. Thus, Buddhism represented a reformation that occurred at a time of crisis in traditional Indo-Aryan spirituality and was contemporary with the crisis that was manifested in other civilizations, both Eastern and Western. With regard to this we find in Buddhism a characteristic opposition, inspired by a pragmatic and realistic spirit, to the mere doctrine or dialectics that became "philosophical thought" in Greece. Buddhism was opposed to the traditional doctrine of *ātman* only inasmuch as the latter no longer corresponded to a living reality and had become an emasculated complex of theories and speculations of the priestly caste. By denying that every human being is endowed with an *ātman;* by denying the doctrine of reincarnation (Buddhism denies the existence of a personal nucleus that remains identical through various incarnations: according to Buddhism, what reincarnates is not a "self," but "craving," *tanha*); and by reaffirming the *ātman* as *nirvāṇa*, as a state that can be achieved very rarely through asceticism—Buddhism promoted a "heroic" theme (the attainment of immortality) over and against the echoes of a primordial, divine self-knowledge that had been preserved in various doctrines of the priestly caste; these doctrines, moreover, no longer corresponded to an experience for the majority of people, due to a process of decline already at work in those times.[26]

A characteristic phenomenon of this situation in more recent times, as the expression of two opposite views, is the opposition between the *bhakti* doctrine of Rāmānuja and the Vedānta doctrine of Śaṅkara. The latter appears to be marked by the spirit of a strict and straightforward intellectual asceticism; nevertheless, it was essentially oriented to the Demetrian lunar theme of the formless *brahman (nirguṇa-Brahma)*, in regard to which all determined forms are nothing but an illusion and a negation, or a sheer product of ignorance *(avidyā)*. Thus we can say that Śaṅkara exemplifies the highest possibility of a civilization of the Silver Age. On the other hand, Rāmānuja may be considered as the representative of the following age, which was determined by the merely human element, and of the new theme that appeared

---

25. *Majjhima Nikāya (The Middle-Length Sayings)*, 1.1.

26. For a systematic exposition based on the texts and on the historical milieu of the early Buddhist doctrine of awakening, see my *Doctrine of Awakening.*

at the time of the decadence of Egypt and among Semitic cycles as well: the theme of the metaphysical distance between the human and the divine, which further removes from man the "heroic" possibility and leaves him mainly with a sentimental and devotional attitude toward the deity. Thus, while Vedānta acknowledged God as a person only at the level of an "inferior knowledge," and while the highest state of supreme unity (ekatabhāva) ranked higher than devotion, which was conceived as a relationship between father and son (pitṛ putra bhāva)—Rāmānuja attacked these views as blasphemous and heretic with a pathos similar to that of the early Church apologists.[27] In Rāmānuja we find the awareness, which humanity had eventually arrived at, of the irreality of the ancient doctrine of ātman and the perception of the distance existing between the empirical self and the transcendent Self, or ātman. The superior and yet exceptional possibility upheld by Buddhism, which was admitted to a certain degree even in Vedānta inasmuch as it upheld the principle of metaphysical identification, was excluded in Rāmānuja's theistic worldview.

Thus, in the Hindu civilization of historical times we find a play of forms and meanings that can be reduced respectively to the Aryan, boreal spirituality (to which I referred whenever I drew examples from India of "traditional spirit" with regard to doctrine), and to various distortions of this spirituality, which betray influences of the substratum of the defeated aboriginal races, their chthonic cults, their unleashed imagination, their promiscuity, and the orgiastic and chaotic manifestations of their evocations and ecstasies. Although in more recent times India appears to be a traditional civilization, since in it life is totally and radically oriented toward a sacral and ritual direction, it nevertheless embodies one of the two secondary possibilities that were originally subsumed in a higher synthesis: the possibility represented by a traditional *contemplative* world. The pole of asceticism as "knowledge" and not as "action" characterizes the traditional spirit of India, despite the presence, rather than the dominance, of many other forms in which the orientation proper to the inner race of the warrior caste arose again in a "heroic" form.

Iran appears to have remained more faithful to such an orientation, even though it did not reach the same metaphysical heights that India achieved by following the contemplative paths. The warrior character of the cult of Ahura Mazda speaks for itself, as do (a) the ancient Iranian cult of fire, part of which is the well-known doctrine of the hvareno or "glory"; (b) the rigorous patriarchical system; (c) the Aryan ethic of truth and faithfulness; (d) the view of the world as ṛtam and āśā, as cosmos, rite, and order, a view connected to that dominating Uranian principle that eventually led to the metaphysical ideal of the empire and the corresponding view of the

---

27. The same type of involution occurred in many versions of Buddhism, notably in Amidism, which eventually became a "religion."

sovereign as "king of kings," once the original plurality of the first conquering stocks was overcome.

Originally, next to the three castes corresponding to three superior castes of the Hindu Aryans (*brāhmaṇa, kṣatriya,* and *vaiśya*), in ancient Iran there was no distinct caste of *śūdras;* it was almost as if in those regions the Aryan stocks had never met at all, or had never encountered as an important social stratum, the aboriginal element of the South that was responsible for the alteration of the ancient Hindu spirit. Iran shares with India the cult of truth, faithfulness, and honor; the type of the Mede-Iranian *atharvan*—the lord of the sacred fire, synonymous with the "man of the primordial law" *(paoriyo thaesha)*—was the Hindu equivalent of the *atharvan* and the *brāhmaṇa* in its original form, which was not yet a priestly one. Even within this aristocratic spirituality, however, there must have been a decline that culminated in a crisis and in the appearance, in the person of Zarathustra, of the figure of a reformer similar to that of Buddha. Even in Zarathustra's life we may detect a reaction aimed at reintegrating the principles of the original cult—which were getting lost even in a naturalistic sense—in a purer and immaterial form, though they were not yet free, in several aspects, of a sort of "moralism." There is a particularly meaningful legend found in the *Yashna* and in the *Bundahesh* according to which Zarathustra was "born" in the Airyana Vaego, the primordial boreal land, conceived in the legend as the "seed of the race of the Aryans," and also as the seat of the Golden Age and of the regal "glory"; it was there that Zarathustra first revealed his doctrine. The precise era in which Zarathustra lived has been debated. The fact is that "Zarathustra," like "Hermes" (the Egyptian Hermes) and other similar figures—designated more a given spiritual influence than a single individual and therefore may be a name referring to several people who in different ages incarnated such an influence. The historical Zarathustra should be considered a specific manifestation of this figure and of the primordial Hyperborean Zarathustra (hence the theme of his birth in the primordial seat of mankind), whose mission was to exercise a rectifying action paralleling that of Buddha in an era that approximately corresponds to that of the abovementioned crisis in other traditions. Interestingly enough, Zarathustra fought against the god of darkness who had assumed the semblance of a female demon, and during his struggle he offered prayers to the good waters of the Daitya River located in the Airyana Vaego.[28] At a historical level we find mention of the bitter struggles Zarathustra waged against the caste of the Magi, who in some later texts came to be considered as emissaries of the *daeva,* namely, of the beings who are sworn enemies of the god of light, Ahura Mazda; this testifies to the involution and decadence the priestly caste had fallen into. Within the Persian tradition, the "dominating" characteristic of

28. *Vendidad,* 19.2.

which was essentially Aryan and regal, a tension arose at one point that was caused by the hegemonic claims of the priestly caste, judging from the attempt of the priest Gaumata, who attempted to usurp the supreme power and establish a theocracy but was expelled by Darius I. This, though, was the first and only attempt of this kind in Persian history.

The original theme, almost as if reinvigorated from contact with altered traditional forms of other people, arose again in Mithraism in the form of a new "heroic" cycle endowed with a specific initiatory foundation. Mithras, the solar hero who overcame the telluric bull, and the ancient god of the luminous ether who was similar to Indra and to the Hindu Mitra, was a figure that stood alone, without those women and goddesses who usually accompany the Syrian gods and the decadent Egyptian gods in an Aphrodistic or Dionysian fashion; thus, he embodied in a characteristic way the Northern-Uranian spirit in its warrior form. Moreover, it is significant that Mithras was identified with Prometheus rather than with the Hyperborean Apollo, the god of the Golden Age; this refers to the luminous transfiguration through which the Titan was confused with a deity personifying the primordial spirituality. Mithras was born from a stone wielding the symbols of the sword and the light (a torch). In a theme also found in the myth of the Titans, we encounter figurations of Mithras using the leaves of a "tree" to cover himself before wrestling victoriously with the sun, becoming his ally, and eventually becoming identified with him.

An antitelluric spirit characterized Mithraism; unlike the views of the followers of Serapis and Isis, Mithraism located the abode of the "liberated ones" in the spheres of the pure Uranian light rather than in the depths of the earth; the blessed would arrive in this "heaven" after the journey through the various planets divested them of all earthly attachments and passions.[29] We should also take notice of the almost universal exclusion of women from the Mithraic cult and initiation; the ethos of the Mithraic community, in which the hierarchical principle was upheld together with the principle of brotherhood, was radically opposed to both the promiscuous feelings proper to the southern communities and to the obscure emphasis on blood that is recurrent, for instance, in Judaism. Rather than being based on the mysticism of love, the brotherhood of the Mithraic initiates, who took on the title of soldiers (milites), reflected more that clear and strongly individuated brotherhood existing between warriors committed to the same enterprise. The same ethos later surfaced both in ancient Rome and in the Germanic stocks.

In reality, although Mithraism began to decline once Mithras was conceived of

---

29. The reason why the ancient Iranians did not practice cremation, unlike several other Nordic-Aryan stocks, was that they believed that the corpse corrupted the sacredness of fire. See W. Ridgeway, *Early Age of Greece* (Cambridge, 1901).

as a "savior" *(σοτήρ)* and a "mediator" *(μεσίτης)* on an almost religious plane, nevertheless, in its central nucleus, it appeared historically (at a time of a deep crisis in the ancient world) as the symbol of a different direction that the Romanized West could have taken instead of the direction represented by Christianity, which eventually prevailed and around which various antitraditional and disaggregating influences crystallized. The last spiritual reaction of the ancient Roman world, represented by the emperor Julian, himself an initiate to the Mithraic Mysteries, drew inspiration from Mithraism.

We shall recall in passing that even after the Islamic conquest of the ancient Iranian regions some themes connected to the previous tradition eventually enjoyed a revival. Thus, from the reign of the Safavids (1501–1722) onward the official religion of Persia has been imamism, which is based on the idea of an invisible leader (imam), who after a period of "absence" will one day reappear "to defeat injustice and to reestablish a Golden Age on earth." The Persian monarchs claimed to be the spokesmen of the Hidden Imam until the day of his return. It is the ancient Aryan-Iranian theme of Saoshyant.[30]

---

30. *Vendidad,* 19.5; *Yasht,* 19.89: "The fiend-smiter will come up to life out of the lake Kasava, from the region of the dawn, to free the world from death and decay, corruption and rottenness . . . the dead shall rise and immortality commence."

30

The Heroic-Uranian Western Cycle

THE HELLENIC CYCLE

When considering the Western world and in particular ancient Hellas, two aspects must be considered. The first is connected to meanings analogous to those I previously detected in the formation process of other great civilizations; these meanings point to a world that had not yet grown secularized and that was still permeated by the general principle of the "sacred." The second aspect refers to processes that anticipate the last humanistic, lay, and rationalistic cycle; it is precisely because of this aspect that many moderns gladly regard Greece as the origin of their civilization.

Hellenic civilization also has a much older Aegean and Pelasgic substratum in which we find the recurrence of the general theme the Atlantic civilization of the Silver Age, especially in the form of Demetrism, together with frequent accretions of motifs of a lower order inspired by chthonic and demonic cults. Over and against this substratum we find the typically Hellenic forms of that civilization created by the conquering Achaeans and Doric stocks and characterized by the Olympian ideal of the Homeric cycle and the cult of the Hyperborean Apollo. The victorious struggle of Apollo against the serpent Python, which was portrayed underneath Apollo's temple at Delphi (prior to this cult at Delphi was the oracle of the Mother, Gaea, who was associated with the demon of the waters, namely, the Atlantic-Pelasgic Poseidon), is one of those myths carrying a double meaning: it describes both a metaphysical event and a struggle between a race practicing a Uranian cult and a race practicing a chthonic cult. We must also consider the effects of the reemergence of the original stratum, which caused the triumph of several varieties of Dionysism, Aphroditism, Pythagoreanism, as well as of other spiritualities connected to the chthonic cult and rite, including their corresponding social and moral forms.

This is also true on the ethical plane. From this perspective we can distinguish three strata. The first stratum is linked to remnants of races that were completely

253

foreign to the races of the northwestern or Atlantic cycle and thus to the Indo-European races. The second stratum probably derives from the branching off of the Western-Atlantic race, which in ancient times reached as far as the Mediterranean basin. This stratum may be called "paleo-Indo-European," though we should not forget the alteration and the involution that it underwent; the Pelasgic civilization is essentially connected with this stratum. The third stratum corresponds to the Hellenic populations of a northwestern origin that migrated to Greece in relatively recent times. This triple stratification and the dynamic of the corresponding influences were also present in the Italic civilization. As far as Hellas is concerned, it is possible that this stratification was reflected in the three classes of the Spartiates, Perieces, and Helots in ancient Sparta. The tripartition, instead of the traditional quadripartition, must be explained by the presence of an aristocracy that had simultaneously a warrior and a sacred character; this was the case with the stock of the Heracleids or of the Geleonts, "the Radiant Ones," who claimed Zeus or Geleon as their symbolic forefather.

Prescinding from the hostile way in which the Greek historians described the Pelasgians and from the connection they often established between the Pelasgian and the Syrio-Egyptian cults and customs, the heterogeneity of the Achaean world, in comparison with the previous Pelasgic civilization,[1] has nevertheless been acknowledged, even by modern researchers, who have also established the racial affinity and the similarities in customs and in the type of civilization of the Achaeans and the Dorians on the one hand, and of the Northern-Aryan stocks of the Celts, the Germanic tribes, the Scandinavian populations, and even the Aryans in India on the other.[2] The following factors clearly illustrate what kind of forces clashed in ancient and prehistoric Greece: (a) the plain linear purity, the geometric and "solar" clarity, the essentialism and simplicity that signify liberation, power, and primordiality that was radically form and cosmos in the Doric style over and against the chaotic organicism and the employment of animal and vegetal symbols prevalent in the traces of the Cretan-Minoan civilization; (b) the luminous Olympian figurations versus the traditions concerned with god-snakes and man-serpents, demons with donkey heads and black goddesses with horse heads, and the magical cult of the subterranean fire or of the deities of the waters. One of the stories of prehistoric Greece was of the demise of the legendary kingdom of Minos, who was enthroned in the Pelasgic land in which Zeus was considered a chthonic demon and thus a mortal being;[3] in which the black Mother earth was the

---

1. Herodotus (*Histories* 1.56; 8.44) regarded the early Ionian inhabitants of Athens as Pelasgians and called their language "barbarous," that is, non-Hellenic.
2. W. Ridgeway, *The Early Age of Greece* (Cambridge, 1901), 1.337–406; 407, 541. This work contains several valuable insights regarding the separation of the Nordic component from the Pelasgic component within Hellenic civilization, even though the author emphasizes the ethnic more than the spiritual opposition between these components.
3. Callimachus, *Hymn to Zeus*, 5.9.

greatest and the mightiest of all the deities; in which we find the predominant cult (still connected with the feminine element and probably related to the Egyptian decadence[4]) of Hera, Hestia, Themis, and of the Nereids; and in which the supreme limit consisted in the Demetrian, lunar mystery characterized by gynaecocratic transpositions in the rites and in the social customs.[5]

On a different plane, a trace of the victory of the new civilization over the old one is found in Aeschylus's *Eumenides*. In the assembly of the gods that is called to pass judgment over Orestes, who killed his mother Clytemnestra in order to avenge his father, the conflict between truth and virile privileges on the one hand and truth and womanly privileges on the other, is clearly exemplified. Apollo and Athena side against the nocturnal female deities (the Erinyes) who want to take revenge on Orestes. If in the *Eumenides* it is declared that it is possible to be a father without a mother (a reference to the symbolical birth of Athena and in opposition to the maternity of the primordial virgins who did not require mates), the purpose was to emphasize the superior ideal of virility and the idea of a spiritual and pure "genesis" free from that naturalistic plane in which the Mother's right and status rule supreme. Thus, the absolution of Orestes marked the triumph of a new law, a new custom, a new cult, and a new right—such was the complaint of the Eumenides, who were chthonic female deities with snake's heads, the daughters of the Night, and the symbols of the ancient pre-Hellenic era. It is significant that where the divine judgment took place in Aeschylus' tragedy was the hill sacred to the warrior god Ares, located in the ancient citadel of the Amazons who were massacred by Theseus.

The Olympian conception of the divine was one of the most characteristic expressions of the Northern Light among the Hellenes; it was the view of a symbolical world of immortal and luminous essences detached from the inferior region of earthly beings and of things subjected to becoming, even though sometimes a "genesis" was ascribed to some gods; it was a view of the sacred associated by analogy with bright skies and with snowy peaks, as in the symbols of the Eddic Asgard and of the Vedic

---

4. Herodotus, *Histories*, 2.50. There are two traditions concerning the Pelasgian Minos: in the first he appears as a just king and as a divine legislator (his name has an interesting etymological similarity to the Hindu Manu, the Egyptian Manes, the Germanic Mannus, and maybe the Latin Numa); in the second he appears as a violent and demonic power ruling over the waters. The opposition between the Hellenes and Minos refers to the latter tradition.

5. Thus wrote Bachofen: "Gynaecocracy is part of the legacy of those races that Strabo (7.321; 7.572) regarded as barbarous and as the early pre-Hellenic inhabitants of Greece and of Asia Minor, whose repeated migrations began ancient history just as the migratory waves of northern populations during later times began the history of our times." *Mutterrecht*, 43. Another historian, Domenico Mosso (*Origini della civiltà mediterranea*, 128) showed that the priestesses of the sarcophagus of Hagia Triada were in charge of the most important functions of the priesthood, while men only had a secondary role in it. Mosso also indicated that the Minoan-Pelasgian religion retained its matriarchical character for a long time and that the privileged status of women, not only in the rites but also in social life (*Escursioni nel Mediterraneo*, 216, 221), characterized both the Minoan and the Etruscan civilizations.

Mount Meru. The ideas concerning: *(a)* Chaos as the primordial principle and its early manifestations, namely, the Night and Erebus, as the principle of a further generation, including the generating of Light and of Day; *(b)* the Earth as the universal Mother who precedes her heavenly groom; and finally, *(c)* the entire contingency of a chaotic becoming, succumbing, and being transformed that was attributed even to divine natures—all these ideas, are really *not* Hellenic, but rather themes that betray the Pelasgic substratum in Hesiod's syncretism.

Ancient Hellas knew both the Olympian theme and the "heroic" theme. Likewise, the "heroes" were perceived to be above mortal and human nature and were regarded as demigods who participated in the same Olympian immortality; the Dorian and the Achaean hero in many cases was defined and forged by *action* rather than by blood ties with the stock of the gods (that is, by an inherited supernatural status). His being was entirely epic, just as in the case of the types that are found in more recent cycles. His being did not know the mystical abandonments of the Southern Light, nor the return to the generating cosmic womb. Victory (Nike) crowns the Doric Heracles in the Olympian dwelling characterized by a pure virility that is "immune" from the Titanic element. The ideal type was not Prometheus—since the Hellenes regarded him as a vanquished foe of Zeus, the latter being the conqueror of Pelasgic deities[6]—but rather the antigynaecocratic hero Heracles, who triumphed over the Titanic element; freed Prometheus after siding with the Olympian gods; destroyed the Amazons; wounded the Great Mother herself; took the Hesperides' apples after defeating the dragon; rescued Atlas after assuming the function of "pole," not as a penance but as a test; and after walking through "fire," passed from an earthly existence to an Olympian immortality. Deities who suffer and die in order to come back to life as vegetal natures produced by the earth as well as deities who personify the passion of the yearning and broken soul were totally foreign to this primordial Hellenic spirituality.

In contrast to the chthonic ritual associated with aboriginal and Pelasgic strata, which was characterized by the fear of demonic forces *(δεισιδαιμονία)*, and by an all-pervasive sense of "contamination," of evil that must be warded off, and of tragedies that must averted *(αποπομπαί)*, the Olympian Achaean ritual knew only clear and precise relationships with the gods, who were positively conceived as principles of beneficial influences and who were dealt with without any fear and with the fa-

---

6. The Olympian Zeus, after defeating the Titans and their allies, confined them to Tartarus or Erebus, which is the location where "Atlas" was kept prisoner and also the seat of Hecate, one of the forms of the Pelasgian Goddess.

7. See J. E. Harrison, *Prolegomena to the Study of Greek Religion* (Cambridge, 1903), 4–10; 120; 162. In this work there are several valid observations regarding the opposition between an Achaean Olympian ritual and a chthonic ritual within the Greek religion.

miliarity and dignity characteristic of an attitude of *do ut des* in a higher sense.[7] The fate (i.e., Hades) that awaited most people living in the "dark age" did not frighten this virile mankind, but was confronted in a calm and impassive manner. The higher hope of the "few" rested in the purity of fire, to which the corpses of heroes and of great leaders were ritually offered (in view of their definitive liberation) in the ritual of cremation, as opposed to the burial practices that symbolized the return to the womb of Mother Earth found among pre-Hellenic and Pelasgic stocks.[8] The world of the ancient Achaean soul did not know the pathos of expiation and of "salvation"; it also ignored ecstasies and mystical raptures. Here too, it is necessary to differentiate the parts in what seems to be one bloc; it is necessary to restore to their respective antithetical origins what refers to each of them within the whole of the Hellenic civilization.

Post-Homeric Greece shows many signs of the reemergence and rebellion of the original subjugated strata against the properly Hellenic element. Chthonic themes typical of an older civilization reappeared, because of contacts with neighboring civilizations, which contributed to their revival. The peak of the crisis occurred between the seventh and the sixth century B.C. During this time, Dionysian spirituality became prevalent—a very significant phenomenon, considering that the feminine element prepared its way. I have already discussed the universal meaning of this phenomenon; therefore, in this context I will only point out that this meaning was preserved even in the passage from the wild Thracian forms to the Hellenized Orphic Dionysus, who was still regarded as an underground god and as a being associated with the chthonic Gaea and Zeus. Moreover, while in the frenzies and in the ecstasies of Thracian Dionysism the real experience of transcendence could occur in a flash, in Orphism we witness the slow but gradual predominance of a pathos similar to that shared by the "all-too-human" religions based on redemption.

Just as a Jew feels cursed because of Adam's fall, which he conceives as "sin," likewise the Orphic follower felt the need to expiate the crime of the Titans who devoured the god. Very rarely did the latter conceive of the authentic "heroic" possibility, preferring instead to await the gifts of health and liberation from the body

---

8. See Ridgeway, *Early Age of Greece* (506 ff.; 521–25), which shows the opposition between the cremation practices of northern Aryan origin and the burial practices of Greek-Pelasgic origin; this difference reflects the Uranian and the telluric views of the afterlife. The cremation of corpses was practiced by those who wanted to remove once and for all the psychic residues of the "deceased," since these residues were regarded as baleful influences, or by those who imagined for the soul of the "hero" a dwelling totally removed from the earth; this dwelling could be reached only after the last connection with the living (i.e., the corpse) was destroyed as if through an extreme purification. The burial ritual expresses the return of "earth to earth" and the dependency on the origins conceived in a telluric fashion. In Homer's times this ritual was virtually unknown, just like the idea of a "hell" and its torments.

from some kind of "savior" (who also was subjected to the same destiny of death and resurrection affecting plant gods and year god).[9]

The "infective disease"—consisting of the guilt complex in conjunction with the terror of punishments in the netherworld and with an undignified yearning for an escapist liberation that is rooted in the inferior and passional part of one's being—never plagued the Greeks during the better period of their history; such a "disease" was characteristically anti-Hellenic and it was caused by extraneous influences.[10] The same applied to the increased emphasis on aesthetics and sensuality found in later Greek civilization and society as exemplified by the prevalence of the Ionian and Corinthian forms over the Doric ones.

The crisis of the ancient aristocratic and sacral regime of the Greek cities occurred almost at the same time as the Dionysian "epidemics." A revolutionary ferment altered the nature of the ancient institutions, the ancient view of the state, the law, and even property. By dissociating temporal authority from spiritual authority, promoting the electoral system, and establishing institutions that became increasingly open to inferior social strata—to an "impure" aristocracy (e.g., the caste of the merchants in Athens and in Cuma), and finally even to the plebs protected by popular tyrants (in Argon, Corinth, Sicion, etc.)—this revolutionary ferment eventually engendered the democratic regime. Regality, oligarchy, bourgeoisie, and finally illegitimate rulers who derived their power from merely personal prestige and who leaned on the demos—these were the descending phases of the involution that took place in Greece, that occurred again in ancient Rome, and that are found on a grand scale in modern civilization.

Greek democracy, rather than a conquest of Greek civilization should be regarded as a victory of Asia Minor and of the Southern Hemisphere over the primordial Hellenic stocks that were too weak and scattered to react.[11] The political phenomenon is strictly connected with similar apparitions that affect the spiritual plane

---

9. Herodotus (*Histories*, 2.81) did not distinguish Orpheus from Bacchus; if Dio (*Roman History*) relates the modifications Orpheus allegedly introduced into the orgiastic rituals, this may be a modification in a Pythagorean sense (Orpheus as musician, or the idea of harmony), which, however, did not alter its fundamental character. According to some Orpheus came from Crete, that is from an Atlantic-Pelasgic center; others, by identifying him with Pythagoras himself, see him as a descendant of the Atlanteans.

10. Harrison (*Prolegomena to the Study of Greek Religion*, 120; 162) identified those festivals in which the feminine theme was predominant with the forms of magical rituals of purification that were typical of the ancient chthonic cult; it is likely that they constituted the germ of a certain aspect of the Mysteries. The notion of purification and expiation, which was virtually unknown in the Olympian cult, was a dominant theme in the inferior stratum. Later on, some kind of compromise and sublimation took place. Once the aristocratic idea of divinity as a natural state was lost (the heroes were mainly such by virtue of their divine origins), what ensued was the idea of a mortal man who yearned for immortality; then the ancient magical and exorcising motif of purification and of expiation was assumed in the mystical form of "purification from death," and finally in the form of a moral purification and expiation, as in the decadent aspects of the Mysteries that presaged Christianity.

in a more direct way, such as the democratization undergone by both the view of immortality and the notion of "hero." Demeter's mysteries at Eleusis may be regarded as a sublimation of the ancient pre-Hellenic and Pelasgic Mysteries by virtue of their original purity and aristocratic exclusivism; this ancient substratum arose and became predominant again once the Eleusinian Mysteries allowed anybody to partake of the ritual that "creates an unequal destiny after death," thus planting a seed that Christianity was destined to develop fully. In this way, the strange notion of immortality arose and spread in Greece as if immortality were a quality any mortal being's soul was naturally endowed with; at the same time, the notion of "hero" was democratized to the point that in some regions (e.g., Boeotia) the title of "hero" was bestowed on men whose only "heroic" deed merely consisted in having died.

In Greece Pythagoreanism represented in many ways a return of the Pelasgic spirit. Despite its astral and solar symbols (including a Hyperborean trace), the Pythagorean doctrine was essentially characterized by the Demetrian and pantheistic theme. After all, the lunar spirit of the Chaldean or Mayan priestly science was reflected in its view of the world in terms of numbers and of harmony; the dark, pessimistic, and fatalistic motif of tellurism was retained in the Pythagorean notion of birth on this earth as a punishment and as a sentence, and also in the teaching concerning reincarnation, which I have previously described as a symptom of a spiritual disease. The soul that repeatedly reincarnates is the soul subjected to the chthonic law. The doctrine of reincarnation exemplifies the emphasis Pythagoreanism and Orphism gave to the principle that is tellurically subjected to rebirth, as well as the truth proper to the civilization of the Mother. Pythagoras's nostalgia for ideas of a Demetrian type (after his death his home became a sanctuary of the goddess Demeter), including the dignity that women enjoyed in Pythagorean sects where they presided over initiations and where the ritual cremation of the dead was forbidden, as well as the sect's horror of blood—are features that can easily be explained on this basis.[12] In this kind of context even the escape from the "cycle of rebirths" has a dubious character (it is significant that in Orphism the dwelling of the blessed is not above the earth, as in the Achaean symbol of the Elysian Fields, but rather under the earth, in

---

11. Bachofen (*Mutterrecht*, 247–49) has brought to light an interesting thing, namely, that popular tyrants usually derived their power from a woman and succeeded each other according to a feminine line. This was one of signs of the relationship between democracy and gynaecocracy that is noticeable even in the cycle of the foreign kings in Rome.

12. According to some, Pythagoras owed his doctrine to the teaching of a woman, Themistoclea (Diogenes Laertius, *Life of Pythagoras*, 5). He entrusted some women to teach doctrine, since he acknowledged their greater propensity to the divine cult; his community had forms that remind us of matriarchy (ibid., 21, 8). Pliny (*Natural History*, 36.46) mentions that Pythagoras's disciples started to practice again the chthonic ritual of burial.

the company of infernal gods)[13] in comparison to the ideal of immortality that was proper of "Zeus's path"; at the end of this path there was a heavenly region or a Uranian world dominated by the "spiritual virility of the light" and inhabited by "those who are," namely, beings who are detached and inaccessible in their perfection and purity. Generally speaking, Pindar's words, "Do not try to become a god" (μή ματένη θεὸς λενέσθαι), already betray a gradual lessening of the tension of the ancient heroic impulse toward transcendence.

What I have mentioned so far are only a few of the many symptoms of a struggle between two worlds that in ancient Hellas did not come to a conclusive end. The Hellenic cycle had its "traditional" center[14] in the Achaean Zeus, in Delphi, and in the Hyperborean cult of the light. Likewise, the Northern-Aryan spirit was preserved in the Hellenic ideals of culture as "form" and cosmos that prevails over chaos; it was associated with the heroic and solar myths and with an aversion for the indefinite, the limitless, the ἄπειρον. The principle of the Delphic Apollo and Olympian Zeus, however, did not succeed in creating for itself a universal body or in ultimately defeating the element personified by the demon Python (whose ritual slaying was reenacted every eight years) and by that subterranean serpent that appears in the oldest stratum of the ritual of the Diasian Olympic festivity. Parallel to these views of culture as spiritual form, to heroic motifs, and to the speculative transpositions of the Uranian theme of the Olympian region, we find *(a)* the inexorable unfolding of Aphroditism, sensualism, Dionysism, and aestheticism; *(b)* the prevalence of the mystic and nostalgic orientation of the Orphic spirituality; *(c)* the theme of expiation; *(d)* the contemplative Demetrian-Pythagorean view of nature; and *(e)* the "virus" of democracy and antitraditionalism.

On the one hand, although traces of the Northern-Aryan ethos were preserved in Hellenic traditionalism, on the other hand, in this context this individualism appeared as a limitation; nor was it able to withstand the influences of the ancient substratum because of which it eventually degenerated in an anarchist and destructive sense; this was destined to happen many times in Italy until the Renaissance. What developed from the same northern path trodden by the Delphic Apollo was Alexander the Great's attempt to organize Hellas in a unitary fashion into an em-

---

13. If we keep in mind the "Dionysization" undergone by the cult of Apollo in Delphi, which led to the introduction of an anti-Olympian ritual of prophecies uttered through ecstatic or delirious women—then the very same traditions that tend to establish a relationship between Pythagoreanism and Apollonism (Pythagoras as "the one who leads the Pythia," or Pythagoras being identified with Apollo through his "golden thigh," etc.) hardly contradict what has just been said.

14. Delphi's value of "pole" was obscurely perceived by the Hellenes since they regarded Delphi as the *omphalos*, or the "center" of the earth and of the world; in any event, they found in the Delphic amphitrionate the sacred bond that united them over and above the particularism of the individual city-states.

pire.[15] In any event, the Greeks were not strong enough to uphold the universality that was intrinsic to the idea of the empire. The πόλις of the Macedonian empire dissolved instead of becoming integrated. In this πόλις too, unity and universality eventually had to confront that which paved the way for the first democratic and antitraditional crises; they acted in a destructive and leveling way instead of integrating that pluralistic and national element that provided a solid foundation for both the culture and tradition of individual Hellenic cities; it is here that the limitation of Greek individualism and particularism became especially evident. The reason for the caducity of Alexander's empire, which could have been the principle of a great new Indo-European cycle, does not lie in a mere historical contingency. When this empire declined, the calm and solar purity of the ancient Hellenic ideal was only a memory of the past. The "torch" of tradition moved somewhere else.

I have already pointed out the simultaneous crises that broke out in various traditions between the seventh and fifth centuries B.C.; all of a sudden it looked as if new aggregates of negative forces had emerged to sweep away a precarious world and begin a new era. Outside the West these forces were neutralized for the most part by reforms, restorations, or by new traditional manifestations; conversely, in the West they apparently succeeded in breaking the traditional dam, rushing forward, and ushering in the definitive collapse. I have previously discussed the decadence displayed by Egypt, the Mediterranean-Eastern cycle, and Israel; this decadence was destined to affect Greece too. In Greece, humanism (a characteristic theme of the Iron Age) made its appearance as a result of the emergence of religious sentimentalism and the decline of ideals typical of a virile and sacral mankind. Humanism eventually affected other dimensions of Hellenic life; it marked the advent of philosophical thought and of scientific inquiry. No traditional reaction worthy of being remembered attempted to block the onslaught of these trends;[16] what occurred instead was a regular process of development of a secular and antitraditional criticism that may be compared to the spreading of a cancer in all the healthy and nonsecular teachings that Greece still preserved.

Modern man may be unaware of it, but the preeminence of "thought" is only a marginal and recent phenomenon in history—though not as recent as the tendency to

---

15. It is significant that Apollonian Delphi, the traditional center of ancient Hellas, did not hesitate to abandon the "national cause" when it came in contact with civilizations that expressed the same spirit that it itself embodied, such as in the fifth century, in favor of the Persians, and in the fourth century in favor of the Macedonians. The Persians, for their part, almost recognized their god in the Hyperborean Apollo; in Hellenism we often encounter the assimilation of Apollo to Mithras, and on the part of the Persians, of Ahura Mazda to Zeus, of Verethragna to Heracles, of Anahita to Artemis, and so on. This was much more than mere "syncretism."

16. In India, Buddhism opposed pragmatism and realism to priestly philosophical speculations around the same time the early Greek philosophers appeared on the scene.

look at nature in purely physical terms. The figures of the philosopher and the "physicist" arose as the products of a degeneration that reached an advanced stage in the last age, the Iron Age. That process of decentralization, which by following the previously mentioned phases alienated man from his origins, was destined to end with the transformation of humankind from "beings" into "existences" whose center is "outside of themselves," mere ghosts or "stumps" who nevertheless still nurture the illusion of being able to achieve truth, wholeness, and life through their own efforts. In Hellas, the shift from the plane of "symbols" to the plane of "myths," with their personifications and latent "aestheticism," foreshadowed the first stage of decadence. Later on, after the gods were reduced to the rank of mythological figures, they were turned into philosophical concepts, that is, into pure abstractions or objects of exoteric cults. The emancipation of the individual from Tradition under the guise of "thinker" and the affirmation of reason as an instrument of uninhibited criticism and profane knowledge arose on the margins of this historical development that found its early characteristic manifestations in Greece.

The abovementioned trend reached a complete development only much later, that is, after the Renaissance; likewise, it was only with the advent of Christianity that humanism in the species of religious pathos became the dominant theme within an entire cycle of civilization. In Greece, however, philosophy had its center not so much within itself but in metaphysical and mysteriosophic elements that echoed traditional teachings; moreover, it always accompanied—even in Epicureanism and in Skepticism—elements of spiritual formation, asceticism, and autarchy. Nevertheless the Greek "physicists" continued to engage in "theology"; only the ignorance of some modern historians could suppose that, for instance, Thales' "water" or Anaximander's "air" corresponded to the real material elements. Some, like Socrates, even attempted to turn the new hermeneutical principle against itself in order to attempt a partial reconstruction of the shattered order.

Socrates believed that the philosophical concept could help overcome both the contingency of particular opinions and the individualistic and disintegrating element of Sophism, and at the same time help people find universal and superindividual truths. This attempt was destined to go wrong, however, and lead to an even more fatal deviation: the replacement of the spirit with discursive thought and the representation as true Being something that, although an image of Being, still remained nonbeing, a human and unreal creation, and a pure abstraction. And while thought openly exhibited its negative characteristics in some writers,[17] so much so as to represent the visible symptom of a fall rather than a danger, the most dangerous seduc-

---

17. Some, like Protagoras, claimed that "Man is the measure of all things" and employed this hermeneutical principle in an individualistic, destructive, and sophistical way.

tion and the most deceptive illusion consisted in thought seeking to situate the Universal and Being in the way that is proper to it (that is, rationally and philosophically) and to transcend through concept and rhetoric[18] the particularism and contingency of the sensible world; this thought eventually became the instrument of that humanism and that profound and corruptive unrealism that centuries later completely seduced the Western world.

The "objectivism" that some historians of philosophy decry in Greek thought was the support this thought derived, whether consciously or unconsciously, from traditional wisdom and from man's traditional attitude. Once this support collapsed, thought gradually became a reason unto itself, losing all transcendent and superrational references—until it eventually culminated in modern Rationalism and Kantian Criticism.

Here I will mention in passing another aspect of the "humanistic" upheaval found in Greece: the development of the arts and literature in a hypertrophic, profane, and individualistic sense. When compared to the strength of the origins, this development should be regarded as a degeneration and disintegration. The peak of the ancient world is found wherever, next to a coarseness of external forms, an intimately sacral reality was translated without expressionism into the greatness of a clear and free world. Thus, the best period of Hellas corresponds to the so-called Greek Middle Ages, characterized by its *epos* and *ethos,* and by its ideals of Olympian spirituality and heroic transfiguration. The civilized and philosophical Greece, "Mother of the arts," which the moderns admire so much and completely empathize with, was a *crepuscular* Greece. This was clearly perceived by those people who still retained the same virile spirit of the Achaean era in a pure state, that is, by the original Romans; see for instance in the writings of Cato (234–149 B.C.) the expressions of contempt for the new breed of "philosophers" and men of letters.[19] In many ways, the Hellenization of Rome, under this aspect of humanistic and almost enlightened development promoted by poets, literatary types, and scholars, was a prelude of its own decadence. Generally speaking this was true, notwithstanding those sacral and symbolic elements that Greek art and literature occasionally retained beyond the individuality of some authors.

The Roman Cycle

Rome was founded during the period of the crises that surfaced everywhere in ancient traditional civilizations. With the exception of the Holy Roman Empire, which was a Northern-Teutonic attempt to revive the ancient Roman ideal, Rome should

---

18. I employ this term according to the sense that Michelstaedter (*La persuasione e la retorica* [Florence, C. 1922]) gave to it; he vividly illustrated the sense of Socratic conceptual decadence and philosophical evasiveness vis-à-vis the doctrine of "being" as defended by the Eleatics.

19. Gellius, 18.7.3.

be regarded as the last great reaction against such a crisis, and also as the attempt—
successful for an entire cycle—to wrest a group of people from the forces of decadence at work in Mediterranean civilizations and organize them into a unitary whole,
thereby realizing on a stronger and more grandiose scale that which the power of
Alexander the Great succeeded in creating for only a short while.

The ultimate significance of Rome will elude us unless we first perceive the
heterogeneity between what constituted the central course of its development and
the traditions proper to the majority of the Italic populations among which Rome
arose and affirmed itself.[20]

It has been correctly pointed out that the pre-Roman Italian peninsula was inhabited by Etruscans, Sabines, Sabellians, Volscians, and Samnites, as well as by
Phoenicians, Siculians and Sicani, Greek and Syrian immigrants in the south—when
all of a sudden, without knowing how or why, a conflict erupted within all these
populations and their cults, views of the law, and claims to political supremacy; a
new principle appeared, powerful enough to subjugate everything in its path, to transform deeply the ancient customs and way of life, and which enjoyed an unrestrained
and almost predestined expansion typical of the great forces of history. No one ever
mentions the source of this principle and the only references to the origins, which still
fail to explain this phenomenon, are confined to an empirical and sociological plane;
therefore, those who stand in awe before the Roman "miracle" as an event to be
admired rather than to be explained, do better than those who attempt to explain it
through secondary causes.

Behind the greatness of Rome we can recognize forces of the heroic Aryan-
Western cycle at work; behind its decadence we can see the alteration of these same
forces. Naturally, in a mixed-up world far removed from its origins, it is necessary to
refer essentially to a superhistorical idea, which is, however, capable of acting in
history in a formative way; in this sense we can talk of the presence in Rome of an
Aryan element and of its struggle against the forces of the South. Our research cannot be based merely on the racial and ethnic plane. It has been ascertained that prior
to the Celtic migrations and the Etruscan cycle, nuclei that derived immediately
from the boreal, Western race made their appearance in Italy; these nuclei, compared to the aboriginal races and the crepuscular by-products of the paleo-Mediter-
ranean civilization of Atlantic origins, had the same meaning as the appearance of
the Dorians and Achaeans in Greece. The traces of these nuclei visibly point to the
Hyperborean cycle and to the "civilization of the reindeer" and "battle-axe." More-

---

20. This opposition was the central thesis of Bachofen's *Die Sage von Tanaquil* (Heidelberg, 1870). In the
next few pages I have borrowed and incorporated into a traditional conceptual framework several ideas
of Bachofen's concerning the meaning and the mission of Rome in the West.

over, it is likely that the ancient Latins represented a surviving vein or a reemergence of these nuclei variously intermingled with other Italic populations; in any event, we must refer to the plane of the "spiritual race." The type of the Roman civilization and the Roman man bear witness to the presence and power within this civilization, and also to the same force that was at the center of the heroic, Uranian cycles of Northern and Western origin. As dubious as the racial homogeneity of Rome in the origins may be, there is no question concerning the formative action this force exercised on the "material" to which it was applied, elevating it to and differentiating it from what belonged to a different world.

There are numerous elements that show the connection between both the Italic civilizations among which Rome arose and the residues of these civilizations in the early Roman world on the one hand, and the type of southern civilizations in their telluric, Aphrodistic, and Demetrian variations, on the other hand.[21]

The cult of the Goddess, which in Greece was typical of the Pelasgic component, most likely played an important role among the Siculians and the Sabines. The greatest deity of the Sabines was the chthonic goddess Fortuna, who reappeared in the forms of Horta, Feronia, Vesuna, Heruntas, the Horae, Hera, Juno, Venus, Ceres, Bona Dea, Demeter—all of which are reincarnations of the same divine principle. The oldest Roman calendar was of a lunar type, and the early Roman myths had plenty of feminine figures: Mater Matuta, Luna, Diana, Egeria—moreover, in the traditions concerning Mars-Hercules and Flora, Hercules and Larentia, Numa and Egeria, as well as in other traditions, the archaic theme of the subordination of the masculine to the feminine principle was also present in the background. These myths derived from pre-Roman traditions such as the Etruscan saga of Tanaquil, in which we find the type of the regal Asian-Mediterranean woman that Rome attempted to purify from its Aphrodistic traits and transform into a symbol of all the maternal virtues.[22] These transformations that the Roman world was responsible for with regard to everything that was incompatible with its spirit, however, still did not permanently remove from underneath the recent stratum of the myth an even older stratum that was connected with a civilization opposed to the Roman one; this stratum can be recognized in the regal succession through the female line or in women's advent to the throne (these being typical features of primitive Rome), especially in relation to foreign dynasties and to kings bearing plebeian names. According to a legend, Servius Tullius, who achieved power thanks to a woman and became a champion of

21. Bachofen's work showed the analogy with civilizations of the eastern Mediterranean. Mosso noticed a general relationship between the Aegean (pre-Hellenic) civilization and the pre-Roman Italic civilization.
22. According to Livy (1.34), in the cult of Tanaquil the Etruscan women exercised the role of priestesses; this is a typical trait of the Pelasgic civilization.

plebeian rights, was illegitimately conceived during one of the many orgiastic feasts celebrated by slaves who devoted themselves to the cult of Southern deities (chthonic Saturn, Venus, and Flora) and who celebrated the return of mankind to the law of universal brotherhood and the promiscuity of the great Mother of Life.

The Etruscans and the Sabines have left traces of a matriarchical system. Their inscriptions often reveal (as in Crete) filiation through the name of the mother instead of the father, and also the attribution of a particular honor, authority, importance, and freedom to women. Numerous Italic cities were named after women. The ritual of burial, as opposed to that of cremation (both of which were found in the ancient Roman world), was probably one of the many signs indicating the presence of two overlapping strata representing a Uranian and a Demetrian view of the afterlife, respectively; these strata were often mixed together even though they retained their unmistakable features.[23] What in Rome was retained as maternal sacredness and authority (*matronarum sanctitas*, or *mater princeps familiae*), rather than being a Roman feature, betrays the pre-Roman and gynaecocratic component that in the new civilization was subordinated to the paternal right and thus put in its proper place. This did not, however, prevent the opposite process from taking place in other cases: while on the one hand the Roman Saturn-Kronos retained some of his original traits, on the other hand he was portrayed as a telluric demon, and as the husband of Ops, the Earth. The same was true for Mars and the often contradictory varieties of the cult of Hercules. In all probability Vesta was a feminine version (due to a Southern influence) of the deity of fire, who always had a prevalent masculine and Uranian character among Aryan populations; this version even led to the association of this deity with Bona Dea, who was worshiped as a goddess of the Earth and secretly celebrated at night. It is said that men were forbidden to participate in this cult and even forbidden to pronounce the name of the goddess.[24] Tradition attributed to a non-Roman king, the Sabine Titus Tatius, the introduction into Rome of the most important chthonic cults such as those of Ops and Flora, Re and Juno Curis, Luna, the chthonic Kronos, Diana, and Vulcan, and even of the *lares;*[25] likewise the *libri Sibillini* (or *libri fatales*), of

23. The Roman gens that remained faithful to the ritual of inhumation was the gens Cornelia, whose characteristic cult was that of the telluric Venus.

24. The most ancient root of the cult of Bona Dea, a deity who at first was venerated in a chaste Demetrian form, reemerged in a decadent period of Roman history during which her cult came to be associated with uninhibited sexual promiscuity. Concerning Vesta, just as the maternal dignity of this goddess was respected and yet subordinated to the authority of the *patres*, likewise her cult was subjected to the *pontifex magnus* first and to the emperor later. After all, the official cult of fire in the time of Romulus was entrusted to priests; it became the legacy of the vestal virgins only as a decision of the Sabine and lunar king Numa. Emperor Julian (*Hymn to King Helios*, 155a) eventually restored its solar character.

25. Varro, 5.74. In this context the *lares* are to be understood in their chthonic aspect. It would be interesting to examine the mixture of the telluric element, which is an Etruscan-Pelasgic remnant, with the "heroic" and patrician element in the Roman funerary cult. Also it would be interesting to analyze the phases of

Asiatic-Southern origin, which were sympathetic to the plebeian component of the Roman religion, were responsible for introducing the Great Mother and other deities of the chthonic cycle: Dis Pater, Flora, Saturn, and the triad Ceres-Liber-Libera.

The strong pre-Aryan, Aegean-Pelasgic, and partially "Atlantic" component, which can be detected from an ethnic and philological view in these populations that Rome encountered in Italy, still remains a fact to be reckoned with; the relationship between these populations and the original Roman nucleus was similar to that which occurred in Greece between the Pelasgian stocks on the one hand and the Achaean and Doric stocks on the other. According to a tradition, after being scattered, the Pelasgians often became slaves of other people; in Lucania and in Brutium they formed the majority of the Bruttians, who were subjugated by the Sabellians and by the Samnites. Interestingly enough, these Bruttians sided with the Chartaginenses in their struggle against Rome in one of the most important episodes in the conflict between North and South; following their defeat, the Bruttians were eventually sold into slavery. Just as in India the aristocracy of the *ārya* stood before the servile caste like a dominating stock stands before an aboriginal stock, in the same way in the Roman opposition between patricians and plebeians we may see an analogous phenomenon and thus consider the plebeians as the "Pelasgians of Rome." The evidence suggests that the plebeians in Rome were inspired by the maternal, feminine, and material principle, while the patriciate derived its superior dignity from the paternal right. The plebs succeeded in becoming part of the state and even participating in the *ius Quiritium,* but never in the political and juridical institutions connected to the superior chrism of the patricians (the reader will recall the saying *patrem ciere posse* in reference to divine ancestors, the so-called *divi parentes,* who were the prerogative of the patriciate and not of the plebs, which instead was considered to be made up of the "children of the Earth").

Even if a direct ethnic relationship between Pelasgians and Etruscans[26] is not

---

the process of purification through which the *lares* lost their original pre-Roman, telluric (the *lares* as the "children" of Acca Larentia, the equivalent of Bona Dea), and plebeian (a characteristic of the cult of the *lares* was that slaves played an important role in it and at times were even the officiating celebrants) character and thus assumed more and more the character of "divine spirits," "heroes," and souls that had overcome death. Augustine, *City of God,* 9. 11.

26. The most widespread classical tradition during the imperial era of Rome attributed an Asiatic origin to the Etruscans, in a way that can be summed up in Seneca's words: *"Tuscos Asia sibi indicat."* According to some, the Etruscans belonged to the stock of the Tursha, seafolk whose dwelling was located in some island or region of the eastern Mediterranean and who invaded Egypt toward the end of the Eighteenth Dynasty. According to a more recent and reliable opinion, the Etruscans were the remnants of a population that preexisted those Italic nuclei that had come from the north; this population was scattered in Spain, along the Tyrrhenian Sea, in Asia Minor and even along the Caucasus (from the Basques, to the Liddi and the Hittites); in that case they belong to the Atlantic-Pelasgic cycle. Other scholars, such as Altheim and Mosso, talk about the kinship existing between the Etruscan and Minoan civilizations not only because of the privileged role that women played in the cult, but also because of affinities that are evident in their architecture, art, and customs.

persuasively demonstrated, the latter people, to whom Rome, according to many scholars, was heavily indebted, display the traits of a telluric and at most lunar and priestly civilization that can hardly be reconciled with the central line and with the spirit of the Roman world. It is true that the Etruscans, like the Assyrians and the Chaldeans, in addition to the telluric world of fertility and of the various Mothers of Nature, also knew a Uranian pantheon of masculine deities ruled by Tinia. Nevertheless, these deities *(dii consentes)* were very different from Olympian deities; they did not possess any real sovereignty and were more like shadows dominated by an occult power that cannot be named, which overshadows everything else and subjects everything to the rules of the *dii superiores et involuti.* Thus, Etruscan Uranianism betrayed the spirit of the South in the same fatalistic and naturalistic way as in the case of the Pelasgic view of the generated Zeus who was subjected to the Stygian king Pluto, ruler of the underworld. The subordination of all beings, even divine ones, to a principle that shuns the light like the womb of the earth and whose law rules supreme over those who arise from it into a contingent life, was typical of the spirit of the South. Thus, we find a return to the shadow of Isis, who warned: "No one will be able to dissolve what I turn into a law,"[27] and to those Hellenic feminine deities, the creatures of the Night and of Erebus, who embodied the destiny and the sovereignty of natural law. At the same time the demonic and magical aspect that played a relevant role in the Etruscan cult through forms that contaminated the solar motifs and symbols reveals the role played in that civilization by the pre-Indo-European element, even in its lowest characteristics.

In reality, the Etruscans living at the time of the birth of Rome had very few redeeming heroic and solar characteristics. They could only view the world in a sad and gloomy way; besides the terror they had of the afterlife, they were so obsessed by the sense of an incumbent destiny and by expiation that they even predicted the end of their own nation.[28] The union of the theme of eros with that of death is found among the Etruscans in a characteristic fashion: they enjoyed with a voluptuous frenzy a fleeting life, dulled by ecstasies dominated by the infernal forces whose presence they were reminded of all the time. The priestly leaders of the Etruscan clans *(lucumoni)* regarded themselves as the children of the Earth; a chthonic demon

---

27. Dio, *Roman History,* 1.27. See also M. Pallottino, *Etruscologia* (Milan, 1942), 175–81. This author, in addition to "an abandonment and almost an abdication of spiritual human activity before the deity," also noticed the gloomy and pessimistic Etruscan view of the afterlife, which did not know any hopes of immortality and heavenly survival for anybody, including the most exalted people.

28. Concerning the pathos of the afterlife, G. De Sanctis (*Storia dei Romani,* 1.147) explained that a characteristic of the Etruscan soul was the "terror of the afterlife, which was expressed through figurations of dreadful demons, like the monster Tuchulcha, and through macabre portrayals that anticipate the medieval ones."

(Tages)[29] was traditionally credited with founding the "Etruscan discipline," or *aruspicina*. This discipline, the texts of which "filled with fear and horror" its students, was part of that type of fatalistic, lunar science typical of the Chaldean priesthood and that was eventually transmitted to the Hittites; the *aruspicina* show evident analogies with the latter science even from the technical point of view of some procedures.[30]

The fact that Rome partially incorporated such elements into the augural science that was the privilege of the patriciate, and that it allowed the Etruscan haruspexes to practice their art and did not disdain to consult them, reveals not only the different meaning that things may have when they are integrated in the context of a different civilization, but also a compromise and an antithesis that were often latent in the Roman world and that sometimes were often actualized and made evident. In reality, the revolt against the Tarquinians represented a revolt of aristocratic Rome against the Etruscan component; the expulsion of that dynasty was celebrated every year in Rome with a feast similar to the feast with which the Persians celebrated the Megaphonia, which was the massacre of the Median priests who had usurped the regality after the death of Cambyses.

The Romans were always diffident to and fearful of the haruspex, as if he were an occult enemy of Rome. Among the many episodes concerning this uneasy relationship, we may recall the time when the haruspexes wanted to have the statue of Horatius Cocles buried because of their hatred toward Rome; however, when contrary to the haruspicium, the statue was erected on the most elevated place and happy events befell Rome, the haruspexes were charged with betrayal and after confessing, were executed.

Thus, Rome departed from the background of the Italic populations of its origins that were still connected to the spirit of the ancient Southern civilizations, thereby manifesting a new influence that can hardly be traced to its background. This influence, however, could only be exercised through a harsh struggle, both inner and outer, and a series of reactions, adaptations, and transformations. The ideal of conquering virility was embodied in Rome. This virility was manifested in the doctrine of the state and in the notions of *auctoritas* and *imperium*. The state was under the aegis of the Olympian deities (particularly the Capitoline Jupiter, who was detached, sovereign, ungenerated, and exempt from any naturalistic myths and generations) and originally it was not separated from the initiatory "mystery" of regality *(adytum et initia regis)* that had been declared inaccessible to ordinary people. The *imperium*

---

29. Ovid, *Metamorphosis*, 15.553.
30. According to Piganiol, in the methods of Roman divination there must have been an opposition between the Uranian and patrician ritual of the augurs and the chthonic ritual of the Etruscan haruspexes.

(not in the hegemonical and territorial sense of the word) was understood in terms of power and the mystical and dreadful force of command that was the prerogative not only of political leaders (in whom it retained its immaterial character, beyond the often irregular and spurious variety of techniques used to attain it), but of the patricians and of the heads of households. The Roman symbol of fire reflected a similar spirituality, as did the strict paternal right and the articulations of a law that Vico did not hesitate to call "heroic law," since it informed the Roman ethic of honor and faithfulness. This ethic was felt so strongly that, according to Livy, it eventually became a trademark of the Roman people; whereas lacking a *fides* and following the contingencies of fate characterized by those whom the Romans referred to as "barbarians."[31] The early Romans characteristically perceived the supernatural as *numen* (as sheer power) rather than as *deus;* this represents the counterpart of a peculiar spiritual attitude. Other characteristics of the Roman world included the absence of pathos, lyricism and mysticism toward the divine, the presence of precise law for the necessary and necessitating rite, and clear and sober views. In their reflection of a virile and "magical" attitude,[32] these themes corresponded to the themes found in the early Vedic, Chinese, and Iranian periods and to the Achaean-Olympian ritual as well. The typical Roman religion had always been diffident toward the abandonment of the soul in God and toward the outbursts of devotion; it restrained, by force if necessary, anything that diminished that serious dignity proper to the relations between a *civis Romanus* and a god. Although the Etruscan component attempted to influence the plebeian strata of society by introducing the pathos of terrifying representations of the netherworld, Rome, at its best, remained faithful to the heroic view proper to early Hellas. Rome had personified heroes, but it also knew the imperturbability of mortal men who had no fear and no hopes concerning the afterlife, and who could not be dissuaded from a conduct inspired by duty, *fides,* heroism, order, and dominion. A proof of this consisted in the good reception accorded to Lucretius' Epicureanism, in which the explanation of reality in terms of natural causes aimed at eliminating the fear of death and the gods and at freeing

---

31. Livy, 22.22.6. Fides—in its various forms, such as Fides Romana, Fides Publica, and so on—was one of the most ancient deities of Rome.

32. In this context "magic" is understood in the higher sense of the word and is referred to the official Roman religion, which according to some, consisted in a sheer "formalism" lacking religious pathos; on the contrary, it expressed the ancient law of pure action. The Roman persecutions against magic and astrology only concerned inferior forms of religion, that were often superstitious or quackish. In reality, a magical attitude understood as an attitude of command and action upon invisible forces through the pure determinism of the ritual, constituted the essence of the early Roman religion and the Roman view of the sacred. Later on, though the Romans opposed the popular and superstitious forms of magic, they continued to have a great respect for the patrician cult and for the figure of the theurgist, who was shrouded with dignity and with ascetical purity.

human life by bestowing upon it calmness and a sense of security. Even in doctrines like Epicureanism we find a view of the gods reflecting the Olympian ideal of impassive and detached essences that the wise regarded as models of perfection.

While next to other peoples such as the Greeks and the Etruscans the Romans may at first have appeared as "barbarians," their lack of "culture" concealed (as in the case of some Germanic populations at the time of the barbarian invasions) an even older force that acted in a style compared to which all cultures of an urban type appeared as decadent and disaggregative. The first account of Rome that Greece ever had came from an ambassador who confessed that although he had expected to sit in the Roman Senate as if he were in a gathering of barbarians, he felt instead like being in the midst of an assembly of kings.[33] Thus, although secret signs of Tradition appeared in Rome from the start in invisible ways,[34] nevertheless, the very epics and history of Rome, rather than its cultural theories and assumptions, contributed to express the truer "myth" of Rome and to give witness in a more immediate way (almost as if through a series of great symbols sculpted by the power in the very substance of history) to the spiritual struggle that forged the destiny and the greatness of this "eternal" city. All the phases of Rome's development represented conquests of the victorious Indo-European spirit; in the greatest historical and military tensions we find the best manifestations of this spirit, even when the life of Rome was already altered because of exogenous influences and plebeian unrest.

From the beginning the myth presents elements that contain a deep meaning and indicate the two opposite forces at work in Rome. There is an interesting tradi-

---

33. Plutarch, *Phyrro*, 19.5. In the episode of the Gallic invasion, the countenance of the elders was described by Livy as "more than human," and as "very similar to the gods'" (5.41).

34. See for instance: (*a*) the "sign of the center," the black stone Romulus put at the beginning of the Via Sacra; (*b*) the fatidic and solar "twelve," which was the number of vultures that gave Romulus the right to name the new city; the number of the lictorian fasces carrying an axe, the symbol of the Hyperborean conquerors; the number, instituted by Numa, of the *ancilia* (sacred shields) which were the *pignora imperii* (the pledge of command); and the number of the altars in the archaic cult of Janus; (*c*) the eagle, sacred to the god of bright skies, Jupiter, and also the *signum* of the Roman legions, which was also one of the Aryan symbols of the immortalizing "glory"; this is why the souls of the deceased Caesars were believed to take the form of an eagle and to fly into solar immortality; (*d*) the sacrifice of the horse, which corresponds to the *aśvamedha* of the Indo-Aryans; (*e*) many other elements of a universal sacred tradition.

In regard to eagles, in ancient traditions we find the belief that the person on whom an eagle came to rest was predestined by Zeus to high offices or to regality and that the sight of an eagle was an omen of victory. The eagle was such a universal symbol that among the Aztecs it indicated the location for the capital of the new empire. The *ba*, the element of the human being destined to lead a heavenly eternal life in a state of glory, was often represented in Egyptian hieroglyphics as a sparrow hawk, which was the Egyptian equivalent of the eagle. In the *Ṛg Veda* (4.18.12; 4.27.2) the eagle carried the magic potion to Indra that consecrated him as the Lord of all gods, leaving behind infernal feminine forces. From a doctrinal point of view, this could be compared to the esoteric meaning of the Roman imperial apotheosis *(consecratio)* in which the flight of the eagle from the funeral pyre symbolized the deceased soul's ensuing deification.

tion according to which Saturn-Kronos created Saturnia, which was regarded as a city and at times as a fortress and was supposedly located where Rome was eventually built; for this purpose, this god allegedly employed a hidden power *(latens deus)* that was present in Latium.[35] Concerning the legend of the birth of Rome, in the story of King Numitor and Amulius we already find the theme of the antagonist couple; Amulius seems to embody the violent principle, evident in his attempted usurpation of Numitor, who in turn corresponds to a great degree to the regal and sacred principle. The duality is found again in the couple Romulus and Remus. Here we have a characteristic theme of the heroic cycles, since the two brothers were generated from an intercourse between a virgin in charge of tending the sacred fire and the warrior god Mars. Second, we find the historical and metaphysical theme of being "rescued from the waters." Third, the fig tree Ruminal, under which the twins take refuge, corresponds to the universal symbol of the Tree of Life and the supernatural nourishment that it grants; in ancient Latin, the attributive *ruminus* was given to Jupiter, and it signified his role as "he who gives nourishment." The twins were fed by a she-wolf. I have already described the double meaning of the symbolism of the wolf; not only in the classical world, but also in the Celtic and Nordic world, the themes of the wolf and the light were often intertwined to the point that the wolf came to be associated with the Hyperborean Apollo. Moreover, the wolf represents a wild force, an elemental and unrestrained power; in Nordic mythology the "Age of the Wolf" designated the age in which the rebellious elemental powers are out of control.

The duality latent in the principle that nourishes the twins corresponds to the duality of Romulus and Remus, Osiris and Set, Cain and Abel, and so on.[36] Romulus marked the boundaries of the city with a sacred rite based on a principle symbolizing order, limit, and law. Remus was disrespectful of this delimitation and was killed by his brother. This was the first episode and the prelude of a dramatic, internal and external, spiritual and social struggle (partially well known, partially represented by silent symbols) on the part of Rome to generate a universal heroic tradition in the Mediterranean world.

The mythical account of the period of the kings of Rome indicates the antagonism between a heroic and warrior aristocratic principle and the element connected with the plebeians, "the Pelasgians of Rome," and the lunar, priestly component (of

---

35. Pliny said: *"Saturnia ubi huc Roma est."* Virgil (Aeneid, 357–58): *"Hanc Janus pater, hanc Saturnus condidit arcem: Janiculum huic, illi fuerat Saturnia nomen."*

36. Set, the dark brother who killed Osiris, was also called Typhon. According to Plutarch: "They called Typhon 'Set'; for this name, which denotes overpowering and violence, also denotes frequent return and overleaping." *De Iside et Osiride*, 49. The enemies of the solar principle (Ra), who were called "the children of the hopeless revolt," were associated with Set.

an Etruscan-Sabine origin); this antagonism was expressed as well in geographical terms, namely, by the Palatine and by the Aventine. It was from the Palatine that Romulus saw the symbol of the twelve vultures that bestowed on him supremacy over Remus, who had chosen the Aventine for himself. After Remus's death, the duality seems to reemerge in the form of a compromise in the pair Romulus-Tatius; Tatius was the king of the Sabines, a people of a prevalently telluric and lunar cult. Following Romulus's death, a war erupted between the Albans (a warrior stock of Nordic type) and the Sabines. Moreover, according to the ancient Italic tradition, it was on the Palatine that Hercules met the good king Evander (who had erected on it a temple dedicated to the goddess Victory) after slaying Cacus, the son of the Pelasgic god of chthonic fire, and after erecting in the latter's cave, located on the Aventine, an altar to the Olympian god.[37] The same Hercules, as "triumphal Hercules" and the sworn enemy of Bona Dea, was destined to play a significant role, together with Jupiter, Mars, and Apollo, in the theme of the Roman Uranian and virile spirituality and thus came to be celebrated in rituals from which women were excluded.[38]

Moreover, the Aventine, the mountain of the slain Cacus and of Remus, was also the mountain sacred to the Goddess; on top of it was the most important temple of Diana-Luna, the great goddess of the night, which was founded by Servius Tullius, the plebeian king and the friend of the people. The plebeians who rebelled against the patriciate took refuge in this temple; in this temple slaves celebrated feasts in honor of Servius Tullius; on the Aventine other feminine cults were also established, such as those of Bona Dea, Carmenta, Juno Regina (392 B.C.)—a deity imported from the vanquished Vejo and of whom the Romans in the beginning were not very fond—or of telluric and virile cults, such as that of Faunus.

The succession of the legendary kings of Rome is a sequence of episodes in the struggle between two principles. After Romulus, who was transformed into a "hero" in the guise of Quirinus—the "undefeated god," of whom Caesar considered himself an incarnation—we find in Numa the reemergence of the lunar type of the regal Etruscan-Pelasgian priest who was guided by the feminine principle (the Hegeria) and who anticipated the scission between the regal and the priestly powers.[39] In Tullus Hostilius, however, we can see the symptoms of the reaction of the characteristic Roman virile principle against the Etruscan priestly principle; this king appeared

---

37. According to Piganiol the duel between Hercules and Cacus may have been a legendary transposition of the struggle between an Aryan or Aryan-like stock and an aboriginal stock of a Pelasgic origin.

38. Macrobius, *Saturnalia*, 1.12.27.

39. After Numa, the king (who originally ranked higher than the *flamines*, who in turn corresponded to the Hindu *brāhmaṇa*) was opposed to the *rex sacrorum*, who during that period was an expression of the plebeian ritual, rather than a priest of the patrician rite; he was the mediator between the people and the great plebeian goddess, the Moon, who did not own the *spectio* (the right to inspect the *aruspicina*, which was an attribute typical of the patricians) and who, according to the ritual, ranked below the vestal virgins.

as the type of the *imperator* and the warrior leader. Although Tully died because he climbed an altar and caused a thunderbolt to rend the sky (which was the prerogative of the priests), the symbolism of his gesture alluded to the attempt to reintegrate the Sacred within the warrior aristocracy. Conversely, in the Etruscan dynasty of the Tarquinians the themes of the woman and of a regality often favoring the plebeian strata against the aristocracy became predominant in Rome.[40]

A fundamental event in the history of Rome was the revolt of the Roman patriciate (509 B.C.), which, after killing Servius, expelled the second Tarquin, put an end to the foreign dynasty, and broke the yoke of the previous civilization—almost at the same time as the expulsion of the popular tyrants and of the Doric restoration in Athens (510 B.C.). After this, it is of little importance to follow the development of inner struggles and the alternation of patrician resistance and plebeian usurpation in Rome. The center shifted from the inside to the outside. Rather than the compromise that some institutions and laws represented until the imperial age, we should consider the "myth" represented by the historical process of the growth of Rome's greatness. Despite the endurance or the infiltration into Rome's social network of a heterogenous and Southern element, the political structures in which this element took a firm hold were nevertheless affected; eventually, they were either inexorably destroyed or swept away by a different, antithetical, and nobler civilization.

To this effect, all we have to do is think about the unusual and significant violence with which Rome destroyed the centers of the previous civilization, especially the Etruscan ones, successfully wiping out all traces of their previous power, their traditions, and even their languages. Like Alba, so did Vejo (the city of Queen Juno),[41] Tarquinia, and Lucumonia disappear from history. In this destruction we find the sense of a destiny fulfilled, being methodically carried out more than merely contemplated, by a race that always believed that its greatness and good fortune were due to divine forces. Next to fall was Capua, which was the center of Southern weakness and opulence, the personification of the "culture" of the aesthetic and

---

40. I will refer the reader to Bachofen's work regarding the relationships between the feminine figures and the kings of the foreign dynasty. I will only add that the name Servius (Servius Tullius) originally indicated a son of slaves, just like the name Brutus (the name of the first tribune of the plebs was Junius Brutus and after the first year this name never appeared again in the consular lists) was given to rebellious slaves of Pelasgic stock. There is also a significant (for the plebeian element) telluric theme emphasized by tradition, according to which after the oracle announced that he who kissed his own mother would become king, Brutus knelt to the ground and kissed the earth, whom he conceived as the Mother of all; likewise, the plebeians and the Etruscan *lucumoni* were regarded as children of the earth. Besides, isn't it curious that centuries later the first person who attempted to usurp the legitimate authority in Rome himself carried the name of the rebellious Pelasgic slaves, namely, Brutus?

41. Piganiol rightly observed that the struggle of Rome against Vejo represented the struggle of Apollo against the Goddess; a similar meaning seems to be given by Livy (5.23.5–8) who related that Camillus, after conquering Vejo, was regarded as a solar deity.

Aphroditized Greece no longer under Doric influence; that civilization was destined to seduce and weaken a segment of the Roman patriciate. The two traditions clashed especially during the Punic wars in the form of political realities and powers. With the destruction of Carthage, which was (146 B.C.) the city of the Goddess (Astarte-Tanit) and the regal woman (Dido) who had tried to seduce the legendary forefather of the Roman nobility—we may say with Bachofen[42] that Rome shifted the center of the historical West from the telluric to the Uranian mystery, from the lunar world of the Mothers, to the solar world of the Fathers. The original and invisible seed of the "Roman race" actualized an inner formation of life with an ethos and a law that consolidated this meaning despite the continuous and subtle action of the opposite element. Truthfully, the Roman right of the conquering arms, together with the mystical view of victory, was radically antithetical to Etruscan fatalism and to any contemplative abandonment. The virile idea of the state took hold in opposition to any hieratic, Demetrian form, nevertheless retaining in all of its structures the chrism proper to a sacred and ritual element. This idea strengthened the soul and made the whole life vastly superior to all naturalistic elements. The asceticism of "action" developed in the traditional forms that I mentioned before; it even permeated the articulations of the corporate organizations with a sense of discipline and military style. Gens and *familia* were organized according to the strict paternal right; the heart of society consisted in the *patres,* who were the priests of the sacred fire, the arbiters of justice, and the military leaders of their own people and of their slaves or clients, and the highly visible elements of the aristocratic Senate. The *civitas* itself, which was the embodiment of the law, was nothing but rhythm, order, and number; the mystical numbers three, ten, twelve, and their multiples formed the basis of its political divisions.

Although Rome did not succeed in shrugging off the influence of the *libri sibillini* (or *libri fatales*), which represented the Asiatic element mixed with a spurious Hellenism allegedly introduced by the second Tarquin (these books met the taste of the plebeian rite by introducing new and equivocal deities in the ancient and exclusive patrician cult), nevertheless, Rome reacted wherever the inimical element clearly manifested itself and threatened its deepest reality. Thus, Rome *(a)* fought against

---

42. In the example of Rome following the *libri sibillini* and welcoming the Phrygian Great Goddess (as it did before with the Asiatic goddess of prostitution, following the defeat at Lake Trasimene) in order to facilitate a victory over Hannibal, Bachofen saw an Aphrodistic city that was almost afraid of having neglected the Mother for such a long time and of having consecrated itself entirely to the virile principle of the *imperium*. This is possible. On the other hand, we should not forget that according to the Romans a war could not truly be won other than by evoking and drawing to their side the gods of the enemy: the great Phrygian goddess was a copy of the Punic Tanit. The cult of that goddess was incorporated into the Roman world only later on and it spread among the plebeian classes especially.

the Bacchic and Aphrodistic influences and banned the Bacchanalia; *(b)* was suspicious of Mysteries of Asiatic origin because they increasingly gravitated around an unhealthy mysticism; *(c)* tolerated exotic cults, among which we often find the chthonic and the Mothers' themes, as long as they did not exercise a harmful influence on the social, virile lifestyle. The destruction of the apocryphal books of Numa Pompilius and the ban of the "philosophers," especially of the Pythagoreans, were motivated by reasons that were more than political and not contingent. Just like the Etruscan remnants, Pythagoreanism too (which in Greece arose as a Pelasgic reemergence), despite the presence of different elements, may be considered an offshoot of a purified "Demetrian" civilization. It is significant that classical authors believed that a close relationship existed between Pythagoras and the Etruscans and that the banned commentaries of Numa Pompilius's books tended to sanction this relationship and open the doors (behind the mask of an alleged traditional spirit) to the antithetical and anti-Roman Pelasgic-Etruscan element.

Other historical events that from a metaphysical view of civilization have the meaning of symbols were the fall of the Isis-like kingdoms of Cleopatra and of Jerusalem, which marked the turning points in the inner Western life, and took place through the dynamics of the archetypal antitheses themselves reflected in the civil war. In Pompeius, Brutus, Cassius, and Anthony we may find the Southern theme in the tenacious but thwarted attempt to slow down and to overcome the new reality. While Cleopatra was the symbol of an Aphrodistic civilization under whose spell Anthony fell victim,[43] Caesar embodied the Aryan-Western type of the conqueror. With the words: "The gens Julia can claim both the sanctity of kings, who reign supreme among mortals, and the reverence due to gods, who hold even kings in their power,"[44] he foretold the reemergence in Rome of the highest view of the *imperium.* In reality, with Augustus—who in the eyes of the Romans embodied the *numen* and the *aeternitas* of the son of Apollo the Sun—the unity of the two powers was reestablished following a reformation that meant to restore the principles of the ancient Roman religion against the invasion of the exotic cults and superstitions. Augustus represented a state that justified itself with the solar-Olympian idea and that naturally tended to implement the ideal of universality. The idea of Rome eventually affirmed itself beyond all ethnic and religious particularisms. Once the imperial cult was defined, it respected and welcomed into some sort of "religious feudalism" the various gods that corresponded to the traditions of the different peoples that were incorporated in the Roman ecumene; above any particular and national religion it

---

43. It is interesting that Cleopatra assumed the name "Isis" and Anthony, "Dionysus," thus reproducing two complementary types of a civilization of "Aphrodistic" type. See Dio Cassius, *Roman History,* 10.5.
44. Suetonius, *Life of the Twelve Caesars* (Julius Caesar, 6).

was given witness to by a superior *fides,* which was connected with the supernatural principle embodied by the emperor, or by the "genius" of the emperor, and symbolized by the Victory as a mystical entity and to which the Senate swore faithfulness.

At the time of Augustus, the asceticism of action characterized by an element of destiny had created a sufficiently vast body so that Roman universalism could also have a tangible expression and bestow its chrism on a heterogeneous group of populations and races. Rome appeared as the "*genitrix* of men and of gods"; as a city "in whose temples one is not far from heaven," and which had made of different people one nation *(fecisti patriam diversis gentibus unam).*[45] The *pax augusta et profunda,* as *pax romana,* seemed to stretch as far as the limits of the known world. It was as if Tradition were destined to rise again in the forms proper to a "heroic cycle." It looked as if the Iron Age had come to an end and the return of the primordial age of the Hyperborean Apollo had begun:

> Now the last age of Cumae's prophecy has come. The great succession of centuries is born anew. Now too returns the Virgin; Saturn's rule returns. Now a new generation descends from heaven's height. O chaste Lucina, look with blessing on the newborn boy whose birth will end the iron race at last and raise a golden through the world: now your [brother] Apollo reigns. . . . He will receive the divine life and see the gods mingling with heroes, and himself be seen one of them.[46]

This feeling was so strong that later on it affirmed itself and turned Rome into a superhistorical symbol; even Christians said that while Rome was safe and wholesome the dreadful convulsions of the last age were not to be feared, but that when Rome fell, humanity would find itself close to the end.[47]

---

45. Rutilius Namatianus, *De red. suo,* 1.49, 50, 62–65.
46. Virgil, *Eclogues,* 4.5–10; 15–18. Among these prophetic expressions of Virgil we find mention of the serpent's death (5.24); of a group of heroes who will renew the symbolic feat of Argon; and of Achilles who will wage a new symbolic war of the Achaeans against Troy.
47. Expressions of Lactantius, *The Divine Institutes,* 7.25.6; Tertullian, *Ad scapulam,* 2.

31

Syncope of the Western Tradition

EARLY CHRISTIANITY

The advent of Christianity marked the beginning of an unprecedented decline. In the previous pages I have emphasized the central force in Rome and its unfolding through a complex development; in the course of this development, heterogeneous influences acted only fragmentarily vis-à-vis the supernatural element that gave to Rome its specific physiognomy.

The Rome that emancipated itself from its aboriginal Atlantic and Etruscan-Pelasgian roots; destroyed in rapid succession the great centers of the more recent Southern civilization; despised Greek philosophers and banned the Pythagorean sect; and outlawed the Bacchanalia, thus reacting against the avant-garde of the Alexandrian deities (persecutions of 59, 58, 53, 50, and 40 B.C.)—that same Rome, that is, the sacral, patrician, and virile Rome inspired by the notions of *ius, fas,* and *mos,* increasingly fell under the spell of the onslaught of the Asiatic cults that rapidly infiltrated the structures of the empire and altered its physiognomy. Rome witnessed the return of the symbols of the Mother and of the most spurious forms of the various mystical and pantheistic cults of Southern deities, which were a far cry from the Demetrian clarity of the origins and were associated with the corruption of the customs and of the innermost Roman *virtus* more than with the corruption of the institutions. This was a process of disintegration that eventually affected the imperial idea itself. The sacred content of the imperial idea was preserved, but only as a mere symbol; it was carried by a turbid and chaotic current as a chrism that rarely corresponded to the dignity of those who were marked by it. Historically and politically even the representatives of the empire acted in a way that ran counter to that which would have required its defense and its reaffirmation as a solid and organic social order. Instead of reacting, selecting, and rallying the surviving elements of the "Roman race" around the heart of the state in order to contain adequately the new forces flowing into the empire, the Caesars began to practice an absolutist centralization and a leveling. Once the senate lost its influence the distinction between Roman citizens, Latin citizens, and the mass of other subjects was abolished and Roman citizenship was extended to everybody. The Caesars thought that a despotism based on military dictatorship and on a soulless bureaucratic and administrative structure could successfully hold together the Roman ecumene, which had truly been reduced to a cosmopolitan and disarticulated mass. Nobody was able to do anything decisive to stem the general process of decadence, not even people who exhibited traits of greatness and ancient Roman dignity, who embodied some features typical of a sidereal nature and the quality of a "stone," who had the sense of what true wisdom was, and who at times even received an initiatory consecration (like the emperor Julian).

The imperial age exhibits, in the course of its development, this contradictory double nature: on the one hand, the theology, metaphysics, and liturgy of regality became increasingly defined; on the other hand, there were plenty of references to a new Golden Age. Every Caesar was acclaimed with the formula *expectate veni;* his apparition resembled a mystical event *(adventus augusti)* and it was accompanied by natural wonders, just like his decline was marked by bad omens. He was the *redditor lucis aeternae* (Constantius Chlorus); he was again the *pontifex magnus* and the one who received from the Olympian god the universal dominion symbolized by a sphere. The crown resembling the rays of the sun and the scepter of the king of heaven were a Caesar's royal insignia. His laws were regarded as sacred or divine. Even in the senate, the ceremony that consecrated him had a liturgical character. His image was worshiped in the temples of the various provinces, portrayed on various military standards, and regarded as the supreme reference point of the *fides* and of the cult of his soldiers and as the symbol of the unity of the empire.

But this was just a ray of light shining in the middle of a dark night of forces, passions, murders, cruelties, and betrayals that assumed epidemic proportions. With the passing of time this background became increasingly tragic, bloody, and fragmentary, despite the sporadic appearance of harsh leaders who were able to command obedience and respect in a world that was weak and falling apart. Eventually, a point was reached when the imperial function existed only nominally; Rome remained faithful to it almost desperately, in a world lacerated by dreadful upheavals. And yet, the throne was vacant, so to speak. The subversive influence of Christianity added its weight to all of this.

If, on the one hand, we should not ignore the complexity and the heterogeneity of the elements that were found in primitive Christianity, on the other hand, we should not minimize the existing antithesis between the dominating forces and the pathos found in these elements and the original Roman spirit. At this point I do not purport to focus on the traditional elements found in this or that historical civilization; I rather intend to assess in what function and according to what spirit the historical currents have acted as a whole. Thus the presence of some traditional elements within Christianity, and more specifically within Catholicism, should not prevent us from recognizing the subversive character of these two currents.

We already know what kind of equivocal spirituality is associated with Judaism, from which Christianity grew, and with the Asiatic cults of decadence that facilitated the expansion of the new faith beyond its birthplace.

The immediate antecedent of Christianity was not traditional Judaism, but rather prophetism and analogous currents in which the notions of sin and of expiation prevailed; in which a desperate form of spirituality emerged; and in which the type of the warrior Messiah as an emanation of the "Lord of Hosts" was replaced with the type of the Messiah as "Son of Man" predestined to be the sacrificial victim, the persecuted one, the hope of the afflicted and the rejected, as well as the object of a confused and ecstatic cult. It is a well-known fact that the mystical figure of Jesus Christ originally derived his power and inspiration from an environment impregnated with this messianic pathos, the size of which grew with time as a result of prophetic preaching and various apocalyptic expectations. By regarding Jesus as Savior and by breaking away from the "Law," that is, from Jewish orthodoxy, primitive Christianity took up several themes typical of the Semitic soul at large. These themes were those proper to an innerly divided human type and constituted fertile ground for the growth of an antitraditional virus, especially vis-à-vis a tradition like the Roman one. Through Paul's theology these elements were universalized and activated without a direct relationship to their Jewish origins.

As far as Orphism is concerned, it facilitated the acceptance of Christianity in several areas of the ancient world, not so much as an initiatory doctrine of the Mysteries, but as its profanation paralleling the onslaught of the cults of Mediterranean decadence. These cults were characterized by the idea of "salvation" in a merely religious sense and by the ideal of a religion open to everyone and therefore alien to any notion of race, tradition, and caste; in other words, this ideal welcomed all those who had no race, tradition, or caste. A confused need started to grow among these masses, in concert with the parallel action of the universalist cults of Eastern origins, until the figure of the founder of Christianity became the precipitating catalyst and the crystallization of what had been saturating the spiritual "atmosphere." When this happened, it was no longer a matter of a state of mind or a widespread influence, but of a well-defined force opposing the world of tradition.

From a doctrinal point of view, Christianity appears as a desperate version of

Dionysism. Modeling itself after a broken human type, it appealed to the irrational part of being and instead of the paths of heroic, sapiential, and initiatory spiritual growth posited *faith* as its fundamental instrument, the élan of a restless and perturbed soul that is attracted to the supernatural in a confused way. Through its suggestions concerning the imminent advent of the Kingdom of God and its vivid portrayals of either eternal salvation or eternal damnation, primitive Christianity exasperated the crisis of such a human type and strengthened the force of faith, thus opening a problematic path of liberation through the symbol of salvation and redemption found in the crucified Christ. If in the symbolism of Christ there are traces of a mysteric pattern (through new references to Orphism and to analogous currents), nevertheless the *proprium* or typical feature of the new religion was the employment of such a pattern on a plane that was no longer based on initiation, but rather on feelings and on a confused mysticism; therefore it can rightly be said that with Christianity, God became a human being. In Christianity we no longer find the pure religion of the Law, as in traditional Judaism, nor a true initiatory Mystery, but rather an intermediate form, a surrogate of the latter in a formulation proper to the abovementioned broken human type; this type felt relieved from his abjection, redeemed through the feeling of "grace," animated by a new hope, justified and rescued from the world, the flesh, and from death.[1] All of this represented something fundamentally alien to the Roman and classical spirit, better yet, to the Indo-European spirit as a whole. Historically, this signified the predominance of pathos over ethos and of that equivocal, deficient soteriology that had always been opposed by the noble demeanor of the sacred Roman patriciate, by the strict style of the jurists, the leaders, and the pagan sages. God was no longer conceived of as the symbol of an essence not liable to passion and change, which establishes an unbridgeable distance between itself and all that is merely human; nor was he the God of the patricians who is invoked in an erect position, who is carried in front of the legions and who becomes embodied in the winner. The God who came to be worshiped was a figure who in his "passion" took up and affirmed in an exclusivist fashion ("I am the way, the truth, and the life. No one can come to the Father except

---

1. Thus, in comparison with historical Judaism, primitive Christianity may be credited with a mystical character along the same lines of prophetism, but not with an initiatory character, contrary to what F. Schuon claimed (*The Transcendent Unity of Religions* [Paris, 1937]) on the basis of sporadic elements found mostly in Eastern Orthodoxy. We should never forget though that if Christianity developed from the ancient Jewish tradition, orthodox Judaism developed in an independent fashion through the Talmud and the Kabbalah, which represents an initiatory tradition that was always missing in Christianity. This is how, later on, true esoterism developed in the West, that is, outside Christianity and with the help of non-Christian currents such as the Jewish Kabbalah, Hermeticism, or movements of a remote Nordic origin.

through me." John 14:6–7) the Pelasgic-Dionysian motif of the sacrificed gods and the gods who die and rise again in the shadow of the Great Mothers.[2] Even the myth of the virginal birth reflects an analogous influence, since it reminds us of the goddesses who generate without a mate (like Hesiod's Gaea); in this regard the relevant role that the cult of the "Mother of God," or the "Divine Virgin" was destined to play in the development of Christianity is significant. In Catholicism Mary, the "Mother of God," is the queen of angels and of all the saints; she is also thought of as the adoptive mother of mankind, as the "Queen of the world," and as the "bestower of all favors." These expressions, which are exaggerated in comparison to the effective role played by Mary in the myth of the Synoptic Gospels, echo the attributes of the sovereign divine Mothers of the pre-Indo-European Southern Hemisphere.[3] Although Christianity is essentially a religion of the Christ, more so than of the Father, its representations of both the infant Jesus and the body of the crucified Christ in the arms of the deified Mother show definite similarities with the representations of the eastern Mediterranean cults,[4] thereby giving new emphasis to the antithesis that exists between itself and the ideal of the purely Olympian deities who are exempt from passions and free of the telluric, maternal element. The symbol that the Church herself eventually adopted was that of the Mother (Mother Church). The epitome of true religiosity became that of the imploring and prayerful soul, that is aware of its unworthiness, sinfulness, and powerlessness before the Crucified One.[5] The hatred early Christianity felt toward any form of virile spirituality, and its stigmatization as folly and sin of pride anything that may promote an active overcoming of the human condition express in a clear fashion its lack of understanding of the "heroic" symbol. The potential that the new faith was able to generate among those who felt the live mystery of the Christ, or of the Savior, and who drew from it the inner strength to

---

2. L. Rougier, *Celse* (Paris, 1925).

3. It is also significant that according to many Catholic theologians, any sign of predestination and election is dubious; the only certain sign is that consisting in devotion to the Virgin. Accordingly, the "true servant of Mary" will inherit eternal life." Concerning this attitude, see J. Berthier, *Sommario di teologia dogmatica e morale* (Turin 1933), 1791–92.

4. Saint Jerome (*Epistula ad Paulinum*, 49) noticed that Bethlehem, significantly, "was once under the shadows of the woods sacred to Tammuz-Adonis; in this cave, in which the infant Jesus cried, Venus's beloved was once mourned." Concerning the feminine element in Christianity, J. de Maistre wrote: "We can see how salvation *(salut)* began with a woman who had been announced from the origins. In all of the evangelical narratives, women have a very important role to play. Also, in all of the famous triumphs of Christianity [as was the case in the Dionysian religion] over individuals and nations, there was always a woman in the background."

5. In pre-Christian Rome the *libri sibillini*, which introduced the cult of the Great Goddess, also introduced the *supplicatio*, the ritual abasement before the divine statue, whose knees were hugged and whose hands and feet were kissed.

pursue martyrdom frantically, does not prevent the advent of Christianity from representing a fall; its advent characterized a special form of that spiritual emasculation typical of the cycles of a lunar and priestly type.

Even in Christian morality, the role played by Southern and non-Aryan influences is rather visible. It does not really make much of a difference that it was in the name of a god instead of a goddess that equality among human beings was spiritually proclaimed and that love was adopted as the supreme principle. This belief in human equality essentially belongs to a general worldview, a version of which is that "natural law" that crept into the Roman law during decadent times; it exercised an antithetical function to the heroic ideal of personality and to the value bestowed on anything that a being, by becoming differentiated, by giving itself a form, is able to claim for itself within a hierarchical social order. And so it happened that Christian egalitarianism, based on the principles of brotherhood, love, and community, became the mystical and religious foundation of a social ideal radically opposed to the pure Roman idea. Instead of *universality,* which is authentic only in its function as a hierarchical peak that does not abolish but presupposes and sanctions the differences among human beings, what arose was the ideal of *collectivity* reaffirmed in the symbol of the mystical body of Christ; this latter ideal contained in embryonic form a further regressive and involutive influence that Catholicism itself, despite its Romanization, was neither able nor entirely willing to overcome.

Some people attempt to see a value in Christianity as a doctrine because of its idea of the supernatural and the dualism that it upheld. Here, however, we find a typical case of a different action that the same principle can exercise according to the function under which it is assumed. Christian dualism essentially derives from the dualism proper to the Semitic spirit; it acted in a totally opposite way from the spirit according to which the doctrine of the two natures constituted the basis of any achievement of traditional humanity. In early Christianity the rigid opposition of the natural and supernatural orders may have had a pragmatic justification motivated by a particular historical and existential situation of a given human type. Such dualism differs from the traditional dualism, however, in that it is not subordinated to a higher principle or to a higher truth, and that it claims for itself an absolute and ontological character rather than a relative and functional one. The two orders, the natural and the supernatural, as well as the distance between them, were hypostatized and thus any real and active contact was prevented from taking place. Thus, in regard to man (here too because of a parallel influence of a Jewish theme) what emerged were: *(a)* the notion of the "creature" separated by an essential distance from God as its "Creator" and as a personal, distinct being; and *(b)* the exasperation of this distance through the revival and the accentuation of the idea, of Jewish origins as well, of "original sin."

More particularly, this dualism generated the understanding of all manifestations of spiritual influence in the passive terms of "grace," "election," and "salvation," as well as the disavowal (at times accompanied by real animosity) of all "heroic" human possibilities; the counterpart of this disavowal consisted in humility, fear of God, mortification of the flesh, and prayer. Jesus' saying in Matthew (11:12) concerning the violence suffered by the kingdom of Heaven and the revival of the Davidic saying: "You are gods" (John 10:34), belong to elements that exercised virtually no influence on the main pathos of early Christianity. But in Christianity in general it is evident that what has been universalized, rendered exclusive, and exalted are the way, the truth, and the attitude that pertain only to an inferior human type or to those lower strata of a society for whom the exoteric forms of Tradition have been devised; this was precisely one of the characteristic signs of the climate of the Dark Age, or Kali Yuga.

What has been said concerns the relationship of man with the divine. The second consequence of Christian dualism was the deconsecration of nature. Christian "supernaturalism" caused the natural myths of antiquity to be misunderstood once and for all. Nature ceased to be something living; that magical and symbolical perception of nature that formed the basis of priestly sciences was rejected and branded as "pagan." Following the triumph of Christianity, these sciences underwent a rapid process of degeneration, with the exception of a weakened residue represented by the later Catholic tradition of the rites. Thus, nature came to be perceived as something alien and even diabolical. Again, this constituted the basis for the development of an asceticism of a monastic and mortifying type, hostile to the world and to life (Christian asceticism), and radically antithetical to the classical and Roman sensibility.

The third consequence concerns the political domain. The principles: "My kingdom is not of this world" (John 18:36) and "Render therefore unto Caesar the things which are Caesar's and unto God the things that are God's" (Matt. 22:21), represented a direct attack on the concept of traditional sovereignty and of that unity of the two powers that had formally been reestablished in imperial Rome. According to Gelasius I, after Christ, no man can simultaneously be king and priest; the unity of *sacerdotium* and *regnum,* when it is vindicated by a king, is a diabolical deception and a counterfeit of the true priestly regality that belongs to Christ alone. It was precisely at this point that the contrast between Christian and Roman ideas escalated into an open conflict. When Christianity developed the Roman pantheon was so inclusive that even the cult of the Christian Savior could have found its proper place within it, among other cults, as a particular cult derived from a schism in Judaism. As I have previously suggested, it was typical of the imperial universalism to exercise a higher unifying and organizing function over and above any particular cult, which it did not need to deny or to oppose. What was required though, was an act demonstrating a superordained *fides* in reference to the principle "from above" embodied in the representative of the empire, namely, in the "Augustus." The Christians refused to perform this very act, consisting of a ritual and sacrificial offering made before the imperial symbol, since they claimed that it was incompatible with their faith; this was the only reason why there was such an epidemic of martyrs, which may have appeared as pure folly in the eyes of the Roman magistrates.

In this way, the new belief imposed itself. Over and against a particular universalism, a new, opposite universalism based on a metaphysical dualism affirmed itself. The traditional hierarchical view according to which loyalty enjoyed a supernatural sanction and a religious value, since every power descended from above, was undermined at its very foundation. In this sinful world there can only be room for a *civitas diaboli;* the *civitas dei,* or the divine state, was thought to belong to a separate plane and to consist in the unity of those who are drawn to the otherworld by a confused longing and who, as Christians, acknowledge only Christ as their leader as they await the Last Day. Wherever this idea did not result in a virus that proved to be a defeatist and subversive one, and wherever Caesar was still given "the things which are Caesar's," the *fides* remained deconsecrated and secularized; it merely had the value of a contingent obedience to a power that was merely temporal. The Pauline saying, "all authority comes from God" was destined to remain ineffectual and meaningless.

And thus, although Christianity upheld the spiritual and supernatural principle, historically speaking this principle was destined to act in a dissociative and even destructive fashion; it did not represent something capable of galvanizing whatever in the Roman world had become materialized and fragmented, but rather represented something heterogeneous, a different current drawn to what in Rome was no longer Roman and to forces that the Northern Light had successfully kept under control for the duration of an entire cycle. It helped to rescind the last contacts and to accelerate the end of a great tradition. It is not surprising that Rutilius Namatianus put Christians and Jews on the same level, insofar as both groups were hostile to Rome's authority; he also blamed the former for spreading a fatal disease *(excisae pestis contagia)* outside the boundaries of Judea, which was under the legions' yoke, and the latter for spreading a poison that altered both the race and the spirit *(tunc mutabantur corpora, nunc animi).*

When considering the enigmatic witnesses offered by ancient symbols, one cannot help noticing the role the motif of the ass played in the myth of Jesus. Not only was the ass present in the Nativity scene, but it was on an ass that the Virgin and the Divine Child escaped to Egypt; most of all, it was on an ass that Jesus rode during his triumphal entrance into Jerusalem. The ass was a traditional symbol of an infernal dissolutive "force." In Egypt it was the animal sacred to Set, who embodied this force, had an antisolar character, and was associated with the "children of the powerless rebellion." In India the ass was the mount of Mudevi, who represented the infernal aspect of the feminine deity. Also, in Greece the ass was the symbolic animal that in Lethe's plain continuously ate Ocnus's handiwork, and that had a relationship with the chthonic and infernal goddess Hecate.[6]

This is how this symbol could represent the secret sign of a force that was associated with primitive Christianity and to which it partially owed its success; it was the force that emerged and assumed an active part wherever what corresponded to the "cosmos" principle within a traditional structure vacillated and disintegrated. In reality, the advent of Christianity would not have been possible if the vital possibilities of the Roman heroic cycle had not been exhausted; if the "Roman race" had not been broken in its spirit and in its representatives (a proof of this was the failure of the attempted restoration promoted by Emperor Julian); if the ancient traditions had not been dimmed; and if, in the context of an ethnic chaos and a cosmopolitan disintegration, the imperial symbol had not been contaminated and reduced to merely surviving in a world of ruins.

6. In the *Ṛg Veda* the ass is often referred to as *rāsabha*, a word that denotes turmoil, noise, and even inebriation. In the myth, Apollo turned King Midas's ears into ass's ears, since the latter had preferred Pan's music to his own—in other words, for preferring the Dionysian, pantheistic cult to the Hyperborean cult. The slaughter of asses was, among the Hyperboreans, the sacrifice that Apollo preferred. See Pindar, *Pythian Odes*, 10.33–56. Typhon-Set (who corresponds to Python, Apollo's nemesis), after being defeated by Horus, runs into the desert riding an ass (Plutarch, *De Iside et Osiride*, 29–32); Apep, the serpent that represents the principle of darkness, is often portrayed in the company of an ass or riding an ass. Dionysus too was believed to have been carried to Thebes by an ass, an animal that was always associated with him. Some of these elements must have been preserved underground, since they later reemerged in some medieval festivals in which the Virgin and Child, led by Joseph, were carried in a procession, in the course of which the highest honors were paid to the ass.

32

The Revival of the Empire and the Ghibelline Middle Ages

The tradition that shaped the Roman world manifested its power vis-à-vis Christianity in the fact that, although the new faith was successful in overthrowing the ancient civilization, it nevertheless was not able to conquer the Western world as pure Christianity; wherever it achieved some greatness it did so only thanks to Roman and classical pre-Christian elements borrowed from the previous tradition, and not because of the Christian element in its original form.

For all practical purposes, Christianity "converted" Western man only superficially; it constituted his "faith" in the most abstract sense while his real life continued to obey the more or less material forms of the opposite tradition of action, and later on, during the Middle Ages, an ethos that was essentially shaped by the Northern-Aryan spirit. In theory, the Western world accepted Christianity but for all practical purposes it remained pagan; the fact that Europe was able to incorporate so many motifs that were connected with the Jewish and Levantine view of life has always been a source of surprise among historians. Thus, the outcome was some sort of hybridism. Even in its attenuated and Romanized Catholic version, the Christian faith represented an obstacle that deprived Western man of the possibility of integrating his authentic and irrepressible way of being through a concept and in a relationship with the Sacred that was most congenial to him. In turn, this way of being prevented Christianity from definitely shaping the West into a tradition of the opposite kind, that is, into a priestly and religious one conformed to the ideals of the ecclesia of the origins, the evangelical pathos, and the symbol of the mystical body of Christ. Further on, I will closely analyze the effects of this double antithesis on the course of Western history; strictly speaking, this antithesis represented an important factor in the processes leading to the modern world.

In a particular cycle, however, the Christian idea (in those concepts in which the

287

supernatural was emphasized) seemed to have become absorbed by the Roman idea in forms that again elevated the imperial idea to new heights, even though the tradition of this idea, found in the center constituted by the "eternal" city, had by then decayed. Such was the Byzantine cycle or the cycle of the Eastern Roman Empire. What occurred in the east, however, corresponded to what had previously occurred in the low empire. The Byzantine imperial idea displayed a high degree of traditional spirit, at least theoretically. For instance, it upheld the ideal of the sacred ruler ($\beta\alpha\sigma\iota\lambda\varepsilon\acute{\upsilon}\varsigma$ $\alpha\grave{\upsilon}\tau o\kappa\rho\acute{\alpha}\tau o\rho$) whose authority came from above and whose law, reflecting the divine law, had a universal value; also the clergy was subjected to him because the emperor was in charge of both temporal and spiritual affairs. Likewise, in the Eastern Empire the idea of the $\rho o\mu\alpha\hat{\iota}o\iota$ (the "Romans") took hold and came to represent the unity of those who were elevated by the chrism inherent in the participation in the Roman-Christian ecumene to a dignity higher than any other people ever achieved. The empire once again was *sacrum* and its *pax* had a supernatural meaning. And yet, even more so than during the Roman decadence, all this remained a symbol carried by chaotic and murky forces, since the ethnic substance was characterized, much more so than in the previous imperial Roman cycle, by demon worship, anarchy, and the principle of undying restlessness typical of the decadent and crepuscular Hellenic-Eastern world. Here too, the Byzantine emperors incorrectly assumed that despotism and a bureaucratic, centralized administrative structure could achieve that which only proceeds from the spiritual authority of worthy representatives who surround themselves with people who had the quality of "Romans," not just nominally, but imprinted in their inner character. Therefore the forces of dissolution were destined to prevail, even though Byzantium lasted as a political reality for about a millennium. What remained of the Byzantine Roman-Christian idea were mere echoes, partially absorbed in a very modified form by Slavic peoples and partially brought together again in that revival of tradition constituted by the Ghibelline Middle Ages.

In order to follow the development of forces that shaped the Western world, it is necessary to briefly consider Catholicism. Catholicism developed through *(a)* the rectification of various extremist features of primitive Christianity; *(b)* the organization of a ritual, dogmatic, and symbolic *corpus* beyond the mere mystical, soteriological element; and *(c)* the absorption and adaptation of doctrinal and organizational elements that were borrowed from the Roman world and from classical civilization in general. This is how Catholicism at times displayed "traditional" features, which nevertheless should not deceive us: that which in Catholicism has a truly traditional character is not typically Christian and that which in Catholicism is specifically Christian can hardly be considered traditional. Historically, despite all the efforts that were made to reconcile heterogeneous and contradictory elements,[1] and despite the work of absorption and adaptation on a large scale, Catholicism always betrays the spirit of lunar, priestly civilizations and thus it continues, in yet another form, the antagonistic action of the Southern influences, to which it offered a real organization through the Church and her hierarchy.

This becomes evident when we examine the development of the principle of authority that was claimed by the Church. During the early centuries of the Christianized empire and during the Byzantine period, the Church still appeared to be subordinated to imperial authority; at Church councils the bishops left the last word to the ruler not only in disciplinary but also in doctrinal matters. Gradually, a shift occurred to the belief in the equality of the two powers of Church and empire; both institutions came to be regarded as enjoying a supernatural authority and a divine origin. With the passage of time we find in the Carolingian ideal the principle according to which the king is supposed to rule over both clergy and the people on the one hand, while on the other hand the idea was developed according to which the royal function was compared to that of the body and the priestly function to that of the soul;[2] thereby the idea of the equality of the two powers was implicitly abandoned, thus preparing the way for the real inversion of relations.

By analogy, if in every rational being the soul is the principle that decides what the body will do, how could one think that those who admitted to having authority only in matters of social and political concern should not be subordinated to the Church, to whom they willingly recognized the exclusive right over and direction of souls? Thus, the Church eventually disputed and regarded as tantamount to heresy

---

1. The origin of the majority of the difficulties and of the *aporiae* encountered in Catholic philosophy and theology (especially in Scholasticism and in Thomism) is essentially due to the spiritual incompatibility between the elements that were derived from Platonism and Aristotelianism on the one hand, and those that were specifically Christian and Jewish on the other. See L. Rougier, *La Scolastique et le tomisme* (Paris, 1930).

2. By divine decree the emperor must ensure that the Church fulfills her function and mission; thus, not only was he crowned with the same symbols proper to the priestly consecration, but he also had the authority and the right to demote and to banish unworthy clergy; the monarch was truly regarded as the king-priest according to the order of Melchizedek, while the bishop of Rome was merely the vicar of Christ. F. de Coulanges (*Les Transformations de la royauté pendant l'époque carolingienne*, [Paris, 1892]) rightly remarked that although Pepin, Charlemagne, and Louis the Pious swore to "defend" the Church, we should not be deceived by the meaning of this expression since in those days it had a different meaning than it does today. To defend the Church meant, in the parlance and in the mind-set of that period, to protect and exercise authority over her at the same time. What was called "defense" was really a contract that implied the state of dependence of the protected one, who was subjected to all the obligations the language of those times conveyed in the word *fides*, including swearing an oath of allegiance to the ruler. Charlemagne, when he took upon himself to defend the Church, also took on the authority and the responsibility of fortifying her in the "true faith."

and a prevarication dictated by pride that doctrine of the divine nature and origin of regality; it also came to regard the ruler as a mere layman equal to all other men before God and his Church, and a mere official invested by mortal beings with the power to rule over others in accordance with natural law. According to the Church, the ruler should receive from the ecclesiastical hierarchy the spiritual element that prevents his government from becoming the *civitas diaboli*. Boniface VIII, who did not hesitate to ascend to the throne of Constantine with a sword, crown, and scepter and to declare: "I am Caesar, I am the Emperor," embodies the logical conclusion of a theocratic, Southern upheaval in which the priest was entrusted with both evangelical swords (the spiritual and the temporal); the *imperium* itself came to be regarded as a *beneficium* conferred by the pope to somebody, who in return owed to the Church the same vassalage and obedience a feudal vassal owes the person who has invested him. However, since the spirituality that the head of the Roman Church incarnated remained in its essence that of the "servants of God," we can say that far from representing the restoration of the primordial and solar unity of the two powers, Guelphism merely testifies to how Rome had lost its ancient tradition and how it came to represent the opposite principle and the triumph of the Southern weltanschauung in Europe. In the confusion that was beginning to affect even the symbols, the Church, who on the one hand claimed for herself the symbol of the sun vis-à-vis the empire (to which she attributed the symbol of the moon), on the other hand employed the symbol of the Mother to refer to herself and considered the emperor as one of her "children." Thus, the Guelph ideal of political supremacy marked the return to the ancient gynaecocratic vision in which the authority, superiority, and privilege of spiritual primacy was accorded to the maternal principle over the male principle, which was then associated with the temporal and ephemeral reality.

Thus, a change occurred. The Roman idea was revived by races of a direct Northern origin, which various migrations had pushed into the area of Roman civilization. The Germanic element was destined to defend the imperial idea against the Church and to restore to new life the formative *vis* of the ancient Roman world. This is how the Holy Roman Empire and the feudal civilization arose, both of which represented the two last great traditional manifestations the West ever knew.

As far as the Germans were concerned, since the times of Tacitus they appeared to be very similar to the Achaean, paleo-Iranian, paleo-Roman and Northern-Aryan stocks that had been preserved, in many aspects (including the racial one), in a state of "prehistoric" purity. The Germanic populations—just like the Goths, the Longobards, the Burgundians, and the Franks—were looked down upon as barbarians by that decadent "civilization" that had been reduced to a juridical administrative structure and that had degenerated into "Aphrodistic" forms of hedonistic urban refinement, intellectualism, aestheticism, and cosmopolitan dissolution. And yet in the coarse and unsophisticated forms of their customs one could find the expression of an existence characterized by the principles of honor, faithfulness, and pride. It was precisely this "barbaric" element that represented a vital force, the lack of which had been one of the main causes of Roman and Byzantine decadence.

The fact that the ancient Germans were "young races" has prevented many scholars from seeing the full picture of earlier antiquity; these races were young only because of the youth typical of that which still maintains contact with the origins. These races descended from the last offshoots to leave the Arctic seat and that therefore had not suffered the miscegenation and the alterations experienced by similar populations that had abandoned the Arctic seat much earlier, as is the case with the paleo-Indo-European stocks that had settled in the prehistoric Mediterranean.

The Nordic-Germanic people, besides their ethos, carried in their myths the traces of a tradition that derived immediately from the primordial tradition. The fact that during the period in which they appeared as decisive forces on the stage of European history these stocks lost the memory of their origins, and that the primordial tradition was present in those stocks only in the form of fragmentary, often altered, and unrefined residues, did not prevent them from carrying as a deep, inner legacy the possibilities and the acquired weltanschauung from which "heroic" cycles derive.

The myth of the *Edda* spoke about both the impending doom and the heroic will opposed to it. In the older parts of that myth there remained the memory of a deep freeze that arrested the twelve "streams" originating from the primordial and luminous center of Muspelheim, located at the "far end of the earth"; this center corresponds to the Ariyana Vaego (the Iranian equivalent of the Hyperborean seat), to the radiant Northern Island of the Hindus, and to the other figurations of the seat of the Golden Age.[3] Moreover, the *Edda* mention a "Green Land"[4] floating on the abyss and surrounded by the ocean; according to some traditions, this was the original

---

3. Considering the fragmentary character and the several strata of the tradition of the *Edda*, it is not easy to orient oneself in it without possessing an adequate preparation in the matter. For instance, we often find in the *Edda* that the Muspelheim (world of fire) was no longer located in the North and therefore made to correspond to the Nordic seat, while the Niflheim and the frost-giants inhabiting it, were. Conversely, after Muspelheim was invaded by the forces of the South, it quickly turned into its opposite, thus acquiring a negative value; it became the seat of Surtr (a fire demon), who will overcome the gods and usher in the end of a cycle. Also, the sons of Muspell became the enemies of the Olympian gods and will cause the Bifrost bridge (uniting heaven and earth) to collapse once they ride over it. See *Voluspa*, 50, 51.

4. In the names "Ireland" and "Greenland" (Grünes-Land = "the green land") we find the idea of "green"; allegedly, up to the time of Procopius Greenland retained a lush vegetation.

location of the "Fall" and of dark and tragic times, since it was here that the warm current of the Muspelheim (in this order of traditional myths, the waters represent the force that gives life to people and to races) met the frigid current of Huergehmir. Just as in the *Zend-Avesta* the freezing and dark winter that depopulated Ariyana Vaego was conceived as the work of an evil god opposed to the luminous creation, likewise this Eddic myth may allude to the alteration that precipitated the new cycle; this is true especially if we consider that the myth mentions a generation of giants and elemental telluric beings, creatures that were defrosted by the warm current, and against whom the race of the Aesir is going to fight.

In the *Edda*, the theme of *ragna-rok* or *ragna-rokkr* (the "destiny" or the "twilight of the gods") is the equivalent of the traditional teaching concerning the four-stage involutive process; it threatens the struggling world, which is already dominated by dualistic thinking. From an esoteric point of view this "twilight" affects the gods only metaphorically; it also signifies the "dimming" of the gods in human consciousness because mankind loses the gods, that is, the possibility of establishing a contact with them. Such a destiny may be avoided, however, by preserving the purity of the deposit of that primordial and symbolic element—gold—with which the "palace of the heroes," the hall of Odin's twelve thrones, was built in the mythical Asgard. This gold, which could act as a source of good health so long as it was not touched by an elemental or by a human being, eventually fell into the hands of Albericus, the king of the subterranean beings that in the later editing of the myth are called the Nibelungs. This clearly shows the echo of what in other traditions was the advent of the Bronze Age, the cycle of the Titanic-Promethean rebellion, which was probably connected with the magical involution in the inferior sense of previous cults.[5]

Over and against this stands the world of the Aesir, the Nordic-Germanic deities who embody the Uranian principle in its warrior aspect. The god Donnar-Thor was the slayer of Thym and Hymir, the "strongest of all," the "irresistible," the "Lord who rescues from terror," whose fearful weapon, the double hammer Mjolmir, was both a variation of the symbolic, Hyperborean battle-axe and a sign of the thunderbolt force proper to the Uranian gods of the Aryan cycle. The god Woden-Odin was he who granted victory and who had wisdom; he was the master of very powerful formulae that were not to be revealed to any woman, not even to the king's daughter.

---

5. It was probably in reference to this that the Nibelungs and the giants were represented as the creators of magical objects and weapons that will change hands and be acquired by the Aesir and the heroes (e.g., the hammer-thunderbolt of Thor; the golden ring and the magical helmet of Sigurd). A rather complex saga explains how these weapons and objects eventually turned into liabilities to the Aesir when they employed them in the reconstruction of the fortress of Asgard, which barred the way to the elementals (*Gylfaginnig*, 42).

He was the eagle; he was the host and the father[6] of the dead heroes who were selected by the Valkyries on the battlefields; it was he who bestowed on the noble ones that "spirit that lives on and which does not die when the body is dissolved into the earth";[7] and he was the deity to whom the royal stocks attributed their origin. The god Tyr-Tiuz was another god of battles, and the god of the day, of the radiant solar sky, who was represented by the rune Y, which recalls the very ancient and Northern-Atlantic sign of the cosmic man with his hands raised.

One of the motifs of the "heroic" cycles appears in the saga concerning the stock of the Wolsungen, which was generated from the union of a god with a woman. Sigmund, who will one day extract the sword inserted in the divine tree, came from this stock. In this saga the hero Sigurd or Siegfried, after taking possession of the gold that had fallen into the hands of the Nibelungs, kills the dragon Fafnir, which is another form of the serpent Nidhoog. This serpent, in the action of corroding the roots of the divine tree Yggdrasil (its collapse will mark the twilight of the race of the gods), personifies the dark power of decadence. Although Sigurd in the end is killed by treachery and the gold is returned to the waters, he nevertheless remains the heroic type endowed with the *tarnkappe* (the symbolic power that can transfer a person from the bodily dimension to the invisible), and predestined to possess the divine woman either in the form of a vanquished Amazonian queen (Brynhild, as the queen of the Northern Island) or in the form of a Valkyrie, a warrior virgin who went from an earthly to a divine seat.

The oldest Nordic stocks regarded Gardarike, a land located in the Far North, as their original homeland. This seat, even when it was identified with a Scandinavian region, was associated with the echo of the "polar" function of Mitgard, of the primordial "center"; this was a transposition of memories from the physical to the metaphysical dimension by virtue of which Gardarike was also identified with Asgard. Asgard allegedly was the dwelling place of nonhuman ancestors of the noble Nordic families; in Asgard, Scandinavian sacred kings such as Gilfir, who had gone there to proclaim their power, allegedly received the traditional teaching of the *Edda*. Asgard was also a sacred land, the land of the Nordic "Olympian" gods and of the Aesir, access to which was precluded to the race of the giants.

These motifs were found in the traditional legacy of Nordic-Germanic populations. As a view of the world, the insight into the outcome of the decline *(ragna-rokkr)* was associated with ideals and with figurations of gods who were typical of "heroic" cycles. As I have said, in more recent times this was a subconscious legacy;

---

6. According to the original Nordic-Germanic view, the only people to enjoy divine immortality were, besides the heroes chosen by the Valkyries, the nobles, by virtue of their nonhuman origin; apparently, only heroes and the nobles were cremated. In the Nordic tradition only this ritual, prescribed by Odin, opened the doors of Valhalla while those who were buried (a Southern ritual) were believed to become slaves of the earth.

7. *Gylfaginning*, 3.

the supernatural element became obscured by secondary and spurious elements of the myth and the saga, as did the universal element contained in the idea of Asgard-Mitgard, the "center of the world."

The contact of Germanic people with the Roman and Christian world had a double effect. On the one hand their invasion resulted in a devastation of the material structure of the empire, while from an internal point of view it turned out to be a vivifying contribution that eventually established the presuppositions of a new and virile civilization destined to reaffirm the Roman symbol. In later times, in the same way, an essential rectification of Christianity and Catholicism took place, especially with regard to a general view of life.

On the other hand, both the idea of Roman universalism and the Christian principle, in its generic aspect of affirmation of a supernatural order, produced an awakening of the highest vocation of Nordic-Germanic stocks; both ideas also contributed to the integration on a higher plane and to the revivification in a new form of what had often been materialized and particularized in them in the context of traditions of individual races.[8] "Conversion" to the Christian faith, more than altering the Germanic stocks' strength, often purified it and prepared it for a revival of the imperial Roman idea.

Many centuries ago, during the coronation of the king of the Franks, the formula *renovatio Romani Imperii* was spoken. Not only did they identify Rome as the symbolic source of their *imperium* and of their right, but the Germanic princes also ended up siding against the hegemonic demands of the Church; thus they became the protagonists of a great new historical movement that promoted a traditional restoration.

From a political perspective, the congenital ethos of the Germanic races conferred to the imperial reality a living, stable, and differentiated character. The life of the ancient Nordic-Germanic societies was based on the three principles of personality, freedom, and faithfulness. This life never knew the promiscuous sense of the community nor the inability of the individual to make the most of himself other than in the context of a given abstract institution; in these societies to be free was the measure of one's nobility. And yet this freedom was not anarchical and individualistic, but it was capable of a dedication that went beyond the person, and it knew the transfiguring value that characterized the principle of faithfulness toward one who is worthy of obedience and to whom people willingly submit themselves. Thus, groups of

---

8. This double influence finds a typical expression in the *Heliand*. In this work, on the one hand Christ is portrayed with warrior and very unevangelical traits; on the other hand, we find the overcoming of that dark view of destiny (Wurd) that in later times will become dominant in German history. In the *Heliand* Christ is the source of the Wurd and this force finds in him its Master, thus becoming the "wondrous power of God."

devoted subjects rallied around leaders to whom the ancient saying did apply: "The supreme nobility of a Roman emperor does not consist in being a master of slaves, but in being a lord of free men, who loves freedom even in those who serve him." Also the state, almost like in the ancient Roman aristocratic concept, was centered on the council of leaders, each member being a free man, the lord of his lands, and the leader of the group of his faithful. Beyond this council, the unity of the state and, to a degree, its superpolitical aspect, was embodied by the king, since he belonged, unlike mere military leaders, to one of the stocks of divine origin; the Goths, for example, called their kings *amals*, the "pure ones," or the "heavenly ones." Originally, the material and spiritual unity of the nation was manifested only in the event of a particular action or the realization of a common mission, especially an offensive or defensive one. And in that circumstance a new condition set in. Next to the king, a leader, *dux*, or *heritzogo* was elected, and a new rigid hierarchy was spontaneously established; the free man became the leader's immediate subordinate. The latter's authority allowed him to take the life of his subject if he failed in his duties. According to the testimony left to us by Tacitus, "the prime obligation of the entourage's allegiance is to protect and guard him and to credit their own brave deeds to his glory: the chieftains fight for victory, the entourage for the chieftain."[9] Once the mission was accomplished, the original independence and pluralism were reestablished.

The Scandinavian counts called their leader "the enemy of gold," since as a leader he was not allowed to keep any gold for himself, and also "the host of heroes," because of the pride he took in hosting his faithful warriors, whom he regarded as his companions and equals, in his house. Even among the Franks prior to Charlemagne, participation in a particular mission occurred on a voluntary basis; the king invited people to participate, he appealed to them; at times the princes themselves proposed a course of action—in any event, there was neither "duty" nor impersonal "service," since everywhere there were free and highly personalized relationships of command and obedience, mutual understanding and faithfulness. Thus, the idea of free personality was the foundation of any unity and hierarchy. This was the "Nordic" seed from which the feudal system arose as the background to the new imperial idea.

The development that led to such a regime began with the convergence of the ideas of king and leader. The king became the embodiment of the unity of the group even in time of peace; this was possible through the strengthening and the extension of the warrior principle of faithfulness to times of peace. A group of faithful retainers (e.g., the Nordic *huskarlar*, the Longobard *gasindii*, the Gothic *palatines*, the Frank *antrustiones* or *convivae regis*), consisting of free men, gathered around the king;

---

9. Tacitus, *Germany*, 14.

these people regarded being in the service of their lord and the defense of his honor and right as both a privilege and a realization of a way of being more elevated than if they were merely answerable to no one but themselves. The feudal constitution was realized through the progressive extension of this principle, originally manifested in the Frank royalty, to various elements of the community.

During the period of conquests a second aspect of the abovementioned development took place: the bestowal of conquered lands as fiefs in return for the commitment to faithfulness. The Frank nobility spread into areas that did not coincide with those of any given nation and became a bonding and unifying element. From a formal point of view, this development appeared to involve an alteration of the previous constitution; to rule over a fief was regarded as a regal benefit contingent upon loyalty and service to the king. In reality, the feudal regime was a principle to be followed rather than a rigid reality; it was the general idea of an organic law of order that left ample room for the dynamic interaction of free forces fighting either side by side or against each other, without attenuations or alterations—subject before lord, lord before lord—and that caused everything (freedom, honor, glory, destiny, property) to be based on bravery and on the personal factor since nothing or virtually nothing was based on a collective element, public power, or abstract law. As it has rightfully been remarked, in the feudal system of the origins the fundamental and distinctive feature of regality was not that of a "public" power, but rather that of forces that were in the presence of other forces, each one responsible to itself for its own authority and dignity. Thus, such a state of affairs often resembled a state of war rather than that of a "society"; it was precisely because of this, however, that a particular differentiation of energies occurred. Never has man been treated so harshly as in the feudal system, and yet not only for the feudal lords who had the responsibility of protecting their rights and honor, but also for the subjects this regime was a school of independence and of virility rather than of servility; in this regime the relationships of faithfulness and of honor played a larger role than in any other Western time period.

Generally speaking, in this type of society, beyond the promiscuity of the Lower Empire and the chaos of the period of the invasions, everybody was able to find the place appropriate to his own nature, as is always the case wherever we find an immaterial catalyst within the social organism. For the last time in Western history the quadripartition of society into serfs, merchants, warrior nobility, and representatives of spiritual authority (the clergy in the Guelph and the ascetic, knightly orders in the Ghibelline system) took form and affirmed itself in an almost spontaneous way.

The fact that the feudal world of personality and of action did not exhaust the deepest possibilities of medieval man was proven by the fact that his fides was able to develop in a sublimated form and be purified into the universal: such was the form that had the Empire as its reference point. The Empire was perceived as a superpolitical reality, an institution of supernatural origin that formed one power with the divine kingdom. While in the Empire the same spirit that shaped the individual feudal and regal units continued to act, its peak was the emperor, who was regarded not as a mere man, but rather as a *deus-homo totus deificatus et sanctificatus, adorandus quia praesul princeps et summus est,* according to the characteristic expression of the time. Thus, the emperor embodied the function of a "center" in the eminent sense of the word and demanded from his subjects and from the feudal lords a spiritual acknowledgment similar to what the Church claimed for herself in order to realize a higher European traditional unity. Since two suns cannot coexist in the same planetary system, and since the image of the two suns was often applied to the duality of Church and Empire, the struggle between these two universal powers, which were the supreme reference points of the great *ordinatio ad unum* of the feudal world, was bound to erupt.

On both sides there were compromises and more or less conscious concessions to the opposing principle. The meaning of such a struggle, however, eludes both those who stop at a superficial level and at everything that from a metaphysical point of view is regarded as a mere occasional cause—thus seeing in it only a political competition and a clash of interests and ambitions rather than a material and spiritual struggle—and those who regard this conflict as one between two opponents who are fighting over the same thing, each claiming the prerogative of the same type of universal power. On the contrary, the struggle hides the contrast between two incompatible visions; this contrast points once again to the antithesis of North and South, of solar and lunar spirituality. The universal ideal of a "religious" kind advocated by the Church is opposed to the imperial ideal, which consists in a secret tendency to reconstruct the unity of the two powers, of the regal and the hieratic, or the sacred and the virile. Although the imperial idea in its external expressions often claimed for itself the dominion of the *corpus* and of the *ordo* of the medieval ecumene; and although the emperors often embodied in a mere formal way the living *lex* and subjected themselves to an asceticism of power[10]—the idea of "sacred regality" appeared yet again on a universal plane. Wherever history hinted only implicitly at this higher aspiration it was the myth that bespoke it; the myth was not opposed to history, but rather revealed its deeper dimension. I have previously suggested that in

---

10. No matter how powerful and prideful, no medieval monarch ever felt capable of performing the function of the rite and the sacrifice (as with the ancient sacred kings) that had become the legacy of the clergy. Although the Hohenstaufen laid claim to the supernatural character of the Empire, they failed to reintegrate in their representative the primordial function of the *rex sacrorum*, even though the Church had usurped the title of *pontifex maximus* that was proper to the Roman emperors. Even in the Ghibelline doctrine of Hugh of Fleury, the sacred primacy of the Empire was limited to the *ordo* (that is, to the external constitution of Christianity) and was excluded from the *dignitas*, which belonged to the Church alone.

the medieval imperial legend there are numerous elements that refer more or less directly to the idea of the supreme "center"; these elements, through various symbols, allude to a mysterious relationship between this center and the universal authority and legitimacy of the Ghibelline emperor. The objects symbolizing initiatic regality were entrusted to him and at times the motif of the hero "who never died" and who had been brought to a "mountain" or to a subterranean seat was applied to him. In the emperor dwelt the force that was expected to reawaken at the end of a cycle, cause the Dry Tree to bloom, and assist him in the last battle against Gog and Magog's onslaught. Especially in relation to the Hohenstaufen, the idea of a "divine" and "Roman stock" asserted itself; this stock was believed not only to be in charge of the *regnum* but also to be able to penetrate the mysteries of God, which other people can only perceive vaguely through images.[11] The counterpart of all this was a secret spirituality (see chapter 14) that was typical of yet another high point of the Ghibelline and feudal world: chivalry.

By producing chivalry that world demonstrated once again the efficiency of a superior principle. Chivalry was the natural complement of the imperial idea; between these two there was the same relationship as existed between the clergy and the Church. Chivalry was like a "race of the spirit" in which the purity of blood played an important role as well; the Northern-Aryan element present in it was purified until it reached a universal type and ideal in terms that corresponded to what the *civis romanus* had originally been in the world.

Even in chivalry we can distinctively see the extent to which the fundamental themes of early Christianity had been overcome and how the Church herself was forced to sanction, or at least to tolerate, a complex of principles, values, and customs that can hardly be reconciled with the spirit of her origins. Without repeating what has been said previously, I would like to recap the main points.

Within a nominally Christian world, chivalry upheld without any substantial

---

11. Ernst Kantorowicz spoke about the "empire breed" in reference to the Hohenstaufen: "A special virtue resided in this race, and to their offspring it was given 'to know the mysteries of the kingdom of God ... but to others only in parables.' . . . The divine stock of the Roman Caesars appears once more in the Hohenstaufen, 'the heaven-born race of the God Augustus, whose star is unquenched forever,' a race which springs from Aeneas, the father of the Roman people, and descends through Caesar to Frederick and his offspring in direct descent. All members of this imperial race are called divine. The predecessors on the imperial throne are *divi* and the living no less, finally all members of the Hohenstaufen family. . . .

The imperial office had been held divine by Barbarossa; now gradually not only Frederick's person but the Hohenstaufen race and the Hohenstaufen blood was Caesarean and divine. But for one half-century of Staufen rule, the longed for Third Frederick whom the Sybils had foretold, and the West would have seen the God Augustus marching in the flesh through the gates of Rome, would have burnt incense on his altars and offered sacrifice. In the Hohenstaufens the son of God had appeared for the last time on earth." From *Frederick the Second,* trans. E. O. Lorimer (New York, 1931), 572–73.

alterations an Aryan ethics in the following things: (1) upholding the ideal of the hero rather than of the saint, and of the conqueror rather than of the martyr; (2) regarding faithfulness and honor, rather than *caritas* and humbleness, as the highest virtues; (3) regarding cowardice and dishonor, rather than sin, as the worst possible evil; (4) ignoring or hardly putting into practice the evangelical precepts of not opposing evil and not retaliating against offenses, but rather, methodically punishing unfairness and evil; (5) excluding from its ranks those who followed the Christian precept "Thou Shalt Not Kill" to the letter; and (6) refusing to love one's enemy and instead fighting him and being magnanimous only after defeating him.

Secondly, the "test of arms" that consisted in settling all disputes through strength (regarded as a virtue entrusted by God to man in order to promote the triumph of justice, truth, and the law here on earth) became a fundamental idea that reached far beyond the context of feudal honor and law into the context of theology, in which it was applied under the name of "God's ordeal," even in matters of faith. This idea was not really a Christian one; it was rather inspired by the mystical doctrine of "victory" that ignored the dualism proper to religious views, united spirit and might, and saw in victory some sort of divine consecration. The theistic watered-down version of this doctrine, according to which during the Middle Ages people usually thought that victory was brought about by a direct intervention of God, did not affect the innermost spirit of these customs.

If chivalry professed "faithfulness" to the Church as well many elements suggest that this was a devotion similar to that tributed to various ideals and to the "woman" to whom a knight committed his own life; what really mattered to the knight and to his way was a generic attitude of heroic subordination of both his happiness and his life, rather than the issue of faith in a specific and theological sense. I have already suggested that both chivalry and the Crusades, besides their outer and exoteric aspect, also had an esoteric dimension.

As far as chivalry is concerned, I have already mentioned that it had its "Mysteries," a temple that most definitely did not correspond to the Church of Rome, and a literature and sagas in which ancient pre-Christian traditions became alive again; among these things, the most characteristic was the saga of the Grail because of the emergence within it of the theme of initiatic reintegration, the goal of which was to restore a fallen kingdom.[12] This theme developed a secret language that often

---

12. See my *Il mistero del Graal*. Though the "Grail's regal character" was the central symbol of the secret Ghibelline tradition, the symbolical genealogy presented by Wolfram von Eschenbach shows the relation existing between this tradition, the notion of "Universal Ruler," and the anti-Guelph aspect of the Crusades. This genealogy connects the Grail's kings with "Prester John" (who happens to be one of the medieval representations of the "Universal Ruler") and with the Knight of the Swan, a symbolic name given to leaders of the Crusades such as Godfrey of Bouillon.

concealed an uttermost disdain for the Roman Curia. Even within the great historical knightly orders, which were characterized by the peculiar tendency to reunite
the types of the warrior and the ascetic, we find underground currents that, whenever they surfaced, brought upon these orders the suspicion and persecution of the
official religion. In reality, chivalry was animated by the impulse toward a "traditional" restoration in the highest sense of the word, with the silent or explicit overcoming of the Christian religious spirit (see for instance the symbolic ritual of the
rejection of the Cross allegedly practiced among the Knights Templar). The ideal
center of all this was the Empire. This is how the legends arose that revived the
theme of the Dry Tree, the blossoming of which was attributed to an emperor who
will wage war against the clergy, so much so that at times he came to be regarded
as the Antichrist (see for instance the *Compendium theologiae*); this was, on the
part of the Church, an obscure and distorted expression of the perception of a
spirituality irreconcilable with the Christian spirituality.

In the period in which victory seemed to be within the grasp of Frederick II,
popular prophecies claimed: "The tall Cedar of Lebanon will be cut down. There
will only be one God, namely, a monarch. Woe to the clergy! If it ever falls, a new
order is ready to be implemented!"

During the Crusades, for the first and only time in post-Roman Europe, the
ideal of the unity of nations (represented in peacetime by the Empire) was achieved
on the plane of action in the wake of a wonderful élan, and as if in a mysterious
reenactment of the great prehistoric movement from North to South and from
West to East. The analysis of the deep forces that produced and directed the
Crusades does not fit in with the ideas typical of a two-dimensional historiography. In the movement toward Jerusalem what often became manifested was an
occult current against papal Rome that was fostered by Rome itself; in this current
chivalry was the militia and the heroic Ghibelline ideal was the liveliest force.
This current culminated in an emperor who was stigmatized by Gregory IX as one
who "threatens to replace the Christian faith with the ancient rites of the pagan
populations, and who by sitting in the Temple usurps the functions of the priesthood." The figure of Godfrey of Bouillon—the most significant representative of
crusader chivalry, who was called *lux monarchorum* (which again reveals the
ascetical and warrior element proper to this knightly aristocracy)—was that of a
Ghibelline prince who ascended to the throne of Jerusalem after visiting Rome
with blood and iron, killing the anti-Caesar Rudolf of Rhinefeld and expelling the
pope from the holy city. The legend also established a meaningful kinship between this king of the crusaders and the mythical Knight of the Swan (the French

Hélias, the Germanic Lohengrin[13]), who in turn embodies symbols that were imperially Roman (his symbolic genealogical descent from Caesar himself), solar (the etymological relation between existing between Hélias, Helios, and Elijah), and Hyperborean (the swan that leads Lohengrin from the "heavenly seat" was also the animal representing Apollo among the Hyperboreans and a recurrent theme in paleographic traces of the Northern-Aryan cult). The body of such historical and mythical elements causes Godfrey of Bouillon to be a symbol during the Crusades, because of the meaning of that secret force that had a merely external and contingent manifestation in the political struggle of the Teutonic emperors and in the victory of Otto I.

In the ethics of chivalry and the harsh articulation of the feudal system that was so distant from the social ideal of the primitive Church; in the resurrected principle of a warrior caste that had been reintegrated in a way that was both ascetical and sacred; and in the secret ideal of the Empire and the Crusades, the Christian influence encountered very precise limitations. On the one hand, the Church partially accepted these limitations; she allowed herself to be dominated—it became "Romanized"—in order to dominate and to remain in control. On the other hand, she resisted by attempting to replace the top of the political hierarchy and to overcome the Empire. The rending of the social fabric continued. The forces that were awakened occasionally escaped from the control of the people who had evoked them. When both adversaries disengaged from the mortal duel in which they were locked, they separately underwent a process of decadence. The tension toward the spiritual synthesis weakened. The Church increasingly renounced its claim to temporal power and royalty its claim to spiritual power. Following the Ghibelline civilization, which we may regard as the splendid spring season of a Europe that was destined to doom, the process of decadence will continue inexorably.

---

13. In the Knight of the Swan, whose homeland is in heaven and who turns down Elsa's love, we find the antigynaecocratic theme proper of the heroic cycles already found in the myths of Heracles, Aeneas, Gilgamesh, Rostam, and so on.

33

Decline of the Medieval World
and the Birth of Nations

The decadence of the Holy Roman Empire and, generally speaking, of the principle of true sovereignty was determined by a range of causes from above and below. One of the main causes was the gradual secularization and materialization of the political idea. As far as the Empire was concerned, the struggle Frederick II waged against the Church, though it was undertaken for the defense of its supernatural character, was associated with an initial upheaval in the following sense: on the one hand, there were (a) the incipient humanism, liberalism, and rationalism of the Sicilian court; (b) the institution of a body of lay judges and administrative functionaries; and (c) the importance given to the Law by legislators and by those whom a rightful religious rigorism (that reacted to the early products of "culture" and "free thought" with autos-da-fé and executions) contemptuously qualified as *theologi philosophantes*. On the other hand, there was the centralizing and antifeudal tendency of some recent imperial institutions. The moment an empire ceases to be sacred, it also ceases to be an empire; the inner vision animating the empire and its authority decline, and once the plane of matter and of mere "politics" is reached they totally disappear, since such a plane, by its very nature, excludes every universalism and higher unity. As early as 1338, King Ludwig IV of Bavaria declared that the imperial consecration was no longer necessary and that the elected prince was the legitimate emperor by virtue of this election; Charles IV of Bohemia completed this emancipation with the "Golden Bull." Since the consecration, however, was not substituted with something metaphysically comparable, the emperors themselves irrevocably compromised their transcendent *dignitas*. From then on they lost "Heaven's mandate" and the Holy Empire survived only nominally. Frederick III of Austria was the last emperor to be crowned in Rome (1452) after the rite had been reduced to an empty and soulless ceremony.

Conversely, it has rightfully been suggested that the feudal system is that which characterizes the majority of the great traditional eras and the one most suited for the regular development of traditional structures.[1] In this type of regime the principle of plurality and of relative political autonomy of the individual parts is emphasized, as is the proper context of that universal element, that *unum quod non est pars* that alone can really organize and unify these parts, not by contrasting but by presiding over each one of them through the transcendent, superpolitical, and regulating function that the universal embodies (Dante). In this event royalty works together with the feudal aristocracy and the imperial function does not limit the autonomy of the single principalities or kingdoms, as it assumes the single nationalities without altering them. Conversely, when on the one hand the *dignitas,* which can rule triumphantly beyond the multiple, temporal, and contingent falls into decline; and when, on the other hand, the capability of a *fides* and a spiritual acknowledgment on the part of the single subordinated elements fails—then what arises is either a centralizing tendency and political absolutism (that attempts to hold the whole together through a violent, political, and state-enforced unity rather than through an essentially superpolitical and spiritual unity) or purely particularistic and dissociative processes. Either way accomplishes the destruction of medieval civilization. The kings begin to claim for their own fiefs the same principle of absolute authority that is typical of the empire,[2] thus spreading a new and subversive idea: the national state. By virtue of an analogous process a variety of communes, free cities, republics, and other political entities that have a tendency to establish their independence, begin to resist and rebel, not only against the imperial authority, but against the nobility too. At this point the European ecumene begins to fall apart. The principle of a common body of laws declines, even though it leaves enough space for the articulations of a singular *ius,* that is a legislation that corresponds to the same language and a common spirit. Chivalry itself begins to decline and with it the ideal of a human type molded by principles of a purely ethical and spiritual nature; knights begin to defend the rights and to uphold the temporal ambitions of their lords, and eventually, of their respective national states. The great forces brought together by the superpolitical ideal of "holy war" or "just war" are replaced by combinations of both peace and war, which are increasingly brought about by diplomatic shrewdness. Christian Europe powerlessly witnesses the fall of the Eastern Empire and of Constantinople at the hands of Ottomans; moreover, a king of France, Francis I, inflicted the first deadly blow to the

---

1. R. Guénon, *Autorité spirituelle et pouvoir temporel,* 111.
2. The French legislators were the first in Europe to claim that the king of a national state derives his power directly from God and is the "emperor of his kingdom."

myth of "Christendom" that was the foundation of the European unity when, in his struggle against the representative of the Holy Roman Empire, he did not hesitate to side with the rebellious Protestant princes, and even with the sultan himself. The League of Cognac (1526) saw the head of the Church of Rome do something similar; Clement VII, the ally of the king of France, went to war against the emperor, siding with the sultan right when the onslaught of Suleiman II in Hungary threatened Europe and when Protestants in arms were about to ravage its heart. Also, a priest in the service of the king of France, Cardinal Richelieu, during the last phase of the Thirty Years War sided with the Protestant league against the emperor until, following the Peace of Augsburg (1555) the treaties of Westphalia (1648) swept away the last residue of the religious element, decreed the reciprocal tolerance between Protestant and Catholic nations and granted to the rebellious princes an almost total independence from the Empire. From that period on the supreme interest and the reason for struggle will not even be the ideal defense of a feudal or dynastic privilege, but mere disputes over parts of the European territory; the Empire was definitely replaced by imperialisms, that is, by the petty attempts of the national states to assert themselves either militarily or economically over other nations; this upheaval was *in primis et ante omnia* promoted by the French monarchy in a very specific anti-imperial manner.

In the context of these developments, besides the crisis suffered by the imperial idea, the idea of royalty in general became increasingly secularized; the king became merely a warrior and the political leader of his state. He embodied for a little longer a virile function and an absolute principle of authority, yet without any reference to a transcendent reality other than in the empty residual formulation of the "divine right" as it was defined in Catholic nations after the Council of Trent and during the age of the Counter Reformation. At that time the Church declared itself ready to sanction and consecrate the absolutism of sovereigns who had lost their sacred inner vocations as long as they were willing to be the secular arm of the Church, which by then had chosen to act indirectly upon European political affairs.

For this reason, in the period following the decline of imperial Europe, we witness in individual states the failure of the ideological premises that justified the struggle with the Church in the name of a higher principle; a more or less external acknowledgment was given to the authority of Rome in matters of religion in return for something useful to the "reason of state." Conversely, there were openly declared attempts to subordinate immediately the spiritual to the temporal sphere, as in the Anglican or Gallican upheaval and, later on, in the Protestant world, with the national churches under state control. With the unfolding of the modern era it is possible to witness the establishment of countries as if they were schisms, and their reciprocal opposition not only as political and temporal units but also as almost mystical entities refusing to submit to any superordained authority.

One thing becomes very clear: if the Empire declines and if it continues to exist only nominally, its antagonist, the Church, after enjoying untrammeled freedom from its ancient foe, did not know how to assume its legacy, and demonstrated its inability to organize the Western world according to the Guelph ideal. What replaced the Empire was not the Church at the head of a reinvigorated "Christendom," but the multiplicity of national states that were increasingly intolerant of any higher principle of authority.

Moreover, the deconsecration of the rulers as well as their insubordination toward the Empire, by depriving the organisms over which they presided of the chrism bestowed by a higher principle, unavoidably pushed them into the orbit of lower forces that were destined to slowly prevail. Generally speaking, whenever a caste rebels against a higher caste and claims its independence, the higher caste unavoidably loses the character that it had within the hierarchy and thereby reflects the character of the immediately lower caste.[3] Absolutism—the materialistic transposition of the traditional idea of unity—paved the way for demagogy and for republican, national, and antimonarchical revolutions. And in those countries in which the kings, in their struggle against feudal aristocracy and their work of political centralization favored the claims of the bourgeoisie and of the plebs, the process ended even faster. Philip the Fair, who anticipated and exemplified the various stages of the involutive process, is often singled out as an example. With the pope's complicity he destroyed the Templar order that was the most characteristic expression of the tendency to reconstruct the unity of the priestly and the warrior elements that was the soul of medieval chivalry. He started the process of lay emancipation of the state from the Church, which was promoted without interruptions by his successors, just as the struggle against the feudal nobility was carried on (especially by Louis XI and by Louis XIV) without feeling any qualms about using the support of the bourgeoisie and without disavowing the rebellious spirit of lower social strata. Philip the Fair also favored the development of an antitraditional culture since his legislators were the true forerunners of modern laicism, being much earlier than the Renaissance humanists.[4] If, on the one hand, it is significant that a priest (Cardinal Richelieu) employed the principle of centralization against the nobility by replacing the feudal structures with the leveling, modern, binomial form (government and nation), on the other hand, Louis XIV, with his formation of public powers and systematic develop-

3. R. Guénon, *Autorité spirituelle*, 111.
4. Ibid., 112.

ment of national unity together with the political, military, and economic strengthening of this very unity prepared the body, so to speak, for the incarnation of a new principle: the people and the nation as a mere collectivity. Thus, the anti-aristocratic action of the kings of France—whose constant opposition to the Holy Empire has been noted—through the marquis of Mirabeau promoted the logical rebellion against these kings and their expulsion from their contaminated thrones. We can argue that since France initiated this upheaval and conferred an increasingly centralizing and nationalist character to the idea of the state, she was the first to witness the demise of the monarchical system and the advent of the republican regime in the sense of a decisive and manifest shift of power to the Third Estate. Thus, in the whole of European nations, France became the main hotbed of the revolutionary ferment and of the lay and rationalistic mentality, which is highly deleterious for any surviving residue of the traditional spirit.[5]

There is another specific and interesting complementary aspect of historical nemesis. The emancipation of the Empire from the states that had become absolutist was followed by the emancipation of sovereign, free, and autonomous individuals from the state. The former usurpation attracted and presaged the latter; eventually, in the atomized and anarchical states (as sovereign nations) the usurped sovereignity of the state was destined to be replaced with popular sovereignity in the context of which every authority and law are legitimate only and exclusively as the expressions of the will of the citizens who are single sovereign individuals; this is the democraticized and "liberal" state, a prelude to the last phase of this general involution, that is, a purely collectivized society.

Beside the causes "from above," however, we should not forget the causes "from below," which are distinct though parallel to the former ones. Every traditional organization is a dynamic system that presupposes forces of chaos, inferior impulses, and interests as well as lower social and ethnic strata that are dominated and restrained by a principle of "form"; it also includes the dynamism of the two antagonistic poles. The superior pole, connected to the supernatural element of the higher strata, attempts to lift up the other pole, while the lower pole, which is connected to the mass or demos, attempts to pull down the higher pole. The emergence and liberation (i.e., revolt) of the lower strata are the counterpart of every weakening of the representatives of the higher principle and every deviation or degeneration of the top of the hierarchy. Therefore, because of the previously mentioned processes, the right of

---

5. Ibid. The fact that Germanic populations, despite the Reformation, retained feudal structures longer than other people is due to the fact that they were the last to embody—up to World War I—a higher idea than that represented by nationalisms and by world democracies.

demanding of one's subjects the double *fides* (spiritual and feudal) increasingly de-generated; thus, the way was paved for a materialization of this *fides* in a political sense and for the aforesaid revolt. In fact, just as faithfulness with a spiritual foundation is unconditional, likewise, that which is connected to the temporal plane is conditioned and contingent and liable to be revoked depending on the empirical circumstances. Also, the dualism of Church and state and the persistent opposition of the Church to the Empire were destined to contribute to lowering every *fides* to this inferior and precarious level.

After all, during the Middle Ages it was the Church that "blessed" the betrayal of the *fides* by siding with the Italian communes and lending her moral and material support to their revolt against the Empire. The revolt of the communes, beyond the external aspect, simply represented the insurrection of the particular against the universal in relation to a type of social organization that was no longer even modeled after the warrior caste, but after the third caste, the bourgeoisie and the merchant class, who usurped the dignity of the political government and the right to bear arms, fortified its cities, raised its battle flags, and organized its armies against the imperial cohorts and the defensive alliance of the feudal nobility. Here began the movement from below and the rise of the tide of the inferior forces.

While the Italian communes anticipated the profane and antitraditional ideal of a social organization based on the economic and mercantile factor and the Jewish commerce with gold, their revolt demonstrated how, in some areas, the sensibility that embraced the spiritual and ethical meaning of loyalty and hierarchy was already at that time on the verge of becoming extinct. The emperor came to be perceived as a mere political leader whose political claims could be challenged. This marked the advent of that bad freedom that will destroy and deny every principle of true authority, abandon the inferior forces to themselves, and reduce to a merely human, economic, and social plane any political form, culminating in the omnipotence of the "merchants" first and of "organized labor" later. It is significant that the principal hotbed of this cancer was the Italian soil that had previously been the cradle of the Roman world. In the historical struggle of the communes, which were supported by the Church against the imperial armies and the *corpus saecularium principium,* we find the last echoes of the struggle between North and South, tradition and antitradition. The truth is that Frederick I—a figure whom the plebeian falsification of the Italian "patriotic" history has repeatedly attempted to discredit—fought in the name of a higher principle and out of a sense of duty, derived from his own function, against a lay and particularistic usurpation that was based, among other things, on unprovoked violations of pacts and oaths. Dante called him the "good Barbarossa" and regarded him as the legitimate representative of the Empire and the source of any true authority. Moreover, Dante regarded the revolt of the Lombard cities as an illegal and biased struggle due to his noble contempt for the "newcomers and upstarts"[6] and for the elements of the new and impure power of the communes; likewise, he saw in the self-government of the individual populations and in the new nationalistic idea a subversive heresy.[7] In reality, the Ottos and the Suevians waged their struggle not so much in order to impose a material acknowledgment or because of territorial ambitions, but rather for an ideal revendication and the defense of a superpolitical right. They demanded obedience not as Teutonic princes, but as "Roman" *(romanorum reges)* yet supernational emperors; they fought against the rebellious race of merchants and burghers in the name of honor and spirit.[8] The latter came to be regarded as rebels, not so much against the emperor, but rather against God *(obviare Deo)*. By divine injunction *(jubente Deo)* the prince waged war against them as the representative of Charlemagne, brandishing the "avenging sword" in order to restore the ancient order *(redditur res publica)*.[9]

Finally, especially in the case of Italy, in the so-called seigneuries (the counterpart or the successors of the communes) it is possible to detect another aspect of the new climate, of which Macchiavelli's *Prince* represented a clear barometric index. During these times, the only person considered fit for government was a powerful individual who would rule not by virtue of a consecration, his nobility, and his representing a higher principle and a tradition, but rather in his own name and by employing cunning, violence, and the means of "politics," which by then was regarded as an "art," a technique devoid of scruples, honor, and truth with religion having become only an instrument to be employed in its service. Dante correctly said: "*Italorum principum . . . qui non heroico more sed plebeo, secuntur superbiam.*"[10] Thus, the substance of such government was not "heroic" but plebeian; the ancient *virtus* descended to this level as did the sense of superiority to both good and evil typically exhibited by those who ruled on the basis of a nonhuman law. On the one hand, we

6. Dante, *The Divine Comedy, Inferno* 16.73.
7. D. Flori, *Dell'idea imperiale di Dante* (Bologna, 1912), 38; 86–87.
8. Dante did not hesitate to criticize the growing nationalist aberration, particularly by opposing the French monarchy and by upholding the right of the emperor. In the case of Henry VII, he realized that if a nation like Italy, for instance, wanted to irradiate its civilization in the world it had to disappear into the Empire, since only the Empire is true universalism; thus, in his view, any rebellious force following the new principle upheld by "cities" and by homelands was destined to become an obstacle to the "kingdom of justice."
9. These are Dante's words. Interestingly enough, Barbarossa, in his struggle against the communes, was compared to Heracles, who was the hero allied to Olympian forces struggling against the forces of chaos.
10. *De vulgari eloquentia*, 1.12. In reference to the Renaissance F. Schuon has rightly spoken of a "Caesarism of the bourgeoisie and of the bankers"; to these I would add the figures of the *condottieri*, who were mercenary leaders who made themselves kings.

see the reappearance of the model of ancient tyrannies; on the other hand, we find the expression of that unrestrained individualism that characterizes these new times according to multiple forms. Here we also find the anticipation, in a radical way, of the type of "absolute politics" and the will to power that in later times will be implemented on a much greater scale.

The cycle of the medieval restoration ended with these processes. Somehow we can say that the gynaecocratic, Southern ideal triumphed again; in the context of this ideal, the virile principle, apart from the abovementioned extreme forms, carried only a material (i.e., political and temporal) meaning even when it was embodied in the person of the monarch; conversely the Church remained the depository of spirituality in the "lunar" form of devotional religion and, at most, in the monastic and contemplative orders. After this scission occurred, the privilege of blood and the land or the expressions of a mere will to power became definitely predominant. An unavoidable consequence of this was the particularism of the towns, the homelands, and the various nationalisms. What followed was the incipient revolt of the demos, the collective element that was at the bottom of the traditional social order and that now attempted to take control of the leveled social structures and the unified public powers that were created during the previous, antifeudal phase.

The struggle that had most characterized the Middle Ages, that of the "heroic" virile principle against the Church, ended. From now on, Western man would yearn for autonomy and emancipation from the religious bond only in the forms of a deviation, in what could be characterized as a demonic distortion of Ghibellinism that was foreshadowed with the taking up of Lutheranism by the German princes. Generally speaking, after the Middle Ages, the West as a civilization became emancipated from the Church and from the Catholic weltanschauung only by becoming secularized under the aegis of naturalism and of rationalism, and by extolling as a sign of conquest the impoverishment proper to a perspective and a will that do not recognize anything beyond man and beyond what is conditioned by the human element.

One of the commonplaces of modern historiography is the polemical exaltation of the civilization of the Renaissance over and against medieval civilization. This is not just the expression of a typical misunderstanding, since this mentality is the effect of one among the innumerable deceptions purposely spread in modern culture by the leaders of global subversion. The truth is that after the collapse of the ancient world, if there ever was a civilization that deserves the name of Renaissance, this was the civilization of the Middle Ages. In its objectivity, its virile spirit, its hierarchical structure, its proud antihumanistic simplicity so often permeated by the sense of the sacred, the Middle Ages represented a return to the origins. I am not looking at the real Middle Ages and at its classical features through rose-colored lenses. The character of the civilization coming after it must be understood otherwise than it has been. During the Middle Ages the tension that had an essentially metaphysical orientation degenerated and changed polarity. The potential that was previously found in the vertical dimension (upwards, as in the symbol of Gothic cathedrals), flowed outward into the horizontal dimension, thus producing phenomena that made an impression on the superficial observer. In the domain of culture this potential produced the tumultuous outburst of multiple forms of a creativity almost entirely deprived of any traditional or even symbolic element, and also, on an external plane, the almost explosive scattering of European populations all over the world during the age of discoveries, explorations, and colonial conquests that occurred during the Renaissance and the age of humanism. These were the effects of a scattering of forces resembling the scattering of forces that follows the disintegration of an organism.

According to some, the Renaissance represented a revival of the ancient classical civilization that allegedly had been rediscovered and reaffirmed against the dark world of medieval Christianity. This is a major blunder. The Renaissance either borrowed decadent forms from the ancient world rather than the forms of the origins permeated by sacred and superpersonal elements, or, totally neglecting such elements, it employed the ancient legacy in a radically new fashion. During the Renaissance, "paganism" contributed essentially to the development of the simple affirmation of man and to fostering the exaltation of the individual, who became intoxicated with the products of an art, erudition, and speculation that lacked any transcendent and metaphysical element.

In relation to this, it is necessary to point out the phenomenon of neutralization. Civilization, even as an ideal, ceased to have a unitary axis. The center no longer directed the individual parts, not only in the political, but in the cultural context as well. There no longer was a common organizing force responsible for animating culture. In the spiritual space the Empire formerly encompassed unitarily in the ecumenical symbol, there arose by dissociation, dead or "neutral" zones that corresponded to the various branches of the new culture. Art, philosophy, science, and law each developed within their own field of competence, displaying a systematic and flaunted indifference toward anything that could encompass them, free them from their isolation, or give them true principles: such was the "freedom" of the new culture. The seventeenth century, together with the end of the Thirty Years War and the fundamental overthrow of the Empire, was the age in which this upheaval assumed a radical form, anticipating what is proper to the modern age.

Thus ended the medieval impulse to pick up again that torch that ancient Rome had received from the heroic, Olympian Hellas. The tradition of initiatory regality ceased to have contacts with historical reality and with the representatives of any

European temporal power; it continued to exist only underground, in secret currents such as Hermeticism and Rosicrucianism, which increasingly withdrew inward as the modern world was taking form—when the organizations that they animated did not themselves undergo a process of involution and inversion.[11] As a myth, medieval civilization left its testament in two legends. According to the first legend, every year on the night of the anniversary of the suppression of the order of the Knights Templar, an armed shadow wearing a red cross on its white mantle allegedly appears in the crypt of the Templars to inquire who wants to free the Holy Sepulcher: "No one," is the reply, "since the Temple has been destroyed." According to the second legend, Frederick I still lives with his knights, although asleep, on the Kifhauser heights inside a symbolic mountain. He awaits the appointed time when he will descend to the valleys below at the head of his faithful in order to fight the last battle, whose successful outcome will cause the Dry Tree to bloom again and a new age to begin.[12]

11. See my *Il mistero del Graal*, chap. 29, especially in regard to the genesis and the meaning of modern Masonry and of the Enlightenment, as prime examples of this inversion.
12. B. Kluger, *Storia delle Crociate* (1887). From the context of the various versions of the second legend what emerges is the idea that a victory is possible but not certain. In some versions of the saga—which were probably influenced by the Eddic theme of *ragna rok*—the last emperor cannot overcome the forces of the last age and dies after hanging his scepter, crown, and sword in the Dry Tree.

34

Unrealism and Individualism

In order to follow the further phases of the decline of the West, it is necessary to refer to what I have previously said about the first crises undergone by traditional civilizations and to assume as a reference point the fundamental truth of the world of Tradition concerning the two "regions" of world and superworld. According to traditional man, these two regions formed one reality; the establishment of an objective and efficacious contact between them was the presupposition of any higher form of civilization and life.

The interruption of such a contact; the centering of all the possibilities in only one of these worlds, that is, in the human and temporal world; the replacement of the experience of the overworld with ephemeral ghosts and with the by-products of a merely human nature—these are the characteristics of "modern" civilization in general; this civilization has reached the stage in which the various forces of decadence, which were manifested in previous times but which had been successfully slowed down either by reactions or by the power of opposite principles, finally reach a complete and fearful efficiency.

In a general sense, humanism may be regarded as the main trait and password of the new civilization that claims to have emancipated itself from the "darkness of the Middle Ages." This civilization will only be limited to the human dimension; in this type of civilization everything will begin and end with man, including the heavens, the hells, the glorifications, and the curses. The human experience will be confined to *this* world—which is not the real world—with its feverish and yearning creatures, its artistic vanities and its "geniuses," its countless machines, factories, and leaders.

The earliest version of humanism was individualism. Individualism should be regarded as the constitution of an illusory center outside the real center; as the prevaricating pretense of a "self" that is merely a mortal ego endowed with a body; and as by-product of purely natural faculties that, with the aid of arts and profane sciences, create and support various appearances with no consistency outside that false and vain center. These truths and laws are marked by the contingency and caducity proper to what belongs to the world of becoming.

Hence, there is a radical unrealism and inorganic character to all modern phenomena. Nothing is endowed any longer with true life and everything will be a by-product; the extinct Being is replaced in every domain with the "will" and the "self," as a sinister, rationalistic, and mechanical propping up of a cadaver. The countless conquests and creations of the new man appear as the crawling of worms that occurs in the process of putrefaction. Thus, the way is opened to all paroxysms, to innovating and iconoclastic manias, and to the world of a fundamental rhetoric in which, once the spirit was replaced with a pale image of itself, the incestuous fornications of man in the form of religion, philosophy, art, science, and politics, will know no bounds.

On a religious plane, unrealism is essentially related to the loss of the initiatic tradition. I have previously pointed out that in the past, only initiation ensured the objective participation of man in the superworld. Following the end of the ancient world and with the advent of Christianity, however, there no longer were the necessary conditions for the initiatory reality to constitute the supreme reference point of a traditional civilization. In this regard "spiritualism" was one of the factors that acted in the most negative way; the appearance and the diffusion of the strange idea of the "immortality of the soul," which was regarded as the natural privilege of each and every one, eventually contributed to the loss of understanding of the meaning and necessity of initiation as the real operation that alone can free a person from all conditionings and destroy the mortal nature. What arose as a surrogate was the mystery of Christ and the idea of redemption in Christ; in this context, a theme that partially derived from the doctrine of the Mysteries (death and resurrection) lost its initiatory character and was eventually applied to the merely religious plane of faith. This surrogate, generally speaking, consisted in a particular "morality" and in leading a life in view of the sanctions that, according to the new belief, awaited the "immortal soul" in the afterlife. If on the one hand the imperial medieval idea was often pervaded by the initiatory element, on the other hand, though the representative of the Church developed a doctrine of the sacraments, revived the "pontifical" symbolism, and spoke of regeneration, nevertheless, the idea of initiation as such, which was opposite to its spirit, remained basically alien to it. Thus, an anomaly was created that lacked something in comparison with every other complete traditional form, Islam included. Christian dualism, in its specific character, represented a powerful incentive to subjectivism and therefore to unrealism in regard to the problem of the Sacred. The Sacred, from a matter of reality and transcendent experience, became either a matter of faith based on sentiment, or the object of theological speculation. The few examples of a purified Christian mysticism could not prevent God and gods, angels and demons, intelligible essences and their dwellings from assuming the form of myth; the Christianized West ceased to have a knowledge of these things as symbols of potential superrational experiences, superindividual conditions of existence, and deep dimensions of integral being. The ancient world had witnessed the degeneration of symbolism into a mythology that became increasingly opaque and mute and that eventually became the object of artistic fantasy. When the experience of the sacred was reduced to faith, sentiment, and moralism, and when the *intuitio intellectualis* was reduced to a mere concept of Scholastic philosophy, the unrealism of the spirit entirely took over the domain of the supernatural. This course underwent a further development with Protestantism, the contemporaneity of which with humanism and with the Renaissance is significant.

Prescinding from its final meaning in the history of civilization, its antagonistic role during the Middle Ages, and its lack of an initiatic and esoteric dimension, we nevertheless must acknowledge a certain traditional character to the Church that lifted it above what had been mere Christianity, because it established a system of dogmas, symbols, myths, rituals, and sacred institutions in which, though often indirectly, elements of a superior knowledge were sometimes preserved. By rigidly upholding the principle of authority and dogma, by defending the transcendent and superrational character of "revelation" in the domain of knowledge and the principle of the transcendence of grace in the domain of action, the Church defended from any heresy—almost desperately—the nonhuman character of its deposit. This extreme effort of Catholicism (which explains much of whatever is crude and violent in its history), however, encountered a limit. The "dam" could not hold and some forms that could be justified in a merely religious context could not retain the character of absoluteness that is proper to what is nonhuman; this was especially true not only because a superior knowledge was lacking, but also considering that the secularization of the Church, the corruption, and the unworthiness of a great number of its representatives and the increasing importance that political and contingent interests acquired within it became increasingly visible. Thus, the stage was set for a reaction destined to inflict a serious blow to the traditional element that was added to Christianity, to exasperate the unrealist subjectivism, and to uphold individualism in a religious context. For this is what the Reformation accomplished.

It is not a coincidence that Luther's invectives against the "papacy, the devil's creature in Rome" and against Rome as the "kingdom of Babylon" and as a radically pagan reality totally inimical to the Christian spirit were very similar to those invectives employed by the early Christians and by the Jewish apocalyptic texts against the city of the eagle and of the battle-axe. By rejecting everything in Catholicism that was Tradition and opposed to the simple Gospels, Luther demonstrated a fundamental misunderstanding of that superior content that cannot be reduced either to the Jewish-Southern substratum, or to the world of mere devotion, which in the Church had developed through secret influences from above.[1] The Ghibelline emperors rose up against papal Rome in the name of Rome, thus upholding again the superior idea of the Sacrum Imperium against both the merely religious spirituality of the Church and her hegemonic claims. Instead, Luther rose up against papal Rome out of an intense dislike for what was a positive aspect, that is, the traditional, hierarchical, and ritual component that existed within the Catholic compromise.

In many regards Luther facilitated a mutilating emancipation, even in the domain of politics. By supporting the Reformation the Germanic princes, instead of assuming the legacy of Frederick II, went over to the anti-imperial coalition. In the author of the *Warnung an seine lieben Deutschen,* who presented himself as the "prophet of the German people," these princes saw one who legitimated their revolt against the imperial principle of authority with his doctrines and who allowed them to disguise their insubordination in the form of an anti-Roman crusade waged in the name of the Gospel, according to which they had no other goal than to be free German rulers and to be emancipated from any supernational hierarchical bond. Luther also contributed to an involutive process in another way; his doctrine subordinated religion to the state in all of its concrete manifestations. Because the government of the states was the responsibility of mere secular rulers; because Luther foreshadowed a democratic theme that was later on perfected by Calvin (the rulers do not govern by virtue of their nature, but because they are the representatives of the community); because a characteristic of the Reformation was the radical negation of the "Olympian" or "heroic" ideal, or any possibility on man's part to go beyond his limitations either through asceticism or consecration and so to be qualified to exercise even the right from above, which is typical of true leaders—because of all these reasons, Luther's views concerning "secular authority" (die weltiche Obrigkeit) practically amounted to an inversion of the traditional doctrine concerning the regal primacy and thus left the doors open for the usurpation of spiritual authority on the part of the temporal power. When defining the theme of the Leviathan, or of the "absolute state," Hobbes similarly proclaimed: *"civitatem et ecclesiam eadem rem esse."*

From the point of view of the metaphysics of history, the positive and objective

---

1. Naturally, this lack of understanding was typical of the representatives of Catholicism as well. Paracelsus was right when he said: "What is this commotion about Luther's and Zwingli's writings? It truly reminds me of a shallow bacchanalia. If I had to make a recommendation about this controversy I would have these gentlemen and the pope himself go back to school."

contribution of Protestantism consists in having emphasized that in mankind living in recent times a truly spiritual principle was no longer immediately present and that, therefore, mankind had to portray this principle as something transcendent. On this basis, Catholicism itself had already assumed the myth of original sin. Protestantism exasperated this myth by proclaiming the fundamental powerlessness of man to achieve salvation through his own efforts; generally speaking, it regarded the whole of humankind as a damned mass, condemned to automatically commit evil. To the truth obscurely foreshadowed by that myth, Protestantism added tints typical of an authentic Syrian masochism that were expressed in rather revolting images. Over and against the ancient ideal of spiritual virility Luther did not hesitate to call a "royal wedding" one in which the soul, portrayed as a "prostitute" and as "the most wretched and sinful creature," plays the role of the woman (see Luther's *De libertate christiana*); and to compare man to a beast of burden on which either God or the devil ride at will, without his being able to do anything about it (see Luther's *De servo arbitrio*).

While what should have followed from the acknowledgment of the abovementioned existential situation was the affirmation of the need for the support proper to a ritual and hierarchical system, or the affirmation of the strictest type of asceticism, Luther denied both things. The entire system of Luther's thought was visibly conditioned by his personal equation and the gloomy character of his inner life as a failed monk and a man who was unable to overcome his own nature, influenced as it was by his passions, sensuality, and anger. This personal equation was reflected in the peculiar doctrine according to which the Ten Commandments had not been given by God to men to be implemented in this life but so that man, after acknowledging his inability to fulfill them, his nothingness, as well as concupiscence's invincibility and his inner tendency to sin, would entrust himself to a personal God and trust desperately in His free grace. This "justification by faith alone" and the ensuing condemnation of the power of "works" led Luther to attack the monastic life and the ascetical life, which he called "vain and hopeless," thus deterring Western man from pursuing those residual possibilities of reintegration available in the contemplative life that Catholicism had preserved and that had produced figures like Bernard of Clairvaux, Jan van Ruysbroeck, Bonaventure, and Meister Eckhart.[2] Sec-

---

2. This is the main difference between Buddhism and Protestantism, which confers a positive character to the former and a negative to the latter. Both movements are characterized by pessimist premises—Luther's *concupiscientia invincibilis* corresponds somewhat to Buddhism's "thirst for life"—and by a revolt against a corrupted priestly caste. However, Buddhism indicated a path to follow since it created a strict system of asceticism and of self-discipline, unlike Protestantism, which rejected even the mitigated forms of asceticism found in the Catholic tradition.

ondly, the Reformation denied the principle of authority and hierarchy in the dimension of the sacred. The idea that a human being, as a *pontifex,* could be infallible in matters of sacred doctrine and also legitimately claim the right to an authority beyond criticism was regarded as aberrant and absurd. According to the reformers, Christ did not give to any church, not even to a Protestant church, the privilege of infallibility;[3] thus, anybody is able to reach conclusions in matters of doctrine and interpretation of the sacred text through a free and individual examination outside any control and any tradition. Not only was the distinction between laity and priesthood in the field of knowledge basically abolished, but also denied was the priestly dignity understood not as an empty attribute, but in reference to those who, unlike other people, are endowed with a supernatural chrism and who carry an *indoles indelebilis* that allows them to activate the rites (these being residues of the ancient notion of the "Lord of the rites").[4] Therefore, the objective, nonhuman meaning that not only the dogma and the symbols but the system of rites and the sacraments could have as well, was denied and rejected.

One might object that all this no longer existed in Catholicism or that it existed only formally or indirectly. But in that case the way leading to an authentic reformation should have been one and one alone: to act in earnest and replace the unworthy representatives of the spiritual principle and tradition with worthy ones. Instead, Protestantism has led to a destruction and a denial that were not balanced with any true constructive principle, but rather only with an illusion, namely, sheer faith. According to Protestantism, salvation consisted in the mere subjective assurance of being counted in the ranks of those who have been saved by faith in Christ, and "chosen" by divine grace. In this fashion, mankind progressed along the path of spiritual unrealism; the materialistic repercussion did not delay its appearance.

After rejecting the objective notion of spirituality as a reality ranking higher than profane existence, the Protestant doctrine allowed man to feel, in all aspects of life, as a being who was simultaneously spiritual and earthly, justified and sinner. In the end this led to a radical secularization of all higher vocations; again, not to

---

3. De Maistre (*Du pape* [Lyon, 1819]) correctly remarked that this situation is paradoxical: Protestantism in fact upholds the idea that God did not bestow infallibility to man or to the Church as if it were a dogma. In Islam, infallibility *(isma)* is not regarded as the natural possession of an individual, but of all the legitimate interpreters of the *tawil,* the esoteric teaching.

4. Within Catholicism, due to a confusion between what is proper to asceticism and what is proper to the priesthood, the clergy never was a real caste. Once the principle of celibacy was established, by virtue of this very principle Catholicism irremediably lost the possibility of connecting the deposit of certain spiritual influences with the deep-seated forces of a blood legacy that had been preserved from any corrupt influence. The clergy, unlike the noble class, was always affected by the promiscuity of the origins since it recruited its members from all social strata and therefore always lacked an "organic" (i.e., biological and hereditary) basis for those spiritual influences.

sacralization, but to moralism and puritanism. It was in the historical development of Protestantism, especially in Anglo-Saxon Calvinism and Puritanism, that the religious idea became increasingly dissociated from any transcendent interest and thus susceptible to being used to sanctify any temporal achievement to the point of generating a kind of mysticism of social service, work, "progress," and even profit. These forms of Anglo-Saxon Protestantism were characterized by communities of believers with no leader to represent a transcendent principle of authority; thus, the ideal of the state was reduced to that of the mere "society" of "free" Christian citizens. In this type of society, profit became the sign of divine election that, once the prevalent criterion became the economic one, corresponds to wealth and to prosperity. In this we can clearly distinguish one of the aspects of the abovementioned degrading regression: this Calvinist theory was really the materialistic and lay counterfeit of the ancient mystical doctrine of victory. For quite a long time this theory has supplied an ethical and religious justification for the rise to power of the merchant class and of the Third Estate during the cycle of the modern democracies and capitalism.

The individualism intrinsic in the Protestant theory of private interpretation of Scripture was connected with another aspect of modern humanism: rationalism. The single individual who got rid of the dogmatic tradition and the principle of spiritual authority, by claiming to have within himself the capability of right discernment, gradually ended up promoting the cult of that which in him, as a human being, is the basis of all judgments, namely, the faculty of reason, thus turning it into the criterion of all certitudes, truths, and norms. This is precisely what happened in the West shortly after the Reformation. Naturally, there were some "germs" of rationalism in ancient Hellas (exemplified in the Socratic replacement of the concept of "reality" with reality itself) and in the Middle Ages (in the theology that was heavily influenced by philosophy). Beginning with the Renaissance, however, rationalism became differentiated and assumed, in one of its most important currents, a new character: from speculative in nature it became aggressive and generated the Enlightenment, Encyclopedism, and antireligious and revolutionary criticism. In this regard, it is necessary to acknowledge the effects of further processes of involution and inversion that display an even more sinister character because they negatively affected some surviving organizations of an initiatic type, as in the case of the Illuminati and of modern Masonry. The superiority over dogma and over the merely religious Western forms—a superiority granted to the initiate by the process of spiritual enlightenment—was claimed by those who upheld the sovereign power of reason. Members of such organizations promoted this inversion until they transformed the groups that they led into active instruments of the diffusion of antitraditional and rationalist thought. One of the most tangible examples of this is the role Masonry played in the American Revolution as well as in the underground ideological preparation of the French Revolution and in the revolutions that occurred in Spain, Turkey, and Italy, among others. This is how the secret front of world subversion and countertradition was formed, not just through general influences alone, but also through specific centers of action.

In yet another one of its "fifth columns," which was limited to the domain of speculative thought, rationalism was destined to develop along unrealist lines and to generate Absolute Idealism and panlogism. The identity of spirit and thought, of concept and reality was upheld; logical hypostases such as the transcendental ego replaced the real ego as well as any premonition of the true supernatural principle within man. The so-called "critical thought that has reached consciousness of itself" declared: "Everything that is real is rational and everything that is rational is real," which truly represents the extreme form of unrealism.[5] Rather than in similar philosophical abstractions, rationalism played a much more important role in a practical way in the construction of the modern world by joining forces with empiricism and experimentalism in the context of scientism.

Again, the birth of modern naturalistic and scientific thought coincided with the Renaissance and the Reformation, since these phenomena were the expressions of the same one global upheaval. Individualism is necessarily associated with naturalism.

With the revolt of individualism, all consciousness of the superworld was lost. The only thing that was still regarded as all-inclusive and certain was the material view of the world, or nature seen as exteriority and a collection of phenomena. A new way to look at the world had emerged. In the past there had been anticipations of this upheaval, but they remained sporadic apparitions that were never transformed into forces responsible for shaping civilizations.[6] It was at this time that reality became synonymous with materiality. The new ideal of science was concerned exclusively with the physical dimension and was eventually confined to a construction; this ideal no longer represented the synthesis of an intellectual intuition, but rather the effort of purely human faculties to unify the multiple varieties of impressions and

---

5. Critical or "epistemological" idealism claimed to be the awareness of all other philosophical systems; in this it was right. It is the unrealism of philosophy in general that becomes aware of itself in the system, whereby the real becomes identical to the "rational," the world to the "concept" of the world, and the "I" to the "thought" of the "I." I have written at greater length about this in my *Fenomenologia dell'individuo assoluto* (Turin, 1930).

6. During the Middle Ages there was a revival of some of the traditional sciences; the view of nature Scholasticism constructed on the basis of Aristotelianism, though constrained in a conceptualist apparatus, still upheld the view of the qualities or of the formative virtues.

sensible apparitions from the outside "inductively," with the sense of touch rather than of sight. The conquests of science merely consisted in the discovery of mathematical relations, laws of consistency and uniform succession, hypotheses, and abstract principles the value of which was exclusively determined by the capability of predicting, more or less exactly, the eventual outcome, yet without providing any essential knowledge and without revealing meanings capable of leading to an inner liberation and elevation. This dead knowledge of dead objects led to the sinister art of producing artificial, automatic, and obscurely demonic entities. The advent of rationalism and scientism was unavoidably followed by the advent of technology and machines, which have become the center and the apotheosis of the new human world.

Moreover, modern science is responsible for the systematic profanation of the two domains of action and contemplation, and also for the plebs' rise to power in the European nations. It was science that degraded and democratized the very notion of knowledge by establishing the uniform criterion of truth and certainty based on the soulless world of numbers and the superstition represented by the "positivist" method, which is indifferent toward everything that presents a qualitative and symbolic character in empirical data. It was science that precluded any appreciation of the traditional disciplines; through the mirage of evident phenomena that are accessible to everyone science has upheld the superiority of lay culture by creating the myth of the scholar and of the scientist. It was science that, by dispelling the darkness of "superstition" and of "religion," and by insinuating the image of natural necessity, has progressively and objectively destroyed any possibility of a subtle relationship with the secret powers of things. It was science that snatched away from man the voice of the sea, the earth, and the heavens and created the myth of the "New Age of Progress," opening doors for everybody and fomenting the great rebellion of the slaves. It is science that today, by providing the instruments for the control and employment of every force of nature according to the ideals of a demonic conquest, has engendered the most formidable temptation ever to confront man: that he may mistake his renunciation as an act of real power and something to be proud of, and mistake a shadow of power for the real thing.

This process of detachment, of loss of the superworld and tradition, of all-powerful laicism and triumphant rationalism and naturalism is identical both on the plane of the relationship between man and reality and on the plane of society, the state, and morality. When dealing with the issue of the death of civilizations, I have mentioned that the inner adherence of humble and ignorant people to leaders and traditional institutions was justified in that it represented a way leading to a fruitful hierarchical relationship with beings who knew and who "were" and who kept alive a nonhuman spirituality of which any traditional law was the embodiment and the adaptation. But when such a reference point is no longer present or when it is present only in a symbolic way, then subordination is vain and obedience is sterile; the final outcome is a petrification and not a ritual participation. And so, in the modern and humanized world that lacks the dimension of transcendence, any law of the hierarchical order and stability was bound to disappear, especially on the outer plane, until the achievement of the state of radical atomization of the single individual, not only in matters of religion, but also in the political domain through the denial of any traditional value, institution, and authority. Once the *fides* was secularized the revolt against spiritual authority was followed by the revolt against temporal power and by the revendication of "human rights"; by the affirmation of freedom and the equality of all human beings; by the definitive abolition of the idea of caste (which came to be understood in socioeconomic terms as "functional class") and of privilege; and by a disintegration of the traditional social structures promoted by libertarianism.

But the law of action-reaction determines a collectivist upheaval to follow automatically every individualistic usurpation. The casteless, the emancipated slave, and the glorified pariah (the modern "free man") has against himself the mass of the other casteless and, in the end, the brute power of the collectivity. Thus, the process of disintegration continues and what ensues is a regression from the personal to the anonymous, the herd, and the pure, chaotic, and inorganic realm of quantity. Just as the scientific enterprise has sought, from the outside, to recreate the multiplicity of particular phenomena (while having lost that inner and true unity that exists only in the context of metaphysical knowledge), so have moderns tried to replace the unity that in ancient societies consisted of living traditions and sacred law with an exterior, anodyne, and mechanical unity in which individuals are brought together without an organic relation to each other, and without seeing any superior principle or figure, the obeying of which would mean consent, and submission to which would represent an acknowledgment and elevation. In this way new collective forms arise that are essentially based on the conditions of material existence and on the various factors of a merely social life, which in turn is dominated by the impersonal and leveling system of "public powers." These collective forms soon overthrow individualism; and whether they present themselves in the guise of democracies or national states, republics or dictatorships, they begin to be carried along by independent subhuman forces.

The most decisive episode in the unleashing of the European plebs, the French Revolution, already displays the typical traits of this overthrow. When studying the French Revolution it is possible to see how these forces soon escape from the control of those who have evoked them. Once the Revolution was unleashed, it seems as if it assumed a life of its own, leading men, rather than the other way around; it eventually devoured its own "children" one by one. Its leaders, rather than real personalities, appear to be the embodiment of the revolutionary spirit and to be carried along as inane and automatic objects. They ride the wave, so to speak, as long as they follow the current and are useful to the goals set by the Revolution; but as soon as they try to dominate it or to stop it, the maelstrom submerges them. Some specific traits of the French Revolution include the speed and the power with which it spread and the speed with which events followed one another and obstacles in its way were overcome; in these traits what is visible is the emergence of a nonhuman element and a subpersonal reality that has a mind and a life of its own and that employs men as mere tools.[7]

This very same phenomenon may be observed, though in different degrees and forms, in some salient aspects of modern society in general, especially after the collapse of the last "dams." Politically, the anonymous character of the structures that credit the people and the "nation" with the origin of all powers is interrupted only to generate phenomena that resemble totally the ancient popular tyrannies; that is, personalities that enjoy a brief popularity by virtue of their being masters in awakening the irrational forces of the demos and in directing their course, all the while lacking an authentically superior principle and thus having only an illusory dominion over what they have awakened. The acceleration that characterizes all falling bodies causes the phase of individualism and rationalism to be overcome and to be followed by the emergence of irrational and elemental forces characterized by mystical overtones. It is here that we encounter further developments in the well-known process of regression. In the domain of culture this regression is accompanied by an upheaval that has been characterized with the expression "treason of the clerics."[8]

The people who still reacted against the materialism of the masses by adhering to disinterested forms of activity and to superior values, and who, by opposing their own faithfulness to higher interests and principles to the masses' passionate and irrational life represented the vestiges of transcendence that at least prevented the inferior elements from turning their ambitions and their way of life into the only religion—these very same people in recent times have extolled that plebeian realism and that deconsecrated and inferior existence, and have conferred upon it the aura of a mysticism, a morality, and a religion. Not only did they began to cultivate realistic passions, particularisms, and political rivalries; not only did they begin frantically to pursue temporal achievements and conquests right at the time their moderating and contrasting role was needed the most to stem the surging power of the

7. Observations by J. de Maistre in *Considerations sur la France* (Lyon, 1860), 5–8.
8. J. Benda, *La Trahison des clercs* (Paris, 1928).

inferior element but—worse yet—they began to celebrate the only human possibilities that are worthy and fit to be cultivated, and the only ones from which man can draw the fullness of the moral and spiritual life. Thus, these people have supplied the passions and the instincts of the masses with powerful doctrinal, philosophical, and even religious justifications with the result of strengthening their power and at the same time covering with ridicule and contempt any transcendent interest or principle that is truly over and above the particularisms of race or nation and free of all human, sociopolitical conditionings.[9] In this we can recognize again the phenomenon of a pathological inversion of polarity; the human person, in his superior faculties, becomes the instrument of *other* forces that replace him and that often use him to bring about spiritual havoc without him even realizing it.[10]

After all, when the intellectual faculties were applied in a systematic and concerted way to the naturalistic inquiry, this represented a "treason." The profane science that derived from this type of inquiry portrayed itself as the true science; it sided with rationalism in the attack against Tradition and religion; and it put itself in the service of the material needs of life, the economy, industry, production and over-production, and the lust for power and riches.

The Law and morals became secularized along the same lines; they no longer were "from above and oriented downwards"; they lost every spiritual justification and purpose and they acquired a merely social and human meaning. It is significant that in some of the more recent ideologies they have claimed the same ancient authority, though with an inverted direction: "from below and upwards." I am referring to the "morality" that recognizes a value in the individual only insomuch as he is a member of a collective, acephalous entity that identifies his destiny and happiness with the latter's and denounces as "decadence" and as "alienation" any form of activity that is not socially "relevant" and in the service of the organized "plebs" that are on their way to conquering the planet. I will return to these considerations when discussing the specific forms with which the present cycle is about to end. At this point I will only mention the definitive overthrow of individualism that originated the process of disintegration, an individualism that no longer exists other than in the residues and the velleity of a pale and powerless "humanism" typical of bourgeois literates. With the principle according to which man, rather than as an individual, must be made to feel part of a group, faction, party, or collectivity, and have a value

---

9. A. Tilgher, *J. Benda e il problema del tradimento dei chierici* (Rome, 1930). The "treason of the clerics," as Benda envisions it, is not a peculiar case of the phenomenon being discussed. The type of the "cleric" as a mere man of letters, philosopher, or moralist (Benda stops at this level) already represents that type of "betraying cleric."

10. In the Chinese tradition (*Meng-tzu*, 3.12) we find indications of this process in which individualism opens the gates to an obsessive phenomenon that puts man at the mercy of subpersonal and irrational faculties.

only in relationship with these units, we find the reproduction of the relationship that primitive and savage man had toward the totem of his tribe, and of the worst type of fetishism.

In general, modern man has looked at the shift from a "civilization of being" to a "civilization of becoming" as a real step forward.[11] The valorization of the purely temporal aspect of reality in the name of history (hence historicism) has been one of the consequences of this shift. Once contact with the origins was lost the indefinite, senseless, and accelerated motion of what has rightly been called an "escape forward" in the name of evolution and progress has become the main feature of modern civilization. Quite frankly, the germs of this superstitious mythology applied to time may be found in Judeo-Christian eschatology and Messianism as well as in early Catholic apologetics, which valorized the "novelty" of the Christian revelation so much so that in Ambrose's polemics against the Roman tradition we can find an early formulation of the theory of progress. The "rediscovery of man" promoted by the Renaissance represented a fertile habitat for the growth of those germs, up to the period of the Enlightenment and scientism. Ever since then the impressive development of the sciences of nature and technology, as well as of inventions, has acted like opium, distracting man's mind and preventing him from perceiving the underlying and essential meaning of the entire movement: the abandonment of being and dissolution of any centrality in man, and his identification with the current of becoming, which has become stronger than him. And when the fantastic ideas of the coarsest kind of progressivism are at risk of being unmasked, the new religions of life and the "élan vital," as well as "Faustian" activity and myth, make their appearance and become new intellectual "drugs" that ensure that the movement may not be interrupted but spurred on, so that it may acquire a meaning in itself, both for man and for existence in general.

Again, the overthrow of the civilization of being is very evident. The center has shifted toward that evasive elemental power of the inferior region that in the world of Tradition had always been considered an inimical force. In this world, the task of anybody who yearned for a higher existence, as foreshadowed in the heroic and Olympian myth, consisted in subduing that force and in subjecting it to a "form," a dominion, and an enlightenment of the soul. The human energies that were traditionally oriented in the direction of disidentification and of liberation, or which, at the very least, recognized the supreme dignity in this approach (so much so as to establish the system of hierarchical participations), after a sudden polar shift, have entered into the service of the forces of becoming by upholding,

---

11. J. Evola, *L'arco e la clava*, chap. 1.

helping, exciting, and accelerating the rhythm of these forces in the modern world.

On this basis, what we find in modern activity, instead of a path toward the superindividual (as in the case of the ancient possibilities of heroic asceticism), is a path to the subindividual; destructive incursions of the irrational and of the collective element into the already shaking structures of human personality are thus promoted and furthered. Nor in some sectors is there a lack of a certain "frantic" element analogous to that of ancient Dionysism—though on a lower and darker plane, since every reference to the sacred is absent and since the human circuits are the only ones to welcome and to absorb the evoked forces. The spiritual overcoming of time, achieved by rising up to the experience of what is eternal, is today replaced with its counterfeit, namely, the mechanical and illusory overcoming of time produced by the speed, immediacy, and simultaneity ("live," the media would say) employed in modern technology. Those who see the part of themselves that is not contingent upon time are able to comprehend it with one glance as it presents itself the stream of becoming; just as one, who by climbing to the top of a tower, is able to gain an overall view and understand the unity of individual things that could otherwise only be perceived had they been experienced successively. Conversely, those who, with an opposite movement, immerse themselves in becoming and delude themselves about being able to possess it will only know the excitement, the vertigo, the convulsive acceleration of speed, and the excesses resulting from sensation and agitation. This precipitation of those who "identify" themselves with becoming, who pick up speed, disrupt duration, destroy intervals, and abolish distances eventually flows into immediacy and thus into a real disintegration of inner unity. Being and stability are regarded by our contemporaries as akin to death; they cannot live unless they act, fret, or distract themselves with this or that. Their spirit (provided we can still talk about a spirit in their case) feeds only on sensations and on dynamism, thus becoming the vehicle for the incarnation of darker forces.

Thus, the modern myths of action appear to be the forerunners of a last and decisive phase: after the disembodied and sidereal certainties of the superworld have faded into the distance like mountain peaks on a cloudy day; beyond the rationalist constructions and the technological devastations; beyond the impure fires of the collective vital substance; and beyond the fogs and the mirages of modern "culture," a new era appears to be coming in which "Luciferian" and theophobic individualism will be definitively overcome and new unrestrainable powers will drag along in their wake this world of machines and these intoxicated and spent beings, who in the course of their downfall have erected titanic temples for them and have opened the ways of the earth.

It is significant that the modern world shows a return of the themes that were proper to the ancient Southern gynaecocratic civilizations. Is it not true that socialism and communism are materialized and technological revivals of the ancient telluric, Southern principle of equality and promiscuity of all beings in Mother Earth? In the modern world the predominant ideal of virility has been reduced to merely the physical and phallic components, just like in the Aphrodistic gynaecocracy. The plebeian feeling of the Motherland that triumphed with the French Revolution and was developed by nationalistic ideologies as the mysticism of the common folk and the sacred and omnipotent Motherland is nothing less than the revival of a form of feminine totemism. In the democratic regimes, the fact that kings and the heads of state lack any real autonomy bears witness to the loss of the absolute principle of fatherly sovereignty and the return of those who have in the Mother (that is, in the substance of the demos) the source of their being. Hetaerism and Amazonism today are also present in new forms, such as the disintegration of the family, modern sensuality, and the incessant and turbid quest for women and immediate sexual gratification, as well as in the masculinization of the woman, her emancipation, and her standing above men who have become enslaved to their senses or turned into beasts of burden. Concerning Dionysus' mask, I have previously identified it with ceaseless activity and with the philosophy of becoming; and so today we witness a revival, *mutatis mutandis*, of the same civilization of decadence that appeared in the ancient Mediterranean world—though in its lowest forms. What is lacking, in fact, is a sense of the sacred, as well as any equivalent of the chaste and calm Demetrian possibility. Rather than the survival of the positive religion that became prominent in the West, today the symptoms are rather the dark evocations proper to the various mediumistic, spiritualistic, and neotheosophical currents that emphasize the subconscious, and are characterized by a pantheistic and materialistic mysticism; these currents proliferate and grow in a way that is almost epidemic wherever (for example, in Anglo-Saxon countries) the materialization of the virile type and ordinary existence has reached its peak and wherever Protestantism has secularized and impoverished the religious ideal.[12] Thus, the parallel is almost complete and the cycle is about to close.

---

12. In my *Maschera e volto dello spiritualismo contemporaneo* (Bari, 1949) and especially in the last chapter of *Cavalcare la tigre* I have discussed the meaning of the most recent kinds of "spiritualism."

35

The Regression of the Castes

As my intent was to offer a bird's-eye view of history, in the previous pages I have presented all the elements necessary to formulate an objective law at work in the various stages of the process of decadence, that is, the law of the regression of the castes.[1] A progressive shift of power and type of civilization has occurred from one caste to the next since prehistoric times (from sacred leaders, to a warrior aristocracy, to the merchants, and finally, to the serfs); these castes in traditional civilizations corresponded to the qualitative differentiation of the main human possibilities. In the face of this general movement anything concerning the various conflicts among peoples, the life of nations, or other historical accidents plays only a secondary and contingent role.

I have already discussed the dawn of the age of the first caste. In the West, the representatives of the divine royalty and the leaders who embody the two powers (spiritual and temporal), in what I have called "spiritual virility" and "Olympian sovereignty," belong to a very distant and almost mythical past. We have seen how, through the gradual deterioration of the Light of the North, the process of decadence has unfolded; in the Ghibelline ideal of the Holy Roman Empire I have identified the last echo of the highest tradition.

Once the apex disappeared, authority descended to the level immediately below, that is, to the caste of the warriors. The stage was then set for monarchs who were mere military leaders, lords of temporal justice and, in more recent times, politically absolute sovereigns. In other words, regality of blood replaced regality of

---

1. The idea of regression of the castes, which I had previously referred to in my pamphlet *Imperialismo Pagano* (Rome, 1927), was detailed by V. Vezzani and by R. Guénon in his *Autorité spirituelle et pouvoir temporel;* finally, it has been expounded in an independent fashion by H. Berls in *Die Heraufkunst des fünften Standes* (Karlsruhe, 1931). This idea has an analogical correspondence with the traditional doctrine of the four ages, since each of the four traditional castes embodies the values that have predominated during the quadripartite process of regression.

the spirit. In a few instances it is still possible to find the idea of "divine right," but only as a formula lacking a real content. We find such rulers in antiquity behind institutions that retained the traits of the ancient sacred regime only in a formal way. In any event in the West, with the dissolution of the medieval ecumene, the passage into the second phase became all-encompassing and definitive. During this stage, the *fides* cementing the state no longer had a religious character, but only a warrior one; it meant loyalty, faithfulness, honor. This was essentially the age and the cycle of the great European monarchies.

Then a second collapse occurred as the aristocracies began to fall into decay and the monarchies to shake at the foundations; through revolutions and constitutions they became useless institutions subject to the "will of the nation," and sometimes they were even ousted by different regimes. The principle characterizing this state of affairs was: "The king reigns but he does not rule." Together with parliamentary republics the formation of the capitalist oligarchies revealed the shift of power from the second caste (the warrior) to the modern equivalent of the third caste (the mercantile class). The kings of the coal, oil, and iron industries replace the previous kings of blood and of spirit. Antiquity, too, sometimes knew this phenomenon in sporadic forms; in Rome and in Greece the "aristocracy of wealth" repeatedly forced the hand of the hierarchical structure by pursuing aristocratic positions, undermining sacred laws and traditional institutions, and infiltrating the militia, priesthood, or consulship. In later times what occurred was the rebellion of the communes and the rise of the various medieval formations of mercantile power. The solemn proclamation of the "rights of the Third Estate" in France represented the decisive stage, followed by the varieties of "bourgeois revolution" of the third caste, which employed liberal and democratic ideologies for its own purposes. Correspondingly, this era was characterized by the theory of the social contract. At this time the social bond was no longer a *fides* of a warrior type based on relationships of faithfulness and honor. Instead, it took on a utilitarian and economic character; it consisted of an agreement based on personal convenience and on material interest that only a merchant could have conceived. Gold became a means and a powerful tool; those who knew how to acquire it and to multiply it (capitalism, high finance, industrial trusts), behind the appearances of democracy, virtually controlled political power and the instruments employed in the art of opinion making. Aristocracy gave way to plutocracy, the warrior, to the banker and industrialist. The economy triumphed on all fronts. Trafficking with money and charging interest, activities previously confined to the ghettos, invaded the new civilization. According to the expression of W. Sombart, in the promised land of Protestant puritanism, Americanism, capitalism, and the "distilled Jewish spirit" coexist. It is natural that given these congenial premises, the modern representatives of secularized Judaism saw the ways to achieve world domination open up before them. In this regard, Karl Marx wrote:

> What are the mundane principles of Judaism? Practical necessity and the pursuit of one's own advantage. What is its earthly god? Money. The Jew has emancipated himself in a typically Jewish fashion not only in that he has taken control of the power of money, but also in that through him, money has become a world power and the practical Jewish spirit has become the spirit of the Christian people. *The Jews have emancipated themselves insofar as the Christians have become Jews.* The god of the Jews has become secularized and has become the god of the earth. The exchange is the true god of the Jews.[2]

In reality, the codification of the traffic with gold as a loan charged with interest, to which the Jews had been previously devoted since they had no other means through which they could affirm themselves, may be said to be the very foundation of the acceptance of the aberrant development of all that is banking, high finance, and pure economy, which are spreading like a cancer in the modern world. This is the fundamental time in the "age of the merchants."

Finally, the crisis of bourgeois society, class struggle, the proletarian revolt against capitalism, the manifesto promulgated at the "Third International" (or Comintern) in 1919, and the correlative organization of the groups and the masses in the cadres proper to a "socialist civilization of labor"—all these bear witness to the third collapse, in which power tends to pass into the hands of the lowest of the traditional castes, the caste of the beasts of burden and the standardized individuals. The result of this transfer of power was a reduction of horizon and value to the plane of matter, the machine, and the reign of quantity. The prelude to this was the Russian Revolution. Thus, the new ideal became the "proletarian" ideal of a universal and communist civilization.[3]

We may compare the abovementioned phenomenon of the awakening and gushing forth of elemental subhuman forces within the structures of the modern world to a person who can no longer endure the tension of the spirit (first caste), and eventually not even the tension of the will as a free force that animates the body (warrior caste), and who thus gives in to the subpersonal forces of the organic system and all

---

2. Karl Marx, *Deutsche-französische Jahrbücher* (Paris, 1844), 209–12.
3. D. Merezhkovsky, *Les Mystères de l'Orient* (24): "The word 'proletarian' comes from Latin *proles,* which means posterity, generation. Proletarians 'produce' and generate with their bodies, but are spiritual eunuchs. They are not men or women, but anonymous 'comrades,' impersonal ants which are part of the human anthill."

of a sudden reacts almost magnetically under the impulse of *another* life that replaces his own. The ideas and the passions of the demos soon escape men's control and they begin to act as if they had acquired an autonomous and dreadful life of their own. These passions pit nations and collectivities against each other and result in unprecedented conflicts and crises. At the end of the process, once the total collapse has occurred, there awaits an international system under the brutal symbols of the hammer and the sickle.

Such are the horizons facing the contemporary world. Just as it is only by adhering to free activity that man can truly be free and realize his own self, likewise, by focusing on practical and utilitarian goals, economic achievements, and whatever was once the exclusive domain of the inferior castes man abdicates, disintegrates, loses his center, and opens himself up to infernal forces of which he is destined to become the unwilling and unconscious instrument. Moreover, contemporary society looks like an organism that has shifted from a human to a subhuman type, in which every activity and reaction is determined by the needs and the dictates of purely physical life. Man's dominating principles are those typical of the material part of traditional hierarchies: gold and work. This is how things are today; these two elements, almost without exception, affect every possibility of existence and give shape to the ideologies and myths that clearly testify to the gravity of the modern perversion of all values.

Not only does the quadripartite regression have a sociopolitical scope, but it also invests every domain of civilization. In architecture the regression is symbolized by the shift from the temple (first caste) as the dominant building, to the fortress and castle (caste of the warriors), to the city-state surrounded by protecting walls (age of the merchants), to the factory, and finally to the rational and dull buildings that are the hives of mass-man. The family, which in the origins had a sacred foundation, shifted to an authoritarian model (*patria potestas* in a mere juridical sense), then to a bourgeois and conventional one, until it will finally dissolve when the party, the people, and society will supersede it in importance and dignity. The notion of war underwent analogous phases: from the doctrine of the "sacred war" and of the *mors triumphalis* a shift occurred to war waged in the name of the right and of the honor of one's lord (warrior caste); in the third stage conflicts are brought about by national ambitions that are contingent upon the plans and the interests of a supremacist economy and industry (caste of the merchants); finally there arose the communist theory according to which war among nations is just a bourgeois residue, since the only just war is the world revolution of the proletarian class waged against the capitalist and the so-called imperialist world (caste of the serfs). In the aesthetic dimension a shift occurred from a symbolic, sacred art closely related to the possibilities of predicting future events and magic (first caste), to the predominance of epic art and poems (caste of the warriors); this was followed by a shift to a romantic, conventional, sentimentalist, erotic, and psychological art that is produced for the consumption of the bourgeois class, until finally, new "social" or "socially involved" views of art begin to emerge that advocate an art for the use and consumption of the masses. The traditional world knew the superindividual unity characterizing the orders: in the West first came ascetic, monastic orders; these were followed by knightly orders (caste of the warriors), which in turn were followed by the unity sworn to in Masonic lodges, which worked hard to prepare the revolution of the Third Estate and the advent of democracy. Finally there came the network of revolutionary and activist cadres of the Communist International (last caste), bent on the destruction of the previous sociopolitical order.

It is on the plane of ethics that the process of degradation is particularly visible. While the first age was characterized by the ideal of "spiritual virility," initiation, and an ethics aimed at overcoming all human bonds; and while the age of the warriors was characterized by the ideal of heroism, victory, and lordship, as well as by the aristocratic ethics of honor, faithfulness, and chivalry, during the age of the merchants the predominant ideals were of pure economics, profit, prosperity, and of science as an instrument of a technical and industrial progress that propels production and new profits in a "consumer society." Finally, the advent of the serfs corresponds to the elevation of the slave's principle—*work*—to the status of a religion. It is the hatred harbored by the slave that sadistically proclaims: "If anyone will not work, neither let him eat" (2 Thess. 3:10). The slave's self-congratulating stupidity creates sacred incenses with the exhalations of human sweat, hence expressions such as "Work ennobles man"; "The religion of work"; and "Work as a social and ethical duty." We have previously learned that the ancient world despised work only because it knew *action;* the opposition of action to work as an opposition between the spiritual, pure, and free pole, and the material, impure pole impregnated only with human possibilities, was at the basis of that contempt. The loss of the sense of this opposition, and the animal-like subordination of the former to the latter, characterizes the last ages. And where in ancient times every work, through an inner transfiguration owing to its purity and its meaning as an "offering" oriented upwards could redeem itself until it became a symbol of action, now, following an upheaval in the opposite direction (which can be observed during the age of the serfs), every residue of action tends to be degraded to the form of work. The degeneration of the ancient aristocratic and sacred ethics into the modern plebeian and materialistic morality is expressively characterized by such a shift from the plane of action to the plane of work. Superior men who lived in a not so distant past, either *acted* or *directed* actions. Modern man *works.*[4] The only real difference today is that which exists between the various kinds of work; there are "intellectual" workers and those who use their limbs and machines. In any event, the notion of "action" is dying out in the modern world, together with that of "absolute personality." Moreover, among all the commissioned arts, antiquity regarded as most disgraceful those devoted to the pursuit of pleasure *(minimaeque artes eas probandae, quae ministrae sunt voluptatum),*[5] this, after all, is precisely the kind of work respected the most in this day and age. Beginning with the scientist, technician, and politician, and with the rationalized system of productive organization, "work" supposedly leads to the realization of an ideal more fitting for a human animal: an easier life that is more enjoyable and safer with the maximization of one's well-being and physical comfort. The contemporary breed of artists and of "creative minds" of the bourgeoisie is the equivalent of that class of "luxury servants" that catered to the pleasure and distractions of the Roman patriciate and later on, of the medieval feudal lords.

Then again, while the themes proper to this degradation find their most characteristic expressions on the social plane and in contemporary life, they do not fail to make an appearance on the ideal and speculative plane. It was precisely during the age of humanism that the antitraditional and plebeian theme emerged in the views of Giordano Bruno who, by inverting traditional values, extolled the age of human effort and work over and against the Golden Age (of which he knew absolutely nothing) in a masochistic fashion and with authentic stupidity. Bruno called "divine" the brutish drive of human need, since such a drive is responsible for producing "increasingly wonderful arts and inventions," for removing mankind further from that Golden Age that he regarded as animalistic and lazy, and for drawing human beings closer to God.[6] In all this we find an anticipation of those ideologies that, by virtue of being significantly connected to the age of the French Revolution, regarded work as the main element of the social myth and revived the messianic theme in terms of work and machines, all the while singing the praises of progress. Moreover, modern man, whether consciously or unconsciously, began to apply to the universe and project on an ideal plane the experiences that he nurtured in the workshops and factories and by which the soul became a *product.*

Bergson, who exalted the *élan vital,* is the one who drew the analogy as only a modern could between technical productive activity inspired by a mere practical

4. O. Spengler, *The Decline of the West* (1918; London, 1926), vol. 1. The term "action" is here used as synonymous with a spiritual and disinterested activity; thus it may be applied to contemplation, which in the classical idea was often regarded as the most pure form of activity; it had its object and goal in itself and did not need "anything else" in order to be implemented.

5. Cicero, *De officiis,* 1.42.

6. Giordano Bruno, *Spaccio della Bestia trionfante,* dialogue 3.

principle and the ways of intelligence itself. Having covered with ridicule the ancient "inert" ideal of knowledge as contemplation,

> The entire effort of modern epistemology in its most radical trajectories consists in assimilating knowledge to productive work, according to the postulates: "To know is to do" and "One can only really know what one does."[7]

Verum et factum convertuntur. And since according to the unrealism typical of these currents, *(a)* "to be" means "to know"; *(b)* the spirit is identified with the idea; and *(c)* the productive and immanent knowing process is identified with the process of reality, the way of the fourth caste is reflected in the highest regions and posits itself as their foundational "truth." Likewise, there is an activism on the plane of philosophical theories that appears to be in agreement with the world created by the advent of the last caste and its "civilization of work."

Generally speaking, this advent is reflected in the abovementioned modern ideologies of "progress" and "evolution," which have distorted with a "scientific" irresponsibility any superior vision of history, promoted the definitive abandonment of traditional truths, and created the most specious alibis for the justification and glorification of modern man. The myth of evolutionism is nothing else but the profession of faith of the upstart. If in recent times the West does not believe in a transcendent origin but rather an origin "from below"; and if the West no longer believes in the nobility of the origins but in the notion that civilization arises out of barbarism, religion from superstition, man from animal (Darwin), thought from matter, and every spiritual form from the "sublimation" or transposition of the stuff that originates the instinct, libido, and complexes of the "collective unconscious" (Freud, Jung), and so on—we can see in all this not so much the result of a deviated quest, but rather, and above all, an alibi, or something that a civilization created by both lower beings and the revolution of the serfs and pariahs against the ancient aristocratic society necessarily *had* to believe in and wish to be true. There is not a dimension in which, in one form or another, the evolutionary myth has not succeeded in infiltrating with destructive consequences; the results have been the overthrow of every value, the suppression of all sense of truth, the elaboration and connecting together (as in an unbreakable magical circle) of the world inhabited by a deconsecrated and deluded mankind. In agreement with historicism, so-called post-Hegelian Idealism came to identify the essence of the "Absolute Spirit" with its "becoming" and its "self-creation"—this Spirit was no longer conceived as a Being that *is,* that dominates,

---

7. A. Tilgher, *Homo Faber,* 120–21.

and that possesses itself; the self-made man has almost become the new metaphysical model.

It is not easy to separate the process of regression along the way of gold (age of merchants) from the regression along the way of work (age of serfs), since these ways are interdependent. For all practical purposes, just as today work as a universal duty is no longer perceived as a repugnant, absurd, and unnatural value, likewise, to be paid does not seem repugnant but on the contrary, it seems very natural. Money, which no longer "burns" the hands it touches, has established an invisible bond of slavery that is worse and more depraved than that which the high spiritual "stature" of lords and conquerors used to retain and justify.

Just as any form of action tends to become yet another form of work, so is it always associated with payment. And while on the one hand action reduced to work is judged by its efficiency in contemporary societies, just as man is valued by his practical success and by his profit; and while, as someone has remarked, Calvin acted as a pimp by seeing that profit and wealth were shrouded in the mysticism of a divine election—on the other hand, the specter of hunger and unemployment lurks upon these new slaves as a more fearful threat than the threat of the whip in ancient times.

In any event, it is possible to distinguish a general phase in which the yearning for profit displayed by single individuals who pursue wealth and power is the central motif (the phase that corresponds to the advent of the third caste) from a further phase that is still unfolding, characterized by a sovereign economy that has become almost independent or collectivized (the advent of the last caste).

In this regard, it is interesting to note that the regression of the principle of "action" to the form proper to the inferior castes (work, production) is often accompanied by an analogous regression with regard to the principle of "asceticism." What arises is almost a new asceticism of gold and work, because as it is exemplified by representative figures of this phase, to work and amass a fortune become things that are yearned for and loved for their own sake, as if they were a vocation. Thus we often see, especially in America, powerful capitalists who enjoy their wealth less than the last of their employees; rather than owning riches and being free from them and thus employing them to fund forms of magnificence, quality, and sensibility for various precious and privileged spectacles (as was the case in ancient aristocracies), these people appear to be merely the managers of their fortunes. Rich though they may be, they pursue an increasing number of activities; it is almost as if they were impersonal and ascetical instruments whose activity is devoted to gathering, multiplying, and casting into ever wider nets (that sometimes affect the lives of millions of people and the destinies of entire nations) the faceless forces of money and of production.[8] *Fiat productio, pereat homo,* Sombart correctly remarked when noticing that the spiritual destruction and emptiness that man has created around himself, after he became *"homo economicus"* and a great capitalist entrepreneur, force him to turn his activity (profit, business, prosperity) into an end in itself, to love it and will it for its own sake lest he fall victim to the vertigo of the abyss and the horror of a life that is totally meaningless.[9]

Even the relationship of the modern economy to machines is significant with regard to the arousal of forces that surpass the plans of those who initially evoked them and carry everything along with them. Once all interest for anything superior and transcendent was either lost or laughed at, the only reference point remaining was man's need, in a purely material and animal sense. Moreover, the traditional principle of the limitation of one's need within the context of a normal economy (a balanced economy based on consumption) was replaced with the principle of acceptance and multiplication of need, which paralleled the so-called Industrial Revolution and the advent of the age of machines. Technological innovations have automatically led mankind from production to overproduction. After the "activist" frenzy was awoken and the frantic circulation of capital—which is multiplied through production in order to be put again in circulation through further productive investments—was set in motion, mankind has finally arrived at a point where the relationship between need and machine (or work) have been totally reversed; it is no longer need that requires mechanical work, but mechanical work (or production) that generates new needs. In a regime of superproduction, in order for all the products to be sold it is necessary that the needs of single individuals, far from being reduced, be maintained and even multiplied so that consumption may increase and the mechanism be kept running in order to avoid the fatal congestion that would bring about one of the following two consequences: either war, understood as the means for a violent affirmation by a greater economic and productive power that claims not to have "enough space," or unemployment (industrial shutdowns as a response to the crisis on the job market and in consumerism) with its ensuing crises and social tensions precipitating the insurrection of the Fourth Estate.

As a fire starts another fire until an entire area goes up in flames, this is how the

---

8. See M. Weber, *Gesammelte Aufsätze zur Religion und Soziologie* (Tübingen, 1924), vol. 3, in which the Protestant roots of such an "ascetical" version of capitalism are discussed. Originally there was a separation between earning as a "vocation" and the enjoyment of riches, the latter being looked down upon as a sinful element of the deification and pride of the human creature. Naturally, in the course of history the original religious considerations were eliminated; today we only find purely secular and unscrupulous forms. [Evola is referring to Weber's *The Protestant Ethic and the Spirit of Capitalism.*]

9. W. Sombart, *Il borghese,* Italian trans. from the French (Paris, 1926), 204–22; 400–409.

economy has affected the inner essence of modern man through the world that he himself created. This present "civilization," starting from Western hotbeds, has extended the contagion to every land that was still healthy and has brought to all strata of society and all races the following "gifts": restlessness, dissatisfaction, resentment, the need to go further and faster, and the inability to possess one's life in simplicity, independence, and balance. Modern civilization has pushed man onward; it has generated in him the need for an increasingly greater number of things; it has made him more and more insufficient to himself and powerless. Thus, every new invention and technological discovery, rather than a conquest, really represents a defeat and a new whiplash in an ever faster race blindly taking place within a system of conditionings that are increasingly serious and irreversible and that for the most part go unnoticed. This is how the various paths converge: technological civilization, the dominant role of the economy, and the civilization of production and consumption all complement the exaltation of becoming and progress; in other words, they contribute to the manifestation of the "demonic" element in the modern world.[10]

Regarding the degenerated forms of asceticism, I would like to point out the spirit of a phenomenon that is more properly connected to the plane of "work" (that is, of the fourth caste). The modern world knows a sublimated version of work in which the latter becomes "disinterested," disjoined from the economic factor and from the idea of a practical or productive goal and takes an almost ascetic form; I am talking about *sport*. Sport is a way of working in which the productive objective no longer matters; thus, sport is willed for its own sake as mere activity. Someone has rightly pointed out that sport is the "blue collar" religion.[11] Sport is a typical counterfeit of action in the traditional sense of the word. A pointless activity, it is nevertheless still characterized by the same triviality of work and belongs to the same physical and lightless group of activities that are pursued at the various crossroads in which plebeian contamination occurs. Although through the practice of sport it is possible to achieve a temporary evocation of deep forces, what this amounts to is the enjoyment of sensations and a sense of vertigo and at most, the excitement derived from directing one's energies and winning a competition—without any higher and transfiguring reference, any sense of "sacrifice" or deindividualizing offering being present. Physical individuality is cherished and strengthened by sport; thus the chain is confirmed and every residue of subtler sensibility is suffocated. The human being,

---

10. The word "demonic" is obviously not to be understood in the Christian sense of the word. The expression "demonic people" found in the *Bhagavadgītā* applies very much to our contemporaries: "Thus they are beset with innumerable cares which last long, all their life, until death. Their highest aim is sensual enjoyment, and they firmly think that this is all" (16.11).
11. A. Tilgher, *Homo Faber*, 162.

instead of growing into an organic being, tends to be reduced to a bundle of reflexes, and almost to a mechanism. It is also very significant that the lower strata of society are the ones that show more enthusiasm for sports, displaying their enthusiasm in great collective forms. Sport may be identified as one of the forewarning signs of that type of society represented by Chigalev in Dostoyevsky's *The Obsessed;* after the required time has elapsed for a methodical and reasoned education aimed at extirpating the evil represented by the "I" and by free will, and no longer realizing they are slaves, all the Chigalevs will return to experience the innocence and the happiness of a new Eden. This "Eden" differs from the biblical one only because work will be the dominating universal law. Work as sport and sport as work in a world that has lost the sense of historical cycles, as well as the sense of true personality, would probably be the best way to implement such a messianic ideal. Thus, it is not a coincidence that in several societies, whether spontaneously or thanks to the state, great sports organizations have arisen as the appendices of various classes of workers, and vice versa.

36

Nationalism and Collectivism

If the apex of traditional civilizations consisted in the principle of universalism, then modern civilization is essentially under the aegis of collectivism. The collective is to the universal what "matter" is to "form." The first step of what in a traditional sense has always been regarded as "culture" consists in the differentiation of the promiscuous substance of the collective and in the affirmation of personal beings through adherence to superior principles and interests. When the single individual has succeeded in giving a law and a form to his own nature and thus in belonging to himself rather than depending on the merely physical part of his being, then the preliminary condition for a superior order—in which the personality is not abolished but integrated—is already present; such is the order of traditional "participations" in which every individual, function, and caste acquire their right place and reason for being through the acknowledgment of what is superior to them and their organic connection with it. At best, the universal is achieved in the sense of the crowning part of a building, the strong foundations of which consist of both the various differentiated and formed personalities, each one faithful to its own function, and in partial organisms or units endowed with corresponding laws and rights that do not contradict each other but rather coordinate and complement each other through a common spirituality and a common active propensity to a superindividual commitment.

From what has been said previously it is possible to see that in modern society the opposite direction is prevailing, that is, the direction of regress toward the collective rather than progress toward the universal, with the single individual becoming increasingly unable to have a meaning other than as a function of something in which he ceases to have a personality. This becomes increasingly evident as the world of the Fourth Estate approaches. Thus, modern nationalism may be regarded as at best a transition phase.

It is necessary to distinguish between nationality and nationalism. The Middle Ages knew nationalities but not nationalisms. Nationality is a natural factor that encompasses a certain group of common elementary characteristics that are retained

338

both in the hierarchical differentiation and in the hierarchical participation, which they do not oppose. Therefore, during the Middle Ages, castes, social bodies, and orders were articulated within various nationalities, and while the types of the warrior, noble, merchant, and artisan conformed to the characteristics of this or of that nation, these articulations represented at the same time wider, international units. Hence, the possibility for the members of the same caste who came from different nations to understand each other better than the members of different castes within the same nation.

Modern nationalism represents, with regard to this, a movement in the opposite direction. Modern nationalism is not based on a natural unity, but on an artificial and centralizing one. The need for this type of unity was increasingly felt at the same time as the natural and healthy sense of nationality was lost and as individuals approached the state of pure quantity, of being merely the masses, after every authentic tradition and qualitative articulation was destroyed. Nationalism acts upon these masses through myths and suggestions that are likely to galvanize them, awaken elementary instincts in them, flatter them with the perspectives and fancies of supremacy, exclusivism, and power. Regardless of its myths, the substance of modern nationalism is not an *ethnos* but a demos, and its prototype always remains the plebeian one produced by the French Revolution.

This is why nationalism has a double face. It accentuates and elevates to the state of absolute value a particularistic principle; therefore, the possibilities of mutual understanding and cooperation between nations are reduced to a bare minimum, without even considering the forms of leveling guaranteed by modern civilization. What seems to continue here is the same tendency through which the arising of national states corresponded to the disintegration of the European ecumene. It is well known that in Europe during the nineteenth century, nationalism was synonymous with revolution and acted in the precise sense of a dissolution of the surviving supernational organisms and a weakening of the political principle of "legitimate" sovereignty in the traditional sense of the word. Yet, when considering the relationships between the whole and the single individual as personality, what emerges in nationalism is an opposite aspect, namely, the cumulative and collectivizing element. In the context of modern nationalism what emerges is the previously mentioned inversion; the nation, the homeland, becomes the primary element in terms of being a self-subsisting entity that requires from the individual belonging to it an unconditional dedication, as if it were a moral and not merely a natural and "political" entity. Even culture stops being the support for the formation and elevation of the person and becomes essentially relevant only by virtue of its national character. Thus in the most radical forms of nationalism, the liberal ideal and the ideal of "neutral culture" undergo a crisis and are regarded with suspicion, though from the opposite perspective to the one in which liberalism and the neutral, secular, and apolitical culture appeared as a degeneration or as a crumbling in comparison to previous organic civilizations.

Even when nationalism speaks of "tradition," it has nothing to do with what used to go by that name in ancient civilizations; it is rather a myth or fictitious continuity based on a minimum common denominator that consists in the mere belonging to a given group. Through the concept of "tradition," nationalism aims at consolidating a collective dimension by placing behind the individual the mythical, deified, and collectivized unity of all those who preceded him. In this sense, Chesterton was right to call this type of tradition "the democracy of the dead." Here the dimension of transcendence, or of what is superior to history, is totally lacking.

According to these aspects, it can be said that modern nationalism on the one hand confirms the renunciation of the pursuit of the upwards-oriented direction and the unification through what is supernatural and potentially universal, while on the other hand it distinguishes itself only by virtue of a mere difference of degree from the anonymity proper to the ideal of the Fourth Estate with its "Internationals," bent, as a matter of principle, on perverting every notion of homeland and of the national state. In reality, wherever the people have become sovereign and the king or the leader is no longer considered as being "from above," or to be ruling "by God's grace," but instead "by the will of the nation" (even where the expression "to rule by God's grace" has been preserved, it amounts to an empty formula)—it is precisely at this point that the abyss that separates a political organism of a traditional type from communism is virtually overcome—the fracture has occurred, all the values have shifted and been turned upside down; at this point one can only wait for the final stage to be ushered in. Thus, it is more than for mere tactical purposes that the leaders of world subversion in the last form, as it has been embodied in Soviet communism, have as their main goal the excitement, nourishing, and supporting of nationalism even where nationalism, by virtue of being anticommunist, should at least in principle turn against them. They see far away, just like those who employed nationalism for their own purposes during the early revolution (i.e., liberalism) when they said "nation" but really meant "antitradition" or the denial of the principle of true sovereignty. They recognize the collective potential of nationalism, which beyond contingent antitheses will finally dispose of the organisms that it controls.

Hence, the difference in degree between nationalism and the tendencies of a democratic and communitarian character that oppose the forces of particularism and spirit of division inherent in nationalism. In these tendencies the regressive phenomenon that is at the foundation of modern nationalism is also visible; at work in it is the impulse toward a wider agglomerate, leveled on a global scale. As Julian Benda said, the last perspective is that humanity, and not just a fraction of it, will take itself as the object of its cult. There is today a trend toward universal brotherhood; this brotherhood, far from abolishing the nationalist spirit and its particularisms and pride, will eventually become its supreme form, as the nation will be called Man and God will be regarded either as an enemy[1] or as an "inoperative fiction." When mankind becomes unified in an immense enterprise and accustomed to organized production, technology, division of labor, and "prosperity," despising any free activity oriented to transcendence, it will achieve what in similar currents is conceived as the ultimate goal of the true civilizing effort.[2]

One final consideration concerning modern nationalism: while on the one hand it corresponds to a construction and an artificial entity, on the other hand, through the power of the myths and the confusing ideas that are evoked in order to hold together and galvanize a given human group, this entity remains open to influences that make it act according to the general plan of subversion. Modern nationalisms, with their intransigence, blind egoism and crude will to power, their antagonisms, social unrest and the wars they have generated have truly been the instruments for the completion of a destructive process: the shift from the age of the Third Estate to that of the Fourth Estate; in so doing they have dug their own graves.

Europe had the chance, if not to stop, at least to contain the disaggregative process in a rather wide geopolitical area after the fall of Napoleon who, though he revived the imperial symbol and yearned for a Roman consecration, still remained "the son of the Great Revolution," the virus of which he helped to spread into the remaining states of traditional and aristocratic Europe as a result of the upheavals brought about by his victorious campaigns. Through the Holy Alliance it would have been possible to create a dam against the fate of the last times. Metternich may rightly be considered the last great European. Nobody was able to see like him with the same far-sighted lucidity and the same overall view the interplay of subversive forces as well as the only way immediately to neutralize them.

Metternich saw all the most essential points: that revolutions are not spontaneous outbursts or mass phenomena, but rather artificial phenomena that are provoked by forces that have the same function in the healthy body of people and states that bacteria have in the generation of diseases in the human body; that nationalism, as it emerged in his own day and age, was only the mask of revolution; that revolution was essentially an international event and that the individual revolutionary phenomena are only localized and partial manifestations of the same subversive current of global proportions. Metternich also saw very clearly the concatenation of the various degrees of revolution; liberalism and constitutionalism unavoidably pave the way for

---

1. Proudhon had already declared that the true remedy does not consist in identifying mankind with God, but in proving that God, if he exists, is mankind's sworn enemy.
2. J. Benda, *The Treason of the Clerics.*

democracy, which in turn paves the way for socialism, which in turn paves the way for radicalism and finally for communism—the entire liberal revolution of the Third Estate only being instrumental in preparing the way for the revolution of the Fourth Estate, which is destined to inexorably remove the representatives of the former and their world as soon as they have completed their assignment as the avant-garde in charge of opening a breach. This is why Metternich saw folly in coming to terms with subversion: if you give it a hand it will soon take the arm and the rest of the body as well. Having understood the revolutionary phenomenon in its unity and essence, Metternich indicated the only possible antidote: a similar supernational front of all the traditional states and the establishment of a defensive and offensive league of all the monarchs of divine right. This is what his Holy Alliance was meant to be.

Unfortunately, the material and spiritual requirements for the full implementation of this grandiose idea were lacking. Around Metternich there were not enough capable men and leaders. The unity of a defensive front on the political and social plane was a clear and evident concept; what was not so clear was the idea that was capable of being a positive reference point and a chrism for this alliance so that it could really be *holy*. To begin with, in the context of religion there was no unity, since the league was not limited only to Catholic monarchs, but it also included Protestant and Orthodox ones as well; thus, this alliance did not even have the direct and immediate sanction of the Catholic Church, the head of which never joined it. What was really needed was a revival of the spirit of the Middle Ages, better yet, of the Crusades; what was really needed was not just the mere repressive action and the commitment to military intervention wherever a revolutionary flame began to flicker within the territories covered by the alliance, but rather something like a new Templarism, an order, a block of men united by a common idea and relentless in action who could give in every country a living witness to the return of a superior human type. Men such as these were needed rather than the courtiers, ministers of police, prudent Church leaders, and diplomats only concerned with finding a "balanced solution." At the same time, an attack should have been launched on the ideal plane for a view of the world and of life. But who were the representatives of the pure traditional spirit who in that period would have been capable of extirpating the hotbeds of the rationalistic, illuministic, and scientistic mentality that were the true ferment of the revolution? Where were those who would have disavowed that culture that, beginning in the 1700s, the royal courts and the aristocracies found it fashionable to be part of, or those who would have been able to cover with ridicule rather than with chains all those who romantically portrayed themselves as the apostles and martyrs of the "great and noble ideas of the revolution" and the "freedom of the people"? Lacking a true soul and having jumped at the center of Europe's attention at the time when the Holy Roman Empire had ceased to exist even nominally—

owing to the voluntary renunciation of the Hapsburgs—Vienna was famous mainly as the "city of waltzes." The Holy Alliance, after ensuring a parenthesis of relative peace and order in Europe, was eventually dissolved and revolutionary nationalisms, which disintegrated the previous political and dynastic units, no longer found any tough resistance to halt their onslaught.

With World War I, the Russian Revolution, and World War II the decisive events of the last age are ushered in. In 1914 the central empires still represented within the Western world a remainder of the feudal and aristocratic Europe, despite the undeniable aspects of militaristic hegemonism and some questionable collusions with capitalism, especially in Wilhelm's Germany. The coalition against the central empires was expressly a coalition of the Third Estate against the residual forces of the Second; it was a coalition of nationalisms and the great democracies more or less inspired by the "immortal principles" of the French Revolution, which some people wanted to replicate on an international scale and which fact did not prevent the humanitarian and patriotic ideology from playing into the hands of a greedy and supremacist high finance. As few other times before, World War I displays the traits of a conflict not between states and nations, but rather between ideologies of different castes. The immediate and willfully pursued results of this war were the destruction of the German monarchy and Catholic Austria; the indirect results were the collapse of the Czars' empire, the communist revolution, and the establishment in Europe of a sociopolitical situation that was so chaotic and contradictory as to contain all the premises of a new conflagration.

World War II was this new conflagration. In this war the ideological line-ups were not as precise as in the previous war. States like Germany and Italy that had appropriated the authoritarian and antidemocratic idea and had sided against left-wing forces, by their initially upholding in this war the right of "nations in need of living space" as they struggled against world plutocracy, almost appeared to espouse Marxism on the international plane by giving to the war they waged the meaning of an insurrection of the Fourth Estate against the great democracies in which the power of the Third Estate had been consolidated. But overall, and especially after the United States entered into the conflict, what appeared to be a prevalent ideology was one that had already shaped World War I, namely, the crusade of the democratic nations bent on "liberating" the people still enslaved to what were looked upon as "back-

3. With regard to the dubious ideological alignments during World War II, one should notice in the two powers of the Axis, Italy and Germany, the negative element proper to "totalitarianism" and the new forms of dictatorial "Bonapartism." With regard to the other power of the Tripartite Pact (Japan), it would have been interesting to see the results of an unprecedented experiment, that is, of an external "Europeanization" coupled with an internal retention of the traditional spirit of an empire of divine right. Concerning the appraisal of both positive and negative elements of Fascism, see my *Il fascismo: saggio di una analisi critica dal punto di vista della Destra* (Rome, 1964).

ward political systems."[3] The latter was destined rapidly to become a mere facade with regard to new political alignments. In their alliance with the Soviet Union, which was willed in order to bring down the powers of the Axis, and in their persevering in a mindless radicalism, the democratic powers repeated the error of those who think they can employ with impunity and for their own purposes the forces of subversion, and who, by following a fatal logic, ignore the fact that when the forces representing two different degrees of subversion meet or clash, those corresponding to the higher degree will eventually prevail. In reality it can clearly be seen how, from the Soviet side, the "democratic crusade" had been conceived only as a preparatory stage in the global plans of communism. The end of the war marked the end of the hybrid alliance and the real outcome of World War II was the elimination of Europe as a main protagonist in world politics, the sweeping away of any intermediate form, and the opposition of America and Russia as supernational exponents of the forces of the Third and Fourth Estates, respectively.

It really does not matter what the outcome of an eventual conflict between these two powers will be. The determinisms of some kind of immanent justice are at work; in any event, the process will reach the end. A third world war in its social repercussions will eventually determine the triumph of the Fourth Estate, either in a violent way, or as an "evolution," or in both forms.

There is more. On the plane of the political powers pursuing world domination, Russia and America appear today in an antagonistic relationship. And yet if one examines in their essence the dominant themes in both civilizations, and if their ideals are closely scrutinized as well as the effective transformations that, following a central tendency, all the values and the interests of life have undergone in both of them, then it is possible to notice a convergence and a congeniality. Russia and America appear as two different expressions of the same thing, as two ways leading to the formation of that human type that is the ultimate conclusion of the processes that preside over the development of the modern world. It may be worthwhile to focus briefly on these convergences. Not only as political convergences but also as "civilizations," Russia and America are like two ends of the same pair of pincers, that are closing in from the East and the West around the nucleus of ancient Europe, which is too depleted in its energies and in its men to put up an effective resistance. The external conflicts, new crises, and new destructions will only be the means to definitely open the way for the varieties of the world of the Fourth Estate.

37

The End of the Cycle

RUSSIA

In the Bolshevik revolution there are some traits worth examining. The revolution had very few of the romantic, stormy, chaotic, and irrational overtones that characterized other revolutions, especially the French one; on the contrary, it was intelligently planned and well executed. Lenin himself, from beginning to end, studied the problem of proletarian revolution like a mathematician dealing with a complex calculus problem by analyzing it in a detached and lucid way in all of its details. He was quoted as saying: "Martyrs and heroes are not necessary to the cause of the revolution; what the revolution needs is sound logic and an iron hand. Our task is not to lower the revolution to the level of the amateur, but to transform the amateur into a revolutionary." The counterpart of this view was Trotsky's activity, which made of the uprising and of the coup d'état not so much a problem of the masses and of the people, but rather a technique requiring the employment of specialized and well-directed teams.[1]

In the leaders of the Bolshevik revolution it is possible to detect a ruthless ideological coherence. They were absolutely indifferent to the practical consequences and the countless calamities that derived from the application of abstract principles; to them "man" as such did not exist. It is almost as if in Bolshevism elemental forces became incarnated in a group of men who coupled the fierce concentration typical of a fanatic with the exact logic, method, and focus on the most effective means typical of a technician.

It was only in a second phase, which these leaders gave rise to and largely maintained within preestablished limits, that the uprising of the masses inhabiting the ancient Russian empire, and the regime of terror aimed at frantically extirpating what was connected to the ruling classes, eventually occurred.

---

1. C. Malaparte, *La Technique du coup d'état* (Paris, 1931), 13.

Another characteristic trait was that while previous revolutions almost always escaped from the control of those who had started them and ended up devouring their "children," this happened only to a small degree in Russia, where a continuity of power and terror was firmly established. Even though the logic of the red revolution did not hesitate to eliminate or remove those Bolsheviks who dared to venture outside the orthodox trajectory, and even though it had no regard for individuals and no scruples about the means to be employed for these removals, still, at the center of the revolution there were never relevant crises or oscillations. This is indeed a characteristic as well as sinister trait; it foreshadows an era in which the forces of darkness will no longer work behind the scenes but come out into the open, having found their most suitable incarnation in beings in whom daemonism teams up with a lucid intellect, a method, and a strong will to power. A phenomenon of this kind is one of the most salient characteristics of the terminal point of every cycle.

As far as the communist idea is concerned, anybody who forgets that there are two truths in communism is likely to be deceived. The first "esoteric" truth has a dogmatic and immutable character; it corresponds to the basic tenets of the revolution and is formulated in the writings and in the directives of the early Bolshevik period. The second is a changeable and "realistic" truth, which is forged case by case, often in apparent contrast with the first truth, and characterized by eventual compromises with the ideas of the "bourgeois" world (e.g., the patriotic idea, mitigation in the collectivization of private property, the Slavic myth, and so on). The varieties of this second truth are usually set aside as soon as they have achieved their tactical objective; they are mere instruments at the service of the first truth. Therefore, those who would fall into this trap and believe that Bolshevism is a thing of the past, that it has evolved and that it is going to take on normal forms of government and international relations, are indeed extremely naive.

However, one should not be deceived about the first truth either; the Marxist economic myth is not its primary element. The primary element is the disavowal of every spiritual and transcendent value; the philosophy and the sociology of historical materialism are just expressions of this disavowal and derive from it, not the other way around, and the corresponding communist praxis is but one of the many methods employed systematically to carry it out. Thus, there is an important consequence that can be arrived at by following this path all the way to the end and that is the integration, or better, the disintegration of the single individual into the so-called collective, which rules supreme. In the communist world an important goal is the elimination in man of everything that has the value of autonomous personality and of all that may represent an interest unrelated to the needs of the collectivity. More specifically, the mechanization, disintellectualization, and rationalization of every

346

activity, on every plane, are the means employed to this end, rather than being, as in the last European civilization, the much deplored and passively suffered consequences of fatal processes. Once every horizon is reduced to that of the economy, the machine becomes the center of a new messianic promise and rationalization appears as one of the ways to eliminate the "residues" and the "individualistic rough edges" inherited from the "bourgeois era."

In the USSR, the abolition of private property and enterprise, which exists as a basic idea in the core doctrines of communism beyond various contingent accommodations, represents only an episode and the means to an end. The goal is the realization of collective man and radical materialism in every domain and with an obvious disproportion with regard to anything that may be deduced from any mere economic myth. It is typical of the communist system to regard the "I," the "soul," and the notion of "mine" as bourgeois illusions and prejudices, fixed ideas, and the principles of all evil and disorder from which an adequate, realistic culture and pedagogy must free the man living in the new Marxist-Leninist civilization. This is how a radical elimination of all the individualistic, libertarian, humanist, and romantic falsehoods of the phase I have called "Western unrealism," is achieved. There is a well-known saying by Zinoviev: "In every intellectual I see an enemy of the Soviet power." The will to turn art into art for the use of the masses, to stop art from doing "psychology" and from busying itself with the private concerns of single individuals, and to prevent art from delighting the parasitic higher classes and being an individualistic production is also well-known. The goal is rather to depersonalize art and transform it into "a powerful hammer spurring on the working class to action." That science may prescind itself from politics—that is, from the communist idea as a formative power—and be "objective" is refuted by communist authorities who see in this a dangerous "counterrevolutionary" deviation. An example of this mentality was the case of Vasiliev and the other biologists who were sent to Siberia because the genetic theory that they upheld, which consisted in acknowledging the factors of "heredity" and of "innate disposition" and in viewing man as other than an amorphous substance that takes shape only through the determining action of the environment, as Marxism would have it, did not correspond to the central idea of communism. The most radical theories of evolutionary materialism and sociological scientism found in Western thought are assumed by communism and turned into dogma and into the "official view of the state," the results being the brainwashing of the new generations and the contribution to the diffusion of a specific mentality. Enough is known about the antireligious campaign waged in the USSR, where it does not have the character of mere atheism, but rather of a real counterreligion; the latter betrays the true essence of Bolshevism mentioned above, which thus organizes the most apt means to eliminate the great disease of Western man, namely, that "faith" and need to "believe" that became his surrogates once the contact with the superworld was lost. An "education of feelings" in a similar direction is also contemplated so that the complications of the "bourgeois man," sentimentalism, and the obsession with eroticism and the passions may once and for all be eliminated. After the social classes have been leveled, and considering that only the articulations imposed by technocracy and the totalitarian apparatus are respected, even the sexes are leveled; the complete equality of women with men is sanctioned in every domain since an ideal of communism is to eliminate the differences between men and women, who are henceforth to be considered as "comrades." Thus, even the family is looked down upon, not only according to what it represented in the "age of the heroic right," but also in the residues proper to the bourgeois period. The so-called ZAGS ("registry offices for documents of civil status") represented a characteristic change in this regard. Anyway, it is well-known that in the USSR education is totally in the hands of the state, so that the child may learn to prefer the "collective" life to family life.

In the first constitution of the USSR a foreigner was automatically regarded as a member of the Union of the Soviets if he was a proletarian worker, whereas a Russian, if he was not a proletarian worker, was excluded from this union, denaturalized, and regarded as a pariah lacking a juridical personality.[2] According to strict communist orthodoxy, Russia was simply the country in which the world revolution of the Fourth Estate triumphed and was first organized in order to expand further. In addition to a mysticism of the collectivity, the Russian people have traditionally been characterized by a confused messianic impulse regarding themselves as a God-carrying people predestined to a work of universal redemption. All this was developed in an inverted form and updated in Marxist terms: God was transformed into the materialized and collectivized man, and the "God-carrying people" became the one attempting to impose its civilization on this earth through any available means. The ensuing mitigation of the extremist version of this thesis, exemplified by the stigmatization of Trotskyism, did not prevent the USSR from thinking it had the right and even the duty to intervene anywhere in the world to support the cause of communism.

From a historical point of view, during the Stalinist phase the myth of the "revolution" in the older sense of the word, which was always associated with chaos and

---

2. M. Sertoli, *La costituzione russa* (Florence, 1928), 67–85. This paradoxical situation occurred: once the pariahs organized themselves into an omnipotent organization, they reduced to the status of pariah anybody who adhered to the values and was faithful to the class principles that traditionally defined the nonpariah.

disorder, is already a thing of the past; a new form of social order and unity is pursued through totalitarianism. Society becomes a machine in which there is only one engine, the communist state. Man is just a lever or cog in this machine for which the value of human life is null and any infamy is allowed, and as soon as man opposes it he is immediately swept away and broken by its gears. Matter and spirit are enrolled in a common effort, and thus the USSR appears as a bloc that does not leave anything outside itself; a bloc that is simultaneously state, trust, and church, as well as a political, ideological, and economical-industrial system. This is the ideal of the superstate as the sinister inversion of the traditional organic ideal.

Generally speaking, in the Soviet communist ideal there are aspects in which some sort of peculiar asceticism or catharsis is at work to attain the radical overcoming of the individualistic and humanistic element and the return to the principles of absolute reality and impersonality; and yet this overcoming is upside down, in other words, it is not directed upwards but downwards; not toward the superhuman, but toward the subpersonal; not toward organicism, but toward mechanism; not toward spiritual liberation, but toward total social enslavement.

For practical purposes it does not really matter that the primitivism of the great heteroclite mass that comprises the USSR, in which all the racially superior elements have been eliminated through mass purges, may postpone to an indefinite future the effective formation of the "new man," and the "Soviet man." A *direction* has been imparted. The terminal myth of the world of the Fourth Estate has taken a decisive form and one of the greatest concentrations of power in the world is at its service; this power is the headquarters of all organized actions, whether covert or open, of the instigation of the international masses and of the colored peoples.

AMERICA

Although Bolshevism, according to Lenin's words, saw the Roman and Germanic world as the "greatest obstacle to the advent of the new man," and although, by taking advantage of the blinding of the democratic nations that willed a "crusade" against the powers of the Axis, it has been successful in eliminating that world as far as the direction of European destiny is concerned, as an ideology it has regarded America as some kind of promised land. With the demise of the old gods, the consequence of the exaltation of the technical and mechanical ideal was a kind of "cult of America." "The revolutionary storm of Soviet Russia must join the pace of American life," and, "The task of the new proletarian Russia is to intensify the mechanization already at work in America and to extend it to every domain," have been the official directives. Thus, Gasteff proclaimed "super-Americanism" and the poet Mayakovski celebrated Chicago, the "electro-dynamo-mechanical metropolis," with his collectivist hymn.[3] Obviously here the hated America, regarded as the bulwark of "capitalist imperialism," faded into the background while America as the civilization of the machine, quantity, and technocracy came into the foreground. References to congeniality, far from being extrinsic, may be confirmed in the elements taken from several other domains.

What and how many the divergences are between Russia and America in an ethnic, historical, and temperamental context is well-known and does not require any further illustrations. These divergences, however, are powerless before a fundamental fact; parts of an "ideal" that in Bolshevism either does not exist as such or is imposed with crude means have been realized in America through an almost spontaneous process, so much so as to acquire a natural and evident character. Thus, in a context much wider than he would have ever imagined, Engels' prophecy has been fulfilled, namely, that the world of capitalism would open the way for the Fourth Estate.

America too, in the essential way it views life and the world, has created a "civilization" that represents the exact contradiction of the ancient European tradition. It has introduced the religion of praxis and productivity; it has put the quest for profit, great industrial production, and mechanical, visible, and quantitative achievements over and above any other interest. It has generated a soulless greatness of a purely technological and collective nature, lacking any background of transcendence, inner light, and true spirituality. America has also put the view in which man is considered in terms of quality and personality within an organic system in opposition with that view in which man becomes a mere instrument of production and material productivity within a conformist social conglomerate.

While in the formation process of the Soviet communist mentality the mass-man who lived mystically in the subsoil of the Slavic race has had a relevant role (the only modern feature is the context in which it can carry out its rational incarnation within an omnipotent political structure), in America this phenomenon derives from an inflexible determinism by virtue of which man, in the act of detaching himself from the spiritual dimension and in pursuing a merely temporal greatness, and having overcome all individualist illusions, ceases to belong to himself and becomes a dependent part of an entity that eventually he can no longer control and that conditions him in multiple ways. The ideal of material conquest that is associated with physical well-being and "prosperity" has determined the transformations and the perversions that America represents.

It has been correctly pointed out that:

---

3. R. Fülöp-Miller, *Mind and Face of Bolshevism* (London, 1927). Stalin himself, in his *Principles of Leninism*, declared that the union of the revolutionary spirit and Americanism characterizes the style of Leninism in the work of the party and the state, as well as the complete type of the Leninist activist.

In its race toward richness and power, America has abandoned the axis of freedom in order to follow that of productivity. . . . All the energies, including those related to the ideals and to religion, lead toward the same productive purpose: we are in the presence of a productive society, almost a theocracy of productivity, which is increasingly aiming at producing things rather than people, or people only as more efficient workers . . .

In the U.S., some kind of mysticism surrounds the supreme rights of the community. The human being, having become a means rather than an end in itself, accepts the role of "cog-in-the machine" *without thinking for a second that in the process he may be somewhat belittled.* . . . Hence, a collectivism which is willed by the elites and acritically accepted by the masses, surreptitiously undermines man's autonomy and strictly channels his actions, thus confirming his very abdication without him realizing it. . . . No protests and no reaction of the great American masses ever ensued against the collective tyranny. They accept it freely, as a natural thing, and almost as if it were expedient.[4]

On this basis the same themes emerge, in the sense that even in the more general domain of culture there is a necessary and spontaneous correspondence with the principles that shape the Soviet world.

And therefore, although America is far from banning the culture of intellectuality, it certainly nurtures an instinctive indifference toward it, and to the degree that intellectuality does not become an instrument of something practical, it is almost as if it were a luxury that those who are intent upon serious things (such as "getting rich fast," "volunteer work," and sundry campaigns and lobbies to promote various social issues) should not indulge in. Generally speaking, in the USA, while men work, women get involved in "spiritual issues"; hence the strong percentage of women in countless sects and societies in which spiritualism, psychoanalysis, and counterfeits of Eastern doctrines are mixed with humanitarianism, feminism, and sentimentalism, as well as with social versions of puritanism and scientism—all things that truly reflect the American understanding of "spirituality." And when we see America acquire with its dollars some representatives and works of ancient European culture for the benefit and the enjoyment of the upper crust of the Third Estate, the true center lies elsewhere. In America any inventor who discovers some new tool that

---

4. A. Siegfried, *Les États-Unis d'aujourd'hui* (Paris, 1927), 436, 349, 350. There is another, opposite phenomenon to be considered, represented by the so-called beat generation and by the "hipsters" in whom an existential rebellion of some youth against American civilization has only an anarchist and destructive character, often ending up without any good causes to fight for and lacking a higher reference point. See my *L'arco e la clava*, chap. 14, entitled "Youth, the 'Beats' and Right-wing Anarchists."

will improve production will always win more social approval and acknowledgment than the traditional type of the intellectual; moreover, anything that is profit, reality, or action in the material sense of the word will always be valued more than anything that may derive from a line of aristocratic dignity. Thus, even though America has not officially banished ancient philosophy like communism did, it has done something better; through a William James it has declared that the useful is the criterion of truth and that the value of any concept, even metaphysical ones, should be measured by its practical efficiency, which in the context of the American mentality always ends up meaning "socioeconomic efficiency." So-called pragmatism is one of the more typical features of the entire American civilization; among others are Dewey's theories and so-called behaviorism, this last being the exact reflection of theories developed from Pavlov's studies concerning conditioned reflexes; it totally excludes the existence of an "I" and of a substantial principle called "consciousness." The consequence of this typically "democratic" theory is that anybody can become anything they wish to be, provided a certain amount of training and pedagogy be supplied; in other words man, in himself, is believed to be a shapeless and moldable substance, just like communism wants him to be when it regards as antirevolutionary and anti-Marxist the genetic theory of innate qualities elaborated in the field of biology. The power that advertising enjoys in the USA can be explained by the inner inconsistency and passivity of the American soul, which in many respects displays the two-dimensional characteristics of puberty rather than youth.

Soviet communism officially professes atheism. America does not go that far, and yet without realizing it, and often believing the contrary, it is running down a path in which nothing is left of what in the context of Catholicism had a religious meaning. I have previously discussed what religiosity is reduced to in Protestantism; once every principle of authority and hierarchy has been rejected and religiosity has rid itself of metaphysical interest, dogmas, rituals, symbols, and sacraments, it has thereby been reduced to mere moralism, which in puritan Anglo-Saxon countries, and especially in America, is employed in the service of a conformist collectivity.

Siegfried has correctly pointed out that "the only true American religion is Calvinism, understood as the view according to which the true cell of the social organism is not the individual, but the community," in which wealth is regarded, in one's mind as well as in others', as a sign of divine election. Thus, "it becomes difficult to distinguish between religious aspiration and the pursuit of wealth ... It is regarded as a moral and even as a desirable thing for the religious spirit to become a factor of social progress and of economic development."[5] Consequently, the traditional vir-

5. Op. cit., 35–36, 40, 51.

tues that are required to achieve any supernatural goal eventually come to be regarded as useless and even harmful. In the eyes of a typical American, the ascetic is regarded as one who wastes time, when he is not looked down upon as a social parasite; the hero, in the ancient sense, is regarded as some kind of fanatic or lunatic to be neutralized through pacifism and humanitarianism, while the fanatical puritan moralist is himself surrounded by a bright aura.

Is all this that far off from Lenin's recommendation to ostracize "every view that is supernatural or extraneous to class interests" and wipe out as an infectious disease any residue of independent spirituality? Does not the technocratic ideology arise both in America and in Russia from the ranks of secularized and all-powerful men?[6]

Let us reflect on the following point. Through the New Economic Policy (NEP) in Russia private capitalism was abolished only to be replaced with state capitalism; the latter consisted of a centralized capitalism without any visible capitalists and it engaged in a mastodonic yet hopeless enterprise. In theory, every Soviet citizen was both a worker and an investor in the all-inclusive socialist state. For practical purposes he was an investor who never received dividends; aside from what he was given to make a living, the fruit of his work went to the party, which in turn invested it in other companies and industries without allowing it to stop circulating and to end up in anybody's pocket. The result was the ever greater power of collective man, though not without a specific relation to the plans of global revolution and subversion. Let us recall what has been said about the role that asceticism plays in capitalism (a typically American phenomenon) and about wealth, which in America instead of being the goal of one's work and the means to display a greatness that transcends mere economic fortunes, becomes the means to generate more work, new profits, and so on in an endless and uninterrupted chain. Once we keep this in mind, we will see that in America, what asserts itself here and there in a spontaneous way and in the context of "freedom," is the same style that the centralized structures of the communist state try to realize in a violent way. Moreover, in the appalling size of the American metropolis, in which the individual (the "nomad of the asphalt") realizes his nothingness before the immense reign of quantity, before the groups,

6. The emergence in America of "atheist Christianity" and of the "theologians of the death of God" (such as T. Altizer, Paul van Buren, and J. A. T. Robinson) is a recent and very significant phenomenon. According to this movement, the idea of God in its aspect of transcendence and supernaturalism ought to be dismissed, since it is no longer operative or acceptable to modern man; better yet, modern man should not even be bothered with the term "god," due to the traditional implications of such a term. The only thing to be spared is a "demythologized" and secularized version of Christianity, amounting to nothing more than a social and humanitarian morality.

trusts, and omnipotent standards, before the jungle of skyscrapers and factories, while the dominators are chained to the very things they dominate—in all this the collective dimension is increasingly revealed in a greater form of anonymity than in the tyranny exercised by the Soviet system over its primitive and abulic subjects.

The intellectual standardization, conformism, and mandatory normalization that is organized on a grand scale are typically American phenomena, though they happen to coincide with the Soviet ideal of the "official view of the state" that is to be imposed on the collectivity. It has rightly been observed that every American (whether he be named Wilson or Roosevelt, Bryan or Rockefeller) is an evangelist who cannot leave his fellow men alone, who constantly feels the need to preach and work for the conversion, purification, and elevation of each and everyone to the standard moral level of America, which he believes to be superior and higher than all others. This attitude originated with abolitionism during the Civil War and culminated with the double democratic "crusade" in Europe envisioned by Wilson and by Roosevelt. And yet even in minor matters, whether it be prohibitionism or the feminist, pacifist, or environmental propaganda, we always find the same spirit, the same leveling and standardizing will and the petulant intrusion of the collective and the social dimension in the individual sphere. Nothing is further from the truth than the claim that the American soul is "open-minded" and unbiased; on the contrary, it is ridden with countless taboos of which people are sometimes not even aware.

I have said before that one of the reasons why the Bolshevik ideology took a liking to America is due to the fact that it fully realized how, in the latter's type of civilization, technology contributes to the idea of depersonalization. The moral standard corresponds to the American's practical standard. The comforts available to everyone and the superproduction of consumerist civilization that characterize the USA have been purchased with the enslavement of millions of people to the automatism of work, as if in their work they have been formed by an extreme level of specialization that narrows the mental field of action and dulls every sensibility. Instead of the type of the artisan, for whom every job was an art and whose production carried the imprint of personality (since it presupposed a personal, direct, and qualitative knowledge of that particular trade), we have today a herd of pariah who dumbly witness the work of machines, the secrets of which are known only to the person in charge of repairing them. Stalin and Ford can be said to meet here, and thus a vicious circle is established; the standardization inherent in every mechanical and quantitative product determines and imposes the standardization on those who purchase them; the uniformity of tastes and progressive reduction to a few types corresponds to what is directly manifested in people's minds. In America everything works toward this goal; conformism in terms of "matter of fact" and "like-mindedness" is the password on all planes of existence. Thus, when the dams are not broken by the phenomenon of organized crime and by other uncontrolled forms of "supercompensation" (I have previously mentioned the "beat generation"), the American soul is protected from any transcendent vocation by its optimistic, sports-minded, and simplistic view of the world.

Thus, the great majority of Americans could be said to represent a refutation on a large scale of the Cartesian principle, *"Cogito ergo sum"*; they "do *not* think *and* are." Better yet, in many cases they are dangerous individuals and in several instances their primitivism goes way beyond the Slavic primitivism of *"homo sovieticus."*

Obviously, the leveling process applies to the sexes as well. The Soviet emancipation of the woman parallels that emancipation that in America the feminist idiocy, deriving from "democracy" all its logical conclusions, had achieved a long time ago in conjunction with the materialistic and practical degradation of man. Through countless and repeated divorces the disintegration of the family in America is characterized by the same pace that we could expect in a society that knows only "comrades." The women, having given up their true nature, believe they can elevate themselves by taking on and practicing all kinds of traditionally masculine activities. These women are chaste in their immorality and banal even in their lowest perversions; quite often they find in alcohol the way to rid themselves of the repressed or deviated energies of their own nature. Moreover, young women seem to know very little of the polarity and the elemental magnetism of sex as they indulge in a comradely and sportive promiscuity. These phenomena are typically American, even though their contagious diffusion all over the world makes it difficult for people to trace their origin to America. Actually, if there is a difference between this promiscuity and that envisioned by communism, it is resolved in a pejorative sense by a gynaecocratic factor, since every woman and young girl in America and other Anglo-Saxon countries considers it only natural that some kind of preeminence and existential respectability be bestowed upon her as if it were her inalienable right.[7]

In the early days of Bolshevism somebody formulated the ideal of a cacophonous, collectivist music that was meant to purify music itself of its sentimental bourgeois content. This is what America has realized on a large scale and spread all over the world through a very significant phenomenon: jazz. In the ballrooms of American cities where hundreds of couples shake like epileptic and automatic puppets to the sounds of black music, what is awakened is truly a "mass state" and the life of a mechanized collective entity. Very few phenomena are so indicative of the general

---

7. This is also reflected in the incredible severity of the penal sanctions that in some states (including the death penalty) are being meted out for "sexual crimes" against women.

structure of the modern world in its last phase as this, since what characterizes it is the coexistence of a mechanical, inanimate element consisting in movement of a primitivist and subpersonal type that transports man into a climate of turbid sensations ("a petrified forest wrecked by chaos," said H. Miller). Moreover, what in Bolshevism was programmed and occasionally realized in theatrical representations of the awakening of the proletarian world in view of a systematic activation of the masses, in America found its equivalent long ago but on a larger scale and in a spontaneous form; I am referring to the senseless delirium of sporting events, which are based on a plebeian and materialistic degradation of the cult of action. These frenzies represent the phenomena of the incursion of the collective and the regression into the collective.

Walt Whitman, the American poet and mystic of democracy, may be regarded as the forerunner of that "collective poetry" that urges one to action, which is one of the communist ideals and programs. A similar kind of lyricism permeates several aspects of the American life: sports, ceaseless activity, productivity, and volunteer work. Just as in the case of the USSR we can only wait for adequate developments to resolve the primitivist and chaotic residues of the Slavic soul, likewise, in America one can logically expect the individualistic residues of the spirit of the cowboys, pioneers, and what is still to transpire from the deeds of gangsters and anarchical existentialists to be eventually reduced and taken up in the mainstream.

If this was the proper context, it would be easy to produce more evidence concerning the similarities between the two countries that would allow us to see in communist Russia and in America two faces of the same coin, or two movements whose destructive paths converge. The former is a reality unfolding under the iron fist of a dictatorship and through a radical nationalization and rationalization. The latter is a spontaneous realization (and therefore more worrisome) of a mankind that accepts and even *wants* to be what it is, that feels healthy, free, and strong and that implements the same tendencies as communism but without the fanatical and fatalistic dedication of the communist Slav. And yet, behind both "civilizations" those who have eyes to see can detect the warning signs of the advent of the "Nameless Beast."

Despite all, there are some who still believe that American "democracy" is the antidote for Soviet communism and the only alternative for the so-called free world. Generally speaking, a danger is clearly recognized in the presence of a brutal, physical attack from the outside but not one coming from the inside. For quite some time Europe has been under the influence of America and therefore has undergone the perversion of traditional values and ideals inherent in the North American world. This has happened as some sort of fatal reaction. America represents a "Far West," and it contains the further and radical development of the basic trends that have been adopted by modern Western civilization. Thus, it is not possible to put up a valid resistance to the modern world while still holding on to the principles and especially to the technological and productive mirage on which this world is based. With the development of this accelerating influence, chances are that the closing of the pincers from East and West around a Europe, which following World War II, has no new ideas to offer and that ceased to enjoy the rank of an autonomous and hegemonic world power even in the political arena, will not even be perceived with a sense of capitulation. The final collapse will not even have the character of a tragedy.

The communist world and America, in their being persuaded of having a universal mission to accomplish, represent a reality to be reckoned with. An eventual conflict between them will be, on the plane of world subversion, the last of the violent operations and will require the beastly holocaust of millions of human lives; and so, the last phase of the involution and shift of power through all four traditional castes and the advent of a collectivized humanity will eventually be achieved. And · even if the feared catastrophe of a nuclear holocaust is averted, this civilization of titans, iron, crystal, and cement metropolises, of swarming masses, statistics, and technology that keeps the forces of matter at the leash will appear as a world that wobbles in its orbit; one day it will wrest itself free and lose itself in a space in which there is no light other than the sinister glow cast by the acceleration of its own fall.

Conclusion

Those who have been forced by the sheer evidence of the facts to acknowledge what they have called "the decline of the West," usually make their considerations follow various appeals aimed at erecting some defenses or provoking reactions. I personally do not have any illusions nor do I want to delude others or abandon what I consider a sober and objective perception of reality for the consolation provided by an easy and cheap optimism.

The only ones who can still harbor some hope are those who have accepted conditioned perspectives, and who are suffering from the very "disease" they are attempting to defeat. Conversely, those who, having assumed as reference points the spirit and forms that characterize every authentic and traditional civilization, were able to travel upstream to the origins and see the phases of the unfolding of history, are also aware of the immense effort it would take not only to return, but even to approximate a normal (traditional) social order. These people are therefore bound to see the future differently from other people.

The reader will have to acknowledge that the transformations and the events the West has undergone so far are not arbitrary and contingent, but rather proceed from a very specific chain of causes. I am not espousing the perspective of determinism since I believe that in this chain there is no fate at work other than the one that men have created for themselves. The "river" of history flows along the riverbed it has carved for itself. It is not easy, however, to think it possible to reverse the flow when the current has become overwhelming and all too powerful. Those who deny that some kind of determinism was at work in the process of the "fall" must also admit that there is no determinism in the opposite sense, in other words, it still has to be established whether, after the end of a cycle, a new ascending phase will be continuous with the previous ones.

In any event, the West can be saved only by a return to the traditional spirit in the context of a new unitary European consciousness. What could possibly be the basis for such a return?

I said: "in the context of a unitary European consciousness." This is the real dilemma. The West needs to return to tradition in a large, universal, unanimous way that encompasses every form of life and of light; in the sense, that is, of a unitary spirit and order that may rule supreme over every man, in every group and people in every sector of existence. I am not referring to tradition in an aristocratic and secret sense, as the deposit entrusted to a few or to an elite acting behind the scenes of history. Tradition has always existed in this subterranean sense and it still exists today; it will never get lost because of any contingency affecting the destinies of people. And yet the presence of Tradition in this sense has not prevented the decline of Western civilization. Somebody has correctly remarked that Tradition is a precious vein, but only a vein. There is a need for other veins; besides, all the veins must converge, although only the central and occult vein dominates by going underground.[1] Unless the right environment is present, there is no resonance. If the inner and outer conditions that allow all human activities to acquire again a meaning are lacking; if the people do not ask *everything* of life and by elevating it to the dignity of a rite and an offering do not orient it around a nonhuman axis—then every effort is vain, there is no seed that will bear fruit, and the action of an elite remains paralyzed.

Today, these conditions do not exist. Man, like never before, has lost every possibility of contact with metaphysical reality and with everything that is before and behind him. It is not a matter of creeds, philosophies, or attitudes; all these things ultimately do not matter. As I said at the beginning, in modern man there is a materialism that, through a legacy of centuries, has become almost a structure and a basic trait of his being. This materialism, without modern man being aware of it, kills every possibility, deflects every intent, paralyzes every attempt, and damns every effort, even those oriented to a sterile, inorganic, artificial construction. The following factors contribute to strengthening this yoke: *(a)* the lifestyle and all the contingencies of daily life from which none of our contemporaries may remove themselves; *(b)* the type of education prevalent today; *(c)* everything that consciously or unconsciously is experienced as a conditioning and an influence originating from the environment and from the collective psyche; *(d)* the idols, prejudices, forms of judgment and feeling of the false conscience and the false action rooted in man's spirit. What is really needed is a total catharsis and a radical "housecleaning" capable of liberating man from his false "self," the things he takes pride in, his works, hopes, and fears. Indeed, the tide of "progress" has been very powerful if this, and nothing short of it, is what is needed for a transcendent reference point to be acknowledged again and for an absolute, traditional *fides* to appear again, bestow on everything (man included) a new meaning, and reabsorb and redeem in a new purity everything

1. Guido De Giorgio, "Ascesi e Anti-Europa," *Introduzione alla magia*, 2.194.

that has been profaned and degraded. But if such a work of inner liberation can hardly be achieved by single individuals, how could it be conceived for the masses? If it is beyond the reach of those who keep playing with the fetishes of science, art, history, faith and philosophy, how could it be within reach of the masses caught in the web of collectivism and swept away by the omnipotence of the economic and technological element, the frenzy of activism, political passions, and everything that converges in a demonic ideal of power or illusory and shallow prosperity?

Moreover, the West seems to be lacking a superior idea capable of becoming the basis for a realization of the traditional spirit, and even of an approach to it.

Among those who have denounced the crisis of the modern world in the most uncompromising way, there are some who have put their trust in the possibilities inherent in Catholicism. By acknowledging that if the West has ever had an order that conformed to tradition it was thanks to the Church, some have thought that Europe's return to a Catholicism integrated with Tradition may be the way leading to a revival of the West. And yet, this too is an illusion.

First of all, how is it possible that Catholicism may have today that strength to operate a radical and universal conversion of which it has proved itself unable even when there existed material, moral, and intellectual conditions infinitely more advantageous? Would Catholicism be able to take again that body it lost so many centuries ago, a body that today has taken a life and spirit of its own and that science and lay culture have profaned in every fiber? Even when Catholicism formally professes the Christian faith, it no longer represents anything essential or decisive in the actual lives of both individuals and entire nations.

It is not a matter of adaptations and of compromises. The "game" of compromises and adaptations has lasted way too long and it did not prevent the decline of the West. Either religion becomes unanimous, absolute, and returns to manifest the live and operating power of transcendence, or it is nothing. Here too, it is not a matter of the possible marginal integrations in the person of this or that exceptional individual Catholic. It is only in the bloc of orthodoxy animated by a totally different spirit that Catholicism, despite its spurious nature, could theoretically provide a reference point to many divided and scattered forces. And yet, how could Catholicism possibly overcome the partisan and antitraditional exclusivism typical of its doctrine and elevate itself to a superior, metaphysical, and esoteric perspective, capable of freeing it from its own limitations? Is it not very obvious that Catholicism today is trying to reconcile itself in every way with modern thought and that the ascetical and contemplative element in it is increasingly neglected in favor of the moralistic and social dimension? Is it not obvious that in the political domain the Church lives day by day, dealing with this or that system, and avoids committing itself to any one and uncompromising direction, being obsessed with keeping up-to-date and staying on top of things, even to the point of engaging in a dialogue with Marxism?

Spiritually speaking, a tradition that merely amounts to a system of faith, scholarly theology, and symbols and rites that are no longer understood in their deepest meaning cannot act in a universal and vivifying fashion. Also, it is problematic to what degree the Catholic clergy still preserves some of the features of a body that is effectively invested with a power "from above." Materially speaking, within the context of European Christianity it would first be necessary to remove the Protestant and Orthodox schisms, itself a utopian prerequisite for a rigorous return to the starting point. Moreover, an eventual defensive solidarity of the Christian churches against the onslaught of militant antireligious forces should not be mistaken for a reaffirmation of a universal idea.

Nor should the issue of power be neglected considering the general conditions of the last age: what is needed is the presence of a bloc of power (economic, military, and industrial) capable of confronting the Eastern and Western forces fighting for world domination and capable of creating a dam and a united front.

Moreover, the idea that the West owes to Catholicism all the elements of Tradition it ever knew cannot be accepted without specific reservations. The composite character of Catholicism should not be forgotten. I have previously remarked that wherever this character manifested itself as a force promoting order and hierarchy, thus providing a support for European society, this was mainly thanks to the influences of the Roman-Germanic world. Conversely, whenever the specifically Christian component triumphed, Catholicism acted in the West in an antitraditional, rather than traditional way. The lunar, priestly spirit, its peculiar dualism, the various views of Jewish origin that became an integral part of the Christian spirit, all these things represented in Catholicism an obstacle that prevented the possibility of its infusing into Europe a spirituality in conformity with and proper to what I have called the Northern Light. Moreover Catholicism has caused the more real forces, after they found the way leading upwards obstructed, to flow into the material domain and realize in it the characteristic values of the Western soul. It is well-known that it was in the terms of a reaction against Catholicism that, beginning with the Renaissance, the reaffirmation of man and life took place. This represented an evident deviation and yet it was largely precipitated by the context I have just described.

Thus, overall, it must be said very clearly that those who think they are men of Tradition simply by virtue of being inspired by Catholicism do indeed stop halfway, and are utterly unable to recognize the first rings in the long chain of causes, and are thus blind to the world of the origins and absolute values. It is possible to see the two antagonistic yet complementary aspects of the same situation in a Western materialism oriented in a virile way and in the presence of a spirituality that cannot be separated from the non-Western, "Southern" elements, and that also lacks the superior, metaphysical, and esoteric dimension.

An analogous structural dualism impairs any attempt at traditional restoration before it starts by channeling it in the wrong direction.

In the actual civilization things are such that any evocation of the spirituality of the origins that could remove the impasse, overcome the scission, transport and elevate to the plane of light the powers of action locked in the dark and barbaric world of modern greatness would unavoidably have a problematic outcome, much more so than it did at the time of the Renaissance. In the modern world, the tendency to conceive virility, personality, action, and autonomy in merely material and human terms is way too strong. Thus, it is extremely unlikely that a doctrine inspired by the original sense that all this had in the light of traditional and transcendent references could avoid being brought back to the same terms, and thus not so much transform the profane into the sacred, but the other way around. In fact, today, when talking about the rights of a sovereign state before the Church, who could conceive anything besides the plebeian and lay claims of temporal power against spiritual authority? Or anything besides the usurping deeds of the new "superstates" and the new nationalist or collectivist mysticisms? When talking today about superindividuality, could the mind possibly go beyond the "superman" notion, which is Nietzsche at his worst? And again, when someone talks today about the "civilization of action" being a possibility as worthy as the "civilization of contemplation," would not everybody recognize in this the triumph in our times of those forms that demonstrate their unquestionable superiority over any past era by virtue of the mechanical, technological, and military superiority that European society has achieved in less than a century precisely through its cult of action? And even the most recent revival of myths, such as the Roman and the Nordic-Germanic myths, and the myths of the race, the Aryan spirit, and so on, have they not taken very questionable directions in the context of the political upheavals that have accelerated the final collapses in Europe?

Therefore we must conclude that the way is doubly blocked. The prison in which Western man is confined is one of the worst ever to be devised because it does not have walls. It is not easy to get up again when there is nothing on which one can lean and push himself up. By increasingly undermining the effective influence of Christianity and Catholicism, the West is abandoning its last references to a spirituality that is not its own; and yet, in the forms that are proper to it, the West is not pure spirit and is also unable to create its own spirit.

Therefore it seems unavoidable that fate will run its course. I have said it before: it is likely that having reached the penultimate step, and being on the edge of the universal advent of the truth and the power of the fourth and last of the ancient castes, mankind is ready to enter the last stage and touch the bottom of the Dark Age or Iron Age (foretold in traditional teachings), the general features of which largely correspond to those of contemporary civilization.

Just like people, civilizations also undergo their own cycle, consisting of a beginning, a development, and an end; the more they are immersed in what is contingent, the more this law is inescapable. This obviously is not enough to frighten those who are rooted in what cannot be altered and what remains as a perennial presence by virtue of its being above time. Even though it may be destined to disappear, modern civilization is certainly not the first to become extinct, nor is it the one after which none will follow. In the life of what is conditioned by space and time, lights are continually being put out and kindled again, cycles end and new ones begin. As I have said, the doctrine of the cycles was known to traditional man and only the ignorance of modern man has induced him to believe that his civilization, which is characterized by the deepest roots in the temporal and contingent element, will enjoy a different and privileged fate.

To those who have a vision in conformity with reality, the problem is rather to what degree can there be a relationship of continuity between the dying world and the world to come; in other words, what elements of the old world will survive and be carried forth into the new one? The predominant view in the ancient traditional teaching is that some kind of gap separates one cycle from the next; the new cycle allegedly will be characterized not by a gradual getting up and reconstruction, but by a new beginning, a sudden mutation brought about by a divine and metaphysical event, just like an old tree does not flourish again, but dies and a new tree grows out of its seeds. This view clearly shows that the relationships of continuity between two cycles are only relative and, in any event, do not affect the masses and great structures of a civilization. These relationships only concern essential vital elements, much in the way the seed is related to the new plant.

Thus, one of the many illusions that needs to be rejected is the one nourished by those who try to see a superordained logic behind the processes of dissolution, and who think that somehow the old world had to die in order to bring forth the new world toward which mankind is heading. And yet, the only world toward which we are heading is simply that which picks up and reassumes in an extreme way that which has acted during the phase of destruction. Such a world cannot be the basis for anything meaningful, nor can it provide the material from which traditional values may be revived again, precisely because it is the organized and embodied negation of these values. There is no future, in the positive sense of the word, for modern civilization as a whole. Thus, it is a mere fancy harbored by those who dream about a goal and a future that somehow may justify what man has destroyed both inside and outside himself.

The possibilities still available in the last times concern only a minority and may be distinguished as follows. Beside the great "currents" of the world there are still individuals who are rooted in terra firma. Generally speaking, they are unknown people who shun the spotlight of modern popularity and culture. They live on spiritual heights; they do not belong to this world. Though they are scattered over the earth and often ignorant of each other's existence, they are united by an invisible bond and form an unbreakable chain in the traditional spirit. This nucleus does not act: it only exercises the function to which the symbolism of the "perennial fire" corresponded. By virtue of these people, Tradition is present despite all; the flame burns invisibly and something still connects the world to the superworld. They are those who are awake, whom in Greek are called the $\varepsilon\gamma\rho\acute{\eta}\gamma\rho\rho\iota$.

There are an increasing number of individuals who experience a confused and yet real need for liberation, though they do not know in the name of what. To orient these people, and shield them from the spiritual dangers of the actual world, to lead them to see the truth and sharpen their will to join the ranks of the first type of people is what can still be done. And yet this too affects only a minority, and we should not delude ourselves that in this way there will be sizeable changes in the overall destinies of the multitudes. In any event, this is the only justification for tangible action that can be carried out by men of Tradition living in the modern world, in a milieu with which they have no connection. In order for the abovementioned guiding action to be successful it is necessary to have "watchers" at hand who will bear witness to the values of Tradition in ever more uncompromising and firm ways, as the antitraditional forces grow in strength. Even though these values today cannot be achieved, it does not mean that they amount to mere "ideas." They are *measures*. And when even the elemental capability to measure was totally lost, then the last night would surely fall. Let people of our time talk about these things with condescension as if they were anachronistic and antihistorical; we know that this is an alibi for their defeat. Let us leave modern men to their "truths" and let us only be concerned about one thing: to keep standing amid a world of ruins. Even though today an efficacious, general, and realizing action stands almost no chance at all, the ranks that I mentioned before can still set up inner defenses. In an ancient ascetical text it is said that while in the beginning the law from above could be implemented, those who came afterward were only capable of half of what had been previously done; in the last times very few works will be done, but for people living in these times the great temptation will arise again; those who will endure during this time will be greater than the people of old who were very rich in works.[2] To make the values of truth, reality, and Tradition highly visible to those who do not want "this" but who confusedly seek something "else," means to offer some reference points so that the great temptation may not prevail in everybody in those situations in which matter seems to have become stronger than the spirit.

Finally, we must consider a third possibility. To some the path of acceleration may be the most suitable approach to a solution, considering that given certain conditions, many reactions are the equivalent of those cramps that only prolong agony and by delaying the end also delay the advent of the new principle. Thus, it would be expedient to take on, together with a special inner attitude, the most destructive processes of the modern era in order to use them for liberation; this would be like turning a poison against oneself or like "riding a tiger."[3]

When regarding the process of decadence in Western society, I identified unrealism as its most typical feature. The individual at a given historical moment finds himself to be totally ignorant of spirituality as a reality. He even experiences the sense of self in terms of thought and reflection; this amounts to psychologism. Eventually his thought and reflection create a world of mirages, phantasms, and idols that replace spiritual reality; this is the humanistic myth of culture, which is nothing but a cave filled with shadows. Together with the abstract world of thought, there arises the romantic world of the "soul." What emerges are the various creatures of sentimentalism and faith, of individualistic and humanitarian pathos, of sensualism and superfluous heroism, of humility and revolt. And yet we have already seen that this unrealistic world is heading to its downfall and that deeper, elemental forces have almost swept away the myths of romantic and individualist man in a world where "realism" prevails over any idealism or sentimentalism and the "humanistic cult of the soul" is definitely overcome. I have indicated currents that see the presuppositions for a new universal civilization in the destruction of the "I" and the liberation of man from the "spirit."

Regarding the way that has been mentioned, it is necessary to establish up to what point it is possible to benefit from such destructive upheavals; up to what point, thanks to an inner determination and orientation toward transcendence, may the nonhuman element of the modern "realistic" and activist world, instead of being a path to the subhuman dimension (as is the case of the majority of the most recent forms), foster experiences of a higher life and a higher freedom?

2. A. Stolz, *L'ascesi cristiana* (Brescia, 1944), 2.

3. In my book *Cavalcare la tigre* I have attempted to outline the existential orientations that may serve this purpose during an age of dissolution.

This is all we can say about a certain category of men in view of the fulfillment of the times, a category that by virtue of its own nature must be that of a minority. This dangerous path may be trodden. It is a real test. In order for it to be complete in its resolve it is necessary to meet the following conditions: all the bridges are to be cut, no support found, and no returns possible; also, the only way out must be forward.

It is typical of a heroic vocation to face the greatest wave knowing that two destinies lie ahead: that of those who will die with the dissolution of the modern world, and that of those who will find themselves in the main and regal stream of the new current.

Before the vision of the Iron Age, Hesiod exclaimed: "May I have not been born in it!" But Hesiod, after all, was a Pelasgic spirit, unaware of a higher vocation. For other natures there is a different truth; to them applies the teaching that was also known in the East:[4] although the Kali Yuga is an age of great destructions, those who live during it and manage to remain standing may achieve fruits that were not easily achieved by men living in other ages.

4. See the *Viṣṇu Purāṇa*, 6.2.

Appendix: On the Dark Age

In reference to what I previously said concerning what ancient traditions called the Dark Age (Kali Yuga), I will now describe some of the features of this age found in an ancient Hindu text, the *Viṣṇu Purāṇa*. I will put in brackets what I consider to be the contemporary applications.[1]

> Outcastes and barbarians will be masters of the banks of the Indus, Darvika, the Chandrabhaga and Kashmir. These will all be contemporary rulers [of this age] reigning over the earth: kings [rulers] of violent temper . . . They will seize upon the property of their subjects; they will be of limited power and will for the most part rapidly rise and fall; their lives will be short, their desires insatiable, and they will display but little piety. The people of various countries intermingling with them will follow their example. . . . The prevailing caste will be the Shudra . . . Vaisyas will abandon agriculture and commerce and gain a livelihood by servitude or the exercise of mechanical arts [proletarization and industrialization] . . . Kshyatrias instead of protecting will plunder their subjects: and under the pretext of levying customs will rob merchants of their property [crisis of capitalism and of private property; socialization, nationalization, and communism] . . . Wealth [inner] and piety [following one's *dharma*] will decrease day by day until the whole world will be wholly depraved. Then property alone will confer rank [the quantity of dollars—economic classes]; wealth [material] will be the only source of devotion; passion will be the sole bond of union between the sexes; falsehood will be the only means of success in litigation. . . .
>
> Earth will be venerated but for its mineral treasures [unscrupulous exploitation of the soil, demise of the cult of the earth] . . .
>
> Brahmanical clothes will constitute a Brahman . . . weakness will

1. [The passages that follow are taken from the English translation of the *Viṣṇu Purāṇa*, by H. Wilson (London, 1868), 4.24; 6.1.]

be the cause of dependence [cowardice, death of *fides* and honor in the modern political forms] . . . simple ablution [devoid of the power of the true rite] will be purification [can there really be anything more in the alleged salvation procured by the Christian sacraments?] . . .

In the Kali age men corrupted by unbelievers . . . will say: "Of what authority are the Vedas? what are gods or Brāhmaṇs? . . . "

Observance of caste, order and institutes [traditional] will not prevail in the Kali age. Marriages in this age will not be comformable to the ritual, nor will the rules that connect the spiritual preceptor and his disciple be in force. . . . A regenerated man will be initiated in any way whatever [democracy applied to the spiritual plane] and such acts of penance as may be performed will be unattended by any results [this refers to a "humanistic" and conformist religion] . . . all orders of life will be common alike to all persons. . . .

He who gives away much money will be the master of men and family descent will no longer be a title of supremacy [the end of traditional nobility, advent of bourgeoisie, plutocracy]. . . .

Men will fix their desires upon riches, even though dishonestly acquired. . . . Men of all degrees will conceit themselves to be equal with Brahmans [the prevarication and presumption of the intellectuals and modern culture]. . . . The people will be almost always in dread of dearth and apprehensive of scarcity; and will hence ever be watching the appearances of the sky [the meaning of the religious and superstitious residues typical of modern masses]. . . .

The women will pay no attention to the commands of their husbands or parents. . . . They will be selfish, abject and slatternly; they will be scolds and liars; they will be indecent and immoral in their conduct and will ever attach themselves to dissolute men. . . .

Men having deviated into heresy, iniquity will flourish, and the duration of life will therefore decrease.[2]

Nevertheless, in the *Viṣṇu Purāna* there are also references to elements of the primordial or "Manu's" race that have been preserved in this Dark Age in order to be the seed of new generations; what appears again is the well-known idea of a new and final epiphany "from above":

2. This prophecy appears to have been contradicted by facts, unless we distinguish the case in which a longer life is due to contact with that which transcends time from the case of artificial "devices" to prolong life (which is meaningless and just a parody of the first type of life), realized through the means of profane science and modern hygiene.

When the practices taught by the Vedas and the institutes of law shall nearly have ceased, and the close of the Kali age shall be nigh, a portion of that divine being who exists of his own spiritual nature in the character of Brahma, and who is the beginning and the end, and who comprehends all things, shall descend upon earth. . . . He will then reestablish righteousness upon earth; and the minds of those who live at the end of the Kali age shall be awakened, and shall be as pellucid as crystal. The men who are thus changed by virtue of that peculiar time shall be as the seeds of [new] human beings, and shall give birth to a race who shall follow the laws of the Krita age, or age of purity [primordial age].

In the same text and chapter it is said that the stock from which this divine principle will be born lives in the village of Shambhala; Shambhala—as I previously suggested—refers to the metaphysics of the "center" and the "pole," to the Hyperborean mystery and the forces of the primordial tradition.

Index